Hanging Around The Big Sky

The Unofficial Guide to Lynching, Strangling and Legal Hangings of Montana

Book One: Legal Hangings

Tom Donovan

Hanging Around the Big Sky:
The Unofficial Guide to Lynching, Strangling and Legal Hangings of Montana. Book One: Legal Hangings

First Printing: Spring of 2007
Set in Bookman Old Style by Portage Meadows Publishing and printed and bound by Data Reproductions Corporation of Auburn Hills, MI.

ISBN 9780976971818

Library of Congress Control Number: 2007924067

Portage Meadows Publishing
POB 6554
Great Falls, MT. 59406

Additional copies of this book are available through local bookstores or they may be ordered directly from the publisher at the above address.

Front and Back Covers

Designed by: Portage Meadows Publishing
Cover photos: by Bonnie Donovan
Front Cover sketch as well as the one on the final page depicting the Weeksville hangings of 1883, by Willis Thorndike from the 12/13/1903 issue of the "Anaconda Standard."
Back Cover sketches:
Gallows, "Anaconda Standard" 9/12/1899;
Portraits from top to bottom:
John Burns, "Missoulian" 12/21/1892; William Gay, "Helena Herald" 6/8/1896; William Biggerstaff, "Helena Herald" 4/6/1896

Dedicated to

To my sister, Roberta Donovan Barrows.

While I love my little sister dearly
and have never considered hanging her,
I have thought about strangling her a few times.

Acknowledgements

Although there are many people to thank for helping with this book, too numerous to mention, I do wish to thank several people and organizations who contributed both advice and support: The Montana Historical Society Library and other public libraries including: Great Falls, Bozeman, Anaconda and Boulder. Museums and historical societies across Montana in particular the Choteau Old Trail Museum, Butte-Silver Bow, Chouteau County Museum, Gallatin County Historical Society Pioneer Museum, Granite County Museum, Treasure County Museum, Western Heritage Center at Billings and the Beaverhead County Museum at Dillon.

Other associations aiding my research were the Old Montana Prison Museum at Deer Lodge; Northwest Montana Historical Society Museum at Kalispell; Central Montana Historical Society of Lewistown; Historical Museum at Fort Missoula; Carbon County Historical Society, Museum of the Beartooths at Columbus, Virginia City and Nevada City Museum and the Wolf Point Museum.

A special thanks goes out to the staffs of several district courts including in the counties of: Missoula, Madison, Chouteau, Teton, Golden Valley, Lewis and Clark and Jefferson and to Larry Stollfuss of Fort Benton, Marcia Porter of Missoula and Justice of the Peace Peter Howard of Choteau who were of particular assistance in my research.

I am indebted to the following individual historians and researchers for making material available to me: Ken Robinson of Great Falls; Ellen Baumler and George Oberst of the Montana Historical Society; Mike Castleberry of Radersburg; Jerry Brekke of Livingston; Ellen Rae Thiel of Boulder and Emma Toman of Sun River.

I am deeply grateful for having an understanding wife and other family members who have tolerated my love of history and obsession with trying to record it. Finally, there are no words that can express my gratitude to my mother, Betty Donovan, who has always given her love and encouragement in all of my endeavors.

CONTENTS

Introduction: vi

Preface: ix

List of Photographs and Illustrations: xi

About the Author: xii

Chapter One: History of Legal Hangings of Montana 1
(The Typical Legal Hanging)

Chapter Two: Territorial Legal Hangings 47
(August 1875-August 1889)

Chapter Three: Nineteenth Century Legal Hangings 127
(November 1889-December 1899)

Chapter Four: Early Twentieth Century Hangings 253
(March 1900 - April 1918)

Chapter Five: Hangings of the Roaring Twenties 383
(September 1920 - November 1929)

Chapter Six: The Last Hangings in Montana 487
(August 1933 - September 1943)

Chapter Seven: The Gallows of Montana 533

Chapter Nine: Extra-Legal Hangings of Montana 559

TABLES:

Hangings by Year: 597
Hangings by County: 605
Hanging Judges of Montana: 613
Reference Index: 619
Execution Case Index: 641

INTRODUCTION

One of the most frequently asked question concerning hangings is why we say a man was "Hanged" by the neck until dead, and not "Hung?" It comes down to respect for human life. No matter how horrific the crime, society displays its concern over taking the life of another human being by stating that rugs, paintings and other "Things" are Hung while a man is "Hanged." The distinction was meant to reflect this respect.

It has been said that the history of capital punishment coincides with the history of revenge it self, and revenge is said to be even older than love. In fact revenge is as old as the instinct of self-preservation. A sign that a society has become civilized is when the government assumes the right and responsibility to exercise revenge. The government proclaims that they alone have the right to punish the criminal. The second stage of the development of a civilization is when the government punishes not in the spirit of revenge but to protect its citizens and to prevent future crime.

The legal executions in the United States, as cruel as they may seem to many, have been better than being dragged by the tail of a horse till life was extinct as was done by the ancient Germans; better than crucifixion where victims could suffer for days, or by skinning alive and boiled in hot lard or oil. During the middle-ages some of the most popular means of execution condoned by the church were the pulling the body apart on the rack, driving spikes into the brain or being crushed in an iron frame with spikes.

Staking a person out to starve to death or be to be eaten by critters was a practice used in Spain and by some North American Indians. For High Treason in England, the violator was first drug by a horse's tail along the streets from the prison to the place of execution; he would then be hanged by the neck until almost dead; his intestines plucked out of his body and burned while he was still alive; beheaded, quartered and then the quarters and head were placed at various location in the kingdom.

These forms of punishment are referred to as "afflictive" punishments designed to prolong death and accentuate the pain and revenge factor. Simple capital punishment merely causes death and minimizes the pain. While the English utilized the prolonged afflictive types of punishment in high profile cases they still simply hanged a person for stealing a sheep.

While legal hangings in this country have been for the most part "simple" capital punishment, there have been many atrocities committed against the slaves mainly of the south that would equal anything of the Dark Ages. The Puritans have influenced most of the capital punishment in this country. Although many of the corporal punishments levied by the early Puritans inflicted extreme suffering, capital punishment was exercised with no intent to provide pleasure for the spectators, as was the case of the barbaric Romans and other Europeans.

In the Big Sky Country there have been examples of revenge executions and atrocities including what could easily be considered barbaric. Montana murderers have been lynched within hours of their crime, and while no one was hanged for stealing a sheep, many have lost their lives for taking another man's horse. A couple of men were hanged for murder only to have their victims recover from their near-fatal wounds. While we have never found any reports of a man being dragged from a horse's tail, an Indian horse thief was roped and drug to his death at Lewistown. We haven't found any examples of a lynching taking place in Montana purely on the basis of race but some of the men might have been hanged with more enthusiasm and zeal because of the color of their skin or nationality.

While most of the famous executions of Montana have been written about in various books and local historical publications, there has never been an attempt made to combine all of these hangings into one publication. Soon after beginning this project we realized that the reason why no one has has taken on this endeavor is because of the sheer number of cases of summary executions. There were so many hangings over the history of Montana and with so varied circumstances that eventually we had to classify them into categories.

We have grouped all of the two hundred and thirty-five hangings of Montana into six categories, those ordered by Miners' Courts, Original Vigilantes of Bannack and Virginia City, the various chapters of "Hometown Vigilantes" across the Territory, Lynch Mobs, "Cowboy Stranglers of 1884" and finally Legal executions. We further broke down the Legal executions into five more categories, those taking place during the days of the Territorial, Nineteenth Century State, Early Twentieth Century, Roaring Twenties and finally the Last Hangings.

The Miners' Courts claimed eleven victims; the Original Vigilantes of Bannack and Virginia City were responsible for thirty hangings while the various chapters of "Hometown Vigilantes" across the Territory held at least thirty-seven executions. Lynch Mob took the lives of another thirty-nine men and the infamous "Cowboy Stranglers of 1884" hanged at least forty-seven while the legal system from 1875 to 1943 executed a total of seventy-one convicted murderers.

After nearly three years of research and successfully organizing the hangings into groups, we were still unable to condense the stories into a single volume, while still giving the individual cases justice. We have elected to publish two volumes, the first covering the legal hangings of Montana in detail while still listing all the extra-legal or illegal executions to make it a complete guide. The second volume will cover in detail the cases of extra-legal hangings while still listing the legal cases. Both volumes will include tables on "Hangings by Year" and "Hangings by County" while the individual publications will have other chapters devoted to their particular emphasis.

In this volume of our unofficial guide, we have described in detail each of the seventy-one legal hangings that took place in Montana from the first one in 1875 to 1943 when the last murderer lost his life on the gallows. We have included a chapter dealing with the history of the judicial system in Montana as well as describing a typical hanging. Another chapter is devoted to the twenty-two gallows that were used along with a table listing the individual "Hanging Judges of Montana."

To complete our unofficial guide to Montana hangings we have included the most comprehensive list of every man illegally hanged in the Big Sky Country by the Miners' Courts, Original Vigilantes of Bannack and Virginia City, the various chapters of the "Hometown Vigilantes," Lynch Mobs and the "Cowboy Stranglers of 1884." Volume two of "Hanging Around the Big Sky" (Book Two) will cover in detail the one hundred and sixty-four extra-legal hangings as will as a section devoted to local stories and rumored hangings that we were unable to substantiate.

PREFACE

While we have researched many court records for the facts, these accounts have mostly been described as they were reported in the colorful newspaper stories of the day. The purpose of this work is not an effort to glamorize crime or the criminals, nor was it written as a social comment on the issue of capital punishment. The hangings like the crimes themselves are described as graphically and brutally as they were reported at the time.

Over the years many of these accounts have been forgotten while others have been exaggerated in the tradition of western storytelling. The old timers passing down the stories have often made polishing the accounts into an art form, which has obviously made it difficult at times to separate fact from fiction.

Disclaimer

The material in this publication has been compiled from published biographical and historical accounts, and while every effort has been made to determine the truth of these stories we cannot guarantee complete authenticity of all the stated facts. In some cases it was impossible to determine even the exact dates, names or other vital information of the incident. Even the descriptions of the most well known executions of our state vary greatly because of different eyewitness accounts and the affects of time and exaggeration.

The versions offered in this unofficial guide to Montana hangings were a result of research from primarily newspaper accounts, local histories and other credible publications. Some references are more complete than others and in some cases a report of a summary execution was merely a sentence or two in an early newspaper. These types of reports rarely indicated the victim's name, their crime or where they were executed or by what means.

In some cases false reports of hangings were made, and while we have tried to confirm all of the cases in this publication, there is always the chance that one or more of our victims had actually survived. Although there have been a few false reports of hangings in the early newspapers, we generally consider theses sources, while often lacking in information and details, accurate and have been included in our publication.

Using this book

As explained in the "Introduction" we have categorized the various Montana hangings into six main groups by type of executioners: **Miners' Courts,** the **Original Vigilantes**, **Hometown Vigilantes**, **Mob Lynching**, the "**Cowboy Stranglers of 1884"** and **Legal Hangings**. While we have covered in detail the legal hangings in this publication, we have included the names of all the extra-legal victims to make this a complete guide.

While it is recommended to read each chapter in order to better understand the history of the early hangings in Montana and how capital punishment evolved over the years, a person can quickly find individual cases by name, year, county or even by type or means of their hangings.

To find out whether or not a hanging has taken place in a particular county, one only needs to refer to the "**Hangings by County"** table, which will provide the names, type of execution and dates. To assist the individual navigate through this book there is also a table listing "**Hangings by Year"**

Each legal hanging case lists the location and specific gallows used as well as the description of the victim, his crime, the judge, prosecutor and defense attorneys and county sheriff involved. If the case was distinctive it is noted as will as any relics or remnants of the hanging are listed. It is recommended that the museums owning the relics should be notified in advance of viewing.

References and Footnotes

Every reference dealing with individual hanging victims are listed in total in the "**Reference Index"** table while items in the narratives, which weren't found in the references of the hanging victims, are in the footnotes at the end of each chapter or section.

Location of Hangings

Montana has gone through many changes including becoming part of Washington and Dakota Territories in 1861, Idaho Territory in 1863, Montana Territory in 1864 and finally statehood in 1889 along with numerous changes in the number and boundaries of counties. From the original nine territorial counties established in 1865, the number had doubled by 1889 and was at twenty-six in 1904. By 1918 the state had forty-three counties and in 1925 Petroleum County became the fifty-sixth and last to be established.

While the hangings actually occurred in the early-day counties, we have endeavored to list them in the present-day county for easier locating. For example, a hanging at Radersberg in 1868, which was at that time the county seat of Jefferson County, is listed in the present day Broadwater County.

Graphic Description

While many of the early-day newspaper articles dealing with crime, criminals and racial groups were very graphic, bordering on gruesome and certainly not "politically correct," we have tried to be sensitive in describing the tragedies but still maintaining some of the original descriptions for their effect. We are not concerned about being "politically correct" and certainly not judgmental as so many others try to be concerning this subject. In this publication we refer to African Americans as "Blacks" and Native American as "Indians" since that was how they were usually described at the time.

Errors and omissions

As was stated in the earlier Disclaimer, it is impossible to verify the names, exact locations and specific dates of many of these hangings (particularly extra-legal) because they are often reported, weeks, months and sometimes years after the fact. In the early mining camps it was actually very bad etiquette to ask a man where he came from or anything about his past.

These attitudes along with miss-information have caused errors in the names and the identities of some of the victims. Delayed reporting of details, omitting or embellishing the facts of the case has either exaggerated the story or the whole affair has been forgotten over time. We have made a concerted effort to get the stories correct, and we apologize for any errors or omissions that we might have made.

Lists of Photographs and Sketches

Photo of Author	xii
First Territorial Legislature Building at Bannack	5
Lewis and Clark County Sheriff Thomas Davidson	10
Fergus County Sheriff Thomas Shaw	11
Judge William Clancy's courtroom at Butte	13
Invitation to a hanging	26
Photo of the hanging of William Gay at Helena	36
Photo of William Biggerstaff in his coffin	43
Pallbearers and coffin	44
The Four Indians before they were hanged at Missoula	134
The Indian, Pierre Paul	145
The Indian, La La See	146
The Indian, Padcale	149
John Burns	153
The hanging of John Burns	159
William Biggerstaff	195
Photo of the hanging of William Biggerstaff	206
William Gay	209
Joseph Allen	233
Gallows used to hang Joseph Allen	238
William Calder	253
Dawson County Sheriff Cavanaugh	263
Joseph Hurst	264
Hanging of Daniel Lucy	282
James Fleming	288
Hanging of Clinton Dotson	303
Hanging og George Rock at the State Penitentiary	344
Photo of the Vigilante hanging of Wilson and Compton	559
The George Ives Trial	560
Moonlight hanging (from "Anaconda Standard" 3/18/1900)	565
"Cowboy Strangler" Posse	592

ABOUT THE AUTHOR
Tom Donovan

The author began working on the subject after learning that one of his ancestors of had been a murder victim and that his assailant was later hanged for the crime. First wanting to write up the story for his own genealogy research, Donovan found it fascinating how the incident played out in the early-day newspapers. The author's ancestor had operated a general store near Whitehall when he was killed in a holdup attempt in 1923 and his murder was found guilty and sentenced to be hanged; he later escaped from the Jefferson County jail at Boulder; then he was discovered at the Missouri State Penitentiary and finally returned to Montana where he was hanged on Valentine's Day in 1925.

Tom Donovan in the Old Deer Lodge Prison Museum

The author couldn't resist turning his interest to other capital punishment cases and while collecting information on those other legal executions he ran across histories about illegal lynching, which caused him to start digging up all sorts of hangings. He gathered stories and accounts from all sorts of sources including of course newspapers, county histories and several books on the history of Montana. It seemed that just about every book about Montana contained one or more hangings and a great deal of the counties of the stat boasted of ancient summary executions but no one had attempted to combine all of these histories into one publication.

Donovan wanted to document each hanging case as completely and as accurately as possible by including the names of the officials, witnesses and members of the juries. With this kind of detail, Tom quickly learned that it was impossible to document all two hundred and thirty five Montana hangings into one publication so he is publishing two volumes in order to adequately record these fascinating histories.

The author has always had a love of history, and in particular, the events that have occurred and changed Montana. Donovan's second volume of "Hanging Around the Big Sky: Book Two" will soon be completed and his love for history drives him to research a number of other projects simultaneously. Besides "Hanging Around the Big Sky" Donovan has written several family histories along with his other successful book, "Dying to Hunt in Montana: Nearly Two Hundred Years of Hunting Related Fatalities In Montana," which has become extremely popular among sportsmen young and old alike.

The History of Legal Hangings of Montana

(And the Typical Montana Hanging)

When the Territory of Montana was created with the Organic Act of 1864, President Abraham Lincoln appointed three judges to administer the law, which in the interim had been taken up by the Miners' Courts, which had successfully carried out mostly the civil matters while the Vigilantes and "Hometown Vigilantes" handled the criminal cases. By the time the justices had arrived in what became Montana Territory the Miners' Courts had already hanged four men in present day Powell and Madison Counties, the Original Vigilantes had executed another twenty-seven road agents and other undesirables in Beaverhead, Madison, Missoula and Ravalli Counties and the "Hometown Vigilantes" of Hell Gate had strung up a rampaging Indian.

The new territorial courts only consisted of a Supreme Court and three judicial districts. The Territorial Supreme Court was made up of a chief justice and two associate justices and these same three judges served on the three District Courts as well. Although this system was often criticized because the Supreme Court justices could obviously confirm their own errors while sitting on the District Courts, the records show that many of the decisions of the lower courts were in fact reversed, and the judgments of the high court were usually affirmed on appeal to the Supreme Court of the United States.[1]

While the Civil War was still raging in 1864, President Lincoln appointed Hezekiah L. Hosmer as Chief Justice and Lorenzo P. Williston, of Pennsylvania and Lyman E. Munson from Connecticut as his Associate Justices. Judge Hosmer arrived at Virginia City in October of 1864, and presided over the First District there. Judge Williston was given the Second District and he lived at Bannack and then he later moved to Deer Lodge and Governor Edgerton assigned Justice Munson to the Third District at Helena. While the Territory had courts, judges and lawyers for a framework of a government, there were no laws to set the whole system into motion until the first Legislative Assembly was held at Bannack in January of 1865. In the meantime Chief Justice Hosmer held several meetings with the lawyers of Virginia City where they discussed the practices of the Miners' Courts and they decided to adopt the statutes of the Territory of Idaho in order to bridge the gap until the first legislative assembly could meet.

Without a courthouse in Virginia City, Chief Justice Hosmer opened the first legal session of court on December 5, 1864, in the dining room of the Planters House, which was the most prominent hotel in town located at the corner of Idaho and Jackson Street. Immediately after breakfast had been served to the hotel guests and the dishes were cleared away, a number of tables were put together and by placing another table on top of them an improvised bench was made for Judge Hosmer. Another table was arranged for the clerk of the court and one more was utilized for the lawyers, both the defense and the prosecution. While the judge was supplied with a chair most of the lawyers, Grand Jury and the spectators were seated on four-legged stools.

At first Judge Hosmer praised the earlier work of the Miners' Courts and the Original Vigilantes in providing law and order to the Territory, after which he made it clear that the legal courts would then take over. It was later reported that after the session was concluded, a member of the new Grand Jury and well-known Vigilante,[2] told Chief Justice Hosmer that the newly formed district court should handle civil cases as the Miners' Courts had done and leave the criminals up to the vigilance committee, who could dispense justice far more efficiently and more economically than the courts could.

The first Territorial Legislature enacted both civil and criminal codes along with authorizing Probate Courts in each county, a Justice of the Peace and Constables in all of the major mining camps and settlements. Governor Edgerton initially appointed these county officials but eventually they were chosen by the vote of the people and the Miners' Courts passed into history except for in the remote mining camps of the Territory. Many of the principles and rules of the Miners' Courts were incorporated into the territorial statutes and they became a permanent part of the law.

By 1865, there was a "Hometown Vigilante" organization in most of the larger communities and they continued to prosecute the alleged criminals. When Justice Lyman E. Munson arrived at Helena on Sunday, July 9, 1865, Last Chance Gulch was a lively mining camp with about three thousand residents. On that particular day, like they did on other such holidays the miners were off and enjoying themselves in the saloons, gambling halls and the noisy hurdy gurdy houses. Judge Munson later said that while he was walking up Dry Gulch he saw a man's body hanging on the famous Hangman's Tree. In a meeting with the other justices, Munson declared that their first duty had to be to put a stop to the nighttime hangings by the various "Hometown Vigilantes," stating that all persons should have the benefit of a jury trial.

According to Judge Munson, at that meeting of the three justices one of his counterparts said that while he too was concerned about the midnight executions he was content to let the Vigilantes continue because their form of jurisprudence was cheaper, quicker and better than the legal courts, especially when there were no adequate jails in the Territory. The other justice warned Munson that if they attempted to try the outlaws their fellow road agents would surely free him and then threaten the witnesses, the officers as well the court itself. Even Judge Munson himself later complimented the swiftness of Vigilante justice and he tried to conduct speedy trials in his own district courts. He said that the courts back East would benefit from trying cases while the witnesses were fresh and not forced to use written affidavits when memories may have faded.[3]

By the time Judge Munson opened his first term of District Court at Helena in August of 1865, another victim of the "Hometown Vigilantes" was found hanging on the famous tree in Dry Gulch. The hanging of this John Doe on July 8 probably prompted Judge Munson's statement to the grand jury explaining that while the patriotic actions of the original vigilance committee at Bannack and Virginia City and various "Hometown Vigilantes" were certainly necessary to bring law and order to the mining camps, the secret trials and midnight executions should be ceased and the legal courts be given a chance to operate. The judges carefully guarded the rights and prestige of their courts and at times they seemed to have been obsessed with trying to gain the confidence of the law-abiding citizens. Unfortunately the justices were looked upon as "carpetbaggers" from the east and their style of justice was considered slow, expensive and inadequate.

It took the legal system of the Montana Territory eleven years to hang its first convicted murderer but during the fourteen years remaining before statehood it managed to execute a total of sixteen men. By the time the first man was legally hanged by order of a District Court in the Territory, four different appointed judges had come and gone, two Chief Justices and two Associates. In the meantime a total of seventy-three men had been hanged by order of remote Miners' Courts or at the hands of Lynch Mobs, the Original Vigilantes and "Hometown Vigilantes." The Original Vigilantes of Bannack and Alder Gulch were responsible for thirty hangings while the various chapters of "Hometown Vigilantes" executed another twenty-eight. Miners' Courts had ordered the deaths of eleven men and Lynch Mobs across the Territory had hanged four more.

By 1875, and with thirty known victims, most of the leading members of the Original Vigilantes were well known and therefore susceptible to prosecution for any additional illegal executions. The Miners' Courts too, because they operated openly found themselves vulnerable when taking the law into their own hands. While the legal justice system had displaced the Original Vigilantes and Miners' Courts in Montana, the more secretive "Hometown Vigilantes," Lynch Mobs and splinter groups the "Cowboy Stranglers of 1884" actually increased their activities. During the fourteen years when the legal courts disposed of sixteen murderers, Lynch Mobs were responsible for twenty-nine hangings, the various chapters of the "Hometown Vigilantes" executed another nine desperadoes and the notorious "Cowboy Stranglers" had strung up forty-seven suspected rustler in 1884 alone.

Since the "Hometown Vigilantes" had hanged their last victim at Miles City in 1883, and the "Cowboy Strangler's'" war on cattle rustlers and horse thieves only occurred during 1884, by statehood in 1889, most of the executions were conducted by the District Courts with only a few isolated cases of Mob Lynching. In total, there were more hangings during the twenty-seven years of Territorial days, one hundred and seventy-four, than the forty-three succeeding years when another sixty-one men were executed mostly by legal authority.

After becoming the forty-first state of the Union on November 8, 1889, the Montana Judicial System went through several more changes. During Territorial days the President of the United States appointed the District Court Judges but after statehood the people of Montana elected the Supreme Court Justices, District and Local Judges along with the other officers of the court. The new state constitution reverted back to the three-justice Supreme Court but the members had no other duties than those of the higher court. Instead of unlimited service, the members of the new state Supreme Court served for six-year terms. This system proved adequate for thirty years until the caseload of the courts had increased until 1919, when the State Legislature increased the Supreme Court to five members. The high court of the state of Montana remained at five justices until the 1979 Legislature authorized two more justices.

The Montana State Supreme Court also adopted a new system of deciding on the cases brought before them. After a case was argued before the high court the Chief Justice assigned one of the judges to make a detailed examination of the evidence, the briefs presented by the attorneys and then he searched for precedents in the law library. Meanwhile the other justices had also studied the evidence and facts of the case and when the judge in charge of the case completed his investigation, the court would convene in chambers where the report was laid out in detail. A discussion was held in chambers, which sometimes lasted for several days, and if a majority agreed with the lead judge's stand he would then draft an opinion. The completed opinion was again heard in chambers where additional changes could be made before the opinion was made final.[4]

Also provided in the new state constitution was the expansion of the District Court System from three to eight jurisdictions. The first eight district judges elected under the new state constitution were:

William H. Hunt, (First District) Lewis and Clark County
John J. McHatton, (Second District) Silver Bow County
David M. Durfee, (Third District) Deer Lodge County
C.S. Marshall, (Fourth District) Missoula County
Thomas J. Galbraith, (Fifth District) Beaverhead, Jefferson and Madison Counties
Frank Henry, (Sixth District) Gallatin, Park and Meagher Counties
George R. Milburn, (Seventh District) Yellowstone, Custer and Dawson Counties
C.H. Benton, (Eighth District) Chouteau, Cascade and Fergus Counties

Statutes Pertaining to Legal Executions of Montana

The home of the first Territorial Legislature at Bannack in 1864
(Sketch from the "Anaconda Standard" 12/22/1901)

The Territorial Legislature of 1865, had passed most of the basic statutes concerning executions, which were almost adopted entirely after statehood. It was in 1865, that "hanging by the neck" was officially adopted as the punishment of death for the Territory and later for the State of Montana. Later on the death penalty was made mandatory for first-degree convictions and second-degree convictions required a sentence of life imprisonment at the penitentiary. This legislature also required that the execution take place not less than four weeks and not more than eight weeks from the time of sentencing. Several other requirements were mandated including the reading of a death warrant, stating the conviction and sentencing to the condemned man.

By statute, all executions in Montana were to be conducted in a private enclosure as near to the county jail as possible. The sheriff was required to invite a specific number of witnesses for the execution and they had to be given at least three days notice. By law the only individuals allowed to witness hangings were the presiding judge of the case, the prosecuting attorney, the clerk of the court, two attending physicians, a minister or priest that the defendant named and up to two friends or relatives of the condemned man. The sheriff was also required to invite twelve "respectable citizens" and he could ask as many visiting peace officers as he deemed proper. Later on the sheriff was authorized to invite most of the officers of the including the complete jury. In order to allow even larger numbers of law officers and other officials to witness executions, the various county sheriffs would often deputize them just before the hanging or specify it on the invitation.

The legislature also specified who could interfere with legal executions. The Territorial Governor could respite or commute the death sentence and he technically had the authority to pardon the condemned man outright. No convicted murderer was ever pardoned before his execution but many of the Governors used the respite to provide additional time so that appeals could be made to the Supreme Court or to review new evidence or extenuating circumstances. The Supreme Court could either order a new trial for the defendant or affirm the decision of the lower court. After the Supreme Court affirmed the decision of the lower court, only the Governor or the presiding judge in the case could stop the execution.

The Governor could stop the execution of the condemned man by commuting his death sentence to life imprisonment at the penitentiary. The framers of the new State Constitution in 1889 took the pardoning power out of the sole hands of the governor and required his decisions to be approved by a board of pardons, which was made up of the Secretary of State, Attorney General and State Auditor. This action was taken to prevent the abuse of the power, which had been charged against a few chief executives but the power was later reinstated.[5]

The legislature eventually passed provisions that allowed the sheriff, if he believed that the condemned man had become insane, to summon a jury of twelve competent jurors, with the concurrence of the presiding judge to inquire into the sanity of the prisoner. The prosecuting attorney was required to attend the hearing in order to produce witnesses before the jury for the people of Montana. If the prisoner was found to be insane at the conclusion of the hearing, the sheriff was to suspend the execution, formerly notify the Governor and then wait for a new warrant from the top executive, the Supreme Court, or the presiding judge to execute the criminal. The new death warrant would either appoint a time and place for the execution or commute the sentence to life imprisonment.

We have found that this provision was used at least on two occasions, the first time by Flathead County Sheriff William O'Connell in 1909, in an attempt to save the life of Frederick LeBeau and then later in 1926, Sheriff Larry Duggan of Silver Bow County requested that the court grant an examination to establish the sanity of Anthony Vettere. At least nine condemned men tried to use the insanity dodge at one time or another during their trials or while awaiting their trip to the gallows. John Douglas who was hanged in May of 1881, stopped appearing insane when all hope was gone while William Brooks began acting mentally ill after loosing his final appeal in the fall of 1899. Calvin Christie tried to gain a commuted sentence on the grounds of epileptic insanity while Rolland Davisson, George Criner and George Hoffman tried to prove that alcohol had made them insane.

Interestingly the legislature even established statutes for consideration of pregnant female criminals facing a death sentence. If the sheriff suspected that the condemned woman prisoner was pregnant, he would first consult with the presiding judge, summon a six-person jury, at least three of the members being physicians, and hold a hearing to determine if she was carrying a child. As in the case of the insanity test, if the woman was determined to be pregnant, the Governor was then notified and the sheriff would suspend the execution until he received a new death warrant from the top executive or the woman's sentenced was commuted to life imprisonment. While there were a number of women in Montana convicted of first-degree murder, and there have been some who were even sentenced to death, there was never a woman in serious danger of being hanged by the Territory or State of Montana.

The Typical Montana Murder Case

Although most of the murder cases varied there were clear steps taken leading up to a legal hanging in the Territory and State. In this section we have illustrated with actual examples how the legal statutes as well as traditional protocols played a part in the Montana hangings. Examples of rules regulating mandatory sentences to the number of witnesses allowed during the hanging as well as describing the condemned man's last meal and their final words are provided. In order for the reader to get a real feel of the legal procedures involved from the time of a murder case to the finished hanging, we have included actual transcripts of some of the formal reports presented by a Coroner's Jury, the judge, jury as well as the Death Sentence, Death Warrant and finally a report filed by the sheriff stating that he had in deed executed the sentence.

The Murderers

In Montana there have been seventy-one men legally hanged who were convicted of murdering a total of seventy-eight victims. We have only counted the victims that were murdered in Montana, as the last man legally hanged, Philip Coleman, admitted he had killed five people before coming to Montana. While Coleman was responsible for the murders of three people in Montana he was only hanged for one.

The average age of the men legally hanged in Montana was thirty-four years old, the youngest, Leslie Fahley was only eighteen when he was hanged in February of 1917. Henry Furhmann was the oldest man legally hanged in Montana when he was executed in May of 1883 at age seventy. Of the fifty-five cases we have data on, there were sixteen men hanged between the age of eighteen and twenty-five; seventeen men between twenty-six and thirty-five and fourteen others were executed who were between thirty-six and forty-five years old. Five of the executed men were between the age of forty-six and fifty-five; two were between fifty-six and sixty-five and only one man was hanged over the age of sixty-six.

Of all the condemned men legally hanged in Montana, nine were black, another nine were of Indian blood, two were Chinese nationals, one was Mexican and the rest were white American, European or Mediterranean. The state required the services of interpreters in at least nine of the murder cases for the German, Henry Furhmann, the four Indians, Antley, La La See, Pascale and Pierre Paul; Norwegian, John Osnes; Lu Sing of China, Juan Cuellae of Mexico and Anthony Vettere of Italy.

These murderers had various backgrounds as well. Most of the murderers hanged in Montana were from poor families like Thomas King who came to America from Italy all alone when he was just eight years old. After spending a year on the streets of New York City, King eventually worked his way west where he was hanged in Montana in 1890. At least nine of the men legally hanged in Montana were career thieves, robbers and con-men. Ten were farm and ranch hands, another ten were common laborers including railroad workers and seven were miners or prospectors. Three of the condemned men were bootleggers or moonshiners, four were vagrants, one was a wolfer and another three individuals were inmates at the state penitentiary at the time the crime was committed. Two of the men disgraced on the gallows were well-to-do ranchers, two were army privates; four were reservation Indians and one successful businessman ran a laundry. Two of the condemned men were woodcutters, while there was also a railroad porter and even an ice cream vendor. As far as trades go, two of the murderers were barbers, two were teamsters and there was a mechanic, house painter and a cook.

Of the sixty-five condemned men who reportedly received spiritual advice, thirty-five of them were Catholic; twenty-four were Protestants; three were reluctant Christians, one was a non-believer and another was a devoted atheist. Harry Roberts confused things a bit when he refused religious counsel but before his march to the gallows he told a priest that he wanted to be buried a Catholic. Seven of the men legally hanged in Montana were veterans of the U.S. Army. William Wheatley, John Clark and Martin Scott had served during the Civil War; William Brooks and Daniel Lucy fought in the Indian Wars while Herbert Metzger served in Cuba. Rollin Davisson was stationed in Yellowstone Park with the Sixth Cavalry where he served along with the man he later murdered. While most of the condemned men had abused alcohol, at least four of them, Daniel Lucy, Louis Mott and Monte and William Harris were admitted dope addicts.

Peter Pelkey, Thomas King, John Burns, William Pepo, James Martin and Frederick LeBeau took pains to hide their true identity to protect their families from disgrace. Four of these men went to their graves with their secret and the other two died believing that they had deceived the authorities. Without his knowledge, John Burns' brother and sister from Duluth, Minnesota attended his trial and never told their father about their sibling's death. James Martin wouldn't sit for a photograph and even requested that the single light bulb be turned off for his hanging in order to prevent his family from learning about his disgraceful death. What Martin didn't know however was that Silver Bow County had located his family and had notified them of his predicament. Martin's family requested that the authorities not inform him that they were aware of his fate and the condemned man went to his grave believing that he had concealed his identity and therefore protected his family's honor.

The Murder Victims

Of the seventy-eight murder victims, sixty-six were male and twelve were of the fairer sex. Sixty-one were shot to death while eight were beaten, seven stabbed to death and one each met their end by strangulation and from a hatchet blade. Robbery was the motive for fifty-two murders, where ten victims were either partners or companions of the murderer and seven of the dead were the assailant's employer. Another thirty murders were crimes of passion including ten fights, four wife killings, three assassinations for revenge and one was a rape and murder case. Ten lawmen were killed in the line of duty, seven while they were arresting the subject, one during an attempted prison break and two were shot during an argument with a man inside of a police station. There were two cases of contract murder, one man had ordered the death of his own father and the other case involved a possible Chinese marriage conflict. Montana even had a political assassination when a disgruntled politician murdered his rival, ironically over the office of county sheriff.

Fifty-one of the murder victims were left where they fell while in some cases the murderer tried to conceal the crime by hiding or destroying the victim's body. Six of these bodies were burned, five buried, four were hidden in nearby foliage and three were thrown into a river or stream. Two victims were burned and their bones tossed into a river while one was left on the vast prairie and another murderer drug his victim into a coulee. After murdering his employer, Peter Pelkey poured lime over the victim and then placed hay over the remains. One murdered man was found in the cellar of his home while another had been hidden in an abandoned cabin. Two murderers attempted to cover their crime by making it appear to have been a suicide while another killer felt that he had committed a perfect crime by throwing his victim down an old mining shaft.

The Coroner's Report:

After the murder was reported to the authorities the prosecuting attorney and the coroner would generally travel to the crime scene where they would conduct a coroner's jury to establish the cause of death as well as name the suspected murderer. The following is the coroner's report concerning the death of Deputy Warden Robinson at the State Penitentiary in Powell County in 1908:

"We the jury find that the person lying dead before us was and is John A. Robinson; that he came to his death at the state prison of the State of Montana, at the city of Deer Lodge, County of Powell, State of Montana, on Sunday, the eighth day of March, 1908, by mortal wounds inflicted upon his head and throat by William A. Hayes and George Rock,

two convicts imprisoned in the said state prison; that said wounds were willfully, deliberately, premeditated and feloniously inflicted by said William A. Hayes and George Rock in the malice aforethought and with the felonious intent to murder said John A. Robinson; the said William A. Hayes and George Rock were assisted by other persons who are to the jury unknown, and was the result of a conspiracy entered into said named persons and the said other unnamed persons for the purpose of murdering said John A. Robinson and others and escaping from said state prison; that said killing was wholly unjustified."[6]

After the coroner's hearing was held, and if the suspected murderer wasn't already in custody, the nearest justice, normally a Justice of the Peace would swear out an arrest warrant and place it in the hands of a lawman. During Territorial days, constables, County sheriffs and or their deputies as well as private citizens arrested the sixteen men who were eventually hanged for their crime. After statehood, law enforcement officers and their legalized posses made the vast majority of the arrests.

Montana Law Enforcement

Law enforcement has obviously changed over the years from the Territorial days and early years of statehood until the last legal execution was conducted in 1943, and beyond. In the late summer of 1864, Governor Edgerton ordered a census of the Territory in order to establish representation for the first legislature and he appointed Judge Tufts to conduct the survey. After the census it was determined that twenty thousand people inhabited Montana Territory. That same September, Governor Edgerton appointed a sheriff, justice of the peace, a clerk and from two to three commissioners for each of the original five counties. After those first appointments, the citizens of the counties elected those officers.

Sheriff Davidson
"Anaconda Standard" 9/12/1899

What most people today don't realize or appreciate is the conditions in which the territorial and first state sheriffs had to conduct their office. First of all there was no real way of collecting taxes and without revenues it was difficult to compensate any of the county officers. Before the communities were able to raise funds in order to build jails, the sheriff was required to house criminals in their own cabins or businesses. Early jails were usually a one-room cabin made from two log structures built one inside the other. The builders then poured sand, gravel and crushed rock between the two log walls making it difficult to cut through or tunnel under. Even with a county jail, the sheriff was generally forced to use his personal residence or place of business as his office from which to conduct his municipal duties.

The early Montana sheriffs received very little or no compensation for the position and they subsidized their poor salaries by collecting various fees and fines along with receiving allowances for the feeding and maintenance of the county prisoners. The sheriffs were also paid an allowance for transporting convicted prisoners to the penitentiary. An example of these fees and allowances was found in the court records concerning the arrest of Thomas King in 1889. Jefferson County. Sheriff Halford received two dollars for serving the arrest warrant on King, one buck for committing him into his jail, thirty cents for mileage and another forty cents in miscellaneous fees for a total of three dollars and seventy cents. As the county governments grew financially, they were able to build newer jails, which not only contained cells for the criminals and offices for the jailer but quarters for the sheriff and his family. With his living quarters provided for by the county, a frugal sheriff who managed his budget well could do alright financially.

Sheriff Thomas M. Shaw
"Anaconda Standard" 3/17/1900

Another misconception about the early-day lawmen in the West is their use of the horse. Very few of our hanging subjects were captured on horseback and even fewer were transported on a saddle horse. The majority of arrests were made on foot and most of the suspected murderers were transported by wagon, buggy, trains and later of course by automobile. Except for the four Indians, Pierre Paul, La La See, Pascale and Antley along with William Gay who were all at large for over a year before they were captured and Seth Danner who's crime wasn't even discovered for a couple of years, most of the murderers who were eventually hanged in Montana were apprehended within days or at most a month or two.

Four of the fugitive murderers left the state and had to be returned to Montana to face justice. In each case the Montana law officers had to get the proper paperwork from the Governor's office at Helena before leaving the state. Then before being able to return to the Montana with their prisoner they had to personally get the approval from the out-of-state authorities. When retuning on public transportation the officers generally kept their prisoners heavily chained up and often employed an "Oregon-Boot," which made even walking very uncomfortable.

Unfortunately nine law enforcement officers were killed while arresting criminals who eventually were hanged in Montana. Meagher County Deputies William Rader and James Macke were both shot and killed in 1893 while they were in pursuit of William Gay; Juan Cuellae shot down Billings Police Officer Enos M. Nelson in 1917, and Albert Yeik murdered the unsuspecting Beaverhead County Sheriff Cyrus Wyman in April of 1920. Joseph Reagin shot and killed Treasure County

Undersheriff Irving Keeler while the officer was guarding stolen property in December of 1921; Livingston Police Chief Peter Holt and Patrolman Martin Zollman were murdered together in the station house in August of 1929. Seventy-six-year old Miles City Police Sergeant James Fraser was killed while answering a domestic violence call in August of 1935, and three years later wealthy rancher, Lee Simpson killed wounded and defenseless Golden Valley County Undersheriff Arthur Burford as if he was an injured horse.

Preliminary Hearing or Examination:

When a suspect was brought into custody he would then be brought before a Justice of the Peace or Probate Judge who would hear the defendant's plea, set bail, and in some cases assign counsel. While some of the defendants later received some support from their families in their appeals, only three of the seventy-one murders that were hanged in Montana, George Bryson, Joseph Hurst and Lee Simpson hired their own attorneys. Just prior to the convening of the District Court, the Grand Jury would meet and if the prisoner was indicted he would be assigned a court date and placed on trial.

The way the justice system of today seems to be strangling on red tape and technicalities, a person would easily assume that in the good-old days when Montana was still a territory the defendants didn't get much of a defense. Actually the facts prove that the defendants received more trials and appeals during the last twenty-five years of the Nineteenth Century than they did during the next forty-three years. For the first sixteen murder cases, which ended in hangings, there were eighteen jury trials, nineteen appeals to the high court of the Territory and one case was even filed with the United States Supreme Court. Of the last six hanging cases in Montana during the 1930's and 40's, only three defendants received a jury trial and there were only three appeals filed.

In all, for the seventy-one men legally hanged in Montana there were seventy jury trials, fifty-two appeals taken to the Territorial or State Supreme Court and two cases were filed to the highest court of the United States. John Hart received three jury trials before he was finally hanged in 1888, and two other men were re-tried, William Sterres who was executed at Helena in 1875, and John Burns who died on the gallows at Missoula in 1892. Four murderers, George Rock, George Criner, Frank Robideau and Philip Coleman pleaded guilty at their preliminary examinations and were sentenced to death by the judge. These four men were among the quickest to be legally executed including Coleman who was hanged the fastest, having only lived forty-eight days from the time of his crime until his execution. Frank Robideau received the second quickest justice, having only lived fifty-one days after he murdered his victims. In contrast, because his murders weren't discovered for nearly two years, Seth Danner didn't pay for his crimes until one thousand and forty-three days.

While at least thirteen of the condemned men attempted to escape from jail, two were successful. James Martin escaped from the Silver Bow County Jail with several other inmates but he was recaptured the following day. Roy Walsh broke out of the Jefferson County Jail and he was at large for three months before being discovered in Missouri and returned to Boulder. Francois Robert, Monte and William Harris all attempted to escape by cutting the bars to their cells while Joseph Koble and Orlando tried to dig their way out of confinement. William Calder made a club from a pipe after taking his sink apart while Anthony Vettere had fashioned a knife from a spoon, which he had sharpened by rubbing it on the concrete floor of his cell. John Douglas had first talked his guards into letting him have a clock in his cell and then attempted to use the mainspring as a saw to cut the bars of his cell. Thomas Harding tried to orchestrate an unsuccessful jail break among the other inmates; Calvin Christie made it as far as the jail yard before he was driven back by a neighborhood dog and John Burns tried to drug his deathwatch.

The Montana Court

Since the first District Courts in Montana had jurisdiction over more than one county, the judges had to travel from one county seat to another accompanied by their recorder, District Attorney and a core of attorneys, which followed the circuit court. Individual County Attorneys eventually replaced the District Attorneys and in time more judges were added and travel was reduced or eliminated.

Before courthouses were built in Montana, District Courts were held in any suitable building available in the county seat including hotels, saloons and even in private residences. In most cases the

Examining a witness in Judge William Clancy's courtroom at Butte in 1900
"Anaconda Standard" 9/25/1900

furniture and fixtures were arranged so that the judge had the advantage of height and comfort. Often his table towered above all others when it was stacked on top of two or more other tables and sometimes he had the only chair in the place. Usually all the attorneys, both prosecution and defense sat at one long table along with the defendant. While the jury was usually provided with chairs, the lawyers generally sat on stools and the folks in the gallery either stood or were accommodated with benches.

Attorneys

While the Judges are discussed in the "Hanging Judges" Table, there have been a few attorneys in Montana's past that are worth noting. The first District Attorney to successfully send a murderer to the gallows was Colonel John A. Johnson or Johnston. After helping to hang William Wheatley on August 13, 1875, the Colonel went on to send four more men to the gallows; William Sterres in October 1875; Joseph Koble and Orlando Marsh, October of 1879, and finally Peter Pelkey in February of 1881. As State Attorney General, Wellington D. Rankin assisted in sending four men to their deaths on the gallows; Joseph Reagin and Glenna Bolton in February of 1923; Seth Danner, July of 1924, and Lee Simpson in December of 1939.

The man who defended more doomed men than any other attorney was John H. Duffy of Butte. He tried to save five defendants including Thomas Harding at Dillon who was hanged in March of 1887; John Hart at Helena, February of 1888; Harry Roberts at Butte, August of 1889; George Rock at Deer Lodge, June of 1908, and William Hayes, also at Deer Lodge in April of 1909. Cornelius B. Nolan helped defend William Biggerstaff who was hanged in April of 1896, and then as State Attorney General he assisted in the prosecution of William Calder who was hanged in March of 1900, and Joseph Hurst who also died on the gallows in March of 1900. James M. Clements helped defend William Gay who was eventually hanged in June of 1896; Joseph Allen, in 1899, and then as District Judge he presided over the trial of James Fleming, hanged in September of 1901, and Clinton Dotson who was executed in April of 1902.

Of the old-time attorneys, Colonel Wilbur F. Sanders successfully prosecuted George Ives in the most celebrated Miners' Court trial and then he went on to help assist in the unsuccessful defense of William Gay who was hanged in 1896. William Y. Pemberton had by far the most experience with the various types of Montana justice having served as recorder during the George Ives Miners' Court trial in December of 1863; consulted with James Brady before he was hanged by the Original Vigilantes in June of 1864; helped prosecute Thomas Harding who was eventually executed at Dillon in March of 1887, and after becoming the Chief Justice of the State Supreme Court in 1893, he was involved with at least ten of the cases, which ultimately resulted in the deaths of Robert Anderson, John Osnes, Calvin Christie, Clay Pugh, Joseph Cadotte, Bill Biggerstaff and Bill Gay.

The Jurors

In Montana only men could sit on juries until 1918, when the laws were finally changed giving women Political rights.[7] That same year the first all-woman jury in Montana served over a civil case at Reed Point but no female ever sat on a capital case where a man was hanged. To serve on a jury a man had to be of legal age, be a citizen of the United States and able to speak and understand the English language. The strategies used in the early criminal trials weren't as elaborate as they are today and for the James Martin trial in 1902, the prosecuting attorney selected any juror who wasn't against the death penalty while the defense attorney only disqualified men that had any dealings with the county attorney or his office.

Over the years in Montana there have been at least eleven men who have had the distinction of severing on more than one jury that had sentenced a man to his death who was eventually hanged. Between 1875 and 1899 there were five citizens of Lewis and Clark County that served on two separate murder cases and in Missoula County there were the same number of jurors doing double duty between 1890 and 1892. One man served on two different juries in Jefferson County sixteen years apart.

Abner Adams of Helena, not only served on William Sterres' first trial in 1875, but he was also on the panel that found Patrick Hart guilty in his third trial in 1888.

William Channel of Jefferson County found George Bryson guilty in 1889 and later served on Clay Pugh's jury in 1895.

C.G. Evans of Lewis and Clark County sat on the juries of both William Biggerstaff and Bill Gay who were both executed in 1896.

James F. Fletcher of Missoula sat on the trial of the Indian, Pascale in 1890, and then later served on the jury of John Burns who was hanged in 1892.

J. McDonald of Missoula sat on the trials of both Antley and Pascale, two Indians who were executed in December of 1890.

Thomas J. McNamara of Missoula, like James Fletcher, served on the jury of Pascale who was hanged in 1890, and then later he sat on the panel that found John Burns guilty sending him to death in 1892.

M.H. Pierce of Missoula served on the same juries as Mr. J. McDonald (See above), which found the two Indians, Antley and Pascale.

Frank Primont of Missoula also served with J. McDonald and M.H. Pierce on the separate juries of the Indians, Antley and Pascale before they were hanged in December of 1890.

Fred Sass of Helena, like Mr. C. G. Evans served on the juries of both William Biggerstaff and Bill Gay who were both executed in 1896.

Henry Schotte of Lewis and Clark County served with C.G. Evans and Fred Sass on the juries that found both Biggerstaff and William Gay guilty before they were put to death in 1896.

Joe H. Smith of Lewis and Clark County sat on the jury that found Peter Pelkey guilty of murder in 1880, and he later served on the panel that sent Joseph Allen to death in 1899.

Judge's Instructions to the Jury before Deliberation

Before their deliberation, the jury is given instructions by the judge and sometimes they were short and at times they were long and detailed. The following is the actual instructions that Judge B.E. Berg made in 1929, to the jurors in the Rollin Davisson case.

"Gentlemen of the jury: The Court gives you the following instructions as to the law by which you will arrive at your verdict. The defendant is charged by an information filed in this Court with the crime of first-degree murder, alleged to have been committed in the County of Park, State of Montana, on or about the twenty-first day of August A.D. 1929.

"To this charge the defendant has entered a plea of not guilty, which plea raises an issue to be tried by the jury and the state is required to prove beyond a reasonable doubt every material allegation charged in the information.

"To guide you in your deliberations in this case the Court gives you the following instructions:

"Murder is the unlawful killing of a human being with malice aforethought, such malice may be express or implied. It is express when there is manifested a deliberate intention unlawfully to take away the life of a fellow creature; it is implied when no considerable provocation appears or when the circumstances attending the killing shows an abandoned and malignant heart.

"The law of this state provides that all murder which is perpetrated by means of poison or lying in wait, torture or by any other kind of willful, deliberate and premeditated killing, or which is committed in the perpetration or attempt to perpetrate arson, rape, burglary, robbery or mayhem, is murder in the first degree.

"The law of the state provides that every, person guilty of murder in the first degree, shall suffer death, or may be imprisoned for life.

"To constitute murder in the first degree, the unlawful killing must be accompanied by a deliberate and clear intent to take the life of a human being, except in cases where the unlawful killing is done in the perpetration, or the attempt to perpetrate arson, rape, robbery, burglary or mayhem, in which case the manner of the killing is held to be conclusive evidence of premeditation and deliberation.

"The intent to kill must be the result of deliberate premeditation; it must be formed upon a pre-existing reflection, and not upon a sudden heat of passion sufficient to preclude the idea of deliberation. There need not be any appreciable space of time, between the formation of the intention to kill and act of killing; they may be as instantaneous as successive thoughts of the mind. It is only necessary that the act of killing be preceded by a concurrence of will, deliberation and premeditation on the part of the slayer; and if such is the case, the killing is murder in the first degree, no matter how rapidly these acts of the mind may succeed each other, or how quickly they may be followed by the act of killing.

"The circumstances from which deliberation and premeditation may be inferred in cases of homicide are various; they may consist of threats, preparation of weapons, search for the victim, absence of provocation,

dangerous nature of the instrument used and the manner of using it.

"The jury are instructed that the deliberate intention called malice aforethought need only be such deliberation and thought as enables a person to appreciate and understand, at the time the act was committed the nature of his act and its probable results.

"To constitute malice aforethought no particular time need intervene between the formation of the intention and the act; it is enough if the intent to commit the act, with a full appreciation of the result likely to follow, was present at the time the act was committed, and that the act was not the result of some sudden heat of passion provoked by some cause calculated to override the judgment and before sufficient time elapsed for reason to resume its sway.

"Malice as used in the phrase 'malice aforethought,' includes not only anger, hatred and revenge, but every unlawful and unjustifiable motive. It is not confined to ill-will toward one or more individual persons, but it is intended to denote an action flowing from any wicked or corrupt motive and thing done with a wicked mind, where the act has been attended with such circumstances as to carry in them the plain indications of a heart regardless of social duty and fatally bent on mischief; therefore, malice is implied from any deliberate or cruel act against another, however sudden.

"The word 'willfully' when applied to the intent, with which an act is done or omitted, implies simply a purpose or willingness to commit the act or make the omission referred to. It does not require any intent to violate law, or to injure another, or to acquire any advantage.

"The word 'deliberately' means in a cool state of the blood, that is not in heat of passion.
'Premeditated' means thought of before hand for any length of time, however short.

"Upon a trial for murder, the commission of the homicide by the defendant being proved, the burden of proving circumstances of mitigation, or that justify or excuses it devolves upon him, unless the proof on the part of the prosecution tends to show that the crime committed only amounts to manslaughter, or that the defendant was justifiable or excusable.

"In every crime or public offense there must exist a union or joint operation of act and intent, or criminal negligence. The intent or intention is manifested by the circumstances connected with the offense and the sound mind and discretion of the accused. All persons are of sound mind who are neither idiots nor lunatics nor affected with insanity. And under the laws of this state when an unlawful act is shown to have been deliberately committed for the purposes of injuring another it is presumed to have been committed with a malicious and guilty intent. The law also presumes that a person intents the ordinary consequences of any voluntary act committed by him. The latter presumption, however, is termed a disputable presumption and may be controverted by other evidence.

"The Court instructs the jury that in their consideration of this case they will only consider the evidence of the witnesses upon the witness

stand and such documentary evidence as has been by the Court admitted in evidence; and they are further instructed that it is their duty to in no wise consider or regard any remarks of counsel in this case which are not supported by the evidence as given by the witnesses on the witness stand, and no juror shall allow himself to be influenced in any degree by anything which he may have read in any book, paper or pamphlet, or other written or printed matter which may have been seen or read by him, outside of the evidence and exhibits in this case.

"The Court instructs the jury that a defendant in a criminal action cannot be compelled to be a witness against himself, but he may be sworn and may testify in his own behalf, and the jury in judging of his credibility and the weight to be given to his testimony may take into consideration the fact that he is the defendant and the nature and the enormity of the crime of which he is accused. If the defendant does not claim the right to be sworn or does not testify, it must not be used to his prejudice, and the county attorney prosecuting must not comment to the Court or jury on the same."[8]

The Jury's Verdict

After the closing arguments and instructions from the judge, the jury retired to deliberate their verdict. Immediately after leaving the courtroom the jury normally took a vote and if the poll wasn't unanimous the panel would debate the case until everyone agreed. When the jury agreed on a verdict they would notify the bailiff who would then call the judge and other officers. Of the thirty-nine cases where accurate deliberation times were reported, they average the juries were out was 5.48 hours. Two juries returned after only ten minutes, the first trial of William Sterres who was hanged in October of 1875, and the third hearing for John Hart who was executed in February of 1888.

Henry Furhmann who was hanged in May of 1883, and Joseph Hurst who forfeited his life on the gallows in March of 1900, were both found guilty of first-degree murder after twenty-four hours of deliberation. During the years between 1875, and statehood the average deliberation was 8.7 hours; after 1890, until the Twentieth Century the average was 4.5 hours. Between 1900, and the Roaring Twenties the jurors were out an average of 2.4 hours and during the 1930's and 40's the juries deliberated for 5.9 hours.

While waiting for the parties to return to the courtroom, the twelve-man jury on the Dan Lucy case in 1900, began singing several popular songs, which could be heard throughout the courthouse. Once the judge and the attorneys were present in the crowded courtroom the deputies brought in the prisoner to hear the verdict. The jury would then take their box and the foreman would hand the verdict to the clerk who would in turn present it to the judge. While presiding over the Clay Pugh case in 1895, Judge Frank Showers was visibly moved after reading the verdict and his hands trembled as he handed it back to the clerk.

There were a number of cases where the defense filed motions for a new trial on the grounds of jury misconduct including the third hearing for John Hart when the jurors were accused of drinking liquor with their meals and openly discussing the facts outside of the courthouse. While Judge McConnell didn't grant another trial, he severely reprimanded the jury and fined eight of the jurors twenty-five dollars each and levied the same fine to both the county bailiff in the case as well as a deputy marshal. John Hart was eventually hanged in February of 1888.

Most of the courtrooms were described as being deathly silent from the time the prisoner was brought into the courtroom and until after the jury's verdict was read. The suspense was almost at a feverish pitch as the clerk of court took the slip of paper from the foreman of the jury and then carefully recorded the decision into his log before he formerly announced the verdict. The tension increased in the Missoula courtroom in 1892, when Clerk John Sloane quietly got up and announced to Judge Marshall that the foreman on the John Burns jury had signed the verdict in pencil instead of ink as was required. After the error was corrected Clerk Sloane then read the guilty verdict.

An example of a typical verdict was that of the Dan Lucy case in 1900, which read:

"State of Montana, plaintiff, vs. Daniel Lucy, defendant: Verdict, We, the jury in the above entitled case, find the defendant, Daniel Lucy, guilty of murder in the first degree. (Signed) A.J. White, foreman."[9]

If the jury came in with a guilty verdict they generally had the option of fixing the penalty at death or they could leave it up to the judge to set the punishment. Later on the State Legislature removed the option from the jury and required the judge sentence the person convicted of first-degree murder to death. Normally after the clerk read the verdict, the defense attorney or the judge would ask that the jury be polled and each man would answer "Guilty" after his name was called.

Eighteen-year-old Miss Vera Anderson became the first woman to ever read a verdict, which sent Lu Sing to the gallows in April of 1906. Miss Anderson was the deputy clerk of Court of Gallatin County and while her father, Clerk of Court Charles Anderson was absent she had the somber duty of recording and reading the verdict and the polling of the jury. It was reported that while the young lady turned a bit pale, she did a fine job. Besides being the first woman to read a guilty verdict to a man who was eventually hanged, she was probably the youngest woman to ever hold the position of deputy clerk of court in Montana.

Court's Pre-Sentencing Statement

Calvin Christie appeared in court before Judge Dudley DuBose as cool and collected as he had during his trial and he gave no outward sign that he was concerned in the proceedings and the sentence, which would send him to eternity. Long before the session was opened the courtroom was filled to overflowing and it came to a hush as the judge entered.

Judge DuBose was visibly affected by the unpleasant duty before him and when asked if he had any legal cause to show the court why judgment should not be pronounced Christie only said he had committed murder. Before pronouncing the sentence Judge DuBose said:

"Christie, on an occasion like this, when we are almost in the presence of death itself, it seems to the court that whatever it might say regarding the enormity of your crime would have no effect. It might seemingly degenerated only in a buzz of a helpless man, and it certainly would not lesson the force of that climax which the law has incorporated into its penal code when it says that any man who maliciously, willfully and premeditatedly takes the life of another shall suffer death. Thus have you broken the law, and thus will you suffer.

"Some four months ago in this courtroom I advised you that you were in a serious predicament, and now you stand on the threshold of eternity. I gave you this advice: Do not let hopes which may prove false prevent you from today making your peace with your maker."[10]

Sentencing

Both Friday and the number "13" were at one time closely associated with capital punishment in British tradition and they were later carried on in the United States. Friday was the standard day for public hangings and because of the tradition of having 13 steps up to the gallows, an execution held on Friday the Thirteenth had particular significance. The Hanging Judges of Montana continued the tradition with most of the condemned men being initially sentenced to be hanged on a Friday. Even with delays and time constraints caused by the appeals process, more than sixty-four percent of the men legally hanged in Montana died on the gallows on a Friday.

By statute, the presiding judges was required to set the date of execution not less than thirty days and not more than sixty days after sentencing. This particular tradition persisted throughout the sixty-eight-year history of Legal Hangings in Montana and it is illustrated by the fact that both the first and last man was hanged on a Friday. Three of these men were hanged on Friday the Thirteenth including the first man legally executed in Montana, William Wheatley on August 13, 1875 and later Robert Anderson and John Osnes were hanged in separate counties but on July 13, 1894.

Judge Decius S. Wade had the unenviable distinction of sentencing the first two men to be hanged in Montana on June 28, 1875. On that day Judge Wade ordered the death of William Sterres and William Wheatley individually with the following death sentence:

"The jurors of the Grand Jury at this term of court presented an indictment charging you with murder of Franz Warl, late of the county of Lewis and Clark and Territory of Montana. Upon this indictment you were arraigned and plead not guilty. Thereupon able counsel was assigned to make your defense. A trial before an honest, impartial jury ensued. Nothing in your behalf was left undone, and a verdict of guilty, as charged in the indictment, of murder in the first degree, was returned into court. You are now at the bar of the court for sentence. Have you anything to say for your life; anything to say why you should not be hanged by the neck until dead, that your crime may be punished and the law vindicated and enforced?"

Sterres who was first sentenced didn't say anything except

to request that the judge give him as much time he could before his execution. The judge continued,

"With the verdict of the jury I am confident. It is the inevitable, unavoidable result of the evidence in the case. Franz Warl is dead, and you, with deliberation and malice helped to kill him. Believing thus beyond a doubt, I go forward unfalteringly to my duty. If life to you is sweet, and you look forward with terror and alarm to the dread hour when it shall be taken from you, you must remember the kind, unoffending old man whom you so savagely murdered; remember that to him the pleasures of living an honest, useful life, serving and obeying the commands of the God whom he loved, brought with it joy and bliss unspeakable; remember that he was an honest man; that he earned his bread by the sweat of his brow; that he feared not the labor, and he lived by the industry of his work; that he trespassed not upon the rights of his fellow men, and least of all had never injured you; remember that he had friends far away who even now are looking for his return to the old home after a long absence in a foreign land: Perhaps his children are there, fondly waiting to embrace and to bless him; perhaps the wife of his youth and his love is still clinging to the hope that soon she will see the father of her children and the husband of her heart, and remembering all this, behold the ruin your bloody hand has wrought! Franz Warl is dead. He to whom the almighty lord gave an immortal soul, and a habitation and a dwelling place upon this earth of His, you had brutally and wickedly murdered for his gold. The hills and valleys that surround the humble house of your victim will never again echo to the sound of his manly voice. The two agonizing cries that he uttered, when you with the fatal slung shot fractured his skull, were his last. The smoke curling from his cabin will no longer admonish the passer by that he lives. No more will he bring upon the streets the products of his toil. He is dead, and you killed him. This life, so precious, so priceless, so sacred, given and bestowed as the bounty of Love and Humanity, disregarding every dictate of right, reason and justice, dead to every impulse of kindness, mercy and honesty, and actuated only by your fiendish love of money, have savagery destroyed, and even now the blood of your victim is dripping from your unholy hands.

"For this crime you must die. Human life is not secure and safe while you live. You have forfeited your right to life and must suffer the penalty that a wise and just law affixes to your crime. And it is better thus. The remembrance of your crime would render all your future life a living agony, when the pricks and stings of an upbraiding conscience would be the gnawing of the worm that never dies. With this terrible burden resting on your soul, haunting the hours when you wake and until you sleep, polluting the very air you breathe, burdening every breath, giving you not a moment's peace or rest, rendering every joy and dissolution, listening even to the pitiful cry of your victim, hearing it even in the light of day and darkness of night. Being reminded of it by every sound, hearing it in the air when all else was still, and as each recurring day brought with it the hour when the fatal deed was done, recalling more vividly than ever the form and the pleading features of him you so wickedly murdered, you

would sooner welcome death as a happy deliverance from the terrors of a life that could no longer be endured. There is no rest for the wicked; there is no peace for the murderer. If the law fails to administer justice for the crime, the criminal himself will be his own executioner: Self-destruction is often the silent confession of murder. And so it is better that you die and thereby escape the agony of life, for in the wise economy of Providence if you could live to ripe old age, you could never live another happy moment. It is better that you answer the demands of the law than to die to satisfy your own conscience.

"What adverse circumstances have so surrounded your life as to bring upon you this overshadowing ruin, I cannot conjecture. Dark and dismal must have been your pathway. Terrible indeed must be the road that leads to murder, and it is only reached by slow approaches. There is a regular progression of crime. Idleness, intemperance, and a desire to get money without honest labor, must have been the commencement of your career and where you now stand is the legitimate end. Your one-year of life in this city has but illustrated this truth. You have spent your time and your money at the gambling table, at the vestibule to the temple of crime, and the insatiable greed for money engendered there has led you on to murder. In this awful moment I know not how to comfort or to console you. I can give you no hope. You must die, and I can only bid you to hasten and repent of your sins, and to implore God of mercy to forgive you.

"It only remains for me to pronounce the dread sentence that inexorable law and even handed justice demands. Only the infinite Lord knows how gladly I would escape the responsibility of uttering these fatal words. But duty commands, and though the hardest task of my life, I unflinchingly obey. Now, therefore the sentence of this court is:

"That you, William H. Sterres, alias 'Red,' be removed from the courtroom and detained in close custody in the jail of the county, and thence taken on Friday, the thirteenth day of August, Anno Domini, one thousand eight hundred and seventy-five, to the place fixed by law for execution, and then and there, between the hours of eleven o'clock a.m., and three o'clock p.m. of said day, be hung by the neck until you are dead. And may God in His infinite goodness have mercy on your soul."

When Judge Wade had completed Sterres' sentence he ordered William Wheatly to stand and again the convict claimed his innocence and then the judge repeated the same sentence for him. Thus ended the first sentencing hearing in Montana that ended in the first two legal hangings. While Sterres and Wheatley were both scheduled to hang on Friday the Thirteenth of August 1875, an appeal postponed Sterres' eventual execution until October of that year.

While Judge Wade's death sentence of Sterres and Wheatley was quite long some like the one rendered by Judge DuBose in the Calvin Christie Case was short and sweet:

"That whereas the said Calvin Christie having been duly convicted in this court of the crime of murder in the first degree, it is therefore ordered, adjudged and decreed that you, Calvin J. Christie be taken to the county jail of Flathead County until Friday, the 28th day of September A.D. 1894,

and that upon that day and between the hours of 9 o'clock in the forenoon and 5 o'clock in the afternoon of that day, you be taken hence to some suitable and private enclosure to be provided by the sheriff so near the said jail as possible and there and then you be hanged by the neck until you shall be Dead, Dead, Dead, and may God have mercy upon you."[11]

Christie listened to the remarks and judgment of the court with apparently cool indifference. He didn't display any nervousness except a minor twitch of his face. Criminals have a great pride in affecting a brave air and meeting their doom gamely, and with the shadow of the hangman's noose before his eyes, Christie still maintained his composure and he did meet his death calmly and without flinching.

Stay of Execution by the Governor

Immediately after the conviction, the defense would generally request a new trial and in every case except for one the presiding judge denied the motion. Justice Wade was the only presiding judge to grant a re-trial to a defendant who was eventually hanged in Montana, that of William Sterres in 1875. As Chief Justice of the Montana Territorial Supreme Court, Judge Wade would have granted the new trial anyway since he reportedly wanted to delay the sentencing in the hopes that the prisoner's co-conspirator would be captured and brought to justice.

When the judge denied the motion for a new trial the defense would then appeal to the Governor for a "Stay of Execution" in order to provide the convicted prisoner enough time for an appeal to the Supreme Court. After 1895, this action wasn't necessary as the mere act of filing a motion for an appeal to the Supreme Court by the defense caused an automatic stay until the case could be heard by the high court.

In 1878, with only two days before the scheduled execution if Michael McAndrews at Radersburg, acting Governor James H. Mills made the following order:

"To Allen M. Easterly, sheriff whereas, you now have in your custody one Michael McAndrews, under and by virtue of a warrant issued out of the district court of the first judicial district within and for Jefferson County, Montana Territory, commanding you to execute the said Michael McAndrews, by hanging him by the neck until dead, on the twenty-fifth day of January 1878, between the hours of ten o'clock a.m. and three o'clock p.m. of said; and

whereas, it further appears to me that the said Michael McAndrews has filed an application in the Supreme Court of Montana Territory for a writ of habeas corpus, which said writ was by said court denied; and

whereas, the said Michael McAndrews has sued out, and been allowed a writ of error from the Supreme Court of the Territory of Montana to the Supreme Court of the United States; and

whereas, good cause has been shown to me for prolonging the time for the execution of said Michael McAndrews, in that his said writ of error would be unavailable to him unless execution of the sentence is suspended during the time he is prosecuting the same; and

whereas the power to suspend or prolong the said sentence is not vested in the judge of said court, or any other person or tribunal except the Governor;

"Now, I, James H. Mills, Secretary and Acting Governor of Montana Territory, by virtue of the power and authority vested in me by law, under section 378, page 546, codified statutes of Montana Territory, do command you, the said sheriff of said county to refrain and desist from executing the said Michael McAndrews, as in said warrant at the time therein provided. And the said execution of said sentence is hereby suspended and prolonged until the first day of March 1878, which day, between the hours of ten o'clock a.m. and three o'clock p.m., you will cause the said execution of the same Michael McAndrews as directed by said warrant, to be had in the manner and form therein directed.

"In witness where of, I have hereunto set my hand and affirm the great seal of the Territory of Montana, this twenty-third day of January 1878."[12]

(Signed) James H. Mills

While we haven't tallied the number of times that Montana Governors have granted commuted sentences, we know that Governor John E. Rickards had declined to act more than any other top executive. As Acting Governor in 1890, Rickards refused to save Thomas King; as Governor he refused to interfere with the executions of Robert Anderson, John Osnes and Calvin Christie in 1894; Clay Pugh and Joseph Cadotte in 1895 and William Biggerstaff and Bill Gay in 1896. Governor Joseph M. Dixon decided not to interfere with the legal hangings of seven condemned men from 1921 to 1924. Governors Joseph K. Toole and Robert B. Smith each denied clemency to six doomed men while the latter top executive had successfully prosecuted to men prior to becoming the head of state.

Notice of Appeal

On the eve of her son's execution, Mrs. Adams drove all night long with the following notice to appeal on behalf of Henry John Zorn:

"To the plaintiff, John Zorn to County Attorney of Custer County. You and each of you will please take notice, and you and each of you are hereby notified that the defendant, Henry John Zorn, hereby appeals to the Supreme Court of the State of Montana. From that certain judgment of conviction made, rendered and entered in the sixteenth District Court of the State of Montana, in and for the County of Custer wherein the State of Montana is plaintiff and Henry John Zorn is the defendant, which said judgment of conviction was made, rendered and entered on the sixth day of October 1934, wherein and whereby the defendant, Henry John Zorn, was convicted of the crime of murder in the first degree and sentenced to pay the penalty of death by execution.

"The appeal is taken upon questions of law and of fact. Dated Miles City, Montana this thirteenth day of November 1934."[13] (Signed) Henry J. Zorn.

The Typical Montana Execution

Since hanging was the legal form of execution in both the Territory and State of Montana, the sheriff would begin his planning by either making arrangements to borrow a gallows from another county or have a scaffold built locally.

Because all legal hangings in Montana were to be private, the sheriff would also order the construction of an enclosure high enough to prevent curious eyes from witnessing the execution. While some sheriffs even took pains in filling the cracks and knotholes in the fences along with posting guards on the scaffolding as a safe guard, other authorities apparently ordered the required barrier to meet the letter of the law and then allowed mobs of people to view the hanging from nearby buildings, trees, railroad cars and other vantage points.

In most cases little was needed to be done other than to build a fence and erect the gallows but in 1904, Sheriff Thompson of Missoula County had to direct his staff and prisoners to first clear the piles of firewood behind the jail to make room for the scaffold. The wood was then stacked along the fence making it perfect seating for the mobs of unofficial witnesses to the Louis Mott hanging in March of 1904.

For the triple hanging of Frank Fisher, John O'Neil and Sherman Powell in January of 1918, the sheriff of Silver Bow County ordered the kitchen building of the old jail torn down so that the trap-type scaffold, ***Gallows No. Sixteen: (Jan. 1918) "Galloping Gallows" No. Five*** could be constructed over the stairway leading down to the basement of the courthouse.

The preparations for the execution of Joseph Vuckovich in February of 1922, also involved extra work because of the frozen ground at Missoula. Small bon fires were required to thaw the soil for the digging of the postholes and small children were often seen playing around the dancing flames while the workers were constructing the tall fence.

Invitations to the Execution

By law, the sheriff was required to be present at the execution, invite a physician, the county attorney and at least "twelve reputable citizens," and at the request of the condemned man, no more than two priests or ministers of the gospel, or any other persons, relatives or friends, not exceed five to be present at the execution along with such officers the officer deemed necessary to witness the execution. Also allowed to attend the hanging was the sheriff's staff, the presiding judge and the officers of the court along with members of the press. No other person than those mentioned was to be present at the execution, nor could women or any person under age be allowed to witness the hanging.[19]

Even with these restrictions some Montana sheriffs had large numbers of witnesses including Sheriff Thomas Shaw who mailed out seventy-one invitations for the hanging of Billy Calder at Lewistown in 1900. Missoula County Sheriff Harry W. Thompson invited one hundred and fifty people at the execution of Louis Mott in 1904, and Sheriff

George Nagues requested the same number of witnesses for the triple hanging at White Sulphur Springs in 1917.

The obvious loophole in the regulations that many of the sheriffs took advantage of was the phrase: "along with such officers he deems necessary to witness the execution." Missoula County Sheriff Charles Berry skirted the rules by making it clear that by accepting his invitation to the hanging of Ah Yung in 1883, each witness agreed to act as a special guard at the execution. Another example of the use of this loophole was in 1896 when Sheriff Jurgens stepped out onto the back steps of the Lewis and Clark County Jail and asked the people in the crowd waiting for the hanging of William Biggerstaff if they were willing to act as deputies in case there was any trouble. The crowd cried out, "We will, Sheriff!"

OFFICE OF SHERIFF

Missoula County, Montana

Missoula, Montana, Dec. 8th, 1890

Mr. Hon. T. L. Greenough

Dear Sir:—You are respectfully invited to be present at the execution of Pierre Paul, Lala See, Pascale and Antley, Friday, the 19th day of December, A. D. 1890, at 10:30 A. M., at the Missoula County Jail.

Yours very respectfully,
W. H. Houston
SHERIFF

From the collection of Jack Weidenfeller of Missoula

At least two legal hangings in Montana were actually crashed by the citizens of the county. One report stated that every miner at Red Lodge turned out to see that nothing interfered with the execution of Thomas Salmon in January of 1899, and the nearly two thousand miners and their wives and children crashed into the enclosure and clustered around the gallows. Later in 1938, a crowd of about three hundred spectators crashed into a building at Columbus to witness the hanging of Frank Robideau.

Invitations were generally printed on three-by-five-inch cards with black-borders and often included a sketch or photograph of the condemned man but Sheriff John Anderson merely used department stationary for the execution of Ferdinand Schlaps in May of 1927. For the multiple hanging at Missoula in December of 1890, Sheriff Houston had the sketches of the four Indians, Pierre Paul, La La See, Antley and

Pascale printed on the backside of the invitations. And o'er its wasted desert blow

The typical invitation to a Montana hanging was like the following one that Sheriff Hubbard issued for the execution of William Brooks at Billings in 1898.

"You are hereby invited to witness the legal execution of W.C. Brooks for the murder of his wife Jennie Brooks on the eighteenth day of November, 1898. The execution will take place in the city of Billings, Montana, on Friday the twenty-fourth day of November, 1899, between the hours of two a.m. and two p.m. signed Sheriff of Yellowstone County."

Not every sheriff mailed out invitations, Gallatin County Sheriff Smith didn't even have any printed up for the Danner hanging in 1924, and instead he reportedly notified the necessary witnesses individually. While Sheriff Thompson reportedly mailed out about two hundred and fifty invitations statewide for the hanging of Louis Mott in the Garden City, he didn't send one to a single resident of Missoula County.

In general, the sheriff conducting the execution invited most every law enforcement officer in the state. He would obviously invite lawmen that had experience with other hangings to assist him and other officers to keep them abreast with the latest technologies and procedures as well as to gain hands-on experience. Lawmen who attended and assisted in executions after having recently conducted hangings in their own jurisdictions were Teton County Sheriff J.C. Billings, Jefferson County Sheriff Daniel Halford, Sheriff Tom Jones of Beaverhead County, Meagher County Sheriff George B. Nagues, Sheriff John J. Quinn of Butte, Gallatin County Sheriff James Smith and Sheriff Daniel Halford of Boulder.

Sheriffs who attended executions to get hands-on experience just prior to hanging men in their own counties were Missoula County Sheriff George Cole, Sheriff Larry Duggan of Butte, Park County Sheriff Clarence Gilbert, Teton County Sheriff William Hagen, Sheriff John Jurgens of Helena and Sheriff Lloyd of Silver Bow County. Other county officers witnessing hangings to learn how it was done were Chouteau County Sheriff George McLaughlin, Sheriff M. Shaw of Lewistown, Yellowstone County Sheriff George Hubbard, Sheriff P.H. Regan of Butte and Missoula County Sheriff Harry Thompson.

These officers became well acquainted with the various gallows of the state and their operation, which most likely helped them decide whether to borrow a scaffold or have one built. Jefferson County Sheriff Dan Halford holds the distinction of being in charge or assisting in the most hangings. Sheriff Halford was in charge of the hanging of George Bryson in August of 1889, and Thomas King in June of 1890; and then he assisted in the execution of the four Indians, Antley, Peirre Paul, La La See and Pascale at Missoula in 1890, and then Clay Pugh in July of 1895.

The sheriff that witnessed the most legal hangings in Montana without ever conducting an execution himself was Joe Hamilton of Cascade County. Sheriff Hamilton witnessed the hanging of six men including Thomas King in June of 1890, and the execution the four Indians at Missoula in December of that same year. Then in July of 1894, the Cascade County sheriff watched John Osnes walk to the gallows at Fort Benton. Sheriff John Conley of Deer Lodge County came in second with five separate hangings, having witnessed Joseph Allen, Joseph Hurst, Dan Lucy, James Fleming and Clinton Dotson die on the gallows between 1899 and 1902.

Last Minute Preparations

Once the death machine was erected the scaffold was thoroughly tested and after the rope was cut to the proper length it would be stretched, lubricated and the noose waxed. In some cases rope barriers would be strung around the gallows the keep the witnesses back and the death straps were cleaned polished and often pre-fitted on deputies for practice and to reduce the time adjusting them on the condemned man.

In 1906, Sheriff John Quinn personally inspected the gallows and strung the half-inch rope through the pulleys at the top of the scaffold for the Miles Fuller hanging and Sheriff Cole and Deputy James Teevan had the hemp stretched with heavy sandbags for several days before the execution of Joseph Vuckovich in 1922. As Sheriff Halford was making his final inspection of the scaffold for the hanging of Thomas Kink in 1890, he noticed a stray playing card lying face down at the foot of the gallows. Upon turning the card over, the ominous Jack of Clubs appeared.

Setting a Deathwatch

Shortly before or immediately after the prisoner was sentenced to death the sheriff would go before the county commissioners for authorization for a deathwatch to be assigned to prevent the inmate from attempting suicide. Generally once the prisoner was officially sentenced a twenty-four hour watch was placed on the condemned man consisting of from three to four guards. Oftentimes while the prisoner was in the courtroom receiving his sentence, the sheriff's staff would prepare a new cell for the condemned man just in case he had a weapon or drugs stashed in his previous quarters. After being returned to the jail, the prisoner would then often be stripped of his clothing; issued another set of clothes and taken to his new cell generally on death row.

Many of the condemned men did attempt to cheat the gallows including George Bryson, Thomas King, James Fleming and Lee Simpson. Jail personal prevented outsiders from passing poison to both Bryson and King while Fleming tried to slit his wrists and hang himself. Lee Simpson had successfully cut his wrist with a broken glass but a guard in the county jail saved his life but because infection had set in, his arm was eventually amputated.

Religious Counsel

The authorities always called in a spiritual advisor for the condemned man to help prepare him even if the prisoner didn't request one. Of the seventy-one men legally hanged in Montana, nearly forty-eight percent of them were Catholic while almost forty-one percent were Protestant represented mainly by the Presbyterian, Methodist, Baptist and Episcopal Churches. Catholic Fathers Follett and Lawrence B. Palladino each served as religious counsel for three condemned men while Reverend J.M. Hard of the Episcopal Church counseled the three men hanged at one time at White Sulphur Springs in 1917.

Living Conditions on Death Row

The Montana prisoners on death row had all sorts of liberties that the regular prisoners and were generally allowed to repaint and decorate their cells. Generally the guards allowed the prisoners to paint the wall in their cell and allowed them to stick photos, news articles and other items into the fresh color. Frederick LeBeau who was hanged in April of 1909, took particular pride in decorating his cell with red, white and blue tissue paper, not only did he blend the American and French colors he also displayed an emblem of Ireland on the prominent wall. He also decorated his quarters with many paper stars as well as pictures of himself along with portraits of the county sheriff and his defense lawyer. Suspended from the center of his cell hung a huge liberty bell and over the door was a hand-painted sign stating: "Gone, but not forgotten."

Other doomed prisoners decorated their cells with the many flowers, which women callers left including James Fleming who was hanged in September of 1901, and James Martin before he died on the gallows in 1904. Daniel Lucy kept his bouquets of flowers on his small table while Monte Harris who left this world in April of 1923, lined a shelf in his cell with potted flowers from his many lady admirers. To prevent the sentimental women of White Sulphur Springs from idolizing Herbert Metzger before he was hanged in May of 1905, Meagher County Sherman intercepted the many flowers, gifts and notes before they reached the prisoner.

The Last Meal

Besides their accommodations at the jail the condemned man generally ate much better than the rest of the inmates. While most prisoners ate twice a day the condemned prisoner usually received three meals. On their visits to the jail many of the family and friends of the doomed men would leave all sorts of goodies including pies, cakes, cookies and candies of all varieties. A sister of William Biggerstaff sent her brother money so that he could have all of his favorite items including Limburger cheese, which reportedly stunk up the Lewis and Clark County Jail something terrible. While Thomas King, William Brooks, William Pepo and George Hoffman refused their last meal most of the death-row prisoners requested and ate fine meals.

Of the thirty-eight meals reported, five men specifically ordered steaks, while oysters, ham, bacon, or chicken tied for second place with four each. Three death-row prisoners had a turkey dinner while others requested crab, pasties and even a Spanish omelet. Six prisoners only wanted regular prison food while Frederick LeBeau requested the most elaborate meal including a duck stuffed with chicken meat and frosted cake decorated with Easter chicken candies. Ironically, the prisoner who had been a cook and who spent a lot of time discussing his meals wasn't granted his choice of main course. James Fleming had requested fried trout but oddly none was available at Deer Lodge in September of 1901, but he was served the rest of his fare of warm biscuits, hot chocolate, potato chips, boiled eggs with cantaloupe, blackberries, sliced cucumbers, toast and coffee.

The Silver Bow Club of Butte prepared and served elaborate meals to Silver Bow County prisoners, Frank Fisher, John O'Neil, Sherman Powell and Anthony Vettere while the Mexican Juan Cuellae ate very little of his last meal at Billings. Although they could have eaten anything they wanted Daniel Lucy had a piece of toast with tea and Peter Pelkey only had a few crackers. George Rock and Rollin Davisson ate prison food before their executions although the latter man finished his meal off with cake and milk.

A last meal wasn't an issue with Lu Sing who had gone on a hunger strike before his execution in April of 1906, but the staff at the sheriff's office ensured that the inmate was fed. Everyday, sometimes twice a day the deputies and the deathwatch would force Lu Sing down on the floor and while a couple of men held the prisoner down, another deputy would hold the prisoner's nose and pour soup into his mouth. Lu Sing reportedly fought like a bulldog but with two or three men holding him down, he ate pretty well. The Chinaman got at least one good meal each day before his execution, and if the boys on the force didn't have too much to do, they even gave Lu Sing a second meal.

John Hart, Martin Scott, Thomas King and Joseph Allen reportedly had a cigar after their meal and a number of the condemned men were allowed to drink alcohol with and after their final meal. Herbert Metzger was given both beer and whisky at White Sulphur Springs but Frederick Lebeau topped his fancy gourmet meal off at Kalispell with none other than a bottle of champagne, which had been sent to him by a friend just for the occasion. LeBeau said that it was the first time he had ever tried the bubbly liquor and he apparently enjoyed it.

Because of the fear that the prisoners would try to cheat the gallows by injuring themselves with their utensils, they were sometimes fed by hand. Since the sheriff's wife was generally in charge of the jail kitchen, doing all of the cooking for the prisoners, they would often be the person who hand fed the inmates on death row. An example of this was in 1922, when Mrs. George A. Cole, the wife of the sheriff of Missoula County personally fed Joseph Vuckovich before he was hanged.

Final Haircut, Shave and a New Suit

A day or two before the scheduled hanging a barber was generally brought into the jail to give the condemned man his last haircut and shave. In most cases the condemned men tried to be humorous during their last visit with a barber. At Dillon in 1887, Thomas Harding told "Brownie the Barber" not to be too particular because it was going to be his last shave and John Burns used pretty much the same line in 1892.

Although Henry Zorn was still hopeful for a reprieve from the Governor in 1935, he stepped into the barber's chair and also told the man that it was going to be the last time he'd need a shave. Daniel Lucy even asked his barber to return on the day before his execution in 1900, for another shave because he wanted to look nice for his big day. In 1925, Roy Walsh joked with his barber by telling him, "Doll me up as pretty as possible, because I want to make a good appearance. First impressions are so important."

With only a few exceptions, the condemned man was always presented with a new suit for his execution and burial. While the family of George Bryson furnished him with a fine new suit, most doomed men were provided with new clothes by the various counties. In most cases the sheriff purchased the suit or suits off the store rack but at times such as the Clinton Dotson case in 1902, a tailor was brought in to custom fit the final wardrobe. Most of the men hanged in Montana wore the traditional black suit while others wore worsted gray, cutaway varieties and Philip Coleman was even dressed in a sharp blue outfit. Lu Sing went to the gallows in his traditional Chinese clothing; Fred LeBeau made the trip in a pair of overalls, Albert Yeik wore a pullover sweater and Frank Robideau died in a green poka-dot shirt with a blue coat.

Before their march to the gallows, two of the doomed men, Thomas King, hanged in June of 1890, and Robert Anderson, executed in July of 1894, were each presented a boutonniere of geraniums by sheriff deputies. After researching the meaning of this particular blossom, it was found that the many varieties of geraniums all have various symbolisms, which might have been relevant to executions including "true friend or friendship," "consolation," "melancholy" and "remembrance."[20]

Refusing to Die with their Boots On

A person dying and being buried with their shoes or boots on usually implied that the individual had met his end violently and made persons wander about the deceased's livelihood and honesty. Many of the early-day road agents who were hanged by the Vigilantes kicked off their footwear before their life was ended as if it were some sort of baptism or shortcut to heaven. The reluctance of the legally condemned men to die with their boots on continued into the Twentieth Century and a great many of the doomed men including Peter Pelkey, Thomas Harding, Martin Scott, Harry Roberts, John Osnes, Thomas Salmon, Dan Lucy and Louis Mott all wore sandals or slippers to the gallows. Nearing the end, Fred LeBeau refused to listen to his death warrant and then frantically tore his shoes from his feet before walking to the scaffold.

The Death Warrant and Emotional Moments

By law, the death warrant, which described the history of the case and ordered the death of the condemned man, was to be read to the prisoner before his marched to the gallows. The sheriff or his undersheriff generally read the warrant inside the jail, normally in the man's cell, the corridor or even in the jail office. The warrant wasn't read to Thomas Harding until he was standing on the gallows. The document was read through an interpreter to at least nine condemned men, the German Henry Furhmann, Indians, Pierre Paul, La La See, Antley and Pascale; John Osnes a Norwegian, Lu Sing, Chinese; the Mexican, Juan Cuellae and the Italian Anthony Vettere.

While listening to his death warrant in September of 1901, James Fleming noticed the document trembling in the hands of Sheriff John McMahon. Fleming quickly stepped forward and grasped one corner of the warrant and told the officer: "Here John, let me hold it, you are too nervous." The two men then commented about how steady the prisoner's hands were under the circumstances. Eight years later, George Rock who was hanged in June of 1908, commented to Sheriff Harvey Fifer that he seemed to be nervous while he too read the death warrant to the prisoner. When the sheriff apologized and explained to the prisoner that it was his first execution, Rock smiled and replied that it was his first hanging as well.

An example of a typical death warrant was the first of two such documents read to Miles Fuller before his execution in 1906:

"In the district court of the Second Judicial District of the state of Montana, in and for the county of Silver Bow, the state of Montana, plaintiff, vs. Miles Fuller, defendant, warrant, the state of Montana to the sheriff of Silver Bow County, greetings: Whereas, on the 18th day of May A.D., 1905, the above named defendant, Miles Fuller, was, by a trial jury, found guilty of murder in the first degree, and thereafter, on the 27th day of May, 1905, the court rendered judgment on said verdict, which judgment and sentence was that the said defendant, Miles Fuller, be taken to a place of confinement and there safely confined by the sheriff of Silver Bow County, Montana, and that on a day to be fixed by this court, within the yard of the county jail, Silver Bow County, Montana, see that the said sentence be executed.

"Now, therefore, this is to command you, the said sheriff of Silver Bow County, Montana, to safely keep the said defendant, Miles Fuller, in the place confined provided by law until Monday, the 24th of July, 1905 and on said day you take him to a place of execution, to be provided as required by law, and there hang the said Miles Fuller by the neck until he is dead, and this shall be your warrant for his execution.
Dated this 27th day of May, 1905"
(Signed) Judge Michael Donlan [21]

Even though these prisoners were convicted murderers, many of the sheriffs and their jailers eventually became emotionally attached to the condemned men during their many months of incarceration. One of the best examples of this was of Missoula County Sheriff William

Houston, one of the toughest lawmen of the time. Sheriff Houston and his men had risked their lives in capturing four murdering Indians but on the day of their execution in 1900, the officer openly weakened. Sheriff Houston was overcome with emotion and tears came to his eyes shortly before he had to hang the four men that he had taken care of for several months. In a touching moment one of the Indians walked up to the officer and told him that everyone had to die sometime. Then the other three men walked up to the sheriff and shook his hand and told him thanks for his kindness.

The wives of the sheriffs reportedly became even more attached to the condemned men over the years. As mentioned earlier Mrs. George Cole of Missoula became close with Joe Vuckovich by feeding him daily before his was execution in 1922. A reporter described Mrs. Cole as being a very kind person who displayed her emotions for the men that she cared for. In an interview Mrs. Cole said that she didn't want Vuckovich to be hanged and that she certainly didn't want her husband to do it but she knew he would certainly do his duty.

A case that was even more poignant was that of Mrs. Marguerite O'Connell, the wife of the sheriff of Flathead County. Mrs. O'Connell was greatly affected by the hanging of Fred LeBeau in 1909, after having spent so much time with the prisoner including helping him decorate his cell. She personally cut out the many paper stars and enjoyed how LeBeau used them to decorate his cell even though he had been convicted of killing two men at their home. It was reported that Mrs. O'Connell's health was so adversely affected by the man's hanging that her premature death was blamed on the case. Flathead County Representative Lincoln cited the death of Mrs. O'Connell when he co-sponsored an unsuccessful bill to have all hangings held at the State Penitentiary instead of the individual counties.

The Execution

While the descriptions and histories of the various gallows used in the legal executions of Montana are discussed in the "Gallows of Montana" chapter, this section is devoted to the protocol, procedures along with the equipment and paraphernalia used in the typical hanging.

The March to the Gallows

After the death warrant was read the ominous "march to the gallows" would begin. In most cases the first step of this march began with the securing of the prisoner's arms and hands. After gaining the respect and trust of Powell County Sheriff John McMahon, James Fleming was the only condemned man ever to be allowed to walk to an outside execution totally unrestricted. When the condemned man was safely secured, the officers would then escort him along with his minister or priest to the gallows.

As soon as the procession came in sight of the waiting crowd of spectators a deathly silence would overtake the enclosure. Although there wasn't even a murmur from the crowd as Clinton Dotson stood on the gallows in April of 1902, a mournful howling of a dog in the neighborhood reportedly sent shivers down the back of many of the spectators. As the sun began to shine through the gray sky on the morning of April 6, 1900, a bird began to sing, which made William Pepo smile just before he was hanged at Choteau.

It was customary that every one present at a hanging remove their hats except the officers in charge of the execution and if they weren't already uncovered they would be ordered to do so by the sheriff as the death party passed towards the scaffold. In most cases the condemned men marched to the gallows gallantly and with a steady step. It was said that no emperor en route to his thrown ever walked prouder, loftier or more independent than John Osnes did as he approached the scaffold. Some of the condemned men were so indifferent that they calmly smoked cigarettes to the gallows as if they were merely walking to dinner. A number of the doomed men were quite inebriated or had to be heavily sedated for their last trip while Anthony Vettere had to be subdued with teargas and carried to the gallows.

The Restraints

When the illegal or extra-legal hanging victims were dropped from a wagon or from the back of a horse, the man's hands were merely tied behind their backs. Then when the executioners began using gallows the hangman found it necessary to prevent the condemned man from trying to straddle the trapdoor. Because of that, the officers began pinioning the prisoner's legs and ankles as well as their hands. Years later specialized restraints were being used which generally consisted of from two to three wide leather straps, one being a heavy waist strap, which had extending straps that secured the doomed man's wrists. Another strap was wrapped around the prisoner's legs and at times another belt, was used to secure the man's arms and shoulders. In at least one Montana execution the officials used a webbing material, which was wrapped around the prisoner from the wrists to above his elbow.

It was a common practice to adjust the belt and straps before hand on a deputy to reduce the time necessary to fit the condemned man and the ankle and knee straps were adjusted after the condemned man had walked to the gallows. In a number of cases the death warrant was read to the condemned man while the straps were being adjusted and usually the prisoners were very accommodating and didn't resist. While the large leather belt was being wrapped around Daniel Lucy's hips in 1900, he took interest in the binding his arms and wrists. At first Lucy tried to assist the officers with the straps but then he admitted that he clearly didn't know how they were to be arranged.

While Daniel Lucy was accommodating, Tony Vettere caused such a fight in his cell in 1926, that he had to be gassed and subdued before the straps could be adjusted and the death warrant was read to him.

On a lighter note, before his hanging in 1894, Calvin Christie jokingly warned Flathead County Sheriff not to tighten his waist belt to tight or the oysters, which he had eaten for his last meal, might get squeezed out of him.

While some officers like Flathead County Sheriff William O'Connell ordered new body restraints for his prisoner, Fred LeBeau in 1909, other officials in Montana borrowed them from other communities for their impending hangings. The heavy leather restraints used for the execution of Thomas Salmon at Red Lodge in January of 1899, were also used by Yellowstone County Sheriff George Hubbard to hang William Brooks in November of that same year. The belts used to secure Roy Walsh in 1925, were one of the same sets utilized in the double hanging of the Harris boys in 1923. After they were used on Roy Walsh, the same straps were employed to secure Tony Vettere for his hanging in 1926, and then they were once again utilized in the execution of Rollin Davisson in 1929.

From the descriptions of the straps used to bind Peter Pelkey in 1881, the same belts were probably used in other hangings in Lewis and Clark and Jefferson Counties including John Hart, George Bryson, Thomas King, Clay Pugh, William Biggerstaff, Bill Gay, and Joseph Allen. They appeared to have traveled with ***Gallows No. Eight: (March 1887): "Galloping Gallows" No. Two*** (See "Gallows of Montana") and in that case these infamous straps were also used in the hanging of Joseph Cadotte and William Pepo. The heavy belts that were employed in the first two legal hangings in Montana, of William Wheatley and William Sterres were reportedly buried with the latter in October of 1875.

Last Words:

While on the scaffold the sheriff would ask the doomed man for his last words as the deputies continued adjusting the straps around the prisoner's legs and ankles. Of course the final statements varied but most of them were gracious, remorseful and sincere. Some like the first to be legally executed, William Wheatley in 1875 said only; "I am ready, God have mercy on my soul." In 1890, Thomas King said that he was prepared to die and John Osnes in 1894, said his good-byes and stated he was ready. While some of the doomed men tried to be humorous at the end like Joseph Koble in 1879, when he said, "Slap it to me," most of them asked for mercy from their maker. After joking with the officers, Calvin Christie became serious and stated: "This is the happiest moment of my life. I would not trade my faith in Jesus Christ for all the gold and pardons that could be stacked up in this jail."

Many of the condemned were concerned about a botched execution including John Burns who in 1892, urged his executioners to do a good and quick job. Both Clay Pugh in 1895, and Fred LeBeau in 1909 urged the sheriff to tighten up the hangman's noose. Several of the doomed men only proclaimed their innocence; forgave their accusers and said good-bye before their deaths including Martin Scott in 1888; William Calder, 1900; William Pepo, 1900; James Fleming, 1901 and Joseph

Black Hood and Restraints on William Gay for his hanging in 1896
From the collection of the Montana Historical Society, Helena

Vuckovich in 1922. Almost every one of the doomed men shook hands and thanked the sheriff before their death with the distinct exception of Tony Vettere in 1926, who only cursed at the officers and the crowd while praising Mussolini of Italy.

A few of the men including John Hart in 1888; George Bryson, 1889; Daniel Lucy, 1900; James Martin, 1904; Louis Mott, 1904, and Lee Simpson in 1939, made long and eloquent statements while in 1917, Harrison Gibson only wanted to have a last bite of an apple. After chewing for a moment he said, “All right, let’s go.” In 1900, Joseph Hurst told the crowd that his hanging was a mistake but he had earlier confided with a minister that he had indeed murdered the victim. Hurst had asked the minister not to disclose his confession until the day after his execution.

The Death Hood or Cap

Except for the cases of Mob Lynching and the various Vigilante hangings where the executioners themselves wore the masks to protect their identity, it was normal to cover the head of the condemned men. The hood was optional but most sheriffs of Montana used them and they were typically made of black denim and some of them were designed with splits on both sides so that it could extend over the back and front of the victim’s neck. The primary purpose of the hoods was to prevent the condemned man from seeing the hangman pulling the lever and moving at the crucial moment but they also spared the witnesses the sight of the dead man’s face, which in the case of strangulation wasn’t very pretty. It was normal to adjust the noose over the doomed man’s neck once the hood had been pulled down to reduce the final discomfort of the rope rubbing against the man’s bare skin.

The first recorded time that a face covering was used in Montana was for Frank Parish at Virginia City in January of 1864, when he was being hanged with the four other suspected road agents by the Original Vigilantes. The Helena “Hometown Vigilantes” used large handkerchiefs to cover the faces of Arthur Compton and Joseph Wilson when they were hanged in April of 1870.

At least two men, Joseph Allen who was hanged in 1899, and George Hoffman in 1933, refused the black caps and four sheriffs were known to forego the tradition in order to catch the condemned men by surprise. After making his last statement on the gallows in 1896, Bill Gay asked Lewis and Clark Sheriff John Henry Jurgens if he would leave the hood above his eyes so that he could see the morning sun for the last time. Thomas Harding, executed in 1887, was talking to a former city marshal of Butte before the hood was employed when Sheriff Tom Jones had the weight released and the condemned man was jerked to death by total surprise. This tactic of surprising the condemned man by making them think they wouldn’t be hanged until the black cap was adjusted was also used on John Hart at Helena, Martin Scott at Deer Lodge as well as Monte and William Harris at Butte in April of 1923.

Joseph Cadotte was reportedly buried still wearing his black cap and the executioner had to wait until Frank Fisher reluctantly relinquished his cigarette before placing the hood over his head on the scaffold. William Biggerstaff requested that his spiritual adviser put the black cap over his head because he noticed the deputy was nervous and might not be able to do the job.

The Hangman's Rope

The standard hangman's rope was either a half, five-eighth or three-quarter inch Manila hemp cord, which generally came in lengths of thirty feet. The various jurisdictions either ordered a custom hangman rope from a specialty house at St. Louis and Philadelphia or the sheriff went down to the local hardware store for a utility strand, which could ordinarily be found on any ranch in Montana. Large cord manufacturing firms normally guaranteed their four-strand, twisted hemp half-inch ropes to jerk a man weighing one-hundred and sixty pounds and their five-eighth variety could hang men up to two-hundred and twenty pounds. These specialty manufactures generally supplied their ropes thoroughly stretched and worked so that they were pliable and smooth along with a standard hangman's knot pre-tied on one end.

In July of 1894, Chouteau County Sheriff O'Neil secured a new hangman rope for the execution of John Osnes from a specialty cord manufacturer in St. Louis but sometimes the companies offered free ropes for hangings in Montana for advertisement purposes. One particular cord manufacturer in Philadelphia provided the special hangman ropes for the execution of Harry Roberts at Butte in August of 1889, William Biggerstaff and Bill Gay at Helena in 1896, as well as for Daniel Lucy at Butte in September of 1900. In 1909, Warden Frank Conley of Deer Lodge went to Seattle personally to purchase the rope used to hang William Hayes, one of the two convicts who had murdered his assistant warden and violently attacked him during a failed prison break.

To eliminate any chance of stretching during the hanging, ropes purchased from the local suppliers were first boiled in water for an hour or soaked over night. After the ropes were thoroughly soaked they were stretched with heavy weights until dry. The hangman's knot was tied at one end of the rope a day or two before the execution and the noose was lubricated with oil, paraffin or even soap so that the rope passed through the knot smoothly. Even with the proper preparations the store bought, off-the-shelf rope often times drew up so tightly around the victim's neck that the noose couldn't be loosened and the cord had to be cut at the noose. One such knot, which had drawn up so tightly around Joseph Cadotte's neck in 1895, had to be cut and he was buried with the noose.

The Noose

The most common hangman's knot was generally called the "Old Knot" and it had from five to thirteen coils. Another popular noose of the day had only three coils and it was called the "Binkley's Knot," after the famous hangman, Daniel F. Binkley of Kansas City, Missouri. The well made noose slid down the rope and delivered a deathblow to the side of the condemned man's neck. The knot was normally placed beneath and slightly behind the doomed man's left ear and the noose was drawn fairly tight. Ideally the victim's neck was broken, which caused rapid unconsciousness, cardiac arrest or quiet strangulation.

Some individuals were known for their ability to tie the all-important hangman's knots. Sheriff Adriel B. Davis of Junction in Alder Gulch was reportedly called upon to prepare the noose, which was used to hang George Ives on December 21, 1863. Another noted executioner known for his noose tying was Harry King who was a member of the Original Vigilantes and was with the party that hanged Sheriff Plummer and his deputies, Ned Ray and Buck Stinson. King reportedly had a peculiar way of preparing the knot, which according to him left an impression on the victim's neck that resembled the letter "K." Some early-day Montana lawmen were also known for their preparation of the dangerous hangman's noose. While a hangman's knot had already been prepared for the hanging of Lee Simpson in December of 1939, one of the visiting sheriffs who had previous experience with executions reportedly undid the noose and retied it in a seven-loop variety.

When there was adequate time to prepare a rope the experts prepared the noose but sometimes the various vigilance organizations and mobs had to improvise. When the Original Vigilantes found that they didn't have enough ropes to execute Plummer and his two deputies on that January night in 1864, Henry Tilden was sent for addition cords and the hangman's nooses were quickly made on the spot with cold and trembling fingers. The "Hometown Vigilantes" at Greenhorn had apparently planned to hang one man on their late night visit but when the opportunity presented itself they found themselves executing two bad characters. The rope found around the primary target was tied with the typical hangman's noose but the other man was hanged with a quickly prepared slipknot.

"Hung with a New Rope"

At least thirty-six of the two hundred and thirty-five known hanging victims in Montana were hanged with a brand new rope. When William Hynson believed that he had been invited to another man's hanging by the Fort Benton "Hometown Vigilantes" he was tricked into purchasing a new rope and probably prepared the noose for his own execution in August of 1868. At least three of these new ropes were reused in other hangings in the state. The strand used to hang Thomas Harding in 1887 was later utilized to take the life of Martin Scott in February of 1888. John Osness' death rope was reused to hang Calvin Christie a year later in 1895.

After hanging William Biggerstaff at Helena in April of 1896, Lewis and Clark County Sheriff Jurgens re-used the rope to take the life of Bill Gay two months later and co-conspirators, James Fleming and Clinton Dotson were hanged with the same rope at Deer Lodge. The rope that was used to execute Thomas Salmon in January of 1899, was going to be used for the hanging of William Brooks at Billings that November but while it was being tested one of the strands broke and the sheriff was forced to purchase a new cord.

"Galloping Hangman Ropes"

Like the various "Galloping Gallows" used across Montana, there have been several ropes, which have been used in more than one hanging. The granddaddy of all of these "Galloping Ropes" used in Montana actually got its start at Chicago, Illinois in 1897. After August Spies, Albert Parsons, George Engle and Adolph Fischer were found guilty of murdering seven Chicago policemen during the Haymarket Riot in that city in May of 1886, Cook County Sheriff Seth Hanchett ordered the four new half-inch ropes for their execution.

When faced with the job of hanging four Indians at Missoula in 1890, Sheriff Houston contacted Sheriff Hanchett at Chicago who was happy to supply the Montana lawman not only the plans for the large gallows but the four used hangman ropes and probably the leather restraints. These ropes were then used to hang Pierre Paul, La La See, Antley and Pascale in December of 1890.

The particular rope that was employed to hang Pierre Paul was later utilized to execute John Burns at Missoula in December of 1892, and then it was sent to Livingston in 1894 where it was used on Robert Anderson. Like most of the other hangman ropes, this most infamous strand has been lost to history.

Out of the hundreds of strands used in Montana hangings, we have only located seven hangman ropes complete with nooses. They include the rope, which was probably used in the John Douglas execution in 1881; the one employed by a Lynch Mob to hang Walter Jackson in 1903; along with the cords utilized on Fred LeBeau, 1909; Glenna Bolton and Joseph Reagin, 1923; George Hoffman, 1933; Joe Robideau, 1938 and Lee Simpson in 1939. These ropes are available for viewing today at various museums across the state.

Rope Souvenirs

Many of the ropes used in Montana hangings never had a chance of surviving because of the custom of being cut up and handed out to the witnesses as souvenirs. A few other strands were buried with the doomed victims while some spectators actually claimed some of the ropes to be use on working ranches. The first recorded instance we have of a hangman's rope being cut into pieces for souvenirs in Montana was after the Lynch Mob hanging of Thomas Stewart in July of 1884 near Choteau. After Stewart's body was cut down the rope was immediately cut up and it was reported that several members of the mob were on hand to retrieve their souvenirs from the night before.

Other examples of hangman's ropes being used as souvenirs are: the one that a Lynch Mob used to hang the infamous Con Murphy in January of 1885, and the cords used in the legal executions of Thomas King in June of 1890; William Gay in June of 1896; Herbert Metzger in May of 1905; Lu Sing at Bozeman in April of 1906; Miles Fuller in May of 1906; the triple hanging of Frank Fisher, John O'Neil and Sherman Powell in January of 1918 and Albert Yeik in August of 1921. Missoula County Sheriff Harry W. Thompson disappointed the souvenir hunters after the Louis Mott hanging in March of 1904, when he ordered the hangman's rope be burned immediately after the execution.

Out of all the souvenir chunks handed out over the years we have only two authenticated, one each from the Miles Fuller hanging in 1906, and Albert Yeik of 1921. Ropes that escaped the souvenir hunters but have been lost over the years are the ones used in the execution of John Clark at Bozeman in December of 1883, and Joseph Hurst at Glendive in March of 1900. The rope used in the Clark hanging was last known to be part of a collection inside the Park County Sheriff's Office in 1897, and the strand that ended the life of Hurst in 1900, ended up going to an unknown collector at Anaconda. If any of our readers know what has happened to any of these lost hangman ropes or if they have any stories related to Montana strands used in hangings, they are encouraged to contact the author through the publisher.

An example of a practical use of a hangman's rope appeared in March of 1883, when after John Jessrang was executed by a Lynch Mob at Dillon a prominent rancher who was known for his thriftiness, carefully rolled up the cord and said that it would come in handy for tying up his horse.

The Executioner:

While it obviously took several officers to pull off a successful execution, technically the executioner was the person who actually tripped the lever, cut the cord, pulled the rope or in some way released the trapdoor or allowed the weight to drop, which ultimately hanged the condemned man. Of the twenty-six cases where the executioner was named, thirteen were the county sheriff, six were either the undersheriff or a deputy and one was a deputy U.S. marshal. An unnamed cook from a hotel in the Mining City received fifty dollars for hanging a convicted murderer there and a Butte railroad express man paid his own expenses to Deer lodge twice to be the executioner for two separate executions. Missoula County Sheriff William Houston executed more men than any other when he tripped the trap on the four Indian murderers in 1890, and then two years later he executed another man there.

The four Jerk-Type Gallows constructed in Montana, which claimed the lives of twenty-seven convicted murders were designed with a small enclosure, which concealed the identity of the executioner. Generally the executioner took his position in the small box next to the scaffold before the witnesses were admitted to the gallows area and he remained until everyone had left the jail yard. About thirty minutes before Miles Fuller was executed in May of 1906, the waiting spectators ceased their joking and talking when they noticed the masked executioner swiftly pass from the rear door of the jail to the box next to the gallows. When the Trap-Type scaffold was employed a screen of canvas was often used to protect the executioner's identity.

Sometimes several men would be assigned as executioners behind the screen so that no one would know which officer had actually pulled the deadly lever. In some cases even the executioners themselves didn't know who was responsible for the condemned man's life. At a given signal all the executioners would pull their ropes but only one of the cords actually released the deadly trap. Because of possible reprisals from Chinese assassins, Gallatin County Sheriff Reynolds reportedly took extra precautions to protect the man who released the weight that executed the assassin, Lu Sing in April of 1906.

Death on the Gallows

Essentially, death by hanging was the result of strangulation or the sudden stoppage of the heart due to pressure on the carotid arteries in the neck. When the execution was botched and the man's neck wasn't snapped he would suffer from asphyxia, as his weight would pull down on the noose causing it to tighten and constrict the trachea. The condemned man would struggle violently for at least three minutes before they would lapse into unconsciousness. If the neck bones were broken in the fall, severing the spinal cord, the victim went into medical shock rendering him unconscious within fifteen seconds. Physicians have stated that the executed man probably only experienced pain when the spinal cord was severed before he lost consciousness and it was measured in milliseconds. The cause of death was still asphyxia but the condemned man would be unconscious and quietly die after two to ten minutes.

Frequently the body went limp from the paralysis but sometimes there were involuntary tremors, which were limited by the body restraints. Typically the brain was dead after about six minutes and the heart generally stopped in about eight minutes but in some cases it has continued to beat for up to twenty-five minutes. Immediately after the condemned man was dropped or jerked the attending physician or physicians would steady the swaying body and begin monitoring the victim's vital signs. Generally one or two physician would grasp a wrist while another doctor might listen to the dying man's heart. The physician in charge would announce to the officials the pulse rate of the doomed man and then finally he would pronounce his death. Of the fifty-seven cases where we have data, the average time till death on the Trap-Type Gallows was 10 minutes, 55 seconds while the end came on the Jerk-Type Scaffold in 9 minutes, 28 seconds. The Chinaman Ah Yung reportedly had the quickest death in just a second and a half while it took a full eighteen minutes for both the Indian Antley and Joseph Allen to finally die.

The doctors would then supervise the lowering of the body to the ground or into the waiting coffin where they would examine the dead man's neck. Of the forty-three cases where the physicians' examinations were published, thirty-nine or 90.6% of the condemned men had their necks broken during their executions while only William Sterres, George Rock, William Hayes and Joseph Vuckovich appeared to have suffered. Although our sample size is clearly inadequate for scientific study, the data indicates that these four victims died quickly despite their obvious suffering. The executed men that had suffered broken necks appeared to have only lived on average less than a tenth of a second less than the four victims whose vertebras remained intact. In fact the men who lived the longest after being hanged all had their necks broken when they were dropped or jerked.

Typically the body of the executed man showed marks of hanging such as bruises and cuts around the neck from the rope and in some cases large amounts of bleeding as will as the release of other bodily fluids including urine and faeces. While we didn't run across any graphic descriptions, we did find accounts where the victim's faces were badly distorted. It was reported that in some cases the faces of the victims appeared to be bluish and had protruding tongues. Facial distortion varied greatly among the hanging victims even during multiple hangings. While all four Indians hanged at Missoula in 1890, had broken necks, three of the victims looked like they were quietly sleeping while one of them had his eyes wide open and his tongue was protruding slightly. Although the face of William Hayes wasn't distorted it reportedly appeared somewhat bluish, Albert Yeik was said to have the same cynical smile on his lips that he had displayed throughout his incarceration.

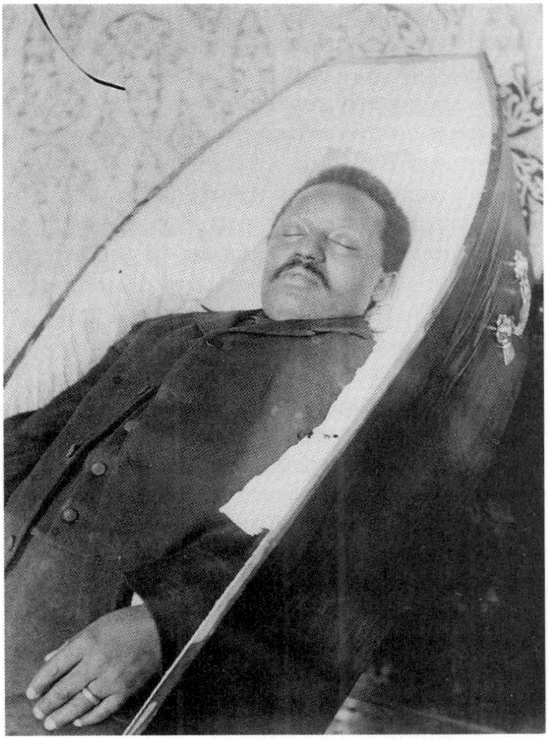

William Biggerstaff in his coffin after his hanging
Photo by J.P. Ball & Son: Montana Historical Society, Helena

In at least three cases where the sanity of the condemned man was in question, physicians conducted an autopsy to determine if there was any brain disease. The brains of Hienrich Furhmann, William Brooks and Tony Vettere were all examined and were found to be normal even after they had acted insane during their time on death row. Dr. Daniel J. Donahue of Butte was the attending physician at probably more executions than any other having attended the triple hanging of Fisher, O'Neil and Powell in 1918, the double execution of Monte and William Harris in 1923 and finally he pronounced Anthony Veterre dead in 1926. Dr. Herbert A. Mailett of Butte attended at least four executions and he officially examined Miles Fuller, Bill and Monte Harris and Tony Vettere. Drs. W.H.A. Campbell and Morris were present for three hangings each.

Burials

While women and children weren't allowed to witness Montana hangings, they were among the huge crowds, sometimes numbering in the thousands to view the remains at the local undertaking establishments after the execution. Among the doomed men who were placed on display after their executions were Harry Roberts, Dan Lucy, Bill and Monte Harris at Butte; William Gay at Helena and Fred Schlaps at Wolf Point. While they were never allowed to view the body, hundreds of men, women and even children waited outside of a funeral parlor at Missoula in hopes of seeing the remains of Louis Mott in 1904.

In most cases the hanging victims who were Catholic were given proper burials in the Church cemetery while the majority of the other condemned men were buried in the Potter's Field of the local graveyard. The bodies of the four Indians hanged at Missoula in 1890, Pascale, Pierre Paul, La La See and Antley were taken to the Flathead Reservation for burial and the final resting place for the remains of Clinton Dotson, George Rock and William Hayes was in the prison cemetery at the State Penitentiary. Before his execution at Kalispell in1909, Frederick LeBeau had taken up a collection to raise money for his own casket as well a portion of the burial plot charges in the Demersville Cemetery.

Pallbearers for James Fleming
"Anaconda Standard" 9/25/1901

Soon after his burial many of the Boulder residents stated their displeasure that Bryson was laid to rest among some of the communities finest citizens. The issue had apparently died down until the execution of Thomas King in June of 1890, when his remains were buried in the cemetery at the county poor farm. There was a call to have Bryson's body exhumed and moved to the Potters Field at the farm but it hasn't been determined whether or not the murderer's body was ever moved. Even with these gravesite controversies most of the men legally executed in Montana eventually rested in peace except for at least two individuals, John Clark and Thomas Harding.

After Clark's hanging at Bozeman in 1883, grave robbers dug up his body and supposedly practiced on by the local physicians. Six months later the papers reported that a human skeleton was found packed in a beer box, which had been thrown in the brush near Bozeman on the road to Story's Mill. A coroner's inquest ruled that the remains were probably of John A. Clark and that unknown medical personnel had dissected the body. The skull of the body was never recovered but the rest of the bones were finally put to rest. Thomas Harding was buried in the Paupers' Field after his execution at Dillon in 1887, but shortly before 1920, his body along with other remains was probably moved to the Mountain View Cemetery.

While George Criner's service as a war veteran was recognized, and the Federal Government paid his burial charges, no military rites were performed over his grave after his execution at Miles City in October of 1935. Criner's last request was that thirty-two dollars and fifty cents, the only money he had in the world, be used to purchase a headstone for the grave of his murder victim and lover, Mrs. Mary Allsup.

Sheriff's Notice: Death Warrant carried out:

After the hanging the sheriff was required to file a statement showing the time, mode and manner in which the death warrant was executed.[22] The following is the filing made by Sheriff John Lloyd of Silver Bow County for the execution of Harry Roberts on August 23, 1889.

"Sheriff's office, Silver Bow County, Montana Territory
I hereby certify that I received the written warrant on the twenty-sixth day of June, A.D. 1889, by virtue of the respite granted in said case, which said respite is hereto annexed, all further proceedings were stayed until August 23, 1889, that on said twenty-third day of August, 1889, the governor of the territory of Montana refusing to pardon said defendant or interfere further in said case, I did in pursuance of said warrant read the same, as also the respite and telegram hereto annexed and made a part hereof, to said defendant, and afterward, to-wit, at the hour of 1:12 p.m., August 23, 1889, in a private enclosure in the jail yard and near the jail of Silver Bow County, Montana Territory, in the presence of two physicians and twelve or more citizens, who were invited to be present by written invitation at least one week before said day of execution, hang the said Harry Roberts by the neck until he was dead, said physicians in attendance pronouncing him dead after examination of him as there hanging. In witness whereof I have hereunto set my hand this twenty-third day of August A.D., 1889."[23]
(Signed) John E. Lloyd, sheriff, Silver Bow County, Montana Territory

(Endnotes)

[1] Montana Territorial Governor Crosby recommended increasing the number of judges and critiqued the penitentiary. "Rocky Mountain Husbandman" 12/13/1883, p2

[2] The first Grand Jury was made up of J.J. Hull, (foreman), Samuel Russell, Henry Thompson, Lester Campbell, L.S. Peck, Thomas Baume, L.H. Davenport, B.R. Martin, James Williams, William Decker, John Ault, J.W. Patte, J. Hilderbrand, George Brandt, Joseph Brown, W.P. Wheeler and John Vanderbilt. "Montana Post" 12/10/1864 (Thomas Baume and James Williams were both members of the Original Vigilantes)

[3] "Pioneer Life in Montana" Lyman E. Munson; Montana Historical Society Contributions: Vol. 5, P200

[4] "Bynum Herald" 8/7/1922

[5] State Board of Pardons "Helena Daily Herald" 9/5/1889, p8

[6] "Silver State" 3/11/1908

[7] "Coffee Creek Herald" 6/24/1918

[8] "Livingston Enterprise" 9/21/1929, p2

[9] "Anaconda Standard" 7/2/1899

[10] "Interlake" 8/24/1894

[11] "Interlake" 8/24/1894

[12] "Helena Daily Herald" 1/24/1878

[13] "Miles City Star" 11/14/1934

[14] "Harlowton Times" 10/19/1939

[15] "Helena Daily Herald" 3/4/1896

[16] "Helena Daily Herald" 3/4/1896

[17] "Helena Daily Herald" 4/10/1896

[18] "Missoulian" 2/6/1922

[19] "Bozeman Daily Chronicle" 7/17/1924

[20] "The History and Language of Flowers and Herbs: origins and meanings" victorianbazaar.com

[21] "Anaconda Standard" 5/28/1905

[22] "Bozeman Daily Chronicle" 7/17/1924

[23] "Anaconda Standard" 9/16/1900

Territorial Legal Hangings
(August 1875 through August 1889)

Up until the first legal execution was conducted in August of 1875, there had already been seventy-three hangings in what would become Montana. Sixty-two of the hangings were conducted by Lynch Mobs, the Original and "Hometown Vigilantes" along with another eleven ordered by various Miners' Courts. Once the legal system of the Montana Territory began successfully hanging convicted murderers in 1875, they executed a total of sixteen men until statehood or a little better than a man a year.

If one thinks that is a high number, consider the fact that during the same period between 1875 and 1889 the "Cowboy Stranglers of 1884" alone was credited with hanging forty-seven men, while another twenty-nine were Lynch Mob victims and nine more died at the hands of the final groups of "Hometown Vigilantes." To further emphasize the impotence of the legal justice system of Montana Territory, of the one hundred and seventy-four men hanged during the period, the government only executed sixteen, or about nine percent of the suspected lawbreakers.

August 13, 1875 (Friday the Thirteenth)
<u>William Wright Wheatley</u>

Other Names: Wheatley was also known by his friends as "Bob."
Location and Gallows: Wheatley was hanged in the Lewis and Clark County Jail yard at Helena on ***<u>Gallows No. Two: (August 1875): "Galloping Gallows" No. One</u>***. A complete description and history of this particular scaffold can be found in Chapter Seven: "Montana Gallows.".
Description: Wheatley was considered a fine looking well formed man about five feet ten inches tall. He looked young, strong and athletic even though he lived a fast life. Wheatley was born in Iowa in 1848, making him twenty-seven years old at the time of his hanging.
Crime: Co-conspirator with William Sterres and Frederick Shaffer in the murder of Austrian born Franz Warl, a charcoal burner between Colorado Gulch and Ten mile, about ten miles from Helena on April 30, 1875.
Judge: Chief Justice Decius S. Wade
Prosecution: District Attorney Joseph Kemp Toole and assisted by Colonel John A. Johnston
Defense: Massena Bullard and Joseph J. Williams
Sheriff: Seth Bullock
Distinction: The hanging of William Wheatley was the first legal execution by the District Court system of Lewis & Clark County as well as the Territory of Montana. This was also the first hanging in Montana utilizing the Trap-Type Gallows. Oddly enough, even though he was the first man hanged by the Territory, Wheatley was actually the second man to be sentenced to death and the warrant executed. William Sterres,

Wheatley's partner in crime was the first of the two men to be sentenced, but because he was granted a new trial, he was hanged later.

On May 2, 1875, men from Ten Mile came to Helena and reported that they had found the body of Franz Warl at his charcoal pit near Colorado Gulch. When the badly mutilated murder victim was found his hands were tied behind his back and the cord was then wrapped around his neck. Warl was between forty-five and fifty years old and was a native of Leibach County, Krain, Austria and he had been in the United States for a number of years. Franz Warl burned charcoal for a number of Helena businesses particularly blacksmiths who didn't have ready access to coal. Mr. H. Frank Tailor of Helena had written several letters for Warl and he reported that the man had a great deal of money in several banks in town.

After securing a wagon, Sheriff Seth Bullock, Dr. C.S. Ingersoll, the county coroner, and Judge Nicholas Hilger accompanied the following jurors to investigate the crime scene:

Jesse Armitage[1]	Moses Morris	D. Jackson
Wes Alexander	Fred Gamer	William Wentworth

The verdict of the coroner's jury wasn't released immediately because it was feared that if it were rendered in advance an impartial jury couldn't be obtained in the county and the first man specifically arrested was William Wheatley who had recently arrived in Helena from the Boulder Valley where he had tended stock for the stage company. In Helena Wheatley made a living by playing the fiddle in local dance halls and while he was considered a bit "slow," he was well liked by the locals.

When he was sixteen years old William Wheatley enlisted as a private in Company "A" of the Twenty-fifth Iowa Volunteers, which was commanded by Colonel J.A. Stoner and was made drummer boy at Chattanooga. His regiment marched with General William T. Sherman on his famous march to the sea and after the war Wheatley was mustered out of the army at Washington D.C. He returned to Iowa but he eventually went to Bismarck to visit an older brother in 1872. He signed on as a bullwhacker for the Diamond "R" Freight Company in the fall of 1873 and came to Montana Territory.

Wheatley had trouble coping with being locked up and soon after his arrest he began talking and his statement along with other clues found at the crime scene led to the identification of two more suspects, William Sterres and Frederick Shaffer. The two men were well known in Helena as they had run a popular barbershop the previous winter at the corner of Broadway and Main Street.

Sheriff Bullock and James H. McFarland left Helena in a buggy and after finally locating Winston Gulch near the Frenchwoman's Ranch, they found William Sterres working with other black miners on a placer mine. When they drove up to the diggings the officers spotted Sterres atop of the sluice boxes separating the coarse gravel with a sluice fork and before he could escape Sheriff Bullock got the drop on him with his double-barreled shotgun and McFarland threw the cuffs on him.

Fred Shaffer left Helena on the stage Wednesday, May 5, 1875 and arrived at Fort Benton the following afternoon where he remained until Monday when he left on a skiff with two other rough characters he had met at the port town. Shaffer had sold a new, gold stem-winding watch worth between one hundred and twenty-five to a hundred and fifty dollars to a lady-of-the-night for thirty dollars, which caused suspicion and the businessmen swore out a warrant for the low-class characters.

Chouteau County Deputy Hardwick and four soldiers from the fort pursued them ten miles down river where the three scoundrels were finally stopped at gunpoint. After a search was made nothing was found on their person and Shaffer and his friends were released to continue down the Missouri. (See: William H. Sterres (10/28/1875) for the full description of the crime and the escape of Frederick Shaffer)

Wheatley's trial began June 6, 1875 and the case went to the jury at four o'clock on the afternoon on June 8. While the jury returned a first-degree murder verdict against Wheatley, Jury Foreman W.T. McFarland presented the judge the following recommendation for clemency signed by each member of the panel:

"We, the jury, find the defendant, William Wheatley, guilty of murder in the first degree as charged in the indictment, in view of the fact that the defendant, Wheatley, made statements to authorities by which the other implicated men were arrested, we, the jury, recommend the defendant to the mercy of the court and the authorities, and that sentence be commuted to imprisonment for life."

Although the jury's verdict was explicit, a first-degree verdict in 1875 called for capital punishment so the court was compelled to pronounce the death sentence because the judge had no power under the statutes to order clemency. The recommendation of the jury was therefore passed onto Governor Benjamin F. Potts who did have the power to commute the sentence.

According to Father Lawrence B. Palladino, neither Wheatley nor Sterres were Catholic but the Church received both of them before they died. While Sterres was resigned to his awful fate and he was contented by making peace with his God, William Wheatley wasn't seeking repentance but instead looking for a way out of his jam. When he was told that there was no hope for him and that he should seek salvation, he replied that salvation didn't trouble him as much as being hanged.

Because this was the first legal hanging in Lewis & Clark County as well as the Territory of Montana, Sheriff Seth Bullock had to have a new scaffold built for the execution of the two men. Prior to 1875, the only other gallows used in the Territory had been a simple Hoist-Type scaffold at Bannack where five men were hanged. (See: ***Gallows No. One: (August 1863)*** in "Gallows of Montana" chapter) A Miners' Court had ordered the execution of John Heron in 1863 and the Original Vigilantes hanged Sheriff Plummer, Ned Ray, Buck Stinson and R.C. Rawley the falling year. The scaffold at Bannack was meant to be a permanent fixture and probably a deterrent to future crime.

By the time Sheriff Bullock was ordered by the District Court to construct the first gallows to be used in a legal execution in Montana, the Helena Hometown Vigilantes had already hanged at least twenty-one suspected criminals. Thirteen of the vigilance committee had been hanged from the limb of the famous "Hangman Tree" in Dry Gulch. Because the basic design of the Hoist-Type Gallows was meant to resemble the branch of a tree, the sheriff probably didn't consider using a scaffold, which resembled the one last used by illegal organizations.

The condemned man had been away from his home for ten years and he hadn't been in touch with his family for six years before he wrote informing them that he had been convicted of murder and he was scheduled to be hanged. In his letter home Wheatley explained to his loved ones that he had associated with some roughs at Helena who first stole three hundred dollars of his money and then persuaded him to join them in a plot to kill a man for his wealth. A few days before Wheatley's execution, Sheriff Bullock sent a dispatch to the condemned man's mother, sister and brother living near Ainsworth, Iowa confirming that their loved one had been convicted of murder and he was going to be hanged. He also informed them that their presence or any other efforts would not change his fate.

Wheatley's brother telegraphed: "Mother and I will come. Is it too late?" The doomed man replied, "Come if you can get here by August 13. I want to see mother." Although Wheatley's widowed mother tried to raise the money for the trip out to Montana, she didn't succeed in seeing her son for the last time. On the day before his execution the prisoner wrote his last letters to his mother, sister and brother. He sent them all a photograph, which had been taken a day or two earlier and he included a lock of his hair for his sister.

Because of the height of the scaffold, a very tall board fence was constructed around the jail yard, which was located on the same ground where the present day courthouse stands in Helena.[2] Evidently in an attempt to reduce the size of the crowds and unauthorized spectators, the sheriff was allowed to change the time of the execution until after midnight. Although the statutes specifically prohibited public executions, the houses and buildings in the immediate vicinity of the county jail yard made it impossible for the sheriff to carry out the law to the letter and more than a thousand people witnessed the hanging of William Wheatley.

At midnight on August 12, 1875, Wheatley was seated in the vestibule of the county jail, and Sheriff Bullock read to him his Death Warrant. The first death warrant read in the Territory of Montana is as follows:

"In the District Court of the third Judicial District within and for the county of Lewis and Clark, Territory of Montana.

"The Territory of Montana vs. William Wheatley, warrant execution. The people of the Territory of Montana to the sheriff of the county of Lewis and Clark, Territory of Montana. Whereas at the May term of the district court of the third Judicial District, within the county of Lewis and Clark, Territory of Montana, held at the courthouse in said county,

the eighth day of June, A.D. 1875, before Honorable D.S. Wade, Chief Justice of the Territory of Montana, and judge of the third Judicial District Court aforesaid, presiding, and by twelve good and lawful jurors duly empanelled, sworn and charged, William Wheatley was duly tried and convicted of having murdered Franz Warl, in manner and form as charged in the indictment, and was thereupon, on the twenty-ninth day of June A.D. 1875, sentenced by the judge of said crime, during said May term, and in open court, to be hanged by the neck on Friday, the thirteenth day of August, 1875, between the hours of eleven o'clock a.m. and three o'clock p.m. of said day, until he should be dead.

"Now, I do, by this warrant, pursuant to the statute in such case made and provided, require appointment that you cause the said sentence to be executed on the day and between the hours therein mentioned and at the place and in the manner prescribed by law.

"Given under the hand of the undersigned, by the judge who constituted the said third Judicial District Court on the twenty-ninth day of June, A.D. 1875, and under the hand of undersigned, the clerk and seal of the said court.

Signed by: Decius S. Wade and Alex H. Beattie, clerk of court"

Father Palladino accompanied Wheatley to the jail yard, and the doomed man showed no weakness as he ascended the scaffold. After his arms and legs had been secured he knelt and said a prayer with the priest and then he asked Sheriff Bullock for permission to address the crowd. "My Friends: You are now gazing upon a very unfortunate man, who is called forth to bid a final adieu to this cheating and sinful world. God of infinite mercy have compassion upon a poor sinner and save me from perdition. My friends, I desire to thank all the good people of Montana, and now ask God to bless you all and those dear ones so far away. I am now about to offer up my life. I make this statement to show you how unfortunate I am and as a warning to you all, just as I go to that awful future, to meet my God. May God bless you all."

At twenty minutes after midnight the black cap was pulled over the prisoner's face, and after he said, "I am ready, God have mercy on my soul," the trap was sprung and the soul of William Wright Wheatley was launched into eternity. Drs. Reece and Holmes checked the man's pulse and reported death after ten and a quarter minutes. At one o'clock Wheatley's body was taken down and placed in a wooden coffin and then it was turned over to Father Palladino for a proper Catholic burial.

October 28, 1875

William H. Sterres

Other Names: "Red" Sterres: Stears, but his real name was John Leonard Nichols.

Location and Gallows: Sterres was hanged in the Lewis and Clark County jail yard at Helena on ***Gallows No. Two: (August 1875): "Galloping Gallows" No. One***.

Description: William Sterres was about forty years old; a mulatto with

reddish hair and he stood five feet, ten inches tall and weighed about 150 pounds.
Crime: Along with William W. Wheatley and Frederick Shaffer, Sterres murdered Austrian, Franz Warl, a charcoal burner between Colorado Gulch and Ten mile, about ten miles from Helena on April 30, 1875.
Judge: Chief Justice Decius S. Wade
Prosecution: District Attorney Joseph Kemp Toole and assisted by Colonel John A. Johnston
Defense: Joseph J. Williams and Harry B. Comly
Sheriff: Seth Bullock
Distinction: Although Sterres was the first man to be sentenced to death and his execution carried out, he was actually the second man legally hanged in Montana because his case was appealed on a technicality. William Sterres therefore also was the first man executed after receiving an appeal as well as a new trial.

The first man place on trial for the murder of Franz Warl was William Sterres on May 18, 1875, and the morning was devoted to the selection of the following jurors:

C.H. Ellis	Hugh Daly	Louis Garcin
Angus McMillen	Charles A. DeWitt	H.L. Clark
John A Keating	R.G. Emerson	D.M. Gillette[3]
John B. LeBeau	Abner Adams[4]	William B. Wright

The packed Lewis & Clark courthouse heard Frank LaBrush, William Blackhall, Jake Shilling and George Reed testify that they heard voices coming from their neighbor's cabin and then of finding the body of Warl. Coroner C.S. Ingersoll told the court that on his first examination he found one eye of the victim missing along with parts of the face and neck partially eaten by the man's dog and his skull was fractured. After further inspection it was determined that the skull had a second fracture and the neck had been dislocated.

William Wheatley took the stand and told the jury that he met Sterres at Professor Smith's cabin on Clore Street and he wanted to go hunting up Ten Mile Creek. The witness said he agreed to go hunting with Sterres but instead he learned that they were going to rob a rich man living nearby. After Shaffer joined them the men approached Franz Warl in the dark of the night but the scene was well lit by the large fire at the pit. He explained how Sterres had come up behind the victim and struck the man on the back of the head and when Mr. Warl didn't go down, the defendant struck him again.

Finally the defendant took the stand in his own behalf and said he was born in Monroe, Michigan in 1837, and that he came to Montana in September of 1874. He was married in Saginal, Michigan in 1865, and his wife and two children were living at Minneapolis, Minnesota but it was later learned that Sterres had another wife and child living at Sioux City, Iowa. Sterres told the court that he worked as a barber at the shop of Johnson & Dutrieuelle during the winter of 1874, and then he had worked for Fred Shaffer at his barbershop during the winter of 1875.

The defendant said that while he was working for Shaffer he was in the process of buying the business from him. While he still owed Shaffer for much of the equipment, Sterres had already sent some of it to Fort Benton where he planned to open his shop.

Sterres explained that in the meantime Shaffer had pointed out Mr. Warl to him and had proposed robbing the rich Austrian. The old fellow worked in his pits and lived in a small hut nearby and it was thought that he was rich because he had the reputation of never spending a cent that wasn't absolutely necessary. Sterres later said that he wanted nothing of the proposition but he feared that Shaffer would cancel the sale of the barber equipment and furnishings.

According to Sterres, Shaffer told him how he once had taken a woman and whisky to Warl's cabin in hopes distracting the man in order to rob him, without succeeding. Since Shaffer had neither the physical ability nor courage to attack Warl on his own, he had approached Sterres to be the "heavy." About that time Sterres renewed acquaintances with William Wheatley who he had known previously at Bismarck. Wheatley had arrived at Helena broke and desperate and was a perfect candidate as a strong-arm man. Sterres testified that he had originally hoped that Wheatley could take his place for Shaffer and he wouldn't have anything to do with the crime.

According to defendant, Shaffer wanted nothing to do with Wheatley unless the defendant came along and at about noon on the day of the murder, Sterres and Wheatley walked out to Colorado Gulch drinking freely from a bottle of whisky and gin. When they got above the Warl cabin they stopped to rest and drink while they waited for Shaffer to arrive. Sterres said that Shaffer had planned to robbery and when he reached their camp the leader was disappointed that the two men hadn't already taken care of Warl.

Sterres said that when he asked Mr. Warl where a Mr. Baker lived, it was Wheatley who clubbed the man with a pick or axe handle. The blow to the neck brought Warl to his knees and the second strike put the man on the ground. Sterres then said he pulled out a sling shot and struck him lightly on the head. While Wheatley and Sterres were tying up the victim, Shaffer was going through the man's cabin for any hidden money. Not finding any cash, Shaffer ordered Sterres to take another look through Warl's cabin but the second search was also unsuccessful. James U. Sanders, the son of Colonel Wilbur Sanders was involved with the crime investigation and he later found a package of bills totaling one thousand and fifty dollars under some old clothes in a corner of Warl's cabin.

Mr. Warl usually ate his meals at the charcoal pits and he kept his coffee pot on the fires and in a last effort to make the old man tell where he had hidden his money, the bandits poured the boiling liquid down the man' throat, which ultimately killed him. As the three men were again going through the old man's cabin, they were interrupted by the screams of two small children being whipped by their father at a nearby cabin. By this time Wheatley was beginning to panic about the crime without any reward and Shaffer began demanding that Sterres control his friend. Sterres told the jury that thought their victim was only unconscious, and they returned to Helena, throwing their sling shot in the big Yaw Yaw Ditch along the way.

A woodcutter, William Blackhall who lived near Mr. Warl, and had worked in the pits for the old man, found the body. The face of Warl was badly mutilated as it was partially eaten away by his big dog, which was still guarding his master's remains. After enticing the animal into the cabin with food and closing the door, Blackhall was finally able to remove the body. It was always a mystery how the three murderers were able to escape injury from the ferocious dog while they killed its master.

Before he was murdered, Warl had been tied up with a cord from a harness and then he was gagged with a barber's apron, which was traced back to Fred Shaffer. The hanging of Wilson and Compton in 1870, by the "Hometown Vigilantes" again became the talk of the town and the folks with feelings against capital punishment, were reminded about the salutary effect on the outlaws of the community after that double hanging.

After closing arguments were given, the case was given to the jury at a quarter to eleven on the evening of May 19, 1875, and after deliberating for forty-five minutes they had reached a verdict. The foreman handed the verdict to Judge Wade who then passed it to the clerk of the court. The courtroom was packed but it was so quiet you could have heard the famous pin drop when in a clear and steady voice the clerk read the verdict: "We the jury, find the defendant guilty, in the manner and form as charged in the indictment."

There was reportedly a collected sigh of relief in the courtroom as well as across the county and territory when the man was found guilty of murder in the first degree. Most of the people of the county had hoped this action would be the end of the Lynch Law and the once all-powerful band of "Hometown Vigilantes" who in the past had been needed to vindicate the law and protect the citizens and their property. Unfortunately the infant territorial justice system would let the folks down and the "Hometown Vigilantes" would again have to take charge several more times.

Judge Wade decided not to sentence Sterres until after Wheatley's trial and the apprehension and hearing of the third conspirator Frederick Shaffer. The stage that Shaffer left Helena on reached Carroll in time to board the steamer "Josephine" and he had been gone four hours by the time the posse had arrived at the port. Deputy Quirk missed his last chance of catching Shaffer at Fort Peck even when the "Josephine" had a long delay at there to load cargo and ore. The county sheriff at Bismarck finally captured Shaffer and he notified the Lewis and Clark County authorities.

Deputy Sheriff Pierce was given Deputy Quirk's warrant for the arrest of Shaffer and he proceeded on to Bismarck where he entered a complaint before Justice Davis. A warrant was issued and Sheriff McKenzie arrested Shaffer and jailed him that same day. In the meantime Deputy Toby of Lewis and Clark County was on his way to Bismarck with the necessary paperwork and to help escort the prisoner back to Montana Territory. During the long delay Sheriff McKenzie went to Iowa with some prisoners and in his absence the mayor of Bismarck, evidently worried about paying the cost of confinement, ordered the jailer to release the prisoner into the custody of Officer Pierce.

Deputy Pierce and his prisoner immediately started out overland to catch a steamer heading west but before they reached the river the Montana lawman was arrested for kidnapping Shaffer. When the party returned to Bismarck Deputy Pierce was jailed and Shaffer was released. There was some suspicion that the corrupt lawmen at Bismarck were more concerned about the five hundred dollars reward than the wanted murderer. Obviously Deputy Pierce's trial resulted in an acquittal but the delay offered more than enough opportunity for Shaffer to escape and he was never heard of again. It was suspected that the Bismarck authorities had actually held the fugitive at an undisclosed location for a higher reward and when none was offered Shaffer was released.

Although Sterres hadn't had any religious background he received the sacrament of baptism in the Roman Catholic Church after several weeks of instruction by Father Palladino. The baptism of Sterres in the county jail was said to have been very impressive and a number of people witnessed it. For the ceremony Sterres requested that one of the jurors who had found him guilty, to assist in the baptism to show that he bore no vengeance. The prisoner took the ceremony very seriously and reportedly was quite subdued during the time when prayers were offered to God for mercy.

When there was little hope that Frederick Shaffer would be apprehended anytime soon, Judge Wade scheduled the sentencing of both Wheatley and Sterres on June 28, 1875, on that same day the judge learned that his aged mother had died at Andover, Ohio. Sheriff Bullock brought the two prisoners into the packed courtroom at nine o'clock in the morning and the judge wasted no time in starting the proceedings. The two men maintained their normal demeanor, Sterres resigned and Wheatley indifferent when the judge scheduled them both to be hanged on Friday the Thirteenth of August 1875. Judge Wade's sentencing statement in its entirety can be found in Chapter One: "History of Legal Hangings in Montana and the Typical Legal Execution."

With the gallows still standing after the execution of Wheatley, Sheriff Bullock only had to mail out the fifty-some invitations for the hanging of Sterres. Two days before his scheduled execution the Supreme Court of the Territory of Montana, which was headed by Chief Justice Wade, Sterres was granted a new trial.

Evidently when the verdict of the jury merely stated that the "defendant was guilty in manner and form as he stands charged in the indictment," they didn't specify either first degree, second degree or manslaughter. The Supreme Court held that the verdict was too indefinite when it came to the death of a man and while the high court found it regrettable that the error had occurred they felt that the delay in justice must be indulged in the "hanging business." It has been speculated however that Judge Wade had granted a second trial for Sterres in the hopes that his further testimony would help bring Frederick Shaffer to justice.

Judge Wade ordered a special term of the district court for September of 1875, for the second trial of Sterres and the jury was made up of the following men:

R.S. Hamilton	George Hale	John E. Vawter[5]
L. Auerbach	J.R Watson	George Booker
William Borbrite	James Dawyer	D.H. Churchill
W.C. Gillette	William Muth	T.R. Dana

The court heard basically the same evidence that was presented during the previous trials including the testimonies of Mr. Grene, the county jailer who overheard Sterres tell Wheatley while in lockup that they were equally guilty of the crime. The second trial lasted for only about two and a half hours and it reportedly cost the county less than a hundred dollars. The jury returned a guilty verdict after only ten minutes and the second sentencing of Sterres was attended by most of the attorneys in the region along with a large concourse of local citizens.

After his first conviction Sterres was said to have called for a priest and confessed his sins and while waiting for his second trial he made several attempts to escape including trying to dig through the cell wall with a stout iron rod from his bunk. After his second trial he tried to negotiate an escape with the jail cook by passing him a note asking him for a small cold chisel but the cook quickly reported the incident. Sheriff Bullock ordered a blacksmith to make a pair of strong ankle bracelets for Sterres and he was not permitted to leave his cell with the others and he passed the time reading and in devotions conducted by the Reverend Father Lawrence B. Palladino. To impress his jailers of his religious faith, he would tumble to his knees and pray every time the sheriff or his deputies walked by and most observers believed that Sterres' religious comments were a put on and that his Christianity was only skin deep.

At midnight, October 28, 1875, William Sterres like Wheatley before him, was seated in the vestibule of the jail and Sheriff Bullock read to him the death warrant. After the reading the prisoner was conducted to the jail yard in the rear of the courthouse to the gallows. Sterres was calm as he ascended the stairs of the scaffold with firm steps and walked to the drop. He then knelt and offered a brief prayer with Father Palladino and then arose. While there was a smaller crowd of witnesses for the Sterres' execution, only about fifty citizens were inside the enclosure, but there were still a good number of spectators perched upon the nearby houses and other buildings adjacent to the courthouse to watch the second legal hanging in Montana.

The black cap was drawn over his face; the rope adjusted around his neck, and at ten minutes after midnight William H. Sterres was launched into eternity. Nine minutes later Drs. Reece and John Bullard pronounced the man dead. Sterres was apparently in agony for about eight minutes as his body made frequent convulsions, and the physicians declared that death was due to strangulation. At one o'clock Sterres' body was taken down and placed in a coffin with the straps still on; then it was turned over to Reverend Father Palladino.

Postscript

By having an error in the very first death sentence case in the history of the Territory, and subsequently ordering a new trial for William Sterres, the confidence of the new district court system may have been eroded and it might have led directly to several more "Hometown Vigilante" actions in Lewis and Clark County and elsewhere in Montana.

The chief prosecutor of the Wheatley and Sterres cases, Joseph K. Tool served as district attorney for the Third District until 1876, and later represented Lewis and Clark County in the territorial Legislature in 1881. Mr. Tool served two terms in the United States Congress before becoming the first Governor of the state of Montana in November of 1889. After completing two terms as governor, Mr. Tool went into semi-retirement but he was again elected as Governor of Montana in 1900, and succeeded Robert B. Smith on January 7, 1901.

Sheriff Seth Bullock moved to South Dakota the following year and became a prominent citizen, marshal, county sheriff and a member of the board of heath there. Mr. Bullock claimed that he was playing cards in the saloon when Jack McCall shot and killed "Wild Bill" Hickock on August 2, 1876. While ranching in South Dakota, Bullock became personal friends with his neighbor, Theodore Roosevelt and they frequently worked and hunted together. Later President Roosevelt appointed Seth Bullock as United States Marshal for South Dakota and he often was the president's personal bodyguard whenever he traveled out West. Eventually Bullock became the supervisor of the Black Hills National Forest and the sheriff who conducted the first two legal hangings in Montana died at his ranch near Deadwood, South Dakota in 1919.

After assisting with the Wheatley and Sterres case, James McFarland became a Deputy U.S. Marshal and was in charge of the execution of Francois Robert at Virginia City in October of 1878. McFarland went on to assist in the legal hangings of Peter Pelkey in 1881, and Joseph Allen in 1899, along with being present to witness the illegal execution of Con Murphy by a Lynch Mob in 1885.

Rumors persisted that the authorities hadn't recovered all of Franz Warl's fortune and that more than fourteen thousand dollars was still buried near Ten Mile Creek. During the summer months treasure hunters searched the old charcoal pits for forty years after Warl's death.

March 1, 1878
Michael McAndrews

Other Names: Micaja McAndrews or John McAndrews
Location and Gallows: McAndrews was hanged on ***Gallows No. Three: (March 1878)*** in the yard of the Jefferson County Jail at Radersburg, which is presently in Broadwater County.
Crime: Murder of George Manor during the first week of September of 1877.
Judge: Henry Nichols Blake
Prosecution: District Attorney James G. Spratt and assisted by Samuel Word
Defense: Thomas L. Napton, John T. Shober and Attorney Sharp
Sheriff: Allen M. Easterly
Distinction: This was the first legal hanging in Jefferson County, and the only such execution in what would later become Broadwater County.

While McAndrews and George Manor were traveling from the Black Hills during September of 1877, they camped in Avalanche Gulch along the Boulder River between Captain Cook's Place and Butte, about twelve miles above Boulder. Sometime during the night McAndrews shot Manor in the head while he was asleep and then left the scene. The authorities first arrested Robert Whitford and Edward Waters in connection with the murder but eventually Samuel P. Alexander arrested McAndrews at Pioneer City, (later called Butte).After McAndrews' preliminary examination at Jefferson City, Sam Alexander escorted the prisoner to Radersburg, which at that time was the county seat of Jefferson County.

During the October 1877, term of district court a jury found McAndrews guilty of first-degree murder. The evidence was reportedly purely circumstantial but the prosecution presented it in such a way that McAndrews' guilt was never in doubt by the jury. Judge Blake sentenced him to be hanged by the neck until dead between the hours of ten o'clock a.m. and three o'clock p.m. on January 25, 1878. McAndrews' counsel petitioned for a new trial with the Supreme Court of the Territory of Montana but on January 14, the motion was denied and the lower court's decision was affirmed in a decision written by Chief Justice Wade. At that point Jefferson County Sheriff Allen Easterly began preparations for the execution including erecting an enclosure behind the jail and the construction of a Trap-Type Gallows.

While there is no description of the scaffold used to hang McAndrews, we have determined that it had a trap and it was probably modeled after the only scaffold in Montana at the time, ***Gallows No. Two: (August 1875): "Galloping Gallows" No. One***, at Helena. For descriptions and histories of these scaffolds or any others, refer to the "Montana Gallows" chapter.

The condemned man received a new lease on life on January 23, 1878, when McAndrews' attorneys successfully lobbied Territorial Secretary James H. Mills, who was acting governor at the time to suspend the execution until March 1. The acting top executive granted the respite in order to provide the defense enough time to prepare a writ of habeas corpus to be argued before the United States Supreme Court. Acting Governor Mill's entire order for the stay of execution of McAndrews can be found in the Chapter One: "History of Legal Hangings in Montana and the Typical Execution." By then all the preparations had been completed for the execution of McAndrews and after the stay the workmen began tearing down the high fence leaving the deathly gallows overlooking the mining town of Radersburg.

The Reverend Father Joseph Guidi counseled McAndrews and he stayed with the condemned man until the end. When Governor Benjamin F. Potts refused to interfere with the execution he was dropped through the trap at 2:30 on the afternoon of March 1, 1878. Sheriff Easterly was given credit for performing a well executed hanging, which reportedly broke McAndrews' neck and he was left hanging for fifteen minutes. McAndrews' body was reportedly taken to Helena on March 2, for a Catholic burial.

October 31, 1878

Francois Joseph Robert

Other Names: Frank Robert; Frank Roberts; Francis Roberts

Location and Gallows: Robert was hanged from a scaffold utilizing the trap mechanism from ***Gallows No. Two: "Galloping Gallows" No. One***. The execution took place inside of an enclosure behind the Madison County Courthouse.

Description: Frank Robert was a thirty-year-old Frenchman with a splendid physique.

Crime: Murder of his prospecting partner, Harry J. Morris in September 1877 along the Big Horn River on the Crow Indian Reservation.

Judge: Henry Nichols Blake

Prosecution: U.S. District Attorney Robert S. Anderson handled the case because the crime was committed on an Indian Reservation.

Defense: Colonel Wilbur F. Sanders

In Charge: U.S. Marshal Alexander C. Botkin

Distinction: While at least eighteen men had already been hanged in the county before 1878, Frank Robert was the first man legally executed in Madison County. The condemned man also had the distinction of being the first foreigner to be legally executed in the Territory as well as the only man hanged in Montana by order of the United States Government.

Frank Robert was a native of central France before coming to the United States in 1866. After first residing at Amador and San Francisco, California Robert worked in the mines near Virginia City, Nevada before going to the Black Hills where he became partners with Harry J. Morris, alias Bob Goudy. Harry Morris was allegedly a rough character and he had spent two terms at a jail at Eureka, California and he was a fugitive of justice from Wyoming Territory for attempting to murder a man between Laramie and Cheyenne.

In September of 1877, the two men left the Black Hills for the gold diggings in Montana Territory when they camped along Rotten Grass Creek near its confluence with the Big Horn River near the present day community of St. Xavier on the Crow Indian Reservation. It was later proven that Morris had been murdered in his sleep as his shoes were off and he was found partially undressed. His skull had been crushed in with either an axe or hatchet and there were no other wounds found on his body.

Further substantiating the theory of the prosecution that the victim was asleep at the time of the murder, the clothing, which Morris had apparently rolled up and used for a pillow was splattered with blood and brain material. After killing his victim the murderer had dug a shallow hole at the foot of a partially burnt tree stump; deposited the body into the depression and then finished burning the trunk. The body of Morris would have remained concealed if it weren't for a pack of coyotes, which had dug it up and partially consumed it.

A few days later a party of emigrants from the Black Hills came upon the gruesome remains, which they quickly recognized as Harry Morris because the dead man and Frank Robert had recently visited their camp on the trail. The party immediately notified General Buell at Fort Custer who ordered them to arrest Frank Robert and return him to the post. With the men from the Black Hills on his trail, Frank Robert made it to Baker's Battlefield, just south of Huntley where he procured a horse for his getaway. After receiving word of the crime, and suspecting that Frank Robert was the murderer, Muggins Taylor turned the man's horse loose during the night so that he couldn't ride out the following morning.

Once again on foot, Robert stole a skiff and started down the Yellowstone River where the party of miners from the Black Hills who were by then reinforced with other local volunteers, eventually stopped him. Robert somehow escaped from that posse and made it on foot as far as McAdow's flourmill near present day Billings where he was finally arrested by a detachment of the Second Calvary from Fort Ellis who had been looking for renegade Indians and illegal whisky traders. First Lieutenant James W. Hamilton and his men delivered their prisoner to Gallatin County Sheriff Silas "Si" Ralston at Dave Carpenter's Trading Post near the Yellowstone Crossing. Since the murder had taken place on an Indian reservation Robert was turned over to the U.S. authorities.

Frank Robert reportedly confessed the crime to Lt. Hamilton and his men during transit but when he was brought before U.S. Commissioner McPherson he denied any knowledge of the murder. The prisoner was denied bail and his case was assigned to the April term of the U.S. District Court at Virginia City and on Monday, October 8, 1877, Deputy U.S. Marshal John X. Beidler arrived in Virginia City with Frank Robert to await his trial.

On Tuesday morning, November 6, the officers at the Madison County Jail detected that Frank Robert was attempting to break jail by cutting through the bars of a window in his cell. Without the prisoner's knowledge Sheriff A.J. "Jack" Edsall slipped around back of the jail building and fired off his six-shooter into the air just inches from where Robert was working on the bars. The prisoner was so terrified that the sheriff and his deputies were able to enter the prisoner's quarters, confiscate the contraband tools, search and inspect the cell before Robert realized that he hadn't been shot. Somehow the prisoner was able to gain possession of the knife, which he had patiently wore down to the thickness of a fine saw blade and then hammered teeth in it with a dull dinner knife provided for his meals.

Undersheriff John Carruthers determined that the suspected murderer had worked on his escape for a number of days as he had managed to cut half way through one of the iron bars and had started on another by the time the officers detected the problem. Before the incident the prisoner was wearing a ball and chain on each foot but after his attempted break for freedom Robert had to drag an additional ball from each ankle. Two months later when the deputies were rearranging the bunks in the jail to increase the number of beds to accommodate additional prisoners, they uncovered evidence of other attempts of jail breaking. The county jail building was built of double logs with stone, gravel, lime and other debris filled in between the two walls. After giving up their attempts of cutting through a wall when they ran into rocks in the inner log wall, the prisoners had almost succeeded in filing down the bolt ends on the hinges of the steel door of the structure.

The prisoner's trial was postponed until the March of 1878, term of U.S. District Court at Virginia City and the counsel, witnesses and prospective jurors had all arrived in the mining camp as required. Then just as the court was about to be opened on Friday, March 15, 1878, it was abruptly terminated when U.S. Marshal A.C. Botkin made a startling announcement that he had no funds to pay the expenses of the juries, witnesses or other court costs at the U.S. Courts at Virginia City, Helena and Deer Lodge.

Apparently the Department of Justice froze the marshal's account in the Montana Territory when Marshall William F. Wheeler wasn't reappointed and it wasn't released soon enough after Marshal Botkin's appointed. Whatever the reason for the mess-up, it was a terrible hardship for the Territory and especially for the people involved in the U.S. Courts at the time. As is the case today, the reimbursements paid in 1878, by the government were more often than not less than the actual expenses incurred by the witnesses and jurors, and when they weren't paid at all, it was a great hardship.

An example of the hardships experienced in March of 1878, by witnesses for the Robert case was when one man had to walk the sixty-some miles to Virginia City from Bozeman because he didn't have the money for the coach fare. He had counted on the reimbursement for his expenses so that he could purchase a ride back to his home after the trial and to pay for his room and board while he was at Virginia City. When the U.S. Marshal lowered the boom on the courts this particular witness ended up having to walk back home and then he was still in debt with the hotel manager in Madison County for his room and board.

Another witness whose actual expenses exceeded what he would have received by over a hundred dollars was forced to go home only to be called back again in September. All of the witnesses and jurors could ask for a voucher at the time but they were required to hold them until redeemable in June. If the person needed the cash before then, the vouchers were transferable but of course at deep discounts.

During his trial, Frank Robert told the jury that he and Harry Morris were prospecting along Rotten Grass Creek when they got into an argument. The defendant did not deny killing Morris but he claimed that he had shot his partner in self-defense. The defendant claimed that when Morris attacked him with a rifle he stepped aside while shooting the man and when his partner went down to the ground Robert shot him again in the back of the head with his revolver. According to the defendant, after the shooting he wandered about the Big Horn River half dazed and after a day or two he returned to the camp where he buried his dead partner. He claimed that he was on his way to report the incident when Lt. Hamilton and his men took him into custody.

The prosecution pointed out that the defendant tried to burn his victim's body for two days in order to conceal the crime and they successfully presented the argument that the victim's head was clubbed in while he was asleep and that he wasn't shot in the manner that Robert described. Lt. Hamilton testified that when Robert was arrested he was in possession of property, which was later identified as belonging to Harry Morris. Other witnesses testified finding the body of Morris; identifying the victim's property later in possession of Robert and told of the defendant's confession. After only a short deliberation on Friday, September 13, 1878, the jury returned a first-degree murder verdict. The defense immediately made a motion for a new trial, which was denied by the court.

Because Frank Robert had insisted so adamantly during his trial that he had killed Morris in self-defense, and as he had no friends, a number of citizens of Virginia City raised enough money to procure a post mortem examination of the victim's remains to determine the truth. The group obtained the services of Dr. L.S. Tesson, the assistant army surgeon at Fort Custer and Joseph Rhinehart the hospital steward for the fort and William A. Allen accompanied them to the gravesite near Fort C.F. Smith on October 7, 1878. The doctor's report indicated that while Morris had been shot in the head, a blow from a blunt instrument was the fatal wound to the skull. In contrast of claims made by the defendant, the victim had no other gunshot wounds to the body.

A scaffold was build in an enclosure directly behind the courthouse and the iron rod or "trigger," which supported the trap on the gallows that was used to execute William Wheatley on August 13, 1875, and William Sterres on October 28, of that same year was borrowed from Lewis and Clark County. Because the United States had jurisdiction in the case, U.S. Marshal Botkin was in charge of the hanging of Frank Robert and he named Deputy U.S. Marshal James H. McFarland of Helena as executioner probably because of his experience with the execution of Wheatley and Sterres in 1875. Colonel Francis C. Deimling, the local post master and Madison County Sheriff Edsall and his deputies also assisted the U.S. marshals in the hanging.

On Monday morning, September 16, 1878, Deputy Marshals Morris and Mitchell escorted Frank Robert into the crowded Madison County Courthouse for his nine o'clock sentencing. The prisoner walked to the courthouse with what was described as a quick and nervous step but except for an occasional twitch of his mouth he maintained an air of bravado during the proceedings. When asked if he had anything to say before his sentencing, the defendant addressed the court in broken English but it was said to have been an eloquent and dramatic plea that he had killed his partner in self-defense. Robert concluded by telling Judge Blake that if he was to be executed he wanted to be hanged at once. At that point Judge Blake sentenced the convicted murderer to be hanged on Thursday morning, October 31, 1878, between the hours of nine o'clock a.m. and eleven o'clock.

The only emotional reaction that Robert displayed was when he quickly snapped his fingers in approval when Judge Blake announced that he would not order the delivery of the condemned man's body to the physicians for dissection. When the condemned man was returned to his cell Robert commented that he would rather be shot than be hung and he immediately asked for a calendar so that he could figure his remaining days. Some of the officials heard the prisoner exclaim in a disgusted tone of voice, "By Damned, I've got plenty of time."

It was said that the condemned man's attitude changed from the bravado demeanor he had maintained before his conviction to a confidence in his salvation with his Maker. This was no doubt with the help of the Reverend Father Frank Kelleher and the Sisters of Charity of the Catholic Church. Father Kelleher had complete faith that Robert had been truthful during his trial and he accompanied the doomed man to the scaffold.

A few minutes after nine o'clock on October 31, 1878, the condemned man was removed from his cell and taken to the sheriff's office where Colonel Deimling read the death warrant in a firm and impressive voice, which reportedly had an effect on everyone present except Robert. The prisoner had prepared a long written statement describing the killing of his partner in self-defense and a description of Harry Morris, which was read aloud in the jail by Father Kelleher. After the reading Colonel Deimling asked Robert if he had anything else to say, and when he answered in the negative the officer announced that the sentence of the law would be carried out.

Robert then shook hands with the officers and asked for alcohol and after taking his last drink he wished everyone present "Good Luck" and then he accompanied the procession to the scaffold. As the condemned man walked with a firm step to the top of the platform, Father Kelleher recited the appropriate prayers of the Catholic Church. At the gallows the officers quickly prepared the doomed man for his execution and at 9:30 that fateful morning the drop fell and ten minutes later Francois Joseph Robert was pronounced dead.

Postscript:

Deputy U.S. Marshal J.H. McFarland eventually left the U.S. Marshal Service and returned to Helena where he became a deputy sheriff for Lewis and Clark County and assisted in the execution of Peter Pelkey in February of 1881. Then when he was running his livery stable at Helena, he was called on to help arrest Con Murphy in January of 1885, only to be over powered by a Lynch Mob and watched his prisoner be hanged. While he wasn't mentioned as assisting with the Furhmann execution in 1883, he helped with the hanging of Joseph Allen in September of 1899.

Judge Henry Blake had already sentenced Michael McAndrews to hang at Radersburg and after sending Robert to his death he went on to order the execution of two more men at Helena, William Biggerstaff in April of 1896 and William Gay in June of that same year.

The Double Execution of Joseph K. Koble and Orlando H. Marsh at Fort Benton

In January of 1879, Joseph Koble, and fellow Third U.S. Infantry Army privates, Orlando Marsh and Frenzler or (Fensler) had planned to desert from the service. They had planned to steal government supplies with the aid of the recently discharged Private Joseph Campbell and then make their escape on stolen army horses. One of the conspirators had written a letter describing the devious plot to a black prostitute who ran a whorehouse at Fort Benton by the name of Lizzie Clark. Instead of delivering the note to Lizzie the messenger gave it to the fort commander, Colonel Moale. The colonel didn't take any action at the time, hoping that he could catch the thieves red-handed in the affair.

On the night of the scheduled crime Colonel Moale and several of his officers staked out the corral but after the prescribed time came and went the officers left the detail to a sergeant and a corporal. Private Paddy Farrell accompanied the sergeant and the corporal to the corral and when the thieves appeared Farrell arrested one of the would-be deserters. Some accounts state that Private Farrell was in on the plot to desert and others have said that he was the person who had delivered the letter to Colonel Moale. Nevertheless which version is correct, Marsh and Koble immediately suspected Farrell of betraying them and had vowed vengeance against him.

It was generally believed that Marsh had planned the murder of Private Farrell and he had convinced Koble, Campbell and Frenzler to assist him. Obviously there wasn't much planning involved in the murder and Marsh merely waited for an opportunity to arise after things had cooled down at the post. One such opportunity arose on February 6, 1879, when Private Farrell was going to attend a party held at the home of another black prostitute by the name of Ellen Martin on upper Main Street. Since Campbell had been mustered out of the army and living outside the garrison he was detailed to steal a razor and a revolver from a Fort Benton resident on the evening of the party and then return the bloody weapons to the owner's home after the crime so that he would be suspected for the murder.

Everyone got rather intoxicated at the party and Koble had gone back to his quarters to sleep it off and Marsh actually had to awaken him and take him back to the ball. Sometime between midnight and two o'clock on the morning of February 7, 1879, Private Farrell was returning to his quarters somewhat intoxicated when the four conspirators intercepted him. The actual particulars of the murder are unclear because of the varying statements of the defendants but it was believed that Koble came up behind Farrell and slit his throat with the razor and Marsh finished him off by beating him to death with the revolver.

The men carried Farrell's body down to the Missouri River where they tried to sink the corpse through an air hole in the ice but failing, the men took the body back to Ellen Martin's house where it remained until the following evening. Campbell was employed as a teamster at the time and therefore had access to a wagon and team, which the murderers used to haul the ghastly load to Nine Mile Coulee some fourteen miles from Fort Benton and buried it in the snow. When Private Farrell was absent from duty for a day or two, Colonel Moale suspected foul play and his body had been tossed down the hole in the ice. The colonel ordered his troops to cut a channel through the ice in order to drag for the body and for two days the soldiers fired blank cannon cartridges into the river in hopes of raising the corpse.

Eventually Sheriff John J. Healy and Colonel Moale arrested army privates, Koble, Marsh, Frenzler and Campbell and took them before Probate Judge John J. Donnelly on Saturday evening, March 1, 1879, and charged them with the murder of Private Farrell. Koble waived an examination but Marsh submitted to a hearing and they were both held without bail. The men were separated and after a few terms in the sweatbox and questioning by the county commissioners, Campbell and Frenzler confessed to the crime. The two men described the murder as was previously described except that they swore that Farrell's body was thrown into the Missouri River. Campbell also acknowledged that he had stolen the murder weapons and that he had attempted to frame an innocent man for the crime.

Months later at the Territorial Penitentiary both Frenzler and Campbell told reporters that their confessions had been illegally coerced, accusing Sheriff Healy, his deputies, the county commissioners and others of forcing them to confess to the murder. Frenzler further claimed that a man by the name of Charles Engle had dictated to him exactly what to say and that Colonel Moale helped revise his confession on two different occasions. Frenzler also stated that he was in bed at the time of the murder and that he was never represented by counsel.

Campbell said that he was taken to the prosecutor's office at night and that the building was surrounded by an angry mob. He was told that the only way he would be protected from the lynch mob was to make a confession that coincided with that of Frenzler's. Campbell later discovered that the mob was only put on in order to deceive him.

Campbell made it clear that Private Frenzler did in deed have counsel as Mr. Jacob A. Kanouse had acted as counsel for both of them. In defense of the state, the reporter pointed out that it would have been difficult to get the U.S. Army the sheriff's department, the county attorney and the county commissioners to all agree to conspire against Frenzler and Campbell. He also pointed out that the two men couldn't explain why they hadn't told the truth about the disposal of Farrell's body or Campbell's securing of the murder weapons little less the attempt to frame an innocent man.

Immediately after the dastardly crime and arrests the "Fort Benton Record" published a fiery editorial for the need of a District Court at Fort Benton. It was pointed out that the method of trying criminals in the past by a people's court or Miners' Court or by the Hometown Vigilantes would no longer be adequate. While there had always been acceptable reasons against holding a District Court at Fort Benton in the past, the increase in crime at the headwaters of navigation called for a formal system of justice. The primary reason against utilizing a court system at Fort Benton had been the heavy tax burden on the county but each boating season left behind more and more of the vile scum thrown off from the communities down river. After the Farrell murder even the leading taxpayers of the county were calling for a District Court for Chouteau County.

District Court Judge Decius S. Wade was assigned to the first term of court held at Fort Benton and he presided over the first murder trial there. District Attorney Colonel John A. Johnston handled the prosecution while Judge John J. Donnelly and Jacob A. Kanouse were assigned to defend Koble and Marsh. The trial began on Monday, April 21, and the jury was made up of the following citizens of Chouteau County:

R.S. Culbertson	Stephen Spitzler	D.G. Rickard
Charles Rowe	W.B. Smith	C.S. Sanborn
William Morris	Al Rogers	Thomas Currie
John Fitzpatrick	Jeff Deveraux	Thomas Haley

The principle witnesses in the case were the defendants' accomplices, Frenzler and Campbell and their confessions and testimonies sealed the fate of the two army privates. Some thirty other witnesses were examined and after long and eloquent speeches by both the defense and the prosecution the jury was out for only thirty minutes, less than the time it took for Judge Wade to explain their instructions. The verdict was guilty in the first degree and Orlando Marsh and Joseph Koble were sentenced to be hanged on September 5, 1879. Frenzler and Campbell were later given life sentences at the penitentiary at Deer Lodge for their part in the murder.

For several months after the murder there were so many reports coming into Fort Benton from down-river ports like Sioux City claiming that they had recovered the body of Private Farrell that the Chouteau County commissioners withdrew the reward for the body of the soldier. Finally during the second week of June of 1879, a stockman who was rounding up his cattle found a decaying body in the uniform of a U.S. soldier near the Highwood Road. Coroner Dr. James W. Wheelock accompanied by Sheriff Healy, Colonel Moale and several soldiers along with a number of Fort Benton citizens that later made up the coroner's jury rode out to investigate the remains.

Most of the man's features were unrecognizable due to the decomposition but after a close inspection of the man's clothing it was positively determined to be the remains of Private Farrell. Along with a slit throat and fractured skull the victim had been shot once in the body. The discovery of Farrell's body on the prairie caused enough uncertainty about the case that Territorial Governor Benjamin F. Potts granted a respite of thirty days to allow for further inquiry but the additional time and investigations only further proved the guilt of the conspirators. Finally on September 18, 1879, the Governor extended the respite by one day and then notified Sheriff Healy that he would refuse to commute the death sentences of the condemned men and that they would be executed on Monday, October 6.

After their arrest Koble frequently boasted of committing every crime on the books except arson and rape. Along with Marsh and another prisoner Koble attempted to escape jail by cutting away the prison door but Sheriff Healy and Undersheriff Talbert detected the plot just in time to prevent the breakout. Koble displayed several times that he could easily escape from any handcuffs placed on him and just four days before his execution he removed both his and Marsh's irons and they were able to cut their way through the floor of the jail but were caught just as they were gaining their freedom. While the two condemned men were trying to escape, Sheriff Healy had ordered a Trap-Type Gallows to be built behind the little log jail, which stood on the corner of Main and Wetzel Street.

While Marsh was usually quiet and resigned to his doom, Joe Koble exhibited a cool indifference and joking spirit throughout his confinement. The sheriff read the death warrant to the two prisoners in the jail and when he finished Koble put on his coat as if he was going to dinner. Both Koble and Marsh maintained their nerve and they walked up the steps to the scaffold with a firm step and without a tremor. Koble displayed a pleasant smile and he disappointed the crowd by not offering a confession. He then shook hands with the sheriff and his deputies and thanked them for their kindness. After again proclaiming his innocence, Marsh also shook the hands of his guards and then took his spot on the platform.

When the ropes were being placed around the necks of the doomed men, Koble requested that his be drawn up tight and after the request was granted, he quietly said, "Slap it to me." With that the trap fell and the two men dropped to their death. Joseph Kobel died without a struggle and there was no visible movement of his body except for a few heavy heaves of the chest, Marsh didn't appear to have struggled. After hanging for about thirty minutes the bodies were taken down and Dr. Wheelock declared that both of their necks had been broken. It was said that no men had ever died braver or apparently with less pain.

Postscript:
Feeling good about the action of their newly formed justice system at Fort Benton, the newly formed Grand Jury began efforts to further "purify the moral atmosphere" of the river community by attacking the Negro prostitutes living there. The "Fort Benton Record" stated that prostitution and unlawful cohabitation were not only against the laws of the Territory but a social disgrace and a detriment to the prosperity of Fort Benton. The editorials pointed out that in the early days when there were few or no white women in the Territory, Indian women were a common feature of every settlement. The paper went on by saying that as long as the Indian women were properly married they were still accepted by the society. As civilization progressed in the country unmarried Indians or any other women had become an obnoxious custom with the newer arrivals to the Territory. Shortly after the trial of Marsh and Koble, the black prostitute, Lizzie was sentenced to the county jail for fifty days for operating a house of ill repute.

The U.S. Army Troops had been stationed at Fort Benton for many years, first being quartered at the adobe fort, later when the walls began to crumble the boys in blue were moved to the old Carroll and Steele building next to the Overland Hotel. Later they were stationed at the old I.G. Baker & Co. store on lower Front Street where they remained until the troops were finally withdrawn. Colonel Moale commanded the last company stationed at Fort Benton.

After the execution of Koble and Marsh, Judge Wade had sent a total of four men to their deaths, having previously sentenced two men to hang at Helena, William Wheatley in August of 1875, and William Sterres in October of that same year. He would go on to be the Champion of all Montana Hanging Judges with six executions when he ordered Heinrich Furhmann to the gallows in May of 1883, at Helena and John Clark in December of the same year at Bozeman.

While serving as sheriff and assessor for Chouteau County during the Marsh and Koble case, John J. Healy was also the local editor and business manager for the Fort Benton "Benton Record." Before serving as the chief law enforcement officer for the county Healy had reportedly rode with the Original Vigilantes at Bannack and had helped organize the Sun River Valley Rangers, a vigilance committee set up to protect the settlers and stock between Fort Benton and Helena.

A few years after being sentenced, Frenzler became insane at the penitentiary and he was transferred to the asylum at Warm Springs where he eventually became a trusty. In May of 1894, Governor Rickards recommended a pardon for Joseph Campbell and in June the State Board of Pardons approved the action and he was released from the penitentiary.

October 6, 1879
Joseph K. Koble and Orlando H. Marsh

Location and Gallows: Koble and Marsh were hanged in the jail yard at Fort Benton on ***Gallows No. Four: (September 1879)***.
Crime: Murder of fellow soldier Private Patrick Farrell in the early morning of February 7, 1879.
Judge: Chief Justice Decius S. Wade
Prosecution: District Attorney Colonel John A. Johnston
Defense: Judge John J. Donnelly and Jacob A. Kanouse
Sheriff: John J. Healy
Distinction: Not only were Joseph Koble and Orlando Marsh the first men to be legally hanged in Chouteau County they were also the first legal multiple execution.

February 4, 1881
Peter Pelkey

Other Name: John O'Brien
Location and Gallows: Pelkey met his death in the jail yard of Lewis and Clark County Courthouse on ***Gallows No. Two: (August 1875): Galloping Gallows One.***
Description: Pelkey was a twenty-four-year-old French Canadian, and a man of great muscular strength on a frame of five foot nine inches tall. He had black hair along with coarse features and he was described as being rather stupid looking.
Crime: Murder of Charles Tacke on August 30, 1880
Judge: Everton Judson Conger
Prosecution: District Attorney Colonel John A. Johnston
Defense: William H. DeWitt and I.B. Porter
Sheriff: Charles M. Jefferies: Before becoming the sheriff of Lewis and Clark County, Jefferies was a blacksmith and had served on the jury of the Miners' Court trial of Arthur Compton and Joseph Compton and he was present for their execution by the "Hometown Vigilantes" in April of 1870.
Distinction: Pelkey might have been the first man hanged in Montana that tried to use the insanity defense. While there had been a five hundred dollar reward offered for Frederick Shaffer for his part in the murder of Warl in 1875, the bounty of a thousand dollars offered for Peter Pelkey was the first ever collected for the capture of a hanged murderer in Montana.

About noon on Saturday, September 4, 1880, Mr. Henry Tacke came to Helena where he informed the authorities that his brother, Charles had been missing for several days. Charles Tacke was a bachelor, somewhat eccentric and kept to himself and seldom visited his neighbors. The missing man was in his fifties and was born in the Dukedom of Brunswick, Germany. He came to America in 1853, and began his 320-acre ranch in the Prickly Pear Valley in 1870. The last time he had been seen was when a neighboring rancher paid him eighty-five dollars on Monday August 30.

Sheriff Charles Jefferies along with some of the neighboring ranchers rode out to Tacke's place, which was about four miles out of town just off the main Bozeman Road. After first searching the man's cabin the men were attracted to the large log stable by a stench, which grew stronger as they approached the building and it became almost unbearable when they opened the door.

The body of Mr. Tacke was dressed in nightclothes and found in a manger covered with lime, which had been emptied from two large barrels. The laborer that Tacke had employed by the name of John O'Brien was missing along with a valuable stallion that belonged to the dead man. Sheriff Jefferies returned to Helena where he dispatched the coroner to the crime scene and he notified the law enforcement officers across the state to watch out for the suspect. County Coroner Dr. William L. Steele left Helena and he secured the following coroner's jury:

Robert Harwood	Fred Rose	Henry Monkmyer
Henry Ward	Henry Pflamme	

The body of Tacke was removed from the manager and it was found in horrible condition. The lime along with the moisture from the corpse had generated additional heat, which hastened the rate of decomposition and the condition of the body was said to be impossible to describe in words. There was an axe clotted with blood and hair near by and the skull was broken in two places indicating that death must have been instantaneous. Tacke's black felt hat had a deep slice in the crown indicating that he had been wearing it when the axe struck him.

The verdict of the coroner's jury was withheld from the public so that its result wouldn't hamper the selection of an impartial jury. The remains of the murdered man was later dressed in a suit of black broadcloth and placed in a rosewood casket and as the body was taken into Helena for burial it led a large number of sympathetic neighbors. Meanwhile Undersheriff Hathaway resigned his recently elected position of honorary Marshal of the County Fair and immediately started in pursuit of the suspected murderer.

It was later determined that John O'Brien or Pelkey had witnessed Mr. Tacke being paid the eighty-five dollars from a neighboring rancher and was also aware of the money that the old man kept in a trunk at his cabin. After killing his employer on Monday, August 30, 1880, Pelkey robbed the body and then took the one hundred and forty dollars from a trunk at the cabin.

The murderer then saddled the stallion and rode to the Dearborn Crossing, arriving there Tuesday, August 31, where he traded the horse to Mr. Thomas, the proprietor of the hotel for eighty dollars and a gray horse. From the Dearborn Pelkey headed for Fort Benton where he met John Largent at Bird Tail Divide along the Benton Road.

At Fort Benton Pelkey acquired a skiff, which he used to get as far as Cow Island where he stayed overnight at the camp of woodcutters, Mike Duvall and Stephen Hodgins. According to Duvall, who had known

Pelkey in Minnesota years earlier, the men spent part of the evening reminiscing about old times. The next morning Pelkey bargained with his hosts for a horse, paying them forty dollars and his small boat. By then it had been about a week since the murder and after asking Duvall and Hodgins the best route for the Yellowstone River Pelkey road off. About the tenth of February Duvall and Hodgins received the details of the murder in Lewis and Clark County and the description of the suspect along with the Governor Potts' one thousand dollar reward.

Believing that Pelkey was the wanted man, the two woodcutters armed themselves and began tracking him southward where a group of Gros Ventres Indians said they had seen the lone man. The chase after Pelkey continued for several days eventual passing near the Snowy Mountains. Duvall and Hodgins went to the Reed and Bowles Ranch on Big Spring Creek in the Judith Basin where John J. Bowles joined in the chase. The three-man posses then headed for the Stevens Ranch some forty-five miles near Judith Gap where they camped for the night.

The following morning the three men rode six miles to the Barrows and Allis' sawmill on Robert's Creek where they found Pelkey working as a laborer. Mr. Duvall positively identified Pelkey as the mill workers were being called for dinner. When his pursuers covered him with their rifles and ordered him to throw up his hands, Pelkey tried to make a run for it, but he stopped in his tracks when the men threatened to shoot him. When arrested, Pelkey had in his possession a Henry Rifle, a Smith and Wesson revolver, a slung shot and forty dollars. At that point Pelkey completely broke down and made a complete confession stating that he was "a murdering son of a bitch" and asked for a French priest, as he was ready to die. He tore open his shirt and begged his captors to shoot him down on the spot.

Instead of granting his wish, the men shackled Pelkey and mounted him upon a horse, which they had procured at the sawmill and rode back to the Reed and Bowles Ranch. At the ranch the party secured a wagon and team and while they were riding towards Diamond City, Pelkey grabbed one of the repeating rifles, placed the muzzle to his head and pulled the trigger three times. Since Pelkey wasn't familiar with the Burgess Patent rifle, he hadn't first levered a cartridge into the chamber before pulling the trigger.

At Diamond City, Meagher County Deputy Sheriff Charles T. Rader met the men and accompanied them to Helena. Along the way Mr. Bowles read a newspaper account of the murder to Pelkey in the presence of the other posse members and the accused man once again admitted that he had committed the crime. He describe how he was first tempted by the money the neighbor had paid Mr. Tacke and that he also knew about the funds in his employer's trunk. The prisoner said that he had struck Tacke in the head and then finished him off by crushing his skull as he was shivering on the ground. Pelkey also explained that he had trouble with Tacke's faithful horse during his escape, saying that the animal appeared to know that his master had been murdered. According to Pelkey, the horse kept trying to bite his leg during the first night and for part of the journey to the Dearborn Crossing he was compelled to lead the animal on foot.

While the Territory was awarding the one thousand-dollar reward for the arrest and delivery of the fugitive to Mike Duvall, John J. Bowles and Stephen Hodgins, Peter Pelkey faced his preliminary examination before Probate Judge Hedges on September 22, 1880. After again confessing his crime, Pelkey was remanded to the county jail without bail to await action of the grand jury in November.

The prisoner was arraigned on Tuesday, December 7, where he pled guilty to the murder charge and it was at that time he claimed his real name was Peter Pelkey. The Third District Court, presided by Judge E.J. Conger opened on December 13, and the following Lewis and Clark County residents were selected for the jury:

James Mason	Joe H. Smith[6]	Gilbert Benedict
J.J. Fant	J.R. Johnson	O.C. Bundy
Abram Collett	F.M. Wood	Henry Monroe
W.H. Kimberlin	Homer Hewins	(unknown)

On the second day of the trial Pelkey took the stand in his own behalf and in his lengthy testimony he described the murder and his escape in a straightforward manner. He claimed that after he had accidentally struck Mr. Tacke with the axe, the sight of the blood made him crazy and then he killed the man. He described how he had first gone through the dead man's pockets and then dragged the body into the stable by the feet. The defendant explained how he disposed the body in the manger and then buried it under the barrels of lime "so the hogs wouldn't get at him and eat him up." Pelkey then said that he was so devastated by what he had done that he decided to take his own life. He went into Tacke's house where he looked for rat poison and when he couldn't find any he took out his revolver but he couldn't bring himself to pull the trigger.

Pelkey skipped over the part about searching the house and taking the money out of the trunk apparently to persuade the jury that he had committed the hideous crime in a state of temporary insanity. The defense then called Dr. Madden to testify on the possibility that the mere sight of blood could actually make a person mad and to rebut Dr. William Steele's testimony that he believed that Pelkey was sane at the time of the murder. Dr. Madden told the court that a physician, referring to Dr. Steele couldn't determine a person's sanity in a thirty-minute interview.

The jury retired at six o'clock Wednesday evening, December 15, 1880, to deliberate the case and they remained all night. At 9:30 the next morning the jury entered the courtroom and asked for further instructions, and after the judge had spoken to them they once again withdrew to their quarters. At ten o'clock the jury returned a verdict of "Murder in the First Degree." Pelkey listened to the verdict and didn't appear to be effected, but as he was being escorted back to the jail he told Deputy Hathaway that he didn't understand what had happened.

On the night of Pelkey's conviction a "Helena Herald" reporter came by the jail to interview the prisoner and found Pelkey sitting on his stool pulling vigorously on his short pipe, but immediately got up and shook the newspaperman's hand and offered him a seat on his cot. While Pelkey was described as being in a dull and listless frame of mind, he didn't seem totally dejected and he could even be cheerful at times. Pelkey said he was born in Canada and had moved to Maine with his family when he was a child.

After working for a lumberman for several years in Maine, Pelkey said he moved to New Hampshire and from there to Minnesota where he worked for four years at several lumber firms in the Minneapolis area before coming to Montana in 1879. The prisoner never gave his actual hometown saying that he didn't want his family to learn about his fate. Pelkey said that the news would kill his mother and he felt that the jury shouldn't have returned a first-degree verdict because the crime wasn't premeditated. He told the reporter that he would prefer prison instead of death but if he wasn't granted a new trial he would die like a man.

Despite the deep snow and cold temperature on the day after Christmas of 1880, the courthouse was crowded with curious people wanting to hear the sentences passed on the various criminals convicted during the last court term. The attorneys were rather late and they staggered in one at a time or in pairs and they gathered in small groups around the heating stoves and cracked jokes and seemed to be best of friends despite their stormy altercations when the courts were in session. At ten o'clock Judge Conger entered the room and shortly afterwards the prisoners were brought in.

After the other prisoners were sentenced, Pelkey was ordered to stand up and although he seemed to be in better health than he did during his trial, he still maintained his sullen indifferent attitude. When asked if there was any reason why sentence should not be pronounced on him, Pelkey answered in the negative. After reading the history of the crime and legal action taken against the convict, Judge Conger sentenced Pelkey to be hanged at the same day and time as the Indian named So-pee. Pelkey accepted the sentence without emotion and at the conclusion he bowed and before taking his seat he thanked the judge.

Pelkey was Catholic and while waiting for his execution he spent most of his time in prayer. He was said to have been in the best of spirits and he joked with the other prisoners as they passed through the corridor. The walls of his cell were elaborately decorated with illustrated papers and fashion plates and on the night stand by his bunk lay a bible along with several other religious books and pamphlets. He later told a reporter: "I know I did wrong and am sorry for it, but it is too late now, and I am willing to die for my crime. I had a fair trial, and I am entirely satisfied with the way I have been treated by the court." He also expressed his gratitude to Sheriff Jefferies and Jailor Peter Tone for their kindness.

The same scaffold used to hang William Wheatley and William Sterres in 1875, was once again erected in the jail yard of the Lewis and

Clark County Courthouse. The high-board fence made the enclosure for the gallows look quite small and dreary especially when the carpenters built scaffolding around the inside of enclosure for the security guards. Although the county still had the two ropes, which had been used for the previous executions, Sheriff Jefferies still ordered a new one for the hanging of Pelkey.

Early on the morning of the execution throngs of men and boys gathered around the jail yard and they began climbing on the roofs of the adjoining buildings. As the hour grew closer to the execution the crowd, which included several women steadily increased and they occupied every available space overlooking the death scene. So thick were the crowds packed on the nearby roofs that three of them reportedly collapsed. The crowd was described as a good-natured and cheerful mob that laughed and joisted noisily while awaiting the hanging.

Although Sheriff Jefferies stated that he had received several hundred requests for admission to the execution, he explained that by law he was only allowed to admit the judge and clerk of the court, the prosecuting attorney, two physicians, a preacher, two relatives or friends of the condemned man and as many peace officers required to preserve order and finally twelve reputable citizens. Many citizens of Helena that didn't receive invitations were calling that the legislature, which was in session at the time change the law and permit public executions in Montana.

Pelkey had always slept well during his imprisonment, but he had a restless night on the eve of his execution and his healthy appetite had also abandoned him and he reportedly only ate a few crackers for his last meal on earth. At ten o'clock Father Palladino arrived at the jail and he engaged in prayer with Pelkey and reporters from both the "Helena Independent" and "Herald" came by to bid the doomed man farewell. From the accounts of the reporters it was learned that, "even condemned men are not ungrateful for the attentions bestowed them by the members of the press." It was reported that a tear came to Pelkey's eyes when the men shook hands for the last time.

While smoking his pipe, Pelkey said that his parents were still living in Canada and that he hoped that they would never learn of his fate. When asked if he had ever served time in jail before, he explained that he had been jailed twice, once for nine days and another for ten both for getting into fights. He said that when he was younger he was quiet strong and he loved to get into fights.

Pelkey's cell adjoined the main corridor of the jail, and while the reporters were interviewing the condemned man several of the other inmates including J.H. Kennedy, So-pee, the Indian and a black man gathered around to listen to the man's story. Kennedy had become friends with Pelkey and had been reading the Bible daily to the French-Canadian who couldn't read English. When asked if he had seen the scaffold and the other preparations made for his execution, Pelkey laughed and said that he hadn't, but he would see them soon enough.

Shortly after eleven a coffin was brought into the jail yard wrapped in a blanket and placed beneath the gallows and at a quarter to twelve the undersheriff and Constable James H. McFarland took the condemned man from his cell and seated him in an armchair in the corridor. The cage door opened and Sheriff Jefferies announced solemnly, "Pelkey, I will read to you the warrant of the court, which is my authority for executing you this day." As the prisoner answered the officer with a polite bow the sheriff read the death warrant in a clear and distinct voice in order that every word of the document was plainly heard throughout the room. The prisoner listened to every word attentively and at the conclusion he bowed his head low and then said with a pleasant smile, "That is alright."

The prisoner was dressed in a new Alpaca wool coat; well-worn pantaloons and new sandals as Father Palladino, the sheriff and several of his deputies and constables escorted him to the gallows. As they entered the jail yard the noisy and boisterous crowd in the enclosure and on the rooftops suddenly became silent and a shocked look came over many of their faces. While every eye was on the prisoner, Pelkey's unflinching gaze was on the scaffold and perhaps his coffin beneath the platform.

Pelkey ascended the steps of the gallows calmly and then knelt on the trap beneath the rope and prayed for a few minutes. Father Palladino read a prayer and Pelkey repeated it and then he kissed a cross that was presented to him. The doomed man arose to his feet and after shaking hands with the priest the officers secured his arms and legs with a large leather band around his waist and smaller straps held his wrists.

During this procedure Pelkey remained calm and shook the hands of the officers and even assisted James McFarland with the proper adjustment of the noose around his neck. By then, McFarland was an experienced executioner having assisted in the hanging of William Wheatley and Bill Sterres in 1875, and Frank Robert at Virginia City in 1878. It was said that at the moment the noose was placed around Pelkey's neck his face paled slightly but the color quickly returned.

The black cap was drawn down over his face at one minute past midnight and upon a signal, Undersheriff J.T. Jefferies cut the cord; the iron lever flew back with a loud clang and the man's body shot through the trapdoor. The body fell about five feet and stopped with a dull thud, a sound, which many of the witnesses later said, "they would not soon forget."

Pelkey's body hung silently for a few seconds, but then it began trembling and the man's hands and feet twitched; then his body went still. The "Helena Independent" referred to the reaction as "The struggle for separation of body and soul, which we call death." The noose reportedly had slipped and the knot ended up at the back of Pelkey's neck but an examination of the remains later indicated that the man's neck had been broken in the fall.

After four minutes Drs. Madden and Morris reported that the man's heart was beating 196 beats per minute, a minute later it had reached one hundred and fifty-six beats. Six minutes after the drop the pulsations were so rapid that they couldn't be counted. After twelve minutes the two doctors detected fifty-six beats and four minutes later the heart had stopped. After hanging for twenty-two minutes the body of Peter Pelkey was cut down, placed in the coffin and it was delivered to the county undertaker.

Postscript:
The "Helena Independent" later published a story stating that ghostly sightings had been seen at the Tacke Ranch in the Helena Valley. According to the story, Tom Darrington, a neighbor of the murdered rancher escorted a reporter along with John B. Sanford and A.M. Walker onto the Tacke farm on March 30, 1881. At the ranch this party met another group of men and women from Helena and they all reportedly saw several lights that night. According to Mr. Darrington and the other neighbors, the strange lights, which sometimes were as bright as a lantern of a locomotive, first made their appearance just before Christmas of 1880. The lights were rather red in color and they usually glided across the surface but the neighbors said that they had also seen them pass over the Tacke farmhouse.

Some of the skeptics were sure that the lights were the work of mischievous rascals but when it was learned that many visitors commonly took pot shots at the lights with rifles and shotguns, it was determined that no one would risk their lives over a prank. Others believed that the lights were phosphorescent flashes caused by ground water, which seemed plausible at first until the fact that the lights were seen over dry ground and in snowing conditions with temperatures of thirty below zero.

On the April 9, 1881, the "Virginia City Madisonian," reported that the account in the "Independent," although thrilling, was merely a yarn for their April fool's Day issue. Some say that the report in the "Madisonian" was published to try and squelch the activity at the Tacke Ranch because there had been so many visitors at the farm that the authorities were worried that someone would get hurt or damage would be done to the property.

Later in the 1920's Reverend Father Lawrence B. Palladino told another story about the lights. The Reverend wrote in his book, "Indians and Whites in the Northwest" that during the first two weeks that he was with the prisoner, "Pelkey was stolid, stupid-like and as devoid of all human feeling." Then one day as he visited the prisoner he was totally amazed when he found Pelkey an entirely different person.

Pelkey told the priest that during the night a strange light came into his cell and that it had struck terror into his soul. He said that his heart was broken with grief for his victim and all he wanted to do was do penance for his sin. Father Palladino said that the jail guards were also shocked by the change in the prisoner's character. Reverend Palladino claims that he never did report the incident about the light to others even when they talked about seeing lights at the Tacke Ranch.

May 27, 1881
John B. Douglas

Location and Gallows: Douglas was hanged at Virginia City from ***Gallows No. Five: (May 1881)***.
Description: Thirty-seven years old
Crime: Murder of Mrs. Celestia Alice Earp on March 24, 1881
Judge: Everton Judson Conger
Prosecution: District Attorney Judge Francis K. Armstrong
Sheriff: Marshall "Mark" D. Plantler
Distinction: Not only was John Douglas the last man hanged in Madison County he also had the dubious honor of being the first man in Montana to be hanged from a "Jerk-Type" gallows. Instead of utilizing a trap and drop, the "Jerk-Type" scaffold used a weight to abruptly lift the condemned man into the air, breaking his neck either on the way up or the fall back down. (See: "Montana Gallows" chapter for more information about the different scaffolds used in the territory and state)

Mrs. Alice Earp was a soldier's widow who had come to Montana from Wharton, in Wyandott County, Ohio, about eighteen months before her death. She was described as being a good looking and enterprising woman who saved her money and worked for some of the best families in Bozeman and as a chambermaid at the Laclede Hotel. She had a sister; Mrs. Bowzier of Bozeman but she lived on her own and during the summer of 1880, Mrs. Earp filed on a piece of land about twenty miles north of town, close to her brother, George Morrison.

Since Mrs. Earp wasn't physically capable of making the necessary improvements on her homestead, she employed John B. Douglas, a bachelor in the neighborhood to do much of the heavy labor. Douglas was born on January 22, 1845, in West Unity, Adams County, Ohio where his mother, a sister and seven brothers still resided. While Mrs. Earp treated Douglas with kindness the employee became infatuated with the woman. When the woman felt that it was no longer safe to live on the ranch because of Douglas' attentions she decided to sell it. Douglas offered to buy the place from the woman, giving up what she already owed him plus thirty dollars and a gold watch and chain.

After accepting Douglas' offer, Mrs. Earp returned to Bozeman where she found work with the Wylie family. When Douglas went to town and discovered that the woman was seeing a gentleman, he reportedly became enraged and began threatening her life if she didn't marry him. By the time Mrs. Earp had gone to work for the family of Mr. Charles Rich in March of 1881, Douglas had also moved to town where he could continue to stock the woman. Finally Mrs. Earp realized that the only way she could rid herself of her nemesis was to leave the territory and return to the States.

On Tuesday, March 22, Douglas once again confronted Mrs. Earp at the Northern Pacific Hotel where she again refused to marry him. At the hotel Douglas drew a pistol to shoot her but the woman was able to wrestle the weapon away and lock it away in a suitcase. Douglas most certainly would have killed Mrs. Earp at that point but the hotel proprietor, Mr. Wakerfield and other men interfered.

About nine o'clock Wednesday night, Mr. George Ash drove the woman by buggy out to Black's Station on the Virginia City Road where she caught the "Virginia City, Bozeman and Pony Stage Line" for Virginia City. Douglas found out where she had gone and he immediately took chase and overtook the stagecoach at the Red Bluff Station, which was about half way to Virginia City. While at the halfway station Mrs. Earp told the proprietor of the hotel that she was afraid of Douglas and she was offered protection.

As the coach was preparing to leave on Thursday morning, March 24, the men at the station confronted Douglas and told him to leave the woman alone and he agreed to return to Bozeman. While the stage proceeded on to Virginia City, Douglas rode away towards Bozeman, but when he was out of sight he doubled back and again overtook the coach near Sterling. Douglas rode past the coach several times to terrorize the woman who was sitting next to Jim Delaney the driver and to find the best place to ambush his intended target.

Douglas finally rode his horse up along side of the coach and he began firing his Smith and Wesson 45-caliber revolver into Mrs. Earp, striking her in the lung, arm, and then a third shot to the head. The murderer then rode ahead of the coach, where he ordered the driver to stop, threatening to kill him too if he refused. After noticing that the woman was still moving, Douglas shouted out: "What, you ain't dead yet!" and then he emptied his weapon at Mrs. Earp. As the gunman was re-loading his pistol, Delaney put the whip to the horses and drove on to Sterling with Douglas in pursuit. When they reached Sterling, Douglas was flashing his weapon and threatening to shoot any man interfering with him.

While the mortally wounded woman was being carried to the house of Richard Goin, Dave O'Brien of Pony arrested John Douglas. After disarming his prisoner O'Brien tied up and escorted Douglas on the stagecoach to Virginia City where a large crowd had gathered to meet the six o'clock stage and followed the prisoner to the county jail. When first arrested at Sterling, Douglas claimed that Mrs. Earp had robbed him at Bozeman, a charge the wounded woman solemnly denied, saying the money she had was the proceeds from the sale of her property.

Mrs. Earp lingered in great agony until about three o'clock on Saturday afternoon, March 26, 1881, when she finally died. She remained conscious right up to the time of her death and was able to give explicit directions for the disposal of her property and the full account of her terrible attack and its cause. The only emotion expressed by Douglas while he was in jail was disappointment when the stage brought in the news that Mrs. Earp was still alive at Sterling. The prisoner was openly relieved when on the next day he was informed that the woman had finally died. Mrs. Earp was buried at Bozeman and the Presbyterian Society handled the service, which was reportedly attended by many people.

The grand jury met on Monday, March 28, and after investigating the facts and interviewing the witnesses, they brought in an indictment against John Douglas for murder in the first degree. The overwhelming evidence was presented and the witnesses stated the facts at Douglas' trial and on Friday, April 1, 1881, the jury returned a verdict of guilty in the first degree. On Monday Sheriff Marshall "Mark" D. Plantler and his deputies escorted Douglas to the spacious courtroom, which was filled to capacity for his sentencing. A deep silence overtook the room as Judge Conger ordered the defendant to rise and then he ordered the sheriff to hang Douglas until dead on Friday, May 27, 1881.

While the judge was reading the sentence Douglas stood motionless except for a nervous twitching of his mouth, and his constant swallowing. When the judge concluded, the prisoner sat down with his head held in his hands. As the sheriff was escorting the prisoner back to the jail it was evident that the man's fortitude had deserted him, and he pulled his hat over his face to avoid the curious gaze of the on-lookers. John Douglas was sentenced along with two Chinese, Ah Wah and Ah Yen convicted of murdering another man from their homeland during a neighborhood China-War but their sentences were later appealed. The Chinese men managed to escape by exchanging places with two other men during visiting hours while the convicted murderers were waiting for their new trial.

A newspaperman interviewed Douglas about a week after his sentencing to learn more about him and get his side of the story. The prisoner told the reporter that he was a native of Ohio, about a hundred miles from where his victim had once lived. Douglas had been living at Flathead Pass for about six years when in July of 1880, Mrs. Earp's brother introduced him to the woman. Douglas explained that Mrs. Earp had filed on a homestead on Pass Creek, which had also been claimed by Ebenezer "Elk" Morse,[7] who was giving the woman a tough time over the property. Douglas took the woman's side and after the property dispute was settled she hired him to help improve her property.

Douglas claimed that he was employed in September, and from that time until March 10, 1881, he and Mrs. Earp had lived together as man and wife. The prisoner said that after he had purchased the ranch from the woman she went ahead to Bozeman where Douglas was to join her. they shared a room for eleven days at the Northern Pacific Hotel and it was there that Douglas claimed that Mrs. Earp was holding four hundred dollars of his own money in a suitcase.

The prisoner explained that the argument at the hotel was about discovering part of his money was missing and Mrs. Earp called him crazy when he confronted her about it. He said she promised to return the money but when he learned that she had left Bozeman he followed her to Sterling. To further damage his victim's reputation, Douglas told the reporter that Mrs. Earp had earlier planned to marry a prominent Bozeman man; and after stealing his money she was going to run off to the Yellowstone country with Douglas.

In mid-April, Douglas began complaining about boredom and he begged to have at least a clock in his cell to keep him company and the officers gave the prisoner a small thirty-hour timepiece, which had been sitting around in the sheriff's office. Douglas appeared to be very grateful and everything went well until Sunday evening, May 1, when the sheriff noticed that the clock had stopped ticking.

When the sheriff inquired about the timepiece, Douglas explained that the clock was out of order even after he had tried to clean it. The sheriff was dubious about the explanation, and after an inspection he discovered that about ten inches or more of the mainspring had been removed, which was going to be fashioned into a saw blade. When the clock was taken to a clockmaker, it was determined that other parts were also missing, and after a search of Douglas' cell was made, several screws, a wheel and several pinions were recovered.

After his plan of escape failed, Douglas played the insanity dodge in an attempt to save his neck from the hemp. The condemned man also began embellishing his past criminal history and his stories of murders and bank-robberies would have filled several dime novels of the day. By the middle of May, Douglas was looking forward to his trip to the scaffold, and his only complaint was that the day of execution wasn't nearer. While he never expressed any remorse for his crime, he was always admitting that he was willing, if not anxious to pay for it on the gallows.

With his time running short and the chance of escape impossible and with no one taking his insanity seriously, Douglas devoted most of his time reading the bible so that he'd be ready to be "swept through the gates." During this period when he was deeply engaged in his religious exercises he recanted all the stories of murders before the killing of Mrs. Earp. He finally admitted to only serving two years in the penitentiary for one sentence, and he was later sentenced to a six-year sentence, but he had escaped on the way to the pen.

John Douglas had the unenviable distinction of being the first man executed in Montana with the "Jerk-Type" gallows. At the time that Sheriff Plantler decided to use this means of execution it was considered the most novel type of hanging since the early days of the Vigilantes when out of necessity the executioners used everything from trees, unfinished buildings and fence poles.

Instead of dropping the victim through a trap, the "Patent Weight System," as it was then called, jerked the condemned man from the ground. The condemned man stood on a small platform on the ground and when a heavy weight was released the doomed man was jerked into the air, rarely failing to break the man's neck causing instant death. (See: Chapter Seven: "Montana Gallows" for more information about this and any other scaffold used in Montana.)

On May 22, 1881, Mrs. Bowzier, the sister of his victim, visited Douglas on the Sunday before his execution and observers said that the interview was brief and not very touching. The woman had nothing but contempt for Douglas while he was hard and insensitive. While Douglas showed no remorse in front of his victim's sister he later told another visitor that he had turned his life around and he had read the Bible from cover to cover and the New Testament three times.

At about 10:30 on the morning of his execution, Douglas was taken from his cell; and after his shackles were removed he was cleaned up and dressed in the suit that he was buried in. While being attended to by the deputies, Douglas began speaking freely about his childhood and his mother, sister and seven brothers who still lived in Adams County. The condemned man told Deputy Hauschild that he was ready to die and gave him directions as to the disposal of his property. He also repeated that he hadn't committed all those crimes he had earlier bragged about, explaining he was only trying to conceal his fear.

Sheriff Plantler read the death warrant to the prisoner at 11:45 in the sheriff's office and Douglas became notably nervous as he was being escorted to the gallows. He was afraid that he would loose his nerve if the affair lingered on, so he practically ran into the temporary enclosure in the courtyard where the scaffold stood. Once he was under the noose, however, he seemed to have regained his composure, and while he was being bound he seemed to be in prayer. The Reverend W.A. Shannon offered a brief but earnest prayer, and at the conclusion the black cap and noose were placed over Douglas' head. The sheriff raised his hand, the weight dropped and John Douglas was whirled into the air, coming back down where his body swung to and fro.

Except for a few slight contractions of the muscles during the first few minutes, there were no other signs of life in the swinging body. Four and half minutes after the weight fell, the man's pulse had ceased.

Postscript:

If departed spirits could return to earth, Bozeman might have had a ghostly visit back in 1881. Just before his death, John Douglas expressed the wish of returning to Bozeman for just an hour or two to put a scare in the many citizens there who feared him. But the "Madisonian" newspaper correctly noted that, "Damned spirits do not return from Hell."

Madison County was again reminded of the recent hanging when the Bozeman postmaster advertised in the "Courier" that there was a letter at the post office for John B. Douglas. At that time, postal patrons were required to pay the postage at the time of delivery and letters had to be picked up at the post office. The "Madisonian" of Virginia City got quite a kick out of informing Postmaster Taylor that the letter would have to be sent to Hell for Douglas to receive it.

Sadly in 1883, Judge Conger was charged with drunkenness and corruption and as a result he was suspended from service.

May 2, 1883
Heinrich "Henry" Furhmann

Other Name: Henry Fohrman
Location and Gallows: Henry Furhmann was hanged inside the enclosed jail yard at Helena from ***Gallows No. Two: (Aug 1875): "Galloping Gallows" No. One***. For a description and history of this scaffold or another see Chapter Seven: "Montana Gallows"
Description: Furhmann was a seventy-year-old German national who weighed under a hundred pounds and generally walked with a cane. He combed his white hair over his head to hide his baldness and he wore a light-gray beard. He didn't speak English and a court interpreter translated the entire court proceedings to him.
Crime: Murder of his son-in-law, Jacob Kenck on December 22, 1882.
Judge: Chief Justice Decius S. Wade
Defense: Thomas H. Carter and Mr. McCutcheon
Sheriff: Steven C. Gilpatrick
Distinction: At age seventy, Henry Furhmann was probably the oldest man hanged in Montana and his execution was the first hanging at Helena where the law prohibiting public hangings was truly enforced. Helena City Marshal Deegan and a special police force were stationed on the rooftops of the buildings in the immediate area to prevent unauthorized spectators from viewing the hanging.

Helena was startled about noon on Friday, December 22, 1882, when the news spread that Heinrich "Henry" Furhmann had shot his son-in-law, Jacob Kenck. The tragedy occurred at the front door of Horsky and Kenck's Saloon on upper Main Street while Mr. Kenck was carrying on a conversation across the street with Mr. Rohrbaugh of the Wicks Stage Line. As the two men were talking, Henry Furhmann walked up behind his son-in-law and shot him behind the right ear, the bullet entering the base of the brain of the victim.

Kenck dropped immediately and when a crowd quickly gathered around him he asked, "Boys, what is the matter? Is somebody hurt?" Apparently Kenck didn't realize he had been shot and then he fell unconscious and was taken to his home on the west side near his brother, Chris Kenck where Dr. Ben C. Brooke attended him. Furhmann was taken straight to the jail and when he was told that Kenck might live he said he was sorry and that he would try killing him again. He told the officers that he wanted to kill his son-in-law on Christmas Day of 1881, but he had broken his arm before he could do the job. He admitted that he had been carrying his old-style 36-caliber Colt, five-shot revolver with a cut-off barrel for over a year just to kill Kenck.

Furhmann had come to Montana ten years earlier from Germany after his daughter had arrived in Helena and saved enough money for her father's passage. Furhmann's face was covered with a light beard tinged with gray and he was often seen walking along the streets of Helena carrying a cane in his hand. Jacob Kenck eventually married Furhmann's only daughter and they had two children. Furhmann lived with his daughter and her family for several years before she became sick and died. The old man brooded over the loss of his daughter and he had always blamed his son-in-law for his loss. When Kenck married his second wife, Furhmann made a big scene refusing to live in the same house and he moved to a small cottage near the smelter.

The day after the murder of Kenck the streets of Helena were reportedly filled with excited mobs with intentions of lynching Furhmann. After the entertainment at the opera house had finished there were several secret meetings at about a dozen saloons on Main Street. The small to medium sized gatherings would be conversing quietly and when a stranger walked up to the plotters they would disperse and then reunite later. Sheriff Steven Gilpatrick was aware of the activity and he stationed a strong guard inside and out of the jail as well as detailing several men to patrol the streets within two blocks of the courthouse.

At about one o'clock in the morning a crowd began to gather at the front of the jail made up of interested citizens trying to maintain law and order as well as angry members of the community who wanted to take care of business with a sprinkling of curious folks wanting to see how it would all turn out. In no time at all, the mob had swelled to perhaps one hundred and fifty men with the individuals who meant business in some sort of disguise, the majority wearing a handkerchief over their faces. There was no direct attempt to break into the jail but the air was filled with shouts of: "Bring him Out!" and "Hang him!"

Before the excitement had reached a great pitch the prominent and more respected citizens began arguing with the leaders of the angry mob and the majority of the crowd listened to the voice of reason and began to disperse. While there were many rumors that the crowd was filled with members of the old-time Helena "Hometown Vigilantes," it was later determined that most of the agitators had only been the good friends of the popular victim.

The funeral services for Jacob Kenck were held at the Catholic Church under the auspice of the Gesang Verein Harmonia and the entire membership attended. The funeral procession was headed by the Helena Silver Cornet Band, which the deceased had been a member. At two o'clock on the afternoon of December 26, 1882, the remains of Jacob Kenck left the family home and taken to the Catholic Church for services and then they were interned in the nearby cemetery. A day later Henry Furhmann was arraigned in probate court for the murder and Warren Toole was initially assigned to his defense.

The trial began on March 26, 1883, and it was presided over by Judge Decius S. Wade who not only held the spring term of court at Helena and Custer County he also conducted the District Court at Bozeman after that. The securing of a twelve-man jury in the Furhmann case took a day and a half to interview the fifty-six prospective jurors and since Furhmann had difficulty understanding English, Mr. Ignatius Miller, an early pioneer of Montana translated the proceedings to the defendant.

Mr. Buchler was the first witness and he told the court that he was with Mr. Kenck at the time and that he had witnessed the shooting and Deputy T.H. Kleinschmidt testified that the defendant had asked him at the jail to go to Furhmann's cabin and retrieve certain important papers, which would justify his killing of Kenck. When the mysterious documents were presented at the trial they proved to be only the newspaper obituary of his daughter's death and other unimportant and irrelevant papers. One witness testified that Furhmann had told him that he didn't expect to be hanged because he wasn't heavy enough to stretch the rope.

The principal feature of the trial was when Furhmann testified on his own behalf and described in detail the circumstances of the crime. The defendant made no attempt to deny that he had killed his son-in-law and that it was indeed premeditated. After Furhmann's testimony the defense called medical experts to explain to the court the mental status of the defendant and after final arguments the case went to the jury at 3:30 on the afternoon of Thursday, March 29, 1883.

After deliberating for a full twenty-four hours the jury returned a first-degree murder verdict at 3:30 on the following day. When the verdict was translated to the defendant all he said was, "It is what I expected." For a moment Furhmann grasped his throat as if he was suffocating, but then he quickly reverted back to his attitude of complete indifference.

The following day the courtroom was filled again with spectators to here the sentencing of Furhmann and the defendant was brought into the courtroom shortly before two o'clock and he didn't appear to be distressed or interested in the least over the serious situation. When the hour of two arrived the court was called to order and Judge Wade instructed the interpreter to tell the prisoner to stand up. Furhmann complied with the order and after the judge read the history of the case he asked the defendant if he had any reason why sentence shouldn't be pronounced. Furhmann only said that there were thirteen witnesses for the defense who were not examined during the trial.

Furhmann told the judge that he could face death as a soldier with powder and ball but not on the gallows, which was not a proper place for any man to die. Judge Wade then asked Furhmann's counsel if they had anything to say and Mr. Carter responded that the case had been quickly tried and he told the court that it was not too late for additional inquiry into the prisoner's mental condition. The judge stated that he could not stop the proceedings and therefore they would proceed. In his sentencing of Furhmann Judge Wade said that a jury had found the defendant guilty by of deliberately killing Jacob Kenck and while he had pity for the prisoner, he had to do his duty. He then ordered that Furhmann be hanged on May 2, 1883, between the hours of ten o'clock a.m. and three o'clock p.m.

After an inspection of the eight-year-old scaffold, Sheriff Gilpatrick found that the support posts had deteriorated and he decided to use only the crossbeam and the hardware of the original gallows. The deep creases worn into the old crossbeam from which the fatal noose was suspended showed evidence of its long service and the re-built gallows was erected on April 30, 1883.

On the day of the execution a "Helena Daily Independent" reporter interviewed Furhmann in the jail office with the aid of Mr. Miller the interpreter. Walking past the rows of cells of the jail, the reporter found Furhmann in Sheriff Gilpatrick's private office where he had been sleeping for several nights under a heavy guard. The prisoner was in excellent spirits as he was dressing himself in a plain black suit. While John Steinbrenner was assisting him, Furhmann was talking with everyone in the office as if he were preparing to take a coach on a journey. As the prisoner was brushing his white hair all to one side to hide his baldness, Mr. Steinbrenner tried to smooth the wrinkles from Furhmann's suit. Furhmann made it clear that death by hanging was a great disgrace and he wanted to be shot by three German soldiers. He told the reporter that he wasn't sorry for murdering Jacob Kenck, but if he could turn back the clock he might not have killed the man.

Although a friend said that he thought Furhmann was a Lutheran, the prisoner claimed that he was not a Christian and that he believed in Pythagoras a belief in reincarnation where the spirit of the dead passed into birds, animals and even into plants. Because of his beliefs, he argued that one's acts in the here and now had little or no effect on his future state and he refused to see any clergymen and never received any religious counsel while in confinement. The prisoner was guarded day and night since his sentence to death and he told the reporter that at one time he had considered suicide to avoid the disgrace of hanging, but he gave up the idea after about a week to ten days. The reporter noted that the rumors of Furhmann's failing health was entirely false and that the prisoner's life in confinement appeared to be comfortable and that he had been eating and sleeping well.

Governor John Schuyler Crosby refused to grant a reprieve stating: "In the rapid growth of our Territory, protection of life is so dependant on the certainty of laws, that I think it dangerous to assume a power of overruling judicial sentences and encouraging any feeling that certain and just punishment may not be safely left to the calm deliberation of properly constituted tribunals. The seventy-year-old Furhmann later said that he had expected the Governor's refusal to pardon or reprieve him and he was fully resigned to die.

After going to the bathroom for the last time Furhmann took a plug of tobacco and he put the rest of it into the right hand pocket of his coat, and then placed a snuffbox in the left pocket. He then reached for a bottle of Rhine wine, which had been placed on ice, and after offering some to those standing around, he took a drink and replaced it to the bucket under the table. At eleven a.m. Furhmann's attorney, Mr. Carter came in and explained to his client through Mr. Miller that all hope was gone and then went over the condemned man's will instructing Drs. C.K. Cole and Charles G. Brown to examine his brain to determine his sanity.

After being marched into the corridor, Furhmann was seated in the same armchair that Pelkey had sat in two years earlier to hear his death warrant. This time Sheriff Gilpatrick read the death warrant to the condemned man in both English and then it was translated into

German and Furhmann listened unconcerned. Ten minutes before twelve Furhmann was led to the gallows where he was assisted up the steps and onto the platform. The prisoner said very little and acted as if he wanted to get the execution over quickly. Furhmann didn't want to be bound but of course the request was denied and while his arms and legs were being pinioned he showed no signs of trepidation and appeared to be completely indifferent. It was said that Furhmann only had a vacant stare as he looked at the sky above. Just before the black cap was placed over his grinning smirk he said, "Now Chris Kenck will laugh."

Meanwhile a large crowd of curious citizens had gathered in the mud outside of the tall fence in hopes of at least being able to hear the trap fall and the twang of the rope as the condemned man fell. Deputy Sheriff George Conrad sprung the trap at four minutes before twelve and the body of Henry Furhmann dropped about seven feet, hung completely still until five minutes after twelve noon when Drs. Morris and Leissen announced that his pulse had ceased. Furhmann's body was then lowered into the coffin that was prepared by George Hermann. According to state statutes, about fifty officials and other invited persons witnessed the execution of Henry Furhmann inside the enclosure.

Postscript:
As was requested in his will, the body of Furhmann was delivered to Drs. Cole and Brown for examination where it was determined that man's brain weighed forty-eight ounces, which was normal for a ninety-five-pound man and nothing was found to indicate that he was otherwise perfectly sane.

Heinrich Furhmann was the fifth man that Judge Decius Wade had ordered to death having already sent two men to the gallows at Helena, Wheatley and Sterres; then Koble and Marsh at Fort Benton. Defense Attorney Thomas H. Carter later became the last delegate to the U.S. Congress for the Territory of Montana and then he won the congressional election of 1889, making him the first state representative to serve in Washington DC.

August 16, 1883

Ah Yung

Other Names: Ah Kee,
Location and Gallows: Ah Yung was hanged inside the jail yard of the Missoula County Courthouse from ***Gallows No. Six: (August 1883)***.
Description: Ah Yung was considered a very bad character having been suspected of killing fifteen Chinese and two white men.
Crime: Murdering paymaster, Chung Yu while attempting to rob him at Horse Plains, present day Plains on January 29, 1883.
Judge: William J. Galbraith
Prosecution: Judge William J. Stephens
Defense: Frank H. Woody; came to Montana in October of 1856 and resided in Missoula County under three Territories, Washington, Idaho

and Montana.
Sheriff: Charles W. "Uncle Bill" Berry
Distinction: Not only was this the first legal execution in Missoula County history, Ah Yung was the first Oriental legally hanged in Montana. His death was also the quickest reported on a Montana scaffold, having been declared dead after only a minute and a half.

Ah Yung was considered a rough thug who loafed around the various camps refusing to work but living off the honest laborers. He had planned to set off explosives at the tent of the Chinese paymaster at Horse Plains, and in the excitement get away with between fifteen hundred and two thousand dollars in payroll along with as much as four hundred dollars worth of opium that was being held in the shelter. While Ah Yung was digging a trench around the tent to place the explosives, another Chinese discovered what he was doing and sounded the alarm. When Ah Yung ran off, Chung Yu, the paymaster of the Wing See Company chased after him. At that point Ah Yung turned and shot and killed Chung Yu and wounded another man.

The authorities immediately posted a four hundred dollar reward for the capture of Ah Yung and during the last week of February he was captured at Frenchtown. Then because of some bizarre reason, there was a question whether or not the reward was going to be paid so his captor released the prisoner. A few days later Andrew Como of Frenchtown arrested the fugitive at Nine Mile and took him to Missoula where he was arraigned before Justice John L. Sloane on Monday, March 5, 1883, but it was delayed until March 12 because of the absence of a key witness. The prisoner was charged under the name of Ah Kee, but he later stated that his actual name was Ah Yung. He was a good prisoner and Undersheriff Robert Lane reported that Ah Yung did well in jail and his appetite was always good.

Sheriff Charles Berry reportedly couldn't find any plans for a scaffold so he designed the gallows himself from scratch. He had an eight-foot square platform erected and at eight-feet off the ground it probably utilized the traditional thirteen steps. Sheriff Berry's scaffold was built inside the standard high-board enclosure behind the jail and with a railing around the gallows platform it looked like a judges' stand at a horse race. However instead of having a canopy over the top of the platform there was a hefty crossbeam erected to support the hangman's rope, which provided for a drop of about six feet. The trapdoor was hinged on one side and it was supported with an iron crossbar. By an ingenious manner the trap was sprung when the sheriff pulled a lever on the platform.

Sheriff Berry requested spiritual counseling for the condemned man and on Tuesday, August 14, 1883, Reverend George M. Fisher of the Presbyterian Church visited Ah Yung and Reverend George Stewart and Father Joseph Menetrey visited the prisoner on Wednesday. Reverend Stewart reported that Ah Yung had no ideal about his future after death and the interpreter explained that Ah Yung was of the lowest class in China and therefore he had not received any instruction of any kind including religious. The spiritual advisers tried to get a confession from the prisoner but all he ever said was the answer he had clung to since his arrest: "Me no kill him."

From the time of his capture until a few hours before his death, Ah Yung remained in the best spirits, whistling, laughing and singing as well as even helping out with the chores around the jail. As time drew near to his execution the doomed man became gloomy but he still marched to the scaffold bravely. After confidently climbed the stairs to the platform he sat for about ten minutes on a common chair where he displayed a pitiful look on his face. Ah Yung generally stared straight down but occasionally he glanced quickly upon the curious onlookers in the enclosure that numbered about a hundred. By accepting the invitations to the affair each of the witnesses had agreed to act as volunteer guards for the Missoula County sheriff. When Sheriff Berry stepped to the front of the platform and asked for the removal of hats, and Reverend George Fisher offered a short but fervent prayer on behalf of the doomed man.

At twenty minutes to two, Sheriff Berry motioned the prisoner to step forward onto the trap and Ah Yung obeyed promptly. Undersheriff Lane fastened the straps around Ah Yung's legs, arms and hands while Sheriff Berry adjusted the noose around the prisoner's neck and carefully pulled down the black cap. As the deputies stepped down from the gallows the sheriff walked to the north side of the platform and quickly pulled the lever and the body of Ah Yung fell through the trap where his toes settled just inches from the ground.

The witnesses reported that there wasn't a single quiver or so much as a twitch of a muscle of a finger detected. Ah Yung's neck was broken and there was no pulse detected after just a minute and an half. After being allowed to hang for a full thirty minutes, the first man legally hanged in Missoula County was then placed in a coffin and buried by the sheriff.

Postscript:

After his defense of Ah Yung, Frank H. Woody assisted his brother Joseph Woody and Missoula County Attorney Frederick C. Webster in the successful prosecution of John Burns who was hanged in December of 1893. Frank Woody later defended Louis Mott who was eventually hanged in March of 1904. Mr. Woody was also the first mayor of Missoula and many people of the law including W.F. Sanders considered him one of the finest attorneys in the Northwest.

December 27, 1883
John A. "Frank" Clark

Location and Gallows: Clark was hanged in the Gallatin County Jail yard at Bozeman from ***Gallows No. Seven: (December 1883).***
Description: Clark was described simply as "not good looking" but he reportedly was well built, standing five foot, seven inches tall and quite husky.
Crime: Murder of Thomas Rodgers at Trail Creek on June 20, 1883
Judge: Chief Justice Decius S. Wade
Prosecution: County Attorney Thomas R. Edwards
Defense: J.L. Staats
Sheriff: Charles P. Blakely
Distinction: Clark was the first man legally executed in Gallatin County

Thomas Rodgers and Peter Lyman had been working for the railroad to raise money for a grubstake to work at the Clarke's Fork mines and after saving up about eight hundred dollars the two men left from Bozeman towards Gardiner with a wagon, a span of horses and a complete camping outfit. They stopped at Rocky Canyon for whisky and when Rodgers pulled out the big roll of green backs it caught the attention of John A. Clark who had been hanging around the bar. Clark started out ahead of the two men and at Mountain House, which was about seventeen miles east of Bozeman he pawned his gun in order to look like he had money. Clark managed to eat with Rodgers and Lyman at the Inn and the two railroaders told him of their plans of going into mining and he convinced them that they would need his services as an experienced packer and guide.

On Wednesday, June 20, 1883, the three men came upon Pine Creek, a tributary of Trail Creek, about eighteen miles from the mines where Clark told the men that the spot was the last best campsite for many miles. After making camp, Clark persuaded Rodgers to go fishing with him up Pine Creek, and because of the abundance of deer in the area he encouraged him to take a rifle. When Peter Lyman last saw his partner alive he was leaving camp with Cark and carrying his Ballard rifle. Not long after the men had left, Lyman reportedly heard three quick shots, and then he waited for the hunters to return with some game.

After waiting several hours at camp Lyman took one of the horses and rode up the creek looking for the men when he met Clark coming down the trail. Clark said that he had shot a deer and he was returning to camp to get an axe to cut up the meat while Rodgers was still hunting in the brush. Lyman continued up the creek for about mile, then crossed the creek and returned to their camp without finding his friend. Convinced that something was wrong, Lyman again rode up the creek searching for Rodgers, and not finding him, he spent the night with Congers Smith at his cabin along the creek. In the meantime Clark hitched up the team and left camp with the wagon and supplies.

The next day the two men organized a search of the area with other residents of the county and the dead body of Thomas Rodgers was found in the brush along Pine Creek. Rodger had been shot twice in the head, his lower jaw was shot away and his skull had been crushed in from being pounded on with the stock of the rifle. The victim had been robbed of about five hundred dollars but there was still two hundred and fifty dollars concealed in his clothing. The murderer had removed the victim's suspenders and used them to strangle the man and then used Rodger's coat and vest to cover his bloody head and face. The victim's weapon was not found but the scabbard for Rodgers' rifle was found about thirty yards from the man's remains and the marks on the ground indicated that the body had been dragged after being shot.

Justice Davis swore out a warrant and Constable Hineman immediately organized a posse, which found the stolen wagon and team at the Andy Ringoldsby Ranch at about midnight. White Calfee soon joined the posse and he offered to help find Clark who had once worked for him near Bozeman. From prior conversation with Clark about his girlfriends, Calfee figured he could be found with Miss Hawks who lived with her family near Livingston and as predicted the suspect was arrested without incidence at the Hawks Ranch. Clark didn't deny committing the crime and the money he was carrying indicated that robbery had been the motive.

Unfortunately the posse didn't take the money from their prisoner and Clark managed to lose the evidence on the way to the jail at Livingston. Clark was returned to Bozeman where a special grand jury was impaneled, which returned a first-degree murder charge against him. Mr. Thompson of the Yellowstone Valley, who had served on the coroner's jury over the remains of Mr. Rodgers, later said that the citizens of the Yellowstone would have certainly lynched Clark if he hadn't been taken back to Bozeman.

After his capture, Clark told the authorities that he was born in Virginia on January 12, 1852, and he lived on his father's farm. Clark joined the Eighth Virginia Cavalry in 1863 and he left home in 1868, for California where he worked the gold fields at Pioneer City until 1870, when he returned home with seven thousand dollars. In May of the following year he went to South America for eleven months where he traveled through Peru, Argentine, Paraguay, Chile and Central America before going to San Francisco.

In October of 1872, Clark moved to Missoula, Montana and for over four years he prospected, cut wood and freighted from Deer Lodge County to Oregon. In May of 1877, he worked on a pack train for General Howard on the Nez Perce Campaign and when the packers were paid off they were sent back to Walla Walla where he spent the winter. Clark bounced around Montana and Idaho until 1882, when he finally went to work for White Calfee near Bozeman.

When District Court Judge Everton Conger of Gallatin County was suspended in 1883, on charges of drunkenness and corruption it left the Territory with only two justices, Judge D.S. Wade and Judge William J. Galbraith. Between the two remaining judges they heard both criminal and civil cases along with divorces and bankruptcy hearings in thirteen counties along with attending appellate courts. Judge Wade volunteered to take on the cases in Gallatin County and in only six-days, he presided over fifteen criminal cases, resulting in seven innocent verdicts; seven men being sent to the territorial penitentiary and after a one-day trial on October 23, 1883, John Clark was found guilty of first-degree murder.

On November 3, Judge Wade sentenced two murderers John Clark and Frank Young to be hanged on December 27, and according to the October 6, 1883, edition of "The Enterprise," trials were conducted with "more regard to the time they occupy than to their general importance." In all, Judge Wade heard twenty-two criminal and one hundred and seven civil cases in the Bozeman court.

Out of his own pocket, Sheriff Charles P. Blakely furnished the twenty-one prisoners including eight convicted murderers at the county jail a fine Christmas Day dinner consisting of ten stuffed roast chickens with a variety of vegetables and all the trimmings. The sheriff furnished the inmates with good-sized "toddies" and a bushel of fresh Michigan apples for their dessert. It was said that everyone, including John Clark, had a great time and they took in the food like a sausage machine. Everyone at the holiday meal behaved themselves with one amusing exception. It seems that one of the prisoners, even with a loaded plateful, reached over and harpooned a large potato off another inmate's plate, illustrating some people have a propensity to steal under any circumstances.

A sturdy eighteen-foot tall scaffold had already been constructed of white pine at Bozeman for the execution of Carl Adolphson who was supposed to have been hanged in August of 1883, before he was saved by acting Governor McCutcheon. The massive structure including its braces took up twenty square feet and the platform was probably twelve-foot-square and since it was about nine feet off the ground it probably had the customary thirteen steps, which were on the south side of the gallows. The five-eighth inch Manila hangman rope was rigged to provide for a drop of seven feet.

The twelve-foot brick wall around the jail yard, which was just west of the jail building, was also completed in August of 1883, for the cancelled execution of Adolphson. The wall was two feet thick and it was topped with imbedded broken glass to discourage prisoners from climbing over and curious spectators from mounting it to observe executions. Besides the brick wall, Sheriff Blakely ordered a large canvas to be spread in such a manner to hide the doomed man and the scaffold from the prying eyes of persons on surrounding buildings.

On the night before his execution, Clark wrote a statement reiterating his innocence to the "Weekly Chronicle" along with three personal letters to his relatives. After writing the letters Clark composed a song and then went to sleep. At about one o'clock in the morning the prisoner awoke and he began singing his new song and then went back to bed. The jailor and Reverend Robert M. Stevenson of the Presbyterian Church who had been counseling the prisoner for the past ten days awoke Clark early on his last day and the condemned man had a light breakfast and then sang and prayed with the Reverend along with visiting with his elderly mother who had come to Montana.

Before making his march to the scaffold at 11:10 a.m., Clark embraced and gave his mother a parting kiss and then he displayed a great deal of courage as he stepped firmly up the steps to the gallows. Only the condemned man's wide-eyed glare and twitching fingers showed that he was considering his awful crime and inevitable punishment. On the gallows he carefully took his place on the trap as if he was posing for a photograph.

After the strong straps had been wrapped around the prisoner and the noose adjusted, the sheriff asked Clark for any last words. When the black cap was about to be placed over his head Clark cleared his throat and in a loud and clear voice he said, "Well gentlemen, I suppose you all know what I am here for, at least you say that I am here for the murder of Thomas Rodgers. Gentlemen of Bozeman I stand here to meet my God, and I say here today, that I am an innocent man. The man who testified against me has sworn falsely but I can meet my God innocent. My mother was brought up in good society. I was raised under a good pious mother and in one of the best families in my state. Farewell to my South, sunny home, my loving mother and the one I love."

As the last words left Clark's lips Sheriff Blakely pulled down the black cap and then motioned to Undersheriff James W. Ponsford, who instantly touched the spring. With a dull thud Clark's body fell through the trap unflinchingly and his toes ended up barely touching the ground. The body made two convulsive moves until it went still before Drs. George W. Munroe and W.H.A. Campbell pronounced him dead after ten minutes. The body was cut down, placed in a coffin and after it was determined that Clark's neck had been broken, the remains were turned over Undertaker J.B. Sennett.

Postscript:

The hangman's noose that was used to hang John Clark in 1883, reportedly ended up in the sheriff's office in the Park County courthouse and it was still there in 1897, but no one knows what happened to it after that. The same can be said about the remains of John A. Clark himself. As ghoulish as it sounds, it appears that the executed man's body was illegally exhumed and the local doctors might have used it to practice on. It was reported that on the very night of Clark's execution, Doctors Monroe and Carroll violated his final resting place and his remains were removed. Later that same evening another party of doctors dug up the same coffin but only found an empty whisky bottle and a cigar butt.

On the way out of the cemetery the disappointed party met a third group of physicians on their way in to dig up Clark's remains. After being told that there was no body in the casket, the two groups consisting of Dr. Campbell of Livingston along with Doctors Foster, Rowe, Chambliss, Waters and Whitefoot all went in search of the first party. While grave robbery was, as it is today a serious offense, the stealing of a body of a man who had suddenly died of a sore throat at the end of a rope was apparently excused because of extenuating circumstances.

Six months later the papers reported that a human skeleton was found packed in a beer box, and discarded in the brush on the road to Story's Mill near Bozeman. A coroner's inquest ruled that the remains were probably those of Clark and that unknown medical personnel had dissected the body. Identification was made by a missing toe on one of the feet of the skeleton and Clark too was missing one of his pinkies at the time of his death. The skull of the body was never recovered but the rest of the bones were finally put to rest.

March 25, 1887
Thomas H. Harding

Location and Gallows: Harding was the first man hanged on ***Gallows No. Eight: (Mar. 1887): "Galloping Gallows" No. Two***. This scaffold was originally set up behind the Beaverhead County Courthouse at Dillon. A complete description and history of this particular scaffold can be found in Chapter Seven: "Montana Gallows."
Description: Harding was a thirty-year old New Yorker who was born near Chohos.
Crime: Murder of George Ferguson near Glendale on May 22, 1886.
Judge: William J. Galbraith
Prosecution: U.S. District Attorney Robert B. Smith along with District Attorney William Y. Pemberton of Beaverhead County with C.W. Turner of Glendale assisting.
Defense: John H. Duffy and Thomas Campbell of the firm Campbell and Duffy
Sheriff: Tom Jones
Distinction: While there had been nine other men hanged in Beaverhead County prior to 1887, conducted by a Miners' Court, the Original Vigilantes and a Lynch Mob; this was the first legal execution in the county.

At about eight o'clock on the evening of May 22, 1886, Harding and two other road agents attempted to hold up the Melrose to Glendale stage and mail wagon, carrying six passengers along with thousands of dollars worth of silver bullion. As the coach driven by George Ferguson was crossing Trapper Creek, a masked man suddenly appeared in front of the team with a double-barreled shotgun and demanded that the driver stop and throw up his hands. Ferguson was described as being a hardened character and his daring bravery often bordered on recklessness and instead of obeying the command he reportedly began to raise his whip when the road agent shouted out: "Stop you son-of-a-bitch" and then discharged one of the barrels into the driver.

The shotgun blast struck Ferguson in the forehead, face and upper body and he immediately fell onto the double-trees of the wagon. At that moment the horses began running up the road out of control for about a mile before Thomas S. Merchant, who had been riding up front with the driver at the time managed to stop the coach. When there wasn't anything that could be done for the driver, Mr. Merchant drove the wagon into Glendale where a posse of angry men was quickly organized and began searching for the road agents between Trapper and Birch Creeks.

After receiving word of the murder, Beaverhead County Sheriff Tom Jones proceeded to Trapper Creek where a shotgun was found along with four facemasks and a handkerchief. In the meantime the citizens of Glendale where the murdered driver had lived for several years had raised a seven hundred-dollar reward for the capture of the killer or killers. With the large reward it didn't take long before two men were arrested and taken to Butte for questioning.

When Sheriff Jones went to Butte on May 27, 1886, to interview the two suspects who were eventually released, he discovered a key witness and strong circumstantial evidence that pointed to Thomas H. Harding. Ex-Deputy Sheriff Shortsleeves of Silver Bow County was given credit for the arrest of Harding and the prisoner remained in the Butte jail a day or two before Sheriff Jones took him back to Dillon.

On his return to Beaverhead County, Harding went before Justice Dr. H. Schmalhausen of Glendale for his preliminary examination on Monday, June 8, 1886. County Attorney W.S. Barbour conducted the examination for the Territory and the defendant; being without counsel, conducted his own defense. Mr. Barbour did a good job of linking together the strong circumstantial evidence while Harding's appearance and conduct in the courtroom was considered very poor.

Because this was merely an examination to establish whether or not there was sufficient cause to hold the prisoner over for action in the district court, Justice Schmalhausen gave Harding a great deal of latitude in presenting facts for his case. It was said that the prisoner contradicted himself several times while trying to account for his whereabouts at the time of the shooting as well as explaining his noted absence from Butte during the same time. After no one in the courtroom could make any sense of Harding's story including the accused, Justice Schmalhausen held the defendant without bail to await the action of the next Grand Jury.

Harding was arraigned on October 30, 1886, and his case attracted widespread attention when the trial opened in November. Besides being difficult to find, the jury was considered by many as a "vigilante type" panel and Mason M. Oliver, a prominent rancher of the Dillon area and one time county commissioner was the foreman of the twelve men. Mr. Merchant identified Harding as the shooter and the prosecution's presentation of the circumstantial evidence was complete and thorough while the defense claimed that an accomplice of Harding's, a man named Michael C. Kennedy had actually murdered the stage driver.

When the jury was given its instructions and went into deliberation, only a handful of people in the courthouse felt that the defendant had a chance. The popular prediction was correct and on November 4, 1886, after a short deliberation the jury came back with a guilty verdict. The following day in front of another capacity crowd,

Judge Galbraith sentenced Harding to be hanged on December 22, 1886. Although Harding's mother, who lived in New York, was rather poor, she raised every dollar she could for the defense of her son.

Harding was given another Christmas when his attorneys submitted formal papers to Acting Governor Webb to suspend their client's sentence of death until the following term of the Supreme Court. On December 8, 1886, after consulting with the Attorney General of the Territory, the acting Governor granted a reprieve for Harding until January 21, 1887. Harding's attorneys argued before the justices that the lower court judgment should be reversed as one of the members of the grand jury, Lambert Eliel was not a U.S. citizen at the time; that District Attorney Pemberton had failed to sign the indictment as was required by law and that the district court had erred by allowing the U.S. District Attorney to prosecute the case. The action by Harding's lawyers was for not as the Supreme Court affirmed the verdict of the lower court.

On January 13, 1887, J.H. Duffy went to Helena asking the Governor for a sixty-day respite to enable him to take the case before the Supreme Court of the United States and Governor Samuel T. Hauser granted a thirty-day reprieve instead and the friends of Harding began contacting wealthy officials in New York where the defendant's family resided.

Along with the respite granted to Harding, the Governor also offered a reward for the apprehension and conviction of the second man involved in the crime. Meanwhile many people of the Territory were questioning whether the return of the surefire Vigilante methods of dispensing justice would be better than the expensive judicial system with all of its delays. Using the Harding case as an example, with its slow and expensive prosecutions and long drawn out appeals, the "Dillon Tribune" published in January of 1887: "The Mills of the gods are grinding slow, too slow one fears."

Harding might have cheated the gallows if an attempted jailbreak on Saturday, February 19, 1887, had succeeded. On that day Sheriff Jones noticed that a pair of his revolvers were missing from his office and feeling sure that the weapons had somehow made their way into the hands of the prisoners, the sheriff knew the inmates were planning a breakout. The sheriff loaded a double-barrel shotgun and hurried to the jail where he found the prisoners eating their dinner under the watchful eye of Jailer Rote. The two officers ordered the prisoners into their cages and before they could begin the search the two pistols were thrown down to the floor. The weapons were dropped so quickly that Sheriff Jones and the jailer couldn't determine which of the prisoners had them.

With only ten days before the hanging of their client, Attorneys Campbell and Duffy finally received permission to file a printed brief, an application for writ of habeas corpus before the United States Supreme Court. Since it would take nearly ten days to prepare and file the brief, the Montana lawyers wired Washington D.C. asking for a further stay of execution but in the end the United States Supreme Court refused to take up the case. Another application was made to Judge Galbraith for a new trial in the district court but it was refused and the State Supreme Court refused to consider the case a second time.

Doctor Pickman of Dillon has been credited with drawing up the plans for the Jerk-Type scaffold used to hang Harding, which was at the time referred to as the "New York" Gallows. The scaffold was erected for the first time on March 24, 1887, and it consisted of a six-by-six inch beam resting upon two twelve-foot pine wood posts, which were placed ten feet apart. Two pulleys were attached to the top beam where the five-eighth inch hemp rope ran from the noose to a weight, which was a 290-pound box of sheets of tin. The large weight and the executioner were both concealed inside of an enclosure near one of the upright posts. The system was designed to jerk the condemned man off of his feet when the executioner severed a small cord, which held the heavy suspended weight. The victim's neck would generally be broken either when the body was jerked upward or when it fell back down.

Dillon was crowded on the day of the hanging with people from the outlining settlements including Glendale, Melrose and as far as Butte to witness the execution. While over the years there have been many different stories told of where the execution was held, in 1920, old-timers of Dillon who had actually witnessed the hanging claimed the scaffold was erected in the old jail yard. The old courthouse and jail at the time were located about where the St. James Guild Hall stood and facing Washington Street. Shortly after the turn of the century the old jail was moved to the north end of town where it was later used as a barn. Some time later the courthouse itself was torn down after serving as a library, paint shop, Salvation Army headquarters and a gymnasium.

The night before the execution at Dillon, Reverend Father Dolls of the Catholic Church at Butte informed Harding that the Governor had declined to interfere, which caused a restless night for the prisoner. Harding awoke early and after having a hearty breakfast at about nine o'clock, "Brownie the Barber" shaved the condemned man. The doomed man told the barber that he didn't have to be too particular because it was going to be his last shave. Harding's first visitor that day was his attorney with news that there was no hope of saving his life and after spending the rest of the morning visiting with his spiritual advisor and lawyer Harding was taken to a corner of the jail yard at 2:30 p.m.

Father Dolls and Sheriff Jones led the condemned man who was dressed in a neat black suit, slippers and wearing no hat to the jail yard. On the way to the gallows Harding asked the sheriff if he could remove his slippers, as he didn't want to die with his boots on. The request was granted and Harding went to his death without his footwear. Although he appeared somewhat pale, Harding appeared cool, collected and he showed no sign of nervousness or fear as he stepped naturally to the gallows where he stopped beneath the noose.

Sheriff Jones secured the prisoner's arms and legs and then adjusted the noose around the prisoner's neck. The officer then stepped in front of the condemned man and repeated the reading of the death warrant. After the reading Harding was asked for any last words and the man replied, "I forgive everybody." By then there was a large crowd of curious people surrounding the enclosure, which were being controlled by armed guards placed on the outside of the barricade.

At 2:35 the weight dropped and Thomas Harding was shot up with a jerk while he was still speaking with Jack Jolly of Butte. The sudden and unsuspecting jerk broke the doomed man's neck and after six minutes Drs. Pickman and Leisson announced that the heart had ceased to beat. After being left hanging for a while longer, the body was cut down and the remains were placed in a waiting coffin that was furnished by the Dillon Furniture Company. Harding's body was turned over to the only undertaker in town at the time, G.T. Paul, and the remains were buried in the Paupers' Field in the old Dillon cemetery, which was located south of Cornell Grove on the east side of the county road. Just before 1920, the bodies were moved to the Mountain View Cemetery, but it wasn't clear whether Harding's remains were moved.

Many invitations had been sent out for the execution and it was said that at least one hundred sheriffs and other officials from all parts of Montana and Idaho Territories were present during the hanging. The hangman rope was later used by Deer Lodge County to hang Martin Scott in February of 1888.

Postscript:
By 1920, there were still many men living in Dillon, who were small boys at the time of the Harding hanging who had vivid descriptions of the gruesome affair. A well-known physician of Dillon who was a small child at the time of the Harding execution said that he had attempted to witness the hanging with some other boys. When the boys were refused admittance into the enclosure they decided to observe the affair from a tall barn that was in the neighborhood. One of the older boys brought some chewing tobacco and the Doctor said that most of the kids became so sick that they wished they could have exchange places with Harding on that day.

February 10, 1888
John Patrick Hart

Other Names: John Hartt
Location and Gallows: Hart was hanged in the jail yard behind the Lewis and County Courthouse on ***Gallows No. Eight: (Mar. 1887): "Galloping Gallows" No. Two.***
Description: Hart was about twenty-five years old, about five feet, four inches tall and he only weighed about 130 pounds. He was described as having a long face with a sharp chin, small nose and mouth, light brown eyes with a grayish cast. Hart had a rather high and broad forehead and a thick growth of glossy brown hair. One of his eyes was on a distorted axis, which gave him somewhat of cross-eyed appearance.
Crime: Murder of John William Pitts on November 7, 1885, in the Jefferson County courthouse

Judge: Hart was tried three separate times, the first two at Boulder and the final hearing was held at Helena. Decius S. Wade presided over the first hearing and Newton W. McConnell heard the final two trials.
Prosecution: Montana Territorial District Attorney William H. Hunt conducted the prosecution for the first hearing at Boulder alone and Jefferson County Attorney Thomas Joyce assisted him during the next two trials.
Defense: John H. Duffy and Thompson Campbell of the firm Campbell and Duffy of Butte defended Hart during all three trials.
Sheriff: J.W. Hathaway
Distinction: While it would only take one rope to hang John Hart, it took three separate trials to stick a conviction on the murderer. Hart was granted the most appeals and received more trials than any other man hanged in Montana.

At the May term of 1886 Jefferson County court, Hart was indicted by the grand jury for murder in the first degree. Fresh from their failed attempt to save Thomas Harding from the gallows at Dillon in March of 1886, the firm of Campbell and Duffy of Butte was selected to defend him. The defense moved for a continuance, which was granted until the October term of court when the trial began on Wednesday the thirteenth. The defense pleaded insanity and they tried to prove to the jury that Hart was suffering from epilepsy at the time he killed Pitts. After the four-day trial the jury, which was led by Foreman Dr. Ben C. Brooke, was given the case on Saturday, and they deliberated for five days. Because one juror, an area rancher by the named of Rogers held out for a second-degree verdict the panel couldn't break the deadlock and Judge Wade discharged the panel on October 18, 1886.

The second trial opened at Boulder on Wednesday, May 4, and lasted until Saturday, May 7, 1887. During this trial the defense called several physicians to prove that epilepsy weakened the mind and when Hart testified in his own behalf he told the court that his father was a crazy epileptic and that he had died in an insane asylum. The defendant explained to the jury that he too suffered from such fits and that they usually occurred at night when he was in bed. The prosecution utilized non-experts as well as Dr. William Steele of Helena who testified that as a rule an insane person normally displayed specific symptoms before they became so deranged that they would commit such a crime. After final arguments were heard, Foreman H.O. Johnston led the other jurors into deliberation at one o'clock on the afternoon of May 7. While it was said that the jury had made up their decision after ten minutes, they didn't report to the courtroom with their first-degree murder verdict until three o'clock.

Defense Attorney Duffy immediately asked for a new trial but Judge McConnell denied the motion but on July 19, 1887, Governor Leslie granted Hart a new lease of life with a respite until August 26, so that he could appeal to the Supreme Court. The Supreme Court's reversed the judgment of the lower court of Jefferson County in May after J.H. Duffy had successfully argued that several errors had been made including the size of the Grand Jury, an alien was allowed to sit on the panel and that he and his client weren't allowed to interrogate the jury. It was the error, which involved the size of the Grand Jury that reportedly led the high court to grant a new trial for Hart.

By then the Hart case, with its two trials and appeals had already cost Jefferson County thousands of dollars and it was faced with the expense of another court hearing. All forty-five witnesses in the case once again assembled at Boulder, but Hart's attorney asked for a change of venue on the grounds that he couldn't get a fair trial in Jefferson County. The court granted the motion and the case was moved to the brand new Lewis and Clark Courthouse at Helena. Hart's third and final trial for his life began on November 21, 1887, and a jury was empanelled of the following gentlemen of Lewis and Clark County:

A.M. Thornburgh (f)	Anton Horsky	C.C. Thurston
E.R. Tandy	Abner Adams[8]	F.M. Proctor
John Steinbrenner	Henry Aggens	E.J. Howe, Jr.
William Dingee	E.D. Willett	Hugh Rogan

(f) Foreman of the jury

Besides the selection of the jury, the first day was involved with the examination of all of the witnesses for the prosecution except for the expert testimony involving the sanity of the defendant. After having his last case against John Hart overturned because of errors, Judge McConnell was livid when it was found that some members of the new jury had gotten together and talked over the case with outside parties while they were in a bar room drinking liquor. The judge spent the first thirty minutes of the next morning expounding the jurors and once again explaining their duties. After reprimanding the jurors the judge turned to Daniel Jewitt who was the officer in charge of the jury and ordered him to keep them together and to not allow them to communicate with any outside parties. The courtroom chuckled when the old guard shook his head and remarked that he would try, but that this jury was a hard lot and it was a big job just keeping them all together.

With the problem with the jury concluded, the witnesses for the defense were all examined including the new testimonies from two men who had recently been released from the state penitentiary. The prosecution asked for and was given time to procure copies of records to substantiate the convicts' assertions and to attempt to impeach their testimonies. On Wednesday, November 23, 1887, with all of the witnesses examined and final arguments given Judge McConnell finally turned the case over to the jury at eight o'clock that evening after giving them his lengthy instructions. In less than an hour the jury returned with a verdict of guilty of murder in the first degree. Mr. Duffy in an effort to save his client immediately gave notice to the court that he was going to ask for a new trial.

The motion for a new trial was argued on Monday November 28, 1887, on the grounds that the verdict was invalid because the jurors had not been under strict surveillance during the entire trial and some of them had talked with outside parties. Defense Attorney Duffy also pointed out that at least eight of the twelve jurors had regularly indulged in cups of liquor as an appetizer before their meals. After listening to the evidence, Judge McConnell overruled the motion for a new trial and then granted Hart's attorney until December 5, 1887, to file his bill of exceptions.

While Judge McConnell didn't consider the action of the jury sufficient cause to overturn the verdict, he severely reprimanded the panel and fined eight of the jurors a fine of twenty-five dollars each for disregarding the court's instructions. The men fined were Abner Adams, Henry Aggens, Anton Horsky, William Dingee, Hugh Rogan, John Steinbrenner, C.C. Thurston and F.M. Proctor. The judge also assessed a twenty-five dollar fine against Deputy U.S. Marshal John A. Quirk and Bailiff Daniel Jewitt who was in charge of the jury.

On November 30, 1887, Judge McConnell's voice echoed from his bench of the large courtroom in the new courthouse sentencing John Patrick Hart to death for murder. The courtroom was filled to its capacity with jurors from a previous case still in the box along with a large number of lawyers who were grouped around the judge and the outside lobby of the courthouse was full of spectators. Hart stood by his attorney wearing a neat plain black suit with the coat buttoned up with a silk neckerchief.

John Hart was in the courtroom while the previous trial was being argued and he sat smiling while resting his head on one of his hands, which was leaning on the table. At about eleven o'clock Judge McConnell delivered his instructions to the other jury and then discharged them to deliberate. Before the jury of the other case had left their box the judge ordered John Hart to stand up. While he seemed extremely interested in the proceedings of this unrelated case he expressed only subtle attention through his own sentencing.

When asked if he had anything to say, Mr. Duffy spoke for his client by saying he had nothing to say. Judge McConnell then ordered the Lewis and Clark county sheriff to erect a suitable gallows in a private enclosure and execute the sentence of death upon John Hart on Friday, February 10, 1888, between the hours of eleven o'clock a.m. and three o'clock p.m. Hart didn't show any emotion when the terrible penalty was pronounced, probably because he has heard it before. As the prisoner was being returned to the jail Mr. Duffy gave notice of an appeal to the Supreme Court and he filed the motion with the clerk of court.

On January 24, 1888, the Supreme Court affirmed the judgment of the district court and therefore John Hart would be hanged. In its twenty-five-page document the high court reviewed the case and took up each point of the grounds taken by the defendant's counsel in his appeal. The only hope left for the condemned man was then the slight hope of an appeal to the Supreme Court of the United States or a commuted sentence by the Governor of the Territory.

On February 6, 1888, a reporter for the "Helena Daily Herald" was allowed to interview John Hart and the newspaperman said that it was a bright sunny day outside when he stepped into the dismal home for lawbreakers. There was a pause at the jailer's office where Jailer Milt Witten inserted a huge key into the massive outer door to the cells and then the men passed through the heavy door before it crashed shut with a double lock.

They first entered the corridor, which was a huge cage in the center, with walls of heavy steel bars and doors. The individual cells all had steel walls, floor and ceiling with sliding doors that all lock at one time with a large lever. There was the constant clatter of the prisoners' feet pacing in the corridors and the dim light struggled to penetrate through the grated windows and the pale faces of the inmates peering through various openings in their cages.

After a "trusty" assisted the jailers pull the lever aside the last heavy door between the prisoners and Sheriff J.W. Hathaway and the reporter slowly opened. The sheriff called out to Hart and the little man with a pale face stepped around the corner and he was introduced to the reporter. Sheriff Hathaway left the cell and once again the bars locked the two men in his cell. Hart's cell was on the southwest corner of the cage and it was about eight feet square. This was his room where he ate, slept and met with visitors.

During the day the prisoners were allowed the freedom of the corridor where there was room to exercise. Hart offered the reporter the only chair while he sat on his bed next to a small table with paper and his writing materials. There was always a deathwatch on duty, and he sat immediately outside the door where he could see and hear everything that went on in the cell. Albert Hanchild was there during the days and "Wash" Kelly stood guard at night.

The prisoner was normally clean-shaven but on that particular day he had about a week's growth. Hart was wearing a black coat and pants with no vest with a blue flannel shirt along with a neatly arranged necktie. For the most part he remained calm during the interview but at times he would grow nervous or excited and would begin to talk rapidly and gesture with his hands. The reporter wrote that the man's manner and conversation didn't show any evidence of an unsound mind and his entire appearance was neat and clean but he had a nervous laugh. The man's face had obviously grown pale from the many months of confinement and while Hart rested his elbow on the table he began telling his life story to the correspondent.

John Patrick Hart was an only child, born to poor but respectable parents in St. Johns, New Brunswick on June 22, 1863. His mother died when he was nine months old and his father passed away when he was only fourteen. The prisoner said that when his father died as a drunkard he was sent to the Sister's convent where he was raised a Catholic. When he was thirteen, Bishop Sweeney sent him one hundred and fifty miles away from the convent to work on the farm of James Noonan in Westmoreland County.

He worked on the farm until he was fifteen when he went to sea as a cabin boy and after one summer he landed in Massachusetts. From there he went to Des Moines, Iowa where he worked on a farm for Louis J. Klemm and other places during the next three years. In 1882 he came to Bozeman where he worked at Phil Skeehan's hotel before moving to Wickes in Jefferson County where he chopped wood and drove a team for Ellis and Barendes.

According to Hart he had always earned an honest living and all of his former employers would vouch for his good character. From the camp at Wicks, Hart moved on to Elkhorn just four months before he got into trouble. While at Elkhorn he drove team, chopped wood, and worked for the mining company before obtaining his own mine, which he signed over to his lawyer for legal fees. Hart explained that he was living at the Foster Boarding House at Elkhorn and it was there that he met Miss Sarah Starkweather, the daughter of Mrs. Pitts and the stepdaughter of John Pitts. He said that he called on the young lady frequently and she was like a sister to him; keeping him out of saloons and on the straight and narrow.

On November 7, 1885, Hart found the young woman crying at breakfast and she told him that her stepfather had deserted her mother. When Hart went to Mrs. Pitts she said that Mr. Pitts had gone to Boulder to have Hart arrested and to begin divorce action against her. The woman said that her husband said that Hart had been frequenting whore houses like Chicago Joe's at Helena and similar places at Bozeman and had called him a "whore-master." Mr. Pitts also said that it was a disgrace for the family to have a man like Hart keeping company with their daughter.

Mrs. Pitts swore that if her husband ever talked about her in such away again she would cut his legs off. At that point the reporter asked the condemned man if Mrs. Pitts had specifically asked him to kill her husband as many people had believed, and the prisoner replied in the negative. Continuing with the story, Hart explained that he told woman that he would go to Boulder and try to straighten things out and to stop the proceedings.

Hart saddled up a horse and went directly to the courthouse where he inquired if Mr. Pitts had been there yet and he was very relieved when he learned that no arrest warrant had yet been filed against him. He explained that he was actually scared because of the false accusations Mr. Pitts had spread about him and he feared that he'd get lynched for seducing the young girl. Feeling safe that he wasn't a wanted man, he set out the find Mr. Pitts at various places in town. He said he found the man at about ten o'clock in the morning at Jerry Smith's Saloon and not wanting to confront him in front of others in the establishment Hart quietly took a drink and then waited outside.

When Mr. Pitts left the saloon Hart started to talk to him about what his wife had told him. Hart asked Mr. Pitts if he had said those things about him and the older man said that he had and then he accused the young man of ruining his daughter and bringing shame on his family. Finally Pitts said that he was on his way to the courthouse to have him arrested and Hart ran off to ponder his situation.

Finally Hart became convinced that he had to take action in order to clear his name and reputation. He and Mrs. Pitts were convinced that her husband had trumped up the charges simply to divorce her. Hart went straight to the courthouse where he found Mr. Pitts in Mr. Wells' office and he thought they were preparing an arrest warrant for him. Hart walked straight into the office and shot Pitts on the spot. Hart told the reporter that he was shaking so much that the first shot only wounded the man, and when Mr. Pitts came towards him he shot him again. Mr. Pitts was wounded in the left side of his breast and he lingered until December 3, 1885, when he died.

Hart explained that he was quite relieved after doing the deed and he immediately turned himself in to Sheriff John McDermott. Hart felt that because he was innocent of the charges against him; since the victim had guilty motives against him and Mrs. Pitts and because his victim tried to assault him after the first shot, the shooting would be considered justified. The reporter asked the prisoner if he was under the influence of liquor at the time, and Hart said that he had only taken the one drink at Smith's Saloon.

When the conversation turned to the upcoming execution, Hart said that he had no fear because his religion had always given him comfort and that he had repented his evil deed and regretted it sorely. The reporter asked the condemned man if he was in love with Miss Starkweather and Hart said that he was, but their relationship hadn't progressed far enough for him to say he would have married her. Hart had written a short note to the young lady and he was working on a special statement for the "Herald" which was to be published after his death. The reporter assured the doomed man that his story would be told faithfully as he had communicated it.

Hart stated that the staff at the jail had been very kind to him and that he was very comfortable. The prisoner received frequent visits from his priest and he had helped him prepare for his death. Hart read his prayer book often and he was seen opening it as the reporter was leaving. While the prisoner didn't have any relatives in Montana, he had two uncles in Maine and one in Iowa. He furnished the reporter with the addresses of these family members and he requested that copies of his article be sent to them. John Hart's uncles were respectable men who were very troubled about their nephew's fate and they had furnished funds for his defense. Hart's family and friends have all offered testimony of his good character before the crime.

On February 9, the carpenters were working in the jail yard putting up the gallows and enclosing the twenty by forty-foot gallows yard with a twenty-foot board fence. This second ever "Galloping Gallows" in Montana was set up for only the second time in the northeast corner of the stockade and a half-inch hemp rope was strung through the two pulleys of the Jerk-Type scaffold. Meanwhile the "Daily Herald" reporter visited the jail where he found the condemned man smoking a cigar and listening to his spiritual adviser, Reverend Father V.J. Van den Broek.

Hart greeted the reporter with a smile and he gave him a manuscript to be published after his execution and he explained that it contained a secret that would be valuable to the public. Hart was cheerful and said that he was done with this world and he spoke of his demise with great composure. He said that he hoped that the Governor would not interfere as he was looking forward to his future. In fact Hart had written a sentimental letter to Governor Preston Leslie asking him to not listen to the pleas of his sympathizers. Finally Hart told the reporter that he didn't need anything and then he walked back to his cell as if he were walking home.

The condemned man past most of his last evening in pleasant conversation with Father Van den Broek and his guards until 10:30 p.m. when he slept soundly. At 12:45 Hart woke up and smoked while he calmly sat on his bed and visited with his deathwatch for a couple of hours. As the chimes at the courthouse rang out the hour of two a.m. over the silent city of Helena, Hart told his guard: "One more hour gone for Jack," and then he rolled over and fell back to sleep. On the morning of the hanging the following diary of the condemned man's final night was found on a table in Hart's cell and it was in his own hand:

9:10 Took a bath
10:30 Went to sleep
12:45 Waked up and smoked a cigar
1:15 Took lunch
2:10 Smoked another cigar
2:30 Went to sleep again

Jailer Witten reported that Hart woke up in good spirits at about seven o'clock and he ate a breakfast of steak and eggs followed by a cigar at eight o'clock. An hour and a half later Father Van den Broek arrived and he heard the man's confession, administered Holy Communion and then prayed with the prisoner. From that point on the spiritual adviser remained at the condemned man's side until the end. Sheriff Hathaway came in and read the death warrant to Hart at ten o'clock the prisoner listened without emotion.

By ten o'clock, the hour set for the hanging a large crowd had gathered on Breckinridge Street in front of the jailhouse and the sidewalks were lined with a mass of men all anxious to witness the execution. Since early that morning hundreds of people had besieged the sheriff's office requesting an invitation to the gruesome affair. Inside the execution enclosure for there were about twenty-five gentlemen including Sheriff McNeil of Jefferson County; Sheriff Tom Jones, Beaverhead County; Sheriff Templeton, Park County; Sheriff John Lloyd, Silver Bow County; Sheriff Charles T. Rader, Meagher County; Ex-Sheriff Churchill, Lewis and Clark; Helena City Marshal Read and Warden McTague of the state penitentiary.

Also among the crowd was Sergeant Bashaw and Officer Sandy Lane of the Helena Police Department; E.D. Weed, ex-deputy district attorney; Leon La Croix, deputy clerk of court; Dr. Morris of Helena; Dr. Joseph C. Hunter of Boulder and Dr. Grant of Yellowstone County. Other persons attending the execution were the officers of the court including the jurors and representatives of the press along with Deer Lodge County Sheriff Lewis Coleman and Undersheriff Hatton who had an execution to conduct of their own a week later.

At 11:10 Sheriff Hathaway, Undersheriff Charles D. Hurd, Deputies George W. Gibbs and George S. Walker, Jailer Witten and the "Daily Herald" reporter all entered the jail. As the party approached Hart's cell the prisoner was on his knees beside his little table praying with his priest. When the condemned man saw the reporter he stood up and stepped forward and shook his hand. Hart's hair was neatly combed he was cleaned shaven and he was wearing a neat black suit with a sack coat and a white shirt. On his right hand Hart wore a cameo ring and on another finger there was band with a large brilliant setting.

After a few minutes the sheriff entered the man's cell and without saying a word to Hart the prisoner followed the officer into the corridor. The procession started through the jail towards the gallows yard with Sheriff Hathaway in the lead followed by Undersheriff Hurd, the prisoner, Father Van den Broek, Deputy Gibbs, Jailer Witten and then the reporter. At 11:20 a.m. the procession went through the back door and into the yard where Hart saw the scaffold for the first time. The sight of the gallows apparently didn't bother the condemned man in the least as he walked with head up and with a firm step. Some spectators said that the condemned man had a smile on his face and he walked to his death like a man about to receive an award for a good deed.

Hart took his place on the small stage under the noose and Father Van den Broek stood by his side while the undersheriff and deputies bound the man's legs, arms and shoulders with the leather straps. Sheriff Hathaway then stepped onto the platform and asked his prisoner if he had anything to say and with quivering lips Hart spoke in a low voice, which was barely audible and only heard by those people standing next to him: "I wish you all a restful conscience and a useful life on this life on this earth. I hope when you come through this door you will bring some little child that has no father and mother on this earth for protection. That is all I have to say on this earth, Good-bye." The reporter later surmised that Hart's reference to the small child referred to his own life as an orphan.

After Hart had finished his address to the spectators who were all as silent as the dead, Sheriff Hathaway placed the noose around his neck. Hart never flinched as the rope was placed over his head and it was drawn up tight around his neck. His only movement was to turn his head slightly towards the priest who whispered something into his ear. The sheriff then said "Ready," the weight dropped at exactly 11:28 a.m., John Hart shot up into the air and after a second his body was swaying to and fro about two feet off the ground. Father Van den Broek immediately fell to his knees and with his hands clasped he prayed for the man's soul.

Hart's body gave three convulsions, and then his feet were drawn up a few inches, and then it hung perfectly motionless except for the swaying of the rope. At that point Deputy Walker placed the black cap over the man's head and it was all over. Eleven minutes later Doctors

Morris, Grant and Hunter pronounced him dead. Drs. Grant and Hunter had been feeling his pulse from the time the drop fell and Dr. Morris listened to the man's heart with a stethoscope.

The witnesses stood around the scaffold in what was described as intense silence and they remained awe-struck until the gallows had done its awful work. At 11:45 the body was lowered into a plain coffin that was waiting in the wings and the spectators quietly dispersed. While in the coffin the doctors determined that the man's neck had been broken in two places. A guard was then placed over the remains and at 2:30 that afternoon they were buried in the Catholic cemetery with Father Van den Broek officiating.

The special manuscript written by John Hart, which he wanted published by the "Daily Herald" was rather unintelligible and it seemed to have been intended as a lesson of sin and repentance as well as an illustration of the conflict between good and evil of man. John Hart was a shrewd man, but he possessed only little education and those two facts were always evident in his conversations and writings. He had always regretted his crime and he faced death as bravely as anyone who had gone to the gallows.

February 17, 1888
Martin Luther Scott

Other Name: "Charlie" Scott
Location and Gallows: Scott was the first man hanged from ***Gallows No. Nine: (Feb. 1888): "Galloping Gallows" No. Three*** between the courthouse and jail building at Deer Lodge, which was at the time in Deer Lodge County but presently Powell County. A complete description and history of this particular traveling scaffold can be found in Chapter Seven: "Montana Gallows."
Description: The fifty-one-year-old Scott had a large build and he stood six feet, four inches tall in his shoes and he weighed about two hundred pounds. Scott was described as having perfect posture with straight broad shoulders. He had a high forehead, blue eyes set beneath prominent bushy brows and his face ended with a narrow chin. Scott was remarkably bright and witty for a man with so little education. He reportedly was a very talented mimic and after just a few minutes he could imitate a person in both voice and actions. While in custody at the county jail Scott had mimicked all the jailers and most of the other prisoners.
Crime: Murder of his wife at Granite on November 17, 1887
Judge: William J. Galbraith
Prosecution: Deer Lodge County Attorney David M. Durfee and U.S. District Attorney Robert B. Smith
Defense: J.R. Boarman of Anaconda and assisted by J.C. Robinson.
Sheriff: Lewis Coleman
Distinction: While there have been a total of five men legally hanged at Deer Lodge, Montana, Martin Scott was the only one to be hanged by

Deer Lodge County. As was stated in the "Introduction" of this work, to better describe where the executions took place, the hangings are listed in the present-day counties. Because of this policy we have listed the hanging of Scott in present day Powell County. The Scott case is one of the most interesting ones as far as jurisdiction goes because he was hanged at Deer Lodge, the crime occurred in what later became Granite County and he was hanged at a county seat of what eventually became Powell County.

Martin Scott was born on April 3, 1837, in Madison County, Indiana, where most of his family still lived at the time of his execution. In 1861, when he was twenty-four years old he enlisted into Company "G" of the Seventeenth Indiana Volunteers, which was en route to West Virginia. Scott served with Generals Milroy and Reynolds and he fought in the battles of Beverly, Rich Mountain, Elk Water, Cheat Mountain and Green Briar River. Later serving under General Buell, Martin Scott fought at New Haven, Bardstown, Bowling Green, Mumfordsville Butte, Nashville, Shiloh, Corinth and Decord Station.

Scott remained in the army until his enlistment was up and then he joined the Quartermaster's Service as a teamster, and in a short time he became wagon master. He also was employed as a miner and railroad worker throughout the west before settling at Butte. At the Mining City he became acquainted with the widow Mrs. McClusky, and after just two months they were married on July 15, 1886. The couple moved to Granite during the summer of 1886, where Scott found work cutting firewood commercially.

While hauling wood for the Granite mine, Scott was injured in the fall of 1886, and suffered through the winter of 1887, with an enlarged liver. His usual weight of two hundred to two hundred and twenty pounds had fallen off to about a hundred and seventy and he was only able to do about half the work he was accustomed of doing and spent a great deal of his time in bed. While he spent much of his time bed ridden his wife, who had a drinking problem, spent much of her time away from their house and at times she never made it home at night.

In September of 1887, four men lived in a tent near the Scott residence and while they were away at work Mrs. Scott would go through their things. The men began noticing certain items missing and witnesses told them that they had seen the woman leaving their shelter with various items. When one of the men confronted Scott about the thefts he supported his wife when she denied the charges. In anger Scott told the man to look around their residence, but when the strange man found an item he had earlier described in their home Martin was devastated with shame. Scott told his wife that if he had fifty dollars to his name he would leave Granite because every one in town will be talking about them.

Mrs. Scott began to drink all the whisky she could get her hands on and Martin Scott realized he could no longer live with her. He was determine to sell everything he had to send her to New Brunswick and on Friday November 12, 1887, he went to ask his neighbors, Mr. and

Mrs. Frowen if they could find a buyer for his house. That evening the neighbors noticed Mrs. Scott returning home drunk and when she began screaming and cursing at her husband Mr. Scott slapped her. The woman ran from the house threatening to have her husband arrested.

The next morning John Hickey came to the Scott house and told Martin that his drunken wife had spent the night with him and his wife. Mr. Scott apologized for his wife's actions, and Mr. Hickey said, "Why don't you leave that woman?" and Scott told the man that he would as soon as he could get his affairs together. While the men were talking Mrs. Scott told her husband that she was going home to get some of her things together and she was going to remain at the Hickey home.

On Monday, November 15, 1887, Constable James Carten of Granite came to Scott's house and told him that he would have to go with him to the office of the justice of peace because there was an assault charge against him. Scott went with the constable to appear before Justice McDonald where his wife had filed a charge and Mrs. Frowen had sworn that he had struck his wife. Scott did not deny the charge and he was fined twenty-five dollars, and was released at ten a.m. so he could raise the money. By Tuesday Scott had earned fourteen dollars and by Wednesday November 17 he had earned the remainder of his fine and was heading home. On the way home he kept an eye out for a bird or rabbit to shoot for his dinner as he normally carried a rifle for that purpose.

It was about seven o'clock in the evening when he was struck on the head as he walked into his dark house and in his weaken state, Scott fell to the ground just outside the front door breaking the stock of his rifle. When he regained his feet he ran into the house and he said someone grabbed him around the waist and he began striking his assailant with the barrel of his weapon. Finally Scott fainted and he fell onto the bed by the door in a stupor. Early in the morning of November 18, Scott was awakened by the sound of moans and after lighting a lamp he found his wife lying on the floor near the door. According to Scott he was too weak to pick the woman up so he turned her over to attend to her. After noticing whisky on her breath he thought that she was drunk and had fallen on the tools by the firewood box.

There was an empty quart bottle of whisky on the table and when asked where it came from Mrs. Scott said that Tom Beach, referring to "Tom the Butcher" had brought it to the house. She told her husband that she had been having an affair with the local butcher along with several other men while Scott was sick during the winter. She said that it was Tom Beach who had waited in the dark and had jumped him as he was entering. Scott later told the authorities that he didn't know who he was swinging at in the darkness; that because of his injuries during the attack he didn't realize how bad his wife was hurt and that he had fallen back to sleep.

The next morning, Thursday, November 18, 1887, Special Constable Thatcher went to the Scott house to collect the man's fine or escort him back to the county jail at Deer Lodge but when no one answered the door he returned to the justice of peace office. Justice McDonald accompanied the constable back to Scott's cabin where one of the neighbors said that he was sure that the couple was at home. Thatcher went to the window and after raising it and pulling back the curtain he saw Mrs. Scott on the floor covered with blood. He immediately told Justice McDonald and then Thatcher was ordered to take out his revolver and kick in the door. After going through the door, Thatcher jumped over the woman on the floor and told Scott to throw up his hand and he complied.

The officials found Mrs. Scott dead, her head and clothing were saturated with blood, and a wound looking like a ball had entered between her eyes and the top of the head was apparently crushed. Scott co-operated with the officers and when he was first questioned, he said that "Tom the Butcher" had probably killed his wife. The officials found the muzzle of the broken Winchester saturated with blood along with the woodchopper's nine-pound hammer and a shovel all smeared with blood and Mrs. Scott's hair. Meanwhile Constable Campbell arrived to help escort the prisoner to the jail at Granite.

A coroner's jury was summoned to the crime scene where they found that the woman's death was caused from either the horrible head injury or the wound between the eyes from some blunt instrument in the hands of her husband, Martin Luther Scott. After inspecting the tools and other items in the house the jury thought the murder weapon was either the barrel of the rifle or the nine-pound hammer.

By the time the coroner's jury had finished its work, the excitement in the little mining camp of Granite was running high and when Constable Thatcher feared that there may be an attempt to lynch his prisoner he quickly notified Deputy Sheriff George Hammond to transport Scott to a more secure jail. It took a lot of guts for Deputy Hammond to lead the shackled and hobbled murderer through the mob of people, place him in his buggy and drive to Philipsburg.

Hammond reported later that even he was surprised that he and his prisoner made it out of Granite and all the way to Philipsburg alive. The deputy drove past the Philipsburg jail and went directly to his own residence, where he hid his prisoner in the cellar until they could board the outbound train. They waited until the train was about to leave town and the deputy and his prisoner jumped on board and made it to Drummond safely.

At Drummond Deputy Hammond received word from New Chicago, which was just south of Drummond, that a party of forty mounted riders from Granite had reached Philipsburg, and after finding that the prisoner was gone, they were on their way to Drummond. Realizing that by the time the eastbound Northern Pacific train from Missoula arrived, the lynch mob from Granite would be at Drummond, Deputy Hammond deposited fifty dollars of his own money to get a locomotive to run him and his prisoner to Garrison Junction where they would get off and wait for the eastbound there. Once they reached Garrison Junction, Hammond only had to worry that members of the lynch mob might have gotten on the eastbound train at Drummond.

The two men hid along the tracks until they were sure that there weren't any of Granite men on board, and then they boarded the train and they arrived at Deer Lodge safely. It was later learned that the lynch mob from Granite had in fact arrived at Drummond before the eastbound had left for Garrison, but evidently the men were so angry that it didn't occur to them to board the train to Garrison Junction. When questioned, Deputy Hammond later said that he didn't have any sympathy for his prisoner, but he said it was his duty to deliver Scott safely to the jail at Deer Lodge.

Just before his arraignment on Tuesday, December 6, 1887, the Deer Lodge Newspaper portrayed Scott as a powerful, quarrelsome bad character who was a wife beater, and the blood on the front of his coat obviously proved that he had clinched his wife. Originally his trial had been set for December 19, 1887, but due to delays on some previous cases his trial was rescheduled for the twenty-third. In the meantime Mrs. Scott was buried at the Philipsburg Cemetery.

The Scott trial, case No. 2446, commenced on Friday, December 23, 1887, with Judge Galbraith presiding; David M. Durfeee prosecuted and J.R. Boarman and J.C. Robinson handled the defense. Most of the first day was spent impaneling the following jury:

Samuel Beaumont (f)	D.A. Morrison	George Adams
John L. Fifer	William Williams	John Gilbert
N.C. Morley	Reuben Cohen	Allen Kimmerly
William Stevens	Fred Garsey	James P. Preston

(f) Foreman

On Saturday morning, December 24, the examination of the witnesses began and Constable Thatcher, Justice McDonald and Mrs. Frowen all testified about the events surrounding the arrest of the defendant. Doctors Dickson and Labrie explained the autopsy performed on the victim and testified that there were four wounds found upon the head of Mrs. Scott, any of which could have killed the woman. The doctors believed that the wounds were made with an iron woodchopper's hammer, which was found near the body, covered with blood and hair. Although her skull was not fractured, the concussion from the blows burst blood vessels in the brain, from which formed clots and were the immediate cause of death. Other witnesses testified that while in custody, Scott admitted to them that he had killed his wife with the barrel of his rifle.

The prosecution then presented witnesses who testified that the defendant was known as a hard cruel man, while the defense didn't offer any witnesses as to Scott's character. Mr. Scott had worked for many important and influential men of the territory; the fact that not one of them was called by the defense and that he never stayed long at any one job, left many people to believe that his employment with those men had been less than favorable.

When the prosecution rested, Martin Scott took the stand and said that he had been ill all winter and most of the summer and that he had been experiencing fainting spills. Scott swore that Tom Beacher, the butcher had struck him as he was entering his own house and he admitted striking out in the darkness, clubbing at whom ever he thought had attacked him. Tom Beacher was called to the stand and he admitted under oath that he had been at the Scott house with the man's wife, but that he had left before her husband had returned from work.

After receiving careful instructions from Judge Galbraith, the jury was given the case at about five o'clock on Christmas Eve, and they returned about 9:30 p.m. with a verdict of guilty in the first degree. The judge thanked the jury and everyone went home to spend Christmas with his or her family and friends while Martin Scott spent his holiday in the Deer Lodge County Jail.

On Wednesday morning, December 28, 1887, Scott's attorney made a motion for a new trial for his client, and two days later Judge Galbraith overruled the motion and sentenced Martin Scott to be hanged by the neck until his death on February 17, 1888, between the hours of eleven a.m. and three o'clock p.m. After the judge pronounced the sentence, Mr. Boarman left for Helena with an appeal to the Supreme Court and on January 18, 1888, at the time the coldest day on record at Helena, nearly fifty degrees below zero, the Supreme Court was listening to the heated arguments in the Scott case. That same day the high tribunal ruled to confirm the judgment of the lower court.

In order to get first-hand experience of an execution, Deer Lodge County Sheriff Coleman checked in at the Cosmopolitan Hotel at Helena on February 8, 1888, to attend and assist the Lewis and Clark County sheriff department with the hanging of John Hart. Sheriff Coleman was present at Helena to observe the construction of the fence around the scaffold and the erection of the gallows. After the execution at Helena, Sheriff Coleman decided to use the same style of gallows that were used to hang Hart and he was able to secure the plans of the scaffold, which had been drawn up by Dr. Pickman in 1887, from the Lewis and Clark authorities.

The twelve-foot tall fence was constructed in a twenty-by-thirty foot enclosure between the courthouse and the jail and the builders reportedly used the same nine-pound hammer, which Scott had used to kill his wife to build the fence and drive the spikes that secured the scaffold. The hammer still had the dead woman's bloodstains on it and with each blow the workers were also driving a point concerning Scott's fate. To save on expense, Sheriff Coleman used the same rope to hang Scott that was used to execute Thomas Harding at Dillon in March of 1887. On Saturday, February 12, 1888, Sheriff Coleman had the hemp rope tested and stretched and the hangman's noose was tried around Scott's neck in order to insure a proper fit on the fateful day.

Mr. Boarman truly believed in his client's innocence and he spent a great deal of his time and money taking the case to the Supreme Court and the many trips to Helena to appeal to Governor Leslie including his final attempt on February 15. On that trip Mr. Boarman hand carried a long personal letter written by Scott explaining his life story and his side of the tragedy. The attorney, while sure of his client's innocence, wasn't trying to win Scott's freedom but merely trying to save his life with a commuted sentence to life in prison, or even a respite to allow more time for him to prepare for his death.

When speaking of his wife's confession of cheating on him, he often showed a lot of emotion, but in speaking of his execution, which he didn't believe he deserved, he reportedly never expressed any weakness. Scott did not request to see any spiritual advisor until the day before his execution and the Reverends McMillan and Dunlap along the Fathers Remigius E. DeRyckere and Peter DeSiere all visited with him. After some consideration the condemned man finally accepted the Catholic faith.

On the same day that Scott was embracing his new faith, Governor Leslie wrote his reply to the condemned man's letter and refused to interfere with the man's sentence. Mr. Boarman telephoned the Deer Lodge courthouse jail and informed his client of the Governor's final decision. After receiving word of his doom, Scott, who had been depressed while following the Hart execution at Helena, became even more dejected. He told his guards that he was afraid he might not be able to meet his fate with the same bravery that Hart had exhibited. Shortly thereafter Father R.E. DeRyckere, the first Diocesan priest of Montana baptized the prisoner as a Catholic and a deathwatch was assigned to Scott.

After dinner, Scott was admitted to the corridor of the jail where he met with his lawyer and other inmates and visitors. Scott jokingly told his lawyer that since he was supposed to be hanged sometime between eleven a.m. and eight o'clock p.m. the sheriff and his men shouldn't be in any hurry on his account. Later he played cribbage with his deathwatch, Al Cain and Deputy Hammond, the deputy who had saved him from the lynching party on the day of his arrest. After playing the game in which the men had wagered cigars, Scott retired to his cell at 10:30 p.m. where he smoked a cigar, read the bible, and then fell asleep at midnight. He reportedly woke up at three o'clock on his last morning and again he began reading the bible until falling back to sleep at 4:30.

Father DeRyckere arrived at the jail at 7:35 and he held Holy Communion with Scott at eight o'clock. After the service Scott ate a hearty breakfast at 8:46 a.m. of oatmeal mush, ham and eggs and coffee. The prisoner then retired to his cell where he enjoyed a cigar and he was joined by Fathers DeRyckere and DeSiere. Scott wrote a letter to his children at 9:25 and then he was shaved at 10:20 and exchanged his prison garb for a neat worsted suit, white shirt with a standing collar, black tie and he wore slippers.

At 10:30 Sheriff Coleman read the death warrant to the condemned man in the presence of Mr. Boarman, Fathers DeRyckere and DeSiere, Deputy U.S. Marshal Thomas McTague, Deathwatch Al Cain, Jailer Bell and the official reporter, Captain James H. Mills. After quietly listening to the warrant without moving a muscle, Scott and the two priests together said, "Thy will be done." Scott and the priests then walked back to his cell where they all knelt in prayer. Scott later told a reporter that he had been wronged, but he had forgiven everybody. He also said that he appreciated the kindness shown to him by the officers, especially Jailer Bell who had always been good to him.

Scott asked for a stimulant at 11:33, which he received four minutes later and then he marched "firm and manly" to the scaffold. At the gallows he shook hands with his attorney without saying a word and then stood with the Catholic priest while Jailer Ross and Undersheriff Hatton were strapping his arms and legs. The condemned man whispered, "I forgive all," to the priests, and when asked by the sheriff if he had anything to say he said, "Gentlemen, I have been wronged today, but I forgive all. Jesus, have mercy on me."

At 11:40 a.m. Sheriff Coleman adjusted the noose around Scott's neck as the priests were talking to him rapidly and in a low tone, and in an instant Deputy Hatton severed the rope, which held the weight. The drop struck the ground with a "Thud," and Martin Luther Scott shot straight up. Scott's face turned deep red for a moment before the sheriff slipped the black hood over his head and except for two or three short convulsions of the stomach the body remained still.

Doctors George C. Douglas and Oliver Lester of Anaconda examined the body at 11:41, and after five minutes they pronounced the man dead. The noose had apparently slipped around to the back of Scott's neck but it still managed to break his neck. The body of Martin Scott hung stiff and ridged for fifteen minutes before it was turned over to the undertaker, who buried the remains that afternoon at three o'clock.

The following is a partial list of spectators at Martin Scott's execution: From Butte, Sheriff Lloyd, Deputies Thomes and Griffith, Chief of Police Meiklejohn and patrolmen Young, Smith, Carver, Carleton, Murray and Price, and a newspaperman for the "Intermountain." About thirty men from Anaconda attended the execution including Mr. Morgan and Evan along with Deputy Sheriff Harver.

Postscript:
The execution of Martin Scott was particularly memorable for the people of the county when at the very time of the hanging at Deer Lodge there was a killing in downtown Anaconda. Billy Martin who managed the Planters' Hotel on Front Street in downtown Anaconda shot and killed a man by the name of Reardon. Apparently the two men had a disagreement over the lodging bill and when Reardon ran from the lobby of the hotel Martin shot him dead in the middle of Front Street.

There weren't very many officers normally assigned at Anaconda in those days but on that particular February day all the lawmen were at Deer Lodge attending the execution of Scott at the time of the shooting. A man in Anaconda was deputized over the telegraph from Deer Lodge and he caught up with Billy Martin at Avon. Martin was taken to the county jail at Deer Lodge but he was eventually acquitted.

In November of 1888, several prospectors found a skeleton in the hills near Fred Burr Lake of a man who had gotten lost while hunting years earlier with Martin Scott. When Martin returned alone he reported that he and his partner had gotten separated and the other man was presumed lost. After the wife-murderer had been hanged many of the residents of the county believed that Scott may have killed the man for his money.

August 9, 1889

George Duncan Bryson

Other Names: J.D. Lunson
Location and Gallows: Bryson was jerked into eternity at Boulder on ***Gallows No. Eight: (Mar. 1887): "Galloping Gallows" No. Two.***
Description: The thirty-two-year-old George Bryson had the look of an educated worldly man who was about five foot, eight inches tall and weighed about 140 pounds. He had dark hair, which he wore short and slicked back. Bryson was always clean-shaven with a dark mustache and he dressed like a debonair sporting gentleman. When dressed in a suit with a Prince Albert coat, Bryson looked more like a polished stage villain instead of a dangerous criminal.
Crime: Murder of his mistress, Anna Lundstrom on August 21, 1888.
Judge: Judge Newton W. McConnell
Prosecution: William Wallace Jr.
Defense: S.A. Balliet
Sheriff: Daniel M. Halford
Distinction: Bryson was the first man legally hanged in present day Jefferson County and the only man hanged in Montana while being defended by the sitting prosecutor of the county that had brought charges against him. S.A. Balliet had been Bryson's attorney before he was elected county attorney and since he had once represented the prisoner he could not prosecute the case.

George Bryson was the son of a wealthy man of Hoosick Station on the Grand Trunk Railway in Canada where he received a good education and had a promising future. In 1881, he married Miss Emma Chase of Montreal and shortly afterwards she became heir to a large amount from her mother. With the newfound wealth Bryson opened a grocery store in his wife's hometown, but because of his extravagant habits he quickly squandered away the funds and he was forced to sell off the business.

Bryson went on to work for various firms in both Canada and the United States from whom he embezzeled but escaped before he was prosecuted. Bryson was finally caught and served several short jail terms for various local crimes and eventually he abandoned his wife and his five-year-old daughter. After leaving his wife in 1888, Bryson met and moved in with Anna Lundstrom who owned and operated the Vulcan Laundry at St. Paul.

After promising to marry the woman, the slick Bryson obtained two hundred dollars from her under false pretenses and he was quickly arrested but after serving sixty days at the county workhouse he once again won Anna's affections and she took him back. Once he got in trouble for stealing from another wholesaler, Bryson talked Anna into selling her business and moving out to Helena, Montana to open some sort of business.

In early August of 1888, the chief of police at Helena received a letter from F.G. Ward, manager of the Union Pacific Tea Company at Minneapolis warning his department that George Bryson was coming to Montana. In the letter Mr. Ward described the traveling salesman perfectly and informed the officer that Bryson would be in company with a forty-year-old woman from Sweden by the name of Anna Lundstrom, who was short, well dressed and wore wigs, had false teeth and spoke in broken English. It was later learned that the woman had two children living in Sweden.

Mr. Ward went on to explain Bryson's notorious history with the law and said that there was any number of businesses and people in St. Paul and Minneapolis who he owed from five to fifty dollars. He told the Helena police about how Anna Lundstrom had Bryson arrested and the rumor that he was going to get even with her. Mr. Ward finally explained that he had learned that the pair was headed for Helena as they had ordered their mail to be forwarded there.

With the valuable tip from Minnesota, Detective Walters located the couple four days later on August 5, 1888, living as husband and wife at the home of Mrs. Sarah Bernett on Bridge Street and two doors west of Rodney Street. In one of those curious and morbid coincidences, this was the same quiet looking little brick cottage in which a Harry Trethowan had earlier committed suicide by hanging himself just a week before.

After staying a few days at the Bernett house, Bryson and Lundstrom moved to Mrs. Mixtur's boarding house at 514 Eighth Avenue where Anna soon made friends with the landlady and several other neighbor ladies. The neighbor ladies were soon told about the woman's troubles with Bryson and they had witnessed several quarrels between the couple. Anna supposedly even consulted Madame Sadie, a local clairvoyant concerning her future with her man.

Bryson hadn't looked for a job or a business and he was satisfied with just living off of Anna's savings and on August 20, when he demanded money from the woman so that he could go out on the town she only offered him twenty-five cents. Bryson became enraged and a huge quarrel erupted before he finally left the house but he came back the next day and made up with Anna, and then talked her into taking a walk with him. Excitedly, Anna told Mrs. Mixtur that she had made up with her husband and they were going on a romantic walk. That was the last time Mrs. Mixtur and the other ladies at the boarding house saw Anna Lundstrom alive.

Later that evening Bryson came home alone and he was heard moving about most of the night packing their trunks. The next morning Bryson told Mrs. Mixtur that Anna had gone to Butte and he was off to meet her there, but he took their trunks to the Lenior House at Helena where he had registered in to room number 50 as Mr. J.D. Lundstrom. Bryson never did go to Butte, but instead he eluded the authorities by checking into different hotels in Helena.

The Helena police department was tipped off that a Mrs. Flora Thompson had been picking up George Bryson's mail at the post office and on September 17, 1888, Special Police Officer A. Dougherty and other detectives were detailed to stake out the post office and trail the lady possibly to where Bryson was hiding out. Detective Dougherty followed Mrs. Thompson from the post office onto a streetcar at the foot of Broadway, and they got off at the train depot where the police trailed her to the Capital Hotel. The woman was also carrying bags of laundry that she had picked up for Bryson and she led the officers to his room where he was captured in his underwear sitting in a reclining chair. After Bryson got dressed and was allowed to take his clean laundry along as he and Mrs. Thompson were escorted to the city jail.

Since the body of Anna Lundstrom hadn't been found the authorities were forced to either find the body or turn Bryson loose. To help speed up things the mayor of Helena went beyond his legal authority and offered a three hundred dollar reward for the discovery of the woman or her body. So sure that Bryson had something to do with the woman's disappearance, Judge J.G. Sanders stuck his neck out and ordered Bryson held over for the grand jury on September 28. It was clear that if the judge hadn't taken the action Bryson would have made his escape.

On October 1, 1888, Duncan Dixon, a miner, prospector, blacksmith and old Indian scout, looking to earn the reward, found the tracks of a woman's shoes near a prospect hole on the top of a mountain east of Dry Gulch, just behind the gun club's shooting range and about a mile south of Helena. With nerve and grit, Dixon lowered himself into the twenty-five-foot hole with a rope and by the light from some candles, he found a lady's hat on top of some boulders. After removing some of the rocks Dixon found the woman's head, then her torso and arm.

After his gruesome discovery Mr. Dixon rode his horse back to town to inquire about his reward from Coroner William C. Morris who quickly organized a recovery team. Later that day the coroner and detectives along with a number of newspaper reporters and a large group of curious citizens were all over the crime scene. The officers uncovered the body, which was covered with a white mold from being in the damp pit, and the authorities found the woman's umbrella and fan along with a rope that was supposedly used by the murderer to hoist himself out of the hole.

The body was wrapped in a blanket and immediately after it was raised from the shaft, Dr. Morris examined the remains and selected the coroner's jury consisting of the following men:

Robert C. Walker (forman)	John Worth (secretary)	
Hugh F. Galen	Otto F. Galen	Otto Peterson
Marcus Lissner	George Bashaw	

The jury made their findings over the corpse and they found that the woman was wearing a white dress; her face was badly smashed in, her jaw was broken and her eyes were bulging out. There was a rawhide strap wrapped around one wrist and marks on the other hand indicated that her hands were tied together before she was killed. After killing the woman the murderer evidently untied her and used the strap to drag the body by the one arm to the prospect hole. The coroner's jury identified the body as Anna Lundstrom from her clothing and jewelry and the panel named George Bryson as the murderer. When word reached the community of Helena there was a great deal of excitement and talk of lynching but finally the people decided to let the law take its course.

Meanwhile the trunks belonging to Anna Lundstrom were located on October 1 at the Wells Fargo Express office at Butte and according to the shipping records Bryson had shipped them there and had planned to claim them at the Mining City as soon as he could safely get out of Helena. When Mrs. Thompson was informed about the murder of Mrs. Lundstrom she broke down in tears and after the authorities were confident she hadn't had anything to do with the crime she was released from custody on October 3.

The Grand Jury took up the case on October 10, 1888, and after interviewing witnesses and examining the trunks of the dead woman they formerly brought two counts against George Bryson the following day. After seeing the sketch of Bryson in the newspaper, Mr. Kartofsky, owner of Uncle Sam's Pawn Shop at Helena reported that the man charged with murder had pawned a gold watch and some ladies clothing at his store about ten days earlier under the name of J.D. Lunson.

At his arraignment before Judge McConnell on October 15, 1888, Bryson led the shackled column of twelve inmates including two accused murderers, five forgers, three held for assault, and two each of burglars and grand larcenists. Bryson seemed out of place dressed in his fancy suit and his hat in his hands as he made his way to his seat where he sat calmly with one leg crossed over the other. His bright eyes gleamed with unusual luster, and they were said to have twinkled.

His darting glances were reportedly the only thing in his whole demeanor that betrayed any nervousness he may have had. The courtroom reportedly buzzed with curiosity as Bryson entered the room and took his place inside the jury box with the other prisoners. In a twist of fate Bryson's attorney, Mr. Balliet won the county attorney position as the Republican nominee less than a month later and because he had served as the defendant's attorney he couldn't prosecute the case and the county had to hire a special prosecutor.

The commissioners of Lewis and Clark County hired a good prosecutor in William Wallace Jr. who had been the successful outgoing prosecutor for the county having recently convicted George Godas of first-degree murder. In another wrinkle in the George Bryson case, Judge McConnell resigned his position on the bench in December of 1888, having sent his resignation to President Cleveland stating that he wasn't content with the three thousand dollar annual salary and he was going into private practice at Helena. He did however state that he would stay on until a suitable replacement was appointed.

Bryson's trial before Judge McConnell began on March 14, 1889, in a crowded courtroom at Boulder after being granted a change of venue from Lewis and Clark County. After a day and a half a jury was finally selected and was made up of the following Jefferson County citizens:

F. Hanlon	J.W. Gilkey	H.C. Shepard
A.C. Dixon	William Channel	George Hubbard
B. Wilson	Thomas Davis	C.E. Hoffen
Lee Haggerty	Adam Dulaney	W.P. Hoopes

On March 16, 1889, the jury after sixteen hours of deliberation returned a guilty verdict of murder in the first degree and later that evening Judge McConnell sentenced George Bryson to be hanged on August 9, 1889. Bryson's attorney immediately filed a motion for a new trial and the defendant later told a reporter that if he was granted a new trial he would make a startling revelation, which would fully exonerate him of the crime. A new trial wasn't in the cards however and Judge Henry Blake, who had replaced Judge McConnell, denied the prisoner's motion for a new trial and later the Montana Supreme Court affirmed the lower court's death sentence.

Defense Attorney S.A. Balliet argued before the Supreme Court for a new trial on the grounds of the incompetence of the jurors, new evidence and because the evidence in the case didn't establish the guilt of his client. After reviewing the case the Supreme Court refused to grant a new trial for George Bryson and on August 2, 1889, they informed the defendant. Bryson's elderly father presented a stoic demeanor throughout the proceedings and he showed no sign of emotion when his son's doom was sealed by the decision of the high court.

While waiting for his sentence to be carried out Bryson made several attempts to break out of jail with the help from the outside. Bryson had sawed a hole through his cell into the adjacent one, from which he could enter the corridor. It was said that the prisoner had planned his break on the Forth of July when the sheriff and most of his deputies would be away. After Sheriff Halford found a butcher knife in Bryson's clothing and two cutting saws concealed in his boots he ordered a continual watch on the prisoner.

In another instance, Jailer Jerry Ellis was asked by a fifteen-year-old inmate by the name of Brown to pass a book over to Bryson to read but when the officer suspected that something was going on he inspected the text and found a folded note containing a suspicious looking powder. A local druggist was called to analyze the powder and he found the substance to be a combination of strychnine and opium. A woman wrote the letter and it read, "Instantaneous poison. George D. Bryson, cheat the gallows. This is quick." Apparently the same mysterious agent who supplied the tools earlier to the prisoner had also shipped the poison. This wouldn't be the only time that the observant jailer would prevent a condemned man from cheating the gallows. A year later Jailer Ellis prevented another woman visitor at the county jail from passing a lethal dose of morphine to Thomas King who was eventually hanged on June 6, 1890.

Bryson passed most of time in reading and playing a violin, at which he was considered quite good. The sounds of the workmen preparing the stockade around the yard and the scaffold reportedly didn't evoke any emotion from the prisoner. He was a very good writer and the Helena "Independent" published a letter of his expressing his innocence. For several days leading up to his execution Bryson spent quietly and nervously, while he waited for commutations from Governor Benjamin F. White. The wait became even more tenser when the Governor commuted the sentence of Peter August Johnson, who was to be hanged at Deer Lodge on the same day as Bryson for murdering a man during a bar fight, to a life sentence at the state penitentiary.

About eight o'clock on Thursday morning August 8, 1889, the Reverend Guiler and Mrs. Reeves arrived at the jail to conduct prayer services with Bryson and he again assured them of his innocence. After the services the prisoner wrote a beautiful and poetic letter to his six-year-old daughter, Maud Chase Bryson who was living at Howyk, Canada. The letter was to be delivered to her by Bryson's father when she was sixteen and old enough to appreciate it. The only time Bryson had shown any emotion during his incarceration was when he received a telegram reporting it was impossible for his daughter to reach Boulder before his execution. After the news, he reportedly broke down completely and sobbed with tears.

After finishing the letter to his daughter and visiting with his father, David Bryson, George asked the sheriff to admit all that wished to see him. Many ladies reportedly called on him during the evening, and then his father called on him before the jail closed for the night. That same evening, Bryson completed the finishing touches on his long statement that he would make on the gallows, stating his innocence and pointing out all of the weaknesses of the case against him. At about ten o'clock Jailer Ellis brought in some oranges for Bryson to eat while he worked on his statement and the two men talked freely for a while. Before the jailer left for the evening, Bryson asked him to pass out cigars to the other prisoners at the jail as he shouted out to them, "smoke heartily." When Bryson asked the prisoner in the next cell to sing for him "The Song Lessons that I Learned at Mother's Knee" he and the other inmates sang along in chorus until one a.m.

Bryson slept soundly until six o'clock on his final morning and then dressed himself carefully in the light suit that he had worn during his trial in March. He then ate his last breakfast of steak, eggs, bread and coffee. While the condemned man's father remained all morning with his son, Bryson spoke with him alone in French about family matters for about an hour right after breakfast. After Bryson's visit with his father, Sheriff Halford informed him that Governor White had sent a message stating that he would not take any action against his execution.

After giving Bryson the word about the Governor's decision Sheriff Halford read the death warrant to him at nine o'clock in the presence of

Professor Brown, Louis De Lestry and Deputy Ellis. When the Reverend Thomas A. Wickes and Mrs. Reeves arrived along with a large line of people wanting to see the condemned man, Bryson was resigned to his fate and he looked haggard and ghostlike. At ten o'clock Leonard Pan, the captain of the Helena post of the Salvation Army visited the prisoner and they prayed together. At 10:20 Bryson changed into another suit, which had been brought in special from Minneapolis. While David Bryson assisted his son get dressed the two men spoke again quietly in private, and then the father left his son for the last time at 10:30, the elderly man crying bitterly.

At 10:45 Bryson began shaking hands with the guards and reporters and the procession started its way to the gallows led by Sheriff Halford. Bryson walked to his execution yard firmly with Jailer Ellis where the executioner had already taken his place in the enclosure. Standing under the gallows and in a firm unshaken voice Bryson read his long statement of several pages reviewing some of the testimony he said was distorted and he dwelt on the story about a hack driver who was seen with bloody clothes that had suddenly left town after the body was discovered. Bryson then denounced the press, particularly the Helena "Independent," which he felt was prejudiced against him. He finished the statement with the words of, "Officers do your duty."

Following the reading of the statement the straps were adjusted around Bryson's arms and legs; the cap was drawn over his head and as the noose was being adjusted he was heard to say, "May God have mercy on my soul." At 10:52 the drop fell with a loud thud and George Bryson's body was jerked into the air. When Sheriff Halford decided to use the gallows, which was originally built to execute Thomas Harding in 1887, at Dillon and then Hart at Helena in 1888, he arranged for the entire contraption to be transported from Lewis and Clark County to Boulder including perhaps the rope.

The hanging at Boulder was nearly botched because Bryson was about four inches taller than John Hart and his toes almost touched the ground. With his neck broken, Bryson's body continued to tremble for about four minutes and after a full nine minutes he was finally pronounced dead by Drs. Fletcher, Leighton and Brooks. The condemned man was cool throughout the affair and it was said that he held up better than any of the officers in charge and spectators. One newspaper later reported that while Bryson said in his statement that he was "going up to heaven," the two or three feet he was jerked up by the weight was probably as close as he was going to get. At three minutes after eleven the body of George Duncan Bryson was lowered into a plain casket and it was buried by the county in the Boulder Cemetery.

Postscript:

Soon after the burial many of the Boulder residents stated their displeasure that the murderer was laid to rest among some of the finest citizens of the community. The issue apparently had cooled down until the hanging of Thomas King in June of 1890, when his remains were buried at the cemetery at the county poor farm. In 1890, there was a renewed call to have Bryson's body exhumed and re-planted in potters' field at the farm but local historians report that because the county cemetery records are inconsistent, it can't be determined whether or not the man's body was ever moved.

After the Bryson hanging the scaffold was placed into storage and in less than a year Sheriff Dan Halford would be using it again to hang Thomas King in June of 1890. After the King execution the gallows again remained just an innocent stack of timbers until it was brought out of retirement to execute Clayton Pugh at the Jefferson County jail yard in July of 1895. In December of 1890, Sheriff Halford was called on to assist in the execution of the four Indians, Antley, La La See, Pascale and Pierre Paul at Missoula and although Halford was no longer in office in 1895, he participated in Pugh's hanging as a deputy sheriff for the county.

August 23, 1889
W.H. "Harry" Roberts

Location and Gallows: Roberts was executed near the county jail building at Butte and he was the second man hanged from ***Gallows No. Nine: (Feb 1888): "Galloping Gallows" No. Three.***
Description: Harry Roberts was born in Whales where his elderly parents and brothers still lived at the time of his execution. The prisoner was in his sixties and he had served two honorable enlistments in the United States Army and participated in sixteen battles and engagements. He never displayed much emotion and he had a peculiar smirking smile about the corners of his mouth.
Crime: Murder of J.W. "Long Tex" Crawford on May 14, 1889 at the Silver Bow House near the Silver Bow Mill about half way between Butte and Meaderville.
Judge: Stephen DeWolfe
Prosecution: Silver Bow County Attorney William H. DeWitt
Defense: Charles O'Donnell and John H. Duffy
Sheriff: John E. Lloyd
Distinction: Harry Roberts was the last man to be legally hanged by the Territory of Montana.

While running a freighting outfit Emanuel Corea employed Harry Roberts as a wagon boss and thirty-eight-year-old "Tex" Crawford as a teamster. Apparently in January or February of 1889, the two men had gotten into a small dispute on the road between Butte and Silver Bow while working together and it eventually simmered into a mean quarrel, and in March it had culminated into a serious battle between the two adversaries in the barn of the freight company.

According to witnesses at the barn at the time of the fight, Roberts had attacked Crawford with a knife but the six-foot, two hundred-pound "Tex" threw his attacker down and then raked his forehead with a pitchfork. Witnesses would later testify that Roberts jumped up with an ugly gash to his head and threatened Crawford that he wasn't finished. Roberts went to Deputy Sheriff Thomes and insisted that he arrest Crawford for assault but the deputy explained to the irate Roberts that he needed a sworn-out warrant before he could take the man in. He told Roberts to come back the next day and fill out a formal complaint so the law could take care of the matter. The officer said that Roberts finally quieted down and agreed to come back the following day, but Deputy Thomes commented that he never saw the man again until he arrested him on May 14 after the murder.

Apparently "Tex" and his friends had continued to torment the wagon master on and off of the job and at about noon on May 14, 1889, Harry Roberts walked into the washroom of the Silver Bow House and shot Crawford while he was bending over a wash basin washing up. There were several men in the washroom at the time and most of them either witnessed the shooting or saw Roberts with a gun standing over the body of "Tex." Immediately after the shooting some of Roberts' friends reportedly convinced him not to shoot any other people in the dining room of the club and to walk up town with them.

The sheriff's office was telephoned and the local officer, Deputy Thomes was dispatched to the scene and he actually passed Roberts and the other men as they were walking to town. When told that the murderer had already left, Deputy Thomes took a witness back to town with him in his buggy to identify the shooter. The deputy had planned to drive to a store on West Park Street where he could use a telephone to call for help in finding the fugitive, but just as he was stepping into the building the witness informed him that Roberts was across the street.

With the heads up, Deputy Thomes quickly ran across the street and arrested Harry Roberts without incident. After searching the prisoner the officer found a double-action Smith and Wesson 38-caliber pistol with two empty rounds on his person. Meanwhile the Silver Bow County coroner, Dr. Howard had arrived at the murder scene where he interviewed witnesses and empanelled a coroner's jury consisting of:

A. Judge	Mr. Thorpy	John Griffin
F.H. Butler	Patrick Regan	James Leach

Besides a pocketknife, the doctor found a plug of tobacco and eighty-five cents on the victim's body. The coroner's jury determined that Mr. Crawford had died from a gunshot wound, the bullet passing through his right arm between the elbow and shoulder and then it entered the body between the fifth and sixth ribs. The round then entered the stomach and finally lodged near the victim's heart. The jury reported that Harry Roberts had premeditated the cold-blooded murder of his victim and Sheriff John Lloyd ordered extra guards over the prisoner because there was talk of a lynching. Meanwhile Judge DeWolfe recalled the Grand Jury to investigate the case.

Four days after the murder, on May 18, 1889, Harry Roberts was indicted for murder in the first degree and his trial began on June 1, in a crowded courtroom at Butte. It required two days to seat a jury, which was made up of the following citizens of Silver Bow County:

A.W. Beuse	P. McCabe	F.A. Wilson
C.R. Burkett	J.M. Albiez	Dennis Simpson
J. Cradlebaugh	H.J. Rothbumlen	J.J. Hammer
Thomas Stees	C.G. Cram	Hugh Harris

Harry Roberts walked to and from the courtroom and jail as erect as a soldier in a parade with his shoulders back and a look of supreme indifference on his face. In the courtroom he sat facing the jury, and if he had experienced any emotion, he never displayed it. The prosecution called more than twenty witnesses while the defense hinged its case on the testimony of Drs. Steele, Todd and Harding to try and convince the jury that Harry Roberts was insane.

The trial ended at ten o'clock on June 6, 1889, when after the first ballot the jury returned and W.L. Clark, deputy clerk of the court read the verdict of guilty of murder in the first degree. Roberts' attorney made a motion for a new trial, which was overruled by Judge DeWolfe and then he sentenced the convicted murderer to be hanged on August 16, 1889. Attorneys O'Donnell and Duffy again called for a new trial and Judge DeWolfe set June 14, 1889, as the day he would hear arguments for the motion. For some time after the trial Roberts refused to see visitors but his lawyers said that he was cheerful and as happy as ever.

The death sentence of Roberts brought out a major rift between the first sheriff of Silver Bow County, John E. Lloyd and the county commissioners. Lloyd had come to Butte in 1874, and was elected as sheriff in 1886, to eliminate the roving bands of Indians who were stealing horses. He had served as territorial sheriff of Silver Bow County and he was eventually re-elected when Montana became a state in 1889. The commissioners appointed S.S. Tice as a special deathwatch for the condemned man but the popular sheriff would not grant him entry of the jail charging that the commissioners had interfered with his duties and felt they should spend the money on the extra jailer his department had taken on at his own personal expense.

Obviously Sheriff Lloyd felt that he needed a larger staff, and to illustrate the point he had hired a man out of his own pocket. When the commissioners hired another part time guard he felt that he should have been spared, even for a short time the loss to his own salary. The same day that the sheriff refused entry to their hand picked guard, the county commissioners ordered the county attorney to draw up a complaint against Sheriff Lloyd. The next day Sheriff Lloyd was in front of Judge DeWolfe facing the complaint but the judge surprised the county commissioners by finding in favor of the sheriff.

Not being satisfied with the judgment of the court, the commissioners quickly passed an order that Silver Bow County would not pay for a deathwatch. In the meantime Roberts was placed in a special cell and Sheriff Lloyd assigned Thomas Richards and J.B. Knight as his deathwatches.

Judge DeWolfe denied Roberts' motion for a new trial in district court, but only minutes before his trip to the gallows on August 16, 1889, the condemned man received a one-week respite from Governor Benjamin F. White. Everyone was convinced that the condemned man was going to hang that day including Roberts who had dressed himself in his death suit and eaten his supposedly last breakfast. The telegram almost didn't make it to Butte in time as the Governor was in Dillon at the time and a message was delivered to the wrong person at Helena in error instead of the Governor's private secretary before being relayed to the Mining City.

After receiving the telegram Sheriff Lloyd read the Governor's message to Roberts in the presence of his attorney, Mr. O'Donnell as well as the District Attorney DeWitt. Tears were seen gathering in the eyes of Harry Roberts but after wiping them away he was soon shaking the hand of the sheriff. The condemned man and the sheriff had known each other for many years and Roberts explained to the sheriff that he was tough enough to handle the hard knocks, but acts of kindness caused him to weaken at times.

Roberts had never asked for a spiritual advisor, saying that he never thought it was necessary to join a church and he insisted that he could prepare himself to meet his God without a public confession or other display of religion. Although he never asked for help, ironically it was the efforts of the clergymen that convinced the Governor to grant the one-week respite. Father Van den Broek and two Sisters of Charity of St. Patrick's Church along with the Reverend Adams of the Baptist Church and others had explained that they had visited the condemned man several times to help prepare his soul but they thought more time would be required. The clergymen and other influential citizens including J.H. Leyson, John Caplice, Jason H. Lynch, M.B. Browler, W.R. Kenyon and J.R. Clark presented a letter to Governor White requesting more time to ready his soul for the other world.

The prisoner was left in suspense once again on August 23, 1889, before he finally learned that the Governor wouldn't interfere again to save his life. Governor White had spent the day before the scheduled execution at Butte reviewing the case and listening to the many pleas on behalf of the condemned man. On the evening before the execution the Governor evoked even more optimism for a commutated sentence for Roberts when he had earlier saved a condemned man's life at Deer lodge. At first it was expected that the Governor would make his decision before midnight but when twelve o'clock had come and gone the supporters felt that the Governor had made up his mind to save Roberts, but at ten a.m. the message arrived announcing that the sentence would be carried out.

On the night before his execution, Roberts sat up until 2:30 talking with Deathwatch Thomas Richards and Jailer Cook and he eventually he fell asleep at three o'clock. Deathwatch Richards woke Roberts up at about eight for his breakfast and because the guard had such a good relationship with the prisoner, Sheriff Lloyd requested he inform the doomed man of Governor White's decision. When Roberts was told about the telegram he stated that he hadn't expected anything else.

Although Roberts had continued to refuse religious counsel, Reverend Father Van den Broek and Reverend Andrews visited the jail on the day of the execution and were available to the prisoner. Reverend Andrews left the building just before Sheriff Lloyd led Roberts to the gallows but Father Van den Broek remained at the courthouse claiming that Roberts had requested a Catholic burial.

After they had both attended the Hart execution at Helena in 1888, Sheriff Lloyd and Deer Lodge County Sheriff Coleman obtained the plans of the Lewis and Clark County gallows and apparently had partnered up to have a new scaffold built. The gallows was built at Butte and it was used for the first time at Deer Lodge to hang Martin Scott in February of 1888. Sheriff Lloyd assisted the Deer Lodge County sheriff with the hanging of Scott and then he brought the most famous of all "Galloping Gallows" back to Butte where it became the property of Silver Bow County. The gallows went on to hang a total of thirteen men, more than any other scaffold in state history.

In addition to the invited spectators in the jail yard, the north windows of the city clerk's office and the county courthouse were lined with men anxious to witness the hanging. There was a continual hum of voices and excitement that filled the air until three minutes after one p.m. when Sheriff Lloyd and Harry Roberts appeared at the east door of the county jail. Following the sheriff and the condemned man through the door was Jailer Richards, Deputy Nichols and Police Captain Sam J. Reynolds. The sheriff's right hand gently held Roberts' left arm as they descended the four or five steps into the jail yard and then the procession made its way to the eastside of the yard where the gallows stood some twenty paces away.

Roberts wore a black suit and a white shirt without a collar as he walked firmly to the scaffold in a pair of slippers instead of shoes. There was a strip of matting or carpeting beneath the gallows and the noose was kept out of the way by being hung upon a nail on the west upright post. Sheriff Lloyd took his place on Roberts' left hand side as he asked the prisoner if he had anything to say. Roberts took one step forward; faced the crowd and then turned his head towards the sheriff and said, "I'd have gotten my reprieve if it had not been for W.A. Clark and W.M. Jack. I forgive them and have prayed God to forgive them and me. I hope He will answer that prayer."

At the conclusion of his statement Roberts took a step back to his former position under the scaffold and then shook hands with his attendants and a number of his friends. He then dropped his hands to his sides and stood at attention, showing both his military training and indicating that he was ready to die. After Deputy Nichols and Captain Reynolds had pinion Roberts' legs and arms with broad soft leather straps, The sheriff placed the noose around the man's neck. Roberts moved his head around as if the rope was irritating him, and in a strong voice, devoid of emotion, said, "Make it a little tighter; it is too loose. It will hurt."

After the sheriff tightened the noose around Roberts' neck he stepped back while he pulled the black cap from his inside pocket and pulled it down over the man's head and face. When the sheriff dropped his hands Harry Roberts was jerked into the air about three feet and then fell back down where his toes came to within five or six inches of the ground. The 340-pound weight dropped at exactly 1:12 and Drs. Howard, Sarchet and J.A. Tremblay immediately examined the suspended body. Dr. Howard grasped the left wrist and Dr. Sarchet took the right hand while Dr. Trembly listened to the heart with his stethoscope.

After one minute Dr. Howard announced that the heart was beating fifty-five beats per minute; after two minutes, sixty; four minutes, one hundred and ten beats; six minutes, sixty-six beats; then it stopped all together but after another minute the pulse returned at twenty-six beats per minute. Eight minutes after the drop Roberts' heart was still beating at seventy beats per minute, but it stopped for good at the nine and a half minute mark. Shortly after 1:21 the doctors pronounced Roberts dead and a few minutes later the body was lowered into a plain dark brown coffin.

The coffin was then carried into the hallway of the courthouse where it was placed on a couple of undertaker stools for public viewing. After several hundred men and women had viewed the remains they were taken to Undertaker Sherman's establishment where a funeral was held officiated by his friends. When it was all said and done it was reported that Roberts was less affected by his hanging than any of the onlookers and he went to the gallows bravely.

(Endnotes)

[1] Jesse Armitage placed the nooses around the necks of Compton and Wilson in April 1870.

[2] Location of 1875 jail yard "Medicine Lake Wave" 1/7/1918

[3] Before serving on the first jury of William Sterres, D.M. Gillette was one of the jurors who found Arthur Compton and Joseph Wilson guilty before the Helena Hometown Vigilantes executed them in April of 1870.

[4] Abner Adams later served on the jury that found Patrick Hart guilty in his third trial and he was eventually hanged in February of 1888.

[5] John E. Vawter supplied the delivery wagon and driver from his grocery business at Helena that was used to hang Compton and Wilson in April of 1870.

[6] This most likely is the same Joe H. Smith that served eighteen years later on the jury that convicted Joseph Allen who was eventually hanged in September of 1899.

[7] "Elk" Morse was instrumental in the capture and hanging of George Ives at Nevada City in December of 1863 along with being an active member of the Original Vigilantes.

[8] Before serving on the jury of John Hart's third trial, Abner Adams had served on the panel that convicted William Sterres who was hanged in October of 1875.

[9] William Channel later served on the jury that convicted Clay Pugh who was hanged in July of 1895.

Nineteenth Century State Legal Hangings
(November 1889 through December 1899)

June 6, 1890
<u>Thomas A. King</u>

Location and Gallows: King was the second man hanged at Boulder and the fourth victim on ***<u>Gallows No. Eight: (Mar. 1887): "Galloping Gallows" No. Two.</u>***
Description: King was a thirty-four-years-old miner who had dark eyes and hair with a black mustache. He had a low forehead and a small ill-shaped head with a large burn scar over his right temple. He was described as not looking very intelligent but he had a pleasant manner and was said to be both sharp as a whip and a smooth talker.
Crime: Murder of Matthew Fogarty in a bar fight at Elkhorn on November 29, 1889.
Judge: Thomas J. Galbraith
Prosecution: Because Jefferson County Attorney Montgomery H. Parker became ill, his law partner, George F. Cowan assisted with the prosecution of King with the help of Allan R. Joy.
Defense: George D. Greene and William L. Hay
Sheriff: Daniel M. Halford
Distinction: Thomas King's hanging was the first conducted by the State of Montana.

On Thanksgiving evening of 1889, Thomas King and a few of his friends decided to celebrate the holiday by attending a dance at Gilliam's Hall. Because there was a lack of women at Elkhorn at the time, King reportedly began dancing with George Peters when Mathews Fogerty, who was the floor manager at the hall ordered them to stop. Apparently King and Peters were offended by the action but they took no action at the dance and they adjourned to the nearby Colberg's Saloon. Sometime before midnight King and Peters left Colberg's and they accompanied others to Lloyd's Saloon to continue their celebration.

When Matthew Fogarty arrived at Lloyd's Saloon on the early morning of November 29, George Peters confronted him. In no time a huge bar fight broke out among just about everyone in the place except for King who just sat back and watched the activity. The fight eventually moved outside where the participants filled the street in a "free-for-all." When Fogarty was getting the better of Peters, Thomas King rushed in to help his friend and during the melee he shot Fogarty. After the shooting, Deputy Sheriff James Mitchell followed King to a nearby cabin where he had barricaded himself inside.

After assigning two men to guard the cabin Deputy Mitchell returned with a Winchester rifle and demanded the fugitive to surrender. While taking King back to Boulder Deputies Mitchell and John H. Forbes overtook George Peters a few miles out of Elkhorn and they quickly arrested him and on Monday, December 2, 1889, the two men were brought before Justice D.G. Warner. Both men waived examination and were held without bail until the Grand Jury was convened when King was charged with murder in the first degree and Peters faced charges of complicity in the murder of Mat Fogarty.

Statehood and a new constitution brought up a controversy over the proper size of Montana Grand Juries, which affected many of the state criminals facing felony charges at the time including two men facing murder charges, Ah Jim in Lewis and Clark and Thomas King at Boulder. On January 12, 1890, Judge Galbraith was called upon to decide the proper size of a Grand Jury and the number of consenting members required to indict an accused criminal. King's attorneys as well as lawyers, Thomas Joyce and Frank Showers argued that the a Grand Jury hearing felony cases were to be made up of sixteen citizens and required twelve to indict. The newly elected State Supreme Court ruled in the test case of Ah Jim that all persons charged with felonies that had been indicted by a Grand Jury of seven citizens could be brought to trial as long as at least five members voted for his guilt.

The King trial opened on January 22, 1890, and because of a delay taken due to the illness of the county attorney it took three days to secure a jury. During the trial five men of Elkhorn, Eugene White, William Powell, N.E. Connor, W.J. Rogers and W.E. Dean testified that they had seen Thomas King shoot Mat Fogarty. Witness Connor said that after he was getting the worst of the fight in the saloon, George Peters ran out into the street with Fogarty chasing him. After a short chase Mat Fogarty quickly dispatched Peters and as he was returning to the bar Thomas King met him, drew his revolver and shot him at point blank.

The court adjourned at seven p.m. for a while, and then returned later that evening to hear the final arguments, which were completed at eleven o'clock that night when the jury retired. The following morning, January 28, King was brought into courtroom looking haggard and tired and Foreman John D. Ripley presented the following verdict: "We the jury in the above entitled cause, find the defendant, Thomas King, guilty of murder in the first degree, as charged in the indictment." It was later learned that the jury had taken two ballots; the first ballot was eleven for and one against the first-degree murder charge. After a short argument the twelfth man reportedly was convinced and they came in with the verdict. While King's face was quite pale, he received the verdict calmly and he was taken back to the jail to wait until the following day for his sentencing.

On January 30, 1890, Judge Galbraith was visibly affected as he pronounced the death sentence on Thomas King for March 27, 1890. All the condemned man said was that he was not guilty of the charge while his attorney asked for a new trial, but the judge overruled the motion. Mr. Greene then prepared a bill of exception for an appeal to the Supreme Court and on March 19, Montana State's First Governor Joseph K. Toole delayed the execution until May 8 for further court review. On May 2, Chief Justice Henry Blake wrote the Supreme Court opinion affirming the decision of the lower court, and Acting Governor John E. Rickards eventually granted Thomas King a respite until Friday, June 6.

King refused to disclose his true identity but said that his father was German and his mother was Italian. He claimed that he was born in a small village in Italy in 1856, and he still had brothers and sisters living there. Because his parents were so poor and couldn't provide for the family, King came to America by himself when he was only eight years old. After living in the streets of New York City without money, friends or family, the boy moved westward earning his living mostly in mines. From Leadville, Colorado King moved on to Butte in May of 1889, and then to Granite where he lived in the boarding house of Mrs. Emma Tusch who he had known earlier at Colorado. King had only been at Elkhorn for a month when he got into the fight with Fogarty, and he had planned to return to Colorado the following day.

While attempting to convince Governor Toole to commute his client's sentence, George Greene presented a petition from Leadville, Colorado with one hundred and five signatures of prominent citizens who exhorted King's good character. The petitioners of Leadville stated that whatever the opinion of the people of Jefferson County, Thomas King's friends in Colorado thought a great deal of him. Since Governor Toole had recently commuted the sentence of Philip the Indian and because most people didn't consider King a "bad man," the general consensus was that he too would be saved from the gallows.

The day before his hanging King tried on his brand new black suit of broadcloth, which the sheriff had purchased for the execution. Among the condemned man's visitors was Maggie Dwyer (or Devere), a notorious ex-vaudeville woman who had been recently released from the jail. After talking for a while she told King Good-bye and then she slipped something into his hand. Fortunately Jailer Jerry Ellis spotted the transfer and the officer and Deathwatch George Graham quickly took the little parcel from the prisoner. A year earlier Jailer Ellis had thwarted another plan to poison an inmate on death row when he prevented George Bryson from receiving strychnine from another inmate at the jail. On examination of the parcel it was found to contain six and a half grains of morphine, which undoubtedly would have enabled King to cheat the gallows. Just days earlier a spoon, which had been sharpened into a knife blade, was found on the prisoner and it was removed before he was able to cut his wrists.

King spent his last night on earth restlessly pacing in his cell on the second floor of the Jefferson County jail and he wasn't able to control his nerves and had a bad night in the little stone jail. Sheriff Halford and two or three reporters stayed up talking with the condemned man until four o'clock in the morning and no matter what subject came up, King seemed to always turn the conversation to his hanging in the morning. He had been told of how bravely George Bryson had met his death in August of 1889, on the same gallows and on the very spot where King would be executed.

While Bryson had read his long statement under the noose, King couldn't read, and therefore had decided to have someone else read his statement, but he made it clear that he wanted to die as bravely as the previous man had. Although King talked like a brave man, the sheriff feared that he would weaken at the first sight of the gallows and he tried to convince the prisoner to have his statement read inside the jail.

King was a model prisoner although he refused to be photographed and he ate sparingly. The day before his scheduled execution the man asked for a plate of soup, which was the most he had eaten for several days. Reverend John Moore of Boulder and Father Follett of Helena were credited with keeping King's spirits up so that he could at least make his way to the gallows.

At four o'clock King was alone with Frank Phinney, the night deathwatch, and the condemned man began pacing the cell, back and forth, slowly and silently. Although the morning sun was blocked from entering King's cell, the reflection poured into the corridor of the jail indicating the condemned man's final morning. Sheriff Halford and the reporters arrived at the jail at 7:30 and they found the prisoner's face had a dark yellowish hue and one newspaperman said that the man's eyes were strained, shrunken with the startled look of a hunted animal.

King didn't touch his breakfast but he did accept a cigar from one of the newsmen and puffed on it with great haste as he continued to pace his cell. He had given away his clay pipe with a bamboo stem hours before to Mike Newman as a memento. At nine o'clock Mr. Greene, King's lawyer, who had at his own expense carried the case to the Supreme Court and did everything a man could have done, called on his client for the last time. The defense attorney was greatly moved and he later said that he had honestly believed that the shooting of Fogarty was purely accidental and that his client shouldn't have to pay for it with his life.

The Reverend Father Follett arrived on the ten o'clock train from Helena and he was brought directly to the jail where he remained with King in his cell for about an hour. The priest administered spiritual advice and consolation to the doomed man along with performing the last sacraments of the Catholic Church. As the priest spoke King listened reverently and he appeared to be comforted by the words.

Meanwhile in the jail yard the preparations were being made for the execution and the 290-pound drop weight had been used to stretch the rope over night. The proper length of rope was determined by hanging a log that was exactly the same height as the condemned man and once the proper length was established, the regulation noose was made. The noose was lubricated with sweet oil under the supervision of Sheriff Quigley of Deer Lodge County, Sheriff Joe Hamilton of Cascade County and Warden Thomas McTague of the state penitentiary.

Another officer present during the preparations of the rope was Lewis and Clark Sheriff Charles Jefferies who was scheduled to execute Albert Jackson in his own jail yard on June 21. It wouldn't be however, as Governor Toole commuted Jackson's sentence to life in prison on June 17, 1890. Also invited to Boulder for the hanging were Sam Tice and Lew Coleman of Butte. Tice's claim to fame came when he and Charles Jefferies captured Con Murphy in 1880 and Lew Coleman had experience with executions while he was sheriff of Deer Lodge County having hanged Martin Scott in 1888.

After the near botched execution of Bryson a year earlier, Sheriff Halford ordered a hole about a foot deep and two feet square dug just under the dangling rope, which extended the death drop by an extra twelve inches. Two boards were laid over the hole and a strip of red and yellow matting covered the wood. These boards would be pulled out from under the condemned man in case the rope stretched and King's feet were touching the ground. As Sheriff Halford was making his final inspection of the scaffold he noticed a stray playing card lying face down at the foot of the gallows and upon turning it over, the ominous Jack of Clubs appeared.

A crowd of curious spectators had been gathering around the jail yard since eight o'clock that morning and the knotholes and cracks between the boards that commanded the best view of the gallows were in great demand. One enterprising individual drove his wagon up against the fence and by placing boxes about the bed of the vehicle he offered several of his friends, comfortable seating for the event. Among the crowd was a little old character that was described as being half lunatic and half idiot. At any rate he was reportedly going crazy that morning demanding entry into the enclosure to insure that the officers did their duty correctly. Well, the officers did do their duty and they picked up the old fellow and locked him away in the most secluded part of the basement of the jail. From that point on there were no further disturbances of any kind within or without the execution enclosure.

At eleven o'clock Father Follett tapped on the iron grating of King's cell and explained to the sheriff that he had finished his work; explaining that religion had done its part to prepare the man's soul and that he was ready to meet his maker. After the priest said that the state could claim its vengeance the prisoner was given a big dose of whisky and wine to brace him but the staff had probably over done it. The door of the cell was opened and King passed through the threshold with the priest at his side followed by the deputies. King was led to the top of the stairs where Sheriff Halford, Undersheriff A.V. Gibson, Mr. Greene and the other deputies were stationed. The many spectators were lined up from the foot of the stairs all the way back into the jail yard.

By then the alcohol had taken its affect and King looked deathly sick and his head leaned over to one side as if he didn't have the strength to hold it up. Everyone who could see the prisoner thought he would faint at any moment as Sheriff Halford read the long death warrant, which included the two reprieves, one by Governor Toole and the other by Governor Rickards. There was no sound except for the low voice of the sheriff as he read the document as quickly as possible since no one knew exactly how long the condemned man would be able to hold up. King made it through the long tedious warrant and at the conclusion he said, "I am prepared to die."

Undersheriff Gibson then pinned a small bouquet of carnations and geraniums to the lapel of King's brand new black coat and then Mr. Greene read King's statement. King's final statement, in part explained that he was being punished for a crime not committed; that although he was guilty of the act he was innocent of the intent. The law required a life for a life and he was going to give his life for the one he had unintentionally taken from Fogarty. He said that he would gladly give up his life, if it would bring back Fogarty, and that God knew that he had nothing against the other man. The statement concluded with a sincere thanks to his attorney and to Sheriff Halford and his staff.

After the reading of the statement the sheriff and his deputies shook King's hand and bade him good-bye. King then whispered something into his lawyer's ear, which was if a certain person (name not given) inquired about his death; Mr. Greene was to send him the true facts. Father Follett held up the crucifix and after King kissed it, the bareheaded procession started down the stairs to the gallows at about ten minutes after eleven. Led by Sheriff Halford, King followed with the undersheriff bracing him by the arm. The priest followed the condemned man down the stairs and he was at King's side as they walked to the scaffold followed by the rest of the deputies and the reporters.

The "Anaconda Standard" wrote that the sun had never shone more gloriously or the sky had never been as blue than on that morning. With slow and steady steps the party marched around the corner of the jail building and it was suddenly confronted by the tall, grim posts of the gallows, with the motionless rope and noose hanging. In the distance the magnificent mountains surrounding Boulder could be seen from the gallows and there wasn't a breath of a breeze stirring that day or a single sound made by either man or nature.

King took his place under the rope and Father Follett stepped to his left side and he whispered a prayer to the condemned man while the sheriff and the undersheriff pinioned his legs and arms with broad leather straps. Meanwhile Mr. Berkins, the local photographer was busy directing the crowd out of the way of his camera. At fourteen minutes past eleven King was still having trouble holding his head up straight as the sheriff pulled the black cap over the man's head.

At 11:12 a.m. the sheriff gave the signal to Undersheriff Gibson who was concealed from view in a sort of tall wooden box to the left of the gallows. There was the sound of a hatchet striking a block of wood as the rope holding the weight was cut and then King's body shot up three feet into the air and then it dropped back down a few inches with an ugly jerk. The body hung motionless for a second or two; then the knees began to quiver; the legs drew up towards the chest and then the body seemed to be going through a terrible struggle. After a few more seconds the body relaxed; the legs slipped to their normal position and then the corpse hung motionless.

Dr. Fletcher of Boulder, Dr. William C. Riddell of Elkhon and Dr. A.F. Judd of Jefferson City, with watches in their hands continually monitored the man's pulse as a plain pine coffin was being brought in through the rear gate and placed under the suspended body. King's pulse continued for nine minutes and it was very faint for another six. Finally at 11:29 the physicians pronounced Thomas King dead and the body was cut down and while it was being placed in the coffin the physicians determined that the first two bones of the spinal cord had been dislocated. They explained that the King's death was painless and the movements of the body were merely reflexive.

There were about a hundred witnesses inside the enclosure including reporters from the "Helena Independent," "Anaconda Standard," "Helena Journal," "Butte Miner" and the "Jefferson County Sentinel." It was reported that Sheriff Halford wasn't strict about people witnessing the body of King and when he was being cut down he ordered the gate of the enclosure thrown opened. Once the noose was removed from the man's neck the hangman's rope was immediately cut into twelve-inch mementos.

Undertaker Paradise of Boulder screwed down the lid of the coffin and it was placed on his wagon and driven to the cemetery at the county poor farm where his resting place would be a pauper's grave. King didn't have any relatives present and there were no tears shed for him. The burial of King at the poor farm once again created a controversy over the grave of George Bryson who was hanged at Boulder in August of 1889. Bryson was buried in the community cemetery among some of the most respected citizens and the recent execution of King caused many in Boulder to call for the remains of the former murderer exhumed and reburied on the grounds of the poor farm.

Postscript:
This was Sheriff Dan Halford's second execution, having had already hanged George Bryson in 1880, and after the hanging of Thomas King the sheriff and his men were given credit for doing their painful duty well. The sheriff was later called to Missoula to assist in the hanging of the four Indians in December of 1890, and although Sheriff Halford had left office, he remained with the department and served as a deputy to assist with the execution of Clayton Pugh on July 1, 1895.

Alex Gilliam who had been an eyewitness to the murder of Matt Fogarty at Elkhorn and testified in court against King later became the sheriff of Jefferson County and he officiated over the execution of Clay Pugh in July of 1895. After the execution of King, the Reverend Father Follett accompanied two other condemned men to the gallows, John Osnes in July of 1895, and Joseph Cadotte in December of 1895, both at Fort Benton.

Maggie Dwyer, the woman who tried to pass King a deadly dose of poison before his execution had originally turned to prostitution after leaving the theater and lived at various disreputable houses on South Main Street. Before the incident with King, Maggie had served nearly two months in jail for aiding the escape of Josie Hopkins who was out on bail for shooting another man at Elkhorn. After trying to help King cheat the gallows, Maggie was arrested at Elkhorn on attempted murder charges.

At her hearing, A.J. Reidel, a pharmacist for the Parchen and Morris Drugstore of Boulder testified that after three different analyses, he found the poison was sulphate of morphine. While the Grand Jury didn't indict Maggie for attempted murder, on July 11, 1890, Judge Galbraith still sentenced her to one hundred days in the county jail for her crime.

December 19, 1890: The Hanging of the Four Indians, Pierre Paul, La La See, Antley and Pascale

This image of the four condemned Indians appeared on the back of the invitation mailed out by Sheriff Houston. (Courtesy of the collection of Jack Weidenfeller of Missoula)

During the 1880's the Missoula County line extended to Canada to the north, Idaho to the east and contained many bands of marauding Indians terrorizing the inhabitants both white and Indian. Killings were frequent among railroad workers, lonely travelers, prospectors and settlers. Many of these Indians were said to have killed for the love of killing as they were taught as small children that the pale face were their natural enemy and many of them sought to redress the wrongs that their people had endured through generations.

On December 19, 1890, four of these outlaw Indians were hanged together from the same gallows at Missoula for three separate murders. Pierre Paul and La La See were hanged for killing two men in the Jocko area during May of 1887; Antley was executed for his involvement in the murder of three prospectors in the Fisher River country in September of 1887; and Pascale forfeited his life for taking a man's life between Demersville and Dayton Creek in 1889.

The arrest of the Indians

In June of 1889, while returning the fugitive half-breed Larry Finley who he had arrested at Great Falls back to the Flathead Reservation, Indian Agent Major Peter Ronan learned about several crimes on the preserve including the murder of two white men on the Jocko River. Although Major Ronan wanted Pierre Paul and La La See arrested and he notified the authorities at Missoula what he had learned from Larry Finley, he refused to assist Sheriff Daniel Heyfron and his men. Without the help of the Indian Police on the reservation Sheriff Heyfron called on a small posse and took the train north to apprehend the renegade Indians. Unfortunately the posse just missed capturing the two Indians as they had headed west along the railroad tracks so they boarded a freight train and eventually overtook a group of Indians.

After ordering the band to stop one of the Indians by the name of Kolchet was bringing his rifle to his shoulder when the crack marksman, James Conley of Deer Lodge dropped the man. Kolchet was reportedly the stepfather of one of the fugitives and he was suspected of murdering a bookkeeper at Demersville as well as the Indian, Koonsaw on the reservation. After being knocked down by Conley's shot Kolchet once again got up and began firing at the posse who returned fire striking him three more times and killing him. After the shooting the Indians threatened the community of Ravalli and most of the residents of that community considered Mrs. Gillett, the acting agent there, the bravest person in the town as she kept the telegraph messages moving to and from Missoula.

Since Indians were big on holding grudges, and because the sheriff and his posse had killed the Indian while getting off of a train, the tribe swore vengeance against the railroad company. The authorities became quite alarmed at Missoula when the Indians started burning off all of the timber near the Jocko Station and they were threatening to burn the railroad bridges on the reservation. Besides the warnings from the reliable half-breed Indians that trouble was eminent, the tribe had also moved all of their women and children into the mountains, which was a practice of the warriors prior to major battles.

Eventually Pierre Paul had terrorized the reservation to the point where Major Ronan finally felt that he really had to do something and in September of 1889, he and his Indian Police captured the renegade only to have him escape custody. In October of 1889 Territorial Governor Benjamin F. White offered a thousand dollar reward for the capture of Pierre Paul and La La See but most people believed that it wasn't a large enough incentive to induce anyone to risk their lives trying to bring in the dangerous fugitives as they traveled under the protection of Chief Aeneas and his tribe near Flathead Lake.

After statehood, the first sheriff of Missoula County, Sheriff William A. "Bill" Houston was determined to put an end to the lawlessness on the reservation. While he was a tough-as-nails lawman, as none other than "Wild Bill" Hickcok had given him a job as a stagecoach guard in 1875, Sheriff Houston concluded that the only way to capture the renegade Indians was to secure the help of men familiar with the reservation and who knew the fugitives. The thirty-seven-year-old sheriff along with about sixty men including William Mooring, Jack Wise and Howard Sprague left Missoula by train to meet with his two deputies, Ralph H. Ramsdell and John J. Grant with a posse from Demersville on Sunday, August 3, 1890, to bring in Antley and the other wanted Indians, Pierre Paul, La La See and Pascale.

The posse from Demersville included Leslie L. Foy and his son, John, Billy Sharp, John and William Elliott, Jack Graves, Jack and William Cummings, Harry Lee, George Blodget, R. Long, Frank Swim, Captain William Ramsdell, Jack Shepard, Lou Shaffer, Jesse Carpenter, Antoine and Charles Therriault. Others from Demersville were Charley Patrick, I. Flinchpaugh, Negro Sullivan, Charles Berry, Bill Boston, Ira Beam, George Blake, Al Neas and James Lang. The forty-man posse from Demersville left Saturday night and at daybreak on Sunday they surprised the Kootenai camp forty-five miles south of Demersville at Dayton Creek on the west shore of Flathead Lake.

Chief Aeneas was enraged that his camp had been invaded and he was about to take action against the Flathead men when Sheriff Houston and his men arrived from Missoula. Chief Aeneas reportedly drew his knife but laid it down when Deputy Ramsdell told him in his own language that if he tried to use it he would be a "very good Indian." When the sheriff said that they were looking for Pascale, Antley and another Indian called Williams, the chief told the officer to look for them himself. When the chief continued to refuse to assist the posse Sheriff Houston threatened to hold him as a hostage, which obviously scared the old Kootenai and he immediately turned over the Indian named Williams.

Not satisfied, Sheriff Houston still arrested Chief Aeneas; sent the main posse back to Demersville and with ten other men proceeded to Missoula with his two Indian prisoners. When darkness fell on the party Houston and his men took their prisoners aboard the sheriff's steamer, the "Tom Carter" and went out onto the lake for safety. That night gunshots and fires were spotted on the shoreline and after investigating, Sheriff Houston told the Indians to deliver Pascale or loose their chief. At daybreak on Monday August 4, Pascale was turned over to sheriff in exchange for their chief.

Besides turning over Pascale, the chief's release from custody was also on condition that Antley would be turned over to the authorities as soon as possible. Chief Aeneas also told Sheriff Houston that Pierre Paul and La La See were among the Pend d' Oreille tribe. While the sheriff and Deputy Ramsdell escorted Pascale to Missoula three other men were left with Chief Aeneas and Williams at the Ravalli Hotel. The Indians on the reservation made a big fuss about the arrest of their chief and Duncan McDonald notified Missoula that the Indians were threatening to attack. Sheriff Houston sent a telegraph back to McDonald at Ravalli telling him to inform the Indians that if the tribe made any trouble the sheriff would bring the troops with him next time.

The next evening Sheriff Houston returned to the reservation and on Tuesday morning he ordered the Indian police to bring all the Pend d'Oreille chiefs and their judges to Ravalli for a meeting. The Indian police apparently feared reprisals from Pierre Paul and La La See and they didn't obey the sheriff's instructions. When the Indians failed to come to Ravalli at the prescribed time and place the sheriff went to the St. Ignatius Mission with three deputies; rounded up all the chiefs and told them: "The people of Missoula County have about concluded that the only good Indian is a dead Indian," and if they didn't produce Pierre Paul and La La See the sheriff would lock up all of the chiefs as an accomplices. This enraged the Indians and while they didn't take on the four lawmen there was much talk of an attack on the white settlers at Ravalli.

Sheriff Houston telegraphed Undersheriff Tom McClury for reinforcements and the officer selected Jim Conley of Deer Lodge along J.H. Bell, I.M. McIntyre, Captain James T. Phillips, M.F. Madison, C. Clapp, "Baldy" Voelker, Charles Bloom and W.S. Crawford, all eager and armed with Winchesters and side arms to accompany him to the reservation. When the posse arrived at Ravalli the sheriff gave the chiefs notice that they must either fight or surrender. The arrival of the men on the train reportedly unnerved the chiefs and they held a big council that evening and on the advice of an ex-chief of Indian police by the name of "Old Joe" (probably Joseph Kotoolayuch), the leaders decided to do their best to cooperate with the whites and to help bring in the two renegade Indians. To compensate Chief Aeneas for his inconvenience throughout the whole incident, Sheriff Houston presented him with a brand new six-shooter, and the two men remained friends for many years.

On Wednesday morning, August 7, a posse under the command of Deputy Sheriff Ramsdell consisting of John Grant, Jim Conley; Special Deputies McVey, Sprague, Wise, Mooring and accompanied by Indian police, Antoine Morijour and Pierre Cottulaye started after the two murderers. At about three o'clock that afternoon they spotted the notorious Pierre Paul and an Indian woman on the Little Bitterroot River. Pierre Paul tossed his rifle to the woman and then rode off but Ralph Ramsdell soon overtook him. The Indian later told his captors that he had heard that the posse was coming but he decided not to escape, as his life on the run had been a great burden. Pierre Paul had made the right decision as Special Deputies Sprague, Wise and Mooring were from the Flathead area, and having had experiences with the Indians they wouldn't have cared if they brought him back dead or alive. As he rode back with the posse Pierre Paul was seen giving away his trinkets to his friends, telling them he wouldn't be needing them any more.

Antoine Morijour, the Indian who along with Dominick and Coosta had cooperated with the authorities in the Antley case was appointed a special deputy sheriff for his good deeds. Antoine Morijour was also placed in command of the Indian posse in search of La La See and Antley before the latter escaped into Canada. On August 19, 1890, after being hounded by the Indian police and the sheriff deputies, La La See sent word to Duncan McDonald at Ravalli telling him that he would turn himself in, but to no one but him. Mr. McDonald honored the man's request and he secreted the fugitive to the County jail at Missoula. The Canadian Mounties eventually arrested Antley and turned him over to Deputy Ramsdell who placed him behind bars on August 29.

Many of the residents of both Missoula and the reservation along with members of the posse were openly upset with Major Ronan for his inaction during the confrontation between Sheriff Houston and the Indians near Ravalli. Major Ronan had refused to assist Sheriff Heyfron earlier and he paid no attention to Sheriff Houston and didn't offer any assistance to the officer. The residents charged that the major didn't take law enforcement seriously as his twelve-member Indian police department had neither arms nor horses while most of the twenty-eight hundred Indians scattered over the reservation were well armed and had many horses. Major Ronan and the rest of the people on the reservation feared the bad Indians, and while they wanted to see them arrested they weren't apparently brave enough to stand with the law.

The Trials

The four Indians were tried in the old county courthouse at Missoula and the courtroom was reportedly packed for the four separate trials presided over by Judge C.S. Marshall. Judge Marshall was the first elected district judge elected at Missoula County and he served from 1890 to 1893. The first trial of Pascale began October 21, 1890, with Frederick C. Webster and Frank H. Woody handling the prosecution while Ilus G. Denney was the chief counsel for the defense aided by H.C. Stiffman and two other attorneys.

Interpreters used by the government in the four trials were Alex Michel and Pete Irvine and the sixty-two-year-old Chief Aeneas reportedly attended each of the hearings. Defense attorneys of today would probably find it particularly interesting that four of the jurors served on two of the trials. M.H. Pierce, J. McDonald and Frank Primont served on the juries of Pascale and Antley's trials while John O'Brien served on the trials of Pascale and La La See. You would think it would take a lot of courage to let a man sit on a jury that had voted guilty in another murder case just days before.

The Hanging of the Four Indians

With only two months to come up with a gallows to execute the four Indians, Sheriff Houston contacted Cook County Sheriff Seth Hanchett at Chicago who had hanged four men on one scaffold in November of 1887. Sheriff Hanchett was very cooperative and he provided plans, sketches and advice concerning the huge gallows as well as presenting Sheriff Houston with the four hangman's ropes and possibly the black hoods as well as the straps used in the 1887 execution. Fireman Robert S. "Bob" Mentrum who later became the first fire chief at Anaconda and state fire marshal was hired to design and build the new scaffold.

While the Cook County Gallows[1] had been built inside the jail building at Chicago, Mr. Mentrum's design was for a freestanding scaffold erected in the yard of the county jail. The gallows consisted of two upright timbers mortised to a crosspiece lying on the ground, and at the top, fifteen feet above the lower cross beam, another beam, which was about twelve feet long was mortised and bolted into the uprights. About three feet up the upright timbers there were braces securing them to the ground reportedly making the gallows strong enough to hoist a locomotive of those days.

The huge platform on the Chicago gallows was accessed from the second tier of cells but for the Missoula scaffold Mr. Mentrum constructed stairs utilizing twelve risers with the traditional thirteenth step being the twelve-foot square platform itself. Judging from sketches of the Chicago gallows, the huge trapdoor was nearly seven feet wide and extended about four feet from the edge of the platform. When released, the large trapdoor on both gallows dropped forward towards the witnesses providing an unobstructed view of the hanging bodies. Supporting the large trapdoor was four heavy hinges on one side and it was held up on the other side by a strong rope, which passed through pulleys underneath the platform.

Mr. Mentrum designed the trap to drop when a cord was chopped with a chisel when the sheriff stepped on a button on one of the steps leading down from the platform. The four hangman ropes passed through individual noose bolts, which were fastened to the underside of the crossbeam and then they were secured to the two uprights. The execution of the four Indians at Missoula was one of the biggest attractions in Montana, and among the many attendees were Doctors William B. Parsons, Hedger, Kneite and Daniel H. Billmeyer, U.S. Marshal William F. Furay and many sheriffs and newsmen of Montana.

The city of Missoula was an exciting place in those days and it was particularly busy the night before the hangings. There were licensed gambling houses located on practically every block of the downtown and they were packed with players. On that night the hurdy gurdy houses were ablaze with lights, laughter and song and there was a continuous procession of wagon and pedestrian traffic up and down West Front Street. The largest group of sheriffs and old-time gunmen from Idaho to the Dakotas to ever gather in the northwest was in town for the hangings. It was said that sheriffs were as thick as clover in the summer and Sheriff Houston's office at the jailhouse was the unofficial headquarters for the old lawmen and it was usually full of gunmen talking. Newspaperman Martin Hutchens of Helena and later editor of the "Missoulian" commented that nothing in the office looked out-of –the-ordinary except for the little pile of four black bundles, which were the cheap black suits purchased for the condemned men.

The other thirty-six county prisoners were all crowded into the upper cells of the two-year-old jail and on their last night on earth the Indians were given the freedom of the full corridor, guarded by Deathwatches, H. Rosensweig and Deputies McVey, Gipe and Harvey

Houston. Some of the family members and friends of the Indians were allowed to remain with the prisoners for part of their last night while singing their death songs. After the last visitors had left about midnight it was said that the jail was so quiet that the only sounds heard were the clunking of keys and chains along with the incoherent mumblings of Pascale, Antley and Pierre Paul.

While the others were chanting, La La See lay on his stomach motionless on the floor and he didn't move until Pierre Paul asked the guards for some liquor. Pierre Paul said, "Me hang good. If I get more whisky I get some more Jesus Christ and will be ready for priest when he comes at seven o'clock. Me die good." The four men were slowly weakening especially La La See and prayers were frequently offered and whisky occasionally given throughout the night.

The prisoners were served lunch shortly after midnight and they all ate heartily except for La La See. After more prayers, Pierre Paul and Antley finally went to sleep but Pascale remained up and requested four candles to be placed in the center of the cell, as he wanted to tell a story. Deputies Ramsdell and Evans translated the Indian's story about the Indians, Anthies and Williams killing Mr. J.M. Dunn and then paying him (Pascale) off to admit he had committed the murder. After telling his story Pascale played solitaire and then prayed until after four a.m. when he went to sleep. At 5:30 Antley and Pascale woke up and asked Deputy Gipe if they were really going to die and after being told that they would indeed die they thanked him for being truthful and then they went back to sleep. Fathers D'Aste and Markman woke the prisoners at 7:30 and they were taken to an upper cell at 8:50 where they were served coffee and then at 9:15 they ate their breakfast.

All but Pierre Paul ate some of their food and Pascale drank a little whisky with his meal. At 9:30 a.m. the men changed into their neat black suits, white shirts with collars, black ties and shoes and then the little white-haired mission priest, Father D'Aste along with Father Jenna of Missoula visited the prisoners. As the hour of execution drew near Sheriff Houston became overcome with emotion and while his resolve remained strong, tears came to his eyes. He found it hard to hang the men who for months had depended upon his care and kindness. Then one of the most touching events of the day occurred when Antley walked up and extended his hand to the sheriff, saying, "You must not be downhearted. We all have to die. You will have to go too some time. So you must not be downhearted."

Pascale then walked up to the sheriff and said, "Good-bye. Don't take it to heart. It is not your idea. Don't feel bad. My heart is good." Sheriff Houston told the men "Good bye" and at ten o'clock he began reading the death warrants with Alex Michel and "One Eye" Riley acting as interpreters. After the reading the priests held a religious ceremony where they sprinkled holy water on the prisoners and each of them kissed the crucifix that was held before them. A few Indian friends visited the doomed men and except for La La See they all stood up well. Meanwhile some of the visiting lawmen and newspapermen were going through downtown Missoula picking up some of their friends who had partied too much the night before. Nearly every one of the old-time gunmen and reporters carried half-pint bottles in their overcoats every where they went just for an emergency.

The procession to the gallows began and it was headed by Sheriff Houston with the smiling Pierre Paul; followed by Father D'Asta of the St. Ignatius Mission with crucifix in hand, Undersheriff McClury and La La See, Deputy Ramsdell with Pascale and Deputy Evans and Sheriff Daniel Halford of Jefferson County accompanying Antley. Reverend Father Jene brought up the rear followed by a large press corps including Martin Hutchens with the "Helena Independent" and John W. Pace, city editor of the "Helena Morning Journal." Other men of the press were Harry O. Collins and B.E. Bradley with the "Missoula Gazette," Harrison Spaulding the editor of the "Missoulian," George Maloney of the "Butte Miner" and Sam Robertson with the "Jefferson County Sentinel."

From the corridor the party went to the office; then through the east door of the jail and through a fenced passageway to the new high-board enclosure, which was filled with the invited spectators. On top of the enclosure were stationed Deputies Ike Abernathy, Gipe, McVey and Klepinger all armed with loaded Winchester rifles to guard the crowd that had gathered in the snow and rain outside. A large encampment of Indians had camped near Missoula and there were many rumors that a band of braves would try to interfere with the execution but there were only about twenty or more Indians and squaws among the large crowd outside of the stockade. Along one side of the fence there was a huge pile of firewood and it was covered with spectators looking down into the enclosure and the two large poplar trees in the jail yard had several small boys perched on their branches, which overhung the enclosure.

Following the condemned men and their escorts to the scaffold was a number of visiting officers from other counties of the state including U.S. Marshal William F. Furay of Deer Lodge, Warden Thomas McTague of the state penitentiary, brothers, James and Frank Conley, Emil Hansen and Alex Brown of Deer Lodge, Sheriff Joe Hamilton and Deputy Sheriff Thomas Wheeler of Cascade County, Deputy Sheriff Gallagher of Silver Bow and Sheriff Ed J. Jones of Custer County. Waiting in the enclosure were Indian Agent Major Peter Ronan and his interpreter, Robert Irvine, Chief Baptiste (Keekasha) who was the Indian Justice of the Peace, Chief Joseph Kotoolayuch (Standing Bear) and a half-breed interpreter, "One Eye" Riley. The two chiefs wore colored blankets while their flowing long gray hair hung from beneath their broad brimmed white felt hats bound with fur.

Another distinguished witness at the hangings and a respected friend of Sheriff Houston was Helena City Marshal Thomas J. Cronin. Marshal Cronin had been a good friend of "Wild Bill" Hickcok and he was marshal of Deadwood at the time of the famous gunfighter's death. Others invited to the hanging were several prominent residents of Missoula including Thomas Leo Greenough.

The doomed Indians took their places under the scaffold and they placed rosaries around their necks as their attendants began to adjust their straps. When Pierre Paul saw his attorney in the crowd he told him good-bye, and Pascale spoke in the Kootenai language as he explained his predicament and that he was innocent. La La See appeared pale and he looked as if he was in pain while Antley's face was described as looking like sunshine as he smiled at the crowd. Chief Baptiste had earlier gathered up the doomed men's blankets in the jail and he had carefully rolled them up for their families.

As the priests continued to pray Pierre Paul kept handling his beads, and La La See pressed the crucifix against his lips as the guards tied their hands behind their backs and their straps were buckled around their arms, thighs and ankles. The nooses were then adjusted around their necks; the caps were drawn over their faces and Father D'Aste remained on the gallows as the sheriff and his deputies stepped down from the platform. As Sheriff Houston stepped down on the button on one of the steps a chisel struck through the rope, which held the trap and at 10:47 the huge trap dropped and the four men fell like rocks, breaking their necks instantly.

On the morning of the executions the sky was heavily overcast with snow clouds and it was still dark at nine o'clock. The heavy snowfall obscured the sun that was trying to lend a few rays of cheerfulness to the tragic scene and large flakes were falling in the cold morning air as the trap was sprung and the four Indians fell with a sickening jerk. The bodies whirled on their ropes for a minute or two and then they each turned towards the crowd. Undertaker James Gallagher reported that it had been a well-managed hanging and none of the men appeared to have struggled.

La La See's pulse went on for seven minutes, Pascale lived for twelve, Pierre Paul's heart continued to beat for fifteen, and Antley was dead after eighteen minutes. Many of the witnesses turned their heads away when the trap dropped including the two old Indian Chiefs. After the bodies were cut down the straps, ropes and caps were removed and the remains were placed in four pine coffins, which were wheeled in later by the undertaker. It was said that the faces of the dead Indians looked life-like and as if they were asleep except for Pascale, whose eyes were open and his tongue was protruding slightly. The witnesses stood around the coffins where they noticed that the ropes hadn't left much of a mark on the victims as the large snowflakes were silently covering the bodies.

After the hangings it was learned that the Indians had camped at the edge of the city not for trouble, but to escort the bodies back to the Mission for burial. Following the execution Indians were seen scattered about Missoula, some on street corners and a number of squaws in colored blankets were seen crying bitterly. The bodies of the dead Indians were turned over to Major Ronan and he had them shipped to Ravalli where they were buried at the St Ignatius Mission.

During the 1890's many Indian tribes in the west were expecting a Messiah to save them by destroying the whites[2] and because of these concerns, Major Ronan allowed Catholic services to be conducted at the gravesites but no Indian rites were allowed to be performed.

Postscript:
Harry Collins, the editor of the "Missoula Gazette" had made arrangements for a twelve-noon edition and not long after the execution young paperboys were barking: "Extra, Extra, Read All About the Hanging Match!" Because of Collins' reporting the paper came out with a graphic description of the hangings and the issue sold very well. After dinner that day, a minstrel band entertained the large departing crowd as they made their way down to the Missoula Depot.[3]

Sheriff Houston said that the four Indians were good prisoners and he saw to it that they were rewarded by giving them a little whisky and a few knickknacks, which they used to decorate their cells. In later years he said that one of the hardest things he had ever done was to read the death warrants to the four men before their trip to the gallows. The sheriff admitted breaking down when he said good-bye to the condemned men and he later said that he had reservations about capital punishment after hanging the four Indians. Two years later the sheriff hanged John Burns, another murderer at Missoula and he eventually became one of the best lawman of the county before he was forced out of office, unfortunately on corruption charges.

Major Ronan was also deeply affected by the hangings of the four Indians since he knew the histories of the four men and he claimed that each one of them had lost family members at the hands of the whites. When one of the doomed Indians said good-bye to him from the gallows, Ronan was obviously choked up and he was unable to answer back. He did keep his promise of returning the men to the reservation for burial but as previously mentioned he wasn't allowed to permit any extravagant or traditional ceremonies over the graves.

Seven years after the state of Montana had offered the one thousand dollar reward for the arrest of Pierre Paul and La La See the money was finally dispersed. Of the seven applicants who applied for the reward, one was denied any portion of it, one of was never located and five were paid their share in May of 1896. The woman of La La See applied for a portion of the reward on the grounds that the fugitive Indian had turned himself in because he was tired of running. While she was turned down, William Mooring received two hundred dollars; James Conley, one hundred; Jack Wise, two hundred; Pierre Cottulaye, two hundred and John Grant also received two hundred dollars.

December 19, 1890

Pierre Paul

Hanged with: Antley, La La See and Pascale
Location and Gallows: Pierre Paul and the other three Indians were hanged behind the Missoula County jail on ***Gallows No. Ten: (December 1890)***. A complete description and history of this particular scaffold or other any other can be found in Chapter Seven: "Montana Gallows."
Description: Pierre Paul had raven-black hair and was a towering Pen d' Oreille Indian who was at least a head taller than the other three condemned men. He had very square shoulders and his appearance was of the typical or traditional Indian.
Crime: Pierre Paul and fellow Pen d' Oreille Indian La La See murdered two white men in May of 1887.
Judge: C.S. Marshall
Prosecution: Missoula County Attorney Frederick C. Webster and assisted by Joseph H. Woody
Defense: Ilus G. Denney and H.C. Stiffman
Sheriff: William A. Houston
Distinction: The hanging of the four Indians at Missoula was the largest single legal hanging held in Montana.

In mid May, Pierre Paul and La La See along with Indians, Larry Finley, Colville Pete and John Paul were all gambling in a cabin near the railroad tracks about five miles west of Ravalli. While the men drank and played their game, La La See said that the group should go out and shoot some white men to avenge the killing of his brother at Arlee by V.A. Coombs. The Indians started down the tracks to a spot near the mouth of the Jocko River where they found two white men eating near their camp. One of the white men had his boots off resting his feet when La La See asked them where they were going. When one of the men said he had a home at Missoula and that was their destination the Indian commented that they probably wouldn't make it.

Being suspicious of the Indian's intensions the white men began preparing to leave, and as they were starting down the tracks La La See ran in front of them and fired his rifle at one of the men. The man grabbed the rifle barrel but La La See wrestled it away from him and shot the unarmed man three times. The man didn't fall until the third shot and then the Indian shot him again while Pierre Paul shot down the second man. The Indians threw the bodies of the two men into the Jocko River where an Indian woman named Mrs. Couture eventually found them. The woman told Duncan McDonald about the unidentified victims and he informed the Missoula County sheriff. Pierre Paul was the last Indian to be tried and the jury was made up of the following men:

C. Betts	Paul Cyr	Robert Kendall
D.R. Maclay	Joseph Deschamps	John Richli
Peter Feddersohn	Thomas Foley	C.C. Pritchett
Napoleon G. Tevis	George Salsig	A.L.D. Hodge

During the testimony of the Indian, Joseph concerning Pierre Paul's confession of the murders, the defendant listened intensely to the evidence and then he stood up, pointed to the judge and stated that it was a lie. Through the interpreter, Michael, Joseph told the court that it was not a lie and then Pierre Paul's answer was that the witness was either lying or he had dreamed it. Joseph said that he hadn't dreamed it; that he saw Pierre Paul's lips move as he told of the two murders.

On the stand on his own behalf Pierre Paul denied that he had anything to do with the murders stating that he had remained at the camp when the others went looking for a white man to kill. It was later learned that Pierre Paul and La La See had shot Chinese as they worked on the Northern Pacific Railroad for the fun of it. The two Indians would hide in the gorges of the mountains and shoot the Chinese workers just to watch them fall and kick around.

Pierre Paul
"Jefferson County Sentinel" 12/25/1890

Two days before his execution Pierre Paul told a "Missoulian" reporter that he was innocent, but after his conviction he had concluded that it was right that the two white men were killed because two of his uncles were killed by whites and his mother died of grief over the incident.

On the scaffold Pierre Paul spoke out to the two Indian Chiefs Baptiste and Joseph who were standing next to the gallows and said, "I killed the men. I do not regret, but they tell me it was wrong. If so, I am sorry. You see how I am here. Try and help my people. If so, tell them how I died, and warn them not to do as I did, or they may die, as I have to die. Be kind to my people and see that they do not want. I am glad you come and I thank you for being here and for what you have done for me. See that I am buried with my people."

Seeing his defense attorney, Mr. Ilus G. Denney in the crowd, Pierre Paul at first said good night to the man but then corrected himself and told him good-bye instead. The big Indian obviously would have preferred dying in a fight, and in a final gesture of defiance Pierre Paul pushed aside one of the deputies who was attempting to pinion his arms. With his freed hand the Indian brushed his black hair from his forehead and his eyes glittered maliciously.

December 19, 1890

La La See

Other Name: Lalachee
Hanged with: Pierre Paul, Pascale and Antley
Location and Gallows: La La See and the other three Indians were hanged behind the Missoula County jail on ***Gallows No. Ten: (December 1890).***
Description: La La See was a member of the Pen d' Oreille tribe and he

had treacherous looking eyes, which some said resembled those of a wide-eyed Indian pony that didn't trust man. He wasn't very tall but he was strong and well built.

Crime: (See Pierre Paul, 12/19/1890)

Judge: C.S. Marshall

Prosecution: Missoula County Attorney Frederick C. Webster and assisted by Joseph H. Woody

Defense: Ilus G. Denney and H.C. Stiffman

Sheriff: William A. Houston

Distinction: The hanging of the four Indians at Missoula was the largest legal execution held in Montana.

Being committed to the capture of La La See, Sheriff Houston offered a five hundred dollar reward for the murderer and after being constantly dogged by bounty hunters both Indian and white, La La See sent word to Duncan McDonald at Ravalli that he would turn himself in only to him and the white man sent word back that he would see that he got safe transportation to Missoula. After turning himself in to McDonald at Ravalli the two men took horses as far as Evaro where they boarded a locomotive to the Missoula. The trial of La La See began on the morning of October 30, 1890, and the jury consisted of the following:

F.W. Gilbert	Edward Rhodes	C.F. Reardon
George Lancaster	Frederick G. Bond	John O'Brien
T.J. McGrade	J.S. Robinson	Pope Catlin
Miles Mix	N.R. Case	Lorenzo Abbott

The trial took all of one day and part of the next with the chief witness for the prosecution being Colville Pete, a man who was present when the murders were committed. The testimonies of John, Joseph and Antoine collaborated Colville Pete's story. Mrs. Canture testified how she found the remains of the two victims and how La La See and Pierre Paul had told her that they had done the killing. Mrs. Larabie and Duncan McDonald were called to support Mrs. Canture's testimony.

La La See
"Jefferson County Sentinel" 12/25/1890

Since the crimes had been committed on the reservation the question of jurisdiction was raised by the defense attorneys who argued that the case should only be tried in the United States courts. Judge Marshall ruled that since the murders had been committed on the right of way of the Northern Pacific Railroad the district court of Montana would have jurisdiction.

On December 17, 1890, La La See told a reporter that Larry Finley, Colville Pete and John and Paul Pierre had killed the two white men. Although La La See maintained his innocence he believed the deaths of the white men were warranted as a white man had killed his brother.

December 19, 1890

Antley

Hanged with: Pierre Paul, La La See and Pascale
Location and Gallows: Antley and the other three Indians were hanged behind the Missoula County Jail on ***Gallows No. Ten: (December 1890)***.
Description: Kootenai Indian
Crime: Antley along with fellow Indians, Little John Annen and Jerome murdered white prospectors, Daniel MacDonald, Ben Tompkins and John Cheley in September of 1887, on the Libby Creek Trail in the Fisher Country. (For a complete history of the crime See: Little John Ann: March 1888, in the "Lynch Mob" chapter)
Judge: C.S. Marshall
Prosecution: Missoula County Attorney Frederick C. Webster and assisted by Joseph H. Woody
Defense: Ilus G. Denney and H.C. Stiffman
Sheriff: William A. Houston
Distinction: The hanging of the four Indians at Missoula was the largest legal execution held in Montana.

After murdering the three white prospectors most of the guilty Indians were captured at Demersville by a posse led by Missoula County Deputy John Clifford. John Annen and Jerome were hanged by a Lynch Mob near Demersville but Antley managed to escape the posse and the rope. Antley avoided capture by hiding out amongst his people on the reservation and he and his friends continued their practices of stealing from and harassing the white settlers.

The Indian Antoine who witnessed the murder of the prospectors cooperated with the authorities by informing them that Antley and the other outlaw Indians would be attending a Sundance at Dayton Creek. On July 19, 1890, a posse organized at Demersville by Deputy Sheriff Jim J. Grant rode at night to the site of the dance and at the same time Company "G" of the Twenty-Fifth U.S. Infantry left by boat for Dayton Creek to rendezvous with the posse. Unfortunately Antley and the others heard the horses of the posse and they once again made their escaped.

The outlaw Indian escaped into Canada but the Mounties eventually arrested him and turned him over to Deputy Ramsdell who took him to Missoula on August 29. That fall Deputy Ramsdell and a posse located the scene of the murders where they panned the ashes of the old campfire and found bones, buttons, buckles and five twenty-five dollar gold pieces that the Indians had obviously overlooked. The remains of the three prospectors were returned to Demersville where they were buried on September 30, 1890. Antley was the second Indian tried and his hearing began on the morning of October 23, 1890, and was it concluded the following day. The jury for the Antley's trial was made up of the following Missoula County residents:

T.C. Sherill	J.A. Jamison	M.H. Pierce
P. McLaughlin	Frank Primont	Henry C. Myers
M. Kirschner	C.E. Atcherson	J. Joule
Hilaire Palin	J. McDonald	C.R. Church

The three unwilling witnesses to the murder on Wolf Creek, Antoine, Dominick and Coosta were the leading prosecution witnesses and they each testified that Antley had shot and killed the third white prospector in the fall of 1887. Chief Aeneas told the court that he had been with the party that found the bodies of the three prospectors and the jury only took ten minutes to return a guilty verdict.

December 19, 1890

Pascale

Hanged with: Pierre Paul, La La See and Antley
Other Name: "Lame Louie"
Location and Gallows: Pascale and the other three Indians were hanged behind the Missoula County Jail on ***Gallows No. Ten: (December 1890).***
Description: Pascale was a Kootenai Indian in his fifties and he dragged his left leg after being crippled from an old gunshot wound.
Crime: Murder of J.M. Dunn of Ida Grove, Iowa in July of 1889
Judge: C.S. Marshall
Prosecution: Missoula County Attorney Frederick C. Webster and assisted by Joseph H. Woody
Defense: Ilus G. Denney and H.C. Stiffman
Sheriff: William A. Houston
Distinction: The hanging of the four Indians at Missoula was the largest legal execution held in Montana.

Pascale had the reputation of being tricky, treacherous and he had even been charged with the murder of one of his own children. He had at least six wives, discarding one at a time and taking or stealing another one along the way. Apparently it was trouble with his last woman, which led to the murder of a white man and Pascale's hanging.

While putting up hay at the Leslie L. Foy's ranch in 1889, Pascale got into a quarrel with his squaw who had left with one of his horses. Pascale mounted another horse and took a short cut to Dayton Creek where the woman supposedly had family. When she wasn't at Dayton Creek Pascale borrowed a fresh horse from Chief Aeneas and he started for Tobacco Plains to find her. While the Indian was camped for the night a white man by the name of J.M. Dunn of Ida Grove, Iowa joined him.

According to the story that Pascale had boasted to his friends: On one evening in July of 1889, he was riding along Angel Hill between Demersville and Dayton Creek when he spotted J.M. Dunn resting while his horse was browsing in a nearby pasture. Pascale approached Dunn and asked him for a drink, which the man objected to as it was against the law to give Indians liquor. Finally after feeling threatened Mr. Dunn gave the Indian a single drink from his small flask, which he carried.

Pascale then insisted on another drink but this time Dunn refused and trying to defuse the situation he proposed a horse trade with the Indian. At first Pascale declined because the horse he was riding belonged to Chief Aeneas, but as the two men started up the hill the Indian said that he would exchange horses with the white man. Mr. Dunn mounted his new horse and started down the grade but after a short time the Indian wanted his horse back and when the white man refused he raised his rifle and shot him through the body below the left shoulder. Pascale told his friends that he had "shot the man as I would a grasshopper."

The murderer quickly took the man's valuables including a money belt with between fifteen hundred and two thousand dollars. Pascale then dragged the body into a clump of bushes; threw it between two logs and then lost the money belt as he was chasing after Dunn's horse. Two other Indians, Anthies and Williams found the money in the spring of 1890, but they quickly lost it gambling and drinking with other Indians including the half-breed, Antoine Finley. Later when Deputy Jim Grant had arrested Antoine for killing his cousin, William Finley at Egan on the Fourth of July 1890, the prisoner wanted to make a deal with Sheriff Houston for information about a murder of Mr. Dunn.

Pascale
"Jefferson County Sentinel" 12/25/1890

In an attempt to save his own neck over the death of his cousin, Antoine turned in Pascale for the murder of Mr. Dunn and agreed to take the whites to the murder scene to recover the man's remains. The story of the murder, which was told by Antoine, angered the settlers in the area because several other men had mysteriously disappeared from the region including the three prospectors murdered by Antley and several other Indians in September of 1887.

In July of 1890, Deputy Grant organized a posse to recover the body of J.M. Dunn consisting of Acting Coroner Clayton O. Ingalls Oscar Boos, Lou Schafer, William Wade, Dr. J.W. Sanders, William H. Mumbrue, Dan English, E.W. Burnham, Hospital Steward C.H. Dodge with the Twenty-Fifth Infantry and Charles Therriault. With Antoine Finley guiding the posse the party found the skeleton of Dunn along with remnants of his clothing and returned them to Demersville where the coroner's inquest was held. At the time of the inquest the name of the victim was not known and Antoine testified that Pascale told him that he had killed the unknown white man because some other white man had killed Chief Aeneas' son the previous fall.[4]

The verdict of the coroner's jury before Justice of the Peace Charles Shepherd of Demersville was, "that the unknown man came to his death from a gunshot wound inflicted by a rifle in the hands of one Indian, known as Pascale, sometime between August 15 and November 15, 1889, at Angel Hill, about twenty-five miles from Demersville, on the road to Dayton Creek, and about one mile in a southeasterly direction from the Little Meadows. The motive for which act we believe to be revenge." Signed, William H. Mumbrue, Oscar Boos, Dan English, Lou Schafer, C.H. Dodge and William Wade.

J.M. Dunn had been a man of wealth and in April of 1889, he went out West to find a new home for his wife and five children. After first visiting J.M. Scott at Post Falls, Idaho he stayed awhile at Spokane and then at Plains, Montana before going to the Flathead country. Mr. Dunn might have been part of the Lowery and Dunn party, which was made up of prospectors, Whips, English and Wrom that had reportedly discovered gold on Wolf Creek in early July of 1890.[5] Mr. Dunn then wasn't heard of until Mr. Scott identified his body in the summer of 1890.

Immediately after the coroner's jury adjourned Deputies Grant and Ramsdell raised a forty-five-man posse to raid the Kootenai Sun Dance on Dayton Creek for Pascale and other renegade Indians. After a dangerous ride through steep mountains, stumps and rocks during the night Deputy Ramsdell, who spoke the Indian language fluently, told Chief Aenas that he must turn over Pascale, Antley, La La See and Pierre Paul. While the chief was considered a friend of the white man he was guilty of allowing the murderers to escape his camp and according to Antoine Finley's statement Chief Aenas had also received a portion of Mr. Dunn's stolen money.[6]

Not only did Chief Aenas receive blood money from Pascale so did a half-breed named George Lineway who got a hundred dollars for a horse worth only thirty bucks. John Curry of Plains said that he saw Pascale in the cabin of Angus McDonald with a bundle of greenbacks and without the knowledge of the Indian he reportedly wrote down the serial numbers of three of the one hundred dollar bills on the window frame of the cabin because he feared that Pascale had obtained the money illegally. Jack Wilson of Thompson Falls also received one of the fifty-dollar bills and Mr. Dunn's gray horse was later located in the Bitterroot Valley on the Baker Ranch.

Pascale was the first of the defendants to be tried and the hearing opened on October 21, 1890. The state relied on the testimony of Antoine Finley who was the first to discover the body of Mr. Dunn and he was one of the four Indians present when Pascale admitted to the murder. Pascale was the only witness for the defense and while he admitted to the killing he claimed it had been self-defense. The jury for Pascale's trial was made up of the following men:

M.H. Pierce	S. Mitchell	Frank Primont
John O'Brien	J. McDonald	G. Simmons
S.P. Swearringen	F.W. Hunton	Thomas McNamara
J.E. Fletcher	S.T. Anderson	C.F. Davis

The jury was in deliberation for only twelve minutes before returning the guilty verdict and when Pascale was sentence to death on October 25, he didn't move a muscle or show any emotion when it was pronounced. Only his sharp eyes peering from under his shaggy eyebrows dropped slightly as he gazed out of the courthouse window towards the west where his home once was.

On the night before his execution Pascale requested that four candles be lit in his cell while he re-told a story of the killing. Deputies Ramsdell and Evans translated Pascale's story about Indians Anthies and Williams having actually killed Mr. Dunn. According to Pascale his friends approached him later and bribed him to admit to the killing for eight horses, a new rifle and a good suit of clothes. Pascale also said that Anthies and Williams had assured him that their friends and families would also protect him from prosecution.

Pascale told the officers that Mr. Dunn had a three-compartment money belt, which he said was about three inches thick. The first compartment contained hundred dollar bills, the second had a pack of twenty's and the third held a package of fives and tens. He said that Anthies and Williams divided up the money at Chief Aeneas' camp, and Tenas, a witness against him took eight hundred dollars as his share. Pascale said that most of the hundred dollar bills were damaged and that they were burned in the chief's campfire.

The Indian boasted that he was not afraid to die, and that his chief had given up his flesh and blood but he would be all right because the priest would be with him in the morning. Pascale would not confess to the priest about the four Indians that swore against him but said he would tell his friends, Deputies Ramsdell and Evans the truth. The condemned man said that he had been treated well at the jail; in fact he said that his life there was the best he ever had. Pascale had been very impressed with the food at the jail and the new blanket and new breechcloth given to him by Sheriff Houston. He sent his old shirt to his people on the reservation so they would have something to remember him by.

After talking about various murders committed on the reservation, Pascale said that although he had a bad reputation he had only killed two head of cattle. He told the guards that he was being truthful and that on the eve of his death he didn't need rest like the others and that he would remain awake until his time of death. At 2:30 a.m. Pascale was playing solitaire while the other three prisoners were asleep until 4:10 when he began to pray, after which he asked a guard how much time he had left and then he too went to sleep.

While the prayers were being offered and the straps were being fastened, Pascale noticed Chiefs Baptiste standing near the scaffold and said, "I come here to stand to die like a man. I will die like one. I did the crime for which I will have to die. They tell me that it is just. I have nothing to say about that."

Postscript:
Antoine Finley was arraigned before Judges Charles M. Shepherd and T.D. Duncan for the murder of his cousin, William Finley at Egan. The judgment of the case was that Antoine was not guilty and that the shooting had been accidental. The court further added that if William and the other Indian, Grotia hadn't confronted Antoine in the first place the incident wouldn't have taken place.

Because he had co-operated with the Pascale murder case he was released and Antoine promised that he would always be the friend of the white man. When asked if he would participate in the Kootenai Indian Sun Dance he quickly replied, "Oh, no! you bet me no dance with Kootenai, they kill me sure." It took Forty-eight years, but a Kootenai Indian finally revenged the betrayal of Pascale and Antoine Finley was murdered in 1938, by a nephew of Pascale.

December 16, 1892

John Burns

Other Names: Hugh J. Hamilton
Location and Gallows: Burns was hanged behind the Missoula County Jail on ***Gallows No. Ten: (December 1890)***.
Description: The thirty-three-year-old Burns was a small thin man with a pointed nose, which was generally red tipped. His hair was described as being "dead" brown and he wore a small thin mustache. At the time of his arrest he was wearing a pair of cheap gray trousers with a black silk or sateen shirt.
Crime: Murder of Maurice G. Higgins on August 15, 1892.
Judge: C.S. Marshall
Prosecution: County Attorney Frederick C. Webster, Assistant County Attorney Joseph H. Woody and assisted by Judge Frank H. Woody
Defense: George W. Reeves along with L.A. Gassoway, T.Q. Barron, Crumbakes and Huddleston
Sheriff: William A. Houston
Distinction: Burns was the third and last man executed after being granted a new trial.

On the early evening of August 14, 1892, one of the most devastating fires ever to strike Missoula broke out at the rear of the Blue Front Saloon on Front Street. The flames eventually destroyed the Rodgers Hotel, the Hawkes Livery Stable and about twelve other buildings. At one point it appeared that the entire town would be wiped out until the fire fighters finally brought it under control. One of the gallant volunteer firemen fighting the flames was twenty-two-year-old Maurice Higgins, the brother of the Missoula mayor and the fourth son of the founder of the city, Captain Christopher P. Higgins.

Earlier that day two tramps, John Burns and a man named Lyons had reportedly rolled into Missoula on a freight train from the coast looking to pawn a watch, ring and other stolen property. While the fire was blazing Burns and Lyons were trying to take advantage of the excitement by stealing from the many people who came to watch as well as to loot the damaged businesses. When the fire broke out many of the nervous businessmen went to their stores and spent most of the night and early morning trying to protect their property from both the fire and looters.

One of those entrepreneurs was twenty-three-year-old former bartender at the Concordia Saloon, Paul Goldenbogen who only days earlier had opened his shoe store in the neighborhood. Because of his experience in saloons he had an eye for the rough characters and he quickly noticed Lyons working the crowd and he notified Police Officer Val Blindorf and after the tip the man was arrested for selling a stolen ring.

At one point Mr. Goldenbogen ran off several men, including the tramp John Burns from stealing goods from the tailor establishment George Houston, which was next to his shoe shop. At about four o'clock on the morning of August 15, the fire had gone its course; the firemen were wrapping things up and the multitude of spectators were still wandering around in the streets when Burns walked up to Mr. Goldenbogen in front of the Exchange Saloon. While berating Goldenbogen for having his partner arrested and for accusing him of being a thief during the fire he pulled out a pistol and shot the unarmed merchant in the right side of his body.

John Burns
"Weekly Missoulian" 12/21/1892

The blast from the weapon sent the wounded man towards the street where Maurice Higgins, was taking a break from fire fighting and talking with Frank Smith, Tom Black and a boy named "Kid" Sheehan. The three men in the street instinctively turned at the noise of the gunshot when Burns fired another shot, which missed Goldenbogen and struck Higgins in the forehead. Young Higgins fell immediately to the sidewalk on his face and Paul Goldenbogen tripped on the fallen body and fell across him.

Burns took off running eastward with Tom Black in pursuit until the murderer ordered him back with his gun, and then disappeared around the Hammond Block heading towards the river. Sheriff Bill Houston arrived at the scene having heard the two shots while he was walking on Stevens Street and he was directed where the murderer had gone. When the sheriff got to the Higgins Street Bridge he saw Burns at the other side getting off near the Fisher's place and turn eastward. The sheriff ran to the flat and along the baseball grounds in the hopes of intercepting his man but when he got to the high ground where South Missoula stood the man was gone.

The sheriff searched the baseball park and then as he was heading back to the bridge he saw the man heading back to town. By the time the sheriff was halfway across the bridge he saw Burns pass the Hammond Block and enter the Concordia Saloon. Tom Black met the sheriff and the two men observed the murderer come out of the saloon and walk towards Main Street. Black positively identified Burns as the shooter and they followed him around the corner and then stopped him on Main Street about two doors west of the "Missoulian" office.

Sheriff Houston called out to the man to halt and when Burns turned around the officer put his gun to his face and ordered him the throw up his hands. The prisoner was then taken to the county jail where he was searched, but no weapon was found on his person. Meanwhile Maurice Higgins was taken to the family residence where he was still breathing and Drs. Daniel H. Billmeyer[7] and Edmond A. Crain cut into the back of his skull to remove the bullet, but it was never located. Maurice Higgins never regained consciousness and he lingered on until a little after noon that day when he finally died.

Paul Goldenbogen was taken to the Sisters' Hospital where at about 11:30 that morning Burns was brought in by a deputy sheriff and the wounded man immediately identified him as the shooter. The Burns trial opened in a crowded courtroom on September 12, and Judge Marshall had to call the sheriff several times to control the spectators. The following jury of Missoula residents was selected on September 14, 1892:

T.J. McNamarra	Jason Crossen	W. Morris
S.F. Coen	G.S. Downing	James E. Fletcher
Jonathon Davis	Peter Whaley	John A. Swanson
H. Lancaster	I.P. Crain	Henry Wolf

Sheriff Houston was the first to be called to the stand where he told the court about the chase and the apprehension of the defendant. Next Tom Black, a waiter at the Arcade Restaurant and Frank Smith identified Burns and testified about the shooting, which took place within sight of the fire engine house. Charles Moore, the night bartender of the Headquarters Saloon also identified John Burns and how he had witnessed the defendant threatening Tom Black to stay back after the shooting of Higgins.

Burns had remained cool and collected throughout most of the testimony until Paul Goldenbogen was brought from the hospital into the courtroom on a stretcher. The defendant took one glance of the pale and emaciated features of the wounded man and then he became visibly nervous and began moving his hands and feet restlessly. In order for the jurors to better hear his testimony, Goldenbogen's stretcher was placed near the jury box where he told the jury how he noticed Lyons trying to sell a ring on the north side of Front Street and that he notified Officer Blindorf; about the arrest of Lyons and how John Burns had gotten mad about him turning his partner in. Finally the wounded man described how the defendant had shot both him and Maurice Higgins on the street.

The defendant testified in his own behalf and he told the court that he came to Missoula with the man named Haywick; that he and Haywick were together during the fire, and that after the fire was under control they visited a house of ill fame and drank beer there. Burns went on to say that he and Haywick started up town before the shooting and that they had reached Stevens Street some one hundred yards from the Exchange Saloon when they heard the two shots. They walked to the large crowd gathering at the scene and in the commotion Burns got separated from his partner.

Burns said that he tried to find his partner and then he spent about twenty minutes in a saloon reading a newspaper before going up the street to the corner of the Hammond Block. When he couldn't find Haywick he walked up Higgins Avenue to check in the Concordia Saloon and then he went up to Main Street where he was arrested by the sheriff. He claimed that the sheriff was about one hundred yards away when he called out to him to halt and he said that he made no attempt to run and he put up his hands when ordered but Sheriff Houston still struck him with his pistol.

The case was given to the jury on the afternoon of September 18, and at ten o'clock p.m. that same evening they returned to the courtroom with their verdict. The clerk of the court, Judge John L. Sloane left the officers and spectators in suspense when he called the attention of the court that the foreman of the jury had signed the verdict in pencil rather than in ink. After the mistake was corrected the clerk read the verdict of guilty in the first-degree. Burns showed no sign of emotion as the clerk polled the jury and two days later the court sentenced John Burns to be hanged on November 11, 1892.

On October 5, 1892, Burn's attorney, Mr. Gassoway argued a motion for a new trial on the grounds that during the first trial the jury was taken to the bridge where the sheriff, also a witness had pointed out the places where he had seen Burns pass the Hammond Block, but the defendant wasn't present and therefore he wasn't able to question the sheriff. The Supreme Court agreed with Burns' motion and on October 12, it granted a new trial. Mr. T.Q. Barron was appointed counsel for Burns in place of George Reeves and the second trial commenced on October 17, with a jury made up of the following men:

Hilare Pauline	John Richli	H.P. Dwyer
George Johnson	W.H. Bovee	Frank Violet
J.M. McIntyre	W. Vanstone	W. Stocking
W.D. Wolcott	W.H. Raymond	Charles Wilson

The second trial lasted for ten days and for the most part the testimony was the same as the first hearing with the exception of John Delaney who was a new eyewitness to the shooting. The jury retired at 4:07 in the afternoon of October 27, and eight minutes later they returned with a guilty verdict. Judge Marshall sentenced the prisoner on November 5, to be hanged on December 16, 1892. Burns showed no more emotion than he had during the trial or his previous sentencing.

Missoula Fire Chief Robert Mentrum[8] was again called on to construct the new scaffold for the county, and he utilized many components of the previous gallows that was used to hang the four Indians in 1890. The newer gallows was built up against the jail and it utilized the original support system, hardware and the overhead crossbeam of the earlier scaffold but the new platform was smaller. The two-foot trapdoor was placed near the center of the platform instead of in front like the 1890 version.

Once again the trap was designed to release as the sheriff stepped onto a button on the fourth of the twelve steps leading up to the platform. When the sheriff stepped on the button a small blade cut the rope and the heavy trap fell against the end of the jail building. Mr. Mentrum installed a light spring on the back of the trapdoor to protect the structure from its impact, yet it wouldn't allow the door from bouncing back and interfering with the falling body. Sheriff Houston was the last man to descend the steps and the spectators were reportedly surprised when the trap fell because only the builder and the sheriff knew about the button and its operation.

Witnesses reported hearing Sheriff Houston's steps as he went down the risers and then a slight chop; a rattle and then Burns dropped to his death before the officer had reached the ground. The hangman's noose hung from the top crossbeam with just the right amount of slack to allow a drop of seven feet, which allowed for a stretch of a fraction of an inch. In the eastern side of the enclosure was a door, which led through an enclosed passage to the east door of the jail. This was provided for the condemned man to have a safe route to the gallows without having to run the gauntlet of curious eyes.

On the day before the hanging Deputy Johnson barely escaped serious injury while he and others were determining the proper drop and testing the system before the execution. To determine the proper drop distance the drop was first lowered so that the rope could hang straight through and then the trap was reset for testing. When Johnson pulled the trigger rope the trap failed to drop because another deputy was holding another rope supporting the trap. When Deputy Johnson went under the platform to investigate, the trap fell and he prevented a dangerous blow with his hands. The trap was very heavy and it bruised the officer's hands badly but it would have seriously injured him if it had struck his head.

While the officers were testing the dangerous gallows a reporter for the "Missoulian" interviewed the condemned man inside the County Jail. Burns thanked the local paper for what he thought was fair treatment and he went on to describe his attempt at suicide after his first conviction. He explained that he had found a package of morphine in some tinfoil under the bed of his cell, which had been recently occupied by a prisoner named Dacey who had been sent to the penitentiary. Burns said that he had been looking for some writing paper to write home with when he discovered the drugs and he knew what it was because he had heard that Dacey was a morphine fiend, and then it dawned on him to commit suicide.

Burns reminded the reporter that he had just been convicted and his lawyers had given him little hope for anything but the gallows and on a whim he swallowed the morphine with the idea of ending his life. He said that later, after making peace with his Maker, he would never attempt suicide again. Although he said that he would never take his own life, he did admit to attempting an escape by drugging Guard Nobles at the jail. Burns had noticed that his night deathwatch was in the habit of taking his lunch at midnight and then the old fellow would wash it down with a glass of water from a pitcher, which Burns had spiked with a drug.

While Guard Nobles never did loose consciousness, Burns was able to work on the cell door with a saw blade while the guard was trying to shake off the effects of the drug. Burns told the newspaperman that the attempt had failed only because he was not familiar with the drug and its potency and he was afraid of killing Nobles but in fact Sheriff Houston had interfered with the jailbreak. Burns was hacking away at the door when the sheriff, who slept above the jail and who was a light sleeper, heard the noise and ran downstairs to his office to get the keys to the cells. When Burns realized that the jig was up he quickly hid the saw blade in a broom in his cell. The handle of the saw was of skeleton iron with a thumbscrew arrangement to hold the blade, which was about nine inches long and reversible, with a screw driven head on the reverse end. After reviving Guard Nobles the sheriff moved Burns to the regular jail and locked him up in the front cell of the lower corridor.

While Burns had confessed his sins and was convinced that he would die a Christian, he never offered a formal confession to the killing of Higgins. When asked if he was going to speak on the scaffold, Burns said that if he saw a certain party among the spectators he would speak out to that person. Burns stated that he hadn't made up his mind about making a speech at the gallows and explained that he had stammered very badly since he was fifteen years old making it difficult for him to speak at times.

The prisoner said that he had no fault with how Sheriff Houston and his men had handled him and said that Day Guard Al Weinrich had treated him very kindly and he thought of him as he would his own brother. He reported that he had been sleeping well and that he would walk bravely to his death.

Burns explained that both of his parents were dead, his mother dying the previous year. He said that he had several brothers and sisters in New York State and he had written to one of his brothers asking him not to inform his other siblings about his trouble. He also asked his brother not to come out for his body, as he didn't want to return home under such dishonorable circumstances. As the reporter was leaving Mr. Simpson, the barber had arrived to shave the prisoner and Burns jokingly told him that this would be the last time he would be shaved. When Simpson asked if he had ever been on the next floor of the building, the prisoner replied that he would be going upstairs tomorrow morning.

The reporter returned to the prisoners' cell at about 7:30 p.m. on his last night and found the condemned man still very brave but when asked if "Burns" was his true name he didn't want to answer that question, but he said he may answer it in the morning. The way the man spoke the reporter was convinced that the name was an alias. Lyons, alias Gannon was arrested at San Francisco for stealing a handbag about ten days before the Burns' execution and while in jail in California he said that he had been in fact a partner of Burns at Missoula.

A diary kept by the "Missoulian" reporter of Burns' final night revealed the following incidents: At ten p.m. the prisoners were all ordered into their cells and a special guard patrolled the corridor. Earlier that evening Burns said that he had something important to tell Mayor Frank G. Higgins, the brother of the murdered young man but when he arrived the condemned man was somewhat despondent and resigned to his fate and he didn't have anything new to say other than his innocence and that another person had committed the crime. Meanwhile the sheriff's office was crowded with visiting lawmen discussing the up and coming hanging including Frank Conley and Tom McTague of the State Penitentiary; D.A. Bishop of Deer Lodge; J.W. Nelson and Emil Hansen of Anaconda, and Sheriff Joel Gleason of Glendive.

Father Joseph Guidi[9] arrived at the jail at 10:30 and he knelt with Burns and prayed. Later Burns refused anything to eat and he began muttering unintelligibly as his attitude varied from despondency to bragging. At midnight Sheriff Houston read the death warrant to the prisoner, after which Burns asked the sheriff if he could smoke a cigar on the way to the scaffold in the morning. At that time he told the reporter that his name wasn't Burns but he didn't offer his true identity. Father Guidi said goodnight and left but Burns declined to go to sleep and sat up and talked with Guard Gipe.

Deputy George Wood offered Burns supper at one a.m. but it was declined and the prisoner only talked with the deputy and Officer Gipe about foreign affairs but he wouldn't speak about his feelings or condition. While the other inmates were sound asleep at the jail, Sheriff Houston came by the Burns' cell to tell him goodnight and that he wouldn't be around again until it was time to lead him to the gallows.

At 1:30 Burns stopped humming in his cell to ask who would be burying his remains. The guards informed him that Barney Flynn would do the honors and then he asked Burns if he wanted a drink of whisky. Burns refused the alcohol and then went into quiet meditation until two a.m. when he promised a guard that he would be giving a sensational speech from the scaffold. He continued talking until about 3:30 when he finally laid down but he got up several times to pace the floor of his cell. He didn't say much but he did wish it were morning so his agony would be over.

Burns finally went to sleep at four a.m. and all of the lights in the jail were turned off except for the one over Burns' cell, which he shared with his constant deathwatch. The prisoner woke up at about six a.m. and he ate a couple of oranges and then partook of a hearty breakfast. The newspaper reporter visited Burns after his meal and they were joined by Father Guidi who remained by the side of the doomed man till the end. Burns was allowed to join the other inmates in the corridor of the second floor where he said his good-byes.

At 9:30 Guard Al Weinrich gave Burns a drink of whisky and when the prisoner handed the bottle back to the guard he commented "that it was pretty good stuff." Promptly at ten o'clock Burns was

The hanging of John Burns "Weekly Missoulian" 12/21/1892

marched to the scaffold and he only required a little help in ascending the steep steps. On the platform Burns looked over the crowd and said, "Well boys, I bid you all good-bye."

The sheriff placed the rope around his neck; adjusted the noose and then fastened his arms and legs. While the sheriff was attending to his prisoner, Father Guidi spoke to him and Burns turned to the priest and smiled. Another smile came on the condemned man's face when he noticed the boys perched on the nearby trees and then he turned his attention back to the priest praying with him.

When the sheriff was finished he said, "Jack is there anything more you wish to say?" "No," he replied, "Let her go," and then in a low voice he told the sheriff, "Make a good job of it Bill." The black cap was then quickly drawn over the man's head, the attendants left the platform and as the sheriff stepped down the steps there was a click; a rattle and John Burns dropped to his death at 10:12 a.m. After fifteen minutes Doctors Billmeyer and Thomas A. Fitzgerald pronounced the man dead and his remains were handed over to Flynn's Undertaking. Burns was buried at two o'clock on Saturday afternoon, December 17, 1892, in the Catholic Cemetery.

Postscript:
After the hanging it was learned that a brother and a sister of Burns from Duluth, Minnesota were both in Missoula for their brother's trial but they never did speak to him. It was revealed that his true name was Hugh J. Hamilton; originally from New York State where his father still lived. He was raised as a Catholic but he had abandoned his faith at seventeen when he left home to become a wanderer.

Years later, L.A. Gassoway, one of Burns' attorneys released a stunning story, which the condemned man had revealed under client-attorney privilege. According to Burns his partner Lyons was actually a man named Gannon and the two along with Paul Goldenbogen (the first shooting victim) were thieves and they had robbed a jewelry store in Spokane. Burns said that he and Lyons took a few pieces of the loot while Goldenbogen was said to have taken the bulk of the stolen jewelry back to Missoula for safekeeping. It was planned that the three robbers would join up again later at Missoula and split up the loot.

Burns told his lawyer that Paul Goldenbogen had no intentions of sharing with his partners and when the two men arrived at Missoula he managed to get Lyons arrested for possession of stolen jewelry. Burns managed to escape the betrayal of Goldenbogen and then he made plans to get even with him. According to the condemned man he started the fire behind the Blue Front Saloon in order to cover his act of killing and robbing Paul Goldenbogen. Burns' plans went astray however as he was never able to locate his target until the fire had been brought under control. Burns said that he and Goldenbogen had words and then he shot the man and one of the shots accidentally struck Maurice Higgins in the head.[10]

Sheriff Houston of Missoula County was one of the most efficient lawman of Montana having had the record of never loosing a man including a man who had fled into Mexico. The sheriff reportedly hired a man to enter Mexico and chase the suspect back into the States where Houston arrested him and brought him back to Montana. During his term of office up to 1892, Sheriff Houston received national attention when he arrested twenty-two murderers, of which eight were sent to the penitentiary, five were hanged including John Burns, seven had been acquitted and two others were waiting for their trials. In all, Sheriff Houston officiated over more legal hangings than any other lawman in Montana and when he was re-elected in the 1920's he was about to hang his sixth victim, Joe Vuckovich when he was ousted from office on corruption charges.

In another one of the many quirky coincidences, John Burns' execution took place exactly two years to the Friday of the same week and months after the four Indian murderers, Antley, Pierre Paul, Pascale and La La See were hanged at Missoula. The rope and probably the black hood used to end Burns' life was the same utilized to hang the Indian, Pierre Paul. Eventually that particular rope was used to hang Robert Anderson at Livingston in 1894.

July 13, 1894 (Friday the Thirteenth)
Robert A. Anderson

Other Names: Robert A. Fields; Robert Mitchell
Location and Gallows: When Anderson was hanged at Livingston he became the first man executed on ***Gallows No. Eleven: (July 1894): "Galloping Gallows" No. Four***. A complete description and history of this scaffold or any other can be found in Chapter Seven: "Montana Gallows."
Description: Twenty-six years old
Crime: The murder of Emanuel Fleming on April 20, 1894.
Judge: Frank Henry
Prosecution: County Attorney Miller and assisted by Allan R. Joy and then later by Edward Cason Day
Defense: M.R. Wilson and Sydney Fox
Sheriff: John H. Conroy
Distinction: Anderson was the first man legally hanged in Park County.

Robert Anderson had lived in Montana for about seven years after coming from Buffalo, Wyoming where he worked at a sawmill and broke horses. His father was Jefferson Anderson but when his mother remarried a man named Fields the boy would often assume that name. Anderson used the name "Mitchell" while living at Castle, Montana before finally moving in with his aged mother, Mrs. Fields on a ranch on the upper Yellowstone in the Shields Valley.

In 1893, Anderson, or Bob Fields as he was known then, began running around with a group of young roughs in the Livingston area who were known to read nickel and dime novels about the exploits of noted desperados and hung around disreputable businesses that sold guns, knives and other customary equipment of outlaws. Anderson became particularly close friends with seventeen-year-old William Mortimer of Livingston and they went into business together cutting and hauling firewood. The two men made their headquarters at a small cabin on the Young Ranch some six miles above Livingston where they planned on making "faster" money than three dollars and fifty cents for every two cords of wood they cut and delivered.

Emanuel Fleming had worked for John Holiday on his ranch for about two years and he had saved several hundred dollars before finally moving to Livingston where he rented a cabin on Urbach's Island just south of town. While at the island Fleming became acquainted with Anderson who would often borrow money from the older man from time to time for what he said were gambling debts. It was during those conversations concerning finances that Anderson discovered that Fleming had a good deal of money.

Anderson and Mortimer planned various schemes in order to relieve the old man of his money including floating down the river to the island and after robbing the man they figured on escaping on the craft but finally the men chose a cross-country attack on horseback on April 15, 1894. The two men rode their horses up the river two miles to attend church at the schoolhouse on Suce Creek to establish an alibi, and before the services were finished they snuck away. Anderson and Mortimer rode towards Livingston and hid their horses in a cabin about two miles from town and then ran to Fleming's cabin.

Finding that Fleming wasn't home yet, the two men hid a short distance away where they put on their gunnysack masks and Mortimer began cutting clubs about three feet long and two inches in diameter. They had intended to use the weapons to club Fleming over the head and then rob him. While Anderson and Mortimer were making their arrangements Mr. Fleming came across the pair about fifty yards away and he shouted out that he was "on to them." The two would-be outlaws quickly ran off across the Lamartine Bridge and back to their horses.

The men rode to their cabin at the Young Ranch above the canyon where they worried about whether or not Fleming had recognized them. The following morning Anderson and Mortimer went to town where they found out that the incident had been reported but Fleming hadn't identified the would-be criminals. Satisfied that they were in the clear Anderson and Mortimer went back to their cabin and continued their wood cutting activities. In the meantime after realizing it wasn't safe to live alone on the island, Mr. Fleming leased a shack in town from William Gay located near Lewis and Eighth Street.

By the following week Anderson and Mortimer had regained their courage and began making plans for another attack on Fleming. Anderson reclaimed a Colt 45-caliber six-shooter that he had first borrowed from his second cousin, R.V. Stumbo and then pawned it off in order to pay off a gambling debt he owed in town. At the same time Mortimer was trying to get bullets for the weapon from various people that he knew in Livingston, finally securing some of .44-caliber rounds.

With the loaded weapon in hand Anderson and Mortimer went to Livingston on April 20, 1894, separately and after an attempt to establish separate alibis in town they met at the White and Ransom's Saloon. While at the saloon they ran into Mr. Fleming and Mortimer confronted the man at about eight o'clock and said, "about time Christians and little boys were in bed," and Fleming answered that he would be going home shortly. At that point Anderson and Mortimer made a point of leaving the saloon alone but they later met at Mrs. Mortimer's barn where their horses were kept. From there they went to Fleming's shack under cover of darkness to wait for their victim.

At the Fleming place Mortimer slammed his body against the door breaking through the bolt and the two men took their places, Anderson on the bed with the six-shooter and the younger man behind the door with a double-bladed axe. The moment Fleming came into the shack Mortimer struck him a glancing blow cutting his scalp on the left side of his head and the man fell to his knees. As Fleming was getting up Anderson shot him in the abdomen, which knocked the man out of the door. The victim began screaming for help as Anderson continued shooting at the man in the night but because of the darkness and improper cartridges, Anderson was only able to strike Fleming in his arm.

Deputy Sheriff Zed H. Daniels heard the shots from his home on Sixth Street and immediately ran to the scene along with others to find the fatally wounded Fleming in the street yelling for help. Meanwhile Anderson and Mortimer ran back to the barn where they both mounted a single horse and rode out of town. As they came to the home of R.V. Stumbo Anderson slipped off the horse and Mortimer continued to the Young Ranch, hiding the murder weapon along the way. Back in town Deputy Daniels, Dr. Robert D. Alton and others carried the injured man back to his shack where the officer questioned him. Because of the darkness Fleming wasn't able to identify his assailants or even determine how many there were. The next morning the injured man was moved to Bill Gay's home where he died that evening.

Shortly after the shooting, Mitchell Askey stopped by the Stumbo home to pick up his small son who had been staying at the place while he was attending a revival at the Hefferlin's Hall. Mr. Askey asked Mr. Stumbo and Anderson if they had heard about the Fleming shooting and the two men answered in the negative but then they agreed to accompany him to the scene of the crime in order to join the posse. Anderson said that he wanted to first find Mortimer and they would then join the posse in the hunt for the murderers.

Anderson went to Mrs. Mortimer's barn, saddled his horse; then road out to the Young Ranch and together they reported to Marshal Mitchell who was directing the search. The posse only managed to round up the usual suspects including a number of hobos, several of which were subjected to a ridged interrogation as to their whereabouts at the time of the crime. After spending the night with his partner in crime at Mrs. Mortimer's house, Robert Anderson had the gall to spend most of his time the following day at Fleming's bedside and it was reported that he was holding the injured man's at the time of his death.

Because of Anderson's unusual display of concern for the victim's condition along with the information provided by a number of people in town concerning the Colt 45, the recent search for ammunition and Anderson's prior financial dealings with the deceased, the two men became the primary suspects in the case. Anderson was immediately placed under arrest while Marshall Mitchell followed Billy Mortimer back to the Young Ranch where he was arrested with the murder weapon.

Coroner W.L. Shawk conducted an inquest over the body of Emanuel Fleming on April 22, 1894, at the Rowe Brothers' Undertakers and he named the following jurors:

J.H. Harris	A.E. Owens	E.H. Hanche
C.E. Collins	H.T. Bingham	J.F. Wittich

The coroner's jury found that Mr. Fleming had sixty dollars on his person at the time of his attack; that Robert Anderson testified that he was at the home of Mr. Stumbo at the time of the shooting and Mr. R.V. Stumbo and William Mortimer confirmed his alibi. Anderson and Stumbo told the jury that William Mortimer had dropped Anderson off at eight o'clock and then he had left for the Young Ranch. After interviewing several other witnesses who placed the two suspects at various points in Livingston just prior to the shooting, the jury rendered a verdict that the victim, Emanuel Fleming had died from a gunshot wound received on April 20, and at the hands of Robert Anderson and William Mortimer.

After the coroner verdict was handed down, warrants were at once issued for the arrest of the two men charging them with murder and another for R.V. Stumbo for perjury during the coroner's hearing. The three men were locked up and questioned separately by the deputies and county attorney and the preliminary examination of Anderson began on Wednesday, April 28, before Justice of the Peace Rose and they concluded on the following day. Justice Rose decided to reserve his decision until after he had examined William Mortimer, which was postponed the following week on request of his attorney, A.J. Campbell.

Several days after their arrest young Billy Mortimer confessed to Undersheriff Hogan that Anderson had killed Fleming and he wanted to make a deal. While he said that he had struck Fleming with the axe and he had loaded the Colt 45 six-shooter with 44-caliber bullets, which was all he could find, it was Anderson who planned the affair and had shot the victim. With news of his partner's confession, Anderson weakened and he told the officers that he was in on the crime but it was his younger partner that had done the killing. On April 30, 1894, Robert Anderson was formerly charged with the murder of Fleming and William Mortimer was the state's primary witness.

The Anderson trial opened on Friday, May 11, 1894, and after exhausting a pool of one hundred and forty names during the first day the following jury was finally sworn in:

Henry F. Nier	John Ray	F.E. Skillman
J.H. Eyman	Frank E. Rich	N.H. Hodgen
J.M. Lutz (f)	J.R. Blackhart	Frank Rife
Grant Keller	F.M. Hicks	T.F. Stevens

(f) Foreman

The jury listened to testimony concerning the death of the victim; his relationship with the defendant indicating the motive of robbery; that Anderson was loaned a Colt 45 long-barreled six-shooter, which he later pawned for money to gamble with, then just before the murder he reclaimed it and that several witnesses had seen the defendant in town just prior to the shooting. After the jury returned to the courtroom they heard final arguments and then at 1:30 Judge Henry read his instructions to the jurors and they retired at 2:40 p.m.

At 5:40 p.m. the jury reported that they had reached a verdict and when Anderson was led back into the courtroom he was very nervous and could hardly be seated by the sheriff. When the court was called to order Foreman Lutz handed the verdict to the judge who in turn gave it to the Clerk of the Court Bailey and he kept everyone breathless as he first entered the verdict into his records and then read the verdict of guilty of murder in the first degree.

Long before the hour of ten o'clock on May 22, 1894, an immense crowd had filled the courtroom and the hallways, all anxious to hear the first death sentence read in the history of Park County. After reviewing the case and the trial, Judge Henry told Anderson that while he had sent the soul of Emanuel Fleming unwilling and unprepared to death, the humane law had fixed a certain amount of time for him to get ready to meet his God. The judge went on to say that he was required to sentence Anderson, not less than four weeks and not more than eight, in which he would pay for his awful crime on the gallows. At that time Judge Henry sentenced Robert Anderson to death and he ordered him to be hanged between the hours of four a.m. and three o'clock p.m. on Friday, June 22, 1894. While Judge Henry was visibly affected by his solemn duty along with most everyone else in the courtroom being deeply impressed, Robert Anderson sat through the fifteen-minute sentencing with a defiant and firm attitude and never once indicated any remorse.

On Saturday, June 2, 1894, Sheriff John Conroy and Undersheriff Hogan went to Bozeman to examine ***Gallows No. Seven: (December 1883)***, which was used to hang John A. Clark in December of 1883. Gallatin County Sheriff White Caldwell had the ancient gallows set up again so that the visiting officers could see how it worked and to draw up its dimensions. The Bozeman sheriff also presented Sheriff Conroy with the rope, which had been used to hang Clark.

The Park County officers might have planned on employing the rope for the execution of Anderson but it was never used again. Upon his return to Livingston Sheriff Conroy ordered an enclosure built in the front and to the right of the entrance of the jail and a scaffold to be constructed at the Gordon Brother's lumberyard. Livingston carpenters Marks, Wolcott and Meredith finished the scaffold in the lumberyard of heavy timbers just before Governor John E. Rickards' announced his respite of Anderson's sentence, which temporarily stopped the hanging.

On Wednesday, June 20, the finished twelve-foot square, eighteen-foot high scaffold was moved to the county jail yard where it was set up and painted a somber black by Joe Briggs. The trapdoor on the death machine was thoroughly tested the following day with bags of sand and the trivia buffs will be interested in knowing that instead of using the rope from Bozeman to hang Anderson, Sheriff Conroy elected to borrow the small hempen cord and black cap, which were used for the hangings in Missoula of the Indian Pierre Paul in 1890, and John Burns in 1892. It should be remembered that the same rope was used to execute one of the four anarchists at Chicago in 1887, for the murder of seven policemen during the Haymarket Riot of 1886. A description and history of this rope or others can be found in the "History of Legal Hangings in Montana; and The Typical Legal Execution" chapter.

Since the defense counsel believed that their client had received a fair and impartial trial they took no action to secure a new trial or an appeal to the Supreme Court but just when there seemed to be no hope for the condemned man, rumors began to circulate among the citizens of the community that an appeal would be made on his behalf. The sentiment came to fruition when the Reverend W.C. Fowler returned to Livingston on June 7, with the news that he had traveled to Helena and made a formal application to Governor J.E. Rickards for a commuted sentence for Robert Anderson.

The application to save Anderson's life was based on the various changes in Mortimer's confession. Governor Rickards promised that he would review the case and travel to Livingston to look into the matter. The Governor kept his promise and he arrived at Livingston on June 15, to go over the petitions and listened to the evidence but the next day he announced that he wouldn't interfere with the sentence. While the gallows was being constructed at the lumberyard, Sheriff Conroy delivered Mortimer's hand written confession, which completely betrayed his partner, Robert Anderson by telling Undersheriff Hogan that his companion had killed Fleming in order to save his own skin. Mortimer later confessed that he and he alone had killed the old man. Judge Henry arranged for a meeting with the young prisoner who confirmed his written statement as being the truth.

Mortimer told Judge Henry that he was with Anderson at the time he made the clubs and masks in preparations for the first murder attempt. It was also confirmed that Anderson had been at the scene of the final crime and Judge Henry was satisfied that the condemned man was still sufficiently guilty because he had the motive, the desire, the intent and the opportunity. Mortimer's story had the necessary effect on Anderson's lawyers that they filed a motion for a new trial on the grounds of the additional evidence.

The motion for a trial was made in district court on Tuesday, June 19, and the arguments were heard two days later when Judge Henry overruled the motion. The Governor was sent a message requesting a respite for Anderson until his attorneys could apply to the Supreme Court and Governor Rickards complied and the hanging was first postponed to July 7, and finally to July 13, 1894, the same execution date for John Osnes at Fort Benton. When the Supreme Court confirmed the lower court decisions for both the Anderson and Osnes cases on July 9, Governor Rickards announced that he would not interfere in either of the executions.

After Governor's announcement Sheriff Conroy began the preparations for the execution, which the statute read: "the sentence of death shall be executed in some private enclosure, as near the jail as possible. The sheriff shall invite to be present at the execution, by at least three days' notice, the judge of the court, the attorney prosecuting and the clerk of the court together with two physicians and twelve reputable citizens to be selected by him. He must also, at the request of the prisoner, permit any minister of the gospel whom the prisoner may name, and any of his relations and friends when he may desire, not exceeding two, to attend the execution, and also such peace officers at the sheriff may deem proper. No person other than those mentioned in this section can be present at the execution, nor can any person underage be allowed to witness the same." Over the years the various sheriffs found a way around this statute by naming all the excess guests as his "temporary" or "special" deputies.

After his re-sentencing, Anderson was immediately placed in solitary confinement and William B. Altimus was employed as his deathwatch. While Sheriff Conroy was walking Anderson in the fresh air on Tuesday, July 10, the prisoner asked to see the gallows and the coffin, which he was going to be buried in. Anderson was in good spirits and he reportedly wasn't any more affected by the sight of the gallows than he was at seeing a visitor at the jail. Later that evening however, the condemned man had become a little more restless and he didn't go to sleep until midnight.

The following morning Anderson woke up at seven a.m. and he became more restless as the day went on. That Wednesday night the doomed man spent the evening talking with his deathwatch and he finally slept from three to eight in the morning. After a light breakfast Thursday morning Anderson had a private interview with his spiritual advisor, Reverend Fowler and later that morning he met with his mother and Mrs. R.V. Stumbo. After the visitors had gone, Sheriff Conroy handcuffed Anderson and escorted him to the jail yard for his exercise.

After spending an hour with the sheriff in the jail yard Anderson returned to his cell where his mother along with Mrs. T.S. Ash, Mrs. V. Walker, Mr. and Mrs. Stumbo and their daughters, Rosa and Lilly greeted him. The visitors remained with the condemned man until five o'clock Thursday evening when he requested that they leave. After they left Anderson's cell Sheriff Conroy again handcuffed the prisoner and the two men walked around the jail yard for the last time before their trip to the gallows the following morning.

At his cell, Bill Altimus shaved the prisoner and then Anderson slept until eight o'clock p.m. when he again entertained his family and friends until eleven o'clock. He spoke with Sheriff Conroy alone until 12:45, after which he slept until two in the morning when he ordered a cup of coffee, smoked a cigar and then had his fingernails trimmed and cleaned. At 3:05 Sheriff Conroy read the death warrant to the condemned man and at 3:15 the prisoner began dressing for the execution. Reverend Fowler arrived at the jail as the prisoner was getting dressed and the spiritual advisor remained by the man's side until the end.

By 4:30 a.m. the grounds outside of the enclosure was packed with a large crowd who were anxious to catch even a glimpse of what was being done inside. Every building within several blocks, which offered even a distant view over the high fence of the jail yard, was covered with people eager to satisfy their morbid curiosity. The mob around the entrance of the execution enclosure was so dense that it was extremely difficult for those people with invitations to gain admission.

Among the invited guests were Sheriff Caldwell and Undersheriff W.R. Brooks of Gallatin County; former Sheriff James W. Ponsford of Bozeman, District Clerk Bailey, attorneys for the prosecution, County Attorney Miller and Allan R. Joy; Defense Attorney Wilson, County Physician G.R. Wells and Livingston doctors, W.H. Campbell, Robert D. Alton and W.L. Shawk. There were many visiting physicians at the Anderson hanging including Dr. Root, physician of the Connecticut State Prison, Dr. Orr of Indiana, Dr. Ingalls of Chicago and Dr. Plummer of Bozeman. Other visitors at the hanging were the brother of the victim, Henry Fleming of Alta, Iowa, several Livingston city officials along with representatives of the local press as well as M.W. Hatch with the "Big Timber Pioneer."

At 4:45 a.m. Sheriff Conroy and Deputy Zed H. Daniels entered the jailhouse and after a few minutes they reappeared as the jail doors swung open with the condemned man. Reverend Fowler preceded Anderson who walked firmly and with a steady step as they ascended the steps to the scaffold. Sheriff Conroy and Deputies Daniels and Charles Millard followed the doomed man who was dressed in his neat black suit. In the left lapel of his long flock coat was a neat bouquet of geranium blossoms. As he stood on the platform of the gallows Anderson had the same defiant, cynical expression on his face that he had maintained since his arrested shortly after the crime. He took his place with Reverend Fowler on his right, Sheriff Conroy at his left and Deputies Daniels and Millard in the rear. The straps were then adjusted about his arms, wrists and feet while the Reverend read a short passage of scripture and then offered a short prayer.

At the conclusion of the prayer Sheriff Conroy carefully adjusted the noose around the man's neck and then he pulled the black cap over his face. Anderson's last words were, "Well, Conroy, Good-bye to you, and tell Daniels good-bye too." The sheriff asked the condemned man if he was ready, and then stepping back to the left side of the platform he said: "Good-Bye." While he was bidding his prisoner farewell, the sheriff pulled the lever releasing the trap and at exactly 5:08 Robert Anderson fell about six feet to his death.

The body remained motionless for a moment and then there were two or three convulsions of the man's legs and arms and then the entire body quivered. Dr. W.H. Campbell grabbed the right wrist as Dr. G.R. Wells checked the pulse on the left side. After six minutes both physicians announced that there was still a slight pulse and three minutes later Robert Anderson was pronounced dead. The body was permitted to remain suspended for twenty-six minutes when it was taken down and examined by the many physicians who determined that the neck had been broken.

At 5:40 a.m. the body was placed in the coffin that had been acquired by the county on the night of June 22, which was the first date set for the execution and it had been kept in the jail yard. The body was taken to the undertaker rooms of Rowe Brothers and from there the remains were sent to the home of Mr. and Mrs. R.V. Stumbo. The

Stumbo had the body buried on July 14, 1894, in the Mountain View Cemetery.

The witnesses were disappointed that Anderson hadn't made a statement on the gallows and when William Mortimer was told of Anderson's death he began to cry. Mortimer said that Anderson hadn't committed the murder and that they had hanged an innocent man. He also claimed that the prosecution had promised that he would be set free once Anderson was hanged and then he walked into the adjoining cell where he completely broke down. A week later the angry Judge Henry sentenced William Mortimer to twenty years at the state penitentiary for his part in the Fleming murder. At the end of his July term of court at Livingston Judge Henry went to White Sulphur Springs to preside over the September term at Meagher County where he disposed of sixty-two civil and ten criminal cases.

Postscript:
R.V. Stumbo, Robert Anderson's second cousin, and the man charged with perjury for lying to save his relative, was released and never prosecuted. The straps used to bind Robert Anderson while on the scaffold were last seen in a criminal exhibit at the sheriff's office in the courthouse at Livingston. The scaffold itself was stored at the courthouse until they were sent to Red Lodge to hang Thomas Salmon in January 1899. The ancient scaffold remained in storage again until September of 1903, when the Park county authorities considered using it for the execution of Martin Zidmair. While the main timbers were reportedly still in good shape, Park County Sheriff A.S. "Harry" Robertson decided to borrow the gallows from Deer Lodge County on which Clinton Dotson had been executed the year before. However, before his execution Zidmair hanged himself in his cell.

July 13, 1894 (Friday the thirteenth)

<u>John H. Osnes</u>

While Osnes was being hanged on that Friday the Thirteenth, Robert Anderson was also being executed at Livingston.

Location and Gallows: John Osnes was hanged in the jail yard at the corner of Main and Wetzel Streets at Fort Benton from ***<u>Gallows No. Four: (July 1879)</u>***.

Description: The twenty-five-year-old Osnes was a heavy-set, burly and powerful Norwegian.

Crime: Murder of Ole Lilledall in Arnoux Coulee on March 31, 1894

Judge: Dudley DuBose

Prosecution: Judge John W. Tattan who later succeeded District Judge DuBose at Fort Benton.

Defense: Thomas W. Murphy and G.W. Sweet

Sheriff: O'Neil

Relics and Remnants: Possible crime scene photographs and a knife, which was probably one of the murder weapons, are currently held at the

Chouteau County Courthouse at Fort Benton.

In late March of 1894, twenty-year-old Ole Lilledall and another Norwegian, Eric Carlson arrived at Fort Benton after their short stay in Illinois. John Osnes had been working at several hotels in Fort Benton at the time when he recognized Lilledall as a younger classmate of his back in Norway. Osnes had lived in Montana for about four years by then and he had the reputation of being absolutely worthless. While he worked in intervals for several sheepmen and for others in the region, none of his employers ever respected his work.

When Lilledall said that he wanted to visit his Norwegian cousin, Peter Testle or Testal in the Highwood Mountains, Osnes agreed to guide him knowing that the newcomer had come to America with a sizable amount of money. Apparently Osnes didn't know that before their journey the young man had deposited all but five dollars of his money in the Stockman National Bank at Fort Benton. Lilledall hired two saddle horses and the men were last seen riding up the Arnoux Hill on Highwood Creek but Osnes reportedly spent that same night at Louis Holland's place, but the boy wasn't with him.

On Sunday April 1, 1894, John Osnes returned to Fort Benton with the horses but without Lilledall. Erick Carlson at once inquired about the where abouts of his friend and Osnes evidently didn't give a satisfactory answer and the Norwegian became very concerned. In broken English, Carter shared his concern with Mr. Burk who had been staying at the same hotel and they reported the incident to the sheriff.

Osnes was arrested on suspicion of murder and he was brought before Justice of the Peace Crane who ordered him to be held. When arrested, Osnes' right arm was cut; his coat was torn and covered with blood. Also in his possession were two dollars and twenty-five cents, a watch and a bloody knife, which was the property of Mr. Lilledall. John Osnes claimed that he had received the watch from Louis Holland, but Lou later denied giving him the timepiece. That same morning a party of men left Fort Benton to try to locate Lilledall and on Wednesday Jailer Lund headed another search party that found the man's body in Arnoux Coulee near Highwood Creek above the James M. Arnoux Ranch.

About twenty miles from Fort Benton the posse found a large pool of blood and after following the drag marks for about three hundred feet the men found the body of Lilledall in a coulee. The victim's throat was cut from ear to ear and his skull was so badly crushed that he couldn't be identified. The murderer then dragged his victim by the heels and dumped him in the brush. When Osnes was informed of the news that the body of Lilledall's body was found all he reportedly said in a very unconcerned tone of voice was; "Is that so?" That same day he told Jailer Lund that when he fought he fought to kill.

A coroner's inquest was immediately called and it consisted of the following men:

Jacob Henderson	G.W. Frieds	Oscar Johnston
W.W. Samples	Chaus Peters	George Shunate

After reviewing the remains and questioning the witnesses the jury ruled that Ole Lilledall had died from injuries received from a rock and knife by John Osnes. On April 6, 1894, Ole Lilledall was buried at Fort Benton with a public funeral and on that same day the prisoner admitted killing Lilledall to Sheriff O'Neil but he said that it was in self-defense. He also offered to show Jailer Lund and Undersheriff Buckley where he had buried the murder weapon, a knife, in an alley behind the Overland Hotel building.

Osnes was brought before Justice Crane for his preliminary examination on April 11, 1894, where it was learned that his father was a fairly well to do farmer near Sondhodland, Norway as well as being first mate on a large sailing vessel. Osnes didn't enter a plea and after being assigned counsel he entered a not-guilty plea on May 17. After exhausting a venire of seventy-two jurors the following men were finally picked to hear Case No. 1077, on Monday, May 21, 1894:

A. Decker (f)	S.B. Anthony	Charles Battles
L. Morsell	William Skillen	Demott Stinson
J.H. Patterson	Jesse Maddox	John P. Cupp
H.W. Stringfellow	W.E. Hiles	Mike Redding

(f) Foreman

Through Interpreter Helsing, Eric Carlson told the court that he and Ole Lilledall had come to Montana on March 29, and John Hammer testified that Lilledall and Osnes had visited his cabin before they headed for the Highwood Mountains. Andrew Engler, also a Norwegian and Louis Holland told how they found the body in the brush in Arnoux Coulee. The men said that the victim's overcoat was used to cover the head of Lilledall and his face had been smashed beyond recognition and a heavy stone was found imbedded into the man's skull.

Photographer Dutro along with M.S. Darling and Undersheriff Buckley identified the photos that were taken at the crime scene. C.M. Fay testified that he was with Louis Holland at the time they found the murder victim and Mr. Sullivan told the court how he remained with Lilledall's body when the others returned to Fort Benton. Dr. C.D. Crutcher told the jury that the first blow to the victim's head was from the rear and it alone was sufficient to produce death and the next blow from a large rock had crushed Lilledall's head and finally the man's neck was cut from ear to ear.

When John Osnes took the stand in his own behalf he told the court that he and Lilledall had been drinking heavily before they reached the Lacy Ranch where they had words concerning his cousin Peter Testle. The defendant said that while they were crossing Highwood Creek and were starting up Arnoux Coulee, Lilledall began cussing and cursing him. Finally as Lilledall was reaching for his revolver Osnes rode up along side and grabbed his arm. In the struggle the weapon discharged and Osnes was struck in the wrist but he was still able to wrench the gun from Lilledall and tossed it into the brush before the two men fell from their horses and landed on the ground. The defendant said that the two men rolled down the hill and when they stopped Lilledall pulled out a knife and Osnes struck him in the forehead with a rock and then cut the man's throat.

After Osnes' hour and a half of testimony, Blanche Brandt was called to the stand where she said that during a party with the men from Norway, John Osnes had proposed that she help him roll the two visitors and steal their money. Judge Tattan found a broken piece of chalk by the body and after a search of Osnes' apartment another piece was found which fit the first chunk perfectly. When all of this evidence was brought out at the trial the defense crumbled.

After closing arguments and following the instructions by Judge DuBose, the jury retired for thirty-five minutes before returning with a guilty verdict. Osnes was then sentenced to be hanged on June 29, 1894, after which the defendant's attorneys filed for a new trial. Osnes' family sent one hundred dollars for his defense and a stay of execution was filed and his case was taken up with the Supreme Court on July 5. Four days later the Supreme Court denied the motion for new trials for both John Osnes at Fort Benton and Robert Anderson at Livingston and both were re-sentenced to be hanged on Friday, July 13.

Sheriff O'Neil secured a new rope for the execution from a firm in St. Louis specializing in hangman cords and as the date of his execution grew nearer, Osnes would pace up and down his narrow little cell like a caged lion while muttering to himself in Norwegian. The condemned man reportedly embraced Catholicism with the help of Father Follett while the Reverends Clowes, Gamble, Carlson had also given him counsel. The night before the hanging, Sheriff Joe Hamilton and Deputies William R. Dwyer and Carrier of Cascade County visited Osnes and he told the officers that he thought his life would be spared. After receiving a letter from Attorney Thomas Murphy, asking that the sentence be commuted to life imprisonment, Governor John Rickards sent a telegraph stating that he would not interfere and the sentence of the court would have to be carried out.

By nine o'clock on the morning of the hanging, a small crowd of spectators had gathered in the improvised execution yard with its high board fence at the rear of the jail. Besides Sheriff O'Neil, Undersheriff Buckley, Deputies Lund, Matthews and Breem of Chouteau County, only those in possession of a black-bordered invitation from the sheriff were admitted. Among the invited witnesses were the sheriff of Cascade County and his deputies, Sheriff McFarren of Flathead County, Alderman McDonald, Ed Maris and T.D. Wright of the "Anaconda Standard." Others in attendance were Mr. Alling of the "Great Falls Leader," George B. McLaughlin of the "Fort Benton River Press" and a reporter for the "Great Falls Tribune" along with various persons from Havre and Glasgow.

Just before ten o'clock Osnes sent word to Judge Dubose asking for an interview and the judge quickly went to the jail where Osnes asked if he had gotten a fair and just trial. When the judge said that he had, the prisoner disrespected the court by turning on his heel and walking to the other side of his cell where he began to talk with the priest. Minutes later Sheriff O'Neil entered the cell and read the death warrant along with the governor's respite in accordance to the law in a loud and clear voice. The doomed man was said to have paid strict attention to the reading and seemed to have been analyzing each word as they left the sheriff's lips.

After the reading of the death warrant the sheriff and his deputies buckled a strap about the man's body to which his arms would be later attached. When asked if he wanted to make a statement, Osnes expressed the hope that no one else from his homeland would be mistreated as he had been. Before he left his cell Osnes said that he had no desire to send word to his father in Norway and at 9:55 a.m. the cell door was opened and the march to the gallows began. Osnes in his neat black suit and Father Follett led the procession followed by the sheriff and his deputies. They passed through a side door of the jail on the north side of the building and then they entered the yard without fanfare by way of a special entrance. It was said that no emperor en route to his thrown had ever walked prouder, loftier or more independent than John Osnes did as he approached the scaffold.

As he walked to the gallows the condemned man scanned the crowd and took in everything with a single glance. Once on the platform he inspected the noose as if he were an expert hangman himself and then he stamped on the trapdoor with his slippered feet to see if it was solid enough while he conducted himself as if it were on a routine inspection. Osnes reportedly told the officers to take their time and keep cool so that they would do a good job with his hanging. Looking down at the crowd, Osnes then recognized his cousin, Sam Arntz, and he told him good-bye and his relative returned the adieu. That was the last public statement made by the doomed man and then he turned to his priest. Osnes pressed a cross to his lips; then he whispered a few words in Father Follett's ear and then he looked straight at the sheriff indicating that he was ready. The black cap was pulled down, Osnes' arms were strapped to his sides and his legs were strapped together.

The sheriff and two of his deputies then stepped to one side of the gallows and disappeared behind a black curtain, which concealed them from the spectators. Someone, no one knows for sure behind the screen pulled a lever controlling the staple that held the trap, and with a sliding noise and a dull crash at exactly 10:02 a.m. the body of John H. Osnes fell through the trap and was dangling at the end of a strong rope. There was a gurgling noise heard when the rope became tight and after about seventeen minutes of convulsive twitches and then a moment without making a sound, Osnes was pronounced dead. The hanging from a hangman's standpoint was a success in every detail, dislocating the man's neck from the shock and he was probably dead within a minute.

When the trap fell a shudder swept over the spectators and many of them immediately turned their heads away. John McGowan of Highwood actually fainted and he had to be carried out of the yard. Seventeen minutes later Drs. Francis Atkisson and Crutcher ordered the body cut down and the corpse was placed in a plain black coffin and Undertaker Claud Peters took charge of the remains, which were buried in the Potter's Field of Riverside Cemetery.

Postscript:
Of the three men executed in America on that Friday the thirteenth of July 1894, John Osnes, Bob Anderson at Livingston and Prendergast at Chicago, it is probably safe to say that the man hanged at Fort Benton was the nerviest of them all. It was said that his exhibition was something very remarkable. His brother, Henry Osnes, who had been working for the Libby and Merrill Sheep Company on McDonald Creek, was discharged about a week after the execution for pilfering and he reportedly left the country. That same week Eric Carlson, the man who had accompanied Ole Lilledall to Montana also returned to Illinois.

Having already provided religious counsel to Thomas King in June of 1890, and John Osnes, Father Follett accompanied another convicted murder to the gallows when he was at the side of Joseph Cadotte at his hanging in December of 1895. Judge DuBose went on to sentence three more men who forfeited their lives on the gallows, Calvin Christie who was hanged in 1884, Joseph Cadotte executed in 1895, and William Calder in 1900.

Friday, December 21, 1894

Calvin "James" Christie

Other Names: Charles J. Black; Chris and Thomas Adams
Location and Gallows: Calvin Christie was hanged inside of a stockade built in the rear of the jail on First Avenue East in Kalispell. Christie was the first man to be hanged from ***Gallows No. Twelve: (December 1894)***. A description and history of this scaffold or any other can be found in Chapter Seven: "Montana Gallows."
Description: The twenty-five-year-old Christie was usually clean shaven and neatly dressed but his medium intelligence; low brows, small black eyes, which were close together, gave him the appearance of being a common thug.
Crime: Murder of Mrs. Lena Cunningham near her ranch house on April 28, 1894.
Judge: Dudley DuBose
Prosecution: County Attorney Sidney M. Logan assisted by William J. Brennen or Brennan
Defense: Henry W. Heideman assisted by Charles H. Foot
Sheriff: Joseph Gangner
Distinction: This was the first legal hanging in the newly formed Flathead County.

Calvin Christie drifted into Kalispell where he worked under the name of Charles Black as a house painter and a common laborer in the summer and he trapped and hunted during the winter months. Sometime after his arrival, Flathead County was established and on election day, November 6, 1894, Kalispell was chosen as the county seat. The first courthouse was a two-story frame building on the corner of First Street and First avenue East, a structure, which had been moved to Kalispell from Demersville.

On April 28, 1894, the body of Mrs. John Cunningham, a wife and mother of four was found partially covered with leaves and brush near the road to her home, which was about two miles northeast of Columbia Falls and ten miles north of Kalispell. While driving his cattle at about six o'clock in the evening, Earnest Miller noticed that his stock was acting strangely at the smell of fresh blood and after investigating he came across the woman who was unconscious but still breathing. The woman's head had been badly crushed and there was brain matter, and a piece of her skull on a heavily blood stained railroad coupling pin found near the body.

Apparently Christie had attempted to rape Mrs. Cunningham and when she resisted he beat her severely with the broken coupling pin that he had found along the railroad tracks. Newly elected Sheriff Joseph Ganger was immediately notified and he and Deputy McFarren or Farlen left Kalispell to investigate the murder. When word of the vicious murder reached Helena Governor Rickards offered a three hundred dollar reward for the capture of the unknown murderer.

The following day Sheriff Gangner and Deputy McFarren arrested Christie walking down a country road carrying a rifle and wearing blood covered shoes and clothing. When arrested he gave his name as Charles J. Black, and he was cool, collected and unmoved by his predicament. The officers took their prisoner to the train station at Columbia Falls for his transfer to the county jail at Kalispell but when the sheriff realized that tensions were running high among the citizens he made a change of plans. When it was determined that there wasn't a train for several hours Sheriff Ganger and his deputy immediately took Christie to a livery stable where they rented two fast horses. The officers placed the handcuffed Christie on one of the horses and as Sheriff Ganger mounted the second animal he ordered his prisoner to ride like hell to Kalispell.

With Christie safely locked up in the county jail Sheriff Ganger continued to collect and analyze the evidence against his prisoner. The bloody tracks of the killer led to the river and the footprints corresponded with the shoes worn by Christie as the heels of his footwear had been cut out for skates and they also had a burn mark from being placed on a hot stove. Microscopic examination also showed the presence of blood on his overalls, which he had attempted to wash off.

The county brought in J.H. Schumaker, a St. Paul detective for his expertise in collecting evidence for the prosecution and he arrived in Kalispell posing as a tramp. After getting himself arrested and lodged in a cell next to Christie, Mr. Schumaker gained the prisoner's confidence in order to obtain a "jail house" confession. While the detective was able to gain knowledge of Christie's previous criminal activity, the suspected murderer never did admit killing Mrs. Cunningham.

While waiting for his trial in August of 1894, Christie managed to break out of the jail at Kalispell once and he was thwarted in his second attempt. First he managed to free himself and successfully escaped from the courthouse building but when he found himself confronted by a barking bulldog in the neighboring yard he retreated back into the safety of the jail and gave himself up. Later he made a key out of a piece of wire with which he unlocked his shackles and then he managed to saw through three of the six by six planks of the floor.

To cover up his activity, Christie secured the cut planks with wire but the end of the boards that ran out into the corridor sagged and that attracted the attention of the guards and the escape was prevented. When a thorough search was made of Christie's cell a pocketknife, with its blade filed like a saw was the only tool found.

Calvin Christie's trial opened on July 30, 1894, and the original courthouse was reportedly unbearably hot as the building had no windows and only two doors for ventilation. Judge DuBose presided with County Attorney Sidney M. Logan and William J. Brennen prosecuting while Henry W. Heideman and C.H. Foot were assigned to defend. After a day and a half the following Flathead County citizens were sworn in as jurors:

Louis Blanchett	Thomas Manuel	H.O. Christenson
William Dewar	T.L. Widdowson	D.A. Carpenter
John Weightman	Charles Smithers	Thomas M. Collins
John Eccles	Alex LeBeau	Robert Bohart

In order to familiarize the jury and the court with the crime scene, Judge DuBose sent the jury and the officers of the court to Columbia Falls under the charge of two county deputies. In all, there were thirty witnesses subpoenaed by the state and the defense called five or six witnesses.

It was learned that before coming to Montana Christie had lived at St Paul and while under the name of Chris Adams he was convicted of grand larceny in October of 1890, and sentenced to a five-year term at the state penitentiary at Stillwater, Minnesota. After arriving at the prison Christie developed signs of epileptic insanity and he was transferred to the state hospital for the insane at St. Peter. During the trial, Dr. B.J. Merrill of the Minnesota State Prison testified through a deposition that Christie's case was the worst example of epileptic insanity that he had ever witnessed and that he had been clearly insane.

The most damaging evidence against the defendant was the blood on his clothing and the perfect match of footprints at the scene of the crime but it was his cold and unflinching testimony in his own behalf that probably hurt his case the most. On the stand Christie appeared totally oblivious to his situation and he was perceived as either a hardened criminal or a man of tremendous will power. He admitted having been convicted of a felony and sent to the state prison in Minnesota and he told the court that he had faked his insanity in order to be sent to the insane asylum where could he easily escape. He further explained that he had assumed various names over the years such as Thomas Adams and Charles J. Black. In the end, the evidence, which convicted Christie, was purely circumstantial, but the volume and relevance was so strong that the jury considered it sufficient to hang him.

Christie took no interest in the trial and he displayed no emotion, which would make one believe he wasn't on trial for his life. The jury only required a few minutes to return with a first-degree verdict and while it was being read and as the panel was polled the defendant appeared unconcerned and was soon seen joking with the deputies as he was being escorted back to the jail. On August 20, 1894, Judge DuBose was visibly affected when he sentenced Christie to be hanged on September 28, and he later overruled the motion for a new trial. Up until that time Christie had refused to reveal his true identity to the authorities but after his sentencing he allowed his mother, Mrs. Joseph Brimley of St. Paul, Minnesota to be notified and his mother came to Montana and made a valiant attempt to save her son.

Governor John E. Rickards granted Christie a respite until October 26, to allow his attorneys to appeal to the Supreme Court but when it was clear that the high court wouldn't be able to hear the case until November the governor extended the reprieve until November 23. When that date arrived without the case being taken up by the Supreme Court the Governor granted another delay until December 21. After finally hearing the case, the Supreme Court refused a new trial for Christie on December 10, 1894, and for the first time the prisoner's nerve began to weaken. The coolness he had exhibited throughout his trial began to fail him and he reportedly said, "Well, I guess that is the last resort and a man can only die once." Christie made no other statement other than that he was innocent and that the newspapers hadn't treated him right.

After the high court had refused a new trial for her son, Mrs. Brimley began circulating a petition asking the Governor to commute the sentence to life imprisonment. She found many folks who were anti-capital punishment, and many people that strongly believed in the guilt of her son, but they generally all signed the petition out of sympathy for the sad mother including Kalispell Mayor Whips. These commutation petitions for the most part were historically well received by the citizens since there was generally several months, or sometimes years from the time of the crime to the execution, and the memory of the victims had faded while the natural impulse to hesitate before taking a man's life intensifies as the execution grows nearer.

The enclosure especially built for the hanging was located between the jail and the alley where the Kalispell Water Department was later located. According to longtime Flathead historian, S.V. Frohlicher in his "Driftwood from the Flathead," the tall ten-foot fence was built during Christie's trial and it was originally used as an exercise yard for the county prisoners. Even after the scaffold was erected inside the enclosure Christie was allowed to roam the yard and he made a habit of dropping heavy bags of sand attached to the hangman's rope through the trap.

Officer Harry P. Stanford, one of Kalispell's first policemen and a witness of the Christie hanging later told Frohlicher why Christie had dropped all those sand bags. The officer explained that when Christie realized that he was a doomed man he wanted to make sure his death on the gallows was quick so he wanted to take all of the stretch out of the rope. According to Stanford, Christie's efforts apparently paid off because on the day of the execution the hangman's rope had the appearance of a piece of ridged iron.

The bravado and indifference that had characterized Christie since his incarceration had definitely weakened within a few days of his execution. The condemned man had also embraced religion just days before his execution with the help of his advisor the Reverend George M. Fisher who had previously walked to the gallows with convicted murderer, Ah Yung at Missoula in August of 1883. Christie broke down on several occasions including on Wednesday, December 19, when he received a letter from a young lady from St. Paul, Minnesota that he had been corresponding with. After finishing the letter the prisoner covered his face with his left arm; grated his teeth incessantly for about two minutes; then closed the letter, rolled a cigarette and smoked it with tears rolling down his cheeks. Several times that night the prisoner told his guards that he wasn't afraid to hang but he dreaded having to face and say good-bye to his poor mother.

Christie then went to bed but he was restless and got up at 3:30 Thursday morning and played cards with his deathwatch. When his mother visited on Thursday afternoon Christie tried to comfort her with the news of his recent acceptance of religion and he kneeled down and prayed for her. Mrs. Brimley paid her son another visit that evening about 8:25 and it deeply moved the prisoner. While he was trying to keep the woman's courage up she was feeling guilty that she had failed him as a mother. Finally he assured his mother that she had always been a good mom; she kissed him; then she completely collapsed with grief and she had to be carried out of the jail. Christie walked to a corner of his cell and burst out crying while he leaned against the wall. Slowly he pulled himself together by shouting that he would conquer his fears and then he began pacing the floor of his cell rapidly.

Mr. Fisher came to the jail at 9:30 and spent an hour praying and talking to the condemned man after which the reverend retired for the evening. After Christie had brightened up a bit he was shaved and spent the rest of the evening restlessly speaking with his guards. When the jailer commented that the prisoner hadn't written a statement about himself or his actions, Christie told him that he would take what he knew with him to the grave.

After being awakened promptly at seven o'clock from a sound sleep by the sheriff, Christie got dressed in his suit and ate a hearty breakfast of a half dozen raw oysters and another six fried along with a couple of eggs. Reverend Fisher joined the prisoner and he remained with him the entire morning in prayer. As the crowd of about one hundred including Mr. Cunningham, the husband of the murder victim, was filing into the jail yard Christie began pacing back and forth in his cell as he waited for the sheriff. Promptly at ten o'clock that morning, Sheriff Gangner opened Christie's cell and after reading the death warrant he removed the shackles from the prisoner's feet.

Christie quickly put on his suit coat and said he was ready to go. After being allowed to say good-bye and shake the hands of the other prisoners and the guards, Christie and the rest of the procession started for the gallows. With Sheriff Gangner and Deputy McFarren at the side of the prisoner followed by Reverend Fisher, Undersheriff Hickernell and Deputy Belifeur the party went out the front door of the jail, around the jail yard and entered the enclosure from the rear. Christie had refused stimulants saying he didn't need anything to brace up his nerves and on the way to the scaffold the condemned man was seen calmly smiling and being as cheerful as if he were leaving on a pleasure trip.

When Christie took his place on the trapdoor he looked over the crowd and waved at several acquaintances from Columbia Falls and said good-bye to a man named Jack. Sheriff Gangner immediately began adjusting the straps on the condemned man, first binding his hands to his side and as the officer buckled the large belt around the man's waist the prisoner said, "That's too tight Joe, you are squeezing those oysters." The feet were then strapped together and everything was ready for the noose when the sheriff said, "Charlie, have you anything to say," to which Christie replied: "This is the happiest moment of my life. I would not trade my faith in Jesus Christ for all the gold and pardons that could be stacked up in this jail yard."

Christie said a brief prayer and then said, "Amen, Let her go." The rope was placed around his neck by the sheriff and Christie remarked jokingly that the noose was too tight and it was choking him. The rope used was the same used to shut out the light of day for John Osnes in July of 1894, at Fort Benton. The black cap was drawn over the man's head and just as Reverend Fisher finished his prayer with "Amen" Calvin James Christie dropped at exactly 10:07 o'clock and he was dangling at the end of a hangman's rope.

Christie's neck was broken clean through and his body didn't even quiver and the coroner, Dr. Cummings and Dr. J.A. Ghent pronounced him dead four minutes later. According to Dr. Cummings, Christie's neck was completely broken and only the skin kept his head connected to his body. After hanging for about ten minutes the body was cut down and placed in a pine coffin and Undertaker Bradley buried his remains in Potter's Field. Christie had left several letters in the care of Mr. Fisher with instructions to deliver them six days after his execution.

Postscript:

After having the misfortune of hanging the first murderer in Flathead County, Sheriff Joe Gangner eventually moved to Dixon. The gallows used to execute Christie were placed into storage until they were once again employed to hang Fred LeBeau in April of 1909.

July 1, 1895
Clayberg "Clay" Pugh

Location and Gallows: When Clay Pugh was hanged behind the courthouse at Boulder he became the fifth man executed on ***Gallows No. Eight: (March 1887): "Galloping Gallows" No. Two***
Description: twenty-three years old
Crime: Murder of Conductor Chauncy W. West near Butte on October 5, 1894
Judge: Frank Showers
Prosecution: Silver Bow County Attorney M.G. Wines of Butte, assisted by George F. Cowan and Mr. Parker of Boulder
Defense: C.L. Campbell of Butte, J.C. English of Anaconda and John B. Clayberg of Helena
Sheriff: Alexander P. Gilliam

While trying to steal a ride on an ore train just pulling out of the railroad yards at Butte on October 5, 1894, Clay Pugh was discovered by Conductor Chauncey W. West. The conductor of the Butte, Anaconda & Pacific Rail Road immediately threw the man off the train but the tramp jumped back on the rear platform and was unnoticed until the train reached the Westside Roadhouse, about a mile out of Butte. When Conductor West discovered Pugh again on the way to Anaconda he stopped the train and put him off a second time. At that point Pugh drew a gun and fired two shots into West's back, and the conductor died from his wounds the following evening.

On February 15, 1895, Pugh's attorneys demanded a change of venue on the grounds that he wouldn't receive a fair trial in Silver Bow County and they produced many affidavits indicating the sentiment at Butte ran strongly against the accused man. Several influential citizens of the mining city, such as C.J. Stevens said that many of the taxpayers and voters expressed a great deal of prejudice against Pugh. Three days later the defense came to the Silver Bow County Courthouse prepared to argue the case when County Attorney Wines surprised them as well as the judge when he consented to the motion for the change of venue. It was later believed that the prosecutor had consented to the change of venue motion after realizing that the jurors of Butte were in the habit of turning murderers loose. After weighing the additional expense to Silver Bow County by hearing the case in another district, Judge Steel ordered Clayton Pugh's trial moved to Jefferson County on February 18, 1895.

The prisoner was moved to Boulder on March 26, and his trial began on April 10, after exhausting the first jury panel a special venire was called and at eight o'clock p.m. the following jury was sworn in:

E.D. Parker, Elkhorn	J.E. Flood, Forbin
R.T. Woliston, Elkhorn	J.M. Tindall, Whitehall
G.E. Coneil, Whitehall	G.C. Dove, Elk Park
R.H. Estes, Basin	S.S. Stewart
James M. Holt, Boulder	Henry Bartelie, Wickes
Tom Borkin	William Channel, Boulder[11]

The great interest in the case was apparent by the large crowds that attended the hearings including a number of ladies. From the very opening of the proceedings Clay Pugh appeared to be cool and calm and he showed absolutely no symptoms of nervousness. The defendant sat calmly throughout the case except on the first day of the trial when he called a witness a liar while he was testifying and Pugh was ordered to “shut up” by his attorneys.

Clay Pugh took the stand and said he was twenty-three years old, that he had a mother, two brothers and two sisters and that his home was in Davis County, Iowa where his mother still resided. He explained that his father was dead and that he had been supporting his mother most of the time while working as a common laborer. He said he was in Butte and on October 5, he had started for Anaconda on the ore train when Mr. West ordered him to get off but he got back on the when out of sight of the conductor.

According to the defendant when the conductor discovered Pugh the second time he threatened him and struck him on the nose and kicked him several times. When the train stopped Pugh said he jumped off and went for his pistol when he saw the conductor go for something in his hip pocket. Pugh explained that he had ridden the train before, but with another crew that didn’t care.

Following the afternoon recess final arguments began and the case was given to the jury at six p.m. when they retired to deliberate. On the morning of April 14, 1895, after deliberating all night long the jury returned with a verdict of guilty of murder in the first degree. Judge Showers was visibly moved and his hands trembled as he handed the verdict to the clerk of the court to be announced. Pugh maintained his usual calm demeanor when the verdict was read and he made no remark of any kind. Only when he was being escorted back to the jail did he say: “Well, they’re giving it to me.”

Back at the jail Pugh was placed in the “cage of death” and a deathwatch was assigned to him. Meanwhile his attorneys were arguing the verdict and were filing motions for a new trial. Judge Showers overruled the motion for a new trial and on April 18, 1985, he sentenced Clay Pugh to be hanged on June 11, 1895. On June 11, 1895, Governor John Rickards granted a respite until July first, so that the defense could apply to the Supreme Court.

Whilegranting the delay the Governor also issued a stern reprimand to the defense attorneys for waiting until the last minute before filing the motion for the appeal before the Supreme Court. Governor Rickards made a point of saying that waiting until the last moment was of no relief to the condemned man but it actually was torture for him. He stated that the justices of the Supreme Court had informed him that they had been waiting to act on the Pugh case but the motion hadn’t yet been filed with the clerk’s office.

Part of the problem with the defense was undoubtedly due to the fact that while fighting for his client’s life, Pugh’s attorney, C.L. Campbell found himself fighting for his own professional life. On April 27, the lawyer was arrested and faced charges in District Court of forging a former client's signature on a power of attorney for his financial gain. Mr. Campbell was quickly released from jail and he was eventually acquitted of criminal charges because the money he received was due him for legal fees, but he was ultimately disbarred in October of 1895, because of the way he obtained it.

The Supreme Court refused to grant a new trial for Clay Pugh on June 26, 1895, because they couldn't find any grounds to overturn the decision of the district court. With the higher court's decision Pugh's last hope was with the Governor and Charles Z. Pond appealed to Governor Rickards on June 29, with two petitions for commutations. The defense also presented affidavits from three citizens of Boulder stating that they had heard jurors say that they had voted for murder in the first degree because they didn't understand that they could have voted on a lesser crime. Guards James Mitchell, Otto A. Riedell and Charles Z. Pond said that they had heard such statements from jurors, F. Tindall, William Channel, S.S. Stewart and James M. Holt after the trial.

Among the many petitioners asking for the commutation of Pugh's sentence were William Deascey and Dan M. Halford, both former sheriffs of Jefferson County along with former deputy, W.B. Tindall. Other influential signers of the petitions from Boulder were Jefferson County Clerk and Recorder Eugene Picot, Sheriff Alex Gilliam, Post Master George Pfaff and jailers, James Mitchell and John J. Bergman. Other signers were Attorney George D. Greene and William Kennedy and the editor of the "Boulder Age." while the supporters of Clay Pugh were asking for the commutation of his sentence, a large number of railroad men at Butte presented another petition opposing any action by the Governor.

The condemned man had an uncle in Iowa, Judge Travis of that state's Supreme Court that did all he possibly could for his nephew. Pugh had also claimed that he was the nephew of W.H. Lockhart of Basin and John B. Clayberg, a lawyer of Helena. Mr. Clayberg later announced that he was not the man's uncle but he eventually helped with the defense during the motion for an appeal.

Mr. Lockhart said that John B. Clayberg might have been the prisoner's relative since one of his sisters, while very young had married a worthless fellow by the name of Pugh against her father's wishes. The father had a very stubborn disposition and after his daughter had married the man he gave her three thousand dollars and told her to leave his home forever. The couple then drifted westward and the Lockhart family lost track of them. Believing that Pugh might have been his nephew, Mr. Lockhart assisted in the efforts to have his sentence commuted, although he had expressed the belief that the man deserved to be hanged.

Clay Pugh himself ridiculed the efforts made to commute his sentence and not only did he refuse to make a statement saying he was remorseful, he refused to even sign the petition to save his own life. Reverend G.W. Blyth, pastor of the First Baptist Church informed the doomed man that the Governor had refused to interfere with the execution and Pugh reportedly took the news well. He appeared to be very anxious to get his execution over with and to some it seemed as though the condemned man had been curious about what it would feel like to have his neck stretched.

Some of the prisoner's friends along with several members of the sheriff department entertained Pugh on his last night on earth and he seemed to be in better spirits than at any time since his trial and sentencing. In addition to Deputy Dan Halford, who was the sheriff of the county when George Bryson was hanged at Boulder in 1889, and Thomas King in 1890; James Mitchell, J.L. Pike, Peter Woolcott and Frank Doyle, better known as "Happy Jack," who was serving a thirty-day sentence were up with him all night long, C.Z. Pond, who had circulated the petition asking for a commutation of his sentence, and other friends of the condemned man dropped in occasionally to say hello. Two other visitors that evening were the Reverend Blyth, and Fred Wolpert, a barber who shaved him.

"Happy Jack" secured a banjo and he played and sang during the night and several of his songs were of the sentimental nature, which seemed to start the condemned man to thinking about his predicament but his many guest didn't allow him to dwell on his fate for very long. When talking about his approaching execution and what lay before him, he would remark to his friends with a smile that it must be a pretty good place because no one ever comes back from there. He would then jokingly ask his friends to be sure and telegraph the winners of future big boxing matches to him.

Deputy Dan Halford called on Pugh early on his last morning, and when asked if there was anything he could do for him the prisoner only said with a smile: "No, let her go as she lays." Deputy Halford once again called on the man just before the hanging and asked him how he was feeling, "As fine as silk," was Pugh's reply. When James F. Bergman, the day deathwatch came in at seven o'clock Pugh greeted him with a smile and said, "Well, Jim, this is your last shift with me." Pugh asked Bergman to write his brother, L.A. Pugh of Walla Walla, Washington, and tell him about his death. "Tell him not to worry about me," Pugh said, "And to forget me as soon as possible."

At 7:45 Pugh had a breakfast of steaks, toast and coffee; fifteen minutes later he lay down and slept peacefully until nine o'clock. Since the judge had set the execution between the hours of ten a.m. and two o'clock p.m. Sheriff Alex Gilliam came by a little after nine o'clock to ask the condemned man what time he would prefer to die. "Make it as soon after ten as possible," said the prisoner as cool as could be, "and let's have it over with." The sheriff asked him if he wanted to speak at the scaffold, whereupon he said, "No, I've nothing to say. I might get up and make an hour's talk, but that wouldn't help me out any,"

The sheriff informed Pugh that there were several pressmen downstairs that want to see him and to get a statement. Pugh said that he had no statement and he didn't want to see a reporter stating that the press had "roasted" him too much and more than he deserved. When the sheriff left Pugh he was joined by the Reverend Blythe who remained with him for more than thirty minutes.

Shortly before ten o'clock the doors of the courthouse yard were opened and about fifty people filed in and surrounded the gallows, which had been originally built for the execution of Thomas Harding at Dillon in 1887. A complete description and history of this scaffold or any other can be found in Chapter Seven: "Montana Gallows." Among the invited guests were Sheriff William R. Dwyer of Cascade County; Sheriff W.H. McKnight, Meagher; Sheriff White Caldwell, Gallatin; Sheriff George B. McLaughlin, Chouteau; Sheriff John H. Jurgens, Lewis and Clark and Deputies E.D. Elderkin and James Hocking of Silver Bow County. Other men from Butte for the hanging were E.E. Congdon, Dominick Salki, James Tickell and J.F. McEvoy.

At precisely ten o'clock Sheriff Gilliam read the death warrant to the prisoner and at the conclusion Pugh said that he was ready. He stubbornly refused to put on the black suit, which had been sent out from Butte along with the coffin saying, "This suit is good enough for me, and I would rather be hung a dozen times in it than to wear anything from Silver Bow County." The doomed man made a point of repeating that statement several times and he expressed his bitterness towards the people and officials of Silver Bow County.

When ordered by the sheriff to wear the clothes provided for him he persistently refused until Deathwatch Bergman, to whom Pugh really liked and respected, persuaded him to don the objectionable suit. Pugh then asked for some whisky as a bracer and he was given three or four stout drinks. When he asked for more he was refused and then he lit a cigarette and started for the gallows with a steady gate with Sheriff Gilliam and Deputy Dan Halford on either side, Undersheriff Henry Sherlock and Deathwatch Bergman bringing up the rear.

Reverend Blythe met them at the door to the courtyard and he took Pugh's right arm while the sheriff walked in front. When Pugh saw the gallows for the first time, he faltered momentarily and his legs became so wobbly that he had to be supported but he recovered quickly and walked under the crossbeam without a second's hesitation. The only other indication of nervousness was in the manner in which he chewed his cigarette.

Pugh glanced up at the dangling noose and pulled off his black hat and threw it to one side with a sarcastic smile. His face was quite pale and there was no sign of blood in his lips, but he stood firm and erect; calmly surveyed the spectators with an unconcerned air that was quite remarkable. He was to all outward appearances the coolest man inside of the courtyard and there was not a visible tremble in either his form or his voice.

On behalf of the prisoner, Reverend Blythe thanked the officers for their kindness and good treatment while he was in jail and then he read the Fourth Verse of the Twenty-third Psalm, "Yea though I walk through the valley of the shadow of death, I will fear no evil for thou art with me, thy rod and thy staff they comfort me." Mr. Blythe then offered another short prayer thanking God that Pugh believed in the Lord and at the conclusion of the prayers Deputy Halford threw Pugh's cigarette stub away and the prisoner watched it burn itself out with an expression of regret.

The prisoner was then bound with straps around his ankles, knees and breast and his wrists were fastened to the straps that passed around his thighs. Sheriff Gilliam asked if the straps were hurting him, to that the prisoner replied, "No, pull them tight." The minister grasped Pugh's hand and bade him Good-bye as the sheriff asked him if he had anything to say. The condemned man only said: "No, let her go." The noose was pulled down and when the sheriff was adjusting it Pugh elevated his head as much as possible to accommodate it. As the sheriff was tightening the noose up as carefully as possible, in a loud voice, which could be heard all over the courtyard Pugh exclaimed, "Tighten her up, old son, tighten her up!"

The big knot of the noose was placed under the left ear, the black cap was pulled down over his head and with a parting, "Good-Bye, Pugh," the sheriff gave the fatal signal to the men in the box and an axe instantly fell and Clayton Pugh's body shot up into the air about a foot and then settled back down with a jerk. There were a few very slight convulsions of the body and then it was all over. The body gradually relaxed until his toes were within an inch of the ground.

The axe fell at exactly 10:28, and at 10:37 a.m. Drs. C.B. Lebcher and L.A. Vawter, who were monitoring the pulse pronounced the man dead. At 10:45 the body was cut down and it was found that the neck had been broken by the fall of the weight so death was practically instantaneous. The remains were placed in a plain casket with a simple inscription of "At Rest" and it was buried at once after a brief service at Potters' Field at the county poor farm, which was about two and a half miles from town. The casket had been purchased by Silver Bow County and it was sent over the day before the execution on the Great Northern and delivered by the local express company.

Postscript:
Sheriff Alex Gilliam was complimented on the manner in which the execution was conducted, and while Clay Pugh was considered a model prisoner, the sheriff was given much credit for the prisoner's actions and attitude because of his administration of the county jail. As a historical side note, Sheriff Gilliam had been an eyewitness to the murder of Matt Fogarty by Thomas King at Elkhorn in November of 1888, and the latter was hanged at Boulder in June of 1890.

Clay Pugh had talked freely with his guards and watches about the murder he had committed and he never did show any regret for it. He had always claimed that he had killed the conductor in self defense; even though he conceded that Conductor West was unarmed and Pugh never could explain how both bullets struck the railroader in the back. Pugh's greatest concern was over his mother, Mrs. Julia Pugh, of West Grove,

Davis County, Iowa and how she would react to his death. As he left for the gallows he gave the woman's address to Reverend Blythe, and asked if he would write her and break the news of his execution as gently as possible.

December 27, 1895
Joseph Cadotte

Location and Gallows: Cadotte was executed behind the jail at Fort Benton and he was the sixth man hanged from ***Gallows No. Eight: (March 1887): "Galloping Gallows" No. Two***.
Description: Cadotte was five feet seven inches tall and weighed about 145 pounds. The quarter-breed Indian had a red birthmark that circled halfway around his neck, which he generally concealed with a handkerchief.
Crime: Murder of Oliver Richards on June 15, 1895
Judge: Dudley DuBose
Prosecution: County Attorney Bernard L. Powers
Defense: Judge John W. Tattan and W.B. Sands
Sheriff: George B. McLaughlin
Distinction: Cadotte was the seventh and last man to be hanged in Chouteau County.

In 1975, Molly Sedgwick[12] wrote about watching the last legal hanging in Chouteau County of Joseph Cadotte. When Molly was ten years old she lived with her family a couple of blocks from the courthouse at Fort Benton and one day when she didn't have anything to do, she walked down to the school to watch the janitors do some renovating during the Christmas school break.

While the men were painting the blackboards in the classroom, Mollie walked past a window on the west side facing the courthouse and noticed a crowd of people in the jail yard. There were horses, wagons and buggies tied up in the vacant lot between the jail and the Episcopal Church and from the second floor she couldn't quite see over the high-board fence into the jail yard, so she climbed up onto the wooden windowsill for a better view.

What little Molly witnessed that December 27, 1895, was only the climax of the tragic life of Joseph Cadotte, known to be part Indian, some said he was a quarter, and others said he was a half to three-quarter-breed. He was described as being an intelligent looking man who spoke English fluently, and though his grammar was a bit lame, his spelling and writing was quite good. The Piegan Indians raised Joseph Cadotte and it's not clear if he was related to either, Louis or Peter Cadotte, both Montana born Indian interpreters of Fort Benton.

Cadotte's troubles began on September 17, 1892, when he shot a cowboy named C.E. Turnbull through the chest while in a drunken row at Big Sandy. There were two versions concerning the dispute; one, that Cadotte shot Turnbull while he was asleep, the other was found in the court records, indicating that Cadotte was asleep and was awakened by the drunken cowboy. The two men began shouting and soon both men began shooting at each other. While there was a dispute over who had fired the first shot, Cadotte fired the last two.

The young Indian was arrested and charged with assault with a deadly weapon with intent to do bodily injury while Turnbull was admitted into the St. Clare Hospital at Fort Benton. Because the pistol round passed completely through his body, Turnbull recovered and he was discharged a few weeks later. On December 20, 1892, Judge Dudley DuBose sentenced Cadotte to a one-year term at the state penitentiary and upon his released in December of 1893, he had a newfound reputation of being a "bad man with a gun."

The convict returned to Fort Benton where he became friends with another half-breed, Oliver Grandchamp, also known as Oliver Richards. Oliver was born to a Frenchman and a quarter-breed Indian woman by the name of Mary at Frenchtown and he grew up in the Missoula area. Oliver's father died when he was a small boy and when his mother married Mr. Grandchamp he took his stepfather's name. The family eventually moved to the Fort Benton region where they homesteaded three hundred and twenty acres on the Teton River.

Cadotte and Richards became good friends and hunting partners for fun as well as profit by going into the wolfing business. When the buffalo were roaming through the country, wolves followed the herds taking mostly the calves and older animals. As the buffalo were killed off the predators found easy pickings among the newly introduced cattle herds and the State of Montana initiated bounties to control the predators. Along with the bounties, the selling of the animal skins became an important industry in Montana. Records for 1898, bounty claims alone, reported that there were 5,869 wolves and 23,754 coyotes taken for total bounties of nearly eighty-nine thousand dollars.

These predator hunters were referred to as "wolfers," and they lived a hard and perilous life on the open prairie. Typically the wolfers' supplies and gear included a pack and saddle horse, blankets, buffalo robe, a good rifle, revolver, ammunition, skinning knife, food and a good supply of strychnine. The wolfer would kill roaming game animals or place large pieces of meat across the blizzard-swept plains and then poison them with the strychnine. The wolves and coyotes would come across the bait and die shortly after eating and their frozen bodies would be found near by. The wolfers would often suffer from the cold while checking their baits, and if a Chinook or warm spell hit the area, the animals might rot before they could be skinned.

On a good season a wolfer could make a very good living, but many of them would take their skins to a trading post; sell them and then drink, gamble and carouse until most of their money was gone. After sobering up, they would have to find work around the trading post communities such as chopping wood or hiring out as freighters in order to raise funds for the next wolfing season.

In the spring of 1895, Joseph Cadotte and his partner Oliver Richards returned to Fort Benton after several weeks of wolfing in north-central Montana to sell their skins and collect their bounties. Apparently the two hunters were typical and they upheld the traditions of true wolfers by drinking and carouse after returning from their hunting expedition.

Although the two young men were known to visit the "Hurdy-Gurdy Houses" in Fort Benton, they both became interested in a pretty quarter-breed Indian girl from Great Falls who had been visiting relatives at Fort Benton. She had been a pupil at the Fort Shaw Indian School before finding employment as a servant for several families at Great Falls. People reported that Cadotte became jealous when it was clear that the Indian girl had favored Richards over him.

While staying at Richards' mother and her third husband on the Stephen Henault Ranch outside of Fort Benton, an argument broke out between Cadotte and his partner on June 15. The two men were staying in the bunkhouse while the Henault's and Oliver's younger half brothers and sisters lived in the main house. The argument was reportedly over the proceeds of the previous season's wolfing and the jealousy over the Indian girl and Cadotte first rode off in an outrage but he soon returned.

After first picketing his horse a short distance from the bunkhouse, Cadotte drew his carbine from his saddle and walked to the cabin. Witnesses said that while Richards was sitting in the bunkhouse mending a bridle, Cadotte thrust his Winchester through a broken window, took deliberate aim and shot his victim in the back at a distance of about fifteen paces. He then walked slowly to the man lying on the ground, and after watching Richards die, Cadotte coolly walked over to his horse, scabbard his Winchester, mounted the animal and rode off to the north as the young victim's mother and sisters were running him.

The rifle bullet had entered the right side of Richards' back, extending through the lower tube of the right lung and pierced the right side of the heart, killing him almost instantly. In minutes the women were covered with the blood of their loved one as they removed his shirt in the attempt to save his life. The ranch hands later told the county coroner that the fugitive was a hard character and that he was armed with a Winchester and a belt full of ammunition.

After the killing, the fugitive rode directly across Sample's Flat to the high ridge to the north, then followed the ridge westward, choosing that ground because his trail couldn't be easily followed. Cadotte also traveled at night and concealed himself during the day in order to avoid human contact, while robbing various sheepherder camps and miners along the way to secure food. Going directly westward, he crossed the Muddy Creek near the five hundred-acre O.G. Cooper's sheep ranch above Bynum, and then to the foot of the Rockies. There he turned south, following the base of the mountains, crossing the forks of the Sun River just west of Augusta.

After crossing the Dearborn River, Cadotte went over the old Pen d' Oreille Pass, ironically known as the "Cadotte Pass," which was an ancient Indian route, later named for the French-Canadian guide, Pierre Cadotte who was with Governor Issac Stevens' Northern Pacific Railroad survey crew in 1853. From the pass the fugitive traveled down the Big Blackfoot River until he reached the Jocko Trail, and then turned northward to the Flathead Indian Reservation.

On Friday, June 28, 1895, Chouteau County Sheriff George B. McLaughlin received word from Teton County authorities that Sheriff Zimmerman had spotted Cadotte near the town of Choteau and he and a posse was in pursuit. With that information, Sheriff McLaughlin notified Colonel Joseph T. Carter, the agent of the Flathead Reservation with Cadotte's description and a request to watch out for the fugitive.

Both Cadotte and Richards were well known on the reservations, especially the Blackfoot Agency, and neither man had very good reputations with the Indians. Most Indians didn't care much for wolfers because they lost a lot of their dogs to the hunter's poison. The fact that Chouteau County had offered a one hundred dollar reward for the capture of Cadotte only made the reservation Indians even keener on capturing the fugitive.

Agent Carter immediately set out his force of Indian Mounted Police to watch the trails for the fugitive, and no sooner had Cadotte crossed into the reservation he was being watched by the police. At about ten o'clock Saturday night, July 7, Cadotte reached an Indian camp, and by two a.m. he was sound asleep with a blanket over his head to ward off the many mosquitoes. The Indian Police waited until four o'clock on Sunday morning, when they cautiously entered the tee-pee and took away the man's Winchester.

When the Indians returned to the lodge and pulled away the blanket, Cadotte reached for his carbine, but it instead he found himself covered by the guns of the Indian Police. After relieving him of his Bowie knife the Indians put Cadotte on his horse and took him to the agency at Arlee. The following day Colonel Carter had the fugitive sent to Missoula where Missoula Jailer Oliver Pichette, formerly of Fort Benton and who personally knew Cadotte, made positive identity. The reward for the capture of Cadotte was wired to the reservation where Colonel Carter waived his share, and the full amount was awarded to his police officers.

When word arrived about Cadotte's arrest, Chouteau County Sheriff McLaughlin was delivering a couple of prisoners to Deer Lodge where he was wired and he proceeded to Missoula to pick up his man. While in the Missoula jail, Cadotte claimed the killing was done over a fit of passion, caused by the fact that Richards didn't want to go hunting with him, nor give up any of the food that they had bought for the proposed trip. During their trip back to Fort Benton, Cadotte told Sheriff McLaughlin that he also got mad at Richards because he had gotten drunk and had spent some of their shared earnings.

Cadotte explained that the dispute continued at the Henault Ranch where he claimed that Richards had threatened him twice with a knife. When Richards started for the house Cadotte called out to him to stop three times, but when he didn't, he shot him. Cadotte told the sheriff that he had shot Richards because he was going to the house to get his shotgun, so he considered the shooting a case of self-defense. Cadotte emphasized that Richards was a bigger man weighing some two hundred and forty pounds and he was afraid of him.

Sheriff McLaughlin and his prisoner arrived at Fort Benton on Friday, July 12, 1895, and Cadotte was housed at the county jail until his trial on Tuesday, September 3. Judge DuBose opened case, No.1175, and on that day the following jury was sworn in:

Frank Linhoff, (f)	Olaf G. Skylstead	J.B. Dority
D.A. Cromley	Fred Prosser	James Griffin
W.D. Smotherman	Moses Pugsley	John Johnstone
Fred Jordan	W.W. Linder	(unknown)

(f) Foreman

County Attorney Powers prosecuted the case while Judge DuBose assigned Judge W. Tattan who had successfully prosecuted John Osnes at Fort Benton the previous year, and W.B. Sands as counsel for the defense. The defense challenged Juror John Johnstone, a brother-in-law of the county attorney, but the judge denied the challenge, as he believed that the man would still be fair and impartial.

While the defendant was on the stand, County Attorney Powers made a dramatic grandstanding courtroom statement that made a tremendous impression on the jury. At one point during his cross examination, Powers pointed out the red birthmark, which circled halfway around Cadotte's neck and stated: "Nature evidently intended the man to die," the county attorney referring to the mark resembling a rope burn proving, "He was born to be hung."

After closing arguments on Friday, September 6, 1895, Judge DuBose gave the jury its instructions and it took less than an hour for the panel to return with their guilty verdict, which came in at about nine o'clock that evening. Saturday morning Judge DuBose reminded the defendant that he had already sentenced him to the state penitentiary for shooting another man and unfortunately the experience had only hardened him. The judge went on and sentenced the defendant to be hanged until dead on October 18, 1895.

During the sentencing, Cadotte never moved a muscle nor gave any indication of emotion. He had no air of bravado nor did he show any reaction to being sentenced to his death, in his quiet manner he just followed Jailer Ford back to the county jail. Judge Tattan announced to the court that a request for a new trial would be filed and on the day before the scheduled execution of their client, the defense attorneys formerly filed a motion for an appeal with the Montana Supreme Court.

Up until July of 1895 when the codes were changed, only the Governor could grant a stay of execution after a man had been sentenced, in order for the defense to appeal to the Supreme Court. Under Section No.2278, of the new 1895 Justice Codes, an appeal to the Supreme Court alone would act as an automatic stay of execution and a respite by the Governor was no longer required. On October 17, the sheriff was notified of the stay of execution and he suspended preparations for the hanging of Cadotte.

At the hearing the defense attorneys brought to the attention of the high court the conduct of the county attorney at the trial when he pointed out to the jury the livid red ring about the defendant's neck. While the Supreme Court determined that although the remarks of the county attorney were certainly reprehensible, they were not enough to reverse the judgment of the lower court. On December 9, 1895, the Supreme Court affirmed the judgment of the lower court and denied a new trial for the defendant.

When Sheriff McLaughlin informed Cadotte of the Supreme Court's decision, he yawned, stretched leisurely, and then said that he wasn't in the least bit interested. On Thursday morning, December 19, Judge DuBose re-sentenced Cadotte to be hanged on Friday, December 27, just a week away.

While Father Follett at the Catholic Mission labored to teach Cadotte the faith, the condemned man tried to couple the Christian religion with the teachings of bravery instilled into him by his first tutors, the Piegan Indians. Cadotte told Jailer Breen that he would die as brave a Christian as those French priests who were referred to as the "Black Robes." When a friend reminded Cadotte of the sheriff's liberal rule concerning whisky for condemned prisoners, he replied that he wanted to die like a Christian and not a drunkard.

During the days leading up to his execution, Cadotte spent most of his time writing letters to several of his friends and acquaintances, the contents of which were never made public. He also wrote a lengthy public statement acknowledging that the crime for which he was going to pay with his life was beyond pardon, but reiterated that it was committed out of anger. He went on by reviewing his past career pointing out that bad influences had induced him to go bad.

On Christmas day, the sheriff spared no expense in making Cadotte's last holiday dinner a veritable banquet. After the meal, the officers made a thorough search of the man's cell for anything that could be used to take his own life and nothing was found. The day after Christmas, and the day before his execution, Cadotte was in the best of spirits and he was quite anxious for Friday to arrive so he could show how brave a man he was. That afternoon the Catholic Sisters spent awhile with him, and by Thursday night Cadotte had everyone convinced that he was calmer than anyone else at the jail.

Sheriff McLaughlin had observed the hanging of Clay Pugh in July 1895, and he apparently made arrangements to use that Jerk-Type Gallows instead of the ancient scaffold at Fort Benton that had been used the year before to hang Osnes. The gallows were set up inside the high stonewall of the jail yard on the corner of Main and Wetzel Streets.

The scaffold was tested Friday morning and the new rope was greased and stretched while Cadotte was getting dressed in a neat fitting suit with a colorful handkerchief around his neck. There was some speculation as to whether Cadotte's neck would stand the strain of the hanging because of the awful scar near his throat. Some folks described the skin over the mark as so thin that the veins were easily seen and for that reason Cadotte had always worn handkerchiefs around his neck.

The prisoner hadn't spoken to the sheriff since the trial because of the accusations made by the officer that Cadotte had threatened his life, so it was quite a surprise when he sent for Sheriff McLaughlin. Then in the presence of the deputies, Cadotte asked for the officer's forgiveness, and then said that not only did the sheriff tell it right he had threatened to kill McLaughlin on several other occasions.

At 10:10 a.m. Cadotte was taken to the place of execution, a space fenced in back of the courthouse and jail, the same place where John H. Osnes was hanged in July of 1894. Just before the hanging, Father Follett was with the prisoner and he prepared him for the tragic end as he had done for Thomas King in June of 1890, and for John Osnes the year earlier. The priest accompanied him to the gallows along with representatives of the "Great Falls Tribune" and the "Helena Herald," Sheriff Zimmerman of Teton County, Cascade County Sheriff Sid Willis, Undersheriff Howell, Dr. Francis Atkisson along with some of the other twelve citizens that the sheriff had invited.

Cadotte kept his nerve to the last and he displayed an indifferent characteristic of his Indian heritage. As he was brought into the enclosure Cadotte appeared to be the most composed man in the crowd and he exhibited no particular fear as he stepped to the gallows with the air of someone going to a dinner instead of his death. Beneath the rope, which dangled ominously in the air, he took occasion to say that the newspapers had written that the murder was over a woman and that this was false and without foundation. In a loud voice he declared, "Gentlemen, it was said that I killed Richards over a girl," holding up his right hand, "that is not so. It was pure passion. I had thought the man wanted to take everything away from me and now I am to pay for his life. Good-bye."

The condemned man then turned and shook hands with Frank Camp, his deathwatch, and Father Follett handed him the crucifix, which he kissed, and then the black hood was pulled over his head. His last words after the black cap was adjusted was a request that the silk scarf around his neck be removed, and it was done. The five-eighths inch hemp rope was then adjusted around his neck with the knot on the left side. Cadotte stood on the ground and at the end of the rope was a weight of window irons weighing 460 pounds. A movement of a lever by Sheriff McLaughlin suddenly jerked the doomed man from the ground about three feet and then he dropped down to within about twelve inches of the ground.

Dr. Atkisson immediately placed his ear to the breast of the man suspended in mid-air, and at the same time grasped the handcuffed wrist with his hand. The jerk apparently ended all sensation, breaking his neck in two places. For two or three minutes after the drop, the attending physician found that the pulse had ceased to beat, and in eleven minutes he was declared dead.

After the rope was cut the body was lowered into a coffin without removing the black cap, which still hid the man's face. Apparently the rope wasn't sufficiently lubricated and the knot had drawn so tightly around Cadotte's neck that it had to be cut at the knot and the noose was buried with the remains. The body was turned over to the friends of the dead man and the remains were buried in the graveyard at Fort Benton. Sheriff McLaughlin was given great credit for the successful manner in which he carried out the sentence of the law.

Several days after the hanging when young Mollie's mother was fitting her with a new dress she told her what she had seen from the school window and asked her why they hanged the man. Her mother told her that the man had murdered another man so he had to pay the consequences for his act.

April 6, 1896

William Biggerstaff

Location and Gallows: At Helena William Biggerstaff became the seventh man to give up his life on ***Gallows No. Eight: (March 1887): "Galloping Gallows" No. Two***.

Description: Biggerstaff was a large forty-two-year-old black man.

Crime: Murder of Richard Johnson on June 9, 1895

Judge: Henry N. Blake

Prosecution: District Attorney R. R. Purcell assisted by Assistant District Attorney Leon La Croix

Defense: Colonel Cornelius B. Nolan was the primary defense attorney and Henry C. Smith helped with the appeal

Sheriff: John Henry "Hy" Jurgens

The cold-blooded crime of murder for which William Biggerstaff forfeited his life was very peculiar, the state was never able to prove a motive for the killing and the defense couldn't establish an excuse for it. Just before five o'clock on the morning of June 9, 1895, the quiet on Water Street in the red-light section of Helena was disturbed by a gunshot and after a few minutes a second shot was heard. About twenty minutes later, just as the sun was appearing over the horizon William Biggerstaff walked into the City Marshal's Office and tossed a revolver into the lap of the young office clerk, William Smith and stated that he had just shot Dick Johnson, the prize fighter, after the boxer had clubbed him on the head with another gun.

William Smith was unnerved by the large black man as he new Biggerstaff was an unsavory type and because they had previous confrontations. Sometime earlier another black man was arrested for some petty offense, he was locked up in the jail and Smith was given strict orders not to allow anyone to visit the prisoner. Biggerstaff called at the jail and when Smith denied him access to the prisoner he became enraged. When Biggerstaff walked into the office this time with a revolver, the clerk was of course frightened but after the black man handed him the small, shinning 32-caliber Smith and Wesson revolver and exclaimed that he had shot a man, Smith became surprised.

After determining that three of the chambers of the revolver contained cartridges, Smith quickly turned the weapon on Biggerstaff and ordered him to throw up his hands. Biggerstaff obeyed and the clerk searched his pockets finding a small pocketknife and several small trinkets. Smith then locked his prisoner up in a room and stepped into the street where he blew a police whistle.

Officer Vanesse was the first policeman to appear and after turning the prisoner over to the officer, William Smith immediately went to the run-down shack at 311 Water Street in time to see Johnson take his last breath. After notifying the coroner the officers began questioning the three primary witnesses about the incident and except for a couple of minor details their stories were practically identical. At about 4:30 Johnson had called on Mrs. Lottie Matthews who was residing in the second-floor apartment on Water Street telling her that he was leaving for Butte that morning. Dick Johnson had known the black prostitute and madam for some time and he had frequently stayed with her when he was in Helena.

Staying with Lottie that evening was a seventeen-year-old white girl, Miss Emma Bowhay, the daughter of another prostitute living next door, Mrs. Annie or "Hannah" Bowhay. Apparently while living with Mrs. Bowhay, William Biggerstaff had been involved with both the older cross-eyed white woman and her daughter Emma. It was later learned that after Mrs. Bowhay had gotten jealous of her daughter she made life miserable for the girl and drove her away to live with Lottie Matthews. Apparently Johnson was also fond of the white woman and her daughter and a rivalry had sprung up between the two men but there had never been any serious trouble until that early morning in June.

The Matthews' apartment was a little two-room affair with plastered walls and it was reached by a flight of a dozen steps. In the front room was a dirty bed where she conducted her business and next to the cot was a dilapidated trunk. Johnson was sitting on the trunk and talking to the women when Dick Smith came in on his way home from work. Lottie Matthews routinely kept Dick Smith's house key for safekeeping and while they were all talking someone began rapping on the door.

When Mrs. Matthews inquired who was at the door Biggerstaff represented himself as a policeman and demanded that the door be opened. When the door was finally opened Biggerstaff entered the room and he began ordering Emma Bowhay to return to her mother's apartment. When Emma refused and Mrs. Matthews' male guests began insisting that Biggerstaff leave he pulled out a large pocketknife and began threatening both Johnson and Smith.

Dick Johnson stepped to the other room and returned with an antiquated handgun and ordered Biggerstaff to leave the apartment, which he reluctantly did. A few minutes later the two men said their good-byes to Mrs. Matthews and Emma and started for the door. Johnson had started out the door when he backed into the room and quickly closed the door, warning that Biggerstaff was returning with a revolver. Wanting to see for himself, Smith opened the door and confirmed that the big man was on his way and was barely able to close the door before Biggerstaff slammed into it. Biggerstaff managed to push the door open far enough to put his arm and handgun through and he fired at Johnson but missed his target when Johnson struck the weapon with his old broken-down handgun.

The blast startled the two men inside the room and in the excitement Biggerstaff forced his way through the door and began struggling with Johnson. The two men had a fierce struggle over the revolver until Biggerstaff gained the advantage and pulled the trigger as they fell to the floor. Biggerstaff crawled out from under the fatally wound man and then ran to the police station where he turned himself in.

William Biggerstaff
"Helena Daily Herald" 4/6/1896

This wasn't the first time Biggerstaff had been involved with the death of a man having shot a man at Great Falls several years earlier and killing a man in Colorado. Because he had been cleared in those other cases, Biggerstaff was confident that he wouldn't get in trouble with the law if he turned himself in to the police immediately after the death of Johnson.

The body of Richard "Dick" Johnson was taken to Undertaker Flaherty's Morgue where before it was examined and eventually prepared for burial it was first put on display so that scores of people could take one last look at the popular black man. Johnson was a twenty-seven-year-old black professional boxer with a great deal of promise and he was looked up to by most of the blacks of the state. He was born at Unionville near Helena where his parents, three sisters and two brothers lived but he had lived for many years at Butte. Johnson had fought and won several fights at Helena, Spokane and a number of cities on the west coast. Exactly one week before his death he had fought Dick Case, the "Yakima Kid" at Helena and had lost the fight and a one hundred dollar purse because of a foul during the third round.

While Biggerstaff was being transferred to the county jail for safe keeping, Coroner T.H. Pleasants held an inquest over the remains of Johnson where it was learned that the deceased and Biggerstaff had known each other for many years and that they had an on going feud over many trivial things including a broken fishing rod and other personal issues involving women. The coroner's jury found that Johnson met his death from a gunshot wound at the hands of William Biggerstaff.

Dick Johnson was buried on June 11, 1895, following the funeral services conducted at the home of his sister, Mrs. Al Marshall at 918 Breckenridge Street. Once the word hit the street about the murder there was a great deal of talk about holding a lynching bee especially among the black population of Helena. The authorities protected the prisoner and on the morning of June 12, 1895, William Biggerstaff was arraigned for the murder of Johnson.

As Deputy Clerk of the Court Casedy read the formal first-degree murder charges against Biggerstaff the prisoner showed no emotion while he only gazed at the speaker as if he were listening to an interesting story. At the hearing the prisoner was sporting two bruises on the right side of his forehead, which he claimed was the result of Johnson striking him with his revolver. When asked if he could secure an attorney Biggerstaff said that Colonel C.B. Nolan had called on him at the jail but he had not yet agreed to take his case.

Although the prisoner was more than willing to speak with a reporter after his arraignment, County Attorney Purcell wouldn't allow Biggerstaff to have any visitors except his legal counsel. The defendant was ordered to appear before Judge Blake on June 26, 1895, and on that day his attorney asked for a continuance. After considering the motion the court granted the continuance until the October term.

There were conflicting stories concerning the background of the defendant; one being that he had been born a slave at Lexington, Kentucky in 1854, and that he was from a Catholic family with six sisters, who mainly lived in Kansas. Other accounts cited that Biggerstaff had been born in the vicinity of Tahlequah, Indian Territory, and it was said that one of his parents had been either Cherokee or Choctaw Indian. He reportedly spent his early years in crap shooting and other petty gambling and when he was twenty years old he was in Denver.

In Colorado Biggerstaff got married and apparently led a relatively straight life until his wife died at Denver in 1881, when he lived a life of destitute spending most of his time drunk and in and out of trouble. He didn't exactly avoid work but he had no ambition and usually lived off the earnings of prostitutes. Most of his time was spent around bawdy houses and other low class resorts where murders were committed frequently and in saloons where drugging and robbing were as common as drinking and dancing. Biggerstaff was arrested after a man was murdered and his body dismembered and placed in a sack but he was eventually acquitted of the charge.

He was later convicted of shooting and severely wounding a man and served a short term in the Colorado State Penitentiary. After being pardoned from prison Biggerstaff joined a traveling "Uncle Tom's Cabin" company that went as far west as San Francisco, California where it finally disbanded. After spending a while in California, Biggerstaff hit the trail and eventually ended up in Montana where he lived at Helena for six years. In the Capital City he went to work doing odd jobs such as painting, carpet cleaning and spending his nights in saloons and whorehouses.

The police register at Helena revealed that Biggerstaff had been arrested for fighting, and other petty offenses including being drunk and disorderly and he quickly gained a bad reputation of being mean and vengeful and was particularly unpopular with the other black people of the city. While he married a respectable black woman living on State Street, he preferred living with white prostitutes. Because of the murder of Johnson and other violent crimes in the red-light district of Helena, City Marshal McCann ordered the arrest of any black men living with white prostitutes or vise versa.

The following day three black men, Ed "Dude" Johnson, J. Wesley and William Allen along with their live-in white girl friends, Louise Forrest, Cora Meyers and Nellie Monget were all arrested and locked up in the city jail. They were all fined twenty-five dollars after being charged for being inmates of houses of ill-fame but since none of them had any money they were all sentenced to twelve days at hard labor. The jailer reported that the three men were dressed in their "Sunday Clothes" and they had to send out for their dirty clothes for the chain gang, which was under the direction of Sandy Lane.

On October 15, 1895, Judge Blake's courtroom was filled with predominately black spectators for the opening of William Biggerstaff's trial and it was reportedly difficult to secure a jury because so many men were prejudiced, not only against the defendant's race but also against capital punishment or the fact that so many people had already formed an opinion concerning the case. Finally the following Lewis and Clark men were selected for the jury.

C.G. Evans[13] (f)	Fred Sass[14]	Charles Stabern
F.H. Fowles	F.S.P. Lindsay[15]	Fred E. Tibbets
S.S. Cook	David Keenan	Ivan Towner
Charles Grossman	Henry Schotte[16]	(unknown)

(f) Foreman

During the five-day trial, even when the case looked bad for Biggerstaff he kept calm and chewed gum as if his life was dependant upon the motion of his jaws. Even when he finally took the stand on his own behalf he was cool and answered questions from both the prosecution and the defense without flinching or hesitation. He rebuffed the testimony of the damaging testimony and he admitted the revolver that was used to kill the victim was his but he said that he carried it occasionally to protect himself from Dick Smith, a discharged black soldier who had threatened him. Eventually the prosecution was able to establish that Biggerstaff had threatened the victim earlier for breaking his fishing rod and the defense failed to prove self-defense or the excuse that he was under the influence of alcohol.

After the closing arguments and instructions to the jurors the panel was turned over to Bailiff John Hudson at five o'clock on the evening of October 18, 1895, and they were escorted to the jury room on the third four of the courthouse. There, the jury deliberated behind closed doors until suppertime when the bailiff took them to the dining room of the Helena Hotel. It was said that the bailiff watched over the jury like a hen brooded over her little chicks and he wouldn't allow anybody to speak to the jurors or let members of the jury hold conversations with anyone but themselves. When they returned to the jury room the men again took up the case until ten p.m. when they retired for the night.

The jury didn't leave the courthouse, but were put up on cots for the night in the jury room and according to Bailiff Hudson; the jurors weren't disturbed by their deliberation as they slept quietly all night. The jury was up early on the morning of October 19, and after they cleaned up, the bailiff escorted them to the Grandon Hotel for their eight o'clock breakfast. Shortly after nine o'clock the twelve men were again discussing the case in the jury room and at ten o'clock there was a knock on the door and they informed the bailiff that a verdict had been reached. The news of the verdict spread through the courthouse like wildfire and in less than five minutes the courtroom was crowded with spectators who had been hanging around for such an announcement.

Despite the size of the crowd and the excitement of the case, there was a death-like silence the moment the jury filed into the room and took their place in the box. The twelve men had barely taken their seats when the doors again opened and Deputy Theodore E. Kleinschmidt brought Biggerstaff into the courtroom. The defendant only had a faint smile and it was clear to everyone who had been following the trial that his nerve and pluck had deserted him as he reportedly trembled slightly as he looked around at the sea of faces as he walked towards his chair. The closer he got to his seat the more frightened he became and a light foam or froth soon gathered around his mouth, giving the appearance that he was about to go into a fit.

When asked to stand and face the jury the defendant was too weak to standup unassisted and he leaned against the table in front of him, his eyes having a far away look while his body was shaking and he seemed to be ready to collapse. When Mr. Evans, the foreman of the jury read the guilty verdict, Biggerstaff weakened even further and his face assumed a ghastly appearance and his fingers began moving convulsively as his arms hung lifelessly at his sides.

After the verdict was read the prisoner was immediately returned to his cell across the street in the jail and as he was leaving the courtroom he displayed somewhat of a smile indicting that he had regained some of his composure. The jury had signed a written agreement, which forbid them from discussing their deliberation and they would only say that they discussed the case before and after supper the previous evening and after breakfast on the morning of the verdict. It was never learned how many ballots the jurors had taken or the results of the polls but many believe that one man had held up the outcome before finally giving in.

After his trial Biggerstaff believed that he had been the victim of circumstances and of a conspiracy claiming that some of the witnesses had been bribed to testify as they did and the fact that he had been living with a white woman was detrimental to his case. Although he felt that Judge Blake and County Attorney Purcell were honest men, he didn't think he received a fair trial because of his own lawyers. In fact he put the blame for all his troubles on whisky and his lawyers explaining that the only distinction between the two was that he truly loved his whisky but he never liked his attorneys.

The courtroom was again crowded with a mass of men and women of all colors, ages and sizes on October 26, 1895, for the sentencing of Biggerstaff and while most of the spectators were making their way up to the courtroom on the second floor others were gathering at the eastern entrance of the courthouse where they knew the prisoner would be entering. About four minutes before ten the door of the jail opened and Deputy Kleinschmidt stepped out followed by the prisoner. The sight of Biggerstaff signaled a great rush and scramble in and out of the courthouse with the cries of: "Here he comes!" The mass of humanity rushed to the doorway and inside the building the crowds pushed their way frantically in order to get a spot in the courtroom or gallery.

Biggerstaff was seated next to Deputy Kleinschmidt as they calmly waited for the appearance of Judge Blake. The prisoner was allowed to speak but he said he hadn't prepared a statement and at that point Colonel C. B. Nolan arose and asked Judge Blake to give his client adequate time for an appeal to be made to the Supreme Court. The judge said that his duty was to sentence the prisoner at once and at that point, Mr. Nolan took his seat and the court proceeded to pass sentence. William Biggerstaff was sentenced to be hanged on December 20, 1895, between the hours of ten in the morning and two that afternoon. William Gay, who was also on "Death Row" at the same time in Lewis and Clark County, was eventually sentenced to be hanged with Biggerstaff on that same day.

Being faced with two potential executions in his own jurisdiction, Sheriff Jurgens had the opportunity of attending the hanging of Clay Pugh at Boulder in July of 1895, on the original Lewis and Clark gallows. Sheriff Jurgens later ordered the ancient gallows be transported back to Helena and instead of having a hole dug beneath the noose he had a wooden platform built, which could be pulled away to increase the drop.

Sheriff Jurgens sent out invitations for the double hanging of Biggerstaff and Gay with the customary photographs of the condemned men but they were unique by having a poetic verse as well.

Underearth its clouds of sin,
The heart of man retaineth yet
Gleams of its Holy origin;
And half-quenched stars that never set,
Dim colors of its faded bow,
An early beauty, linger there,
And o'er its wasted desert blow
Faint breathings of its morning air
O, never yet upon the scroll
Of the sin-stained, but priceless soul,
Hath heaven inscribed "Despair!"
By Sheriff Jurgens

Biggerstaff was saved from his first date with the hangman's noose in December with a stay of execution, which was granted just three days before the fateful day. It was said that no attorney had ever worked as hard for a client as Colonel Nobles did for Biggerstaff, and he never received a dollar for his work other than the small fee provided by the state. The condemned man's sister, Mrs. Laura E. Ross of Tallequash of the Cherokee Nation, paid Henry C. Smith one hundred dollars to help with the case during the appeal to the Supreme Court.

On December 16, 1895, Biggerstaff's attorneys presented a notice of appeal, and on the December 19 they submitted a one hundred and thirteen-page transcript. At first when Chief Justice William Y. Pemberton began reading his opinion on February 17, 1896, most everyone in the courtroom thought the Supreme Court had decided to grant Biggerstaff a new trial but by the end of his statement it was known that the convicted murderer was doomed. Before receiving the bad news Biggerstaff reportedly told William Gay who was locked up in the cage next to him that he was probably going back upstairs to death row.

Once Biggerstaff was convicted and sentenced to death in October of 1895, he was assigned a deathwatch and placed on "Murderer's Row," which was made up of a row of cells on the upper tier in the left hand side of the jail. William Gay joined him there after his conviction in November of 1895, but they were both moved to the lower level once their appeals had temporarily stayed their executions and their deathwatches were suspended. After the Supreme Court's decision Jailer Martin and Deputy Kleinschmidt entered Biggerstaff's cell and told the prisoner he was going back upstairs. The condemned man quietly got his coat and accompanied the officers upstairs and as his cell door closed behind him on "Murderer's Row" he told the officers that he had expected the decision of the high court.

The courtroom was crowded on March 5, 1896, for the re-sentencing of Biggerstaff, as most of the spectators were curious to hear the defendant's final plea for his life. Just before ten a.m. Biggerstaff was removed from his cell and escorted to the courthouse by Undersheriff Fred E. Hoss, Deputy Kleinschmidt and one of the deathwatches. The handcuffed prisoner walked between the officers in order to prevent the crowd of spectators from approaching him as they entered the courtroom. Biggerstaff didn't appear to be the slightest bit nervous and he was talking and laughing with the deputies before the judge entered the room.

Every seat in the courtroom was taken and the gallery was filled to capacity and among the large audience were many blacks and a few women. Although most of the people thought the defendant or his attorneys would present something startling, they were soon disappointed by Biggerstaff's rambling. He spoke for an hour and fifteen minutes and finished at just about the same place he had started and during his statement a number of people left the courtroom disgusted and didn't stick around for the sentencing. Biggerstaff said that Mr.

Henry C. Smith didn't act in good faith and he accused Mr. Nolan of selling him down the river by conspiring with the prosecution.

In his long statement Biggerstaff claimed that his friends had also abandoned him in his greatest hour of need and he complained about his treatment in the jail and particularly about the mice running about his cell. After his client's rambling statement Henry Smith, who had conducted Biggerstaff's case during the appeal stood up and said a few well-chosen words for the prisoner. Judge Blake then ordered Biggerstaff to stand and then he sentenced him to be hanged on April 6, 1896. The condemned man took the death sentence without a change of expression.

Soon after his re-sentencing one of his sisters sent Biggerstaff some money so that he could eat anything he desired and for three weeks up to his execution the prisoner gorged himself with Limburger cheese, chicken, oysters and other delicacies. The prisoner gained a great deal of weight as well as notoriety by his enormous appetite and the officers at the jail reported that the man consumed more food, beer and whisky in one day than his fellow prisoners could eat in a week.

His attorneys prepared a petition asking for the Governor to spare his life and one of the condemned man's oldest friends, George D. Johnson, no relation to the victim, promised to circulate the petition. The two men had been best friends for fifteen years while they worked and traveled together in Colorado and Montana and several years earlier Biggerstaff had saved Johnson's life while they were hunting and he nursed his friend back to health for three months. When Mr. Johnson received the petition he promised Biggerstaff that he would quit his work and devote all his time gathering signatures.

Every few days Johnson would drop by the jail and tell his old friend that he was getting all kinds of signatures; that some people were coming out of their houses in order to get an opportunity to sign the petition. Johnson gave Biggerstaff the impression that hundreds of people had signed the petition to save his life but on the day that the petition was to be turned in, the so-called friend reportedly caught the Northern Pacific train for Des Moines, Iowa, leaving his friend and petition behind. After learning that Johnson had skipped town Biggerstaff instituted a search for the missing petition at Mrs. Johnson's residence, and there it was found; instead of finding hundreds of names there was but eight signatures.

It was learned that Johnson had indeed made an effort to save his friend, but because he met with so much opposition and poor success he quit and didn't have the heart to tell his friend, so he kept lying to the prisoner. The lie had gotten so large that he couldn't tell his friend the truth so he left town. Before leaving, Johnson told his friends that if Biggerstaff hadn't made that long speech at his sentencing, it would have been easier to acquire signatures on the petition.

Discouraged by the desertion of his best friend, Biggerstaff gave the petition to another of his black friends along with five dollars with instructions to get as many signatures as he could get as his life depended on it. The friend took the money and the petition and he got as far as the nearest saloon where he got good and drunk. The condemned man never did see that friend again and he eventually gave up on the rest of his friends and became contented by drinking beer and whisky, eating Limburger cheese and playing cribbage with his deathwatch.

The office of Governor John E. Rickards was flooded with petitions, letters and many people asking for executive clemency for Biggerstaff and wo days before the execution his lawyers presented a petition from their client asking for another month in order to circulate his petition while they asked for another appeal on the grounds that the jury in the case had been prejudiced because the defendant had been living with a white woman. They also stated that their client was drunk at the time of the murder; that because the state of Montana sells alcohol it should accept some of the responsibility for the crimes it causes. Attorney J.P. Ball met with the governor that same afternoon on behalf of Biggerstaff after taking interest in the case and the Governor had assured him that he had gone over the petitions carefully and had checked off the influential signers in red ink. Governor Rickards explained to Mr. Ball that unfortunately there were very few red marks.

Some of the special visitors of the condemned man at the jail included the murder victim's mother and his sisters. Biggerstaff had lived seven years with Mrs. Johnson and her family and she came to the county jail to pray for the man and to tell him she had forgiven him for killing her son. Along with these special visitors, about three hundred other people, carrying petitions for executive clemency visited Biggerstaff and his fellow death-row prisoner, Bill Gay at the county jail. Biggerstaff's supporters were hoping for a reprieve of a month but the condemned man promised the people that if the Governor didn't interfere he would die bravely.

Mrs. A.T. Koldrup and Miss Grace Miller were among the last to call on the condemned man and he asked them to purchase a bottle of cologne for him. Later that evening a bottle of Hoyt's German Cologne was delivered to him compliments of the ladies. Then Lucy Biggerstaff, the black wife of the condemned man walked up the iron steps to say good-bye to her husband but all she had to say was that she hoped that she would see him in heaven and that she would take good care of his body. As the woman walked down the noisy iron steps with tears in her eyes, Biggerstaff took the cigar stump from his teeth; flipped it in the woman's direction and said, "There goes a mighty fine little woman."

Three black women of the A.M.E. Church and members of the elite Black Society of Helena offered Biggerstaff their affectionate farewell. During the last couple of nights on earth, Biggerstaff became moody and didn't indulge in as much joking and loud singing as he had before and the guards were getting concerned that one of his friends would try to pass him some poison. At about 6:30 that evening Biggerstaff ate one of his typical suppers of a whole stewed chicken, plum duff and some of his favorite Limburger cheese.

At three o'clock on the afternoon of April 4, 1896, Governor Rickards announced that he would not interfere with the execution but it wasn't until after six that evening that Biggerstaff finally heard the news that his fate had been sealed. Jailer Martin and Deputy Kleinschmidt had decided earlier not to tell the prisoner the news while the jail was full of visitors and they didn't want to upset him since he was enjoying the company.

The sheriff had given strict orders not to admit any more visitors after six o'clock p.m. and it was strictly enforced even though there were still about a hundred people waiting to see the prisoner. The officers were hoping that one of the doomed man's attorneys would come by and break the news to Biggerstaff as none of the deputies relished the task. Jailer Martin, Deputy Kleinschmidt and three newspapermen looked at each other, as if to say, "Will you do it?" "No, you do it."

At last it was decided that Deputy Kleinschmidt would have the dirty job but he insisted that the three reporters accompany him. As the four men slowly climbed the iron steps leading to the upper tier of cells, Biggerstaff was talking and laughing with William Gay and the two deathwatches. When they reached the grating in front of Biggerstaff's cell, Kleinschmidt didn't know how to break the news to the prisoner. Bill Gay reportedly looked up at the four men and he seemed to be able to read the news off of the solemn faces of the messengers standing outside of Biggerstaff's cells.

At that point Gay stopped talking and again glanced at each of the faces of the officers and then a peculiar expression came over his own face, which told plainly that he knew what was up. For the rest of the evening Bill Gay remained depressed and he sincerely felt sorry for Biggerstaff, as he was keenly aware that he was subject to the same fate. After several unsuccessful attempts of tactfully breaking the news to the prisoner, one of the reporters handed a copy of the "Helena Herald" to Deputy Kleinschmidt who in turn passed it through the bars to Biggerstaff. The newspaper was folded in such a way that the headline was displayed prominently and it read, "Biggerstaff Will Hang."

Without looking up at the men, Biggerstaff began to read the article and all eyes were on him expecting that he would show signs of weakness but instead of weakening he was cool and collected and without showing any uneasiness he only said that he had expected it. After just a few minutes he began talking to everyone about how he was never given a "fair show" and at 11:30 p.m. Biggerstaff asked his deathwatches, George Cressap and Joe Genzberg for a nightcap. After a drink of government whisky in his tin cup, the prisoner jokingly told his handlers to keep the rest on ice because he'd need some later. He then sat down at the little night stand in his cell and began playing cards with a newspaperman. While he spoke freely with the reporter, Biggerstaff paid close attention to his hand and displayed his great skill at the game of cribbage.

After winning eleven out of fifteen games with a newspaperman, Biggerstaff went to bed at two o'clock a.m. and fell right to sleep, snoring loudly and keeping many of the other inmates in cellblock awake. He woke up at six a.m. and the first thing he asked for was a big drink of whisky while he read the morning papers. He dressed him self with great care in a black suit, a soft black shirt and a necktie fastened with a plain gold ring. Breakfast was delivered at seven o'clock of ham and eggs, potatoes, coffee, bread and butter and fruit, the last meal being topped off with a large glass of whisky. As he was finishing the meal Father Day arrived to perform the last rites of the church and the priest stayed with him until the end.

The morning started out being cloudy and cold and by eight o'clock the crowd had gathered at the big stone jail on the hill, those with invitations including, Sheriff Jake L. DeHart and Undersheriff Sam Jackson of Sweet Grass County and Sheriff Sam Reynolds and Undersheriff Young of Silver Bow County. Also in town for the hanging were Sheriff Sid Willis of Teton County, Sheriff George A. Berky of Yellowstone County and Meagher County Sheriff W.H. McKnight.
A detachment of police arrived just before ten o'clock to secure the enclosure but they also admitted late arrivals, Cascade County Sheriff William R. Dwyer, Sheriff Baldwin of Flathead County, Sheriff White of Fergus County and Jefferson County Sheriff Alex Gilliam.

The gallows were given a last minute test and then at 9:30 Sheriff Jurgens stepped out onto the back steps and asked the crowd of witnesses if they were willing to act as deputies in case there was any trouble and the crowd cried out, "We will, Sheriff!" City Marshal McCann offered as many of his policemen as he could and Sheriff Jurgens placed four outside, one on each side of the jail yard and at least two assisted his deputies with controlling the crowd within the enclosure.

The jail yard was surrounded on three sides by an eighteen foot-stonewall and the fourth was blocked by the jail itself. The jail building blocked the view from the west and the execution couldn't even be observed from the clock steeple of the courthouse. The tall stonewalls effectively hid everything from the north and the east but on the south, the execution could be observed from the rooftops of the Episcopal parsonage and the residence of Mr. N.H. Webster and from a corner of his barn. Special policemen were assigned to prevent spectators from using those vantage points as well as gathering outside of those private residences.

The invited witnesses entered the jail yard through a heavy iron gate, which opened into the alley on the south side of the jail and as they entered the enclosure they saw the gallows in the northeast corner of the yard near the whitewashed stonewall. The top crossbar of the scaffold was almost as tall as the wall itself and to prevent the witnesses from crowding the gallows a heavy rope was strung over several two-by-four posts driven into the ground. Besides the barrier around the death machine, order was further maintain by a number of deputies and city policemen with Winchesters patrolling inside the rope fence. To the right of the gallows was a light frame covered by heavy canvas where Sheriff Jurgens and about six of his deputies were concealed so no one would know who actually pressed the lever that released the weight sending Biggerstaff to eternity.

Sheriff Jurgens received two hangman's ropes from a cord manufacturer in Philadelphia for the execution of both Biggerstaff and William Gay. The specialty firm sent one five-eighth inch, four-strand hemp for the heavier Biggerstaff and a half-inch rope for the smaller Gay. Both ropes came from the factory pre-stretched and worked until they were smooth and pliable. The rope passed through two pulleys on the crossbeam of the scaffold that were held in place by a wire, which drew their lower end nearer each other and allowed the smoothest possible movement of the noose. There was about two feet of slack in the rope as it passed down the inside of the right upright post of the scaffold to where the 470-pound weight was suspended.

As the hour of execution approached, the waiting crowd showed obvious signs of nervousness and at 9:45 Sheriff Jurgens climbed the iron steps leading to the balcony directly across from the condemned man's cell and read the death warrant, which ended with the words, "and you shall execute the sentence of this court between the hours of ten o'clock a.m. and two o'clock p.m." Biggerstaff absorbed every word and when the sheriff finished the reading he asked if the time had been set. The sheriff answered his prisoner with, "Yes, it will be just as soon as you are ready." The doomed man then told the sheriff that he was ready.

Sheriff Jurgens offered the man a drink of whisky and urged him to drink up. As the sheriff was about to leave, Biggerstaff said: "Whisky's all right, but I would rather have a beer." It was too late to request beer so Biggerstaff took his drink and then continued talking with Father Day as the big clock in the courthouse chimed ten o'clock. At six minutes past, Sheriff Jurgens and Undersheriff Hoss entered the man's cell with the shackles, which were leather straps with large black buckles. Biggerstaff stretched out a hand to Bill Gay, who was in his cell with Guard George Henry and said, "Well, Bill, I've got to say Good-Bye." Bill Gay became emotional as he shook the man's hand and he could hardly speak.

After that emotional farewell between the two condemned men, the march to the gallows began, with the sheriff and his undersheriff leading the way with a deputy on either side of the prisoner. The procession went down the stairs and then around to the rear of the jail with Biggerstaff needing no assistance even with his arms bound to his body. The prisoner walked directly to the scaffold, took his place on the board platform under the gallows and then he calmly gazed over the spectators.

In a normal voice Biggerstaff thanked the crowd for their kindness and he asked for their forgiveness; then he told them that he had forgiven everyone and announced that he was going home. When the man was finished Undersheriff Fred Hoss adjusted the strap around his feet. Noticing that the deputy was a bit nervous and shaking, Biggerstaff asked Father Victor Day who was praying, to put the black cap over his head.

Hanging of William Biggerstaff, 1896
Photo by J.P. Ball & Son: Montana Historical Society

Sheriff Jurgens adjusted the noose; there was a slight pause as the officer stepped behind the screen; a shudder ran through the spectators when the signal was given to the executioner behind the canvas. The weight fell with a thud and the body of William Biggerstaff bounded into the air about fourteen inches and then it fell back as the deputies removed the platform, which allowed the body to hang off the ground. The drop fell at precisely ten minutes after ten a.m. and after a twitching convulsion and eight and a half minutes Biggerstaff was pronounced dead by Drs. N. Salvall and Dogge.

After hanging for fifteen minutes, Undertaker Flaherty lowered the body into a black casket when the black cap was removed it was revealed that Biggerstaff's facial features weren't distorted in the least. The body was then taken to the morgue and the remains were buried the following day in Potter's Field. Sheriff Jurgens saved the rope that was used to hang Biggerstaff and used it to execute William Gay on June 8, 1896.

Postscript:
William Biggerstaff was the second man that Judge Henry Blake had sent to the gallows, having earlier ordered the death of Francois Robert to hang at Virginia City in October of 1878. The judge would also order the death of William Gay in June of 1896. Jurors C.G. Evans, Henry Schotte and Fred Sass that found Biggerstaff guilty also sat on the jury that convicted William Gay a month later.

Lead defense attorney, Colonel Cornelius B. Nolan eventually became the Montana State Attorney General and he was involved with the successful prosecution and execution of William Calder and Joseph Hurst in two separate cases in March of 1900. Lewis and Clark County Attorney R.R. Purcell assisted in successful prosecution of William Gay who was hanged in June 1896; successfully convicted Joseph Allen, executed in September of 1899. Then after leaving office Mr. Purcell helped to secure the release of the primary suspect in the Mob Lynching of James Brady at Helena in October of 1901.

June 8, 1896

William M. Gay

Other Names: George Leroy
Location and Gallows: When Bill Gay was hanged at Helena he became the eighth victim to die on ***Gallows No. (March 1887): "Galloping Gallows" No. Two***.
Description: Gay was about five foot, nine inches tall and weighed about 160 pounds. He was about fifty-three years old at the time of his execution and his dark mustache was turning gray. Although he was known for his piercing dark gray eyes, he never looked into a man's eyes while talking.
Crime: Murder of Meagher County Deputy James Macke on May 19, 1893, and he was involved earlier with the gunning down of Deputy William Rader on May 9.
Judge: Henry N. Blake
Prosecution: Meagher County Attorney A.C. Ghormley and assisted by Lewis and Clark County Attorney R.R. Purcell
Defense: Mr. Max Waterman of White Sulphur Springs, Lewis Penwell and Judge James M. Clements handled the defense during the trial in November of 1895, and Colonel W.F. Sanders was brought in to assist with the appeals
Sheriff: John Henry "Hy" Jurgens
Distinction: Although Deputy Sheriff Donald Dillingham was the first lawman killed in what later became Montana, William Gay was the first man legally hanged for the murder of a peace officer in the state.

Bill Gay was born in Wheeling, West Virginia on October 20, 1847, to a farmer and slaveholder. When he was four years old Gay's mother died and he moved with his father to Noble County, Ohio where they remained for seven years. The boy and his father later moved to Gentry County, Missouri, which Gay explained on the eve of his execution, as a move that was grounds enough to hang any man. After living in Missouri for seven years, Bill ran away from home and enlisted in the Union Army as a drummer boy with the Twenty-Fifth Missouri Volunteers, only to desert after six months complaining of hard treatment.

At Atchison, Kansas Bill Gay joined a wagon train led by Mart Bowler bound for Laramie, Wyoming where he had his first brush with the Sioux Indians at Plumb Creek. The Indians had just massacred a wagon train killing ten men; running off with one of the white girls while another woman escaped by hiding in the brush and being rescued by the Bowler train, which ran off the hostiles. In that Indian battle young Bill Gay was shot and slightly wounded in the chest and on his second trip out west, the Sioux attacked his wagon train on the way to Denver and the men were forced to abandon their wagons. The Indians killed two of the white men; one being shot the other burned to death by being placed in a pit and covered with a fire. The survivors of this engagement, which was later referred to as the Battle of Cottonwood Creek were forced to catch another train to Denver.

That fall Bill and John Nelson went into the mountains where they traded and lived among the Sioux. The following year after a short visit back to Missouri Gay traveled west again where he joined the Seventh Cavalry under Colonel Custer as a scout. Gay served with distinction in Kansas and Nebraska particularly at Sand Creek and Wichita. After serving with the Army for two years Bill took a herd of cattle from Aberdeen, Kansas to the Dakota Territory and became Dell Paxton's trail boss out of Omaha, Nebraska for two years before he began hauling mail from Spottail Agency to Fort Randell, Dakota.

In 1878, Bill traveled to Grand River where he helped to develop a coal field and then spent a few more years between there and Deadwood. Bill and his family came to Montana in 1889, and settled in Castle while his brother-in-law Harris "Harry" Gross moved into a cabin a short distance from the mining camp. Gay purchased land that was not only valuable for the mineral wealth but because it lay on the proposed route of the Montana Midland Railroad. It was the only piece of property that the Castle Land Company hadn't acquired and it was desired by many including Mr. N.E. Benson, owner of the "Castle Reporter" who reportedly spread rumors about Bill Gay and his brother-in-law having committed numerous robberies in the Castle area along with parts of northern Wyoming.

Finally charges were brought against Gay for incest of his daughter, Ella and he was brought before Judge Henry at White Sulphur Springs and when the charges were dropped Judge Henry criticized the men who had instigated the action. Over time Gay and Gross were both charged and later released for several other offenses and the authorities and so-called vigilance committees routinely searched their homes. When Mr. Benson's printing shop burned to the ground and other burglaries occurred in and around Castle, warrants were sworn out on April 4, 1893, for the arrest of Bill Gay and Harry Gross.

One of the most deadly manhunts in Montana history began when Harry Gross was arrested in Castle and was bound over on the various charges. Undersheriff Fred W. Lewis accompanied Gross out to his cabin where he was supposed to secure enough money for his bail. Bill Gay was at the cabin at the time and while Gross went into the house for the money Deputy Lewis remained outside where he had a clear view of both doors of the cabin.

After waiting several minutes for his prisoner to come out the officer entered the house and found that Gross had escaped with Gay through a side window and ran into the nearby timber behind the cabin. Nothing was heard of the fugitives for some time, but finally on April 26, 1893, the Meagher County authorities received word that the two men were seen hanging around the Gross Ranch, which was about six miles from Castle.

Undersheriff Lewis and two men rode up to the Gross Ranch where they found two men unloading hay about two hundred yards from the house. After riding down to the house the officers concealed themselves thinking that the fugitives would return to their cabin when they were finished with their work. Apparently the fugitives detected the posse at the house, and Gay and Gross hitched up their horses to another wagon and started down the creek away from the cabin.

Seeing their quarry escaping, Deputy Lewis ran out into the open and ordered the men to stop and throw up their hands at which Gay reportedly jumped off the wagon and started to use the spokes of a wheel to steady his Sharp's 45-120 caliber Buffalo Rifle. Just before he fired on the officers, Lewis quickly drew his revolver and fired at the wagon and several shots were exchanged between the posse and the outlaws before Gay and Gross escaped into the brush.

William Gay
"Helena Daily Herald" 6/8/1896

After that encounter the fugitives weren't seen or heard of until May 8, 1893, when Ed Westbrook ran into them while running down some of his missing horses. He later said that when he first came across the two men, Gay stepped off of his horse and pulled his big rifle on him. After that threatening gesture, Westbrook quickly turned and rode off but sometime later he again found the fugitives at a small cabin and on that meeting Westbrook was invited into their camp. Bill Gay and Gross offered Westbrook some coffee as they told him where they had seen his missing horses. The fugitives told the rancher that they were on the run and they were getting tired of their situation and that they would start killing their pursuers.

Bill Gay told Westbrook that the people of Castle and Meagher County in general had been hounding him and his family for a long time; taking shots at him several times; searching his house without warrants and he had received threatening letters signed with "3-7-77," the familiar mark of the Vigilantes. Finally Gay announced that he and Harry Gross would be at the Durst Ranch, which was about four or five miles from the Gross Ranch and if the authorities wanted them they could come out and get them there. As Westbrook was leaving, Gay told him that there weren't enough men in Meagher County to take him and Gross.

Ed Westbrook rode to Castle and informed the authorities where the outlaws could be found and a posse was quickly organized and a second group was formed at White Sulphur Springs. Although he and his wife were both quite ill at the time, ex-sheriff, and current Meagher County Deputy William Rader was urged to help lead the posse. The two posses met on May 9, at the Thompson Ranch, which was about a mile from the old Gross Ranch where two of the posse members, Deputy Sheriff William Rader and Constable Pete Westbrook (Ed's brother) were sent to check out the Gross Ranch.

At the ranch the two officers saw two men leaving the house and going into the brush where Westbrook and Rader trailed them for several miles until they reached a slight ridge above a willow-fringed creek. The deputy and constable dismounted and cautiously climbed to the summit of the ridge where they observed Gay and Gross standing next to the creek about a hundred yards away. Will Rader called out to the men, ordering them to throw up their hands and surrender but the two wanted men quickly jumped behind a large pile of fence post and a gunfight began.

After a short time, Rader again ordered the fugitives to surrender but there was no response and the deputy told Constable Westbrook to stay on the ridge while he made his way to a high point, which commanded a view of the outlaw's position. When next seen by Westbrook, Rader was climbing up the hill when Harry Gross suddenly came out of the brush about fifty yards behind the unexpected officer and shot him in the back with his rifle.

After hearing Rader cry out and watching him fall backwards, Westbrook quickly ran back to their horses and rode back to the Thompson Ranch for help. The full posse returned to the scene where they found the dead body of William Rader hidden in some brush about five hundred yards from where he had been shot but Gay and Gross had escaped during a terrible hailstorm. William Rader's funeral was held at his residence at White Sulphur Springs on May 11, 1893, and after Reverend Lenhart conducted the services there was a line of carriages a mile long to the cemetery. Acting Governor Alexander Botkin immediately placed a one hundred dollar reward each for the capture of the two killers.

On May 12, the authorities at Castle received a telephone call from the Musselshell stating that the wanted men were seen about eighty miles from where Rader was killed. It was learned that the fugitives had gone to the Fitzpatrick Ranch where they had breakfast on the twelfth and a large posse led by Meagher County Sheriff James J. O'Marr went in pursuit of the fugitives and they reached the Ralph Berry Ranch, which was about ten miles below the Fitzpatrick place and near present day Harlowton. At the ranch the posse learned that they had just missed the outlaws by only a few hours and one of the posse members rode ahead to locate the fugitives and he soon returned with word that Gay and Gross were camped on a horseshoe bend on the Musselshell River.

The scout reported that the two men were heavily armed and they were traveling with a packhorse and a dog. After noticing the dog tied up near the camp on the river, Sheriff O'Marr split his posse into two groups to cut off the outlaws' escape and then led the larger party to the river bottom. Undersheriff Lewis and Deputy James "William" Macke and George L. Williams of Martinsdale, who had been deputized by Sheriff O'Marr, went further down stream and then advanced along an old cattle trail to the river.

With Deputy Lewis leading the way through the willows, George Williams second and then Macke bringing up the rear the officers were about twenty yards apart when Williams and Macke reportedly heard a noise coming from the large stand of trees. Seeing that he had been discovered, Gay shot Macke in the hip and the bullet passed through the man's abdomen. Deputy Macke fell to the ground but he managed to return fire and as he did so Williams saw a man lying on the ground with a smoking rifle.

The two outlaws had each dug a rifle pit in the willows and it was Bill Gay who Williams saw with the smoking rifle after Macke went down. Williams tried to shoot the sniper, which he described as having black piercing eyes but his ancient needle gun kept misfiring. Undersheriff Lewis wasn't in a position where he could see the shooters but he began firing his weapon in the general direction that Williams was pointing his rifle in. Meanwhile the wounded Macke crawled into the brush and the gunshots had attracted the rest of the posse to the scene. Posse member, E.N. Edwards joined Macke in the brush where he remained with the injured man until the others arrived to take him out.

Realizing the danger of rushing straight into the brush after the armed fugitives, Sheriff O'Marr ordered that Deputy Macke be taken to the Berry Ranch in a wagon while the rest of the posse circled the area and the underbrush set on fire. While the sheriff and his men recovered the outlaws' saddles and horses along with their two rifles and gear, Bill Gay and Gross escaped the fire and gave the posse the slip during the night. Deputy Macke had known Bill Gay in the Black Hills and he also had dealings with the man at Castle so on his death bed he identified him positively as the man who had shot him along the river.

James Macke died from his wounds at the Berry Ranch on Friday, May 19, 1893, and it was reported that Sheriff O'Marr had later sworn over the graves of both William Rader and Macke that he would bring in the murderers of his brave deputies. The state had already offered one hundred dollars for the capture of the fugitives and Meagher County matched that amount plus the residents raised another four hundred making the total reward of six hundred dollars for the two men dead or alive.

The State of Montana eventually increased the reward for the two outlaws from one hundred to two hundred and fifty dollars and many of the citizens believed that Sheriff O'Marr and his posse had executed the murderers and they were cremated in the fire. The "Inter Mountain" later reported that many people of Butte had read between the lines of the official report and believed that the two outlaws were the kind of men that would never relinquish their horses and weapons without a fight to the death. The handling of the Bill Gay and Gross affair in 1893, clearly upset many of the residents of Meagher County and it most assuredly cost Sheriff O'Marr's his re-election and W.H. McNight defeated him in November of 1894.

While on the lamb there was always speculation concerning the whereabouts of the two murderers, some thought that Bill Gay and Gross would surely head for Deadwood, South Dakota where his murderous friends there would give them the same reception that they had given him after his short stay at Detroit Prison in the 1870's. In June of 1893, a man originally from Castle reported that he had spotted Bill Gay and Harry Gross in front of the Bozeman Post Office but when Gallatin County Sheriff White Caldwell and Sheriff Joe Haines from Madison

County investigated the lead they only ran across a couple innocent civilians, David Van Horn and Jim Howell.

Finally on December 17, 1894, Governor John E. Rickards received a letter from Justice of the Peace Jason Carrol of Needles, California reporting that William Gay had been arrested under the name of George Leroy as he was entering a blacksmith shop. The justice said that Gay believed that he would be lynched by a mob if he was returned to Meagher County and he had requested to be taken to Helena. Sheriff James O'Marr began his journey to bring Gay back to Montana by first going to Helena for the necessary requisition papers and while Governor Rickards was at Virginia City on business, his secretary Mr. Keith made out the papers and the sheriff met the Governor at Dillon for his signatures. Before taking custody of Bill Gay from Sheriff Frank Keyes of San Bernardino, County on December 24, 1894, Sheriff O'Marr first had to travel to Sacramento to get the necessary papers signed by the Governor of California. After all the paperwork was complete the Montana sheriff took his prisoner first to Albuquerque, New Mexico then on to Denver and two days later they arrived in White Sulphur Springs.

Shortly after his capture at Needles, California Gay reportedly made a full confession to Sheriff Keyes who he had known twelve years earlier in the Black Hills. On the way back to Montana William Gay told Sheriff O'Marr that after the gunfight on the Musselshell River where Macke was killed, he and Gross returned to their place at Castle by a roundabout way a week later. After obtaining needed supplies and assistance from their friends in Meagher County the fugitives split up, Gross going to Livingston while Gay rode to Butte where he sold his gun for five dollars. Jumping a southbound freight out of the mining city Gay went to Pocatello, Idaho where he met up again with his partner. The two men traveled together until they reached Ogden, Utah where they again separated and Gay said he never saw his partner again.

Gay said he knocked around the mining camps of Utah and Nevada until he heard about the rich strike in the Mojave Desert in southern California. He apparently got tied up with another partner in the Southwest and they got into trouble after a shootout at Vegas, Nevada and the pair had to separate. As Gay was on his way to the rich mines along the California-Nevada border, Sheriff Jason Roseborough of Vegas and Sheriff Keyes of Needles arrested him.

While temporarily housed at the Silver Bow County Jail at Butte, the prisoner had a number of callers including his son, William Gay Jr. who was a printer in the Mining City. Gay had sent for his son and while the young man at first had no desire to see his outlaw father his friends finally persuaded him to visit the jail. As young Bill Gay walked into the courthouse his father was in handcuffs and shackles while he was waiting to be taken to the depot. The two men shook hands with little emotion and they were engaged in small talk when Sheriff O'Marr interrupted them so they could get into a hack for the train station.

Gay's son was a highly thought off citizen of Butte who later said that he neither had love or respect for his father. He explained that his mother had died many years earlier and his father was a cruel man who had often beat him as a child. Eventually Gay and his son reconciled their differences and the younger man worked for his father's defense and helped write the man's memoirs.

Another visitor at the jail was one that Gay probably didn't care to see, a half-breed Indian by the name of "Little-Bear." It seems that the Indian was on his way to Blackfoot, Idaho when he heard that the notorious outlaw was locked up at the Butte jail and he wanted to make sure it was the William Gay that he knew of. After taking a look at the prisoner the Indian told the sheriff that if Gay beats the murder charge at Meagher County he was wanted in Idaho for raping a pretty young Indian by the name of "Little-Dove" two years earlier. "Little-Bear" told the authorities that before Gay had his way with the young girl he nearly beat her to death with his revolver until she gave into his demands. The Indian said that his sister, "Pretty-Eagle" was offering a fifty-dollar reward for the return of Gay and according to "Little-Bear," Gay had been one of George Custer's army scouts and he later gained a bad reputation for murdering several Indians and white men.

After he was taken to White Sulphur Springs there were rumors of a possible jailbreak by Gay with the help of his many outlaw friends and various groups of people across Montana as well as Needles, California and the Black Hills. These interested parties were concerned that the prisoner wouldn't get a fair trial or could possibly get lynched at White Sulphur Springs. At Judge Armstrong's first term of district court in September, Gay stated that he had no counsel or funds to hire any and the court appointed Max Waterman of White Sulphur and Lewis Penwell of Helena for his defense. When faced with difficulty in securing a jury in Meagher County, Judge Armstrong granted a motion for change venue and Gay was taken to Helena where he was arraigned before Judge Blake on September 24, 1895. When Judge Blake asked the prisoner how he pleaded after his attorney, Lewis Penwell had already entered an innocent plea for his client Gay startled the court by yelling out loud: "Yes sir, that's my plea!"

Finally after years of searching and waiting on the part of the Meagher County authorities and the constant eluding of capture of the fleeing fugitive whose head had large rewards, the trial of William Gay finally began on November 3, 1895, in Judge Henry Blake's court at Helena. In a crowded courtroom a jury was secured out of the regular panel without much trouble with only seven men being excused by the state, three by the defense and another three disqualified on the grounds that they didn't believe in capital punishment. The final selection of jurors included the following Lewis and Clark County residents:

E.A. Macrum (f)	Ulysses S. Jones	Henry Schotte[17]
Jerome D. Hayes	A.P. Dorrance	Louis C. Henry
C.G. Evans[18]	W.C. Hickey	George B. Child
E.C. Babcock	W.B. Thompson	Fred Sass[19]

(f) Foreman

Incidentally jurors, C.G. Evans, Henry Schotte and Fred Sass had also served on the jury that found William Biggerstaff guilty of first-degree murder only a month earlier. At the single attorneys' table directly in front of Judge Blake's bench sat Meagher County Attorney Ghormley, R.R. Purcell of Lewis and Clark County for the state, Lead Defense Attorney Max Waterman, Lewis Penwell and Judge J.M. Clements for the defense along with the defendant, Bill Gay. Mrs. Abernethy, Mary Drucet both of Castle attended the trial daily along with Gay's wife, his daughter and mother-in-law, Mrs. P. Gross. During the trial Bill Gay sat calmly and on occasion he would whisper to his attorneys and take notes during the testimony of the witnesses.

During the proceedings, testimony concerning the land dispute between the defendant and Mr. Benson and the Castle Land Company was ruled not allowed, which obviously placed Gay at a disadvantage. On the stand Justice of the Peace W.W. Parker of Castle read the records of the trial and conviction of Harry Gross for stealing certain goods, which had brought about the deadly affair when Deputy Lewis took the convict to his ranch for his bail money.

The defense opened its case by putting Gay on the stand and he was considered a good witness. The prosecution was unsuccessful in their attempt to mix the defendant up as he confidently told the court that it had been Harry Gross who shot both William Rader and James Macke. The witness told the court that he had arrived at Castle in 1890, and a year later he became involved in a lawsuit with Benson who was the editor of the local newspaper as well as a member of the powerful Republican Central Committee of Meagher County. Gay claimed that Mr. Benson used all of his wealth and power to destroy him and he had the defendant arrested for incest but he was released several weeks later when there was no proof of the charges.

The defendant then told the jury about a systematic process that certain parties of Castle and Meagher County had waged against himself and his family, explaining that his home had been broken into, that he had been shot at on sight by many residents and that when the various posses had approached and shot at him and Harry Gross he assumed that they were only violent mobs. The prosecution then recalled Henry Durst who testified that Bill Gay had said that he had recognized several of the posse members, which rebuffed the defendant's earlier statement that he thought they were an unknown mob of assassins. After being pressed by the prosecution on cross examination, Gay admitted that he had been convicted of second-degree manslaughter in the Black Hills and that he had served ten months in a prison in Michigan before the Governor of the Dakota Territory pardoned him.

The May 19, 1893, "Helena Daily Herald" reported that in 1878, Gay had murdered a young man by the name of Forbes who was still living with his family at Gayville, which was about two miles from Deadwood. Apparently Gay was married to a woman who enjoyed flirting with younger men and after young Forbes passed her a note Gay found it. Without saying a word the older man walked up to the boy and shot him in the head, killing him instantly. Gay was arrested, convicted and sent to Detroit Prison for three years but like many cutthroats and cold-blooded murderers he was pardoned after only serving a few months. The honest citizens of Deadwood were shocked when the local outlaws and horse thieves all welcomed convicted killer back to town with a brass band and a big party in the streets.

Soon afterwards Gay was involved in another shootout at Hay Creek some fifty miles from Deadwood and when the newspaper was about to run the story he reportedly threatened the publisher. Gay had been one of the old timers in the Black Hills, having arrived in 1865, and for that reason his activities had been tolerated. But even Deadwood tired of the outlaw's ways and he and Harry Gross ended up together at Dickinson, North Dakota where they began stealing horses and killing range stock. In 1889, they were ran out of North Dakota and they moved to Castle where they were accused of stealing goods and caching them in the mountains.

The defense then called other members of Gay's family including his wife and their thirteen-year-old daughter Maude. They both testified that Constable Pete Westbrook and about four other men had searched their home on April 24, 1893, while they held a gun to the head of Gay's wife and then left a threatening letter on the doorknob. Twenty-one-year-old William Gay Jr. of Butte, the defendant's son was called to testify to a conversation he had with Harry Gross at Livingston after the shootings. The young witness testified that Harry Gross had told him that he had shot Macke but the prosecution quickly objected sighting the statutes prohibiting conversations with co-conspirators for or against the defendant.

Probably the most important witness for the defense was Henry Durst, who was originally subpoenaed by the prosecution but under cross-examination he told the jury that he had met with the two outlaws after the deadly shooting on the Musselshell and Gross had told him that he and not Gay had shot James Macke. The witness continued by saying that Gross stated that he would have killed more of the posse if Gay hadn't interfered but when he was questioned by the prosecution Mr. Durst said that Bill Gay had also told him that "we" had shot Macke.

Many folks in the courtroom had come to listen to Meagher County Attorney Ghormley give his three-hour final argument because the young attorney had been born and raised in the county and he had a huge following. After final arguments on November 12, 1895, the case was turned over to the jury for deliberation at 12:50 and at 3:30 p.m. the jurors returned a first-degree murder verdict. Three formal ballots had been taken, the first two being eleven votes for hanging and one for second degree.

Before the verdict was read Bill Gay was brought into the courtroom handcuffed to Deputy Lewis and Sheriff Jurgens and the room was deathly silent as the jury entered. The defendant was totally confident that he was going to be acquitted and as the verdict was being read he had bent over to pick at a raveling from his trouser leg.

Immediately after the trial Gay said the verdict was the greatest surprise of his life and although he was surprised by the decision that doomed him to the gallows, he never displayed any sign of fear or nervousness. The convicted murderer was moved to the upper tier of the jail next to William Biggerstaff on "Death Row" who was hanged on April 6, 1896. The day before a small package of morphine was found in Gay's original cell and the authorities never did find out how it had been smuggled into the prisoner.

The Lewis and Clark County Courthouse was filled to its capacity on November 16, 1895, for the sentencing if William Gay with all available standing room was taken and the jury box was filled with attorneys as well as the jurors. The gallery was jammed with men and boys and many of the spectators were clearly disappointed at the sight of the defendant since he didn't match his reputation of being a dangerous looking desperado. All they saw was a little man whose tired eyes had long lost their well-known piercing appearance.

When Judge Blake began to speak the defendant stood with his hands clasped behind his back and he appeared to be perfectly cool and collected. When asked if he had anything to say, Gay said that he had intended to give a long speech and to swear before God that he was innocent, but upon the advice of his attorney he would say nothing. When defense attorney Judge J.M. Clements asked for a later sentencing in order to prepare for their client's appeal Judge Blake told him that it was his duty to sentence the defendant and at that point the judge sentenced Bill Gay to hang on the same day and time that William Biggerstaff was scheduled to be executed, on December 20, 1895.

On November 29, 1895, Lewis Penwell filed shocking affidavits charging gross misconduct of the jury and errors of the district court, which if proved would have certainly resulted in a new trial. In one affidavit, juror A.P. Dorrance claimed that one of the other jury members was saying that Bill Gay's oldest stepdaughter, Ella had died during childbirth or during an illegal abortion and that the defendant was the father of the unborn infant. Another affidavit was produced, which stated that Juror Fred Sass had told others about an alleged contract between Gay and his stepdaughter concerning her cover-up of the incest charges.

Another sworn affidavit filed was that of Judge J.M. Clements, which charged that while the court was in recess, members of the jury would mingle freely among the spectators without being admonished by the court not to converse with themselves or anyone else. Judge Clements charged that while the jury was scattered throughout the courtroom and hallways the jurors could not possibly help overhearing conversations about the case. He also claimed that juror Jerome Hayes was seen reading about the case in a Helena newspaper.

Even after the prosecution had presented counter affidavits like the one from Jerry Hayes who had denied reading a newspaper while serving as a juror and from Bailiff John Hudson, Deputy Kleinschmidt and Undersheriff Lewis who all swore that the jury wasn't allowed to talk with outsiders, there was a great deal of mixed feelings about the case.

The city of Butte took a particular interest in the Bill Gay case and they worked hard to secure a commutation of his sentence. The sentiment aroused was due to the fact that the condemned man had a son and a daughter living there who were well thought of and many of the residents at the Mining City believed that the state was hanging an innocent man. They noted that Undersheriff Lewis had practically admitted that he had fired the first shot in the skirmish at the Gross Ranch and it was said that Constable Peter Westbrook confirmed that the posse started the fight in which Deputy William Rader was killed.

The friends of Bill Gay explained that the fugitives had been hunted down like animals without due process until the "Battle of the Musselshell" as it was being called, where Deputy James Macke met his death. While Gay's supporters conceded that one of the men had certainly killed the two deputies, they didn't think it was right to hang a man on circumstantial evidence.

Thomas J. Fowlie swore in an affidavit that he was with James Macke after he had been shot and he said that the wounded man had said that if he lived he would never again meddle in other people's business, referring to Gay. One particular supporter was Mrs. Emma Lyons of Butte who at one time lived near Bill Gay's residence at Castle and she told the press that the defendant had killed a man in a fight while intoxicated but he had been accused of killing as many as nine men in his day. Mrs. Lyons said that Gay was cleared of the charge in a court of law but it cost him a small fortune.

Mrs. Lyons said that when Bill Gay first came to Castle he worked as a carpenter and he saved enough money to build himself a small house across from her home. Gay's seventeen-year-old daughter lived with him before he sent for his family and Mrs. Lyons reported that many of the evil-minded residents of Castle spread scandalous talk about the father and daughter. The man was arrested on suspicion of being the father of a child that his daughter was about to have but no evidence was ever presented and his daughter testified that the father of her child had left Castle before her father was arrested.

After the incident concerning his daughter, just about crime in the mining camp was blamed on Bill Gay. When a cabin caught fire, Gay was blamed for it and when a millinery shop was broken into and the goods stolen he was again the number one suspect. Mrs. Lyons said there was a lot of talk about lynching Bill Gay and a "white-cap band" of men had approached her husband before he died to help hang the man.

Mrs. Lyons explained that after Gay and Gross had escaped from the law, both of their families were arrested and taken to the jail at White Sulphur Springs. Besides having their house ransacked and burned to the ground the sixty-two-year-old and feeble Mrs. Gay was kept locked up in jail for a crime her husband and her brother-in-law were accused of committing. When she was finally released she and her family had no money or home to go to.

In mid-December of 1895, Bill Gay receive a supportive letter from an old friend he knew at Deadwood in 1876-1877, Postmaster

James H. Lynch of Butte and Colonel Wilbur F. Sanders agreed to assist in the appeals. The defense attorneys had gathered affidavits stating that Sheriff O'Marr in his zeal to capture the murderers of his friends and deputies had ordered his posse to shoot the fleeing outlaws on sight, in effect forcing Bill Gay and Harry Gross to act in self-defense.

All the hard work of his lawyers and friends had apparently paid off when on December 19, just fourteen hours from his execution, Governor Rickards granted Bill Gay a reprieve until January 22, 1896. The action taken by the Governor was necessary because the motion for a new trial couldn't have been submitted in time to prevent the execution.

During arguments for a new trial in Judge Blake's court, Gay's attorneys, Lewis Penwell and Wilbur F. Sanders entered an exception that the district court's instructions to the jury because they didn't include considerations for murder in the second degree or for manslaughter. Mr. Penwell had over twenty law books on his desk along with hundreds of pages of testimony and affidavits while the attorneys for the prosecution wanted the motion presented without arguments. Because the defense insisted on arguing the case the hearing couldn't be settled in time for a stay of execution so a reprieve was required. Although Governor Rickards at first refused to grant a reprieve, he finally approved it after consulting with both sides of the case. While his attorneys were rushing around on his behalf Gay sat coolly in his cell and took in the whole matter very philosophically.

As the lawyers were working to save their client's life, Sheriff Jurgens had started to prepare for the double execution of William Biggerstaff and Bill Gay on December 20. Every half hour or so the two prisoners on death row heard the dull thud of the weight falling as the gallows was being tested for their hanging. The ropes had been soaped and all the preparations were made to carry out the executions when Biggerstaff was granted his stay on December 17, and Gay was saved two days later. Before his reprieve was granted Gay had told the sheriff that he had been in tighter places than the one he was in.

During the first week of January of 1896, Sheriff Jurgens received a package by express mail containing two new ropes from a large cord manufacturer in Philadelphia. Apparently the firm had heard of the two pending hangings in Lewis and Clark County in Montana and they had sent the free thirty-foot ropes as an advertising ploy.

Since the county commissioners of Meagher County had refused to pay the extra expense of maintaining a deathwatch over Bill Gay after December 31, 1895, he was placed in his old cell on the lower tier where the jailers could watch him easier. He had been ill for the prior ten days having lost his appetite and his spirit. His cell was reportedly too dark to read in; he had received very few visitors and Gay told his guards that being locked up for over a year with nothing to do but think, think, think from morning to night was driving him crazy.

By the end of January of 1896, Judge Blake had explained his refusal for granting Gay a new trial in a lengthy statement by saying he concurred that Gay had committed no crime greater than manslaughter if he had immediately turned himself in after the shooting of Deputy Rader, but instead he traveled sixty miles and he mortally wounded James Macke. The court pointed out that while a member of the posse, Macke was an officer and he was not shot while attempting to arrest Gay but he was searching for the fugitives and was shot down in ambush.

After Judge Blake refused the defendant a new trial, Gay told the officers at the jail that he had expected that decision from the lower court and in an attempt to discredit and humiliate the cour Gay said, "The lower court was so small that you couldn't have seen it with a microscope." Gay's attorneys were able to stop his execution once again by filing an appeal with the Supreme Court with County Attorney Purcell and Clerk of Court A.C. Gormley

Biggerstaff was in a cell about thirty feet away from Gay's compartment and while Bill Gay had been given hope of getting a new trial the black convicted murderer took his predicament more philosophically and was certain of his death. Biggerstaff was described as being as "cheery as a light-hearted hobo in a free-for-all" and he said that he was comfortable; had plenty to eat and drink, so why worry? By then both men had turned to religion, while Biggerstaff had completely accepted the Catholic faith, Bill Gay had not gone that far yet, but it was said he wasn't swearing as much as he had earlier.

Gay received another unsolicited character reference from none other than Frank Conley, warden of the state penitentiary at Deer Lodge. While in Helena Warden Conley told reporters that he knew Bill Gay in the Black Hills and at the time he was considered a great man in that region. Conley recalled one cold winter when he was after a horse thief when he stopped at Gay's cabin at three in the morning. The warden said that Bill Gay not only let him into his cabin he also prepared him breakfast and furnished him a fresh horse. Conley explained that Gay was the type of man who would stand up for his rights and when pushed into a corner would certainly fight. The warden said that while he didn't know anything about Gay's present trouble, he credited the prisoner for the quick apprehension of the horse thief back in the Black Hills.

On March 23, 1896, the Supreme Court announced its fifty-six paged decision delivered by Associate Justice Hunt that the omission of jury instructions concerning second-degree murder and manslaughter were not prejudicial to the defendant and affirmed the judgment of the lower court in its denying of a new trial for Gay. In the opinion the high court stated that the resistance of Gay and Gross at their Ranch by firing at the officers was regarded as evidence of defendant's threat that "there weren't enough men in Meagher County to take him alive."

The killing of Deputy Rader was regarded by the high court as evidence of the deliberation and intent of Gay and Gross to resist arrest by shooting those who would attempt to take them into custody. The court said that it was evident that William Gay was determined to kill any man he saw first or who had seen him, and that James Macke was a victim and that Williams would have been if Gay hadn't missed him.

The Supreme Court stated that it considered Gay liable for arrest for resisting an officer at Castle, for resisting the posse at the Gross Ranch, for aiding in the killing of Rader, for stealing the fallen deputy's horse and for resisting arrest thereafter. The court continued by saying that it is evident that Gay saw and knew the law officers, and that, where a party was endeavoring to evade arrest and when ordered to submit himself deliberately aim a rifle at an officer, the necessity for the reading of a warrant is dispensed with. The Supreme Court said that the instructions by the lower court were carefully laid down concerning self-defense and justifiable homicide, and the jury rejected the theory of self-defense and found William Gay guilty of first-degree murder.

The decision of the high court was a terrible shock to Gay because he was sure that he would be granted a new trial. While his attorneys tried to cheer him up, nothing seemed to bring the man out of his shock and he was moved to a cell closer to Biggerstaff and a deathwatch was placed over him. Gay's outlook on life dimmed even further when fellow death row prisoner Biggerstaff failed to be saved by executive clemency and he was executed on April 6, 1896. In the meantime Colonel Sanders and Lewis Penwell began efforts to secure a commutation of sentence for their client but Governor Rickards had never before interfered with an execution.

Judge Blake's courtroom was once again crowded on the morning of April 10, for Gay's re-sentencing and when Undersheriff Hoss brought in the defendant he was seen nervously tapping on the arm of his hardwood chair while waiting for the judge. After court was in session Gay was conferring with Colonel Sanders and then he began looking over some papers that he had in his pocket. When he was asked if there were any legal reason why he shouldn't be sentenced he began reading from his notes about how he and his family had been persecuted by the people of Meagher County. Gay told the court that following the shooting of James Macke, County Attorney Powell Black had ordered Sheriff O'Marr to arrest his wife and daughters along with his sixty-five-year old mother-in-law for being accessory to the crime of larceny. At one point the townspeople were threatening to lynch the women in order to entice Gay and Gross to turn themselves in.

The defendant explained that his younger daughter and mother-in-law along with his wife and oldest daughter who were both sick, were thrown into the calaboose at Castle, which was filthy and full of vermin. Gay said that there were only a few dirty old quilts and the bare floor for his family to sleep on and the convicted murderer said that his sixteen-year-old daughter, Ella had died a few months later because of the experience. As Gay spoke his mouth twitched and his voice trembled and most of the people in the courtroom thought he would break down altogether.

Finally after a delay of about two minutes the defendant mustered up his feelings and he continued by telling the judge that after the townspeople ransacked their home they set it afire and they wouldn't let anyone fight the blaze. His family was later transferred to the county jail at White Sulphur Springs where they were kept for ten days until they were released because the cells were needed for several male prisoners. Gay's ten-year-old daughter, Maud was placed in the poor house until Mrs. Gay was cleared of any wrongdoing and was discharged.

When Gay was finished speaking Colonel Sanders arose and in his usual well-polished manner asked that the court give the defendant as much time as possible in order that his defense would have sufficient time to present the case before the Supreme Court of the United States. Judge Blake granted the request for more time than the normal thirty days and fixed the execution for May 25, which gave the defense forty-five days to prepare the appeal. Gay was obviously thankful for the additional time and when a friend commented on his chances of beating the wrap he said he was hoping for the best.

A transcript of Gay's case was sent to Washington D.C. and on Thursday, May 21, 1896, an application was made to Justice Harlan of the United States Supreme Court for a writ of error. Meantime the defense attorneys applied to the Governor for another respite to provide sufficient time for the justices of the highest court of the land to consider the case. As Governor Rickards was considering the request word came to Helena that Justice Harlan had refused to grant the writ, and the hope of Gay being saved by the United States Supreme Court was lost.

Even when the Supreme Court refused to hear the case, the Governor still granted a respite of two weeks so that he could consider the issue thoroughly himself. Meantime Gay's attorneys began preparing petitions and papers in order to try and get the other justices of the Supreme Court to grant the writ of error, but the other six members including Chief Justice Fuller refused to interfere with the Montana case.

Once again petitions were circulated by Gay's attorneys in Helena, Butte and in Meagher County asking for a commutation of sentence by Governor Rickards. The Governor had never before interfered with such a case and most observers felt it was unlikely that he would help Gay. One of the condemned man's strongest supporters was the famous western poet scout, J.W. "Captain Jack" Crawford of Omaha, Nebraska who wrote a letter to the "Anaconda Standard" asking for space in the paper to defend his old friend.

"Captain Jack" stated that twenty-two years earlier he knew Bill Gay as a pioneer in the Black Hills who was a generous and brave man who had risked his life several times to protect men, women and children from marauding hostile Indians. He said that Gay's cabin was a safe haven for many weary footsore travelers who received generous hospitality. Mr. Crawford had been assured by the sheriff of Lewis and Clark County and several other prominent people that the public sentiment was with Bill Gay and that there was too much justice in the great state of Montana to allow him to be executed so he didn't take as much interest in the case as he should have earlier.

Mr. Crawford wrote to the people of Montana so that they would support the petitions to the Governor and contribute to Bill Gay's defense fund. In all it was estimated that about four thousand people had signed petitions asking to save the life of William Gay.

Ten days after Biggerstaff was hanged, representatives of the Crow Indian Reservation including "Scolds-the-Bear" and his interpreter, Tom Laforge, and A.A. Campbell visited the Lewis and Clark County Jail accompanied by a reporter from the "Helena Daily Herald." "Scolds-the-Bear" was a prominent member of the Indian Police force of the reservation and he was eager to tour the county jail where in his words, "Where the man with black face that killed the other man with the black face lived," referring of course to William Biggerstaff. After Jailer Martin admitted the four men they had to log in for security reasons. While one of the white men wrote in the names of the Indians the Crows carefully looked over his shoulders with great interest.

After registering at the front desk the tour of the jail began with a visit to the cell of William Gay and the prisoner immediately stood up and greeted the Indians with a hearty handshake. Although Gay was able to converse in Sioux he wasn't able to speak to his guest in the Crow language but that certainly didn't lesson the Indian's curiosity or the prisoner's cordiality. The look on Gay's face was easily interpreted as saying that he wished he could go back with them to the mountains of the Reservation. As the tour proceeded down the iron stairs towards the corridor Tom Laforge and "Scolds-the-Bear" remarked that Gay was a nice man. They later entered the jail yard to visit the scaffold that was used to hang Biggerstaff and would soon be employed to execute their newfound friend, William Gay.

As Gay's execution date got closer and closer his attorneys were finding more and more people willing to speak up for their client. On May 25, George Densmore came forward and swore that two days after William Rader was killed he was in the telephone office at White Sulphur Springs when Meagher County Sheriff James O'Marr placed a call to his deputies on the Musselshell River searching for Gay and Gross. Densmore said that the sheriff told his men there was a hundred dollar reward for the fugitives, dead or alive, and the deader the better.

Mr. N.E. Benson, who was also in the office with the sheriff at the time, and after hearing the reward, immediately said that the community of Castle would throw in another hundred dollars and after hearing that pledge, the excited sheriff relayed the news to his deputy on the other line: "Two hundred dollars reward dead or alive, and the deader the better." Also on May 25, 1896, Daniel S. Riggs swore that on the night Gay's home was on fire armed men threatened him if he attempted to fight the blaze.

Mr. M.N. Hines swore that while he was a range rider in Meagher County he came across Bill Gay and Gross at their camp in the hills and he told them that Sheriff O'Marr had arrested their family, burned down their house and ordered his posse to shoot the fugitives on sight. Former

Sheriff James O'Marr went public and he stated that there was nobody in Meagher County by the name of M.N. Hines. and this generated a great deal of controversy and many citizens of the county reported that Mr. Hines existed including Burt Marsh of Castle who took the man's affidavit.

Hines had been a range rider for five or six different Musselshell cattle outfits including the "Two Dot," Wilson, Fitzpatrick and Sanford Moore. Clearly the former sheriff of Meagher County was caught with egg on his face after several residents confirmed that the officer had even been seen together with the man in question.

Having just experienced the large volumes of appeals concerning the Biggerstaff case two months earlier, Governor Rickards and his private secretary A.B. Keith again found themselves carefully reading and examining great piles of letters, affidavits, manuscripts and petitions containing thousands of signatures. The Governor's decision to either commute Gay's sentence or let his execution proceed got even more complicated when former sheriff James O'Marr wrote to the Governor and denied ever saying he wanted Gay and Gross dead or alive while many more citizens and even some of the deputies who participated in the posse including John Miller who swore that the sheriff told him not to let the two men surrender.

Finally at two o'clock on the afternoon of June 5, 1896, Governor Rickards pulled down his roll-top desk; picked up his broad-brimmed white hat and a few papers and told Mr. Keith that he would not interfere with the execution and then he walked out of his office. While the Governor was climbing into a waiting carriage Mr. Keith was telling a reporter of the "Helena Daily Herald" of the executive order.

The statement was only divulged to the newspaperman after he promised not to tell anyone else until it was published in the following day's issue of the paper. The extra precaution was taken because Bill Gay had said that he would never be hanged and the authorities were afraid that he would attempt suicide. As soon as Sheriff Jurgens received word of the Governor's decision he quickly ordered Gay to undress and to take a bath while the guards made arrangements to place him in a new cell.

The prisoner's clothes were not returned to him and while he was being outfitted in a new outfit he asked why he was being put into a new cell. Without telling Gay that they wanted to eliminate any chance of him taking any drugs that he may have stashed in his old cell, the guards told the prisoner that the new quarters were larger and would be more comfortable. Gay was happy that the cell had a nice window from which he could once again stare upon the mountains, knowing that his days were numbered.

After considering the history of his case, Gay later told a "Helena Independent" reporter that the biggest mistake he had made was to push for the change of venue to Lewis and Clark County where he had no friends. He said that he would have received more support in Meagher County and he pointed out that by the time his trial took place the citizens had begun to believe he had been persecuted.

When Gay told his daughter Maud farewell for the last time on the eve of his execution he told her to never come back to Montana because he considered it a land of "stranglers." He asked her to keep all of the affidavits and petitions that had been presented to the Governor in his behalf and she apparently took them with her when she boarded the morning train for Salt Lake.

Mr. William A. Boots of Great Falls presented one of the most extraordinary letters in behalf of the doomed man to Governor Rickards, which was delivered only days before the hanging of Gay. In his letter Mr. Boots explained that he ran a pharmacy in Great Falls and that he had owned a similar business at Castle during the Gay trouble. Boots said that he wasn't a friend of William Gay but that he only had made his acquaintance. One night in the spring of 1892, Mr. Boots attended a meeting of the citizens of Castle for the purpose of discussing the question as to whether or not Gay should be hung on account of his reputed intimacy with his stepdaughter. At the meeting it was advocated by several parties that they immediately go to his house and lynch him and some of the men had even brought a rope to the meeting for the job.

Although Mr. Boots was new to the mining camp and wasn't familiar with the case, he stepped forward and strenuously opposed the mob action and insisted that Gay be given a chance to defend himself in a court of law. The majority of men at the meeting objected because no one wanted to sign the complaint against Gay and then, in an attempt to quiet the mob, Mr. Boots offered to sign the complaint himself if the others would dispense. The mob broke up and Mr. Boots was obliged to sign the complaint along with seventeen other men of the mining community. A thorough court hearing was held and there was no evidence found against Bill Gay and after the trial Judge Henry lectured those who had brought the charges against the defendant from his bench. After his acquittal Gay brought a five thousand dollar damage suit against the citizens of Castle who had caused his arrest.

Mr. Boots wrote that he and others weren't included in the lawsuit, as he had signed the complaint against Gay for the purpose of saving him from being a victim of mob violence. The citizens of Castle became incensed, and their hatred for Gay intensified until Mr. Boots sent word to him warning him to leave the county. The community turned against the pharmacist as well and he was warned to remain in his house on the night that the community burned Gay's home to the ground. Feelings ran so high against Mr. Boots that he apparently was forced to move to Great Falls. Obviously Mr. Boots' letter didn't have the desired effect of saving Bill Gay from the gallows, but it illustrated the character of the Great Falls pharmacist.

During his last day on earth Bill Gay was cool and collected and most people at the jail said that no one would have thought he was about to be hanged. In the early part of the evening the prisoner spent in quiet conversation with his close friends his lawyers and a reporter from the "Helena Daily Herald." While his thoughts were undoubtedly on his impending doom, Gay took pains in recounting little incidents of his past life that his listeners found entertaining if not interesting. During those few hours Gay reportedly reviewed his whole life from his early childhood to his present predicament and the only sign that Gay was nervous was his frequent blinking of his eyes and the constant running his fingers of his left hand through his scarce hair.

Reverend Father Van Clarenbeek visited with Gay earlier and the prisoner listened attentively and bowed respectfully as his spiritual counselor prayed for his soul. Later County Attorney Purcell called on the prisoner at Gay's request and they talked for about an hour. Gay next greeted his attorneys and a "Helena Herald" reporter warmly but he refused to see a representative of the "Independent" saying that particular paper had treated him unfairly. He had also refused to see Meagher County Sheriff McKnight earlier that day and the prisoner asked the "Herald" reporter to publish his thanks to Colonel Sanders for all that he had done.

Gay said that while he appreciated what Mr. Clements and Penwell had done, he felt that if Mr. Sanders had represented him from the start things might have been different. The condemned man also had praise for his keeper, Sheriff Jurgens, for being kind and considerate. The sheriff did everything in his power to make Gay's time in the county jail as pleasant as possible and the prisoner said that if there had been such a good and fair officer in Meagher County a few years earlier he wouldn't be facing the gallows today.

When Colonel Sanders arrived at the jail Gay asked him if there was any news from the Governor's office and the attorney said no, but added that most of the people in town wished that this wasn't going on. "So do I" said Gay and then he told the Colonel that he had sent the manuscript of the book of his life that he had been working on to his son, William Jr. and said he was sorry he wasn't able to finish it. Gay said that unfortunately he had lots of things on his mind for the last two months and he held his first attorney, Max Waterman mostly to blame. He explained to Mr. Sanders that Waterman had refused to subpoena Sam Allbaugh and John Bacon as character witnesses but his biggest regret was not leaving his family with some security.

Late on Gay's last night his daughter, Maude called on her father and the last meeting between father and daughter was described as being very touching and there wasn't a dry eye among even the most hardened deputies. Maude had worked tirelessly to save her father and her farewell was very difficult for them both. The time seemed to fly by as Gay listened to the striking of the big courthouse clock in the steeple, each strike meaning less time to live. The prisoner hadn't eaten anything for two days but at about eleven o'clock on his last evening he asked the sheriff for some coffee.

As the new dawn was breaking Gay was still sitting in his chair and with the morning sun he listened hard for the sorrow notes of a robin knowing well that it was his last day and he would never again behold another rising sun. After midnight Gay completely broke down and the officers didn't think he would be able to walk to the gallows. The man's eyes were bloodshot, his hair was matted down and great drops of perspiration were beading on his forehead. This was not the William Gay that had stood up so defiantly before the law and his prosecutors, but a weakened not yet broken man.

Gay was watched closely all night long by his deathwatch along with additional deputies that had been assigned to remain at the jail in case they were needed. Sheriff Jurgens had taken every precaution to keep his prisoner safe so that his sentence could be carried out as the court had ordered it. The sun rose in a cloudless sky over Helena and its warmth and glow renewed the life of the outdoors. About nine o'clock the skies became cloudy and a light rain began to fall as if tears of sorrow. As the march to the gallows began the sun reportedly reappeared but as if a freak of nature, when the noose was adjusted about the man's neck it disappeared behind a big cloud.

As Sheriff Jurgens climbed the stairs from his office up to the second floor near the women's department the great clock in the tower solemnly struck off ten o'clock. When he reached Gay's cell the prisoner was stretched out on his cot having totally collapsed from nervousness and malnutrition. Although he hadn't tried to starve himself his nervous stomach was unable to hold anything but liquids. In the cell sat Father Van Clarenbeek soothing the feverish brow of the semi-conscious Gay, and speaking reassuring words to him.

The sheriff removed his broad-brimmed hat as he entered the cell and he said that he had a legal document that he was required to read to the prisoner. There was no response from the prisoner who was twisting and turning on the cot but the sheriff began reading the death warrant anyway. While the sheriff read the warrant the Catholic priest stepped from the cell and into another room where he put on his large black robe. As the priest left the cell Dr. Charles B. Miller took his place on the chair at the head of Gay's cot and took the prisoner's left hand.

When a reporter asked Father Van Clarenbeek if the prisoner had made a confession he said that he had and that Gay was all right. According to the priest Gay had made peace with God but the reporter said that he had meant if he had confessed to the crime. Father Van Clarenbeek told the man that Mr. Gay had become a Catholic and that he was baptized the day before and he wasn't in any position to make a statement about the prisoner. Meanwhile Sheriff Jurgens finished reading the death warrant and he asked Gay to get up and get dressed so that they could carry out the instructions of the court. The condemned man didn't move an inch and it appeared as though he would have to be carried to the scaffold.

The sheriff went to his office where he asked Drs. Carmichael and N. Salvall to assist Dr. Miller to brace up the prisoner so that they could avoid having to carry him to the scaffold. The physicians entered Gay's cell where they injected him with some medication just below his elbow and it didn't take long for the drug to take affect and Gay was able to sit up on his bunk. While sitting in his cell Gay presented a pitiful sight, which touched the other men deeply. His hair was messed up, he had a compress bandaged around his head to control his fever and all of his limbs trembled like a leaf.

The man was helped to a chair in the corridor where he was dressed in a black suit, vest and slippers while Gay was saying that he wanted to make a statement but he couldn't because he was too sick. By the time he was completely dressed including his brown Fedora hat he was demanding to make his statement but the sheriff told him that the doctors thought it best that he not expend his energy by speaking. Gay insisted however, and he was given the opportunity to write down what he had wanted to say and he turned the statement over to Colonel Sanders for safekeeping. As he began speaking with his attorney about the statement the others gathered around the two men until Gay asked them for some privacy.

Minutes later Gay asked if his daughter, Maude was there, and he was told that she had already gone. At that point Dr. Salvail administered another injection into Gay's arm and the prisoner took a sip of whisky. The prisoner asked Sheriff Jurgens to delay the execution until one o'clock in order for him to do some more writing but the sheriff denied the request and when Father VanClarenbeek began to plead with the officer, Gay interceded by saying it was his own fault for neglecting to write when he had the opportunity. Gay then pleaded for a short time more to straighten himself up and to finish his affairs with his attorney.

Once again the sheriff refused to grant any delay in the execution and this time Colonel Sanders asked the officer for only one more hour and Gay asked the sheriff to telephone Governor Rickards so that he could speak to him personally for five minutes. The sheriff told the prisoner that if he were trying to get more time it wouldn't work and he probably couldn't locate the Governor anyway. Sheriff Jurgens finally agreed to compromise with the doomed man and gave Colonel Sanders five minutes to try and contact the Governor.

While Colonel Sanders was gone Gay continued to write his letters and he was still busy when his attorney returned. When the prisoner asked his attorney what the Governor had said, Sanders told him that he hadn't telephoned but he had gone to see him personally. Mr. Sanders reported sadly that the top executive said he would not come to the jail or speak with the doomed man. After the unfortunate news Gay continued to write when he noticed a dime on the table and he paused and asked the sheriff it was his. When Sheriff Jurgens said it must be the prisoner's, Gay picked it up and as he handed to his lawyer he said it was his fee. The joke seemed to really please Gay and he had a little chuckle.

When Gay finished his manuscript he handed it over to the sheriff with instructions for it to be given to his son and then presented his final statement to a reporter from the "Helena Herald." At that point Gay announced that he was ready and the march to the scaffold began. Although he was still very weak, Gay refused assistance but he had to hold onto the handrail and the iron grating as he went down the stairs within the jail. Sheriff Jurgens took the lead, next came the priest and then Gay followed by Deputies Fred Hoss and Marten who were supporting the prisoner. Following the main group were several newspapermen, the doctors and a few other civilians.

The deputies had to assist the prisoner as the procession went up and down the short pair of steps, which led to the jail yard and finally the solemn march ended under the fatal noose, which Gay glanced at and then looked away. To the condemned man's right stood Father Van Clarenbeek and Sheriff Jurgens was on his left as the crowd of witnesses stood around with their heads mostly uncovered. Kootenai County Sheriff William Ryan of Idaho stepped up and shook Gay's hand warmly as the two men had been good friends and had been in more than one skirmish with hostile Indians together.

The sheriff asked the doomed man if he wanted to address to the crowd and after several attempts Gay cleared his voice and began to speak in a hoarse and husky voice. He began to protest his innocence and when he displayed his bitterness with the use of profane language the sheriff tried to interrupt him several times but he wouldn't stop until Sheriff Ryan finally asked his old friend to cut it short. The straps were quickly placed on Gay, his hands bound to his sides, then his arms and then his feet. Finally when the final strap was placed around his knees the black cap was pulled down over Gay's face but then he asked to have the hood pulled up for another minute.

After saying he thought it was wrong that he be hung like a dog, Gay asked that the mask be kept up so that he could continue to watch the morning sun. Sheriff Jurgens granted the request and then he adjusted the noose, carefully pulling the knot snug and under Gay's left ear. As the clock in the courthouse tower began to slowly strike eleven the sheriff stepped back; raised his hat and before the crowd had complied with the officer's order to remove their hats the ground trembled from the shock of the dropping weight. As the clock struck its eighth stroke of eleven Gay's body shot up into the air about a foot and then settled back under the scaffold where it remained suspended in the air.

Drs. Salvail and Dogge, the attending physicians stepped forward at once and grasped the wrists of the man and felt for the pulse of Gay's heart. The only visible signs of movement were the contractions of the muscles in the back and Gay's chest as the air escaped from the lungs for the last time. Seven minutes and twenty seconds after the weight had dropped, the doctors pronounced William Gay dead. When the weight was raised and there was slack in the rope, the body was cut down and it was removed to the Flaherty's Undertakers on Broadway where a large crowd later viewed the remains.

Among the visiting sheriffs from around the state were Missoula County Sheriff H.W. McLaughlin and his deputy, T.H. Corbett; White Caldwell of Gallatin County; G.B. McLaughlin of Chouteau County; Meagher County Sheriff W.H. McKnight, Cascade County Sheriff William R. Dwyer and Sheriff George T. Young of Livingston. After the hanging of Gay the rope was reportedly cut up into pieces by the witnesses for souvenirs as a chunk of it was later seen in Park County Sheriff Young's office in 1897.

Postscript:
William Gay was the third and last man that Judge Blake had sentenced to death having already ordered the legal execution of Francois Robert at Virginia City in October of 1878, and William Biggerstaff at Helena in April of 1896. Auxiliary Sheriff Deputy George Williams who missed his chance at killing Bill Gay on the Musselshell because of a miss-firing rifle, later became the undersheriff of Meagher County and he helped arrest Herbert Metzger who was hanged in May of 1905.

Harry Gross was eventually located at St. Louis, Missouri where he was working on the St. Charles Bridge but when two deputies approached him he suddenly pulled two guns; ordered them back and escaped into the underbrush at the rivers edge. he was never captured nor was he ever heard of again.

Defense attorney, James M. Clements later conducted the unsuccessful defense of Joseph Allen who was hanged in September of 1899, and he eventually became a district judge and presided over the trials of James Fleming and Clinton Dotson at Deer Lodge. Fleming was hanged in September of 1901, and Dotson was executed in April of 1902. Prosecuting Attorney R.R. Purcell successfully convicted Joseph Allen of first-degree murder and then while out of office in 1901, he helped secure the release of the leading suspect in the Mob Lynching of James Brady that October.

One man obviously absent at the execution of William Gay was one of Sheriff Jurgen's top men, Deputy Theodore E. Kleinschmidt who was on his honeymoon in Alaska. Five days before the scheduled execution date Sheriff Jurgens gave his daughter, Miss Frances A. Jurgens away to the popular deputy. While some folks claim the wedding was performed at the county jail, the June 4, 1896, issue of the "Helena Daily Herald" reported that the ceremony was conducted at the Episcopal Church on Warren Street but the couple left from the courthouse where the reception was probably held at the county jail.

January 27, 1899
Thomas Salmon

Location and Gallows: The execution of Thomas Salmon took place in the yard of the old stone jailhouse, which stood where the Carbon County High School stands at Red Lodge. Salmon was the second man hanged from ***Gallows No. Eleven: (July 1894): "Galloping Gallows" No. Four.***

Crime: Murder of Superintendent William O'Connor on September 10, 1898.

Judge: Frank Henry

Prosecution: County Attorney Ludlow B. Reno

Defense: George N. Bailey and L.O. Caswell

Sheriff: John Dunn

Distinction: Tom Salmon was the only man hanged in Carbon County.

According to one of his final statements, Thomas Salmon came to Montana in 1883, where he first went to work in the mines at Timberline. Eventually he became involved with the Knights of Labor and in 1888, he was traveling the mining camps recruiting and raising funds for the union. The executive board sent Salmon to the state of Washington where he worked at several locations and he organized several others. By 1890 he was vice-president of the Miners and Mine Laborers Protective Association in Canada where his top priority was preventing Chinese labor in the mines of British Columbia.

While in British Columbia, Salmon was hospitalized with rheumatism and he moved to Red Lodge in May of 1892, because of the dryer atmosphere. He found work in the mines of the Rocky Fork Coal Company but he avoided union activity until 1897, when he helped organize the Accident Benefit Fund and was its chairman for nine months. In January of 1898, Salmon helped organize the workers of the company and he was elected its first president. He was the president of the union when a strike was called in June of 1899, which lasted for a few weeks before the men finally broke ranks and returned to work. According to Salmon the strike was called after a secret vote of the membership that he had not authorized.

Superintendent O'Connor was back east when the strike was called and upon his return to Red Lodge he accused Salmon of ordering the work stoppage. Superintendent O'Connor settled the disagreement and the miners went back to work but when Salmon reported to Martin Woods, the pit boss of the mine he was ordered to report to the superintendent. Salmon claimed that when he went to O'Connor asking for work the superintendent told him that he didn't want to work but wanted a fight. O'Connor accused Salmon of being dirty and the instigator of the strike and therefore he wasn't welcome at the mine.

Without a job at the mine Salmon lost his position as president of the union but he was eventually elected as the president of the new co-operative store, which was started by the workers. After a couple of months he got an entry-level job at the mine but he reportedly lost that job after just one month because of absenteeism. According to Salmon the two times that he had missed work it was for official union business. On the morning of September 10, 1898, Salmon walked up to O'Connor who was standing in the doorway of the mining office and demanded to know why he was discharged from the company. Salmon claimed that the superintendent told him that he was fired because the foreman had reported his poor performance on the job.

After the conversation Salmon pulled out a Derringer pistol and shot Mr. O'Connor in the body and then the assassin went straight to the courthouse and surrendered himself to Sheriff John Dunn. By the next morning O'Connor's friends had begun talking about lynching the man and the sheriff and Deputy Mike J. Kerrigan quickly secured a team and buckboard and drove the prisoner the twenty-eight miles to Joliet where they obtained a fresh team and with the help of Sam Oliver who hid the lathered horses they headed for Billings. Minutes later a group of riders arrived at Joliet looking for the sheriff and Salmon, but not finding the used up horses they decided that they had gone to Columbus.

The defense tried to secure a change of venue but the Salmon trial opened on December 7, 1898, in the general store of J.H. Conrad, which was serving as the courthouse at Red Lodge at the time. County Attorney Ludlow Reno who had served with General Sherman on his march to the Atlantic had an easy case to prove and while on the stand in his own defense, Salmon reportedly convicted himself while under cross-examination. The defendant first said that the killing of O'Connor was in self defense, but under cross he admitted that he had borrowed a gun just two hours before the shooting for the express purpose of demanding an explanation for his recent discharge from the company.

On the second day of the trial the jury reportedly reached a decision immediately after they had retired but for appearance sake they waited for almost two hours before announcing their verdict. When Clerk of the Court J.E. Mushbach announced the first-degree murder verdict, Salmon took the decision with the same demeanor he had shown throughout the trial. Salmon had been resigned to his fate since the union had forsaken him and he even told his attorney that there would be no use in applying for a new trial or appealing to the Supreme Court.

The preparations for the execution were made during the third week of January of 1899, with the construction of a high board fence on the east end of the jail yard and the erection of the scaffold. A complete description of this scaffold or any other can be found in Chapter Seven: "Montana Gallows." By the time construction had begun on the gallows, Sheriff Dunn had already ordered the hangman's rope for the hanging from St. Louis and it was prepared and tested when it arrived.

After eating a hearty supper Salmon took a bath and went to bed at eight p.m. and he was sound asleep by eleven o'clock. The prisoner woke up at five a.m. on Friday, January 27, and he dressed himself in a light gray cutaway suit, white shirt, collar and cuffs, satin necktie and black leather slippers. When asked by Sheriff Dunn what he wanted for his last breakfast, Salmon said that he wasn't particular. After eating a breakfast of beefsteak, eggs, boiled rice, baked apples and coffee, Salmon laughed and joked with his deathwatches, Harry Cain and Thomas Donohue and then visited with friends and a reporter. The prisoner then handed his watch to Jimmy Dick with instructions to sell it and send the funds to his friends back in Illinois.

Salmon turned to Sheriff Dunn and announced, "Mr. Dunn, I am at your service at any time, and if 7:30 is the hour fixed I do not wish to delay your arrangements in the least." Since the weather was cold that January morning, the condemned man asked that the execution come off as quickly as possible so that people wouldn't think he was trembling because of cowardice. While the sheriff went to the courthouse for the straps, Salmon preached his own funeral sermon, since he was an admitted atheist and didn't see a priest.

As the hour of execution arrived a very large crowd had gathered about the courthouse and one report stated that every miner in Red Lodge turned out to see that nothing interfered with the execution and the nearly two thousand miners and their wives and children crashed into the enclosure and clustered around the gallows. Salmon stood calmly as the sheriff, Undersheriff Kerrigan and Deputy Dick Hiaks were adjusting the straps. While the other officers were buckling the heavy strap around Salmon's waist and the small straps to the wrists, the sheriff explained to the prisoner that the straps for his feet would be secured on the scaffold.

It was said that no man had ever faced death more fearlessly or with as much nerve as Tom Salmon who ran up the steps of the gallows ahead of the officers to take his place facing east on the scaffold. As the officers were buckling the straps around his feet, the condemned man looked up to see that he was directly under the beam and the hangman's noose. Sheriff Dunn placed the black cap over his head, and then drew the noose about his neck placing the large knot behind his left ear.

Before the crowd realized the sheriff's movements, he had pushed the lever springing the trap and Thomas Salmon's body dropped six feet three inches. Drs. McClanahan and Kelly of Red Lodge and Dr. Allen of Joliet stepped forward and checked the pulse, and pronounced the man dead after twelve minutes. After dangling for about fifteen minutes longer the body was finally cut down and placed in a coffin and it was interred in Potter's Field without services.

Salmon had gained about ten pounds since he was returned from Billings and he probably tipped the scales at about one hundred and seventy pounds on the day of his hanging and he had always told his guards that he was going to be a good meal for the worms after he was dead. After the hanging, the wooden scaffold was dismantled and it remained a pile of lumber for many months in the county jail yard.

Postscript:

Although Tom Salmon had no family in Red Lodge, it was rumored that he was in love with the superintendent's wife, Katie O'Connor and for several months some unknown person tended to his grave in the potter's field on the bench over looking the town.

September 14, 1899
Joseph H. Allen

Location and Gallows: When Joe Allen was hanged in the jail yard at Helena he became the ninth victim of ***Gallows No. Eight: (March 1887): "Galloping Gallows No. Two***.

Description: Allen was a twenty-one-year-old handsome, stoical quarter-breed Indian who was born on June 7, 1878. Although he had Indian blood, the casual observer may not have suspected it. While he had brown eyes and his hair was straight, it wasn't as black as the typical Indian. The five feet, nine inch tall, 155-pound young man had high cheekbones and dark complexion like an Indian's but his conversation was that of an ordinary white American lad of the day.

Crime: Murder of Jess S. Reynolds on the Keller Ranch on July 23, 1898.

Judge: Henry C. Smith

Prosecution: County Attorney R.R. Purcell

Defense: Judge James M. Clements

Sheriff: Thomas J. Davidson

Distinctions: This was last legal execution of Lewis and Clark County although the last hanging in the county was the Mob Lynching of James Edward Brady on October 2, 1901, for the brutal assault of a little girl in Helena.

Joseph Allen was either the victim of circumstances, or a criminal of extraordinary purpose and ability. His case was such that there was no gray area; either he was innocent of the crime, or he was a murderer who assassinated his victim for a paltry sum or to satisfy a lingering hatred.

Joseph Allen
"Anaconda Standard" 9/12/1899

Allen was born just two miles from Oakland, Oregon to a poor laborer and his half-breed wife. He was the oldest of seven children, six boys and one girl, and from his earliest childhood he knew nothing but poverty. After his first eighteen years in Oregon, Allen and his family moved to Shoup, Idaho where he was a mail carrier through the mountains through the North Fork of the Salmon River during the winter of 1896-97. It was in this Idaho community that Allen first met Jess S. Reynolds while they worked together at a mining camp.

Against his mother's wishes, Allen left Shoup, Idaho with his new friend and partner on June 1, 1898, to work their way to a fortune in the Klondike. The men first traveled to Salmon, Idaho and then to Montana, where Reynolds had sheared sheep for a number of years. The older man and his young helper found work in Lewis and Clark and Teton Counties for William Gillette, O.G. Cooper, Edmund A. LaRock and William W. Martin. After working on the Martin Ranch, which was four miles west of

Mitchell's at the head of the Wolf Creek Canyon, Mr. Martin wrote them a check on July 23, 1898, for twenty-six dollars and fifty-eight cents and made it out to J.S. Reynolds.

While camping on the Martin Ranch some of their horses had wandered off and they road double as they traveled through Emil D. Keller's property in search of the missing animals. The two men stopped at the Keller Ranch and asked the owner for permission to camp on the property. That evening they camped at the base of a high hill about three-quarters of a mile above the Keller residence where Stephen Arnold, who was employed by Mr. Keller, noticed the men's camp on his way home Sunday evening and before he came in sight of the men, he overheard them in a heated argument.

From the conversation, Mr. Arnold had gathered that the men had lost some of their horses, and Reynolds was blaming Allen for letting the animals escape. As the man approached the camp the two men stopped their quarrel and began talking about the weather. Mr. Arnold offered the men a warm bed at his cabin but Reynolds declined. About 8:30 the next morning Arnold was driving some of Mr. Keller's cattle to the upper end of the property and on his way to Sheep Creek he past the camp that he had visited the evening before. The man noticed a hat lying near the fence and as he was dismounting he recognized it as the hat Reynolds was wearing the night before. As he picked it up he was startled when he saw it splattered with blood and brain fragments.

Arnold didn't see anyone as he approached the camp but he found the campfire still smoldering; the matted down grass where the blankets had been and at the head of one of the beds was a pool of clotted blood and more brain matter. Following a blood trail, Arnold went into a thicket about forty feet where he found the body of Reynolds. The gruesome corpse was wrapped with two blankets and a gunnysack was covering the man's badly crushed head.

Mr. Arnold quickly rode to the Keller Ranch and reported the murder to his employer and the two men returned to the scene to search the brush. They surmised that the victim had been shot in the head with a heavy caliber weapon at close range, as there was powder burns in the scalp. The body had been stripped of a pair of blue trousers, their horse was gone and the camp had been quickly abandoned. Arnold and Keller knew that the two men had a complete camping outfit stored at the Martin Ranch and that they were only carrying a few essential items with them while they were looking for their lost horses.

As the men were searching the brush near the camp they found the camping items, which had been hurriedly tossed into the thicket by the murderer including a blood-soaked sack of flour. After their search they rode to M.A. Mitchell's ranch and from there they notified Sheriff Thomas J. Davidson, who in turn contacted twenty-six-year-old Coroner Ben C. Brooke[20] and County Attorney Purcell. The County Attorney along with Deputy Ed Andrews, Dr. Brooke Jr. and County Stenographer James Deering left Helena on the noon train for Mitchell's. From there W.W. Martin, Stephen Arnold, M.A. Mitchell and Mr. and Mrs. Keller accompanied the officers to the crime scene.

After visiting the tragic scene at about three o'clock on Monday, July 25, 1898, a coroner's jury was empanelled consisting of the following men:
Stephen Arnold (The last person other than the murderer to see Reynolds alive)
Emil D. Keller (The first to investigate the crime scene with Mr. Arnold)
William W. Martin (The last employer of Reynolds)
M.A. Mitchell (Had talked to Reynolds and his partner two weeks earlier)
Deputy Sheriff Ed Andrews
County Stenographer James Deering

County Attorney Purcell determined that all of the jurors except the officials had spoken to both the victim and the suspect during the last three weeks but none of them could recall Allen's name at the time. The jury found that Reynolds had been murdered by his partner; that he had been shot through the head, the bullet entering over the right eye and then traveled down the neck, cutting off a piece of the spinal cord; the right side of the victim's face had powder burns, indicating he had been shot at very close range. It was the opinion of the jury that robbery was the motive as the victim's trousers and a check for twenty-six dollars and twenty-eight cents were both missing. The murderer had made his escape on a buckskin pony with a black stripe down the back and only had shoes on the front hoofs.

Following the inquest, Deputy Andrews followed the tracks of the pony north to the Martin Ranch where the buckskin pony was found picketed near the ranch. The deputy returned to Mitchell's at midnight where he telephoned Undersheriff Haley reporting what he had found and then joined the other officials back to Helena, arriving there at three o'clock in the morning. The authorities believed that Allen would make for the Canadian boundary and Sheriff Davidson and his staff began notifying all the stations between Helena and Great Falls, then they telephoned the fugitive's description to every community in the state.

After shooting his partner, Allen rode his pony to the Martin Ranch where he unsaddled the animal and then walked the fifteen miles to the William Johns Ranch on the Great Northern Railway line north of Helena. Mr. Johns spotted Allen next to his barn at about 6:15 a.m. on Monday morning, July 25, and the stranger told the rancher that he had been shearing sheep and he could pay for some breakfast if he could cash his paycheck. After breakfast Allen presented a check and when Mr. Johns recognized it was written on Mr. Martin's account he didn't hesitate honoring it. Allen claimed that he was J.S. Reynolds and was given over twenty-six dollars in change. Mr. Johns last saw Allen boarding a freight train slowly pulling up the grade on its way toward Helena.

By the time Sheriff Davidson had learned of the murder on Monday morning, Allen had already arrived at Helena on the Montana Central freight train and by Tuesday afternoon the sheriff had received word that his suspect had been captured at three different locations in the state. One report stated that a man had been captured at Marysville and another suspect was being held at Anaconda, but the most promising lead was from Sheriff Patrick H. Regan saying that a man answering the description of Allen had been arrested in the train yards at Butte. The Silver Bow officers were convinced they had the right man because he was wearing blue trousers and he claimed to be William Allen Reynolds.

After checking out the false leads, Sheriff Davidson realized that Allen had probably left the state and he instructed his undersheriff to mail out five hundred postcards to various parts of the northwest particularly locations where the fugitive had once lived, stating the two hundred and fifty dollar reward offered by the state along with the following description: “Allen is dark complexioned; shows Indian blood; aged about twenty-two; height about five feet, nine inches; weighs about one hundred and fifty-five pounds. Has black Indian hair and good teeth. Is smooth-faced, slim built and stands with head bent forward. At the time of the murder he wore blue overalls, old dark soft hat, and light brown shirt, with miner’s shoes with hobnails.”

Just three days later, on Saturday, August 13, 1898, Sheriff Davidson received a telegram from T.G. Ruth, deputy constable at Oakland, Oregon reporting that he had captured Allen, and the prisoner had admitted killing Reynolds but said it was in self-defense. After securing Governor Robert E. Smith’s signature on the proper paperwork, the sheriff left on the Northern Pacific Railroad on Tuesday morning for Oregon. Mr. Ruth and his prisoner met Sheriff Davidson at the Salem depot and after obtaining the necessary warrant from the Oregon state capital the sheriff escorted Allen back to Montana. A few days later it was announced that Mr. Ruth would indeed receive the reward for the capture of the Montana fugitive.

On the way back to Montana Allen told the sheriff that he had killed Reynolds in self-defense; that he concealed the body, threw the 45-70-caliber rifle that he used into Prickly Pear Creek and then caught the train to Helena. Actually Allen had taken the train through Helena for about sixteen miles before jumping off at Clancy and grabbing another freight train to the capital and from there he walked to Elliston where he caught another freight into Missoula. At Missoula he was almost captured by the police but he managed to slip the officers and caught a ride on another train to Sprague, Washington where he purchased a ticket for Portland and then he walked to Oakland, Oregon.

Once Allen was captured, Coroner Brooke returned to the murder scene on August 17, 1898, where with the help of Emil Keller and Stephen Arnold he exhumed the body of Reynolds, which had been buried in a lonesome nook about one hundred yards from where he was murdered. After removing the man’s head it was placed in a rusty tin bucket; the grave was again filled in and the doctor returned to Helena.

The trial of Joseph Allen started on Wednesday, November 9, 1898, and it was presided over by Judge C. Smith. The murder of J.S. Reynolds had been well publicized in Lewis and Clark County and the trial attracted large crowds of spectators including the victim's two brothers from Michigan. Most of the first day was taken up with the selection of the jury and by four o'clock the following panel was sworn in:

William H. Taylor	John Ahues	Joseph Bowers
Allan Gilmour	Thomas Cooney	Joe H. Smith[21]
A.G. Religman	W.M. Biggs	Joseph Ernst
Jacob Tonn	M.F. Root	D.B. Henry

The evidence against Allen was overwhelming and the prosecution established that Reynolds had been shot while sleeping and Coroner Brooke's testimony probably sealed the case when he placed an odd-shaped bundle wrapped in a newspaper on the desk of the stenographer. As the witness was describing the fatal wounds he picked up the newspaper bundle, unwrapped it and as he turned he presented the head of J.S. Reynolds to the jury. After describing the course of the bullet and the vivid damage to the skull it was placed on the table in front of the county attorney, and from there it seemed to be grinning at the jurors through the remainder of the session.

Allen took the stand in his own defense and asserted that Reynolds was violently dangerous when he drank and he denied the killing was over money. He told the court about the argument between the two men over their horses and how Reynolds had threatened him. He claimed that Reynolds attacked him with a club and he shot him to protect himself. Allen explained that he took the check from Reynolds because half of it was his and the man owed him for other jobs but he couldn't explain the missing pants and suggested that someone else had stolen them. The defendant went on to tell how he concealed the body, cleared the campsite and then described his escape and capture. Allen concluded by telling the court that he didn't think anyone would believe his story because he was part Indian.

The defense then called two witnesses who testified that Reynolds was in fact a mean character and one of them said he was almost killed by the man. They both said that Reynolds was a cranky man that was hard to get along with and was threatening to whip someone every other day. After final arguments on Saturday, November 12, 1898, the jury retired at 2:30 p.m. to deliberate the case and after deliberating over the fate of Joseph Allen the jury returned their verdict of guilt of first-degree murder at 10:15 that evening. On Tuesday, November 15, Judge Smith sentences Allen to be hanged on January 12, 1899, in the yard of the Lewis and Clark County jail.

Returning to his cell after his sentencing he wrote to his parents at Shoup, Idaho about his situation and explained to the jailer that his folks wouldn't be able to help him. Although Judge Smith later denied Allen's motion for a new trial there was a ground swell of interest and support by many prominent citizens of Helena. With the support of the community, Judge J.M. Clements was able to secure a stay of execution in order to make an appeal to the Supreme Court.

When the high court didn't reverse the district court's decision in July of 1899, Judge Smith re-sentenced Allen to be hanged on September 14, 1899. Although Governor Smith was presented with many letters and petitions from virtually a list of "Montana Who's Who" and after personally meeting with many more including the grieving mother of the defendant, he graciously declined to interfere with the execution. Sheriff Davidson then began making the arrangements for the execution by mailing out the invitations and on September 11, the sheriff appointed A.O. Becker as the first deathwatch over the prisoner.

The gallows on which Joseph Allen was hanged.
"Anaconda Standard" 9/12/1899

The scaffold that was used to hang both William Biggerstaff and Bill Gay in 1896, which had been taken apart and put away in the basement of the jailhouse was brought out for the execution for the young condemned man. While Allen reportedly showed no sign of concern, his friends and family were weeping and praying during his final day on earth. The prisoner started his day at seven a.m. when he donned his brand new suit except for the jacket and he ate a breakfast of fried chicken, fried potatoes, bacon and eggs, fruit, oatmeal with cream, and he washed it down with coffee. After breakfast, Allen played cribbage with his deathwatch until the many visitors interrupted the game.

While Allen was having his breakfast, Sheriff Davidson was once again testing the gallows in the jail yard with sacks of shot weighing about the same as the prisoner and a large bag of sand weighing about a hundred and eighty pounds had been attached to the hangman's rope to take the stretch out of it. William H. Taylor, one of the jurors at Allen's trial arrived at the jail with his camera and asked if he could photograph the condemned man and his mother. The request was granted and it was the last photograph of Allen as Sheriff Davidson made it clear that there would be no cameras allowed inside the jail yard during the hanging.

While visiting with his mother the boy did most of the talking because the woman seemed almost speechless. After being with her son Mrs. Allen spoke with the officials and requested that as few people as possible view the body of her boy after the execution; that the grave be marked with a cross and a board with her son's name. She said that she would not attend the services and Mrs. Charles Dahler promised to attend to the details.

Allen's dinner was served at 3:30 p.m. and he had fried chicken, bread and butter, corn on the cob, sweet potatoes, cantaloupe, pie, sliced peaches with cream along with ice cream and cookies for dessert. The young man ate so much that fifty-six-year-old deathwatch, George F. Ingram jokingly commented that Allen had lost his own appetite and found a wolf's. When Father Michael T. O'Brien, who was sitting with Allen, remarked about him being left-handed, the condemned man argued that he could eat with either hand, proving it by eating his peaches and cream with both a fork and spoon at the same time.

At four p.m. Mrs. Allen again met with her son before the prisoner made his press statement in which he thanked the many people who had tried to save his life and that he bore no ill will against anyone. While Alen was signing photographs for some of his friends a deputy placed a silver dollar into the prisoner's hand, explaining that it was from one of the Sisters of Charity. Allen looked at for a few moments and then handed it back to the officer saying he didn't have any use for money anymore. When the deputy wouldn't take the dollar back, Allen slipped it into his pocket and reportedly gave it to his mother later.

All day long and as late as ten p.m. the sidewalks in front of the jail on Breckenridge Street had a crowd of curious men, women and boys surrounding the building and every excuse possible was attempted to gain admittance for just a single look at the condemned man. Men and boys even climbed up to the covered windows, hoping to find some loophole through which they might see inside the jail. Shortly after ten p.m., it began to rain slightly and the crowd around the jail began to disperse.

Sheriff Davidson allowed Mrs. Allen to visit her son in the alcove of the jail office where they could have some privacy. The mother and son were together but they talked very little, as Mrs. Allen seemed to have been at a loss for words as the hour of ten o'clock approached. As the clock in the courthouse tower across the street tolled the hour, Mrs. Allen arose to her feet sobbing and her son fell into her arms without saying a word. After embracing his mother Allen walked across the floor followed by Deathwatch Ingram and he entered his cell without looking back or saying anything.

The woman stood in the corner of the office and watched her son walk to his cell, and as he disappeared around the corner she burst into tears. Reverend Father O'Brien led the grief-stricken woman to the door and accompanied her outside where he said a few words to her and then he went to Allen, who was waiting to pray. Mrs. Allen was last seen that evening walking into the darkness of the night with a friend of the family.

Reverend O'Brien remained with Allen for about an hour while the deathwatch and Jailer George Mahrt remained nearby. At 11:30 p.m., the prisoner went to bed after enjoying some cold chicken, bread and butter. When asked by his deathwatch if he wanted some cake with it, Allen said all he wanted was meat. After the late night snack Allen pulled the blankets over his shoulders and he was sound asleep within a half an hour and he slept as a child might have after a hard day's play while Deathwatch Becker sat quietly in the cell.

Among the many invited guests to witness the hanging were several county sheriffs that had pending executions in their respective jurisdiction including: Sheriff George W. Hubbard of Yellowstone County, who later hanged William C. Brooks on November 24, 1899; Sheriff M. Shaw of Fergus County who executed Bill Calder in March of 1900; Deer lodge County Sheriff Jack Conley, who eventually executed James Fleming in September 1901, and Clinton Dotson on April 4, 1902.

Other law enforcement personnel present at the hanging were Sheriff William D. Hagen of Teton County who would later execute William Pepo in April of 1900; Sheriff William J. Fransham of Gallatin County; Sheriff G.E. Pool of Broadwater; Sheriff James Jobb, Meagher County; Sheriff D.J. Curran, Missoula County; Sheriff Henry Sherlock, Jefferson County; Sheriff C.C. Proctor, Cascade County; Sheriff W.S. Pyle, Beaverhead County; Undersheriff Murphy of Silver Bow County and Colonel Thomas McTague of the state penitentiary.

A few minutes before five a.m. Jailers Thomas Conlon and George Mahrt entered Allen's cell and aroused the sleeping man and minutes later Father O'Brien cheerfully greeted the prisoner. As Allen was donning his white collar and his plain black suit Jailer Conlon ordered a light breakfast of bacon and eggs, toast cantaloupe, peaches with cream and coffee. While eating his breakfast Allen commented on the "rubberneck" watching him from the jail office and the jailer laughed and said that people would spring out of the corners to steal a glance at the condemned man, and the prisoner only smiled as he resumed his eating. On the table in front of the prisoner was a jar containing three Great American roses, which had been sent to him by a young woman who had occasionally visited him at the jail.

When Allen finished his breakfast he lighted a cigar, and while sitting back in his easy chair he puffed away and calmly read a paragraph or two from a newspaper. A few minutes later he received his last spiritual consolation from Father O'Brien who had been at the jail since 4:40 a.m. Two minutes after six, Undersheriff Haley read the warrant of execution to Allen as Sheriff Davidson entered the cell with the straps. When the sheriff indicated that the white collar should be removed Allen smiled and placed it on the little table next to the roses. As the sheriff and Deputy Hendricks were adjusting the straps Allen spoke his final words when he said, "Now, Tom referring to Sheriff Davidson, let's get out and have this thing over as soon as possible." The sheriff acknowledged the request with a slight nod of his head.

The prisoner didn't require any stimulants and at five minutes after six the sheriff emerged from murderer's row into the corridor of the jail, holding Allen by the arm. The prisoner's arms were bound to his sides and his wrists were held by the straps that passed around his thighs. Strapped down as he was, Allen walked as though he was going almost anywhere other than to his death. The procession formed as had been prearranged with Father O'Brien leading the way through the narrow passage way. Allen walking alone a few feet behind the sheriff and J.H. McFarland following just behind him. Sheriff Davidson later reported that Allen never flinched as he was led through the window to the jail yard and bound as he was, with only his feet free, he climbed the five steps, crossed the windowsill and then stepped down the other side without faltering.

The rain was beating down and the sky had a dark overcast, as the sun hadn't yet raised high enough to dispel the gloom of that September morning. The condemned man walked alone towards the scaffold where he would forfeit his life for the life he had taken and he took his place upon the square of carpet under the scaffold. There priest touched the prisoner's shoulder and he obediently moved directly beneath the noose. The man's feet were quickly bound and the noose was brought down and it rested on his shoulder. Mr. J.H. McFarland, who had been involved with the execution of Wheatley and Sterres in 1875, Frank Robert in 1878, and Pelkey in 1881, drew the noose tight directly under Allen's left ear.

By his own request, the black hood, a usual feature of the hangman's paraphernalia to hide the suffering was not placed over the prisoner's head. Allen's face was calm with his eyes down cast, as he stood unsupported, never looking at the crowd of about one hundred spectators, who had removed their hats in the presence of the condemned man. Many of the witnesses had hoped all along that Allen would at the last minute say something to relieve any doubt about his guilt but he neither affirmed his innocence or admit his guilt, and just stood there for a second or two as the morning rain beat upon his bare head.

At 6:07 a.m., the sheriff gave the signal and the 450-pound weight dropped, the thud of the weight and the rattling of the links through the sheaves of the pulleys wasn't noticed by the audience as the body of Joseph Allen was thrown about forty inches into the air, then it rebounded by its own weight and remained suspended motionless. A slight tremor shook the body once or twice as the muscles moved involuntarily; Allen's eyes were closed and his mouth was open a little. A vertebra was dislocated under the right ear and the man was probably dead before most of the crowd realized that the execution had taken place.

Dr. W.C. Riddell, the county physician and Dr. A.C. Fleming of Augusta held the man's pulse, and eighteen minutes after the jerk Joseph H. Allen was pronounced dead. After giving the signal for the body to be lowered into the waiting coffin, Dr. Riddell said that death was instantaneous and there was probably a loss of sensation as soon as the noose tightened around the veins in the man's neck. Father O'Brien removed the crucifix from the clenched hand of the young man while he was being placed into the coffin.

Many of the people including most of the visiting law enforcement officers remained to watch the scaffold being dismantled and once again placed in the basement of the jailhouse. Dr. Riddell told Sheriff Davidson that the execution was successfully conducted and the praise was repeated by most of the visiting sheriffs. The sheriff said that a great load had been lifted from his mind, and he commented that only a man who had experienced what he had gone through could know how he had felt during the last three weeks. What most people didn't realize was that the sheriff was concerned all morning after receiving a letter written in red ink with a picture of the devil stating: "You'd do anything for money, but you will meet your maker some day." Even under these threats, Sheriff Davidson conducted his duties like a true professional.

Joseph Allen's funeral was held three hours after the body was removed from the jail yard and it was conducted as Mrs. Allen had directed. There were only four people at the Hermann and Company funeral parlor and the Reverend Fathers Mueller and O'Brien conducted the brief service over the plain casket of imitation rosewood. After the service the casket was placed on a spring wagon where it was driven to the Catholic Cemetery. Mrs. Allen was deeply affected when the grave sight service was completed and she was assisted to a carriage and driven to her hotel. The women left on the noon train over the Northern Pacific Railroad for Red Rock, Montana and from there she took a stage to Shoup, Idaho where she worked as a cook at a nearby mining camp.

Postscript:
In the shadow of the hills, about a hundred yards from the spot where he was murdered, there is a lonely grave in which the headless body of E.C. Leech, better known in Montana as Jesse S. Reynolds rests. It was said that he was not a kind man but a man of many faults and few friends. His life had more than one tragedy in it and at the time of his death he was thirty-seven years old and a decade earlier an unfaithful wife had driven him from his home.

Leech was then a prosperous man in the lumber business at Six Lakes, Michigan where his brothers and sisters still lived. When he discovered that his wife had cheated on him he gave up everything he had in Michigan, including his name and left for the West. His wife tried to locate her husband and had prayed that he would someday forgive her and come back to his home state. Until his death no one in Montana and Idaho ever knew the real tragedy in his life, which had probably made him a bitter man.

Before defending Joseph Allen, James M. Clements had represented William Gay who was hanged for murder in June of 1896. Eventually Mr. Clements became a district judge and presided over the cases of James Fleming who was hanged in September of 1901, and of Clinton Dotson, executed in April of 1902.

Joseph Allen was the third defendant that County Attorney R.R, Purcell had helped send to the gallows, having previously prosecuted William Biggerstaff and Bill Gay. Then after he had left office Mr. Purcell helped secure the release of the leading suspect in the Mob Lynching of James Brady at the Capital City in 1901.

Jailer George Mahrt was later found "totally incompetent" by the Lewis and Clark County Grand Jury after a Lynch Mob broke into the county jail while he was guarding accused child abuser, James Brady who was taken out and hanged in Helena in 1901. No one was ever charged in the lynching and while County Sheriff O'Connell was criticized and a couple of Helena city police officers were found to be negligent in their duties, Jailer Marhrt was apparently the only official discharged in the affair.

George Felix Ingram who was one of Allen's deathwatchs was described as a mountain man who had done his share of hunting and trapping and before coming to Montana he had been a partner in a gold mine near Deadwood with William Gay who was eventually hanged at Helena in 1896. Coincidentally Ingram also testified in Clinton Dotson's first murder trial before the killer was finally hanged in 1902.

November 24, 1899
William C. Brooks

Location and Gallows: Brooks was hanged inside the Yellowstone County Jail yard at Billings and he was the third man executed on ***Gallows No. Eleven: (July 1894): "Galloping Gallows" No. Four***. This scaffold was originally designed as a Trap-Type Gallows but it was converted to a Jerk-Type for the Brooks hanging. For a description and history of this scaffold or any other can be found in Chapter Seven: "Montana Gallows."

Description: Brooks was a forty-two-year-old black man who weighed about 185 pounds.

Crime: Murder of his wife, Jennie Brooks on November 18, 1898.

Judge: Charles H. Loud

Prosecution: Yellowstone County Attorney W.M. Johnston

Defense: C.L. Harris

Sheriff: George W. Hubbard

Distinction: William Brooks was not only the first man to be legally hanged in Yellowstone County but he was also the last person executed in Montana during the nineteenth century. During its first sixteen years of existence Yellowstone County had charged seventeen men with first-degree murder but Brooks was the first verdict rendered.

According to the army discharge papers signed by Captain William Davis, William C. Brooks was born in Culpepper County, Virginia in March of 1857. Nothing is known about Brooks' early years other than he had been married in Virginia and his wife and two children were living in the D.C. area. Evidently Brooks left or divorced his first wife and enlisted in the Tenth Regiment of the U.S. Cavalry in Texas on March 30, 1883. After serving his five-year term Brooks re-enlisted with the same outfit on May 1, 1888, and he was eventually promoted to sergeant and transferred to Fort Apache where he met and married his second wife, Mrs. Jennie Jefferson.

According to Brooks' stepson, William Jefferson, who worked as a porter at E.L. Brown's Barbershop at Billings, his family moved to Fort Custer where his stepfather was discharged from the Army in March of 1893. According to his commanding officer, Lieutenant Colonel D. Perry, Sergeant Brooks was a good soldier and had served his enlistment well. Will Jefferson told the authorities that after living at Butte for a couple of months the family moved to Billings where his stepfather became an ice cream vendor and he and his wife ran a restaurant. In February of 1898, Brooks was granted a military pension of eight dollars a month because of his bronchitis and injuries to his hip and back that he had sustained while in the army.

On Friday, November 18, 1898, Brooks shot and killed his wife, Jennie in her home on Twenty-seventh Street, a brick four-room cottage on the south side of Billings. The neighborhood was startled by several pistol shots and the cry of "murder, murder!" on that afternoon at about 4:30. In no time at all a large crowd had congregated at the house but by then the husband had accomplished his terrible deed and the woman's body lay dead across the street from her home having tried to get away from her killer while Brooks was trying to take his own life with the weapon.

Brooks told the large crowd that he would not let the law hang him and he shot the pistol a couple of times near his head, but several witnesses said that the man took particular pains to move his head away each time he pulled the trigger. No one dared approach the man as long as he had the gun and was in such a frenzied state but when Policeman Sawyer arrived the murderer turned the weapon over to Charles R. Stoll.

Coroner E.P. Townsend had the woman's body moved to her home where he questioned about six people that had witnessed the shooting. Several of neighbors said that the couple had been separated for some time and they had recently started fighting again over a Mrs. Range at their restaurant business near Swim and Brewer's Saloon. Brooks had thrown his wife's things out of the restaurant and then he followed her to their brick home where they continued the argument. Brooks reportedly stormed from the house and he didn't return for four or five days until the afternoon of the murder.

On that Friday afternoon Brooks returned to the house while his wife was outside hanging up some clothes and the only person in the house was Charley Powers, the twelve-year-old grandson of the woman. According to the young boy, Brooks, who he referred to as "papa," accused Mrs. Brooks, "mama" of having a man over a couple of nights, which she denied. When Brooks didn't believe his wife she called out to Joe and Luke, two men who were standing nearby and asked them if a man had been around.

The jealous man didn't believe the men who had confirmed Mrs. Brook's statement and he began calling his wife an "old whore." The woman had a small switch in her hand and when she began hitting him he threatened to kill her. The woman then picked up the broom and tried to strike him a time or two but he slugged her with his fist and the twelve-year-old boy ran outside and jumped on the man's back and Brooks threw the boy off threatening him as well. When Brooks began dragging his wife into the kitchen her grandson began striking the man's head with a piece of firewood.

Meanwhile Brooks removed a pistol from the inside pocket of his overcoat and as they entered the kitchen he pulled the trigger two or three times but the weapon didn't discharge. He kept pointing the pistol to her head and pulling the trigger until it finally went off and Mrs. Brooks broke away running out of the house holding her head, screaming that she had been shot. After stopping outside to lean on the fence, she then ran out into the street as Brooks came out of the house shouting "are you shot?" She answered, "yes, I'm shot" and kept running. The man followed the woman into the street and he shot his wife and she fell as the boy ran up town as fast as he could run, crying "murder."

Dr. J.H. Rinehart assisted the coroner with the autopsy on the remains of Mrs. Brooks on Saturday morning and they found two bullet wounds, one had entered the left breast about four inches above the left nipple, passing through the aorta just where it left the heart and then it lodged in the lung. The other bullet had entered the left ear, passing through the base of the brain and then it was lodged in the right side of the skull. The coroner's inquest was held at the county courthouse on Saturday morning at 10:30 with the following jurors:

Will Calhoun	Charles Spear	F.L. Mann
H.F. Clement	J.F. Sleeper	W.B. Ten Eyck
E.S. Holmes		

County Attorney Johnston conducted the examination of the witnesses during the inquest and he interviewed Charley Powers, Luke Bryant, Jon Johnson, Mary Turner, Albert Brunswick, Jesse Van Wagonen, Charles Stoll and Dr. Rinehart. After hearing all of the testimony the jury returned a verdict that Jennie Brooks came to her death from gunshot wounds inflicted at the hands of William C. Brooks.

Brooks seemed indifferent when he was taken before Justice Fraser Saturday afternoon at 1:30 where the murder charge was made against him and when asked if he wanted to consult an attorney before pleading Brooks said that nothing could save him and only asked when his trial would begin. After being told it would convene in January or February of 1899, Brooks seemed disappointed saying that they couldn't erect a scaffold on the prairie and swing him soon enough. Justice Fraser bound Brooks over to the district court and he refused bond after the prisoner waived a preliminary hearing and Brooks told the judge that he didn't care how soon he was hanged.

The prisoner explained that all he wanted to do was to see his wife, Jennie's grave, but Sheriff George A. Berky refused the request because he couldn't guarantee the safety of the prisoner from a Lynch Mob. Reverend Jacob Mills of the M.E. Church conducted funeral services for Jennie Brooks at the family home on Sunday afternoon, November 20.

In a brief interview with a "Billings Gazette" reporter after his hearing, Brooks said that he was sorry for what he did and he expected to plead guilty to second-degree murder and spend the rest of his life in prison. There were numerous rumors that Brooks had killed two men before coming to Billings but his stepson explained that while in the Army at Fort Apache, Arizona his father had shot a deserting soldier who later died. After a military investigation Brooks was cleared of any wrongdoing as he was fulfilling his lawful duty. In another incident at Fort Apache, Brooks was involved in a quarrel with another soldier who sustained a gunshot wound to the leg but it wasn't fatal.

William Brook's trial began on Friday, February 3, 1899, in the fourteen-year-old Yellowstone County Courthouse, which was described as being sorely inadequate. The business in the courtroom was often interrupted by the noise of heavy wagons passing on the nearby street and even by pedestrians merely talking on the sidewalk. The courtroom was terribly hot in the summer and it required three coal stoves to keep warm in the winter. The air in the room was said to be very foul by the end of each day's session but even with these poor conditions inside the courtroom, it was still crowded every day of the Brook's trial where the following twelve men made up the jury:

Almond G. Redding (f)	Jacob Dahlstrom	C.C. Steers
C.D. Prather	George Lacy	John Partington
George Gamble	John A. Miller	John McCann
Henry Caldwell	E.F. Sullivan	Robert Steele

(f) Foreman

Having failed to convince the jury that his client was insane at the time of the murder Defense Attorney Harris told the jurors that a first-degree verdict would put a stain on Yellowstone County. Finally Mr. Harris, who had only recently been admitted to the Montana State Bar, tried an unusual defense strategy of first describing a dreaded execution including the noose, black cap and then warning the jurors that their dreams might be haunted by figure in the black mask. Even with the threats of ghostly haunted dreams, the jury returned a first-degree verdict just twenty minutes after being presented with written instructions by Judge Loud.

While awaiting his trial, Brooks was heard saying that the state could dispose of his body but God would take care of his soul. he reportedly showed no visible sign of surprise and only kept his eyes on the court clerk as he read the verdict. Attorney Harris on the other hand immediately gave notice of his intentions of filing a motion for a new trial. On Friday, February 10, 1899, the crowded courtroom was so quiet that a pin could be heard as Judge Loud sentenced William Brooks to be hanged by the neck on March 17.

Members of audience said that the condemned man wasn't affected in the least by the sentence and he didn't show any emotion as he was being led away by Jailer Harding. While Judge Loud immediately overruled the motion for a new trial for Brooks on February 13, he did order a stay of execution for the condemned killer when his attorney said that he was going to appeal the case to the Supreme Court. Although the stay offered the defense enough time to prepare and for an appeal the higher court eventually affirmed the ruling of the lower court.

Immediately after the Supreme Court affirmed the judgment of the lower court in July of 1899, William Brooks began acting insane by singing and yelling continuously at the jail. His handlers reported that the prisoner would increase his crazy antics whenever strangers were at the jail and he caused constant trouble for the jailers and everyone including the other inmates were annoyed with his constant singing and ranting.

Eventually it was necessary to gag and handcuff the prisoner most of the time and because he refused to clean himself the staff would provide the prisoner a cold shower with the use of a fire hose, which also had the side effect of stopping his singing while he was taking on the water. When Brooks was gagged and handcuffed, he was allowed to roam freely in his cell but at night he was tied down on his bunk.

On October 27, 1899, Deputy Sayers and Jailer Harding brought William Brooks into Judge Loud's court for his re-sentencing and by then the prisoner was thinner and had grown a heavy mustache and a go-tee since last being in the court. On the way from the jail Brooks reportedly kept rubbing his handcuffed hands together and in the courtroom he began singing loudly before the officers placed a gag in his mouth. At that point the prisoner refused to take his seat and as he stood before the judge, Brooks continued to step from side to side and swinging back and forth while Jailer Harding held his arm.

When the prisoner was asked for any reasons why he shouldn't be sentenced his attorney objected to the sentencing by claiming his client was obviously insane. Mr. Harris then asked the court to impanel a jury to inquire into the man's sanity and Judge Loud told the attorney that he had anticipated the request of the defense so he personally had visited Brooks at the county jail along with the county attorney to determine his sanity. While the judge and the county attorney believed that the prisoner was sane, the court still had appointed three licensed doctors of Billings to examine Brooks. In separate affidavits Drs. E.P. Townsend, Baxter and Armstrong all declared that the convicted murderer was perfectly sane.

Sheriff Hubbard, Deputy Sayles and Jailer Harding also had entered affidavits stating that Brooks had acted normally before the Supreme Court affirmed his conviction and he had been simulating insanity ever since. According to Jailer Harding, who had constant charge of the prisoner, Brooks had constantly read his bible, sang spirituals and prayed during his time at the jail until his appeal to the high court. When he wasn't granted a new trial, he began singing continuously, refused to speak or bathe, wash his hands and face or to do other chores including washing his dishes or sweeping out his cell.

The jailer stated that when Brooks began ripping up his bedding and throwing the blankets and mattress off of his cot he was threatened with a whipping with a rubber hose. Since the prisoner didn't require a second warning, it was concluded that Brooks was in deed sane enough to understand consequences of his actions. Brook's attorney engaged Drs. Rinehart and Hogan to determine whether or not his client was insane but soon after their examination they recommended that he drop the case because they felt the prisoner was sane and that the public sentiment was in favor of hanging the murderer.

When the prisoner was returned to the jail after his re-sentencing a deathwatch was placed over Brooks, with Harry K. Fish taking the night shift while Benjamin watched the condemned man during the day. Brook's last hope faded away on November 13, 1899, when Governor Robert B. Smith refused to commute his sentence, saying he believed that the condemned man had received a fair and impartial trial.

Sheriff Hubbard was besieged daily by curious people from all parts of Montana and Wyoming wanting an invitation to the execution but because of the limited space, only about one hundred spectators were admitted including Sheriff Patrick H. Regan of Silver Bow County;

Sheriff George T. Young, Park County; Sheriff John Dunn and Deputies Fred Bacheider and Dick Hicks of Carbon County and Custer County Deputy Crashaw. Because Sheriffs G.E. Pool of Broadwater and William J. Fransham of Gallatin County arrived late into Billings they were unable to witness the hanging.

The invitations issued for the Brooks hanging read: "You are hereby invited to witness the legal execution of W.C. Brooks for the murder of his wife Jennie Brooks on the eighteenth day of November, 1898. The execution will take place in the city of Billings, Montana, on Friday the twenty-fourth day of November, 1899, between the hours of two a.m. and two p.m. signed Sheriff of Yellowstone County."

After observing the hanging of Joseph Allen at Helena two months earlier, Sheriff Hubbard apparently had planned to use a Jerk-Type gallows built using the same pattern of ***Gallows No. Eight: (March 1887): "Galloping Gallows No. Two***. Later on he decided to borrow the Livingston Trap-Type death machine that was used to hang Thomas Salmon at Red Lodge in January of 1899, but he had the scaffold converted to a Jerk-Type Gallows. The sheriff ordered the two pine uprights reduced from the original eighteen feet down to twelve to match the Lewis and Clark death machine and a "T" frame was added to the bottom of the uprights for support. Two pulleys were then attached to the bottom of the overhead beam, which the rope passed through and the suspended 450-pound weight was secured with a pin.

Sheriff Hubbard had the option of using either the rope that had been purchased by Custer County to hang the Indian, Spotted Hawk before Governor Robert B. Smith had commuted his sentence or the one used to execute Thomas Salmon at Red Lodge. Finally the sheriff decided to use the same noose and straps that were used at Red Lodge because the rope had already been treated and stretched but while testing the cord on the day before the execution a strand broke and a new one-half inch Manila rope had to be used.

The restraints consisted of three straps, one to secure the legs together, another was used around the waist, which fastened the arms tight, and one out bound the hands. The new rope was stretched and both the weight and lever were thoroughly tested before the execution. From his cell Brooks was able to see a portion of the scaffold, which was erected in the rear of the county jail and the first board fence around the enclosure wasn't built high enough to obscure the gallows so it had to be extended several more feet.

Brooks had really shown signs of uneasiness over his impending doom and he lost a great deal of weight. When first arrested he weighed about 185 pounds but at the time of his execution he was barely 160 pounds even though he continued to eat with the same appetite. Since the time the deathwatch was assigned, Brooks had become very restless, paced up and down his cell all day long, and he would have done it all night if Jailer Harding didn't have him tied down on his bunk each evening. The prisoner was kept gagged nearly all the time, but his special mouthpiece didn't hurt or inconvenience him and it was removed for about three or four hours a day.

The entire day before his execution Brooks was permitted to sing and pray all the time and the night deathwatch, Harry Fish said that the prisoner wasn't a bit concerned on his last night and he was quiet all night long. While Brooks may have been unconcerned before the day of his execution, there was a steady stream of people going up and down the street in front of the jail trying to see the gallows and perhaps hear the condemned man singing.

After waking up at five a.m. the prisoner continued his singing as he put on his new black suit with the assistance of Jailer Harding. At 5:30, Jailer Burding brought in the good breakfast Brooks had requested consisting of oatmeal with cream, oyster stew, fried chicken and spiced currents, buttered toast, fruit, coffee and ginger snaps, which he refused to eat or even taste. The Reverends Opie and Clark arrived as the meal was being served and his attitude had changed towards them as well and he refused to have anything to do with the two ministers.

Just moments before seven o'clock that morning Sheriff Hubbard along with his deputies, the two ministers, attending physicians and newspaper reporters went to Brooks cell where the officer told the prisoner he was going to read the death warrant. Brooks instantly stopped singing so that the officer could do his duty, but after a minute or two the condemned man began singing again and he continued throughout the reading of the warrant. When finished, Sheriff Hubbard asked Brooks if he had anything to say, and the prisoner only began singing louder. Reverend Opie asked Brooks if he would stop singing, but the man paid no attention to the minister as the sheriff and his deputies began placing the body and arm braces on the man.

The crowd of nearly three hundred people began gathering at the jail on Twenty-Seventh Street at about five a.m. and by seven o'clock there were hundreds more on top of the nearby boxcars of the Burlington Railroad, telephone poles, trees and other nearby vantage points. The execution enclosure was kept locked until the sheriff, his deputies and the condemned man reached it, and as they passed through the gate the crowd rushed in behind the procession and when the people atop the boxcars realized that the crowd was being allowed into the enclosure there was a mad rush of humanity, fighting their way towards the gallows. A man with a camera was also admitted into the enclosure but because the lighting was so poor a photograph was never taken of the hanging.

Since some of the authorities had feared that the condemned man would weaken and have to be carried to the gallows a special rope harness had been designed and suspended from the scaffold in order to support him until the weight was dropped. To most people's surprise Brooks met his death calmly and he walked to the gallows as straight and as firm as the officers had. When the gallows was reached the prisoner took his place under the noose and he stood on a piece of carpeting that Jailer Harding had placed on the ground.

After stepping on his designated spot under the scaffold, Brooks motioned to Sheriff Hubbard that he wished to pray and he was permitted to fall to his knees. After a few moments of silence he arose to his feet, faced the sky and began singing as his feet were being strapped together. When the sheriff adjusted the noose around his neck Brooks stopped singing and as Jailer Harding pulled the black cover over the man's head Sheriff Hubbard stepped to the lever. The signal was given at 7:03 a.m. and the heavy weight fell to the ground; the body of William Brooks rose about fifteen inches off the ground and when it came back down the toes were about a half an inch from the ground.

The execution happened so quickly that most of the witnesses at the scene didn't realize what had happened. Doctors Townsend and Rinehart went forward and while one of them grasped a wrist, the other pressed his ear to the man's heart. There were no tremors visible on the body and at 7:15 a.m. the physicians pronounced the man dead. Although the man's heart had continued to beat for twelve minutes before he was pronounced dead, the physicians were sure that Brooks had met a painless death.

The body was lowered into a nearby coffin and it was taken to the morgue where a day after the execution Doctors Rinehart, A. Clark and Hogan later assisted coroner E.P. Townsend with an autopsy on the brain of William Brooks. A portion of the skull was removed and the brains were taken out and were found to be in perfect condition showing no sign of mental disease and indicating that the man was simulating insanity. The remains were later interred in the Potter's Field in the Billings City Cemetery.

Postscript:
Sheriff Hubbard later attended the hanging of William Calder at Lewistown in March of 1900, and the execution of William Pepo a month later at Choteau. Prosecuting attorney, W.M. Johnson later became mayor of Billings and coincidentally he was in office when the second and last hanging took place in the Magic City, that of Juan Cuellae in April of 1918. In another twist of fate, former Sheriff Hubbard was the day jailer at the county jail during the Cuellae hanging.

(Endnotes)

[1] The Cook County Gallows were built in 1897 for the hanging of the four anarchists, August Spies, Albert Parsons, George Engle and Adolph Fischer for the murder of seven Chicago policemen during the Haymarket Riot in 1886. The gallows eventually hanged a total of eighty-six men before being retired in June of 1927. They remained in storage for fifty years until Mike Donley purchased them in 1977 for an undisclosed amount for his "Wild West Town" amusement park located northwest of Chicago. The ancient gallows were auctioned off in December of 2006 for over sixty-eight thousand dollars to the Ripley's Museum. "Seattle Times" 12/8/2006

[2] "Jefferson County Sentinel" 11/13/1890

[3] "Missoulian" 2/12/1922, p1, Section 2

[4] Chief Aeneas' son was shot and killed while he was breaking into a house at Demersville in the fall of 1888. While Chief Aenas' son, Samuel was trying to open a window of the house a small boy clubbed him his hands and arms while his mother and another women were yelling for help. Hearing the screams a man came out of Johnny Foy's Saloon and shot the Indian dead. "Kalispell Montana and the Upper Flathead Valley" by Henry Elwood

[5] "Missoula Gazette" 7/2/1890

[6] Chief Aeneas probably accepted the money as compensation for his son's death in 1888 (see 4)

[7] Dr. Daniel Harrison Billmeyer had earlier been an attending physician at the hanging of the four Indians at Missoula in December of 1890.

[8] Robert Mentrum designed and constructed the large gallows used to hang the four Indians, Antley, Pierre Paul, La La See and Pascale at Missoula in December of 1890.

[9] Before counseling Burns, Father Guidi was with Michael McAndrews when he was executed in March of 1878.

[10] "Missoulian" 2/19/1922 p1, Section 2

[11] Before serving on the Clay Pugh jury William Channel sat on the panel that convicted George Bryson who was eventually hanged in August of 1889.

[12] Letter to Joel Overholser, "River Press" dated May, 1975 from Mollie Sedgwick

[13] C.G. Evans later served on the jury that convicted William Gay and who was eventually hanged in June of 1896.

[14] Fred Sass was one of three men serving on the William Biggerstaff jury that later served on the panel, which convicted William Gay who was eventually hanged in June of 1896.

[15] After serving on the Biggerstaff jury in 1896, Mr. Linsay was named to the Lewis and Clark County Grand Jury that investigated the Mob Lynching of James Brady at Helena in October of 1901.

[16] Henry Schotte was one of three men serving on the William Biggerstaff jury that later served on the panel, which convicted William Gay who was eventually hanged in June of 1896.

[17] Henry Schotte was one of three men on the William Gay jury that had earlier sat in judgment of William Biggerstaff who was hanged in April of 1896.

[18] C.G. Evans had earlier served as foreman on the jury that convicted William Biggerstaff who was executed in April of 1896.

[19] Fred Sass was one of the three men serving on the William Gay jury that had earlier served on the panel that convicted William Biggerstaff who was hanged in April of 1896.

[20] Dr. Brooke later examined the body of James Brady after a Lynch Mob hanged him at Helena in October of 1901. "History of Montana" by Tom Stout Vol.2 p 619

[21] This is most likely the same Joe H. Smith that sat on the jury eighteen years earlier that convicted Peter Pelkey who was hanged for murder in February of 1881.

Early Twentieth Century Legal Hangings

(March 1900 through April 1918)

March 16, 1900

<u>William Wallace Calder</u>

Location and Gallows: While ***<u>Gallows No. Thirteen: (March 1900)</u>*** was originally designed to jerk two men to their deaths at Lewistown; Billy Calder was its only victim. A description of this scaffold or any other used in Montana can be found in Chapter Seven: "Montana Gallows."
Description: At the time of his death Calder was one month shy of his twenty-sixth birthday. Billy resented the fact that he only stood five foot, six inches tall and he always tried to make up for his lack of stature by being over bearing, extra cocky and dirty mouthed.
Crime: Double murder of John Allen and Farquhar McRea on Box Elder Creek on September 24, 1898.
Judge: Dudley DuBose
Prosecution: County Attorney Frank E. Smith aided by Montana State Attorney General Cornelius B. Nolan
Defense: William E. Cort
Sheriff: Thomas M. Shaw
Distinction: The Calder execution was not only the first ever hanging in Montana to take place in the Twentieth Century it was also the last to occur in Fergus County. Of the thirty-two known hangings that took place in that county, Calder was the only man legally executed within its boundaries.

Billy Calder was born in Steubenville, Ohio in 1872, and after his parents divorced, Mrs. Calder took her two sons to Montana in 1888, where she married Sam Smith. The family lived on Box Elder Creek and William immediately resented his mother's new husband and he began making trouble. Billy threatened his stepfather on several occasions and during one quarrel he kept Mr. Smith under a bed for several hours with a shotgun. Billy's younger brother, Jimmy lived peaceably with Mr. Smith and he never did cause the family any trouble.

William Wallace Calder
"Anaconda Standard" 3/17/1900

Calder moved from town to town along the Northern Pacific Railroad where he held various cooking jobs but at Billings he was arrested for a minor offense and served a term at the county jail. From Yellowstone County Calder moved to Bozeman where he befriended James Eli "Dee" Fisher who had come out from Wisconsin and was playing piano at a local whorehouse. In September of 1898, Calder invited his new friend back to the Smith Ranch on Box Elder Creek to hunt big game while some people later speculated that he meant deer a man named McRea and his sheep instead.

Farquhar McRea was an elderly man with a good reputation who lived on Box Elder Creek where it emptied into Flatwillow Creek. His cabin was twenty miles from the Musselshell River, and about seventy miles southeast of Lewistown. As it still is today, the country was very sparsely settled, rough and devoted to the raising of stock. To help work his some seven hundred head of sheep Mr. McRea had hired John Allen as a herder.

Calder went back to the Smith Ranch in advance and because he had been thrown out of Billings, he sent his brother Jimmy there to meet Fisher and to purchase a new gun. When Fisher and Jimmy arrived at the ranch the three men made plans for a hunt, but Billy was scheming to kill McRea and steal his sheep. Saturday morning, September 24, 1898, the three young men, with only two guns started down Box Elder Creek to hunt antelope but they returned later that morning. That same afternoon they went to where McRea and his herder were cutting out some ewes to take to the Elisha Clark Ranch where they were to be exchanged for some wethers. Along with his own herd of sheep, McRea was caring for Mr. Hidebrant's nine hundred-head, which he owned a partial share in.

When the three men were about halfway to the McRea place they sat down to rest in a clump of willows and it was there that Billy supposedly told the other boys about his scheme of making some easy money. Calder explained that after killing the two men and running off with the animals they could sell the sheep for about three dollars a head. While Jimmy later testified that he protested the idea and Fisher remained quiet, Fisher told the court that he and Jimmy were both against the deal, but Billy had threatened to kill them both if they didn't go along with the affair.

When they were near the ranch of Lou Lewis, a half brother of Sam Smith, the three men met Mr. McRea and his horse on the prairie about a mile from his cabin. Billy had worked for several of the area ranchers the year before including Mr. McRea so the old gentleman didn't hesitate to approach the men. John Allen and the rest of the sheep were out of sight as Billy started talking to the old man while Fisher and Jimmy were holding the two guns. As Billy talked with McRea he kept motioning to his companions to kill the old man, and after about twenty minutes he grabbed the gun away from Fisher and shot the man in the middle of the forehead. Billy turned to the other two and told them they were too slow, and that it wasn't any different than shooting a dog.

After searching the man's body, the only things of value found by the assassins was a knife and a silver watch that Billy quickly took for his own. Billy ordered his little brother to wrap the body up in a blanket, which was on McRea's horse and then they dragged the corpse to the old man's cabin. Once they had concealed McRea's body inside of an outdoor chimney near the building the three men retraced their route covering up the tracks.

From that point the testimonies varied between the three suspects. At first Jimmy and Fisher said that they stayed at the cabin and Billy shot and killed Allen, but during the trial Jimmy testified that he and Billy remained at the cabin while Fisher killed the herder. All that was certain was that John Allen was killed with one shot and his body was disposed in the same manner as was Mr. McRea's.

After all of the sheep were rounded up and placed in a corral, the three men returned to the Smith Ranch where they spent the night. The next morning they left early with Jimmy's horse and as they approached McRea's place Billy went to the Lewis Ranch where he made up a story in order to borrow a wagon and team from his stepfather's relative. When the prosecution later asked Fisher and young Jimmy why they didn't escape while Billy was gone, they explained that they were still afraid of him coming after them.

The men loaded the two bodies into the wagon, covered them with a tarp from McRea's cabin and after stealing everything of value from the place, the party left with one man driving the wagon as the other two herded the sheep. They took a southeasterly course to Miles City where they had planned to sell the herd, which numbered from fifteen to seventeen hundred head. Meanwhile Sam Smith had become suspicious of the boys and he rode after them, catching up to Billy who was driving the wagon.

Billy explained to his stepfather that McRea had hired them to drive his sheep along with Hidebrant's herd to the railroad. Calder also told Smith that McRea had decided to steal Mr. Hidebrant's herd and share the proceeds with the three young men. When Smith asked where McRea was, Billy told his stepfather that he was hiding in the wagon because he didn't want to be seen leaving by his neighbors. As Sam Smith continued questioning his stepson, Billy motioned to his gun and the older man knew he'd better back off.

Not believing Billy's story, Smith rode to the Lewis Ranch and his stepbrother accompanied him to the McRea's Ranch where they found the house emptied out and a pool of blood nearby the structure. The next morning the blood trails were found along with the location where the two bodies had laid over night and Smith wrote a letter to Fergus County Sheriff John D. Waite. Because the letter from Smith didn't contain all of the pertinent facts the officer at first believed the rancher's suspicions were groundless and so he didn't take immediate action. Why Mr. Smith didn't inform the sheriff of all the facts led many people to believe that he may have been covering up for his stepson.

At first Smith and Lewis expected the law to track the boys down, but when no officers had arrived after two days, Special Deputy T.J. "Jeff" Sherman organized a posse to pursue the young desperados including Smith and Lou Lewis along with J.W. Woods, E.H. Messenger and Mr. Wilkerson. Meanwhile on Monday afternoon, September 26, 1898, the murderers had reached the Musselshell River on the old Miles

City to Fort Maginnis trail at a point, which was then referred to as the Hude Ranch. That night the boys gathered a pile of driftwood and built a huge fire and through the bodies of their two victims onto the flames.

The fire was still burning the next morning and the men cooked their breakfast over the embers and cremate remains of John Allen and Mr. McRea. After eating their meal the men went through the dying coals and raked up the remaining bones, belt buckles and buttons and then tossed them into the stream. Confident that the evidence of their crime was lost in the river, the murderers rounded up the sheep and instead of continuing on their journey to Miles City they left the road and went down Big Porcupine Creek of the Yellowstone in the direction of Forsyth.

Deputy Sherman and his posse left Flatwillow that Monday and reached the Musselshell on Tuesday evening where they found the remnants of the fresh campsite. Trying to escape while herding a large band of sheep was slow going and the posse was able to spend the night and still catch up with the boys at about nine o'clock Wednesday morning. When the posse inquired about McRea and Allen, Billy told them that they had gone ahead and were waiting at Miles City.

After searching Calder, Sherman and his men found incriminating evidence including money, a pocketknife and the watch belonging to Mr. McRea. Without Billy's knowledge, Jimmy Calder and Fisher had agreed upon a story, claiming that they had expected to be captured and they had gone along out of fear. While one man remained with the sheep the rest of the posse took the captives to Forsyth some thirty-five miles away, where they were lodged in the jail. From Forsyth Sherman wired Sheriff Waite at Lewistown, but the officer had already hit the trail.

Because of the poor condition of the jail at Forsyth, Sherman took the three men to Billings by train where Sheriff Waite met up with them. When captured Fisher and Jimmy said they didn't know where the bodies were, claiming Billy had driven the wagon over a hill and returned later without the remains. While at the jail in Billings however, Jimmy broke down and he confessed that they had burned the bodies and then dumped them into the river. Deputy Sherman and his posse were sent back out over the trail to locate the bodies and to look after the sheep.

Sherman had already presumed the bodies had been thrown into the river because the crime was similar to the 1889 case when James Wilber murdered four adults and child near Lewistown and then threw their bodies into the Judith River. When Sherman's posse returned to the campsite along the Musselshell they searched the ashes and the streambed where they found human bones and teeth along with the belt buckles and other items from the victims' clothing.

At Billings Jimmy Calder and Fisher were being treated as witnesses and while they were in custody they had the freedom within the jailhouse while they were being questioned. While in custody an old girlfriend of Billy's from Billings slipped him some paper and a pen and he wrote a letter, which he post-dated from Miles City stating: "Sheriff: Turn them boys loose, they haven't done anything. F. McRea." Billy gave this letter to his little brother to be mailed in an attempt to get out of jail, but instead Jimmy turned the correspondence over to Deputy Sherman.

Great praise was showered on Jeff Sherman and his conduct during the pursuit of the murderous band, and while many other posses would have quickly lynched the assassins on the trail, Sherman and his men protected them from violence. Deputy Sherman's only reward for his heroic work was only to have his personal expenses reimbursed by the county.

When Sheriff Waite received word at Billings that an attempt would be made to lynch the three men if he returned cross-country by wagon, he decided to transport them by train to Helena, then to Fort Benton and then take a stagecoach to Lewistown. At about midnight on October 10, 1898, Sheriff Waite arrived at Lewistown with Billy Calder in irons while the other two boys returned with the officer without any problem. The boys were all locked up in the six-cell jail at the Fergus County Courthouse, which was a three-story building surrounded by a fence. Calder was arraigned on October 29, 1898. and his hearing was scheduled for the March 1899, term and his trial began on March 24, before a crowd of over three hundred and fifty people including seventy-five women to witness the selection and swearing in of the following jury:

C.P. Colver	George Gilpatrick	Jacob Knerr
Daniel Bean	George Carolus	A.N. Weydent
C.M. Goodell	C.H. Evers	J.T. Evans
Albert Schneider	A. Meyers	(unknown)

During the three days including evening sessions, Calder's demeanor was that of a tough guy who truly believed that he was a hero. It was said that Calder was naturally bad and he never wanted to become better, and instead he actually aspired to get worse. Before the murder of McRea and Allen, Calder wasn't an experienced criminal but he had been in and out of jail and in the police court news. He later said that he would have done anything, even be hanged to have his name and picture in the "Police Gazette," the leading crime magazine of the time.

While the jury was deliberating on March 25, 1899, Calder reportedly told the bailiff that if he were found guilty it would be the biggest thing that had ever happened in that court. After about an hour and fifteen minutes the jury returned a verdict of guilty in the first degree and Calder's earlier prediction was correct, no other trial had ever attracted, as much attention in Fergus County and the courtroom was reportedly crowded with hundreds of men and women day and night. Calder and James Fisher were both sentenced to be hanged on May 12, 1899, and the people in the courtroom said that Billy's eyes welled up with tears but he quickly recovered and he was seen smiling as he was being escorted back to the jail.

Because of scheduling difficulties with the Supreme Court, Governor Smith granted respites for the two men until June 5, pending their appeals. Judge DuBose actually joined both boys' defense counsel in their request to the Governor for a stay of execution and the Supreme

Court heard the two cases separately. On January 29, 1900, the justices found no errors in the William Calder case and therefore affirmed the judgment of the lower court but Fisher's appeal resulted in a new trial.

After the Supreme Court rulings, Calder managed to loosen a large section of pipe from his sink, which he had intended to use to knock out Jailer Theodore Nichols as he brought in his meal. Calder told Fisher that after his escape he would first kill his brother then do away with Sheriff Waite and then burn his stepfather before disappearing into the Dakota Badlands. A permanent rift arose between the two condemned men when Fisher warned Jailer Nichols and then told his lawyer about Calder's entire plan.

Before his re-sentencing on Monday, March 12, 1900, Calder had made the statement that he would "roast," or cuss out the judge and the other officials in the court when asked to speak. When Jailer Nichols and Deputy Mike Riser escorted the handcuffed Calder into the courtroom with his usual swagger and cunning smile Judge DuBose told Billy that the first word of abuse he uttered he would order the deputy sheriff to gag him on the spot with a wet sponge, which he had carried in specifically for the purpose. After finishing his own threat to the prisoner, Judge DuBose told the young convict that if he had any legal reason why sentence shouldn't be passed he would listen.

Calder stated that he didn't have any legal reasons why he shouldn't be sentenced but he wanted his handcuffs removed. When the cuffs weren't removed Calder then started to list all of the reasons why he shouldn't be sentenced including that his brother had lied, that he wasn't cross-examined fairly and that he had been separated from Fisher and Jimmy. The judge listened to Calder patiently and then he passed the death sentence while Billy stood through the entire pronouncement without expressing any emotion, not even a quiver of an eyelid.

To be sentenced on a Monday and hanged on the following Friday was something very unusual and in his sentencing of Calder, Judge DuBose explained that: *"It has been my unpleasant and unfortunate duty since I have been on the bench to sentence a good many men to be hanged, more than I wish it had been, and therefore I have necessarily thought a good deal of what is humanity and what is not humanity in this matter, and I do not believe that to give a man who is under sentence of death, as you are, a long time to live is any kindness to him at all. He knows that he must die, and I believe that the shorter the time is the better for him and the better for the state. Viewing it in the light of a kindness to you, I have made the time very short. The sheriff of Fergus County will have you in his charge and on Friday, the sixteenth day of March, between the hours of nine a.m. and two p.m., will in the yard of the Fergus County jail, on a scaffold there erected, hang you by the neck until you are dead, may God have mercy on your soul."*

The short time between the sentencing and execution didn't leave new Fergus County Sheriff Thomas M. Shaw much time to prepare but a high-fence enclosure was built in two days and the gallows, which had already been constructed, were erected in the back corner of the yard just outside of Calder's cell. As for the invitations for the affair, the sheriff was really at a disadvantage as the time constraints severely hampered the possibilities of visiting law enforcement officers to witness the execution but Cascade County Sheriff C.C. Proctor, Sheriff George W. Hubbard of Yellowstone County and Meagher County Sheriff James Jobb were in attendance.

Billy Calder was a very difficult criminal to handle since his arrest and Sheriff Shaw and his staff were reportedly glad to get rid of him. Calder was a foul-mouthed little man who took delight in entertaining the other inmates at the jail with his dirty stories and poetry and he never wrote a letter or held a conversation that was free of profanity or cussing. Even in conversations with his mother during the last days of his life, he didn't refrain from using awful language, which always bothered Jailer Nichols and the other officers. Billy even openly blamed his mother in a cruel hearted manner for the crimes, which had eventually led him to the gallows.

Calder had always considered himself an infidel and the first time a minister visited him at the jail he received a very discourteous reception from the prisoner. Even with all the abuse, Sheriff Shaw felt that the condemned man should still have the opportunity to speak with a spiritual advisor and on March 14, 1900, the Reverend Albert Pfauss of the Presbyterian Church met with him. Although Calder made it clear that he hadn't requested or appreciated the meeting with the minister, he asked to see Mr. Pfaus the following morning. After those first two meetings, Reverend Pfaus visited the prisoner frequently and he was with the man at his death. While Calder obviously respected the reverend he refused to allow any praying, and the only concession he made was stating if there was a God, he hoped for something better than he had gotten on earth. Reverend Father James A. Vermaat saw Calder at the last hour but the prisoner refused to confess his sins.

Calder's demeanor changed during his last three days in both attitude and abusive language toward those who had been active in his capture, conviction and detention. His previous relationship with his mother had been terrible, but on the morning of his execution Calder freely asked for her forgiveness in front of Mr. Colt and Reverend Pfaus. Three days earlier Calder had a tearful parting with his younger brother, Jimmy although he still claimed that he and James Fisher had conspired against him. Before the two men parted, Jimmy seemed to be embarrassed by his brother's show of emotion and he seemed rather cold himself when all he said to his sibling was, "Well, so long, Billy. That unaffectionate response hurt Calder and he refused to say good-bye to his little brother.

During Calder's last two nights of incarceration he was constantly watched over by Deputies Clyde Osgood, John Foster, Mike Fraiser and one other officer. The prisoner didn't go to bed until 3:30 on Thursday morning still complaining that he couldn't sleep. Calder claimed that he had a lot on his mind and he asked if the lights could be shut off at night. Minutes after the officers had explained that they couldn't turn them off due to safety and security reasons Calder was sound asleep and he didn't wake up until seven o'clock.

On Wednesday Calder had requested oysters, but none could be found so he was served eggs instead. By Thursday morning the oysters had arrived on the stage from Great Falls and Calder was treated to a half dozen along with halibut and a plate of buckwheat pancakes, honey and other extras for his breakfast. Later the prisoner asked for some fruit and he was given oranges, which he reportedly enjoyed. The only request he made concerning his execution was that Jeff Sherman, who had captured him and Halsey P. Watson of the "Fergus County Argus" not be allowed to witness his hanging. While both men witnessed the hanging they respected the sheriff's request of standing in the rear of the crowd and the newspaperman had good reason to stay clear of Calder, as the prisoner had thrown stale soup at him the previous fall at the jail.

The condemned man slept soundly after midnight on his last night and he didn't rise until a little after seven o'clock when he woke up pleasantly and greeted every one with a "Good morning." After his breakfast, Calder once again met with Reverend Pfaus and he reiterated his innocence and agreed to see his mother for the last time. His mother was escorted into the jail where she first presented her son with a new shirt and socks and then she made peace with her child and they both wept openly. After his mother had left Calder took a bath and then Mr. Johnson the barber gave the prisoner his last shave and haircut.

Sheriff Shaw then read the seven-page, typewritten death warrant including his conviction, the reprieves from the Governor, Supreme Court findings and the second re-sentencing. Although Calder joked and used profane language concerning the length of the warrant he listened to the sheriff. Upon finishing the reading Calder got into his dark black suit while the sheriff and his deputies adjusted the straps on the prisoner. While the officers were attending to the prisoner, the crowd inside the enclosure, which numbered about seventy-five, were notified and ordered to make room for the procession. A minute a or two before eleven o'clock the march to the gallows began which consisted of Calder, the sheriff, Undersheriff Lincoln P. Slater, Deputies Riser, Scovel, John Foster and Clyde Osgood as well as Dr. Henry H. Wilson, Clerk of the Court Edmund Wright, Attorney William Cort, and others.

Witnesses with invitations included T.J. Johns of the "Lewistown Democrat," and "Fergus County Argus" reporter, H.R. Watson, began arriving at the jail early that Friday morning as the deputies were testing the gallows. Another three hundred people were reportedly outside the enclosure eager to catch even a sound of the awful affair. The scaffold was a lift or "jerk-type" and it was originally built for two victims as James Fisher had been originally sentenced to hang with Calder in May of 1899.

The contraption was the thirteenth death machine built in Montana and it consisted of three beveled six by six-inch black timbers; a crossbeam supported twelve feet off the ground by two upright posts. Four pulleys like the ones used in a barn to hoist hay were attached to the bottom of the crossbeam, which two ropes were to pass through to hang two victims. For the Calder hanging only two of the pulleys were utilized and the rope was allowed thirty inches of slack, but in order to provide against error, a hole was dug beneath the noose with a board covering to allow for additional distance.

The rope was five-eighths of an inch in diameter and it ran through the pulleys and fastened to a box of scrap metal weighing 308 pounds. The weight was held up at the left of the scaffold by a pin, which was pulled by the executioner who was hidden behind a sheet of canvas. On the signal from undersheriff, the executioner removed the pin, which dropped the weight and the condemned man was jerked upward and then his body fell downward from its own weight. Before the hanging the gallows was tested three times and to make the rope pliable it was stretched and soaped.

Calder had that familiar smile on his face as he marched with a swagger to the gallows and he nodded at the people in the crowd he recognized. Since his last sentencing he had shown signs of possibly breaking down and confessing but on the day of his hanging he bore himself up and was nonchalant throughout the whole affair. As Billy stepped under the scaffold his head brushed the noose and the deputy directed him to the proper position. After taking his place on the boards beneath the noose, Calder looked up to the sky for the last time, and he remarked that the sun was in his eyes. At 10:55, Undersheriff Lincoln Slater adjusted the noose and then he gave Calder a last opportunity to speak. Although it was expected that the man would make a long statement, he only proclaimed his innocence and bid the boys good-bye.

The black cap was pulled down over the man's face, the signal was given; Sheriff Shaw pulled the pin holding the weight and at eleven a.m. the body of William Wallace Calder shot upward and then settled to within four inches of the ground. It was reported that the sight of the execution stunned most of the spectators and a couple of the men even vomited in the enclosure.

The body gave a few slight tremors after the jerk, but they were involuntary and death was presumably without pain and at 11:14 attending physicians, Stone, Lindsay and Wilson declared Calder dead. Ten minutes later the body was lowered into a coffin and it was turned over to the undertaker and Calder's mother. That same morning the heart-broken mother accompanied the remains of her son to the Lewistown Cemetery, west of town where the Reverend Pfaus held a short service. After the execution Sheriff Shaw went to the jail and broke the news to Jimmy Calder and James Fisher. While Fisher showed no interest in the matter Jimmy broke down crying.

Postscript:

Since young Jimmy Calder had turned state's evidence against both his brother and Fisher, and it was through his confession that led to location of the bodies of McRea and Allen it was first understood that the charge against him would probably just go away. About a week before his brother was executed however, Jimmy began making statements that contradicted his previous testimony, which would have cleared Fisher of the murder charge.

It was a great surprise to everyone in the courtroom when James Calder's name was called and it was announced that he would stand trial for first-degree murder. Judge DuBose explained that it had been agreed between the county attorney, the state attorney general and Calder's counsel that if Jimmy told the truth in the case against his brother he would be let off with only two years imprisonment.

When the court made that statement Jimmy Calder's attorney, Rudolf VonTobel asked to withdraw from the case and he was given permission. It had been James Calder's testimony on the stand that hanged his brother and later saved the neck of Fisher, but on April 28, 1900, the witness himself was found guilty of perjury. Judge Dubose sentenced Jimmy to six years but since he was a model prisoner at Deer Lodge he was discharged on July 30, 1904, after serving just over four years. For Fisher's new trial he was granted a change of venue to Fort Benton and on April 27, 1900, he was found not guilty and was freed. After James Fisher was acquitted he wore a smile as big as the one worn by Billy Calder under the gallows, but Judge Henry V. Smith warned the young man to return to Indiana and never return to Montana.

March 30, 1900
Joseph C. Hurst

Location and Gallows: Hurst was hanged at Glendive in Dawson County and he was the last man to be executed on ***Gallows No. Eleven: (July 1894): "Galloping Gallows" Four***. This gallows had the distinction of being the only scaffold in Montana to have been converted from a trap-type to a jerk style scaffold. A complete description and history of this scaffold can be found in Chapter Seven: "Montana Gallows."
Description: Hurst was a handsome looking man with a stylish moustache
Crime: Murder of Sheriff Dominick Cavanaugh on December 23, 1898.
Judge: Charles H. Loud of Miles City was a personal friend of the defendant, Joseph Hurst.
Prosecution: County Attorney Thomas C. Holmes assisted by Custer County Attorney T.J. Porter of the firm, J.W. Strevell & Porter of Miles City along with, State Attorney General Cornelius .B. Nolan of Helena
Defense: C.R. Middleton and Henri J. Haskell assisted by George W. Myers of Miles City and William Wallace Jr., of Helena
Sheriff: Alfred Euclid Aiken
Distinction: Hurst was the only man ever hanged in Dawson County and he was one of the few defendants who forfeited their lives on a Montana gallows who could afford his own attorneys.

The citizens of Glendive had never been more shocked than they were just two days before Christmas in 1898, when the news that Sheriff Dominick Cavanaugh had been murdered within fifty feet of his home holding a little wrapped gift for his small daughter. J.H. Ray Jr. was the first to discover the body first thing in the morning on the way to his business. Not recognizing the victim at first he went at once to the sheriff's residence, which was at the nearby courthouse. Mrs. Cavanaugh answered the door and she reported that her husband wasn't home and that she had waited up all night for his return.

Mr. Ray then went to the home and office of Dr. J.H. Hunt who accompanied him back to the alley to examine the body, which was lying face down in a large pool of blood. There were two large fractures in the back of the man's skull and the impressions in his hat were clearly visible and matched the wounds on the head. When the body was turned over the men were shocked to find it was the sheriff. Apparently it was the sheriff's habit to visit the stable before going to his house each night, and he was last seen alive at the W.B. Foster Store, where he had made a small purchase for one of his children. Dr. Hunt then remembered hearing someone cry out the night before but he thought it was some boys playing outside.

Sheriff Dominick Cavanaugh
"Anaconda Standard" 3/30/1900

Sheriff Cavanaugh was born at Hamilton, Canada, on April 4, 1854, and when he was two his family moved to Fayette County, Iowa. He came to Dawson County in 1883, where he entered the cattle business and then he went into horse-trading. In 1894, he was elected as county sheriff and he was re-elected in 1896, and again in 1898. Cavanaugh was considered a fearless officer, who discharged his duty fairly and was highly respected by the honest citizens as well as the suspicious characters and outlaws. The entire county mourned his death and grieved for the bereaved wife and her three children.

Deputy Coroner G.N. Burdick conducted a coroner's jury at ten o'clock on the day before Christmas where several citizens were questioned including the murderer, Joseph Hurst and several arrests of suspicious characters in the community were made. The coroner's jury was made up of the following citizens of Dawson County:

Henry Dion	H.B. McCure	James C. Brooks
G.D. Hollicker	W.F. Jordan	Elmer S. Herrick

The Knights of Pythias and the Woodmen of the World conducted the funeral for Sheriff Cavanaugh on Tuesday afternoon, December 28, and many people including Judge Charles H. Loud of Miles City who would presided over the murder trial attended the services. Before that though, on December 27, 1898, the county commissioners of Dawson County named the murderer, Joseph C. Hurst to complete the remainder of Sheriff Cavanaugh's term because he was the Republican candidate for the office in a loosing effort during the 1898 election.

Two days later on Friday, December 30, at a special meeting the county commissioners rescinded their previous decision and appointed Alfred Euclid Aiken as the county sheriff after Joseph Hurst was named as a suspect in the murder of the sheriff. On January 10, 1899, the coroner's inquest concluded its twelve-day investigation and on the strength of the evidence a warrant was issued for the arrest of Joe Hurst. The jury was assisted by Chief Detective Gallin of the St. Paul Union Bureau, Stock Detective W.D. Smith, Custer County Attorney T.J. Porter and State Attorney General C.B. Nolan.

The arrest of Hurst for the murder of Sheriff Cavanaugh came as a great surprise to the citizens of Glendive as he had always been highly regarded and he enjoyed the confidence of everyone who knew him. Hurst had been a resident of Glendive for twenty years and his friends were sure that when the examination was concluded the charges against him would be found groundless.

Joseph C. Hurst
"Anaconda Standard" 3/30/1900

After County Attorney Holmes presented the evidence with the aid of Custer County Attorney T.J. Porter, Justice Thomas F. Hagen remanded Hurst over to the district court because the prisoner's testimony at his preliminary hearing apparently didn't agree with the statements he had made earlier at the coroner's jury and because he couldn't account for his whereabouts at the time of the murder. Judge Loud convened the case of the State of Montana vs. Joseph C. Hurst on Monday Morning, February 27, 1899, and the defendant and his friends and attorneys were so sure that they would get a fair trial that they didn't ask for a change of venue in fact they refused it and was satisfied with the following jury:

Orville Jones	John Maycock	Henry Louis
Charles Lovering	Samuel Kernick	H.C. Spencer
J.W. Brooks	Homer Squirer	A.H. Thomas
Harry N. Newell	George Mitchell	L.N. Allen

The chief witness for the prosecution was Frank Gillmore, who swore positively that on the evening of the murder he saw Hurst follow Sheriff Cavanaugh into the alley and other testimonies introduced evidence that the defendant had threatened the life of the victim immediately after the election. The counsel for Hurst relied heavily on the fact that the evidence was circumstantial and they didn't think it was sufficient to warrant a verdict of guilty.

The Hurst case was one of the most bitterly fought murder trials in the eastern part of Montana and while the state did their utmost to convict him, Hurst's attorneys didn't leave a stone unturned to clear their client. After deliberating for a full twenty-four hours the jury returned a first-degree guilty verdict on March 21, 1899. At the time, Dawson County was considered quite liberal and very few people believed that a person could ever be convicted of murder in the first degree there.

On Wednesday, March 22, 1899, Hurst was brought into court for sentencing where he told his friend, Judge Loud that he was innocent but the court said that the jury had found him guilty, and if he was innocent, he hoped that an appeal would be taken to the Supreme Court. But with no legal cause why judgment shouldn't be pronounced Judge Loud sentenced Joseph Hurst to be hanged on Friday, May 19, 1899.

Hurst's execution was temporarily cancelled because of an appeal to the high court and in December of 1899, the high court scheduled to hear the case during their January term along with that of William Wallace Calder and James Fisher at Fergus County. On January 29, 1900, the Supreme Court affirmed the convictions of William Calder and Joe Hurst while ordering a new trial for James Fisher.

On Friday, February 23, 1900, Judge Loud re-sentenced Joe Hurst to be hanged on March 30, between two a.m. and two o'clock that afternoon. Hurst's conviction and sentencing caused quite a stir throughout the state and a great effort was made to convince Governor Robert B. Smith to prevent the execution. Among those championing the cause of Hurst was Silver Bow County Attorney C.P. Connolly along with the "Anaconda Standard," "Butte Miner" and the "Minneapolis Journal." The largest newspapers of the state charged that the Dawson County court had failed to prove Hurst's guilt and his conviction had been the grossest abuse of the law ever known in Montana criticizing Judge Loud, the county attorney the firm of Strevell & Porter as well as the twelve-man jury. Put another way, the newspapers charged that the people of Dawson County were guilty of attempted judicial murder.

Ten days before Hurst's date of execution the Governor's private office was transformed into a courtroom with executive officer being the judge and jury while the various attorneys argued their cases. Right up to the memorable execution, groves of people pleaded with Governor Smith for the convicted man's life including his father, W.S. Hurst of Vancouver, British Columbia, his wife and some of the most prominent citizens of Montana. After hundreds of personal interviews, reviewing the trial records, examining seventy-seven petitions with about five thousand names from all over the state especially from Silver Bow, Missoula and Deer Lodge counties, Governor Smith finally decided not to interfere with the execution of Joe Hurst.

Besides declining to commute the condemned man's life, the Governor thoroughly criticized the Silver Bow County Attorney's statements and the other editorial attacks on the process, the officers and the people of Dawson County. Governor Smith also pointed out that in the paperwork sent to him from the defense there was a damaging letter by Attorney Meyers, which had been accidentally presented, explaining why the defendant wasn't placed on the stand. Smith pointed out that Judge Loud along with most of the jury and witnesses all knew and liked the defendant therefore they had no reason to railroad him.

The family and friends of Hurst held out hope until the final hour that the Governor would change his mind and commute the sentence. While at Butte the Governor was again asked to grant a short respite to go over some new evidence, which the defense claimed to have possessed but that same afternoon he again expressed that he would not interfere.

The gallows used for the Hurst execution had been used three times previously, the last being for the hanging of Brooks at Billings in November of 1899. It consisted of two upright pine posts twelve feet long and a cross piece, set on large six by six-inch sills. The noose was a half-inch rope, which ran through two pulleys and was attached to three granite blocks weighing nearly four hundred pounds.

Prior to the execution there was talk that the hanging of Hurst would be prevented by his friends and the threats were given credibility when it was reported that four boxes of blasting powder had been stolen from the warehouse of the Northern Pacific Railroad just a few days before the big day. Some people believed that the reason why the execution was re-scheduled at 2:30 o'clock in the morning was to prevent any attempts of Hurst's friends to interrupt the hanging but according to visiting sheriff, Jack Conley, the unusual hour was chosen by the condemned man, as he wanted the ordeal to be over as soon as possible.

So mixed were the feelings about the hanging at Glendive that some of the authorities felt that if Governor Smith had commuted Hurst's sentence or interfered in any way the officers of the county probably couldn't have restrained the crowd from pulling off the hanging themselves. Sheriff Aiken had appointed a number of special deputies in case of trouble from either group but fortunately everything went quietly.

Hurst spent his last afternoon with his family and friends and after a light supper he went to sleep and slept until one a.m., when he got dressed into a black suit, soft shirt, underwear, socks and shoes, which were all furnished by the county. On his lapel of his new suit the prisoner wore a photo button of his wife and two children. The condemned man held up wonderfully during his long confinement and Father Claude M. Ebner told the press that in his twenty-three years of ministry he had never seen a man as unconcerned or in a better frame of mind on his way to his death than Joseph Hurst.

Father Ebner of Dickinson, North Dakota, came to Glendive after the condemned man had telegraphed him to be baptized a Catholic at 1:30 a.m. and then he administered the last rites of the church to Hurst as he was being marched to the gallows. Sheriff Aiken read the death warrant to the prisoner only moments before the officers escorted him to the gallows and Hurst walked between Deputies George B. Williams and George Twible, followed by Father Ebner. On the way, Hurst said to Deputy Twible, who was holding his arm, "You need not hold me, George; I can stand alone."

As he took his place on the scaffold, Hurst recognized one of the doctors in the crowd and he greeted the man. After the noose was adjusted and before the black cap was drawn over the face of the condemned man was asked if he had anything to say. "It is all a mistake," Hurst called out in a clear voice. "I forgive you all, as Jesus did." Deputy Twible again asked if he anything further to say, to which Hurst said: "That is all."

The black cap was pulled down and at 2:28 a.m. the weight dropped and Joseph Hurst was jerked about eighteen inches off the ground. Those close enough to the gallows reported hearing a convulsive sob from Hurst as Dr. Francis G. Gray of Miles City held the left wrist while Dr. J.H. Hunt grasped the right, and they pronounced him dead eleven minutes later. The body was cut down a minute later and it was quickly placed on a stretcher where after an examination, the doctors reported that his neck had been broken. The body was first taken back to the jail where the undertaker placed it into a casket and then it was taken to the Hurst family home. The wife and parents of Hurst accompanied the remains to Wadena, Minnesota for burial.

The day after the execution Reverend Henry Warman, pastor of the Methodist Episcopal Church at Glendive reported that Joseph Hurst had confessed on Tuesday, March 27, 1900, that he did in fact kill Sheriff Dominick Cavanaugh. Hurst told the minister that after talking to the victim he waited until the sheriff turned to shut the door to his stable and then he struck him with an iron bolt. Cavanaugh fell to the ground moaning, which caught the attention of a woman in the alley, but she couldn't see anything because of the darkness. Hurst continued by saying he then struck his victim several more times. Reverend Warman said that Hurst requested that he keep the statement from the public until after he was dead and to not contradict any statement he might make on the scaffold before his execution.

Reverend Warman had an excellent reputation in eastern Montana and he had always been considered to be a conscientious and honest man whose word was as good as his bond. When he came out with the statement of Hurst's confession most of the people believed that the question of his guilt had been answered but the Hurst family understandably protested by pointing out the unsupported statement of the reverend was inconsistent with Joseph's previous claims of his innocence and his final words on the gallows.

A day or two after Hurst's execution some state newspapers published what was allegedly the condemned man's final letter denying his guilt and many people tried to discredit Reverend Warman's statement by pointing out that Hurst hadn't signed the confession. After receiving Hurst's confession, Warman said that he wrote it down and waited for an opportunity to obtain the prisoner's signature without alerting the guards. The Reverend explained that he stayed at the jail until nine p.m. on the condemned man's last evening to secure the signature but Hurst was with his family the entire time and he felt he shouldn't interrupt them.

Mr. Warman also pointed out that everyone including the Hurst family, his friends and the authorities all knew that he believed in the prisoner's innocence until he made his confession. While in jail Hurst was always glad to see Mr. Warman, his brothers attended the reverend's church and his sister had been singing in the church choir. Sheriff Aiken wasn't surprised in the least about the contradicting letter left in Hurst's cell, saying the prisoner would often make a statement one day, and then stoutly deny it the next. The sheriff pointed out a number of falsehoods in his so-called final letter that differed from his own testimonies during his preliminary hearing.

Of the one-hundred and twenty-five people who witnessed the hanging there were only three outside officers able to take advantage of the invitation because of such short notice between the time of Governor Smith's decision and the execution date. The only visiting lawmen able to attend were Sheriff Cato and Undersheriff C.A. Tizer of Custer County and Sheriff Jack Conley of Deer Lodge County who managed to return to Anaconda with most of the half-inch rope that was used for the hanging as a memento. Mr. Conley had left Glendive with the entire noose but an enterprising newspaperman from Butte reportedly cut off a portion of the rope when the sheriff wasn't looking. The knot remained, as well as the noose that had encircled Hurst's neck and it reportedly was presented to one of the many collectors at Anaconda.

Sheriff Conley said that Sheriff Aiken, although a young and inexperienced officer, carried out the execution as well as anyone could have. The Deer Lodge officer also reported that after talking with many Dawson County residents before the execution he had determined that about sixty percent of the folks believed that Hurst was guilty and should have been hanged while the remaining forty percent was evenly divided between those believing he should have received a life sentence and acquittal.

The confession made by Hurst, which was made public the day after the hanging removed almost all doubt of his guilt. The Deer Lodge County sheriff recounted a pathetic occurrence at the hanging when Hurst was holding a crucifix while the noose was being adjusted and he asked that if it fell out of his hand that someone would replace it. The crucifix did fall from his hand when he was jerked but as he was suspended the crucifix was replaced as he had requested, and he died holding the image.

Postscript:
The Hurst case was talked about for many years because the lines were so distinctively drawn between those believing in the man's innocence and his guilt. On Memorial Day 1900, at Glendive the Woodmen of the World and the Knights of Pythias jointly conducted a special parade including the city brass band to the Cavanaugh residence where they escorted the family in a carriage to the sheriff's gravesite and unveiled a monument erected to the fallen officer. Senator T.P. Cullen addressed the impressive crowd and spoke of the virtues of the deceased sheriff and friend.

April 6, 1900
William Pepo

Location and Gallows: William Pepo was hanged at Choteau in Teton County and he was the last man to give up his life on ***Gallows No. Eight: (March 1887): "Galloping Gallows" No. Two***. A complete description and history of this famous scaffold, which claimed the lives of ten men, can be found in Chapter Seven: "Montana Gallows."

Description: Pepo was about forty years old, a German native with a large frame, standing about five foot ten inches tall and weighing about 180 pounds. By the end of his long imprisonment Pepo lost considerable weight and had become very weak. He had iron nerves as well as a pleasant and intelligent looking face and it was said that he was witty, well read, which indicated a good manners and education.

Crime: Murder of Julius Plath on June 15, 1898

Judge: D. F. Smith

Prosecution: County Attorney John Edward Erickson assisted by Jason Sulgrove

Defense: John G. Bair of Choteau and Major D. Baldwin

Sheriff: William D. Hagen

Distinction: The execution of William Pepo at Choteau was the first legal hanging in Teton County.

On June 29, 1898, a farmhand found a badly decomposed body in an abandoned cabin on Muddy Creek about twenty miles from Choteau. The corpse was on a bunk with most of the flesh rotted away, and what hair remained was dark brown. The man had been wearing a black coat and vest with a shirt and dark blue overalls with stripes. A fractured skull indicated that some blunt instrument had been used to kill the man probably in his sleep and a heavy iron bolt covered with bloodstains was found near by.

A notebook and other papers found in an overcoat along with a watch charm, which was lying nearby on the floor helped identify the man as Julius Plath. Area residents reported that Plath had been seen in the company of William Pepo and after further investigations the authorities discovered that the suspect had served two sentences in the Penitentiary of Canada. When it was learned from Plath's family that Pepo and their relative had left Lethbridge Canada together the Teton County officials immediately suspected him as the murderer.

Nine months after the body of Plath was found the Teton County authorities were beginning to think they would never find the murderer, when Pepo was found in Washington State. Apparently a schoolteacher had seen the fugitive working on a farm near her home at Davenport, Washington and she remembered him from her original home in Canada. Although the woman didn't know Pepo was a wanted man, she wrote to her relatives in Canada that she had seen the man and slowly the news leaked out and it finally reached Sheriff Hagen at Choteau. The sheriff went to Washington in May of 1899, and arrested the fugitive who was living under the name of William Ferris and denied knowing anything about the crime.

Julius Plath and Pepo had been friends in Canada and they had traveled together on the train as far as Pondera and then they walked through Teton County. When he left home, Plath was reportedly wearing a black coat and was carrying one hundred and twenty dollars along with a watch with a charm hanging from a chain. Several ranchers from Shelby to Choteau had identified both men from the photograph and one of the farmers claimed he had directed the two men to the small log cabin on June 14, 1898. William Pepo was seen alone several weeks later near Great Falls inquiring the route west through the mountains. On May 24, 1899 William Pepo was arraigned before Justice of the Peace H. Beaupre and his trial opened on May 31, 1899, when the following jury was selected:

H.A. Gillette (f)	Ed Bollrud	William Lillard
B.B. Rogers	Ed Stonehouse	Henry Ryan
Adolph Fellers	Pat A. Knowles	William McDonald Wright
John E. De Haas	John Jackson	John W. Kerr

(f) Foreman

The weakest point of the state's case against William Pepo was the identity of the deceased man because when found the body was little more than a skeleton and at first the coroner's jury couldn't even determine whether the remains were those of a man or a woman. The only proof of identification of the deceased and connection between Plath and Pepo was a photograph of the two men, the testimony of local residents who had seen them together at the cabin along with a few personal effects found on and around the body.

When arrested in Washington, Pepo was wearing a watch chain, which he said a man on the farm had given him but when everyone at the ranch was questioned no one claimed presenting it to the fugitive. Pepo always maintained that he didn't kill Plath, and in fact he didn't believe the dead man in the Montana cabin was friend. Several witnesses identified the deceased man's coat and Plath's brother of Toronto also pointed out a hole in the garment, which had been sewed up by their mother before Julius left Canada.

Purely on circumstantial evidence the jury eventually found Pepo guilty of first degree murder and after Judge Smith sentenced the man to be hanged on July 26, the defense filed a motion for a new trial on the grounds that the bailiff, Thomas J. Moore had remained overnight with the jurors and had influenced the jury's verdict. Each member of the jury filed affidavits that Thomas Moore had only delivered blankets and a meal to the members of the jury and that he did not discuss the case with any of them. Judge Smith denied the motion for a new trial on July 6, and the defense then appealed to the Supreme Court. Finally when the high court affirmed the judgment of the district court on February 10, 1900, Pepo was brought before Judge Smith on March 5 when he was re-sentenced to be hanged on April 6, 1900.

With no friends, no money and no hope, Pepo became devoted in saving himself from the most disgraceful manner of death, that of being hanged and he immediately attempted to starve himself to death. When his attorney filed for a new trial and during the time that the Supreme Court was considering his case, the condemned man began eating freely again but when the high court affirmed the decision of the lower court he once again refused to eat. When he was re-sentenced he was reportedly so weak that he had to sit down while the judge made the pronouncement and for the first time Pepo desired to see a minister and it was feared that his condition had deteriorated to the point that he would indeed cheat the gallows.

On September 14, 1899, Sheriff Hagen went to Helena to attend the hanging of Joseph Allen in order to get first hand experience of an execution and make the necessary arrangements with Lewis and Clark County Sheriff Thomas Davidson to have the famous scaffold transported to Choteau. Even while Pepo and his attorneys were working on the appeals, Sheriff Hagen went on with the preparations for the hanging by hiring the services of Charles Wymer of Choteau to construct an enclosure in the jail yard and to assemble the gallows.

By using his own money, Mr. Bair carried on Pepo's appeals and he traveled to and from Helena to personally appear before Governor Robert B. Smith in an attempt to save his client's life. During this time, Joseph Hurst had just been hanged at Glendive after presenting petitions containing seven thousand names asking the Governor for clemency. Mr. Bair was pleading for a client that had been convicted on purely circumstantial evidence but because Pepo was totally unknown, without money and without a single friend in the state he couldn't get any support for a commuted sentence.

In the end, the results were the same for both convicted murders as the Governor refused to interfere with either case. In a letter to Mr. Blair, Governor Smith stated that the evidence in the Pepo case was convincing and clear and he felt that the jury couldn't have reached any other conclusion. The Governor described the crime as being a cold-blooded murder and he emphatically refused to interfere with the sentence of the court.

By mid March, Pepo had given up his hunger strike and he was interviewed by a reporter for the "Dupuyer Acantha" who described the doomed man as being composed and taking his impending doom as an "ordinary transaction of life." Pepo maintained his innocence pointing out that Plath had blue eyes while the murdered man who was found on Muddy Creek had brown. He also claimed that on the day before Plath left the Northwest Territory he was clean shaven and he couldn't have grown a beard as thick as the one on the murdered man in that short of time. The prisoner explained that the watch chain in his possession, which was similar to the one owned by Plath was presented to him by a young man that he had named at his trial but the man couldn't be located to verify his story.

On the day before his execution Pepo had his beard nicely trimmed up and he was presented with his brand new clothes, which he would wear to the gallows. A reporter from the "Anaconda Standard" visited with the prisoner and he was greeted very politely. The prisoner was smoking and he politely passed his pack of cigars out through the iron bars, stating that there were more than enough to last him until his hanging. There were many other visitors to see the condemned man, and those that he recognized he shook hands heartily with and talked pleasantly with each of them. A small white kitten romped around the floor of Pepo's cell and the prisoner was quite concerned about what would happen to his little pet after he was gone. One of the officers finally promised to look after the kitten and the condemned man appeared very relieved.

Pepo spent most of his last night smoking, writing, talking and playing cards with his guards and the newspaperman. While he refused to argue his case over again, he maintained his innocence and several times expressed his belief that Plath was still alive. Although the condemned man talked about many subjects he refused to divulge his true name or disclose anything about himself or his family. There had been indications that he might have been a black sheep of an aristocratic German family but all the officials ever knew about the man only went back ten years.

At about 2:30 o'clock on his final morning Pepo finally went to sleep and slept soundly until 4:30 when the sheriff woke him up for his breakfast. He told the officer that he didn't want any breakfast, saying that, "sleep would do him more good." He then slept until five o'clock when he was awakened by Deputy McDonald and again the prisoner refused breakfast but asked to see his attorney and his spiritual advisers, Father Snell of the Catholic Church and Reverend C.E. Cunningham of the Methodist Church. Pepo told the two ministers that he had professed religion but he wouldn't commit to either church, saying that he would go "straight to Jesus," and assured them both that he was innocent of the crime. When Mr. Blair asked his client to tell the truth, Pepo became disappointed that his lawyer didn't believe in his innocence in the end.

Shortly before six o'clock Undersheriff Haggerty read the death warrant to the prisoner and Pepo, in his brand new suit of clothes listened to it attentively. After the reading Pepo said that he wanted to be hanged at once and the deputies began adjusting the harness while the condemned man said good-bye to the guards in the corridor. When his arms were strapped down the march to the gallows began, and Pepo walked steadily and unassisted between Deputies Devlin and Armstrong, followed by Sheriff Hagen, Undersheriff Haggerty and Reverend Cunningham.

As the procession walked down the north side of the jail through the alleyway formed by the high board fence built around the yard the morning air was crisp and cold, and the condemned man turned to one of the officers and jokingly said, "This must be like the weather they tell about in North Dakota." As Pepo turned the corner of the building and headed for the gallows he had a smile on his face and his eyes looked straight ahead.

When he reached the gallows Pepo looked into the faces of nearly every one of the uncovered spectators and several members of the crowd admitted that the condemned man was the most calmest and self-possessed man present as he bowed pleasantly three or four times to men that he recognized. Among the fifty witnesses included Sheriff George Hubbard of Yellowstone County who had recently executed William Brooks in November of 1899. The sun was beginning to shine brightly through the gray morning sky and its rays fully illuminated the condemned man as the birds began to sing, which made Pepo smile. When asked if he had any last words he stood silent for a moment and then said, "Gentlemen, you are hanging an innocent man."

Pepo then turned his head towards Sheriff Hagen who was adjusting the straps around his knees and the condemned man assisted by carefully placing his feet together. The noose was placed around his neck and Pepo didn't flinch an inch while Reverend Cunningham was reciting a prayer in a low tone while the prisoner's eyes were closed. Suddenly a meadowlark in the nearby field whistled its morning song loud and clear; Pepo quickly opened his eyes and looked over the crowd of awe struck faces as if to say, "Did you hear that?"

After making the final adjustment to the noose and pulling down the terrible black cap over the man's head, the sheriff gave the signal by moving his hat and a concealed deputy released the trap. At 6:09 a.m. the four hundred-pound weight dropped and William Pepo's body was jerked about three feet and then it fell back down. With his neck broken, there wasn't even a quiver noticed and the hanging form reportedly showed as much life as a block of wood.

The drop fell at 6:15 and ten minutes later Drs. Thomas Brooks and A.J. Cooper reported that the man's pulse had ceased and at 6:30 the body was cut down and placed into a coffin. It was reported that there was a smile on face of the body as it lay in the coffin and the remains were buried at three o'clock that same afternoon. Pepo left behind several letters of thanks including the one to the Reverend Cunningham, in which he once again stated that he was innocent.

Postscript:
William Pepo protected his true identity to the very end, and he prevented any attempt to be photographed by always pulling his collar above his neck and shielding his face with his hands. He told his attorney and closet friend, Mr. Blair that nobody knew who he was and that he would never bring disgrace upon his family by letting them know he had died a felon's death.

Teton County Attorney E.J. Erickson later became a district judge at Kalispell where he presided over the trial of Frederick LeBeau who was convicted of murder and hanged in April of 1909. Erickson was then elected as the state's seventh Governor and he was in office to review and consider the cases of Roy Walsh, Anthony Vettere, Ferdinand Schlaps, Rollin Davisson and Henry Zorn who were all eventually hanged.

September 14, 1900

Daniel Lucy

Other Names: Dan Sullivan, Daniel Reagan

Location and Gallows: Daniel Lucy was the second man legally hanged in Silver Bow County and the third man hanged on the most infamous ***Gallows No. Nine: (Feb. 1888): "Galloping Gallows" No. Three***.

Description: The forty-two year-old Lucy was an Irish born miner.

Crime: Murder of Patrick L. Reagan on September 2, 1898 in Silver Bow Canyon about three miles east of Gregson Springs.

Judge: William D. Clancy

Prosecution: County Attorney C.P. Connolly assisted by Chief Deputy County Attorney Cornelius Francis Kelley

Defense: Z.T. Cason and J.M. Hinkle and later Lucy's sister hired B.S. Thresher

Sheriff: Patrick H. Regan (no relation to the victim)

Daniel Lucy worked in the mines of Butte off and on for a number of years when he became acquainted with Patrick L. Reagan while they worked together at the Never-Sweat Mine. The younger Patrick Reagan was a hard working man that had managed to save between five and six hundred dollars even though he had the one bad habit of doing things on a whim. Lucy apparently took advantage of Reagan's weakness and talked the man into going to Coeur d'Alene to work in the mines there. Reagan lived with his brother, Michael and his family in a little cottage at 131 West Cooper Street just two blocks almost due north of the county jail where Daniel Lucy eventually was hanged.

After telling his sister-in-law that he and Lucy were headed for Idaho, Patrick went to his trunk and took out a certificate of deposit for five hundred and fifty dollars to cash at his bank. About five o'clock that evening Reagan returned to his brother's home with the certificate saying that he hadn't yet cashed it and put it back in the trunk. It is believed that Lucy thought Reagan had cashed the certificate and had figured Patrick was carrying over five hundred dollars when in fact the young man was only carrying about one hundred dollars.

At eight o'clock Lucy came by the house for Reagan and the two men said good-bye to Pat's sister-in-law and left to catch the nine o'clock train for Anaconda. When questioned why they were going to Anaconda to catch a train to Idaho, Lucy apparently convinced them that transportation was cheaper if booked outside of Butte. The next day, September 3, 1898, the dead body of Patrick Reagan was found by some section hands for the Butte, Anaconda Pacific Railroad in the Clark Fork River about three miles east of Gregson Hot Springs

At first the men believed that the man had been struck and killed by a passing train and was thrown into the river but about a hundred yards up the tracks towards Butte, the men found the man's hat and necktie along with evidence of a fierce struggle. The acting coroner was at Gregson at the time and E.J. Lauran Dean rushed to the site where he found the dead man's face crushed into a mangled mass. The only portion of the victim's skull that was still intact was the back part of the head. The lining of the victim's coat and vest had been cleanly cut open and all the pockets had been turned inside out indicating that he was murdered for his money.

About a quarter of a mile further up stream the authorities located a large pool of blood several yards from the tracks and two jagged rocks with blood and tufts of human hair clinging to them. The body had been dragged through a barbed wire fence and pieces of the victim's garments were still clinging to the sharp points. From the murder scene, footprints were found indicating that a man had carried the victim's body some forty yards to the river where it was then thrown in and it floated to the location where it was found. Along the gruesome trail the authorities found several silver coins and the key to Patrick Reagan's trunk.

When word of the murder reached Butte, Reagan's sister-in-law immediately declared that Daniel Lucy was the murderer and further investigations proved the theory correct. Somehow the murderer convinced Reagan that they should walk to Anaconda and shortly after leaving Butte they were noticed walking together near Rocker and at about six o'clock on the morning of September 3, Lucy was seen alone at Gregson carrying the dead man's handbag. After spending several hours at the saloon near the hot springs getting drunk and flashing money around, Daniel Lucy left town and he wasn't seen again until he was arrested seven months later at Cripple Creek near Victor, Colorado.

It was learned that Lucy's motive for the murder was to raise money so that he could marry his sweetheart on Labor Day, which was two days after the murder. After Lucy was hanged it was reported that Margaret Gallagher was the name of the girl he was going to marry. The young woman was a domestic working in a westside household and she told the authorities that Lucy had told her that he came across the money for their marriage but he wouldn't tell her where he had found the funds. He told her that he had gotten a room for her in an apartment house and he wanted her to wait there until the day of the wedding.

Miss Gallagher said she went to the room and waited there for Lucy but she never saw him again until she later visited him on several occasions at the Butte jail. Her name was originally kept out of the newspapers and even when she refused to obey a subpoena as a witness at the murder trial the prosecution didn't press her. Although the authorities were certain of the motive, the prosecution didn't bring up the marriage in court because they didn't want to drag the name of the innocent women into the nasty case.

After running from Butte, Lucy worked on a thresher crew in the Gallatin Valley and drove team at Manhattan. He told the Butte authorities that while in the Gallatin Valley he considered re-enlisting in the army and go to the Philippines but he was afraid he would be recognized. During the winter of 1898-99, Lucy traveled and worked at Salt Lake City, St. Louis, Nashville and New Orleans. Lucy went to the Denver area to work in the mines where he then turned up at Cripple Creek, Colorado.

A former Butte bartender had recognized Lucy at Cripple Creek and he quietly sent for the authorities and the fugitive was arrested under the name of Daniel Reagan. After the proper requisition papers were drawn up, Silver Bow County Undersheriff Murphy went to Colorado for the prisoner and on the return trip Lucy practically confessed to the murder. At one time he considered making a plea-deal with the prosecution but he reconsidered after he was assigned counsel. Dan Lucy's trial, Case No.1051, opened on June 29, 1899, when the following men were sworn in as jurors:

Hugh Morrison	A.J. White (f)	Abe Phillips
Joseph Roberts	Ernest Rodgers	R.W. Sampson
W.H. Griffiths	J.W. Phariss	Enoch H. Giberson
G.S. Holbrook	Chris Christensen	Daniel Johnson

(f) Foreman

While the evidence heard at the Lucy trial was wholly circumstantial it was truly overwhelming, but many observers said that if the defendant hadn't taken the stand in his own defense he probably wouldn't have been convicted. Although some of the jurors had initially sworn that they would never convict any man on circumstantial evidence, Lucy's testimony was considered so damaging that the jury was out just a little over an hour.

Closing arguments began at four o'clock on the afternoon of July 1, 1899, in a crowded courtroom and they concluded at 8:30 when the jury retired at nine o'clock after receiving their instructions. Although the jury had sent out word at about eleven o'clock that they had agreed on a verdict, J.M. Hinkle with the defense didn't arrive at the courthouse until midnight. While waiting for the defense attorney the jury was heard singing the songs, "I'm Tired Now and Sleepy, Too, So Put Me in My Little Bed;" "God Be With Us Till We Meet Again;" "In the Morning by the Bright Light" and other popular tunes of the day.

The singing could be heard all through the courthouse and many of the spectators were sure that the jury would acquit Lucy while the county prosecutor interpreted the songs as displaying that the jurors were satisfied with their work and had convicted one of the worst criminals that Silver Bow County had ever seen. When the jurors filed back into the courtroom it was clear to most observers that the jury had "Guilty" written all over their foreheads.

When the guilty verdict was read it was said that Lucy appeared to be the coolest man in the courtroom and he only turned to his attorney and calmly asked what would be the next step. Mr. Hinkle told his client that he would consult with his associate, Mr. Z.T. Cason and they would plan for an appeal. After hearing Lucy told his attorneys to do their best and then he returned to the jail. Because of various motions, Lucy wasn't sentenced until September 26, 1899, when he was ordered to be hanged on November 24, but his attorneys were able to stave off the execution with his appeals.

On July 16, 1900, the Supreme Court refused to grant Lucy a new trial and it affirmed the lower court's decision. When Sheriff P.H. Regan received word of the high court's decision he removed Lucy from the corridor with the other prisoners and placed him in the long narrow solid iron cage known as the "box car." While he wasn't specifically told why he was being moved, the frightened look on Lucy's face indicated that he knew what had happened. Later that evening Lucy was given the official word of the court's decision and he made no comment. At about six o'clock that same evening his attorney stopped by the jail to discuss the future of the case and he explained that he would apply for another hearing and possibly appeal to the United State Supreme Court.

Lucy's sister living in Providence, Rhode Island had retained the services of Mr. B.S. Thresher as counsel after the original trial and to handle the appeals. About two weeks earlier a troublemaker at the jail had started a nasty rumor that the Montana Supreme Court had granted Lucy a new trial and he was so elated that he wrote to his sister the good news. No sooner than it was in the mail Lucy learned that he had been fooled and he was ashamed to tell his sister the truth and then when he really lost his bid for a new trial he didn't know how to tell her.

The prisoner decided not to write to his sister again until he and his lawyer knew exactly what the status of his case was but on August 1, the highest court of the state refused to re-hear Lucy's case and his attorney wasn't able to raise a federal question in order to present it to the United States Supreme Court. In the meantime the sheriff and his men were preparing a more pleasant cell for Lucy and he was moved out of the "box car."

At ten o'clock on the morning of August 14, Lucy was brought before Judge William Clancy for re-sentencing in a crowded courtroom at the courthouse. The prisoner was under heavy guard and he appeared very pale and was showing the effects of his long confinement and mental strain. Lucy looked over the courtroom full of spectators and then he sat next to his counsel. He only spoke one word to Mr. Thresher and then he stared at the judge's bench and hardly took his eyes off of it. After hearing from the attorneys, Judge Clancy ordered the prisoner to stand and then he sentenced Daniel Lucy to be hanged on September 14, 1900. After being sentenced to death for the second time, Lucy sat perfectly still for a few minutes while he spoke with his attorney and nervously pulled at his mustache. He reportedly had broken down earlier that morning when the officers went to his cell to take him to the courtroom.

Attorney Thresher attempted to have the execution stayed by getting a bill of exception and an application for a certificate of probable cause signed by either the district court or a member of the Supreme Court, which was not in session at the time. If a question could be raised whether the execution should go forward the hanging could once again be postponed until the Supreme Court met again. Unfortunately for condemned man, Judge Clancy refused to issue the certificate on August 29, and Chief Justice Brantley of the Supreme Court passed on the application on September 8, 1900, on the constitutional grounds.

While being visited by several members of the Rocky Mountain Medical Association Lucy used the opportunity to demonstrate to the physicians the extent of his morphine addiction. While the delegation led by Dr. Cole of Helena presented the prisoner with several fine cigars, Lucy told the physicians that he took two tablets of morphine three times daily. Dr. Murray commented later that after taking that quantity of the drug, the fourteenth of the month (Lucy's hanging date) would look the same as the sixteenth to the prisoner.

A firm at Philadelphia provided the rope and had prepared the traditional hangman's noose free for the execution of Lucy as it had done for all sheriffs who requested them. The same firm had supplied the rope and noose used to hang Harry Roberts in 1889, and Sheriff Regan received the specialty rope on September 5, 1900, and two days later he was sending out invitations for the execution. Sheriff Regan had witnessed the hanging of William Brooks at Billings in November of 1899, to gain first-hand experience and on Monday, September 10, 1900, he ordered the scaffold taken out of the courthouse cellar. A carpenter reported that the gallows was in better shape than it was when it was constructed eleven years earlier because it was thoroughly seasoned and had hardened over time.

Lucy was able to observe the work on the scaffold from his cell window and he got a kick out of all the people he noticed sneaking into the yard to see the gallows. By the time the preparations for the execution were well under way Lucy had gone through some changes in his actions and attitudes. He had ceased to talk flippantly and carelessly about the future and he devoted more time in prayer. Whereas before he had offered animosity towards persons who were active in his prosecution he no longer showed ill feelings towards those parties, even though he hadn't forgiven them.

At first Lucy was very selective in his visitors but within a week of his execution he expressed a willingness to see anybody and everybody. The condemned man also expressed the fact that he preferred death to life in prison and he wasn't disappointed when Governor Robert Smith announced that he wouldn't interfere with the execution. On September 10, the Governor had left Helena to go hunting and fishing in Deer Lodge County and before leaving he said that he wouldn't interfere with the judgment of the courts.

On September 10, a barber called on the jail to give Lucy a shave and a haircut and the condemned man asked the man to return Thursday afternoon for another shave because he wanted to look nice for his big day. In his roomy cell on the east wing of the jail, Lucy talked about being born in Kerry County, Ireland and moving to Boston where he learned the plumber's trade. After serving his three-year apprentice, he moved to Kansas where he was going to farm but instead enlisted in the Thirteenth U.S. Infantry and went to Texas from 1882 to 1886. While in the southwest Lucy was attached with the Sixth Cavalry where he served two years in the Geronimo Indian Campaign under General Chaffee who was then just a captain.

Lucy deserted from the army in 1886, at Fort Wingate, New Mexico because he felt he was being taken advantage of because he was being paid as a regular soldier but asked to work as a plumber and he wasn't compensated for the extra duties. While on the run he changed his name to Daniel Sullivan and went to work in the mines in Arizona and New Mexico before eventually coming to Butte. Lucy's only known relatives in the United States were two or three brothers and sisters residing in Rhode Island and there was much speculation whether any of them would meet with their brother before his death.

Several years earlier Lucy had been run out of Pony for getting into trouble and in 1898, he served time in the county jail for obtaining goods under false pretenses from the Hennessy Company. Lucy tried to convince everyone that would listen that a man named Gilligan had actually murdered Patrick Reagan. He claimed that Gilligan was with Reagan last, and there was actually a man named Luke Gilligan who reportedly left Butte about the same time of the murder and he was known to have worked with Lucy at Deadwood and several other places. The missing Gilligan said that he would return to Butte and he had in fact left personal property of value there, which caused speculation that he might have killed Reagan but the vast majority of the people feared that Lucy had probably murdered him as well.

Before Lucy was executed it was speculated that he had also murdered another miner named Timothy Leary who had mysteriously disappeared in 1896, under the same pretenses of leaving town. A body of a dead man was found two months later just a stone's throw away from where Patrick Reagan was later murdered, but the remains were so decomposed that they could not be positively identified as Leary. Lucy always denied any involvement in that murder and pointed out the fact that they had been very good friends. He said that the last time he saw Leary was when they parted company at the Butte Brewery Saloon on North Wyoming Street.

On September 11, 1900, Lucy held sort of a public reception where a large number of callers crowded the corridor near the jailer's office all afternoon. The condemned man seemed glad to see the crowd and he really enjoyed the notoriety and the curiosity he had aroused. Several of the women callers brought him flowers and openly wept for the prisoner and among the crowds around the jail were many little school children who were permitted to inspect the gallows in the courtyard.

County Physician Sheeran visited the prisoner every day to check on him and to dispense two grains of morphine and all of the whisky he could drink. All day long Lucy proudly displayed a letter he had received from his young niece at Providence, Rhode Island telling him that his brother cried for him everyday and that the whole family felt very bad for him. While he was obviously proud of his family, Lucy reportedly didn't want any of his relations to come out for his execution.

September 13, 1900, was reportedly Lucy's forty-second birthday but he didn't celebrate it and barely mentioned it to anyone as he appeared very nervous all day and walked about his cell in a disturbed state. The sheriff restricted the crowds that day and he reported that the prisoner's air of bravado had deserted him and he was resigned to his fate. The prisoner ate a very light breakfast and he barely touched his dinner of roast veal, fruit, pie and cake. For his last supper the prisoner had ordered a nice porterhouse steak but he hardly touched it.

Lucy spent his last night restlessly, staying up till midnight praying and talking with the Catholic priests who had stayed with him the last two days. The condemned man sent for Dick Butler, and he was asked to remain with the prisoner all night and his good friend consented to the request. A little after midnight the prisoner retired to his cot and slept uneasily until twenty minutes before four on his last morning when he was awakened and got dressed. It had been the intention of the sheriff to have the execution as soon after the hour of eight as possible, but at Lucy's request it was postponed until eleven o'clock in the morning. The prisoner explained that he always had a bad stomach in the morning and Lucy told the sheriff that he probably wouldn't be able to walk to the gallows until about eleven o'clock.

Sheriff Regan provided Lucy with an entire new outfit of clothing for the execution including underwear, socks, a black suit with a black flock coat, white shirt and a lay-down collar and a black bow tie. Mr. E.H. Sherman had fitted Lucy for the new suit of clothes and he was said to wear a size thirty-eight coat, thirty-two trousers, size sixteen collar and eight and a half slippers. After Lucy had finished getting dressed, Fathers Peter DeSiere, James P. Harrington, McGlynn and Batens celebrated mass at eight o'clock and the doomed man had a little tea and some toast.

Although he had a bad night's sleep, he appeared in better spirits than he had for several days and some said that Lucy was the coolest man in the courthouse on his last morning. The man then shocked everyone by asking that he be photographed and the murderer's image was captured as he was sitting at the little table in his cell with some flowers. Until that morning the prisoner had steadfastly refused to be photographed stating that he didn't want the "Anaconda Standard" to get hold of a photo of him.

As early as six in the morning the people were gathering around the courthouse and in the vicinity of the courtyard and a large number of policemen and sheriff deputies were required to keep the crowds out of the building except for those carrying valid invitations. Early that morning the weather was cloudy and shortly before the execution there was a slight sprinkling of rain, but the sun broke through the clouds and the day was bright at the hour of the hanging.

As the bell in the courthouse tower was tolling the hour of eleven, Sheriff Regan and Undersheriff Murphy entered Lucy's cell with the death warrant along with the straps, which were wrapped in a newspaper. The straps had been pre-fitted on one of the deputies downstairs to expedite the final adjustments and while the deputy was placing them on Lucy the sheriff read the warrant. While the large leather belt was being wrapped around the man's hips Lucy listened to the sheriff read as well as took an interest in the binding of his arms and wrists. Lucy continued to joke with everyone around him while he was being prepared for the scaffold as if to ignore the grim seriousness of the situation. At first he tried to assist the officers with the straps but then he admitted that he clearly didn't know how they were to be arranged.

The cell door was opened and the march to the gallows began through the corridor, down the steps and into the rotunda of the courthouse. In the lead were two Catholic priests without gowns followed by the condemned man supported by Father DeSiere and Harrington in their robes along with Sheriff Regan and Undersheriff Murphy followed by the deputies and Lucy's attorney and a few newspapermen. The gallows had been tested the day before when a one hundred and eighty-pound sack of sand was jerked up twenty inches by the four hundred-pound weight. While walking down the two flights of stairs to the jail yard Lucy didn't appear to overlook one detail of the scene including the huge crowd on the hills to the north and the thick crowd in the yard parting so that the procession could pass through to the scaffold.

At the gallows the priests finished reading the supplications to the saints and the condemned man made the appropriate responses. Father DeSiere closed his Bible and then whispered into Lucy's ear as he looked over the spectators with bared heads including visiting sheriffs, George T. Young of Park County, Jack Conley of Deer Lodge County, Summers of Madison County, Henry Sherlock of Jefferson County and Ravalli County Sheriff B.S. Chaffin. Other witnesses at the hanging were County Attorney Connolly, his deputy attorneys, Mr. Kelley and Alley along with Lucy's attorney, and Deputy Evans who had fitted the straps and oiled the fatal noose. There was a masked and concealed man inside the gallows box, where he was ready to cut the cord on the signal, which released the weight jerking the condemned man to his death.

It was only a few minutes after eleven when Lucy stepped on the carpeted platform under the dangling noose and the crowd of spectators closed in around the scaffold as the officials on the platform stepped back and allowed the condemned man to speak his final words. Lucy raised his head defiantly and looked around as the people on the far off Gagnon Hill strained to catch the slightest sound of the hanging. Lucy spoke in a very nervous tone and his last words were, "Well, gentlemen and ladies, the only statement I have to make is that I was convicted by the "Anaconda Standard," through prejudice between it and County Attorney Connelly. I blame them for sending me to the gallows. I am very thankful to friends for kind treatment, more over, the Catholic Fathers and Sisters. It is something remarkable the attention they paid me. I am ready and willing to die and I forgive all and beg to be forgiven. That is all I have to say."

After his speech the priests kissed Lucy's pallid lips and then knelt about the scaffold while the sheriff and his men stepped forward and bound the prisoner's legs and ankles. The noose was quickly adjusted about the man's neck and just as Undersheriff Murphy was pulling down the black cap the sheriff noticed that the condemned man

Daniel Lucy walking to the gallows, (Note: executioner behind wooden sheild)
"Anacoda Standard" 9/14/1900

was about to faint and the sheriff quickly signaled for the weight to be dropped. Just as the condemned man was about to fall to the ground at 11:11 a.m. he was jerked into the air and he kicked convulsively as he came back down. The black-capped form hung swaying before the gaze of thousands as he clutched a crucifix in his clinched fist. The doctors steadied the swaying body and pushed up the straps to reach for the pulse, Dr. Sheeran holding the left hand and Dr. T.J. Murphy kept tally on the right wrist. At first the pulse was so rapid that the heartbeats couldn't be counted but after a minute it was running normal. Three minutes later the heart was beating forty-five per minute and two minutes later it stopped for good.

The rope had cut deep into the front of Lucy's throat and the doctors reported that the neck was cleanly broken. When Sheriff Regan announced to the witnesses that the doctors had reported that the neck was broken and death ensued in five minutes it was the first sound that broke the stillness. The priests arose from their knees and the men in the crowd put on their hats and one of the spectators commented: "it's an awful deal to give a man." "It's as square a deal as he gave the man he murdered," was an answer from another man in the crowd, and it was clearly the view of the majority of the witnesses.

The body was allowed to hang a full twenty-one minutes and then it was cut down and placed in a black coffin with silver handles. An undertaker wagon was backed up to the scaffold and the corpse was taken to Sherman's establishment on Park Street, where it was viewed all afternoon by a throng of curious sightseers. Laying in the silk-lined casket the body of Dan Lucy was a magnet that drew about twenty thousand curious people including many women and children until eleven o'clock that evening. The rope used to hang Lucy was saved as a number of other men were currently under the sentence of death including the brutal wife-murderer, Peter Dempsey who eventually escaped from the county jail and was never recaptured.

More than five thousand people witnessed the execution from the huge dump of the Gagnon Mine and from many housetops surrounding the jail, which were said to be "black with people." While Lucy didn't breakdown as many had predicted, he certainly didn't "die game" either and as the murderer swung in the open air the people outside the enclosure began shouting and cheering. It was reported that a female relation of Lucy was in Butte at the time of the execution but she was never located and the family came forward and provided a formal Catholic funeral for the condemned man.

It was a silent funeral and only one carriage with four passengers followed the hearse to the cemetery while men and women lined the sidewalks to catch a glance of the somber vehicle as the hearse passed through the streets of Butte towards the Catholic Cemetery. At the church, Father McGlynn conducted the services and then a simple ceremony was conducted at the gravesite. Hundreds of curious people who had never seen Daniel Lucy in life continued to visit the Catholic Cemetery where he was buried and what attracted the most attention of the people was the nearness of Lucy's fresh grave to that of the man he had murdered, Patrick Reagan. The two graves were about a stone's throw apart and within plain sight of one another.

Postscript:

Nearly five months after the execution, Lucy's attorney produced a written and signed confession of his client, which had been dictated to a friend of the murderer while he was in the county jail in February of 1900. The statement was taken down in pencil and Lucy signed every page of the manuscript and left directions to turn it over to the lawyer after the execution. While in the confession Lucy did not admit the killing of Reagan in the way the authorities believed, the statement clearly indicated that he had taken the man's life in what he considered to be in self-defense.

Lucy's confession indicated that not only did he kill Reagan but he killed a black man on a Mississippi riverboat while he was on the run as a fugitive. According to his statement, while working on one of the Diamond Joe steamers near St. Louis he got into a fight with the man one night over a game of poker. Lucy claimed that he hit the man over the head with a stick of wood and then kicked him into the river.

In his confession he said that when he was arrested he intended to tell how Reagan was killed but when he got to Butte he changed his mind because he felt the circumstantial evidence was too weak to convict anyone.

After the hanging of Daniel Lucy was witnessed by several thousands observers and because of all of the commotion in the streets of Butte before and after the execution, many law officers called for all capital punishments to be held at the state penitentiary. Sheriff T.C. Hand of Flathead County and Conley of Deer Lodge were also asking that the state adopt electrocution instead of hanging.

Execution of James Fleming and Clinton Dotson

Part One: Clinton Dotson's first murder

In 1899, Clinton Dotson traveled from his home in South Dakota to work with his father, Captain Oliver Dotson on his gold claim in Washington Gulch near Avon. While Dotson had a good reputation in South Dakota he apparently was looking to make his fortune in Montana without working for it. Also working at Captain Dotson's claim was Charles Oliver Benson, the nephew of Clinton and by August the two men were planning to rob sixty-five-year-old Eugene Cullinane at nearby American Gulch.

Mr. Cullinane was one of the first residents of the area and had done very well and had banked his riches over the years. Thinking the old man was carrying lots of cash, Dotson and his nephew planned to establish an alibi by first going to Helena with great fanfare and then secretly return to American Gulch, traveling by night, carry out the robbery and then return to the capital city.

At Helena the two men befriended a man named Ellis Persinger who was a big, happy but reckless out-of-luck Missourian. He had left his wife and family to find good employment and Persinger had made his way to Helena from Nebraska and Wyoming working on cattle ranches. Dotson mailed two or three postcards to his father at Washington Gulch from Helena to reinforce their alibi and then on the early morning of August 5, 1899, the three men left Helena in Dotson's wagon drawn by two horses and after traveling nights for two days they arrived near American Gulch.

Before daybreak of August 8, Dotson and Persinger left Benson with the horses and ambushed Cullinane on the trail; buried his body and then ransacked the old man's cabin to only find a gold watch and fifteen dollars. Even though the murderers had traveled at night and purposely avoided being seen, a number of people had observed them traveling to and from Helena. Along with evidence found at the scene of the crime the Deer Lodge County officers soon tracked the gang to Gallatin County where with the help of Sheriff William J. Fransham they were captured and returned to Deer Lodge.

The three men received separate trials presided over by Judge W.B. Napton and prosecuted by County Attorney Duffy. The case against Clinton Dotson and his gang members was purely circumstantial until Charles Benson made a full confession to the affair. While Dotson's court-appointed attorney, William H. Trippet managed to save his client from the gallows the murderer was sentenced to ninety-nine years at the state penitentiary and Persinger and Benson drew ten-year terms each for their part in the murder. Normally that would have been the end of the tragic story but unfortunately Clinton Dotson became a cellmate to James Fleming who was serving time under the assumed name of James McArthur.

Part Two: Dotson's plan for freedom

Fleming was a strong and daring criminal but he lacked in intelligence and he was easily influenced by others. In 1895, while serving another term at Deer Lodge, Fleming had successfully escaped from the penitentiary but he was quickly captured and Dotson's goal was to gain his liberty without the risks involved with a jailbreak. Since intelligence wasn't one of Fleming's strong points, Dotson had no problem impressing his cellmate with his own outlaw adventures and he soon gained his cellmate's loyalty and the big lug would and even did kill for him.

Dotson's evil scheme was to have his own father killed, making it appear to be a suicide; produce a suicide note stating that he, (Captain Dotson) had murdered Cullinane in 1899. When Dotson discovered that Fleming was eligible for a pardon by the end 1900, he convinced his cellmate that he and his gang had robbed a rich train in Wyoming and in the flight from the authorities, one member of the gang was killed and the others went off in different directions and have never been heard from again. Dotson explained that he was carrying the stolen fifteen thousand dollars and though he was hard pressed he managed to elude the posse and buried the money.

Dotson promised Fleming half of his buried treasure if he carried out the deadly deed and then he began educating his new partner in crime the important facts concerning the Cullinane case, how they would implicate Captain Dotson and then described the lay out of his father's property including the man's cabin. Fleming was instructed to first force Captain Dotson into writing a confession that he had killed and robbed the prospector and then framed his own son.

Fleming was released from the penitentiary on December 30, 1900, and that evening he took the train to Avon where he spent the night. The stranger spoke with several people at Avon and then got a free ride up Washington Gulch with the mail carrier. As planned in their cell, Fleming introduced himself to Captain Dotson and after a couple of days he offered to buy the place from the old gentleman, who was eager to sell out. Since the homestead had not yet been proofed up, Captain Dotson asked Fleming to accompany him to Helena to finalize the paperwork.

After spending New Years Eve at the cabin the two men went to Helena where they were later exposed to smallpox and were placed in quarantine. After informing the authorities that he was an ex-convict from the penitentiary, where the inmates were all vaccinated, he was released from the pest house but not before robbing Captain Dotson. Fleming returned to Avon and then walked to Washington Gulch where he broke into Dotson's cabin. While waiting the return of old man Dotson, Fleming cut a hole in a wall of the cabin to accommodate his rifle, did some target practice outside the house and then set up a rifle with a string attached to the trigger to make it appear to be the suicide weapon.

Fleming apparently had abandoned the plan of trying to force a confession out of the old man and decided to write the statement himself just as Clinton Dotson had instructed. Unfortunately for Fleming the ink at the cabin had froze and it was difficult to use so he went next door and asked a neighbor for some to finish the suicide note. It just so happened that Fleming visited one of the few neighbors who didn't like Captain Dotson and so he made a big deal out of the loan of the ink. Finally after securing the ink with great difficulty, Fleming completed the suicide note using two kinds of inks and obviously in his own hand.

On February 15, 1901, the Captain arrived at Avon and he made it known to everyone he came in contact with that Fleming had robbed him at Helena and Dotson was seen going to his cabin and a shot was later heard by some of the neighbors. Fleming assassinated the Captain as he entered the cabin and the old man dropped immediately to the floor. In order to properly match the body with the apparent suicide weapon attached to the wall, Fleming had to drag the body to the correct position. To prevent the blood from streaking across the floor during the movement of the body, the murderer placed some underwear beneath the victim's head. After leaving the suicide note on the small table, mounting the murder weapon on the wall and properly positioning the body, Fleming quickly left the cabin.

Not only did Fleming not straighten Captain Dotson's clothing or even remove the blood soaked underwear under the dead man's head, he was also seen leaving the cabin by several of the neighbors. Others also later testified that they saw Fleming walking back to Avon including two men who were carrying a brand new clock, which they all commented about the time they had observed the stranger.

It should go without saying that the authorities realized it was a murder case as soon as they walked into the cabin but they first reported it as a suicide in the hopes that it would slow the murderer's escape by making him think he was in the clear. The strategy worked and Fleming was captured down in the Bitterroot Valley at his girl friend's family place. Clinton Dotson was eventually charged for the murder of his father and becoming him the first prisoner in a penitentiary convicted of murdering a person outside the facility.

September 6, 1901
James Fleming

Other Names: James McArther
Location and Gallows: Fleming was hanged in the jail yard of Powell County at Deer Lodge and of its unlucky thirteen victims, he was the fourth man jerked to death on ***Gallows No. Nine: (Feb. 1888): "Galloping Gallows" No. Three***. A description and complete history of this or any other scaffold can be found in Chapter Seven: "Montana Gallows."
Description: The thirty-five-year-old Fleming had red hair and beard with dark blue eyes, a sandy complexion, coarse features, low forehead, large flat nose and a large mouth full of decayed teeth. He had a short square chin, hollow cheeks, small ears, large head, big neck, square shoulders and a small scar on the right side of his head.
Crime: Murder of Captain Oliver Dotson on February 15, 1901, in Washington Gulch.
Judge: James M. Clements
Prosecution: County Attorney J.M. Simpson and assisted by William H. Trippet of Anaconda
Defense: C.J. Walsh and assisted by Joseph C. Smith
Sheriff: John McMahon
Distinction: Fleming was the first man legally hanged in the newly formed Powell County and the only prisoner allowed to walk to the scaffold without any restraints.

Fleming was born in 1866, in Milwaukee, Wisconsin and raised by a quite respectable family at Lisbon, North Dakota. After leaving home at age eighteen, Fleming didn't keep in touch with his family and he soon became a professional criminal and served time in the North Dakota prison at Bismarck before moving to Wyoming where he soon fell into trouble there as well. He was suspected of killing a man there and he skipped to Montana where he changed his name to McArther.

In June of 1892, he was again on his way to prison, this time it was to the penitentiary at Deer Lodge for robbing a cabin after being tracked down and arrested by Deputy Sheriff John Robinson, the lawman who also arrested the Dotson gang in the Gallatin Valley after the Cullinane murder. Robinson later became deputy warden of the prison at Deer Lodge where he was killed during an attempted prison break for which George Rock was hanged in 1908, and William Hayes paid with his life on the gallows in 1909.

In June of 1892, Fleming entered the state prison for five years under his real name, and claiming that he was married and that he was a barber by trade. While he was at the prison, the massive stonewall at Deer Lodge was being built to replace the wooden security fence and the new maximum-security cellblock was started in 1895. After accumulating good time, Fleming only served less than four years of his sentence and he was released in February of 1896. After his discharge from the pen, Fleming was under suspicion for the murder of a man in the Flathead County and he moved to the Gallatin Valley where he befriended Minor Berry and became even friendlier with one of his daughters. Fleming terrorized and stole from the adjacent ranchers while he lived with the Berry family who eventually moved on to the Bitterroot Valley where Fleming was eventually arrested after the Captain Dotson murder in 1901.

Fleming allegedly killed an unknown prospector near Central Park and after stealing a couple of sleds in February of 1897, he fought off a posse and escaped to the Highwood Mountains in Chouteau County. While there he talked a rancher into selling his place and without making a down payment, Fleming rode to Fort Benton and filed a phony deed for the property at the courthouse. When a friend met the rancher at Fort Benton, he asked the man why he had sold his property and the landowner rushed to the county seat and filed a complaint with Chouteau Sheriff Tom Clary who eventually arrested the outlaw.

The prisoner was returned to Gallatin County where Fleming should have alao been charged with assault for shooting at a posse but Judge Armstrong was lenient and he was only sentenced to a one-year term at the state penitentiary, this time using the alias of James McArther. In March of 1897, the prison wasn't the same facility that Fleming had left a little more than a year before. Where the old penitentiary was barely able to contain the inmates, the upgraded facility had added a new cellblock, which was considered escape proof.

James Fleming
"Great Falls Tribune" 9/7/1901

By November of 1897, the three-time convict had become cellmates with another hard case, a twenty-four-year-old half-breed Indian named William Mosney who was serving time for horse stealing. Just as Clint Eastwood and his mates did in the motion picture, "Escape from Alcatraz," Fleming and Mosney chipped their way through the roof of the escape-proof cell block; left dummies in their beds and successfully escaped over the tall stone wall. But instead of escaping across water the Montana men stole away on the Warden's own horses.

The snows were heavy during April of 1898, and the two escaped convicts almost froze to death as they made their way through the Wolf Creek Canyon on their way to Canada. A deputy captured the two men when their horses had given out but Fleming appeared to be seriously ill when he purposely swallowed a large chunk of chewing tobacco making him throw up profusely. Not being able to carry one man and watch the other, the lawman decided to leave Fleming behind; then take Mosney back to the horses and the other deputies, and then return for the other prisoner.

The ruse worked and Fleming made his escape from the posse only to be captured along the railroad tracks near Mid Canyon on his way to Great Falls between Craig and Hardy Creek. At the time of his escape, Fleming only had eleven days to serve on his prison time, but he said that he was really excited about Mosney's plan of being the first to escape from the so-called escape-proof prison. He also pointed out that Mosney would have gone without him and by doing so he would have had his term extended for not informing on his cellmate anyway. Fleming obviously decided to take his chances on the jailbreak since he would never "rat" on a fellow convict.

After murdering Captain Oliver Dotson and his subsequent arrest in the Bitterroot Valley James Fleming was returned to Deer Lodge, which by then was the new county seat of Powell County. Fleming's trial opened Monday morning, July 8, 1901, and after Judge Napton excused himself, having presided over the earlier Dotson case, Judge J.M. Clements heard the case. None other than William H. Trippet who had first saved Dotson from the gallows in 1899, and then had arranged for Fleming's pardon prosecuted the murder case.

Although Trippet's efforts for the defendant earlier were both perfectly legal and honorable, they ultimately made the murder of Captain Dotson possible and the attorney probably felt somewhat responsible to prosecute Fleming for the deed. Attorneys Mr. C.J. Walsh and Joseph C. Smith were appointed the counsel for the defense and by the end of the first day the following jury was sworn in:

John Eliason	John Lancaster	Peter Assgard
R.S. Burdess	Hiram Jones	Erick Hill
Mat Hansen	Ovando Hoyt	William M. Davis
Rasmus Hansen	Edward Donnie	E.P. Schumacher

The trial of Fleming had been a huge expense for the brand new county, it having cost at least five thousand dollars to secure the conviction, but many of the local businesses in Deer Lodge benefited by the large army of witnesses and visitors attending the affair. With all of the witnesses that had followed the defendant's movements from the time he had left the penitentiary to Avon and to Washington Gulch; the trip and the stay over at Helena and then his return to Dotson's cabin; the two different inks in the suicide letter and the gunshot with the defendant leaving the scene, there was but little question of the outcome of the verdict. After less than two hours of deliberation the jury returned a first-degree murder verdict.

On July 17, 1901, Judge Clements for the first time in his career sentenced a man to his death when he ordered James Fleming to be hanged on September 6, 1901. The huge crowd that had gathered to hear the sentence pressed closely to the railing and they watched for some sign of emotion from the condemned man, but they were all disappointed. Some in the courtroom later reported that they had actually seen a smile on the Fleming's face as the judge was speaking. When he took his chair after the sentence was read Fleming did show some emotion and his face turned purple as though he was choking, but it quickly passed.

Because of the widespread attention to the Fleming and Dotson cases most of the sheriffs and other law enforcement officers of the state were interested in attending the hangings and by the end of July, Sheriff John McMahon had received hundreds of letters from people who wanted to be present for the executions. The sheriff provided ample opportunity for the press and officials of Powell County to attend but because of the limited size of the jail yard he was forced to limit the number of outside visitors to mainly officers of the law.

The defense attorneys for both Fleming and Dotson held a meeting at Anaconda on August 11, 1901, to examine the court records and transcripts to determine their chances for new trials for their clients. When Fleming heard about the meeting he joked about his approaching death and didn't care about a new trial while Dotson was delighted with the efforts of the attorneys as he had begun to develop a terrible fear of the gallows.

Although it was the normal custom in nearly all cases for counsel of convicted murderers to make an appeal to the Supreme Court, Attorney C.J. Walsh decided that it would be useless to try to secure a new trial for Fleming, as there had been absolutely no errors in the trial run by Judge Clements. In the case of Dotson however, his counsel felt that since he was locked up in the state prison at the time of the crime and because there were many discrepancies, they could pursue a new trial, and at least gain a delay in the sentence.

Attorney C.J. Walsh informed Fleming of their decision on August 20, and his client acted as though he had expected it. Mr. Walsh later published a letter in the newspapers explaining his decision; saying that he believed that Fleming had received a fair and impartial trial; and that Judge Clements had correctly decided on all of the legal questions, and that he didn't want to burden Powell County with the expenses of a useless motion. Walsh concluded that if Fleming wasn't satisfied with his defense, he (Walsh) would give any other attorney all the assistance he could for an appeal.

By September 3, 1901, three days before the hanging of Fleming, everything was in readiness including the gallows, which had been brought over from Butte. The scaffold was erected near the center of the east wall of the jail-yard enclosure and it was given a fresh coat of black paint, which made it look even more grim looking. The rope was pre-stretched with a weight of 165 pounds and the 312-pound drop and its release was tested thoroughly.

As time grew short for Fleming, everyone around him watched very closely for any sign of weakening, but if he had, no one ever knew about it. He had always maintained an air of indifference to his situation and he seemed to talk freely of his impending hanging as he would of any other occurrence. He continued to joke and carry on with his fellow prisoners as well as his guards and although he thoroughly realized his awful fate, he didn't seem to care about his future, and he was satisfied to let the consequences be what they may. The man's nerve was remarkable; and his speech was always calm and deliberate.

The condemned man insisted on having a varied menu three times a day and he explained to Sheriff McMahon that nothing should be denied him, inasmuch as he only had a few more meals left. He showed by his conversations that he was somewhat of a cook and he enjoyed the time he spent explaining to the sheriff just how he wanted the dishes to be prepared. Sheriff McMahon reported that when Fleming was first captured he was a bit unruly, but he soon changed under kind but firm treatment and he became a model prisoner at the county jail.

On the morning of August 4, the Sisters from St. Mary's Academy visited Fleming and he paid close attention to what they had to say and a reporter for the "Anaconda Standard" also visited the prisoner and he talked willingly about his upcoming execution when he would die like a man while he still protested his innocence. He explained that his eighty-three-year-old mother was still living in Wisconsin and he was hoping that she would never learn how he had died. When asked about his faith, he said that his parents were Catholics and that he had adhered to Catholic ideas, although he had not professed religion.

Fleming was given a bath that afternoon, which he seemed to have really enjoyed, and he joked about it being his last. The prisoner was then shaved and he looked very neat and clean with his red mustache, which he was allowed to keep quite long but it was very well groomed. More and more visitors came to the county jail to see Fleming, and the women brought along many gifts of flowers as well as fruit for the prisoner. He seemed to really enjoy all of the notoriety that he was receiving and he acted as though it was sufficient compensation for his death on the gallows.

The day before the hanging, Fleming's nerve had still not deserted him, although he appeared more fidgety and more excitable than before. At one o'clock in the afternoon Fleming met with his brothers, William, who was in the transfer business at Lisbon, North Dakota and John, a stationary engineer at a mine at Butte. While John Fleming had visited the jail recently, William had not seen his brother for many years and the men talked for about forty-five minutes under the close watch of the sheriff and his deputies. As Fleming clasped William's hand he broke down and wept; the first exhibition of any emotion he had ever displayed since he had been imprisoned.

The condemned man, like an eager child poured out the tale of his troubles to William, protesting his entire innocence in the whole affair. He declared that he had been railroaded into his fate, that he had been prevented from getting witnesses to prove his alibi, and that the jurors had been prejudiced against him by the newspapers. He tried to convince his brothers that the witnesses, including his so-called friend, Minor Berry had mistaken him for another man.

Fleming's brothers were sympathetic, but they declined to commit themselves and they avoided publicity in order to preserve the family name and keep the news from reaching the ears of their elderly mother.

When his brothers left that afternoon, Fleming gazed long and hard through the bars of his cell as they walked away, and then he sighed and then continued writing his farewell statement to the world.

It was later learned that the prisoner had planned to kill himself Thursday night, the eve of the hanging by poking his wrists with a surgeon's probe. Although there was an empty cell between them, Dotson had learned of Fleming's promise of cheating the gallows, and obviously knowing he was capable of keeping his promises, Clinton passed a note of warning to the sheriff. Early Thursday morning after the prisoner was given medical treatment and while the deputies were searching his cell, Fleming gave the probe to Deputy Charles E. Aspling. How and when the prisoner had obtained the surgical instrument remained a mystery, but it was believed that some sympathetic woman had smuggled it inside the stems of some flowers.

That last plan of suicide was but one of the many attempts made by the prisoner to cheat the gallows. Two weeks earlier on Saturday night, August 17, Fleming had tried to pick open an artery in his wrist with a small needle. Again it was never learned how the prisoner had gotten the needle but the tiny instrument could only inflict a small wound and although the wound bled profusely at first, it would always stop due to coagulation. He tried again and again to make the wound larger but finally he abandoned the attempt after only succeeding in soaking his blankets and bedding with his blood.

Fleming had been able to conceal his bloody attempt from the officers for several days by acting sick and refusing to leave his bunk until it was time for his regular weekly bath, and when he still objected to leaving his cell the officers became suspicious. After the discovery of the blood, Fleming told the story of his attempted suicide and when his cell was searched the deputies found a long strip of blanket that the prisoner had torn from his bedding in order make a rope in order to strangle himself. The crude hangman's rope was found tucked away in the ventilator pipe in his cell.

At six o'clock in the evening of September 5, Sheriff McMahon ordered that the two-man deathwatch to be placed inside of Fleming's cell instead of in the corridor so that every move of the prisoner would be seen. Dotson said that he was glad that Fleming wasn't able to take his own life; maintaining that such an action would have been considered an admission to the crime, even though he could understand why a person might want to avoid death on the gallows.

On his last night on earth, Fleming did not sleep but sat up the entire night talking with his deathwatches, Deputies Aspling and Frank Comstock. The prisoner just sat in his cell and joked, laughed, told dirty stories and didn't seem a bit dismayed about his impending death. Several times during that night, as his courage was beginning to fail him, Fleming asked for and was given some whisky. After each drink of liquor he was strengthened and continued to joke and laugh with his guards.

Fleming had declared that he would die game and innocent like a man that had been recently hanged at St. Louis. Fleming had often compared their two cases, both being convicted on circumstantial evidence, and in the case of the Missourian, it was later proven that he was innocent. Fleming explained to the guards that the Missourian went to the gallows without a tremor and that he would be the way he would go down.

At about 1:30 in the morning, Fleming was sitting on a stool smoking a cigarette when a reporter from the "Anaconda Standard' was admitted to the condemned man's cell. After greeting the reporter, Fleming told the man that he had not slept, as it was the day of his slaughter. When asked about his lack of sleep, the prisoner explained that he would soon be sleeping good and sound. Fleming said that he was pleased with the two men that the sheriff had picked for his deathwatch as they were both splendid storytellers and he always had a good time with them. Although he told many of his visitors that he and his guards were supplied with plenty of booze, the condemned man consumed very little whisky and it was never permitted in his cell.

Fleming had requested fried trout for his last meal, but for some unknown reason none was available although his other fare of warm biscuits, hot chocolate and Saratoga chips, which were the precursor of today's potato chips were served to him at nine o'clock. Along with his requested items Fleming was also served boiled eggs, cantaloupe, blackberries, sliced cucumbers, toast and coffee. The prisoner appreciated his last meal and he talked and joked while he ate, kidding about being able to play four different musical instruments so that he would surely get a job in a dancehall in hell. Fleming had apparently been a member of the Deer lodge Prison Band at one time as he mentioned that the guard and band conductor at the state penitentiary, Mr. Kline was going to be one of the witnesses to his hanging to "direct him off."

At the conclusion of his breakfast, Fleming pushed the untouched pieces of cantaloupe, the only thing he didn't eat, towards Deputy Comstock and he said that he was full and that the officer should eat it. Fleming finished off his meal with a glass of water filled with toothpicks, which he used to pick his poor teeth. Undersheriff Richard Dee presented a silk handkerchief to Fleming but the prisoner declined it with sincere thanks, saying that although it was a good "wipe," he didn't have much use for one, and it should be given to someone who was going to roam around for while longer.

Since the prisoner had already been shaved the day before, on the morning of the execution Fleming only had to get dressed into his new suit for his execution. He considered putting on and adjusting his collar and necktie as very important work and he displayed a great degree of vanity, as he was as concerned about how he had his hair parted, as a woman would be in having her hat on straight. While Fleming was struggling with his collar, Colonel Tom McTague of the State Penitentiary entered the jail corridor, and the prisoner told him the standing joke; of being abused by his guards; and how he had tried to go to sleep, but the sheriff had put a couple of rubbernecks in with him who kept him up all night. Then he told McTague that he had been a fair warden and that he, (Fleming) had always been treated well at the prison as he extended his hand through the bars to shake the man's hand. At last Fleming and the sheriff had decided that the collar wouldn't fit his thick neck, and the officer said he would find another one.

As more visitors entered the corridor, Fleming commented that there were a lot of rubbernecks about that morning, and he told one deputy that half of the world wanted to put the other half under the ground. The prisoner also remarked that it was a dark day as he glanced through the jail window at the dull gray skies outside. Although he made those remarks in sarcasm he was obviously proud of all the attention he had attracted.

The weather on Fleming's last day really did seem to agree with the somberness of the occasion as the air was chilly and an icy wind was blowing while the sky was overcast as though a great dull curtain had been drawn to screen the rays of the sun. The ground was wet, and the tree branches were dripping as they swayed to and fro in meek submission to the winds. It had snowed the previous night from about nine p.m. until four o'clock in the morning, but there was no sign of the white stuff on the ground that morning. Off in the distant the tall mountain peaks had white caps, which served to remind everyone that morning of the previous night's storm.

When the sheriff returned with the new collar, Fleming pronounced that it wasn't as tall as the first one making it just his style and Deputy Aspling assisted him in buttoning it on. After they were finished with the collar the two men sparred for a second or two in fun, which Fleming seemed to really enjoy. About that time the two brothers of the condemned man appeared in the corridor along with County Attorney Simpson. The prisoner had several minutes of quiet conversation alone with his brothers out of the earshot of the others. Fleming then bade his brothers a good-bye, then he kissed them affectionately, and then he turned away crying softly.

Father William Patrick Phelan had heard Fleming's confession earlier that morning and then he administered the sacrament and baptized the condemned man. Later the priest returned and he had a quiet conversation with Fleming after his final visit with his brothers. Following their talk, the prisoner and the priest renewed their request to the sheriff that Fleming be allowed to walk to the gallows without his arms being bound. Together they pleaded earnestly for the favor and finally the sheriff consented and he told the prisoner that he would be taken out without a single strap on. That delighted Fleming and he exclaimed to the sheriff, "All right, you'll find that I can be a man." Father Phelan later told the reporters that Fleming was the bravest man he had ever known, and that the country would not see another like him for many a day.

The next to visit the prisoner was Attorney C.J. Walsh, the man who had defended him during his murder case and Fleming quickly turned on him accusing him of selling out to Warden Frank Conley, referring that he didn't want to burden the county with his appeal. Fleming was referring to the fact that Mr. Conley was also the mayor of Deer Lodge at the time and one of the largest taxpayers of Powell County. While he had just treated his attorney with disrespect, Fleming then greeted Warden Conley pleasantly and shook his hand when he arrived. After the incident with the lawyer and warden, Fathers Aken and Phelan took Fleming by the hand and prayed with him and administered words of consolation.

When Fleming noticed Dotson in a nearby cell crying, he nudged Sheriff McMahon quietly and pointed at Clinton, evidently taking satisfaction in the other prisoner's weakness. For several weeks Dotson had been pleading for his former cellmate's forgiveness, but Fleming had persistently refuse and on the night before the hanging Dotson went so far as to get down on his knees and begged and cried for forgiveness for getting him in trouble. As the condemned man was being led to the gallows, Dotson made another tearful plea, and then Fleming told him that he forgave him and then shook his hand. Dotson grasped Fleming's extended hand; held it strongly and then sank down onto his cot and began weeping bitterly while the smiling Fleming walked off.

Outside in the enclosure under the gloomy scaffold the crowd shivered as they moved about nervously below the ominous clouds, which had hidden the blue skies. Inside of the jail the mood was also gloomy, but Fleming was easily the most cheerful man present. While listening to the death warrant he noticed the document trembling in the sheriff's hands as he was reading and Fleming stepped forward and grasped one corner of the warrant and said: "Here John, let me hold it, you are too nervous." Sheriff McMahon and Fleming then talked about how steady the prisoner's hands had been under the circumstances.

Carrying a crucifix and attended by his spiritual advisors, Fleming was then led into the blustering air of the outside world. When Sheriff McMahon took Fleming gently by the arm, the prisoner asked the officer if he could walk without any assistance. In front of the procession marched Father Aken of Philipsburg and Father Thompson of Boulder, then came Fleming with the sheriff on his right and Father Phelan to his left. The priest wore a black cassock and purple stole and as he walked he read in a low tone from a prayer book into Fleming's ear. Following the somber procession from the jail was Undersheriff Dee, several other deputies and officials.

From the jail the death parade marched slowly into a narrow passageway between the building and the high fence that surrounded the building, through a gate and then into the execution enclosure. As they entered the yard the crowd cleared a lane through its midst to let the party pass to the gallows. Chilly and cold though the day was, every man took off their hats as the condemned man appeared, as was the custom. Reaching the gallows, Fleming took his place, with the noose resting upon his shoulder, while the priests and the officers stepped back. Fleming had earlier requested to make a few remarks and the privilege was granted. At first he had planned to "bawl out" all those who he felt had wronged him, but Father Phelan had talked him into softening and shorten his statement. Fleming's voice rose clear and true above the whistling wind and the rustling trees overhead.

"Friends, I want your attention for a few moments. I am about to meet my Maker. I am here to die, an innocent man. I have been brought to this unjustly, and God knows it. I hope that the officers now here will be able some time to find and catch the parties who are guilty of the crime for which I have to suffer death. I forgive everybody. I go with a clear conscience to meet my Maker. I thank you for your attention and am ready to meet my Maker. Good-bye all."

Since Fleming had been allowed to walk to the scaffold with his arms untied, it took a few minutes for Sheriff McMahon to strap his arms behind his back and to secure his legs, knees and finally his ankles. Father Phelan continued to read in a low voice the litany for dying and Fleming repeated the responses after him while he positioned himself for the sheriff. The sheriff placed the noose around the neck of the prisoner followed by the black cap.

With the litany concluded, Father Phelan stepped to one side and the sheriff pulled a string that signaled the operator within a square canvas booth to cut the cord that dropped the 312-pound weight, which then jerked James Fleming into eternity at 10:17 a.m. Still clasping the crucifix in his hand, Fleming's neck was broken, and after fifteen minutes, Doctors S. Glass and E.F. Dodds declared that the man's heart had stopped. Four minutes later his body was lowered into a casket and it was turned over to Undertaker M. Bein.

An hour later the remains were buried with a simple ceremony attended by Father Phelan and Fleming's two brothers in the Catholic Cemetery at Deer Lodge. Soon after the funeral, the brothers left Deer Lodge and asked E.W. Knight of Anaconda, who had known the boys in Lisbon, North Dakota, to say that the two men wanted to thank the residents of Powell County for the treatment they had received during the trying ordeal. The brothers of the executed man also said that they were deeply touched by the kindness they had received at the hands of the people of Deer Lodge.

Among the two hundred witnesses at the hanging were Deer Lodge County Sheriff Jack Conley and Undersheriff Morgan, as well as former sheriffs, Fitzpatrick and Nelson and Anaconda Assistant Police Chief Frank O'Brien. Other sheriffs in attendance were H.E. Benner of Cascade County, Hadley of Beaverhead and William F. Furay of Silver Bow County. Others present were Tom McTague, Warden Frank Conley and Band Conductor Kline, all from the state penitentiary, as well as Attorneys C.J. Walsh and J.G. Smith.

From Anaconda came Mr. Pratt, the manager of the Rocky Mountain Telephone Company along with W.J. Johnson, Frank Tucker and Rod Williams. Before the crowd had left the enclosure the sight of the stiff and motionless object hanging from the rope had sickened one of the spectators, Ed Ellert of Anaconda who had fainted and had to be carried out.

Witnesses from Butte included former lawmen, Chief of Police Jack Lavell and Sheriff P.H. Regan who hanged Dan Lucy in September of 1900, on the same gallows. Also from the mining city were Hugh Wilson, William Gemmell and the well-known character known as "Fat Jack" Jones. Mr. Jones was actually over six feet tall and as skinny as a beanpole, who had been a "hack" or carriage driver for hire at Butte since 1878. Because of his connections and seniority he had the honor of hauling the most distinguished visitors to the Mining city such as William Jennings Bryant, Theodore Roosevelt and William Howard Taft, as well as being invited to many area functions including hangings.

The execution of James Fleming was considered to have been a perfectly planned event and the crowd management had prevented small children and other morbidly curious people from peeking through the cracks of the tall fence. It was an easy death for the man, who, in cold blood, murdered an aged miner, but he died game, as he had declared he would, and he was as good as his word. Few others had shown more nerve in the face of impending death and James Fleming was cool, calm and collected.

Postscript:
Before becoming a district judge, James Clements unsuccessfully defended William Gay who was hanged in June of 1896, and Joseph Allen who was executed in September of 1899. Clements would go on to preside over the trial of Clinton Dotson who was himself executed in April of 1902.

April 4, 1902
<u>Joseph "Clinton" Dotson</u>

Location and Gallows: Dotson was hanged at Deer Lodge, the fifth man jerked to his death on the infamous ***<u>Gallows No. Nine: (Feb. 1888): "Galloping Gallows" No. Three</u>***.
Description: The thirty-nine-year old Dotson was a good-looking man about five feet, ten inches tall and 163 pounds. According to prison records, he had a dark complexion, blue-gray eyes, iron grayish hair and moustache. His teeth were good and he had a heart, anchor, cross and two spears tattooed over his left nipple on his chest. There was a five-inch scar across his left instep, which caused his foot to look deformed and presented him with a limp.
Crime: Accomplice to the murder of his own father, Captain Oliver Dotson on February 15, 1901, in Washington Gulch.
Judge: James M. Clements
Prosecution: County Attorney J.M. Simpson and William H. Trippet
Defense: Joseph C. Smith and assisted by C.J. Walsh
Sheriff: John McMahon
Distinction: Clinton was the first man legally hanged in Montana who was convicted of a murder that was committed while he was serving a sentence in the state penitentiary.

Apparently Clinton Dotson had once been on the high road to prosperity, but unlike his brother and brother-in-law, he had lost his wealth and he and his wife and nine children had a hard struggle to stay afloat at his home at Crook City, South Dakota. When Clinton entered the state penitentiary on October 14, 1899, for the murder of Cullinane he stated that he had been born in Denver, Colorado and that he was a stonemason by trade. His wife Mary lived with their children at Whitewood, South Dakota and he had a brother and sister at Spearfish. Dotson's conspiracy to murder trial opened on July 17, 1901, and the following jury of Powell County residents was empanelled:

J.S. Turner	Jeremiah Brodshaw	Chris Nelson
G.W. Dasa	Louis Gosselin	B.F. Harrison
Henry Sharp	H.W. Evans	Christian S. Church
John Manning	A.W. Sager	Ben D. Lear

Dotson sat through the trial calmly and never once displayed the slightest emotion even while witnesses like Ellis Persinger testified that the defendant had told him of his plan and that he was elated at the news of his father's death. Six other convicts told the court of conversations with Dotson about the planned murder and Charles Benson explained how the defendant had threatened him if he didn't deny his earlier confession in the Cullinane case. Dotson apparently remained calm since Fleming would not testify against him even though Clinton admitted on the stand of talking with him about the plan of killing his father, but the defendant claimed that he later tried to stop his cellmate from doing the crime.

After just one hour of deliberation on July 20, 1901, the jury returned a verdict of murder in the first degree and Judge Clements sentenced Dotson to join Fleming on the gallows on September 6, 1901. As he was being escorted to the county jail Dotson was informed that he had finally gotten his wish; he had been officially released from the state penitentiary by order of the district court. While Dotson wanted to be executed in the state prison, Warden Tom McTague made it known that the prisoner was not wanted at the facility and his presence there would have an undesirable effect on the other prisoners.

While Dotson was being escorted to his cell after his sentencing, his attorneys, Smith and Walsh began filing notices of their intentions for new trials for both of their clients. The two attorneys were co-counsel with Walsh being lead for Fleming and Smith was in charge of Dotson's defense. The filings allowed the attorneys thirty days, in addition to the statutory time, to prepare their motions, and for the county stenographer to prepare the court transcripts of the two cases, which comprised over a thousand pages.

The defense attorneys decided that an appeal for Fleming would be impossible so they decided to put all their efforts into trying to save Dotson's neck. With merely filing the motion for an appeal, the lawyers had given their client at least another sixty days to live, and for them to study the court transcripts to try and save him. Dotson would not hang beside his previous cellmate and co-conspirator, James Fleming on September 6, 1901.

Dotson was informed of James Fleming's death immediately after the hanging and he again began crying and told a reporter that he was hurt by the news but he was glad that Fleming had died bravely. Again Dotson became choked up and stopped the interview entirely by throwing himself into a chair in his cell and he went into despondency. A week later there was a noticeable change in the prisoner and he had shed his somber and morose appearance, which he had worn during the last few days of Fleming's life, and became more cheerful after learning that there was a chance of gaining a new trial. Dotson had always maintained his innocence and he said he was never afraid of Fleming confessing on the gallows because he didn't have anything to confess to.

On December 1, 1901, Attorney J.C. Smith mailed a brief to the Supreme Court alleging ten errors in the district court's ruling and urged the high court to hear the appeal. During the months of December and January, Dotson had become convinced that he wouldn't be hanged and that he would remain a prisoner at the penitentiary for the rest of his life. In fact he became quite a jailhouse lawyer, as he had become very familiar with a lot of the legal precedents and many of the state statutes. Not only did he take an active interest in the legal phases of his own case, Dotson had also advised other prisoners and Sheriff McMahon commented that the condemned man was the most enthusiastic amateur lawyer he had ever known, and that he could easily recite many court decisions and was literally giving legal advice to everybody at the jail.

On February 24, 1902, the Supreme Court removed the last hope for Dotson of getting a new trial when it decided not to overturn the judgment of the district court. After getting the telephone message from Helena at noon, Sheriff McMahon went to the jail and told Dotson of the court's decision. The prisoner was devastated by the news and the sheriff tried to calm the man down by telling him he could still be saved by the Governor but he became deeply depressed and explained that he was a doomed man because he was without wealth, friends or influence.

After that episode, the sheriff became concerned about Dotson so he ordered an entire change of clothing and his cell was thoroughly searched for items in which he could harm himself. Even though Dotson assured the sheriff that he would never attempt suicide, and that the county would have to end his life, Sheriff McMahon assigned a deathwatch outside of the prisoner's cell day and night.

In March of 1902, Dotson wrote to Governor Joseph K. Toole asking for executive clemency, stating that Charles Benson and Persinger had killed Cullinane while he was still in Helena; that Persinger and Fleming had hatched the conspiracy, which took his father's life. His story of the planned conspiracy also involved the planned assassination of Warden Conley by a gang of men on horseback, all friends of Fleming and after the breakout the convicts were all going to hide out at Berry's place in the Bitterroot. Trying to appear as a hero in the scenario, Dotson claimed in the letter to the Governor that he had foiled the scheme to kill the warden but Persinger and Fleming then decided to kill his father instead.

Although he read the fantastic letter from the prisoner several times and listened to pleas to commute his sentence from others including the condemned man's brother from South Dakota, Governor Toole still declined to interfere with the judgment of the courts. On Monday morning, March 24, 1902, Clinton Dotson was again in a courtroom, not for a new trial, but for his re-sentencing. He reportedly didn't display the least sign of emotion as Judge Clement sentenced him to be hanged on April 4, but afterwards he sank into his seat without saying a word. When he was returned to his cell he just sat on his cot and lit a pipe, which he began smoking as hard as he could.

By the end of March many observers had agreed that the condemned man had aged considerably since his murder trial, and especially since the Supreme Court's decision. Sheriff McMahon told a group of people at Butte that the prisoner had grown a full beard, and that both his beard and hair was quite gray and that the prisoner may have to be carried to the gallows. While the sheriff was at Butte, Warden Conley was keeping a promise with Dotson by going before Governor Toole on the condemned man's behalf. While the authorities were searching for Fleming after the murder, it was Dotson who informed Conley that they might find the fugitive at the Berry's place in the Bitterroot and the warden told the Governor what Dotson had done, but he also added that Fleming would have been captured anyway.

As the date of execution approached Sheriff McMahon reported that Dotson had been holding up well, that he had become resigned to his fate and that he was a model prisoner. Dotson had professed a belief in Christianity and that he had daily talks with his spiritual adviser, Reverend A.B. Martin of Deer Lodge. The sheriff explained that while it was an established custom or rule to grant the condemned man whatever they wanted to eat, Dotson's tastes were very simple. When told he could have anything his appetite craved the prisoner first didn't want anything special but later he surprised the officers when he requested some oranges and green onions. The request was of course granted and he was served the requested items with his regular supper.

During the last couple of days of his life, Dotson was calm and collected as he sat in his cell smoking his pipe and reading the daily papers. His appetite remained good and he reportedly slept like a small child. His spirits were noticeably raised when he was presented some photographs of himself, which had been taken a few days earlier and he eagerly had some sent to his family.

Because the scaffold was still standing in the jail yard after the Fleming hanging, everything was in readiness for the hanging by April 2, but the hour of the execution had been changed from ten a.m. to just before noon in order to accommodate the many invited visitors from Butte and Anaconda who were unable to travel to Deer Lodge until the morning of the hanging.

At three o'clock on the afternoon of April 3, while Dotson was being fitted for his new suit of clothes, Mr. Smith shattered the last ray of hope for executive clemency when he informed his client that he had just finished talking to the Governor on the telephone at Missoula and he said that while he had great sympathy with the relatives and friends of the prisoner, he would not interfere in the decree of death. At first Dotson couldn't speak, but after he realized that everyone was watching him, he partially regained his composure.

On the eve of his execution, Dotson created quite a sensation when he calmly admitted that he had conspired with James Fleming, Benson and Persinger to murder John Chadwick, a neighbor of Captain Dotson, and then later to have his own father killed instead. In the presence of his attorney, Joseph Smith, Day Guard Henry G. Evans and a reporter from the "Anaconda Standard," Dotson stated that he later refused to continue with the conspiracy but the other men went right on with the plan. He said that he didn't expose the scheme to the authorities because he had been sworn to secrecy and that he had been honor bound not to betray his fellow convicts.

Dotson then thanked his attorney and said he was ready to die and that he would try to be brave when he faced the crowd at the gallows. Finally he declared that he hadn't been treated right by the courts and the newspapers, but that he forgave everybody. He went on to say he would prefer to hang than be imprisoned for life, but he expressed that his hanging would certainly disgrace his family. Attorney Smith later said that he was glad that a newspaper reporter was present so that the truth would be published for the sake of the Dotson family. He felt that it was best that his client had admitted his guilt, and not have been executed while a doubt was on the minds of those who loved him. Soon after his confession, Dotson told the sheriff and his staff that he had a knife concealed where he could easily get to it, and could cheat the gallows if he wanted to. The knife was never found in Dotson's cell but his deathwatches were more diligent after his threat.

The prisoner sent for several people including Deputy Warden John Robinson of the state penitentiary, the man who had arrested him for the murder of Eugene Cullinane and later assisted in the arrest of Fleming for the murder of Captain Dotson. The condemned man assured everyone that he had forgiven them for anything they may have done against him. The Reverend Martin agreed to go to the scaffold with Dotson but Father Phelan had previously announced that he couldn't go with him unless he had embraced the Catholic faith. Even though Father Phelan couldn't see himself accompanying Dotson to the gallows he did promise to visit him on his last morning along with the Sisters of Mercy, Sisters Hilaria and Bertina.

Later that evening, Dotson began speaking freely of other crimes that he had committed over the years and admitted that he had served time at the Wyoming Penitentiary for murder but he was pardoned by the Governor. At about midnight the prisoner ate a meal with his deathwatch, Deputy Aspling and Undersheriff Dee, where he was served a mixture of whisky and port wine. He drank the concoction in large glasses and at frequent intervals and the alcohol finally got to him and he finally fell asleep after asking to be awakened early enough to greet the Sisters of Mercy.

On his last morning, Dotson couldn't be awakened in time to meet the Sisters and the guards decided to let the doomed man sleep in until Father Phelan gently woke him up at 10:50. When the prisoner finally opened his eyes, he groaned a little but he wasn't in a talkative mood. At first he declined to choose which spiritual advisor would accompany him to the scaffold, but then he finally announced that he would not die a Catholic. Apparently Dotson was afraid to face his accomplice, James Fleming who was buried in the Catholic Cemetery even after death, so Father Phelan left the condemned man and Reverend Martin was admitted into the man's cell.

By eleven o'clock Sheriff McMahon was helping the prisoner put on his clean linen shirt and new black suit while the condemned man was very nervous and was crying. He composed himself long enough to neatly brush his hair and then he sat down and wept for several more minutes. Reverend Martin did all he could do to console his charge and he advised him to have some breakfast, but Dotson only wanted a cup of coffee. When Dotson finished his coffee he listened intently to the words of his spiritual adviser and he occasionally sobbed and whimpered. The prisoner eventually ate a breakfast of fried eggs, toast and crisp bacon and he remained seated while the sheriff read the death warrant but he was so totally occupied with his own thoughts that apparently he didn't hear a single word that the officer had said.

When ordered to stand, Dotson got up slowly so that the straps, which had been used earlier to bind Fleming to be adjusted. When he realized that his time was short, Dotson tried three or four times to say something, and finally, in a trembling voice he asked for some alcohol, which he drank from a tin cup. After having his favorite mixture of whisky and port wine he didn't speak another word until the black cap was placed over his face at the gallows. Dotson walked to the gallows with an unhesitating step and he kept his eyes intently fixed on the scaffold and not the five hundred or so people present to witness his death.

The condemned man took his place beneath the scaffold and stood there unusually pale but he didn't appear nervous as he faced the crowd and calmly looked into their faces. His face was described as livid and expressionless until a man in the crowd shouted out, "Farewell, Clint" when he looked up and a faint smile was visible on his face. The slight smile turned into a sneer as he lowered his eyes, and they were never raised again.

When he felt the black cap being drawn over his head at 11:27 he asked the sheriff to hold him up as his trembling knees were beginning to fail him. After a moment of being supported by the sheriff and Reverend Martin, Dotson regained his balance and he stood alone as the same noose that had been tightened about the neck of Fleming was

Clinton Dotson being escorted to the gallows at Deer Lodge in April 1902.
Sketch by staff artist, Willis Thorndike: "Anaconda Standard" 4/5/1902

around his throat. The sheriff gave the signal and at 11:29 the weight fell and Clinton Dotson was jerked to his death.

There was scarcely a tremor as Dotson's body settled at the end of the rope and then Doctors J.H. Owings and E.F. Dodds stepped forward, each taking a wrist to feel for a pulse. Fifteen minutes later the physicians announced that the heart had ceased to beat and declared that the neck was broken. There was not a murmur from the crowd until the mournful howling of a dog in a neighboring yard broke the awful silence and sent cold shivers creeping down the spines the spectators.

Among the large crowd were Warden Frank Conley and Deputy Warden John Robinson, the warden's brother, Sheriff Jack Conley of Deer Lodge County and his deputy, Joseph Daly; Deputies Pellatier and Charles McGarvey of Silver Bow County; Chief of Police Reynolds and Patrolmen Sullivan, Byrne and Hines and Former Chief of Police Jack Lavell of Butte, the first game warden of Montana, W.F. Scott and his deputy, Henry Avare. Also present at the hanging was John Fleming of Butte, the brother of the late James Fleming, Dotson's partner in crime.

The body was cut down and it was placed in a coffin, which had been waiting in the courthouse hallway. Dotson's remains were prepared for burial at the expense of the county and they were interned at the convict burial ground by request of the condemned man since the prisoner had said that he felt that because he was a convict, he was entitled to rest among his fellows. Reverend Martin later described the execution as a perfectly clean, easy hanging in which every consideration had been shown a murderer and a fellow man.

Postscript:
After her husband's hanging in Montana, Mary Dotson went on and raised her nine children alone in South Dakota. When her children had grown and scattered across the country she eventually moved to Casper, Wyoming where she finally died at the age of sixty-nine at the home of her daughter on May 3, 1932. Dotson's nephew, Charles Oliver Benson was released from the state penitentiary on January 10, 1906; got married, became a prospector in the southwest and died in 1943 at Shoshone, California. Ellis Persinger was released from prison in June of 1906, but nothing else is known of him.

February 23, 1904
James Martin

Location and Gallows: Martin was hanged in the yard of the Silver Bow County jail at Butte from the infamous ***Gallows No. Nine: (Feb. 1888): "Galloping Gallows" No. Three.***
Description: Thirty-seven-year old Martin was five foot eight inches tall and weighed about 135 pounds. He had a dark and swarthy complexion and at the time of his arrest he had a scab on his unusually large nose. Martin had an old wound, a bullet scar that crossed the full length of his chest, which he jokingly claimed he had received from a jealous husband.
Crime: Martin and another tramp, Charles Lennox murdered John R. Williams, a fireman and brakeman for the Butte, Anaconda & Pacific Railroad on May 17, 1902.
Judge: John B. McClernan
Prosecution: County Attorney Peter Breen assisted by Deputy County Attorney Mackel
Defense: Thomas A. Morrin
Sheriff: John J. Quinn

For several days during the second week of May 1902, two tramps, Charles Lennox and James Martin were seen hanging around the railway station and saloon at Silver Bow Junction. No one paid them any more attention than to any of the other many hoboes resting between depots as they stole rides on the various freight trains. While attempting to rob John R. Williams on Monday evening, May 17, Lennox and Martin mortally wounded the railroad man.

When the wounded man was found he was taken to the saloon and he placed on the billiard table where he was given medical aid but he eventually died at the St. James Hospital at Butte. Between gasps and withering in pain the victim said that he had been shot by two men, a large man and a smaller one and he went on to describe his assailants. From Williams' description of the men, the saloonkeeper and others recognized the men as the two tramps that had been hanging around the place for several days. Public sentiment ran high about the murder and there was considerable talk about lynching the men when caught.

The sheriff's office at Butte was notified immediately and the description of the two suspects was telegraphed along the line of the Oregon Short Line and it was this quick reaction and the notification of the conductors on the trains that resulted in the quick arrests. The next morning a crew on a freight train reported seeing the two suspects riding the brakebeams heading southbound. It was very cold out and Conductor Daniel N. McNamara told the two suspected fugitives they could ride in a boxcar where they would be more comfortable. Being more than thirty-five miles from the scene of the crime and thinking they were safe from the authorities, Lennox and Martin accepted the invitation to ride in the empty car.

When the fugitives were safely in the boxcar on Train Number 28, to Dillon, the conductor locked the door and because the report stated that the two men were heavily armed, Special Deputy John Gelhouse boarded the train at Melrose and guarded the car into Dillon. After stopping at Dillon the conductor threw open the car and although the fugitives had tried to cut their way out of the car with their knives, they presented no resistance at the time of their arrest by Police Chief F.L. Stone and his men. When searched the two men were unarmed and they had a total of fifty-five cents between them. They said that they had no knowledge of the crime or the reason for their arrest but they gave conflicting stories of their whereabouts during the previous evening.

Two days later on May 22, 1902, Coroner Johnson conducted an inquest into the murder of John Williams and the jury named Charles Lennox and James Martin as the murders. At the hearing Lennox made a full confession that his partner, James Martin had fired the fatal shot and told the authorities where they could find their guns. Martin, who was also a witness at the inquest, denied everything even when he was shown a telegram from the Dillon authorities stating that the guns had been found in the boxcar where Charles Lennox had said they would be found. Lennox eventually made a full and complete confession of the hold-up and subsequent murder claiming that it was Martin who had fired the bullet that killed Williams but there was no direct evidence to corroborate his accusation.

In early June of 1902, the two men were arraigned, formerly charged and assigned counsel, Thomas A. Morrin for James Martin and J. Bryce Kemmer representing Lennox. On July 7, Martin's attorney argued for a change of venue claiming that his client couldn't get a fair trial at Butte because County Attorney Breen had such great influence with the general public there. Most of the observers at the time felt that the defense was using the argument as a ploy in order to delay the action since Martin was believed to have fired the fateful bullet. After considering the concerns of the defense, Judge McClernan promptly overruled the motion for a change of venue and then informed the defendant that his rights would be protected. The judge went on to assure the defense that no man would be permitted to sit in judgment of the defendant who was biased and prejudicial in any manner by what he may have read in the newspapers.

After County Attorney Breen calmly and impassionedly outlined the charges against James Martin on July 8, 1902, the work of impaneling a jury began and because of the cold-blooded character of the crime and so many of the prospective jurors were against the death penalty only eleven men were selected on the first day. While the county attorney accepted every juror that wasn't opposed to the death penalty, the defense rejected anyone who had any dealings with the prosecuting attorney whether personal, business or professionally. After ordering another venire of one hundred and twenty-five men the following jury was finally selected who swore that they could "try the case fairly, impartially and render a verdict according to the evidence and the law:"

James Graney	William Burg	James Brogan
John E. Wheeler	J.N. Lees	Matt Mooney
E. Wilcox	John Hurley	William H. Thomas
Samuel Pipes (f)	J.C. Freeman	James Gavin

(f) Foreman

Throughout the trial Martin sat next to his attorney, Thomas Morrin and reportedly paid close attention to everything that was said and done. The defense wanted to prove that on the night of the shooting the defendant thought he and Lennox were on their way to catch a freight train to California but his partner had planned the crime. Dr. Turner testified that he attended Mr. Williams at St. James' Hospital before he died and that Dr. Bertha Mackel[1] had assisted him during the autopsy. He said that the bullet entered William's back about two inches to the left of the backbone, then it passed through the left kidney, the left part of the liver, stomach and then it was lodged just under the skin of his belly.

Charles E. Brooks, chief clerk of the Oregon Short Line testified that he searched the Denver and Rio Grande Railroad car No.12047, at Pocatello, Idaho and in the south end of the car he found two revolvers hidden between the inside lining and the exterior sheeting. He described one of the weapons, as a Colt's 41-caliber and the other was the American Bulldog 32-caliber revolver. Also found in the cache were twenty-one cartridges and a dirty silk handkerchief, which had traces of blood. J.E. Lindsay, a reporter for the "Anaconda Standard" told the court that he was present at the hospital when Mr. Williams described the attack and the men to the authorities. In his deathbed statement the victim claimed he had knocked the tall man down before he was shot.

When Lennox was called to the stand he first told the court that he had not been promised any immunity from prosecution for his testimony and then he repeated the same confession that he had told at the coroner's inquest and to the county attorney. He said that he had met James Martin at Spokane just a few days prior to the shooting and he identified the large 41-caliber revolver as belonging to him and he told the court that the Bulldog looked like the one that James Martin was carrying on the night of the murder.

James Martin then took the stand in his own behalf and for the first time since his arrest he admitted that he was present when Williams was shot but he stated that it was the intoxicated Lennox who did the shooting after he had been knocked to the ground. Martin was obviously uncomfortable on the stand and he contradicted himself several times and he candidly admitted that he had lied to the coroner's jury. He tried to stick to his story and he smiled whenever he thought he had successfully had stood his ground against the prosecution. Martin told the jury that after the shooting they ran to the Freeley Station where they rested until the next morning when they caught a freight heading south. When asked why he had lied at the coroner's inquest he said that he was trying to save Lennox, but that he was telling the truth in court.

The first witness for the defense was Ed Duffy who testified that he was serving in the county jail with Al Stack, William Perry, a prisoner by the name of "Scotty" and Charles Lennox." Duffy said that Lennox told them all that he was going to hang because his partner (Martin) would probably squeal on him, and that he should have killed him the same time he finished the other fellow. To help prove Martin's claim that Lennox had shot Williams, the defense called Dr. Frank E. Donaldson who testified that the bullet wounds on the victim indicated that he had been shot by a man on the ground. While the argument was possible, many observers in the courtroom later said that the physician was a poor witness and the prosecution found it easy to confuse him.

While waiting for the jury to return, Martin didn't seem to be concerned about his fate and he was seen laughing and joking with deputies. He wore a sneering smile throughout the trial but he quickly lost the old smirk on his face when he heard that the jury had agreed on a verdict. The jury received the case at 3:20 on the afternoon of July 11, 1902, and they deliberated for about five hours before returning a guilty verdict at 8:50 that evening. Martin reportedly turned pale as the clerk was stamping and filing the verdict, which he had received from the foreman and when Clerk Vogler announced the first-degree verdict in the courtroom the defendant was ghostly white.

Attorney Morrin immediately asked that the jury be polled and as each juror answered to his name by replying "Guilty." It was reported that there had been twelve ballots taken in the jury room before the jurors had finally agreed upon their verdict. The court was then adjourned and Undersheriff William McGuigan along with Deputies Dobbin, Proebstel and Quinn escorted Martin back to the jail. Most observers of the trial said that the case against Martin was so circumstantial that it was doubtful that he would have been convicted without the testimony of Charles Lennox.

The judge announced that the sentence would be passed in a week and the defense didn't give notice that they would appeal to the Supreme Court. When the news of the verdict was posted in the window of the "Anaconda Standard" there was a general expression of approval by those who had been following the case closely. The general comment was that while the trial was short, the prosecution had presented the evidence in such a way that the result couldn't have been otherwise.

Four days later Charles Lennox was placed on trial and the same evidence offered in the Martin case was again brought into court with the addition of Miss Martha Fish, the county stenographer who had recorded the defendant's confession at the county attorney's office. The twenty-seven-year-old Lennox who was described as being non-threatening, told the court that he had a wife and an eighteen-month-old baby at Hancock, Michigan. After a five-day trial, Lennox was also found guilty of first-degree murder for the murder of John Williams.

On July 26, 1902, Martin and Lennox were both originally sentenced to be hanged on October 29 but the court postponed their sentences indefinitely when a stay was granted in order to provide time for their attorneys to prepare their appeals to the Supreme Court. On the way back to the jail after their sentencing, the two defendants were seen joking and laughing together and with the deputies, one of the prisoners asking outgoing-Undersheriff McGuigan if he was buying the drinks. Since most prisoners hated "Rats" and looked up to "bad characters," Lennox told his fellow inmates that it was Martin who had confessed and testified against him in order to protect himself while awaiting his appeal.

On the evening of August 9, 1903, the same day that the famous convicted murderer, Tom Horn attempted his escape from the jail at Cheyenne, six desperate men successfully broke out of the county jail at Butte including convicted murderers, James Martin and Charles Lennox. At about seven o'clock that evening, convicted robber, Frank Ortoff faked an illness and when Jailer William Dolan opened the door to the corridor of the east cage so that Dr. Ignatius Donnelly could examine the prisoner a revolver was pushed into his face.

Ortoff held Jailer Dolan and the doctor at bay while the other prisoners in the corridor made their escape. The break occurred so quickly and quietly that Deputy John Wyman who was in the sheriff's office at the time didn't hear anything but when he finally noticed four prisoners running down the stairs of the courthouse he gave chase and fired two shots at the escapees.

It was later learned that Frank Ortoff and Charles Lennox were the only two men involved in the planning of the jailbreak and it was executed at that particular time and day because Sheriff Quinn was out of town, and because it was so quiet around the courthouse in the evening, there were only three or four officers on duty. Although unarmed, Jailer Dolan reportedly stood firm and refused to turn over the cell keys even under the threat of loosing his life. Even while Dr. Donnelly begged him to surrender the keys and save his life, Dolan declared that he would die first before submitting but in the end he was eventually overpowered by the prisoners and the keys were removed from him.

The original plan of Lennox and Ortoff's was to lock up the jailer and the doctor in a cell, free the other inmates and then leave in the mass escape making it difficult for the officers to pursue everyone. Evidently the cowardly Lennox got cold feet and as soon as the jailer was overpowered he immediately made his escape leaving Ortoff alone with the two officials. After getting out of the corridor Charles Lennox went to the jailer's office where he took Dolan's revolver from his desk and then ran out with the other inmates. Only one other inmate, Joseph Rogers stuck around to help Ortoff and they quickly surrendered to the officers.

Both Rogers and Ortoff were fitted with Oregon boots and while the former was locked up in the "boxcar," the latter was heavily grilled by the officers and then placed in the dungeon of the jail. The stubborn Swede refused to divulge how he had obtained the revolver, which he had used during the escape and the names of the prisoners involved in the planning. Ortoff had robbed two stagecoaches in Wyoming and he was apprehended at Butte when he was trying to sell a large number of postage stamps, which had been stolen during one of the holdups. A few days after the jail break he apparently hanged himself in his cell after leaving a suicide note for the newspapers, which in pencil stated that he had gotten the revolver from his cellmate, Charles Lennox and that the two men had planned the escape alone.

In his suicide note, Frank Ortoff said that he was leaving this world to look for a better one and then he finished by writing: "Well, I have to stop writing, as I am rather curious to see what the other world would look like. I leave in good spirits. Tell Undersheriff McGarvey there is no need to put me in irons any more, as this is the last break I will make." Of course the incident and the note brought accusations that the sheriff's office personnel had either murdered the prisoner outright or had pushed him into ending his life after torturing him for information.

At about 10:30 on the morning after the jailbreak, while searching a road at the head of Hail Columbia Gulch, about fourteen miles north of Butte, Deputy McKenna and Special Deputy John Colligan came to the cabin of wood chopper, John McGlynn. When the officers stopped their buggy in front of the cabin, Deputy Colligan asked McGlynn if he had seen any suspicious persons in the neighborhood and the man said that he was serving breakfast to a stranger in his cabin.

With rifles ready the officers entered the cabin and Deputy Colligan recognized James Martin and ordered him to throw up his hands. With a slight smile on his face, Martin gave no resistance and the officers even allowed the man to finish his breakfast of eggs, meat and bread before handcuffing and taking him back to Butte. Before the jailbreak the prisoner had a black mustache but while on the run he had cut most of it off by sawing it with the blade of a pocketknife and while at McGlynn's cabin he borrowed the old man's scissors and clipped it down where it looked like a three-day's growth.

When Martin was returned to the county jail he was limping and was obviously fatigued and he told the officers that while he regretted being caught he was glad to be back in his old cell. When questioned about the escape, Martin said that he didn't know anything about the planning of the break and said he was getting ready to retire when someone told him to hurry and get dressed. At first he thought there was a visitor calling on him so he put on his collar and tie along with his vest and coat.

When he stepped out of the open cell door, Martin realized an escape was in progress and he ran out of the jail with Lennox, Llewellyn L. Felker, convicted of manslaughter and Patrick and Joseph Rogers, two brothers who were in custody for robbing saloons. In the meantime Frank Ortoff was stuck all alone holding a gun on the jailer and so Joe Rogers returned to the corridor to assist the other convict. Knowing there was no hope for his escape, Frank Ortoff insisted that Joe Rogers make a run for it too but Deputy Wyman managed to quickly apprehend him.

Later that day after eating and resting up, Martin laughed and joked about the whole thing and spoke with a reporter telling him that after the breakout he broke into a small cabin at Butte where he remained until after nine o'clock and then he headed for the lowlands intending to eventually take refuge in Canada. The fugitive didn't make it very far and by the time he reached John McGlynn's cabin he was cold, tired, hungry and thirsty. The prisoner explained that his low endurance and weakness was due to his lack of exercise while in custody but it was later determined that Martin was actually suffering from tuberculosis and for that reason he wasn't able to put much distance between himself and the Butte authorities.

Martin said that Lennox was running north about four blocks ahead of him when he went around a corner and he was never seen again. He told the reporter that Deputy Wyman might have shot Lennox during the escape as his arm hung limp at his side as he ran. It was later determined that Lennox had been shot in the hand and he made his way to Walkerville where he broke into a house when the family was gone. The fugitive left a pool of blood on the floor and he stole some bacon and two loaves of bread along with a piece of muslin from a china closet in which he bandaged his gunshot wound.

Like Martin, Llewellyn Felker was captured the day after the jailbreak but Lennox made good his escape and a reward of one hundred dollars was offered for his capture and law enforcement officials in the surrounding states were all notified of his escape. Over the years there had been reported sightings of the Charles Lennox in and around Butte but they were all disproved by the authorities including one as late as 1919.

On December 21, 1903, the Supreme Court affirmed the judgment of the district court and denied the motion for a new trial for Martin but Governor Toole postponed the execution so that the prisoner, who was suffering from late stages of tuberculosis, could become stronger. On February 13, 1904, Undersheriff Charles McGarvey handed Martin a letter from Governor Toole stating that he wouldn't interfere further with the edict of the courts and the prisoner carefully opened the envelope and after reading the letter he placed it on his table and didn't talk about it further.

Throughout the appeals process the condemned man maintained a cheerful manner with his daily visits with the Reverend Mr. C.L. Bovard of the Mountain View Methodist Church and two ladies of the Crittention Circle. Another special visitor was ex-sheriff John McMahon of Powell County who had executed Fleming and Dotson a couple of years earlier. Then on January 22, 1904, Judge McClernan re-sentenced Martin to be hanged on February 23, and Sheriff Quinn began preparing for the execution.

For the hanging of Martin, the “Galloping Gallows” of Silver Bow County, which were last used to end the life of Clinton Dotson in April of 1902, were brought back to Butte. After the Dotson hanging the scaffold was sent to Livingston for an hanging there but Martin Zedman's death sentence was commuted. The death machine was later transported to Hamilton but the scaffold was again cheated when an angry mob lynched Walter Jackson in October of 1903. The rope, which had been purchased by the Ravalli County to hang Jackson at Hamilton, was presented to Sheriff Quinn by Sheriff Joshua Pond and it was safely locked away until it was needed for Martin.

The gallows was erected in the northwest corner of the jail yard and because they were placed against the north wall, the large crowd within the walls could witness the execution but it was impossible for the crowds outside to observe the hanging. The scaffold had been set up in the center of the yard for the Lucy hanging in 1900, and thousands of Butte residents thronged the hills north of the courthouse to witness the execution. The same executioner that sent Lucy into eternity was selected to officiate over the Martin hanging and he reportedly had no connection with the sheriff's department.

A few days before the execution, Martin began to show signs of nervousness and he began having difficulty sleeping and his appetite had begun to fail him. Former Sheriff John E. Lloyd who had executed Harry Roberts in 1889, visited the condemned man along with former Undersheriff James B. Gallagher and the men chatted and laughed for about ten minutes before they shook hands and said good-bye. The only request Martin had concerning his hanging was that he be allowed to have as quiet an execution as possible; that his body be given a decent

Christian burial and that it wasn't dissected. Martin came out with a written statement that reviewed his case and warned other young men not to follow in his footsteps.

After eating a hearty breakfast, Martin met with his lawyer, who knew his true name, and instructed him to write to his father, telling him that he was in jail for a miner offense, but that he was seriously ill and probably wouldn't recover. Martin was terrified at the possibility that his family back east would find out about his predicament and he refused to be photographed or sketched. There was nothing published about the mystery man other than he was born in New Jersey, he was a pipe fitter and that he had met Lennox in Spokane on his way to Butte from California.

When the visitors left the jail Sheriff Quinn suggested Martin take a bath and when he was finished the officer presented him with an immaculate starched linen shirt and black tie. Martin was very careful with his tie and he took pains in arranging it properly. Later he asked to see the gallows on which he would be hanged and Sheriff Quinn reluctantly granted his request. The incident received considerable coverage in the newspapers and it was considered a sensational feature of the execution because a preview of the gallows by a condemned man before a hanging wasn't often done.

The sheriff escorted Martin to the jail yard where the condemned man became fixated on the black frame of the gallows. Martin's gaze was not riveted on any one particular spot; instead it slowly shifted from the gallows, to the large weight, which he knew was to jerk him into eternity to the black enclosure where a trusted man stood out of sight to cut the rope that released the drop. The men didn't say a word and when the prisoner had satisfied himself he mechanically turned towards the sheriff and they walked back to the jail.

At seven p.m. Martin said he was hungry for crab and they were served to him with bread and butter along with hot coffee. This was the prisoner's third meal of the day and he finished one crab and almost a second before he began eating his bread and butter. Judge McClernan had ordered the execution to take place between the hours of one o'clock a.m. and ten in the morning but Sheriff Quinn decided to leave the exact hour up to the doomed man

At 9:30 that evening the sheriff asked his prisoner if he had decided the hour of his execution and after Martin was told that the newspapers went to press at four a.m. he exclaimed that he would die at 4:30, so his hanging would be too late for the papers. People had been calling the jail all day long and into the night to find out the hour of the execution but when Martin set the hour the word spread over town like wild fire.

As the hour of his execution neared Martin grew visibly more nervous and he was obvious anxious to get it over with. The prisoner didn't drink alcohol excessively during the days leading up to his death and he only had a glass of wine during his last day. At one o'clock in the morning he became hungry again and a message was sent to a restaurant with an order for a special lunch for the condemned man. For his final meal Martin ordered hot tamales, a piece of lemon pie and a pot of strong coffee. The prisoner also ordered a tamale and coffee for his favorite deathwatch, David Keefe who he had become quite close. While incarcerated at the jail, Martin had made a handmade whiskbroom holder for the deputy so that the officer would have something to remember him by.

Mrs. Johns and Mrs. Wedlake along with the deathwatch remained with the condemned man from two a.m. to four o'clock in the morning the women sang hymns such as "What a friend we have in Jesus." Martin joined the ladies in perfect harmony and his voice could be distinctly heard in the jailer's office. When Reverend Bovard arrived at the jail that morning he was immediately escorted to Martin's cell and during his final religious ceremonies tears reportedly came to the prisoner's eyes several times. At four o'clock Martin sent for County Physician Donnely just to thank him and to bid him good-bye.

At 4:15 the two ladies left Martin's cell after bidding the him good-bye and they carried out the bouquets of flowers that he had presented them. Martin then said good-bye to each of the deputies and then at 4:30 Sheriff Quinn read the death warrant and the straps were placed around the prisoner's arms and legs. The original plan to lead Martin to the gallows through the front entrance of the jail was cancelled at the request of the condemned man, as he wanted to avoid as much publicity as possible and he expressed his preference of using the rear exit.

Martin was taken down the stairs and then through the hallway of the living quarters of the sheriff and then they went through the kitchen door to the scaffold. Martin asked to have his execution as soon as possible so that it would take place in the darkness of the night, and at 4:40 James Martin stepped from the jail into the yard with Sheriff Quinn and Reverend Bovard at his sides followed by the deputies and the newspapermen.

As the condemned man reached the small platform beneath the scaffold he turned and faced the crowd and asked that the light, which hung on the side of the jail be put out, and when it was turned off the condemned man was in almost total darkness. He first turned to his spiritual advisor and said he was ready to die and then he spoke to the crowd saying, "Bless these people, Oh, God. Bless them all. Teach them the right way that this might be a lesson to them from what they see. Bless them all. Good-bye, everybody, Good-bye. God bless you."

The condemned man then turned back to Mr. Bovard and said that thank God, it would soon be over. He asked God to forgive his sins and that the Lord bless the sheriff. Martin turned to the sheriff and said, "Good-bye Jack, God bless you." The Reverend Bovard started the Doxology, in which Martin joined in a trembling tone. During a slight delay in the proceedings the minister began singing the hymn "Praise God, From Whom All Blessings Flow" and the condemned man sang along in a strong clear voice.

After singing the song, Martin offered a prayer with his head bowed beneath the cross bar, "It is now time for you, my brethren, to see what befalls a man in my place. Pray to God; see that you do not do as I have done. Glory be to God! I am ready." After the prayer Mr. Bovard began the hymn, "In the Sweet Bye and Bye," which many of the men in the crowd joined in. At the conclusion of the hymn Martin was asked for any last words, to which he replied with a strong voice, "No, I have nothing to say except that I am sorry and that I hope all my friends will profit by my experience. Good-bye friends, good-bye all. God bless you all." Some of the men in the crowd began to lobby to have the light turned back on, which Martin objected to. Fearing that someone might recognize him and his true identity divulged, Martin asked the sheriff to act quickly in order that he be hanged in the darkness.

The sheriff quickly placed the rope around Martin's neck; pulled down the black cap; then two raps were heard and at 4:46 a.m. the weight dropped. After James Martin's body flew into the air and fell back down to within two feet of the platform there was a faint quiver evident through the strong leather straps. The body stiffened, the head swung forward, his hands clenched, the arms lifted somewhat and then a slight muscular contraction was observed as the life slowly left the body.

The body swayed slowly in the dim light as Dr. Donnelly and his assistant checked for signs of life and at 4:59 the county physician pronounced Martin was dead. A few minutes after the yard had been cleared of spectators; the body was cut down and placed in a casket. The remains were then carried to the Richard's Undertakers on West Park Street, where they were prepared until they were buried at eleven o'clock in the Mountain Moriah Cemetery. The representatives of the W.C.T.U. kindly offered to provide a Christian burial for the deceased murderer and Mr. Richards donated his services, the casket and the use of his hearse. The Reverend Bovard read appropriate words from the Bible, after which the women of the W.C.T.U. sang "I am thine, O Lord; I have heard thy voice," said to have been a favorite hymn of the deceased.

Among the many witnesses at the hanging were F.L. Stone, chief of police of Dillon who had captured Martin and Lennox; Sheriff George Storrar of Anaconda, Undersheriff Dart and Deputy Remington of Beaverhead County, Undersheriff Larson of Dawson County, Sheriff J.C. Barnden and Deputy William Britt of Powell County along with Sheriff Harry W. Thompson and Undersheriff Edward Sterling of Missoula County. Also attending the execution were ex-sheriff Pat Regan and U.S. Marshal William F. Furay along with ex-Undersheriff William McGuigan of Silver Bow County, Undersheriff E.M. Reynolds and County Attorney George D. Pease of Gallatin County and County Attorney Peter Breen, Commissioner Pat Peoples, Stock Inspector John W. Collins of Butte.

The pallbearers at Martin's funeral were all attached to the sheriff's office and included Sheriff John Quinn, Undersheriff Charles McGarvey, Deputies Dave Keefe, Charles White, Horace Merkle and W.J. Rowe. Immediately after the hanging of Martin the scaffold was dismantled and placed into storage.

Postscript:
It was later reported that James Martin went to his grave believing that his disgrace upon the gallows had been successfully concealed from his family but in fact his sister and father knew of his predicament for a year and a half. The authorities of Silver Bow County along with Martin's attorney were all aware of the ruse and they kept it from the prisoner in order to protect his feelings. The family's request of protecting his true identity from the public was also honored by the officials at Butte.

March 18, 1904
Louis H. Mott

Location and Gallows: Louis Mott was hanged behind the jail at Missoula and he was the seventh man jerked to his death on ***Gallows No. Nine: (Feb. 1888): "Galloping Gallows" No. Three*** A description and history of this infamous scaffold can be found in Chapter Seven: "Montana Gallows."
Description: Tall and gaunt
Crime: Murder of his wife, Leah H. Mott January 4, 1903
Judge: Frederick C. Webster
Prosecution: County Attorney Charles H. Hall assisted by H.C. Stiffman
Defense: Firm of Asa L. Duncan and Draffen, Joseph K. Woody and Frank H. Woody as well as S.G. Murray
Sheriff: Harry W. Thompson

For the better part of a year Louis Mott had been fighting with his wife over his drinking and drug addiction as well as his failing business, the Troy Steam Laundry on North First Street. During his absence to Mandan, North Dakota Mrs. Mott had sold the business and the rest of their property to the Jones Brothers of Spokane, Washington. Her disposing of the property only made Louis Mott even angrier and he began to drink heavier and started to threaten his wife in public.

Living with the Mott's above their laundry at the time was a Mrs. L.G. Lockhart and Jesse and Leroy Jones, the new owners of the property. At the noon meal on Sunday, January 4, 1903, Mott was blaming the world for his many problems and became angry at everyone present. When finished with his meal, one of the Jones brothers got up and kissed Mott's one-year-old daughter and then made a reference that she wouldn't have to listen to the abuse for much longer. The act enraged Mott who made a great scene and then went downtown and secured a revolver.

When Mott returned he started in on his wife accusing her of cheating on him and for plotting against him with the Jones boys. Mrs. Lockhart was in the kitchen as the Mott's were quarreling in the other room, when Leah Mott came through the kitchen and passed to the rear door, which led down the back stairs. An instant later the witness saw Mr. Mott pass through another room to the rear door where he drew a .38-caliber pistol from his pocket and shot his wife five times. Seeing Mrs. Mott lying at the bottom of the stairs Mrs. Lockhart ran to Louis

Mott and demanded to know why he shot his wife.

At first Mott implied that he would also take his own life, but instead he went out into the street and told people passing by to call the police as he had killed his wife. Officer John Wilson and City Detective Walter Hogan were on the scene in a matter of minutes and placed the man under arrest without incident. The prisoner was very drunk at the time and he reportedly walked unsteadily to the county jail.

A week earlier while drunk, Mott had fired at a man with his rifle who was standing across the street at the Keim Building. Mott was arrested for that incident as well but unfortunately he was only charged with disturbing the peace. County Attorney Hall had urged that Mott be given jail time for the offense but probably because he was an established businessman he was only fined twenty-five dollars and released.

After the deadly shooting, Doctors George T. McCullough, Edward W. Spottswood and John J. Buckley attended the dying woman, who was taken to the Sisters' Hospital. Mrs. Mott was shot four times, three of the bullets being lodged near her spine and the fourth round had struck her arm near the elbow, another shot was diverted by the woman when she grasped his arm. All of Mrs. Mott's wounds were serious, and any of the three bullets to the spine would have proved fatal. The woman was conscious most of the time and had suffered intense pain for about six hours until her death at 9:25 p.m.

Before dying Mrs. Mott made an ante-mortem statement to County Attorney Hall charging her husband with the crime while he was under the influence of drugs and liquor. While the murder was a great shock to the community, people familiar with the couple were not really surprised over the crime. Mott was considered a savage man when under the influence and he was generally oblivious to his actions. While his sanity was questioned by many people, most believed his awful actions were largely due to the influences of liquor.

Louis Mott was born in Kentucky where his parents died while he was still a small boy and Lemoine Mott who owned a large flourmill in Des Moines, Iowa along with property at Lemon Grove, California adopted his nephew. When Louis was about eighteen years old he got itchy feet and left his uncle's home to go to California to make his own fortune. He went to Walla Walla where he worked several years at a hotel and then on to Yellowstone National Park where he ran the company laundry. When he first came to Montana in 1888, he was described as being a bright, energetic young man with a great future. Somewhere along the way he developed a drinking problem and went to Boulder Hot Springs where he took the "Gold" or "Keeley Cure" and became an exemplary citizen for several years before falling once again off the wagon.

The attorneys for the prosecution were so committed in the guilt of Mott and the case against him was so strong that they wouldn't give the defense any break at all. Mott's first two attorneys withdrew before the case went to trial and their motion for a continuance was denied and the hearing was scheduled for the March term of 1903.

S.G. Murray and Joseph Woody conducted a hard battle for Mott's life basing their defense on the fact that their client was insane at the time of the crime, that he was addicted to morphine and on alcohol, which caused him to be deranged at the time. The Mott trial drew great crowds including a large number of women and young girls and because of all the publicity the selection of the jury took several days and finally consisted of the following men:

Charles E. Coleman	A.C. Vanderpool	Theodore Loveland[2]
William Neal	Walter B. Butler	Jacop Herman
W.F. Hutton	Jacob Rehder	John Maloney
Joseph Wagner (f)	T.J. James	James Prichard[3]

(f) Foreman

Detective Hogan testified how he had arrested Mott and while they were on the way to the jail the defendant had told him that he had killed his wife. According to the detective Mott said, "Be careful how you handle me, I'm not all together." Officer John Wilson then told the court that he was present at the time of Mott's arrest and that he had also heard Mott confess to the crime.

At one point Mott's nine-year-old daughter, Alice was called to testify against her father and the unusually bright young girl didn't appear nervous in the least as she told the court how she was playing with her younger sister, Ethel in their living room when she first heard the gun shots. She then explained how she found her dying mother on the family's back steps and how she ran to the hospital to find Dr. Buckley. The girl's testimony had a great affect on the jury and the defense chose not to cross-exanimate the young witness and she was excused.

After final arguments the case was presented to the jury on Monday evening, March 2, 1903, and after being out for twenty-three hours the jury returned a verdict of guilty in the first degree. The expression on Mott's face never changed as Jury Foreman Joseph Wagner read the panel's verdict and after hearing the decision the defendant addressed the panel by saying: "Gentlemen I thank you for your verdict. I believe it was rendered in accordance with your honor and your belief. I hold no animosity against any of you." One of the members of the jury reportedly turned and thanked the convicted murderer.

Two days later Mott was brought into court for sentencing and he maintained the perfect composure that he had displayed throughout the trial. As the judge sentenced him to be hanged on May 4, 1903, Mott stood with his arms folded in front of him and his head was erect. S.G. Murray withdrew from the case when Mott asked for a new trial and Frank H. Woody replaced him and he presented sensational affidavits for a new trial on the grounds of jury misconduct.

Theodore Loveland and James Prichard swore that their fellow juror, Charles E. Coleman was intoxicated on February 25, 1903, and Frank Sherman swore that he was in Dan Feightner's saloon in January of 1903, when he overheard Coleman discussing the case saying: "That son-of-a-bitch ought to be hung." In another affidavit John Doll swore that juryman William Neal also said that Mott should be hung.

At first the appeals process pleased Mott and he was given permission to fix up his cell by neatly painting it. He greeted visiting reporters cheerfully and on one visit in March of 1903, he was fixated with how the fourth day of the month ran through his life. The prisoner pointed out that his birthday fell on the fourth; the crime for which he was occurred on the fourth day of January and he was convicted on the fourth day of March and finally he was sentenced to be hanged on the fourth day of May. Mott made it clear however, that he didn't think he would be hanged on that day.

When the court overruled the motion for a new trial, Mott's attorneys filed a notice of appeal to the Supreme Court on April 27, 1903, and on December of that year the high tribunal denied the appeal. Mott's uncle, Lemoine Mott of Des Moines came to Missoula and he personally spoke with the Governor Joseph K. Toole for an appeal but his efforts were fruitless. Many folks made it clear that Mott should have been granted a new trial solely on account of his children and another appeal was made to the Governor for clemency within a week of Mott's execution but once again he refused to interfere.

Mott went through the disappointing appeals process with a forgiving spirit and his bad luck had apparently changed his demeanor gradually during the last weeks of his life. The prisoner's vindictive and vengeful frame of mind changed to a more kindlier and temperate attitude and during his last few weeks he received spiritual counsel and encouragement from different religious advisers. After that the prisoner was visited daily by Catholic priests and Evangelical pastors as well as the Sisters of Charity. Up to the day before his death, the doomed man was firm in his declaration that he would make his own peace with God even though several zealous Christians worked hard to influence Mott to accept one faith or another. During his last afternoon on this earth, Mott seemed to waver in favor of the Catholic Church and Father Macklin attended the condemned man during his last night.

On the day before Christmas of 1903, Mott's cell was thoroughly cleared and everything thing was removed and the prisoner was issued new clothing. During the search of the man's cell a hypodermic syringe was found hidden in the water closet, which he was using to maintain his morphine addiction. Mott admitted that he had been using five grains a day and said that he would go crazy if he was cut off. It is believed that the sheriff saw to it that the unfortunate man's cravings were satisfied, but the syringe was under guard and given to the prisoner only once a day. From that time on a twenty-four-hour deathwatch was ordered over the prisoner, Ed Larson, former Missoula police chief, during the days and John Wilson, former night chief of police, watched him at night.

The first preparations for the hanging was made when Sheriff Harry W. Thompson made arrangements to borrow Butte's "Galloping Gallows" and to attend the hanging of James Martin at Butte in February of 1904, with his chief deputy, Undersheriff Edward Sterling to get first-hand knowledge of the death machine's workings. The first visible evidence of Louis Mott's approaching execution appeared on March 4, when Sheriff Thompson and his staff selected the location for the enclosure for the gallows and directed the prisoners of the jail clear the area of the piles of fire wood.

The forty by sixty-foot stockade was then built directly behind the county jail out of sixteen-foot rough-cut boards. Even the cracks in the fence were intentionally covered with overlapping boards, which shut out the view to the interior except from the upper floor and roof of the courthouse. The gallows arrived in Missoula on March 5, and they were placed in storage until a couple of days before the execution and when they were erected on March 16, the black scaffold was located at the north end of the stockade directly under the shadow of the jail.

While the preparations were being made for his execution, Mott remained busy with his correspondences with several people including Governor Toole and Congressman Joseph M. Dixon. By March 11, Sheriff Thompson had mailed about two hundred and fifty invitations statewide and it was reported that he hadn't mailed a single invitation to a resident of Missoula County arguing that if he had invited one person of the county he wouldn't be able to draw the line.

Mott woke up at two o'clock on his last full day feeling fresh and during the afternoon he received several visitors and that evening a newspaperman joined Mott while he was preparing his dinner in his cell. The prisoner had started a small campfire in the middle of the cell floor and he was warming his meal over the fire. He chatted with the reporter while he was tearing pages out of an old magazine to feed the blaze, and said that it reminded him of camping out but he missed the trees and the small stream flowing by.

Mott believed that if he had been a rich man he would have been acquitted, but his wealthy uncle had withheld his aid until it was too late to help him. As he was eating his dinner the five o'clock whistle blew at the jail, and Mott announced that he only had thirteen more hours to live. Many visitors desired to talk with the prisoner but only Judge William Hayes and Father Macklin were admitted and the condemned man was baptized into the Catholic faith shortly after midnight on the eve of his death.

The prisoner made no effort to sleep during his last night and he just sat or walked around his cell the entire evening. At two o'clock in the morning Sheriff Thompson sent a fine supper of raw oysters to Mott's cell and two Sisters of Charity visited him at five o'clock for twenty minutes. By that time, those invited to witness the hanging had begun to arrive or had gained entry to the stockade through a doorway nearest the courthouse. Among the visiting sheriffs were H.E. Benner of Cascade County, J.C. Barnden of Powell County and Park County Sheriff Harry Robertson.

The death march began a few minutes after six with Father Macklin in the lead followed by Mott and the sheriff and his deputies.

The condemned man faced the crowd with a frank and open face with no sign of fear and after a few whispered words to the priest, Mott made a brief speech in which he said that he was willing to pay for the crime but stated that there were extenuating circumstances. He said that he bore no malice toward anyone and he would die at peace. Undersheriff Sterling and Deputy Jack Gannon began strapping up the prisoner and when they were in place the undersheriff placed the noose around the man's neck. Mott closed with a short but eloquent prayer: "Almighty God, into Thy hands I now resign my spirit. Citizens of Missoula, Good-bye."

The man's voice rang out clear and distinct and there wasn't a single nervous tremor and when the last words passed from his lips the black cap was pulled down; the signal was given, the executioner in the secret enclosure severed the cord and at 6:08 a.m. Louis Mott's body was shot into the air. At 6:13, Doctors Buckley, Brown and McCullough pronounced him dead, stating that his neck had been broken and after allowing the body to hang awhile Undertaker Charles H. Marsh cut it down and the remains were placed into the casket.

The day before his execution Mott had gone over his own funeral arrangements with C.F. Marsh and instructed the undertaker that he wanted to be laid to rest in the Missoula Cemetery with a quiet Christian service. He left the time of his internment and other details to the undertaker but he didn't want to be buried in the suit of clothes furnished by the county and wished to meet his maker in the garments he had bought and paid for himself. Before saying good-bye to Mr. Marsh the condemned man said, "I've only got two things left in the world, my hat and my boots. You take my hat and give my boots to Billy Wilson." The undertaker complied with Mott's last request and he was buried at ten o'clock on the morning of his execution with the services conducted by a Catholic priest.

Mott was buried in his nightshirt in compliance with his orders and two small button portraits of his two children were pinned over his heart. While it was the wish of the condemned man to be buried next to his dead wife, his stepson would not give his consent and Louis Mott was interred in a private lot arranged for by the undertaker.

One commendable step taken by Sheriff Thompson, which disappointed the relic hunters, was his order to disallow the reprehensible practice of cutting up the hangman's rope and distributing the pieces among the witnesses as souvenirs. The sheriff did not allow anything to be removed from the gallows and he gave specific instructions that the rope be burned immediately after the hanging. The slippers worn by the condemned man were also cremated with the rope leaving nothing for the relic hunters.

All day long men, women and children loitered around the stockade at the county courthouse after the hanging and the undertaking establishment was another center of attraction, and at least one hundred people reportedly hung around in hopes that they would be permitted to view the dead man. At one point there were sixty men, women and children lined up at the front door of the establishment.

Postscript:
Before making her deathbed statement Mrs. Mott made County Attorney Hall promise to look after her daughters, Ethal, one, and nine-year-old Alice. Mr. Hall was good to his word and he placed the girls into a well-to-do-family who raised them.

A little more than a year later Sheriff Thompson went to White Sulphur Springs to assist Meagher County Sheriff Charles Sherman with the hanging of Herbert Metzger. Mrs. Mott was fatally shot just one hundred feet from where Joe Vuckovich later shot and killed Mrs. Shea in February of 1921, for which he too was hanged.

May 5, 1905

Herbert Henry Metzger

Location and Gallows: Metzger was hanged at White Sulphur Springs and he was another victim of ***Gallows No. Nine: (Feb. 1888): "Galloping Gallows" No. Three.***

Description: Twenty-nine years old

Crime: Murder of Homer E. Ward in his cabin on Sheep Creek about twenty-five miles from White Sulphur Springs on Thanksgiving Day, November 23, 1904.

Judge: Edwin K. Cheadle

Prosecution: Meagher County Attorney, Napoleon B. Smith and assisted by Gallatin County Attorney George D. Pease of Bozeman.

Defense: Powell Black

Sheriff: Charles H. Sherman

Distinction: While Metzger was the first man legally executed in Meagher County, he was actually the fourth convicted murderer sentenced to die there. The Chinaman, Henry Lee, the first to be sentenced to die and Joseph W. "Toe String Joe" Hanna managed to escape from jail before they were executed and Charles J. Wooster cheated the gallows in 1892, by hanging himself in his cell.

Relics and Remnants: The battered hat of Metzger, which played a part in his murder conviction, is currently on display at the Castle Museum at White Sulphur Springs.

Twenty-two-year-old Homer E. Ward was born at Eau Claire, Wisconsin and he had settled on Sheep Creek in 1901, after leaving his father's home at Bozeman. The hard-working young man worked for area ranchers and his cabin was six miles above the Mumbrue Ranch and three from Mr. William Woolsey's Stage Station on the Neihart Road. When Ward hadn't been seen for several days and his team of horses was running loose, Mr. D.P. Mumbrue sent his foreman, John Payne to check on the young man on Thanksgiving morning, November 24, 1904.

After knocking on Ward's door at about nine o'clock, Payne noticed that the key was still in the lock and he entered the cabin. When his eyes became accustomed to the darkness he saw a body on the floor and not wanting to disturb the crime scene he immediately rode off to report his discovery to his employer.

Before leaving for White Sulphur Springs to report the murder, Mr. Mumbrue detailed his foreman and Leroy "Roy" Ward, the victim's brother to guard the crime scene until the arrival of the coroner. About one o'clock on Thursday afternoon, December 1, 1904, the coroner's jury and officers left the Mumbrue Ranch for the Ward cabin passing the William Woolsey Ranch about halfway through the wild and thickly timbered region. Before entering the well-constructed cabin, which faced to the north, two photographs were taken of the structure. There were two small windows with four small panes of glass in each on the east and west sides of the cabin, which was built of hewn logs. The barn was about thirty-five feet to the southwest and there was a log hitching post thirty feet in front of the cabin. The first officers to enter the Ward cabin were Coroner Dr. John D. Shorey, Major James Keown, a detective from Bozeman and Gallatin County Attorney George D. Pease.

After taking preliminary photos of the crime scene the jury and the officers found the body of the victim, which was quickly identified by Leroy Ward by his pants and shoes. The victim was on his back with his feet extended under the table, the head and upper body of Ward were badly burned when they had been covered with a burning quilt and old newspapers in an attempt to cremate the remains. The spilled bowl of lamp oil and an empty five-gallon can of coal oil were also found near the charred body indicating that they had been used to fuel the fire.

On the rough hewn table were dishes and food including a full cup of coffee suggesting that Homer Ward had just sat down to eat his supper when he was shot in the back of the head. There was toast by the tin plate and a frying pan near where his elbow would have rested and fragments of Ward's skull were found on the dishes and the tablecloth, which was soaked with blood while more brain tissue was splattered on the broken panes of the window and even on the log rafter above the table. A 30-30 Winchester bullet had been fired through the east window and after penetrating Ward's head it exited out of the west window. The bullet entered the back of Ward's head near the center of the skull and it emerged just above the man's right eye.

It was believed that when Ward was shot his head fell forward onto the table and when the murderer pulled the chair out from under the victim he fell to the floor. Next to the body was an empty 30-30 Winchester cartridge indicating that after killing Ward the murderer ejected the empty round as he stood over his victim. After plundering the cabin, the murderer covered the body with the coal oil-soaked bedding and newspapers and then ignited them in an effort to cremate the remains. Another gruesome find by the officers were two dead kittens, which had died from starvation and neglect after their master had been murdered.

Among the many items stolen from the cabin was a 32-caliber Harrington and Richardson revolver, which Ward kept in his hip pocket, a 30-40 Winchester rifle and a gold watch. The unknown assassin had also stolen a sack of flour, a package of Arbuckle's coffee and other groceries and sundries, which the victim had just purchased in town including several razors, a double harness, a fur overcoat with a white collar and a fairly new Stetson cowboy hat.

After taking his victim's Stetson and overcoat, the killer left behind a light jumper coat and an old odd looking white hat. The peculiar styled hat was found on the floor and it had a pronounced burn mark on the crown and when it was worn the brim drooped. The hat was considered an important clue in the murder case as the murderer had obviously discarded the worn head cover in favor of the newer Stetson hat.

When Homer Ward's remains were being placed on a canvas stretcher a small purse was found under the body containing a five-dollar bill and a dollar and five cents in change. Some of the witnesses recalled that at about four o'clock on the afternoon of Wednesday November 23, 1904, Homer Ward had stopped at the Mumbrue Ranch complaining about being sick. He said that he had been battling a fever and that he wasn't able to work for about two weeks. The wagon he was driving was loaded with hay and he was last seen alive passing the Woolsey Stage Station.

Apparently Ward had un-harnessed his two horses and tied them to the wagon wheels so that the animals could eat the hay from the box. After preparing his supper Ward was murdered as he sat down to eat and after the murderer stole everything of value in the cabin, the buildings were set on fire to destroy the evidence of his crime. As the barn was burning to the ground the two horses managed to drag the wagon about eight feet from the blaze, which saved their lives. About a day later the animals somehow broke away from the wagon and Mr. and Mrs. Woolsey saw them roaming the nearby foothills.

Dr. Shorey held the coroner's inquest at the Mumbrue Ranch on the same evening that the body was found and the jury was made up of the following men:

C.W. Cook	James Chamberlin	Charles Mixer
Edward Allen	Cliff Tipton	John Butler

Assisted by Attorneys George D. Pease and W.L. Ford along with detective Major Keown and Undersheriff George L. Williams, the coroner's jury found that Homer Ward had been murdered by a person or persons unknown. After the hearing Undersheriff Williams, Detective Major Keown and John Payne rode to the Patrick Petit Ranch where they obtained a description of a man who had been wearing a similar white hat that was found at the murder scene and from there the posse headed far into the wild and lonely region of the Little Belt Mountains before they reached Neihart on Saturday night, December 3, 1904.

The posse spent all day Sunday checking out fruitless leads and then on Monday, December 5, they were instructed by Fred Walker to a small hunting camp at the head of O'Brien Creek about seven miles from Neihart. Inside the empty hut the men found most of the articles that had been taken from Ward's cabin except the gold watch. Among the cache of stolen items hid under a bunk was the fur overcoat with a white collar, the double harness, and the 30-40 Winchester.

The posse decided to stake out the temporary shelter for the occupants' return and while Payne took their horses out of sight, Major Keown and Deputy Williams hid in the darkness of the hut. At about 3:30 that afternoon a man named Alex Oriet entered the abode where he was ordered to remain quiet and about an hour later another man approached the camp.

This second man noticed the extra horse tracks in the new snow and he entered the camp warily and he had his Winchester ready as he opened the canvas flap that served as a door to the small cabin. Immediately the man and Undersheriff Williams both covered one another and before a round was fired Major Keown jumped forward and grabbed the fugitive's rifle barrel. The quick action of Major Keown in disarming the fugitive in the hut probably saved the life of the outlaw, as Deputy Williams would have surely killed the young man on the spot.

The cool-nerved Undersheriff Williams had earned a reputation for his bravery and fearlessness when he helped track down William Gay and Harry Gross back in 1893, along with his dealings with other outlaws. George Williams was eventually elected as sheriff of Meagher County in 1906, and he served three terms. The second prisoner was identified as Herbert Metzger and after they were both put into irons, Major Keown went for John Payne and the horses while Williams guarded the two captives. Night was falling as the quiet procession headed for Neihart, with the men in irons walking ahead of the party.

After a short night's rest at the San Francisco Hotel at Neihart, the party secured a team and wagon and drove over the mountain range towards White Sulphur Springs where Sheriff Charles H. Sherman met them on Sheep Creek. The expanded posse with their prisoners arrived at White Sulphur Springs about midnight on Tuesday, December 6, 1904, where Metzger and Oriet were placed in separate cells at the county jail. The jail at White Sulphur Springs at the time was a thirty by forty foot single-story structure that had been built in 1884.

The jail contained offices for the sheriff and undersheriff along with what was then a state-of-the-art "Canary Cage" consisting of two cells along with a lattice corridor that held another eight prisoners with automatic doors and locks manufactured by the Pauley Brothers of St. Louis. All day Wednesday the prisoners were questioned behind closed doors and they reportedly talked freely about their activities while camping on Sheep Creek, but when they weren't being grilled a large number of people were allowed to see them through the bars of the cages.

Also on Wednesday the two men had their preliminary hearing at the county courthouse where Attorney Freeman represented Alex Oriet while Herbert Metzger was without counsel. At the hearing Leroy Ward, the brother of the murder victim, identified many of the articles found at the suspects' camp including the harnesses, the rifle, revolver, fur coat and other clothing items and trinkets. Dr. J.M. Kumpe described the wounds of the murdered man and Patrick Petit said that he had seen Metzger wearing the old white hat found at the murder scene. Fred Walker and Albert Bronson also identified the same hat along with many of the stolen items found at the camp when they stayed at the hut with Oriet and Metzger after hunting grouse on November 29, 1904. At the conclusion of the hearing Judge Hartfield held the two prisoners over for the March 1905, term of the district court.

Eventually Alex Oriet was released because of lack of evidence but Metzger's trial began Thursday morning, March 23, 1905, with Judge Edwin K. Cheadle presiding. The two-story courthouse was built in 1882 and the clerk of the court and probate judge offices were located on the lower floor while the courtroom that could accommodate up to three hundred people was upstairs. For a while it appeared as though the entire venire of about fifty men would be exhausted before a jury could be seated.

One disqualified juror was Sam Scott who expressed his opposition to capital punishment by saying he didn't believe it was severe enough. After telling the court that he believed that the convicted murderer should be placed in an oven and cooked to the edge of his life; revived and then the punishment repeated, Mr. Scott was quickly excused and at half past four a jury was finally made up of the following Meagher County citizens:

James Christensen	J.B. Campbell	William Jennizen
John I. Conway	I.M. Hensley	L.H. Vanalstine
Sanford Holliday	H.C. Klock	W.H. Cartwright
Ole Eike	Charles Bryan	O.N. Kennard (f)

(f) Foreman

Each time Metzger was brought into the courtroom he wore steel bracelets on his wrists and a short chain was connected to Undersheriff Williams and at least two other deputies closely followed the two men. Sheriff Sherman had taken the extra precaution to prevent an escape or suicide since there had been so many other prisoners who had cheated the gallows in the county. Earlier in Meagher County a Chinaman by the name of Henry Lee escaped from the county jail before the sheriff had started on a gallows and the murderer Joseph "Toe String Joe" Hanna had also escaped just before his execution and a thousand dollar reward was put on his head. Although he was located some years later at Crawfordville, Indiana the county commissioners didn't want to go through the expense of bringing him back to Montana including the reward.

Then in December of 1892, Charles J. Wooster was in the county jail for the murder of Martin O'Brien, the marshal of Neihart when he cheated the gallows by hanging himself with a cord in his cell. Meagher County lost another chance of hanging a man when William Gay was granted a change of venue and he was executed at Helena in 1896.

At half past seven on Wednesday night, March 29, 1905, after deliberating for two hours, Foreman O.N. Kennard handed the verdict to Judge Cheadle and after Clerk of the Court Grande recorded it, which caused a delay that must have seemed an eternity to the many spectators, it was read: "guilty in the first degree." When the jury had first announced it had reached its verdict Metzger had to be awoken from a sound sleep to return to the courtroom. After the verdict was announced, the courtroom was described as being as quiet as a funeral parlor and while most of the audience showed signs of being nervous, Metzger didn't show any sign of emotion except once to wipe a single tear from his eyes. When he was ordered to stand by the judge Metzger's stoic indifferent attitude had disappeared and his manner had turned to resignation and penitence rather than defiance.

On Thursday morning, March 30, 1905, the prisoner was brought back into the crowded courtroom fastened by a steel bracelet to Undersheriff Williams as he faced Judge Cheadle for his sentencing. Judge Cheadle sentenced the prisoner to death but he didn't specify the date although it had to take place within thirty days by law. When the prisoner was returned to the jail a day and night deathwatch placed over him.

There was a scaffold in storage at the county jail, which had been built by R.S. Price[4] and Dan Hurd to hang Joseph W. Hanna or "Toe String Joe" in 1884, but the prisoner escaped from the jail the night before his execution date. The scaffold was the old style with a trap door and it was again erected to execute Charles J. Wooster in 1892, but he too managed to cheat the gallows by hanging himself in his cell. After an inspection of the ancient gallows revealed that it had been warped out of shape, Sheriff Sherman decided to use the scaffold constructed to hang William Wallace Calder at Lewistown on March 18, 1900.

When it was learned that the Fergus County scaffold had been damaged during the construction of the new courthouse in Lewistown, Sheriff Sherman then requested the tried-and-sure circulating gallows of Silver Bow County that was last used to hang Louis Mott at Missoula in March of 1904.

The big frame of the Silver Bow County gallows was securely braced to the wall of the jail and the top of the scaffold was even with the twelve-foot wooden security fence. A canvas enclosure next to the gallows concealed the weight and the unknown parties assigned the unpleasant duty of severing the cord that launched the condemned man to his death. In side the forty-two by thirty-two foot enclosure the witnesses were kept from the gallows by a stout railing, which was placed about ten feet from the scaffold. The 310-pound weight, which measured only ten by seven by thirteen inches, was composed of molten lead encased in a tin or sheet-iron covered.

By the middle of April workmen had dug holes and set posts for the enclosure around the jail yard while the gallows were temporarily stored at Dorsey, which was about twenty miles south of town. Eventually it was set up close to the west side of the jail building, which obstructed the view from the schoolhouse and the courthouse. The big fence around the enclosure, which Metzger nicknamed as the "Bull Pen," didn't have a single crack or knothole for prying eyes and guards were still stationed outside of the wall to keep the curious crowds back. The rope used to hang Metzger had been previously stretched by a two hundred-pound bag of sand and then it was made more flexible with a soap and water mixture. The pulleys were carefully oiled and tested and a deputy sheriff from Silver Bow County helped with the assembly of the gallows and then returned to White Sulphur Springs to assist in the operation of the scaffold on the day of execution.

The condemned man was up until one a.m. on the night before his execution drinking, singing and dancing. Musicians were at the jail with a banjo, guitar and a harmonica playing all of the old, favorite tunes of the day. Metzger remained in a festive mood even during the tender tunes, which ordinarily would make a man think of the folks back home with glistening eyes. Once when the carpenters were hammering on the fence Undersheriff Williams found Metzger crying on his bunk and when confronted the condemned man stated he was only thinking of his family back home.

The following morning he jokingly told his guards that he was putting his shoes on for the last time and a long-time friend of the Metzger family, D.L. Dilworth was allowed to remain with the condemned man during his last night and they talked about their lives back in Canton, Ohio. Mr. Dilworth later told reporters that Herbert Metzger was the "black sheep" of the triplets, one of which coincidentally was named Homer, the same as the murder victim.

It was learned that Metzger had enlisted in the United States Army in 1892, under the assumed name of Bert J. Bartlett and then deserted while he was serving in Cuba. The convicted murderer had been a suspect in another similar crime several years earlier but the cremation of the victim was so complete that no evidence was ever found. Metzger openly stated that he had shot and killed men during wartime but swore he had never taken another life since. While Metzger initially resisted the services of a clergyman, the Reverend Mr. Wakefield eventually consoled the condemned man.

During his confinement, sentimental woman weren't allowed to idolize Metzger, as was frequently the case in other executions. The sheriff had wisely guarded against such displays and he carefully screened messages and gifts to the prisoner. Special notes and bouquets of flowers never got past the sheriff's office and with no pitiful "thank you" notes from the condemned man the women wouldn't call again.

One woman was allowed to visit the condemned man and as she was pouring her heart out to him and making him out as a martyr she said between sobs, "I wish I might take your place." "I wish you could too," was Metzger's cool response. "It would be a great relief to me." Metzger had two women friends who were frequent visitors, and they were his only sincere sympathizers. These women were considered outcasts of society but they had tender hearts and could sympathize with the condemned man as they too had been forsaken by humanity.

A letter from Metzger's sister, Mrs. Ida Young of Pierce, Ohio reportedly had an effect on the condemned man with its pitiful appeal to come back home and to stay with his family. She was a sister that Metzger had often spoken of in terms of endearment, and like the rest of his family, he had never informed her of his immanent fate. In the correspondence his sister included a photograph a baby in the woman's arms and although the letter was dated February 10, the authorities had withheld it until the day before the execution. Metzger returned the photo in a letter to his sister dated May 6, and it was given to Reverend Wakefield to forward to the woman.

During his last day Metzger was well supplied with whisky and he continually ordered more. As the day wore on he seemed less hilarious and when he began to settle into a somber mood the musicians would cheer him up again. While drunk, Metzger spoke freely of his past, about being from a well-to-do family in Ohio, and leaving when he was just fifteen years old. He had traveled over a great deal of the country; mingled with good people and he was even engaged to a nice girl before she ran off with another man. After that he started running with a lower class of people and he got into trouble and had finally reached the end of a rope in Montana. Leroy Ward, the murdered man's brother was also in town for the hanging, but Metzger refused to talk with the man.

At about midnight Metzger ate a hearty chicken dinner while he drank whisky and beer until he went to sleep but he was awakened at 2:30 a.m. for the reading of the death warrant. When asked by an "Anaconda Standard" reporter if he had slept well, Metzger said yes, and that he never lost any sleep over being hanged, and that he never would. He said he felt sorry for the officers as he had been cracking jokes at their expense and he asked the reporter to tell his friends good-bye for him, and that he didn't blame anyone but his own foolish talk for his conviction.

Undersheriff Williams entered Metzger's cell with the leather straps and asked the prisoner if he was ready, and then offered him another drink. "I don't give a damn," was Metzger's calm response. "What have you there; are you going to put a harness on me?" Metzger put on his coat and the leather strap was placed around his waist. "George, God bless you," he said, "Good bye, sheriff." "Metzger, I hate to do it," said Deputy Williams, "but I have to." The condemned man then asked for and received another glass full to the brim of whisky and the march to the scaffold began.

While he was obviously drunk, Metzger still walked with a steady gate and he displayed no sign of nervousness. There was no terror in his eyes, his hands didn't tremble, his lips did not quiver, and although he was pail, it wasn't as white as most of the other faces in the crowd. Undersheriff Williams fastened another strap around the doomed man's ankles and one about his knees and the suspense was at a pitch as the noose was adjusted behind his left ear and lightly drawn up by the sheriff. One photograph of the hanging shows that Dr. Jonathan Stephens had also adjusted the noose around Metzger's neck while the undersheriff was still adjusting straps around the prisoner's legs.

The sheriff stepped behind the screen and after asking Metzger if he had any last words, the support cord was cut and the weight fell to the earth with a dull thud and at 2:45 in the morning the body of Herbert Henry Metzger shot into the air and then dangled in convulsions. The man's shoulders drew up uncontrollably, his fists turned purple as they clinched and after eleven minutes Drs. J.M. Kumpe and Stephens pronounced Metzger dead.

There was no large crowd around the jail and only about fifty men witnessed the hanging including Sheriff Munden of Broadwater County, Fergus County Sheriff Fallon, Silver Bow County Sheriff John J. Quinn and Sheriff Harry W. Thompson of Missoula. A plain coffin painted black with white metal handles was brought into the yard and as Metzger's body was being placed in the box the hangman rope was cut up into pieces by the crowd and retained as souvenirs.

Postscript:
In the next edition of the "Meager Republican" it was reported that "Herbert Metzger had been fatally injured in an endeavor to unravel a knot tied by the sheriff in the county jail last Friday and he was quietly buried by the undertaker the evening after the mishap."

April 20, 1906
<u>Lu Sing</u>

Location and Gallows: Lu Sing was hanged inside the jail yard on Main Street at Bozeman and he was the ninth man to die on ***<u>Gallows No. Nine: (Feb 1888): "Galloping Gallows" No. Three</u>***.
Description: Lu Sing was described as being fat and quite ugly.
Crime: Murder of laundryman, Tom Sing on October 3, 1905 in the kitchen of the China Restaurant next to the Willson Company building on the corner of Main and Bozeman Streets.
Judge: W.R.C. Stewart
Prosecution: County Attorney A.J. Walrath
Defense: J.L. Staats
Sheriff: E.M. Reynolds
Distinction: The death sentence for the Lu Sing case was the first ever read in a Montana courtroom by a woman, then Deputy Clerk of the Court Vera Anderson and at eighteen years of age she was probably the youngest clerk to have ever read such a verdict as well.

It was believed that a Chinese woman was at the center of this sad tragedy at Bozeman. Six-year-old Annie Kum Chee was brought over from China to San Francisco in 1880, for immoral purposes and she was later sold to a rich Chines at Astoria, Oregon. The girl eventually escaped her enslavement and was rescued by the Presbyterian Mission at San Francisco where she received an education and embraced the Christian faith. Apparently Tom Sing helped pay for her upkeep and education at the mission and eventually he married the young woman and they moved to Butte and later to Bozeman.

The rich Chinese man in Oregon was so insulted by the loss of his property that he supposedly put a price on the couple's heads and it was believed that Lu Sing was intending to earn the six hundred dollar reward when he located the pair at Bozeman. Apparently Lu Sing wasn't able to catch both Tom and his wife together so he decided to take out the husband first and then find the wife.

The story about the Chinese reward gained credence at the time of Lu Sing's arrest when he reportedly told Chief of Police Robertson texcitely hat he had "heaps of money." The powerful Chinese family never came to the aid of Lu Sing however, and as far as anyone knew he never did receive a cent for the murder. Other people who were knowledgeable about such customs explained that Lu Sing's family in China or in California had probably received the reward for the apparent assassination.

At the time of Lu Sing's incarceration in the county jail a member of Governor Toole's committee to evaluate all of the city and county facilities of the state had recently inspected the facilities. Reverend M.L. Rickman found that while the county jail, which was in the basement of the courthouse on Main and Third Streets was terribly inadequate to handle the volume of inmates, it was considered clean and that the walls were free from obscene and immoral pictures and drawings. The trial of Lu Sing opened in the November term of court of Judge W.R.C. Stewart and the jury was made up of the following citizens of Gallatin County:

John H. Foster	E.M. Knadler	Louis Kruger
John Eschenbacher	Lester Mickleberry	Henry Nelson
R.A. Nunnelly	C.E. Rowland	Albert Brandley (f)
J.H. Stiff	Lewis P. Lay	W.E. Crowley

(f) Foreman

The proprietor of the City Restaurant, Yung Sing and one of his waiters, Mar Quong, other wise known as Charlie, and a cook named Chen Yuen all testified that they had either seen or heard Lu Sing murder Tom Sing. Chen Yuen testified through an interpreter, Um Yeck of Butte, that he and Lu Sing were peeling potatoes on the morning of October 3, 1905, when they saw the defendant strike Tom Sing with a meat hatchet while the victim was eating his breakfast on a meat block in the kitchen. When placed on the stand on his own behalf Lu Sing testified through his interpreter that he remembered being at the restaurant that day, but he didn't recall anything about the killing. It was reported that Lu Sing didn't show any sign of nervousness throughout the proceedings until the jury came in with their verdict on Friday November 10.

When the jury returned the verdict the clerk of the court, Charles B. Anderson was absent from the office and the duty of polling the jury and reading of the verdict fell on the deputy clerk and daughter of Mr. Anderson. Eighteen-year-old deputy clerk of the court, Miss Vera Anderson read the guilty verdict, making her probably the first woman to have ever read such a verdict in the state of Montana. Miss Anderson read the verdict without a tremor although she had turned a little pale when she discovered that she had the unpleasant duty to perform. Not only was she probably the first woman to read a murder verdict in the state, she was probably the youngest person to hold the office of deputy clerk of the court in Montana.

Because the district court term of Judge Stewart ended Saturday evening, he scheduled the sentencing of Lu Sing on the afternoon of Saturday November 11, 1905. In a courtroom crowded with men, women and children trying to catch a look at the condemned man, Attorney J.L. Staats announced that he had filed his objections to the sentencing because: Under the statute, Judge Stewart could not pronounce sentence until two days after the verdict was rendered, his client was insane, and that the defendant had good cause to offer the court for an arrest of judgment.

The judge quickly overruled the motion pointing out that in his sentencing statement the court had endeavored at every point to protect the defendant's rights and counsel was appointed to insure that the man's rights were in no way infringed upon. Although the judge didn't initially set a date for the execution a twenty-four-hour deathwatch was assigned over the prisoner and George Herndon was assigned days and Edward Scott stood guard during the nights. Four days after sentencing Lu Sing to his death, Judge Stewart and Court Stenographer Garver left Bozeman for Townsend where he held the November term of the district court for Broadwater County.

Lu Sing appeared to realize that his life was drawing to a close, as he made every effort to escape including trying to slip past the jailer every time he delivered his meals.While Lu Sing had taken most of his trial proceedings nonchalantly he became more and more nervous as the time of his execution approached. According to the deathwatches Lu Sing would jump at the slightest sounds and he would fall to the ground with the slightest push or gesture like a badly beaten-down dog. On the day that he was being photographed he told the sheriff his prediction of the day of his own execution and he was within three days of the original date of December 21, 1905.

The prisoner was given a bath on November 16 and he was presented with a complete set of American clothes, which he wore until the day of his hanging when he wore his native attire. On Saturday November 25, 1905, Sheriff E.M. Reynolds went to Butte to make the arrangements to have the famous "Galloping Gallows" transported to Bozeman for the hanging and the scaffold was erected just west of the sheriff's office in the county jail yard, which was already surrounded by a tall brick wall.

J.L. Staats presented a motion for a new trial on December 9, but his argument was overruled and later that day the defense attorney served a notice of an appeal to the Montana State Supreme Court, which resulted in a stay of execution. Most of the Chinese residents at Bozeman were astonished at the time it took for justice in America explaining that if Lu Sing were in China his head would have been chopped off the day after the crime. Finally the prisoner was re-sentenced on December 9, for his date with the scaffold on April 20, 1906

On April 9, Sheriff Reynolds mailed out the invitations to the hanging and by law, the executions were to be private except that at least twelve citizens had to witness the hanging. It was customary to invite the sheriffs and other peace officers of the state, members of the press, the lawyers involved in the case, the jury and officers of the court and the friends and relatives of both the victim and of the condemned man.

Unfortunately this wasn't the first hanging that Sheriff Reynolds had ever witnessed. As a boy of about eight years old in Missouri, Kansas or Arkansas, he couldn't quite recall which one, he was playing with several of his friends in a barn when the hired man came in, sharpened his razor, shaved, washed and slicked himself up as though he was going to visit his best girl. The boys had seen him do this act several times before and they didn't think anything of it until he said, "Well, boys, come on out if you want to see me hang myself."

At first the boys were a bit surprised by the stement but they were intensely interested and so they quickly followed the man out of the barn. The children thought the hired man was going to show them a new trick or two and make them laugh and scream like he had done so many times before and they followed him to the wagon shed and then walked close behind him as he carefully selected a convenient place for his execution. Finally the man found a place where he could stand on the end of a ladder, or some other piece of farm machinery from which he could easily launch himself into eternity. He took a halter rope, tied it carefully to the cross beam of the shed, climbed upon the binder, slipped a noose around his neck and then swung off.

As the little boys watched the man twist, squirm, kick, swing around and gasp for air they all cheered with delight and begged him to keep it up, believing he was doing an act just for fun. When the man stopped struggling and one of the boys pointed out that the man's tongue was swollen and sticking out of his mouth, the youngsters got scared and ran to a neighbor and reported the incident but unfortunately by the time help arrived the poor man was dead. Apparently the young man and his girl friend had a falling out and she reportedly told him to go and chase himself, but instead he decided to end it all.

During the second week of April Lu Sing went on a hunger strike but the staff at the sheriff's office ensured that he still got fed. Everyday, sometimes twice a day the deputies and the deathwatch would get Lu Sing down on the floor and while a couple of the men held him another deputy would hold the prisoner's nose and pour soup into his mouth. Lu Sing reportedly fought like a bulldog but with two or three men holding him down, he ate pretty well. The condemned man got at least one good meal each day and if the boys on the force didn't have too much to do, they gave Lu Sing a second meal when they had time.

About three days before the execution Lu Sing became very nervous after hearing the preparations being completed for the hanging including the construction of the gallows in the jail yard, the stretching and testing of the rope and the trials of the mechanism of the scaffold. Few people of Bozeman knew the murdered Tom Sing by sight, and virtually nobody knew the murderer, who had come all the way from the Pacific coast to do the killing, but hundreds of the residents wanted to see a man die. Because the hour of the execution wasn't announced publicly some morbid people sat up all night, perched on piles of lumber in an adjacent lumber yard to peer over the wall of the execution yard.

On the eve of his execution Lu Sing was allowed to don a suit of Chinese clothes and shortly after one o'clock in the morning of April 20, Sheriff Reynolds, Undersheriff Sales and several of the deputies entered the man' cell. The death warrant was read through a Chinese interpreter who was attached to the Federal Court at Helena and then while he was very nervous and trembling visibly, Lu Sing didn't object to Sheriff Deputies Keown and Battenfelder adjusting the straps during the reading of the warrant.

After that the sheriff and his men conducted their prisoner to the jail yard where one hundred and fifty men and two women were waiting. The two women were said to have been waitresses, and after the unpleasant affair, most of the witnesses said that the ladies had wished that they hadn't come. Among the other witness at the hanging were Sheriffs John Quinn of Silver Bow County, A.S. Robertson of Park County and his deputies, Robertson and Belles, Chief of Police Nelson of Livingston, Sheriff Munden of Broadwater County, two newspapermen and a number of city and county officials.

While climbing the stairs from the basement of the jailhouse Lu Sing became faint and he had to be helped up by the deputies. Five minutes later the condemned man was standing under the gallows and while adjusting the noose around the prisoner's neck, the sheriff asked if he had anything to say. Speaking through the interpreter, Lu Sing spoke in a rather rambling manner trying to give his story of the murder of Tom Sing. Just as the interpreter had spoken the last words of Lu Sing's statement, Undersheriff Sales pulled the black cap over the condemned man's face, Sheriff Reynolds raised his hand and the unknown man beneath a blanket covering released the 320-pound weight of bags of hardened cement and at 1:10 a.m. the murderer went into the air with a jerk. The hanging wasn't considered a clean one by most observers, as the jerk wasn't sufficient to break the man's neck. Either there was too much slack in the rope or it hadn't been properly stretched the result was that the prisoner wasn't jerked severely enough and he suffered a slow death by strangulation.

Following the jerk the body trembled violently several times for about fifteen minutes and after it had been hanging for about ten minutes it appeared to squirm and Lu Sing's pulse grew stronger for a second or two before it gradually grew weaker. Doctors Safeley and Ragsdale each tracked Lu Sing's pulse and from time to time Doctors Blair, Patterson, McCoy, W.H.A. Campbell and other members of the medical fraternity of Gallatin County examined the executed man. At 1:25 Lu Sing was pronounced officially dead by the many doctors there.

Three minutes after the doctors had made their pronouncement Lu Sing's body was taken down and placed in a coffin and Paul Reichert on behalf of the undertaker, Dr. Fafley took charge of the body and it was buried in the cemetery before daylight. When the rope was removed from the dead man the spectators crowded in and began struggling for a piece of the rope as a souvenir and within a few minutes there wasn't a single threat remaining. When some of the disappointed people began chipping off pieces of the gallows the deputies immediately cleared the yard.

After everyone was removed from the yard there was nothing left to tell of the affair except for the tall, black gallows, which stood ghostly in the light from the single electric lamp. Only Sheriff Reynolds knew the identity of the man who released the weight that executed Lu Sing and it wasn't divulged to the public in order to protect him from possible reprisals from the dead Chinese man's friends and family.

Postscript:
It was rumored by many that Sheriff Reynolds had received five hundred dollars for the hanging of Lu Sing. That belief may have originated from the fact that the sheriff of the miners' court, Robert Hereford had received five hundred dollars from the first territorial legislature for his services in the hanging of the notorious George Ives on December 21, 1863. The Gallatin County sheriff didn't receive such a fee but the total cost of avenging the murder of Tom Sing was reported to have been still about two thousand dollars.

Annie Kum Chee, the widow of Tom Sing was later ordered to be deported after the murder case had exposed her classification in this country and Reverend R. M. Donaldson of the Presbyterian Church of Bozeman traveled to Washington D.C. on behalf of the thirty-two-year-old Chinese born woman who had spent the last twenty-six years of her life in America. At this time it is not clear what the outcome of her case was.

May 18, 1906
Miles Fuller

Other Name: "Lizzie Bloch"
Location and Gallows: When Fuller was executed in the jail yard at Butte he became the tenth man hanged on ***Gallows No. Nine: (Feb. 1888): "Galloping Gallows" No. Three*** .
Description: The old prospector walked bent over with squinting eyes and generally he wore his white hair down to his shoulders and his beard was at least a foot long. During his trial he persuaded his guards to take him to a barbershop where he had his head practically shaved but he left his beard intact.
Crime: Fuller killed a neighboring prospector, Henry J. Gallagher on October 24, 1904, by first shooting him and then he later cut his throat.
Judge: Michael Donlan
Prosecution: Deputy County Attorney Thomas J. Walker[5] and assisted by I.G. Denny and Mr. Lamb

Defense: James H. Baldwin and Judge John Lindsay assisted by E.S. Booth
Sheriff: John J. Quinn
Relics and Remnants: A souvenir piece of the hangman's rope is available for viewing at the Gallatin County Historical Society Museum at Bozeman.

Miles Fuller and Henry Gallagher were both lone prospectors in their sixties living in neighboring cabins on the outskirts of Butte about where the School of Mines now sits. Fuller was very quarrelsome and he had reportedly threatened his neighbor's life on several times and was suspected of placing ground glass in Gallagher's flour and strychnine in his sugar. Fearing for his life, Gallagher was forced to build up his cabin like a fortress and to avoid his angry neighbor all together.

On the evening of October 24, 1904, Fuller hid in a gulch near the McKinley School and after Gallagher passed by he followed him and shot him in the back. At first the assassin ran off after the shooting but he returned and cut the dying man's throat with his pocketknife. Sheriff John Q. Quinn followed the tracks of the murderer until they led him to Fuller's cabin and the old man was arrested because the suspect's shoes matched the tracks in the snow right down to the broken nail in one of the heels.

Not much was ever known about the victim and very little was learned about Fuller's past life other than J. Galloway of Texas had adopted him where he received a little formal education and some religious training. He eventually got married and was known to have had children. The old man was a loner and about the only real friend he had in the world was a black prisoner named Horace Dwyer who he had met while being in the county jail. The Fuller trial began on May 8, 1905, and he was assigned a defense consisting of James H. Baldwin, Judge John Lindsay and E.S. Booth who assisted them later. The jury was made up of the following Silver Bow County residents:

W.H. Arnold (f)	Fred Hubert	M.L. Mustard
G.H. Giles	William J. Simpson	A.E. Cully
Philip Haskins	R.H. Hocking	Arthur Dessault
A.N. Patterson	John Morgan	E.H. Bruce

(f) Foreman

Several physicians including Dr. W.H. Haviland and Dr. J.C. Schapps were called on to describe the bullets and knife wounds on the body of Henry Gallagher and three witnesses testified that they had actually witnessed the shooting. The men explained that they had watched the two men exchanging a number of shots and then the one still standing went over and cut the other man's throat. While the circumstantial evidence had piled up against their case, the most difficult job of the defense attorneys was to keep Fuller from discussing his case with anyone and everyone who would listen. During recesses, or the few minutes he was in the courtroom before the opening of each session or after adjournments, Fuller took advantage of the opportunity to talk with anyone including the prosecuting attorneys, about the mistakes in some of the testimonies of the various witnesses.

From the time his attorneys took their eyes off of him or if they had to leave the room Fuller would wander off to another part of the courtroom and engage in conversation and more than a few times Mr. Baldwin had to physically drag his client by force away from the prosecuting attorneys. During the trial Fuller was very cheerful and he would be frequently seen laughing and joking around with everyone including Judge Donlan on the bench.

Final arguments were concluded at 1:30 on the afternoon of May 18, 1905, and then the jurors were taken to dinner before they began deliberating at 2:20. While the jury was out, Fuller complimented the jurors and was confident that they would acquit him and that he would be walking down the steps of the courthouse a free man by five o'clock that same afternoon. Fuller also told Judge Donlan that if the jury didn't hang him, he would be bringing up cases before the court himself after hearing stories about his property while he was in the jailhouse.

Fuller told the judge that he had heard that tons of ore had been removed from his claim, over three hundred dollars worth of gold was stolen from his sluice box and another hundred and fifty dollars of personal property had been taken from his cabin. A man serving with him in the county jail told Fuller that he had been one of the men that had robbed his claim and that he had been arrested for an unrelated crime. According to Fuller, he had told Sheriff Quinn about the crimes and he asked that the prisoner be held until an investigation could be conducted but the officer refused to take any action.

When he was first brought into courtroom to hear the verdict, Fuller insisted on sitting among the spectators handcuffed to the deputy instead of taking his usual place at the table with his lawyers. While waiting for the jury to file into the courtroom the deputy sheriff had given him a cigar, which Fuller had lit up and was smoking. While Fuller had complimented the jury earlier, when the jurors returned after only thirty-five minutes with a verdict of first-degree murder, the prisoner said that they were a prejudiced bunch of son-of-a-bitches.

After the jury came in the foreman handed their verdict to Judge Donlan who glanced at it and then handed it over to Clerk Wedekind who recorded it into the records and then read it in a loud clear voice. Fuller continued to calmly smoke his cigar as Judge Lindsay asked that the jury be polled and to the man the jurors answered guilty. The defense then gave notice that they would ask for a new trial and they were granted thirty days to prepare their motion.

During the time he was in the county jail, Fuller had been allowed to keep an old pocketknife, which he used to clean and trim his fingernails but upon returning to the jail on May 27, 1905, after Judge Donlan had sentenced him to be hanged on Monday, July 24, his knife was taken from him. For further precautions against suicide it was decided to move Fuller into the cell that was formerly occupied by James Martin before he was hanged in 1904.

While the officers were preparing his new accommodations and establishing a deathwatch, Fuller was held in the jailer's office where he smoked his old pipe. Meanwhile Judge Donlan was signing the death warrant for the condemned man and it was presented to the sheriff and Undersheriff Mike Quinn assigned Charles White, William Quinn, Joe DeFour and Charles Murray as personal guards or deathwatches.

Fuller's execution was stayed and his case was eventually appealed to the Supreme Courton on March 19, 1906, and the high court affirmed the judgment of the district court and after re-sentencing the prisoner was scheduled to be hanged on May 18, nearly nineteen months after he had murdered his victim. Fuller had boasted of being a member of the Vigilantes at Virginia City and while in jail he had even threatened vigilante action against some of the witnesses who had testified against him during his trial.

Some of the men in the Mining City claimed that Fuller hadn't been a Vigilante but a tinhorn gambler at Virginia City and in Judge Sullivan's Police Court, Fuller had been fined fifty dollars after being arrested for pulling a big gun on a Negro on West Park Street. He had also been suspected of murdering the miner, Adolph Schwade in his cabin southwest of Butte and while in jail he had boasted of shooting a man between the eyes in Texas. The condemned man also said that while he was working on a lumber boat on the Mississippi River he had killed a black shipmate.

The day before the hanging there was a stream of visitors passing by Fuller's cell door from ten in the morning until five o'clock in the evening. While most of the visitors were just curious citizens some were the condemned man's neighbors and friends including the Reverend Father Follett and two Sisters of Charity along with his primary spiritual adviser, Reverend Dr. F.H. Gwynne of the Immanuel Presbyterian Church. County Physician J.A. Tremblay dropped by to examine the prisoner and found his pulse to be normal and he didn't require any stimulants. The guards reported that Fuller had enjoyed the jail food and he refused a glass of beer with his final meal. At 4:15 in the morning Reverend Gwynne and Reverend R.E. Williams of the Welsh Church awakened Fuller from a sound sleep and they said that he was hard to wake up. Religious services were commenced by the reading of the Scriptures, followed by the administering of the holy sacrament.

During the sacrament, Fuller stretched out on his cot with his arms folded saying "amen" repeatedly during the offering. The condemned man then prayed in an incoherent manner and asked forgiveness for all his evil and for those who had sinned against him. He thanked the Lord that his earthly troubles were nearly over. The condemned man remained silent about the crime for which he was convicted but on the day of his execution he reportedly made a secret admission to his spiritual adviser.

The final preparations for the execution started at 4:30 that morning when Sheriff Quinn personally inspected the gallows and strung the half-inch rope through the pulleys at the top of the scaffold. After witnessing the execution of Lu Sing at Bozeman in April of 1906, Sheriff Quinn made arrangements to have the trusty old scaffold returned to Butte for the hanging of Fuller. The Manila rope had been thoroughly tested but the authorities had another cord on hand just in case the first one failed.

With the help of his deputies, the sheriff lifted the heavy weight in place and arranged everything in readiness for the gruesome task. As early as two o'clock the crowd had stretched along the brick wall even though the structure was topped with large chunks of glass and sharp nails. The sharp objects on the fence apparently didn't bother the spectators but a few were seen sitting on the stockade wall with bandaged hands. Two women came to the jail demanding to be allowed to witness the hanging and when they were refused they were later seen at the window of a nearby two-story building observing the execution.

It was a cold, damp and gray morning, but as time passed it gave promise of being a beautiful day and at 5:05 o'clock a masked man was seen passing swiftly from the rear door of the jail to the box beside the scaffold. Everyone knew that he was the executioner who would send Fuller into eternity and suddenly the crowd ceased their joking around and realized the seriousness of the affair. It was later reported that the concealed hangman was a cook from a local hotel and it was learned that he was paid fifty dollars for the job. Among the many visiting officers were Sheriff David Graham[6] and Undersheriff John Gannon of Missoula County, Madison County Sheriff Charles Kadell, Deer Lodge County Sheriff Tom Fleming, Cascade County Sheriff Ed Hogan, Beaverhead County Sheriff Duke Gist, Jefferson County Sheriff A.V. Gibson and Sheriff A.S. Robertson of Park County.

After the sheriff had read the death warrant the fateful procession emerged from the jail by the rear door of the building at 5:21 a.m. and two minutes later the prisoner was hanged, making the execution of Miles Fuller one of the quickest ever. The aged prospector walked bent over and he had a surprised look on his face when he first encountered the large crowd of spectators that had partially blocked his path to the scaffold. Sheriff Quinn, Deputy Frank Burke and others quickly strapped Fuller's arms and legs and the sheriff adjusted the rope with quick and steady fingers.

Before the crowd realized what had happened the victim's body shot up about two feet and then fell back down swinging slightly at the end of the rope. The body twitched slightly and the fingers began to twitch followed by the trembling of his limbs and shoulders. Retaining opes had been stretched around the scaffold to keep the witness away but scores of the morbid crowd trampled it down and gathered around the body as it hung quietly until the guards cleared the spectators away. As Sheriff Quinn and a deputy steadied the swinging body, Dr. Tremblay stepped forward and grasped one wrist while Dr. Herbert A. Maillett and Maginn also monitored the man's pulse and heartbeat. They announced shortly after the drop of the weight that the man's neck had been broken and in eight minutes he was pronounced dead.

What seemed like a terribly long time, the carriage with the casket finally arrived and then the big gate was opened; the body was cut down and it was taken to the undertaking room of White and Krebs. The spectators again crowded around the platform and gallows and the men began fighting for a piece of the hangman's rope for souvenirs. The main portion of the rope disappeared in a matter of moments while the noose and a number of feet of the strand were distributed to the visiting sheriffs. About two thousand people reportedly witnessed the hanging from the execution yard as well as from the windows and rooftops of the surrounding buildings. The main doors of the courtroom on the second floor of the county courthouse were crushed by a large mob of citizens who had pushed and jammed their way in order to get to a window to observe the execution.

June 15, 1908

George J. Rock

Location and Gallows: When George Rock was hanged in the northeast corner the State Penitentiary yard at Deer Lodge he became the eleventh victim of ***Gallows No. Nine: (Feb. 1888): "Galloping Gallows" No. Three***. A complete description and history of this infamous scaffold can be found in Chapter Seven: "Montana Gallows."

Description: The thirty-five-year-old George Rock was rather undersized but he was described as being very strong with remarkable will power and determination. Many prisoners and officials at the time considered him one of the most dangerous inmates at the state prison.

Crime: Murder of Deputy Warden John A. Robinson of the State Penitentiary during an escape attempt on March 18, 1908.

Judge: George B. Winston

Prosecution: County Attorney S.P. Wilson, assisted by State Attorney General Albert J. Galen

Defense: John H. Duffy of Anaconda and O.B. O'Bannion of Deer Lodge

Sheriff: Harvey Fifer

Distinction: George Rock was the first person to be sentenced to death and hanged without a jury trial. In all there were four men who went to the gallows without a jury trial, after the Rock case there was George Criner in 1935, Frank Robideau in 1938, and Philip Coleman in 1943. Rock was also the first man executed inside the walls of the State Penitentiary.William Hayes was the only other man hanged inside the facility when he was executed there in April of 1909.

George Rock was serving a ninety-nine-year prison term at the state penitentiary for the murder of Edward Curl in a saloon at Jordan on October 19, 1904. At the prison Rock proved to be a troublesome inmate and the guards generally disliked him and so did the majority of his fellow prisoners. He was nearly always disobedient and he served many days in the dungeon for breaking prison rules. He spent all of his free time planning for an escape and he was able to gain the confidence of three other prisoners, William Hayes, who was finishing a ten-year term; another named Oram Stevens, also a ten-year man, and Clarence Young who was doing fifty years for holding up the mail train at Bearmouth.

The four convicts contrived a plan of escape, which resulted in the murder of the deputy warden and seriously wounding of the warden. They're planning was done so well that none of the guards had any suspicion that anything was afoot and the prisoners were able to manufacture and conceal four knives and none of the men ever told the authorities how they were secured. According to the deadly plan, all four men would break a prison rule for which they would be brought before Warden Conley at his weekly tribunal. The original plan called for the locking of the office; two of the convicts would attack and kill Deputy Warden Robinson while the others would do the same to the warden. After the two officers were killed the inmates would secure the keys to the doors of the stone walls through which they would make their getaway.

According to Warden Conley, the convicts probably hid away several large bolts during the summer of 1907, when additional buildings were being constructed at the prison and the new boilers were installed. One of the knives was made from a one and a quarter inch square-headed bolt and it had a handle made from braided leather and twine. The other knives had similar handles and were manufactured by binding several smaller bolts together and all of the deadly weapons had been ground down thin and sharpened to razor sharpness.

What the prisoners didn't factor in their escape plan were the two armed officers guarding each wall with 30-40 Winchester rifles, a 10-bore shotgun and a Colt 45-caliber revolver. On the morning of March 18, 1908, the four men as planned managed to be brought before the warden and for some unknown reason, instead of going behind the prisoners; the deputy warden went in first. As the last prisoner came in, he locked the door to the prison office and then Rock and Hayes attacked Deputy Warden Robinson, cutting and stabbing him. At the last second Stevens and Young got cold feet as the attack began and they managed to get back to their cells, throwing away their knives on the way.

While Hayes was finishing off Officer Robinson, Rock entered the warden's office and demanded his keys to the gate. Frank Conley told the convict that he had no keys and then he jumped over the railing surrounding his desk and began grappling with the younger prisoner. Although being cut viciously, Warden Conley still managed to knock Rock senseless and then he threw him out of his office. Robinson with his neck nearly severed from his shoulders managed to get away from Hayes and staggered into Conley's office where after trying to speak with his throat badly cut he fell on the desk and then rolled to the floor.

Conley immediately attacked Hayes who was slashing at him as he had done with Robinson. Reaching into his pocket Conley pulled out a small pocket gun and tried to shoot his attacker a number of times but the cartridges weren't very effective. While the bullets didn't cause the desired damage the noise from the warden's weapon alerted a trusty who alarmed the other guards.

The warden managed to wrestle the knife from Hayes and he tossed it into the hallway and then began beating his assailant with his pistol. In the meantime Rock regained consciousness and continued his attack on Robinson until Conley shot him through the lungs with one of the weakened bullets. When Guard E.M. Carver Finally broke through the locked doors he clubbed Rock unconscious, and then found the deputy warden dying with his throat cut from ear to ear and Warden Conley covered in blood with over fifty stab wounds still clubbing Hayes with his revolver.

After another guard struck Hayes with a Billy club, the warden was rushed to the prison hospital and a doctor was summoned to dress his many wounds on his face, neck, chest and legs. Officer Carver remained with Robinson who eventually died in the guard's arms. The injured inmates were also treated at the prison hospital, Hayes being shot in the ear with the round still lodged in his skull; the second broke his collarbone and a third in his arm while the last three rounds from Conley's pistol were extracted from Rock's body.

Prison physician, Dr. Edgar C. Lee and Dr. W.G. Dye examined the dead officer's body before the remains were taken to the Bien Undertaking Rooms. Powell County Coroner Dr. Albert Bien held an enquiry over the body with the following jury:

N.J. Bielenberg	John Bielenberg	M.W. Task
Charles Frint	Tobias Schurtz	William Coleman

County Attorney Wilson and State Attorney A. J. Galen conducted the examination of the witnesses and when it was completed the jury found that Deputy Warden John A. Robinson died of knife wounds at the hands of William A. Hayes and George Rock. Two theories offered for the shots from Conley's gun not being fatal were that the ammunition was old and secondly because the barrel of the gun had been cut off to make it easier to handle and carry in a pocket.

For their arraignment on Thursday, April 9, 1908, the four convicts were brought into the crowded courtroom handcuffed in pairs, Rock and Hayes and Stevens with Young. Wardens Conley and Thomas McTague along with six prison guards escorted the prisoners to the courthouse and they were all transported from the prison in James Beaton's closed bus. Inside the courtroom the handcuffs were removed from the prisoners and along with the officers in the courthouse there were four other well-armed guards stationed about the grounds outside.

Court was called at about ten o'clock that morning and after the defendants stated that they had no means of employing counsel, Judge Winston assigned them attorneys. At that point Rock's assigned attorney, O.B. O'Bannon asked the court that the statutory time be granted in which the defendants could enter their pleas and the date for that hearing was set for April 22, 1908.On that day and in front of about one hundred and fifty curious spectators, the defense attorneys asked for separate trials and that their client's cases be set for after the

May term. The defense claimed that since the crime was so fresh in the public's mind it would be most difficult to secure an impartial jury and if the cases couldn't be put off until later a change of venue would be asked for. After considering the matter Judge Winston ordered the prisoners to stand up and after the charges were read to the men they each entered not guilty pleas.

Judge Winston then set George Rock's trial for May 18; William Hayes' hearing was scheduled for May 22; Young, May 25; and Stevens would see the judge on May 28. After the hearing the convicts were returned to the prison on the Beaton's bus. A week later it was determined that since the crime was committed against state officers, inside of a state institution, on state property, and because the State Board of Prison Commission had complete charge of the facility, the State of Montana was called upon to pay all the expenses of the prosecution of the defendants.

While Rock's attorneys had advised their client to plead innocent and stand trial, George Rock caused quite a commotion on Wednesday, May 6, 1908, when he sent word to Judge Winston that he would be pleading to the charges. The judge immediately sent Deputy Robert Sellens to the penitentiary to bring the prisoner before him and in a short time he was brought into the courtroom handcuffed to Guard Patrick Tuohy and accompanied by Guard Will Gleason. Since Frank Conley, the principle witness in the case was out of town, Judge scheduled the hearing for Monday, May 11, and he informed Rock and his counsel that he wouldn't accept his plea until then.

At the hearing the defense attorneys made it clear that they wanted their client to plead innocent but finally George Rock stood up and pleaded guilty to the first-degree charges and then asked Judge Winston to sentence him as soon as possible. When asked by the judge, Rock said that he had no family living in the state and that he was aware of the consequences of entering the plea and that he was anxious to have his execution as quickly as possible. The judge accepted Rock's plea, but also told the prisoner that if he changed his mind and wished to withdraw his plea he would be given an opportunity to do so.

Judge Winston asked for the evidence in the case and the prosecution called Warden Conley and Guard E.M. Carver to testify to the facts and Dr. E. C. Lee, the prison physician, told the court as to the nature of the wounds inflicted on the victim. After reviewing the case Judge Winston made a short statement concerning the bloody crime, the prisoner's history at the penitentiary. George Rock was considered one of the craftiest, most dangerous and unmanageable inmates at the prison and Judge Winston sentenced him to be hanged by the neck until dead on June 15, 1908. After Judge Winston completed the sentencing the defendant simply thanked the court he was then handcuffed to Sheriff Harvey Fifer who returned him to the state penitentiary for safekeeping and a three-man deathwatch was placed over him.

Sheriff Fifer was instrumental in having the hanging held within the walls of the penitentiary in order to provide an example to the other convicts. In passing sentence on Rock, Judge Winston stated that the prisoner was to be executed in some enclosure in Powell County and the sheriff explained to the press that the penitentiary walls would form the enclosure and he believed that a good lesson would be impressed on the other inmates by the sight of a hanging.

After he was ordered to death, Rock requested a meeting with Sheriff Fifer inside the penitentiary and the two men talked over the upcoming hanging and the condemned man was both cordial and in good spirits. While the prisoner preferred to get the whole matter over with as soon as possible he accepted the sheriff's execution time of 1:30 in the afternoon. The last day of George Rock's life was quite uneventful and the prisoner retired at nine o'clock that night and slept until six o'clock without even turning once on his bunk. During his last night, prison officers visited the condemned man and a basket of fruit was sent to his cell, which Rock barely touched. That morning Rock partook of the regular prison fare, and he refused anything extra for his final meal.

Rock eventually accepted the Catholic Faith and Reverend Father McCormick, the local priest administered Holy Communion and the sacrament of penance. The shackles and handcuffs were removed from the prisoner at noon and he was dressed with a neat black suit, white shirt and collar and black necktie. He conferred with Father McCormick until about 12:30 p.m. when he asked to speak with the newspapermen telling them that he didn't like them even though he didn't know any of them personally and he had only taken offense to what they had written about him. Rock asked the reporters that they not mention anything about his family in Michigan and that he was glad he wasn't killed during the escape attempt.

Rock expressed to the newsmen that he had since made peace with God, and that he knew he deserved his fate. He admitted that he hadn't lived a model life but he promised that he would die like a man. The reporters later described the prisoner as being a bit pale, he was perspiring slightly and that his hands were cool. A few minutes before the appointed time, Sheriff Fifer read the death warrant to the prisoner and when he finished Rock commented that the sheriff seemed a bit nervous. When the sheriff explained that it was his first execution, Rock replied with a smile that it was also his first hanging.

Meanwhile the witnesses were congregating near the gallows including Sheriff E.M. Reynolds and Undersheriff Sales of Gallatin County, Deer Lodge County Sheriff Tom Fleming and his deputies, Dr. Orton of Anaconda, Sheriff Dedmond and Deputy James of Granite County Sheriff Charles S. Henderson. Invited guests from Butte included Mayor Corby, John "Fat Jack" Jones, Sergeant Sinsel, ex-Sheriffs John Quinn, John Berkin, Deputy Tom Richards, George Forsythe, D. Phalan, Mr. Ryan, Jerry Murphy and Bryon Cooney.

Rock's arms were then strapped to his sides and he started for the scaffold with a steady step and with downcast eyes. Father McCormick and Father Moran of Anaconda walked besides the prisoner as they chanted the Penitential Psalms and Sheriff Fifer, Undersheriff

The hanging of George Rock: from the "Dillon Examiner" 5/25/1921

Joseph Larson and Deputy Sellens followed the trio as they walked through the hall of the penitentiary office where Deputy Warden Robinson was murdered during the attempted prison break. The procession was followed out the front door into the prison yard and to the foot of the scaffold by Reverend George O. Jewett of the Methodist

Church, one of the penitentiary contractors, two prison guards and Colonel Thomas McTague who Rock had personally requested to be with him at the gallows. Just before 1:30 the procession reached the rectangle in the northeast corner of the prison yard where Rock took his place on the grassy plot just beneath the noose.

The executioner for the Rock hanging was reportedly an express man from Butte who later acted in the same role for the execution of William Hayes in April of 1909. It was said that the un-named Butte man had paid his own expenses for the honor of executing the two convicted murderers. The noose was placed around the condemned man's neck and before pulling the black cap down Sheriff Fifer asked Rock if he had anything to say. Although he told the warden the day before that he would have a statement to make at the gallows, Rock apparently had lost his nerve, and all he could manage was to shake his head and say: "No Sir." Just as the sheriff pulled the cap down Rock began to falter and he was saved from falling by the 300-pound weight, which jerked him about three feet off the ground at 1:30 p.m. For some reason the noose failed to tighten and although he was rendered unconscious he was strangled to death.

Ten minutes later Drs. Edgar Lee and Dye of Deer Lodge and Dr. Girard of Garrison declared George Rock dead and after that announcement he body was lowered and six prisoners wearing convict outfits brought out a plain black casket and placed the remains into it. The remains were then buried in the prison graveyard, which was located adjacent to the city cemetery. Rock was the second inmate buried in the prison cemetery after being hanged, Clinton Dotson was interred in 1902, after being executed and William Hayes joined them in 1909. The gallows remained in position inside the prison yard in anticipation for the July hanging of William Hayes but his attorneys were successful in securing an appeal and the Deer Lodge authorities had the scaffold dismantled and placed into storage until the Supreme Court affirmed the sentence by the district court and he was hanged in the prison yard on the morning of April 2, 1909.

Postscript:
While all four convicts were initially charged with the murder of Deputy Warden Robinson, only George Rock and William Hayes paid with their lives. After Clarence Young' attorneys recommended that he plead guilty and ask for mercy he received a life sentence. Stevens pled innocent and only lost his good behavior time and served out his original term. After being released from prison in 1913, Stevens brought civil action against Warden Conley for his treatment while at the penitentiary. One trial was held in Powell County and another in U.S. District Court with both cases being thrown out of court on the grounds that the warden of the state prison was an arm of the state government and therefore not subject to damages for acts done while in the performance of his duties.

Clarence Young never wrote to his family about being in prison for life but apparently they learned of his troubles and with the help of some of his previous employers at Missoula a petition was circulated and he was eventually paroled from Deer Lodge. Young returned to his home state of Oklahoma where he took over his father's farm and he once told a friend that there wasn't a perfect crime; he said he knew many men inside the big gray walls at Deer Lodge that had figured on perfect plans.

April 2, 1909
William A. Hayes

Location and Gallows: When Hayes was executed in the southeast corner of the State Penitentiary yard at Deer Lodge he was the last man hanged from the complete ***Gallows No. Nine: (Feb. 1888): "Galloping Gallows" No. Three***. Thirteen years later, portions of the most famous of all gallows was used in the execution of Joseph Vuckovich at Missoula. T
Description: Hayes was about thirty years old, he had blue eyes and at the time of his hanging he was still carrying two bullets in his body, which Warden Conley had fired into him along with a bad powder burn near his left ear.
Crime: Murder of Deputy Warden John A. Robinson during an attempted prison break with George Rock on March 18, 1908. (See: George Rock 6/15/1908 for account of the attempted prison break, coroner's jury and preliminary hearings.)
Judge: George B. Winston
Prosecution: Powell County Attorney S.P. Wilson and assisted by State Attorney General Albert J. Galen and his assistant, W.H. Poorman
Defense: John H. Duffy of Anaconda and O.B. O'Bannon of Deer Lodge
Sheriff: Joseph E. Neville
Distinction: While there have since been three convicts executed at the State Penitentiary, Hayes was the last man hanged in the facility.

According to prison records, William Hayes was born at Cripple Creek, Colorado and was received at the penitentiary on December 11, 1905, from Chouteau County after being sentenced to a ten-year prison term for robbing a saloonkeeper by the name of Wellwoll at Zortman. According to Hayes, he had always been a hard and honest worker and when his boss refused to pay him he took what he was owed. At the time of the attempted prison break in 1908, Hayes was considered a trustee and due to be released on March 11, 1912.

Hayes' murder trial began on May 18, 1908, and after a great deal of difficulty in securing a jury the following jurors were sworn in and watched over by Bailiff E.G. Fox: John W. Blair, Michael Geary, John O'Neill and William McElwain from Helmville; William Y. Elliott, A.G. Backlund, William Johnson and Afred S. Peterson of Race Track; E.L. Skines and Frank C. Willox from Elliston; William J. Marshall of Ovando and John Hoffman from Avon.

In the hard-fought case, the prosecution brought in civil engineer, Lee Williams to explain a map of the penitentiary along with two convicts, William Brown and Charles Comment who testified that Hayes was a part of the conspiracy to escape. The defense tried to prove that Hayes had not actually attacked John Robinson since he was assaulting Frank Conley at the time, but it was pointed out that he had been a member of the conspiracy from the time it was first hatched. While the defense brought to Deer Lodge several character witnesses from Hayes' former residence of Malta including Bob Smith, James Wilson, Philip Caselburg and Fred Smith, none of them were called. Instead of calling any of the men from Malta the defense rested their case after being satisfied after cross-examination of the state's witnesses and J.H. Duffy agreed to send the case to jury without presenting final arguments.

On May 22, 1908, after deliberating overnight for seventeen hours the jury found Hayes guilty of first-degree murder and recommended the death penalty. While waiting in the courtroom Hayes appeared unperturbed and although the prisoner had previously indicated that he preferred death over life imprisonment, he was clearly affected as the color reportedly left his face for a few minutes after the verdict was first read. Four days later the prisoner was sentenced by Judge Winston to be hanged on July 3, 1908. Immediately after the judge had pronounced his sentence the defense attorneys asked for time to prepare a bill of exceptions and they were given until July 1. While the motion for a new trial was overruled the hanging was stayed with an appeal to the Supreme Court. In February of 1909, in an opinion written by Associate Justice Henry Smith, the high court affirmed the judgment of the district court and denied Hayes a new trial. Shortly after Hayes lost his appeal for a new trial an "Anaconda Standard" reporter interviewed the condemned man who talked freely about many subjects except about the crime.

Hayes explained that he was resigned to his fate and he was glad that his family didn't know about his impending execution. The prisoner said that he was quite young when he left home and no one in his past could identify him from the recent photographs taken of him. The prisoner declined a cigar from the newsman saying that he hadn't smoked since he was kid when he got sick after his first time under a large apple tree back home.

Warden Conley went to Seattle to personally purchase the hangman's rope used to hang William Hayes and after securing the fine strand he sent it directly to Sheriff Harvey Fifer at Deer Lodge. When Sheriff Fifer left office he handed the death rope to incoming sheriff Joseph E. Neville who personally prepared it for the hanging of Hayes. While the sheriff prepared the rope the condemned man made his own preparations by embracing the Catholic faith with the help of Father Moran of Phillipsburg and Father T.F. Landy of Deer Lodge who also accompanied the prisoner to the gallows.

When a newspaperman suggested to the condemned man to do his best to meet the end calmly, Hayes replied that the advice was easy to give, but it was sometimes hard to follow. Hayes never did reveal his true identity, saying that the fact that his relatives weren't aware of his imprisonment and death on the gallows was his only consolation. Hayes' last day of life was much like the ones he had spent during his last several weeks at the prison with the exception of being constantly guarfed by a deathwatch. After Hayes had eaten a hearty supper in the evening he told his deathwatch, Charles E. Aspling that he was happier than he had been in years because he had learned his sins; had found his God and was ready to suffer for the wrongs he had done.

The guards said that the prisoner had a good night's rest and he woke up at six o'clock on his last morning and from seven to seven-thirty he was visited by three Sisters of Charity along with Mrs. Cahalin, the mother of Warden Thomas McTague, Miss Edna Wells, his niece and Father Landy. When he met his visitors Hayes was wearing a somber black suit with a white shirt, collar and a plain black tie and before leaving for the scaffold he told his spiritual adviser the following statement: "Pray for the repose of my soul Father. I need all the prayers you can say. And if you know others who are willing, ask them to pray for my soul. I am not afraid to die, for I am nearer at peace with myself and my God than ever before. I have no word but this for any one. Good-bye Father." It was understood that Hayes also gave Father Landy his true name and confidential information concerning his family.

A Catholic Mass for the dead was held in the large prison office, ironically near the exact spot where the brutal murder had taken place the year earlier. At 7:45 Sheriff Neville read the death warrant to the condemned man who stood between Colonel McTague and Father Landy. While the warrant was being read, Hayes was moving his lips in prayer but there was no sign of nervousness in his face or body. When the sheriff was finished with the reading he and Undersheriff Tom Mullen began adjusting the straps on the prisoner's arms and hands.

When leaving the office, the reporter pressed the button for the guard to open the door, and Hayes jokingly asked if he was ordering for room service. Hayes enjoyed that joke but the large number of invitations that had been printed and mailed out annoyed him, as he was still concerned about his relatives finding out about his fate. There were reports that some four to five hundred people attended the hanging and among the witnesses were Sheriff Reynolds of Gallatin County and his undersheriff, Deer Lodge County Sheriff Tom Fleming and a number of his deputies along with Dr. Orton from Anaconda. Attending from Butte were Sheriff Charles S. Henderson, Mayor Corby, "Fat Jack," Sergeant Sinsel, ex-Sheriff John J. Quinn, Deputy Richards, John Berkin, George Forsythe, D. Phalan, Mr. Ryan, Jerry Murphy, Byron Cooney and Sheriff Dedmond and Deputy James of Granite County.

At ten minutes before eight the death march began with Father Landy on Hays' right and Colonel McTague was to his left followed by a small procession of prison officials, newspapermen and several plainclothes detectives from the Butte police force along with the Powell County sheriff's staff. Under the scaffold Hayes' feet were secured; the black cap was placed over his face; the noose was adjusted and then Sheriff Neville stepped back and when the signal was given the same express man from Butte that acted as the executioner at the George Rock execution severed the line dropping the weight. Just five minutes after the party had left the prison office, the condemned man was jerked into eternity and for the second time in a row the trusty scaffold, which had been used since 1888, failed to break the victim's neck and like George Rock before him, Hayes died slowly from strangulation. His body twitched spasmodically and his legs drew up to his chest twice while his secured hands were seen clenching and relaxing several times.

For five minutes the twitching body of Hayes swung listlessly in the air as it fought for life in vain and the witnesses could see the man's lungs struggling for a breath that was not there. At two minutes after eight the body was finally still and Drs. W.G. Dye and J.H. Garberson examined the man and they determined that he was still alive. Three minutes later, exactly ten minutes after the drop had fallen the physicians pronounced him dead. The body was allowed to swing in the cool morning breeze for a few more minutes before two convicts, L.O. Howell who was serving fifteen years for murder and Isaac Erickson, doing ten years for assault came out of the prison carpenter shop with a black coffin. The convicts laid the coffin below the dead man and slowly the corpse was lowered into the box. After the noose was removed, Dr. Dye inspected Hayes' neck and declared that the man had died of strangulation as he pulled off the black cap and closed the man's staring eyes. The dead man's face wasn't distorted but it was reportedly blue-white and his lips were without color. After the examination was completed by the physicians the two convicts screwed down the lid of the coffin and with the help of two other prisoners they carried it to the penitentiary graveyard for burial.

Postscript:
Powell County Sheriff Joe Neville later became the deputy warden at the state penitentiary at Deer Lodge and attorney General Albert J. Galen eventually became a justice on the State Supreme Court. He was later found drowned on Lake Hauser near Helena in 1936, and sadly Judge George B. Winston also died that same year.

April 2, 1909
Frederick LeBeau

Other Names: Jim Sharkey
Location and Gallows: Fred LeBeau was executed at Kalispell, the second and last victim to be hanged from ***Gallows No. Twelve: (December 1894)***.
Description: LeBeau was a French Canadian by birth and about forty-three years old at the time of his execution. He stood five feet, ten inches tall and weighed 205 pounds. He was described as being a big, brawny fellow with massive shoulders and a kind face. Observers said that LeBeau spoke broken English and he was very bright.
Crime: Murder of William Riley Yoakum and his son, Frank about four miles from Fortine on June 19, 1908
Judge: John E. Erickson
Prosecution: Flathead County Attorney W.T. McKeown assisted by

Judge D.F. Smith
Defense: Senator Thomas D. Long assisted by Mr. Nash
Sheriff: William Henry O'Connell
Relics and Remnants: After the execution of LeBeau the hangman's rope and the murder weapon was presented to Mr. Douglas Johns as a Christmas gift and he displayed the ghastly relics along with many other ancient revolvers, rifles and other memorabilia on the walls of his downtown Kalispell hardware store. After the death of Mr. Johns his unique collection, which also included an invitation to the LeBeau hanging was presented to the Montana Historical Society in 1959. Along with the items mentioned at Helena, another invitation to the hanging, which was originally presented to Fred Rogers, is on display at Northwest Montana Historical Society Museum at Central School at Kalispell.

During the first quarter of the twentieth century Montana as well as the rest of the nation was overrun with tramps who tramped up and down the railroads without money and without motivation other than living without work and to annex as much property as they could find. Frederick LeBeau was one of those many "men of the road" who was hanging around a little shack near Whitefish. When not getting in trouble he sat around watching freight cars and sketching various railroad couplings and other mechanical parts of trains with the dream of inventing newer technology. He barely had enough money to survive on when he met Joe Hobbins, who had just sold two bicycles he had stolen at Kalispell on June 13, 1908. Hobbins at the time was twenty-two years old and ran with a bunch of "big talking" tramps and two-bit thieves who were always planning jobs to score big.

The Whitefish gang had planned to make some "easy money" by robbing the bank at Somers, but when LeBeau and Hobbins figured that they couldn't reach that community in time for payday on the fifteenth, and because they didn't want to hang around in the valley another month, the two men decided to head west on a freight. They made it to Rexford near the Kootenai River about seven miles from the Canadian border where they "vagged" or panhandled around for a day. In that day and age alot of people used bicycles for local transportation and stealing "wheels" or bicycles was more common than car thefts of today. One of the tramps in the gang named Willie swiped a wheel; sold it, bought a new hat, got good and drunk and then jumped a later freight out of Kalispell and met up with LeBeau and Hobbins at Rexford. Willie tagged along with the two older tramps like a puppy dog, talking about his big spree and his new hat as they walked down the tracks toward Eureka.

LeBeau and Hobbins didn't think much of the young tramp and when they were far enough out of town they tied a large rock to the boy and tossed him into the river. The water was only waist deep though and Willie scrambled back to shore and begged for mercy and after being satisfied that they had sufficiently scared the boy, Hobbins took the lad's new hat, gave him his old one and then warned him to "keep shut" and "back track." According to Hobbins, Willie left without hesitation and he was never seen again.

After leaving Eureka the two men worked a day for a man piling a load of logs and were paid with a fine meal and a place to sleep. The next day Hobbins figured he needed some new underway so as they were walking towards Fortine he "hunted a clothesline" where he obtained a suit of black shorts for himself and found socks for both. Then on June 18, the two men stopped at the Campbell place where they asked for some food and while Mr. Campbell was obliging, his wife got upset and told the tramps to get off the property. As they left the Campbell home, Hobbins was outraged and he wanted to return and shoot Campbell and then have his way with the woman before killing her too. The more he thought about how the woman had disrespected them the madder he got until LeBeau quieted him down by changing the subject. By then they were nearing the Yoakum house where they were hoping they could get a bite to eat. In order to break the ice, LeBeau asked the Yoakum's for only a drink but the father and son weren't in the least bit hospitable and called them hobos and then told them to leave the property.

LeBeau and Hobbins went back to the tracks where they sat in an old shack and argued over what to do next. With empty stomachs and only fifty cents between them they finally went back to the Campbell place where they purchased a loaf of bread and some milk for fifteen cents and probably had to listen to more abuse from the lady of the house. Hobbins was still starving and he was suggesting all kinds of plans of robbery and revenge but LeBeau with a cooler head, convinced the younger man that they should sleep it off on the railroad right of way until the next morning.

On the morning of June 19, 1908, the men decided that since LeBeau had the Colt 45 and about sixteen rounds of ammunition he would go down to the Yoakum house while Hobbins remained on the tracks as a lookout and would come to his pal's assistance if needed. When LeBeau neared the house he asked seventy-year-old William Riley Yoakum if they had some bread and the old man told the stranger that they didn't have any but they could sell them some biscuits for twenty-five cents. LeBeau then asked the man for ten cents worth of onions, after which Yoakum agreed to get the produce but told LeBeau to stay out of his garden. According to LeBeau's confession, when he commented about the high price of the food, the old man threatened him with his hoe and when he saw the son, Frank Yoakum coming out of the house with a rifle he quickly shot both of the men in the abdomen. To end the old man's agony LeBeau said he put another shot into the old man as Frank Yoakum began shooting at him from the house.

LeBeau ran for the nearby fence where he tookf cover and after shooting three shots from his rifle, Frank Yoakum ran into the cabin. Not knowing that the younger Yoakum was mortally wounded or not, LeBeau laid in the bushes the rest of the day fearing he would be shot if he made a run for the railroad tracks. Actually the mortally wounded Yoakum boy crawled back into the cabin where he eventually shot himself in the head to end his agony. Meanwhile after hearing the gunshots at the Yoakum place, and thinking LeBeau had been killed, Hobbins hit the tracks and went back to Whitefish. After hiding out all day in the brush, LeBeau left the Yoakum place under the cover of darkness and made his way across the Canadian line where he pawned his pistol to a saloonkeeper for fifty cents and then took the Canadian Pacific Railroad to Fernie. There LeBeau found work and stayed with an old acquaintance by the name of Duffy.

Scott Grubb discovered the bodies of William and Frank Yoakum and Sheriff William H. O'Connell and Coroner Sherman were called to the scene and after a thorough investigation it was first determined that the father and son had gotten into a quarrel, which culminated in a shooting affray. The authorities surmised that the father had shot his son first in the abdomen before his son took the weapon away from him and shot his father. After killing his father, the young man returned to their cabin where he committed suicide. LeBeau found a Flathead County newspaper at Fernie where he read the coroner's verdict that the deaths of the Yoakum's was a case of murder-suicide and after breathing easier and lounging around a few days he figured it would be safe to return to Eureka. Hobbins also read the coroner's report at Whitefish and because he received a certain amount of notoriety by knowing more about the incident than anyone else, he began to talk while he was drinking. When he was taken in for questioning, Hobbins figured he would name the dead LeBeau as the murderer and by explaining the incident he could come off as some sort of a celebrity.

When the body of LeBeau wasn't found the authorities quickly notified all points and LeBeau was arrested at Eureka by Deputy Frank Baney. Realizing that the "game was up," LeBeau made a long confession to Deputy County Attorney Mark Conrow in the Flathead County sheriff's office on July 1, 1908, and the following morning Joe Hobbins made his confession. The two confessions brought out about the same facts but the stories only varied on the main instigator of the crime. When arraigned, LeBeau pleaded guilty and he asked for immediate sentence, but he later withdrew that plea and entered one of not guilty. LeBeau's trial began Monday morning, December 7, 1908, and the jury was composed of the following men:

A.M. Webster	W.P. Fox	A. Stowell
Henry Reimer	N.W. Searles	Robert Wells
C.J. Crossley	Clarence Chope	Andrew Madsen
Carl W. Lund	Charles Bjork	J.S. Coverdell

While the defendant claimed self-defense, he admitted firing a bullet into the old man's brain while he was on the ground explaining that he wanted to put him out of his obvious misery. After the prosecution presented the state's testimony including the defendant's own confession the only thing that the defense could do was to introduce witnesses to show that LeBeau was mentally unbalanced at the time. After a two-day trial the jury found LeBeau guilty of first-degree murder and on December 19, 1908, Judge Erickson sentenced him to be hanged on Friday, February 5, 1909. Mrs. Phoebe Lang attended the hearing with her nine-year-old son Delbert, and later said that her boy tensed up when Judge Erickson announced the sentencing.[7] LeBeau too was affected by the sentence as his face twisted and he looked dazed as Sheriff O'Connell took him back to the jail.

Since so many citizens believed that the prisoner was mentally insane, Governor Edwin L. Norris granted a reprieve until April 2, 1909, in order that LeBeau's condition could be evaluated. After Governor Norris sent Dr. J.M. Scanland of the state insane asylum to examine LeBeau the prisoner was declared sane but morally degenerate. As for LeBeau's past life and his actual identity, nothing was ever discovered other than he had been known in Minnesota for nine years as Jim Sharkey while he did some prize fighting there. He also told the authorities that his mother and a sister were still living but he had used his current name for over twenty years. After he entered a plea of guilty he sent a letter to a so-called soiled lady at Grand Forks, North Dakota and the authorities interviewed the woman and she claimed to have been a childhood friend of LeBeau and said that he had proposed marriage to her several times. The woman was of no help with discovering LeBeau's true identity as she was from various foster homes and she never knew anything about his family.

LeBeau took great pride in decorating his cell with red, white and blue tissue paper, not only blending the American and French colors but he also displayed an emblem of Ireland on the prominent wall. There were also many stars on the wall as well as a few pictures of himself, the sheriff and of his lawyer hanging about. Suspended from the center of his second-floor cell was a huge liberty bell and over the cell door was a hand-painted sign in what was described as perfectly proportioned letters, "Gone, but not forgotten, Frederick LeBeau." The decorations were remarkable when it is considered that the prisoner did all the work himself, without a knife or a pair of scissors. Mrs. Marguerite O'Connell, the wife of the sheriff, cut out the stars for him, but outside of that, LeBeau did all the work himself. Shortly before his last day on earth, the condemned man ordered fifteen oranges so that could arrange them around his cell, to give it the "proper tinge."

Up to a week before the hanging Sheriff O'Connell was still presenting invitations to special guests for the affair including the entire staff of the county courthouse. That same week at his own request, LeBeau was shown the gallows along with all the other hanging paraphernalia including the rope, black cap and straps, which had been especially purchased for his execution. The condemned man even tried on the black cap for size and after inspecting the hangman's rope he suggested it be waxed to insure its proper action.

The condemned man kept busy with his plans and designs for a number of inventions dealing with the railroad industry including a combination freight car door lock and seal, which was designed to lock the door automatically when closed and it would also slide a seal in place. Another of his ideas was a coupling device that operated without any slack between the cars as well as an extra step on passenger cars, which was designed to retract once the train was in motion.

For about a week before his execution LeBeau had placed little "Toll" plates at the side of his cell and asked for a fee from his many visitors and he had already collected forty-seven dollars and sixty cents. Declaring that he did not want to be buried in an executed murderer's clothing, he spent thirty-two fifty for a new suit of "citizen's clothes" to his own liking. Along with the purchase of his own clothing for his execution, LeBeau also bought the casket and a portion of the lot charges at the Demersville Cemetery. On March 24, 1909, Governor Norris officially notified Sheriff O'Connell that he would not commute LeBeau's sentence and when the prisoner learned the news he ordered his last meal of duck stuffed with chicken with frosted cake, which was decorated with Easter chicken candies. A jar of jelly-filled candies with fruit chips and nuts was provided for snacking and the prisoner washed it all down with a bottle of champagne sent to him by a friend. LeBeau later said that it was the first time he had ever tasted the bubbly liquor and he thoroughly enjoyed it. The condemned man was also allowed the use of the small corridor outside of his cell and one of his favorite activities was rocking in a chair there.

Not only was the scaffold for the hanging of Fred LeBeau the same gallows used to hang Calvin Christie in 1894, the same man who had built the original death machine was called in to erect it for its second execution. The gallows was a drop-type scaffold, and for a man of LeBeau's size it required a seven-foot fall to do its job. On the day before it was to be used, an armed deputy was assigned to guard it while a constant line of curious spectators filed through the enclosure to inspect the gruesome contraption. The day before the execution several hundred people visited the jail each with a word of cheer for LeBeau who was by then showing the effects of the strain. Many of the visitors were women who took an interest in his misfortune, and to repay them for their kindness he would present them with simple mementos, which he had used to decorate the walls of his cell. The prisoner was shaved at about 4:30 that afternoon and then he was presented with his new clothing that he had purchased himself consisting of a pair of blue overalls and a light cotton shirt. LeBeau was excited about his new outfit but he remarked that he would not die with his shoes on.

A correspondent from the Great Falls "Tribune" accompanied by a lady called on the prisoner and he became quite talkative and he handed the lady a copy of the newspaper, pointing to an article in it concerning himself. As the woman began unfolding it to read the story she suddenly dropped the paper and let out a scream. The prisoner was pleased that he had startled yet another person with one of his homemade devices. The newspaper vibrated and produced a buzzing sound as it was being unfolded, which was caused by flapper made of a piece of cardboard and a rubber band. The young lady's fright amused LeBeau but he quickly apologized and hoped that she wouldn't take offense to his little trick and after he was assured that she had forgiven him, he again started telling different stories about his life.

During the evening Reverend Morris of the Baptist Church called on the doomed man and then LeBeau spent a restless night. Later that night he woke up and he made out his will, which he sent to Senator Long his attorney and then he resumed work on the manuscript that had he had been working on for several days, stopping a few times to ask the guard for the proper spelling of various words including “murder” and “funeral.” He also frequently consulted the little Bible, which had been presented to him by a local pastor. After finally managing to fall asleep, LeBeau was awoken at 5:15 in the morning by Father O’Farrel who visited him for about twenty minutes. By that time the sidewalk in front of the jail was crammed with people, waiting for the gate to be opened as the sheriff and his deputies were busy getting things ready for the hanging. The guards spotted a few cameras in the crowd and they were quickly confiscated from their owners and the rest were warned against taking any photographs of the execution or of the scaffold. The newspapermen were summoned to the corridor just prior to seven to record any final remarks of the condemned man who by then was on the verge of having a nervous breakdown and refusing to make a statement to the press.

Dr. Campbell, the attending physician, and Death Watch Albert Adams stepped into the cell to examine the prisoner and Sheriff O’Connell soon joined them with the death warrant. When LeBeau spotted the document in the sheriff’s hand he said that he wanted it and that he would read it himself. When his lawyer explained to him that it had to be read by the sheriff, he jumped onto his cot and threw a towel over his face and ears. As the word “murder” was read the prisoner jumped to his feet; slapped at the paper and then asked that the word be left out of the reading, saying he was no murderer. The word “murder” evidently reminded him of not wanting to die with his boots on, and he started to untie his shoes while the sheriff continued with the warrant. Because of his nervousness LeBeau was unable to loosen the knots and he began tugging at the laces and soon he had them torn to pieces. No sooner had he completed that he cried out that he was sick; ran out into the corridor and to the bathroom where he tried to vomit. The sheriff merely followed the prison and kept on reading of the warrant while LeBeau’s head was bent down over the toilet.

LeBeau returned to his cell where he sat back down on his cot and placed the towel back over his head and ears. As the sheriff came to the end of the page and paused, the condemned man jumped up and pleaded with the officer to stop reading. As the sheriff continued the prisoner got behind the officer and placed his arms around him and continued to plead. When the sheriff spoke the last word of the warrant the prisoner exclaimed that he was ready to hang. When the straps were being fastened around his waist and the cuffs were buckled, LeBeau reached through the bars and shook hands with his lawyer, Mr. Long, whom he had asked to accompany him to the gallows. The attorney had first declined, but he was finally persuaded to do so as a favor to the sheriff. LeBeau didn’t want anyone to take his arm, saying he was able to go by himself and on the way down the stairs to the outer steps LeBeau paused a moment and kicked off his shoes, once again avowing that he was not a murderer and therefore he would not die with his shoes on.

Contrary to what he had promised, LeBeau gave no speech but only went up the scaffold and greeted the crowd of about two hundred and fifty by promising that his execution would be the grandest of them all. Senator Long joined him on the platform where they shook hands for the last time and the condemned man announced that he was not a murderer. As the straps were secured around his legs and the noose was being placed around the hooded head of LeBeau he shouted several times to make it tighter. He then requested that Mr. Long, who was visibly affected, to see that he was given a good funeral and about that point a young man in the crowd fainted and was carried out of the enclosure.

At 7:23, Sheriff O'Connell calmly waived his hand and then pulled the lever that caused Frederick LeBeau to pay for the murder of Frank and William Yoakum with his life. Those standing near the scaffold reported hearing the snap of LeBeau's neck followed by a slight quiver and then a convulsive heave of his chest. After about eight minutes Doctors Campbell and Taylor pronounced the man dead and fifteen minutes later the body was taken down and placed into the casket along with the rope. LeBeau had left specific instructions for his execution and burial, requesting that Sheriff Connell himself adjust the hangman's rope, pull down the black cap and pull the death trap. He requested as big a funeral as possible with heaps of flowers on his grave and designated the following pallbearers for his funeral: Senator Thomas D. Long, Former County Sheriff Baldwin, N.C. Arseneau, Ross Young, former County Attorney Sidney M. Logan, and Sheriff O'Connell.

LeBeau told the sheriff and his lawyer that he would leave a written statement with Mr. Long detailing his history and activities prior to coming to Montana while living in Michigan, Illinois, Wisconsin, Minnesota and Canada. The document consisting of several pages did exist and it was seen by most of the staff as well as his attorney. The prisoner had obviously destroyed the document before his attorney had arrived at the jail most likely fearing that the information would have revealed his true identity.

Postscript:
On December 15, 1908, Joseph Hobbins was sentenced to ninety-nine years imprisonment at the State Penitentiary at Deer Lodge and when war broke out in Europe, he asked for and received permission to return to Canada to fight with the Canadian Expeditionary Force in April of 1916. While some publications have reported that he was killed in action he was actually discharged after the war and returned to his hometown in Canada.In January of 1925, while introducing a bill to have all Montana executions held at the state penitentiary, Representative Lincoln of Flathead County stated that the LeBeau hanging had broken down Sheriff O'Connell and blamed for the death of his wife.

The Triple Hanging of Leslie Fahley, Harrison Gibson and Henry Hall

During the summer of 1916, Claude C. Campbell and his partner Michael Freeman had worked hard at Judith Basin helping to install the city water system and to put up the new school building. On the night of October 6, the two men boarded a fast eastbound Great Northern freight train to Billings known as the "hot shot" where they met farm laborer, Earl Fretwell of Oklahoma. The three men were on a gondola loaded with lumber when their train overtook a local freight train at Nihil and while the two trains stood along side one another the three white men saw nine black railroad workers climb aboard their train in the bright moonlight.[8]

Normally, Judith Gap was one of the most peaceful towns in Montana but when the many railroad workers, sometimes numbering a hundred or more arrived to work on the Milwaukee Railroad there were numerous fights including shootings and knifings. Because most of the toughest railroad trackmen carried guns and knives the three white men became concerned, and when seven of the black men started to muster as the train pulled out of Nihil, Campbell told Freeman that they were about to be robbed. Just then two of the blacks jumped Earl Fretwell who was the closet to them, and then all seven of them pulled automatic revolvers and ordered the three white men to put up their hands. The three complied and the blacks went through their pockets, taking everything they had.

By then the train was traveling thirty to thirty-five miles an hour on a downgrade when the blacks ordered Fretwell to jump off. The boy begged to be allowed to remain but they forced him down the ladder and then they began shooting at him and one of the thieves, Mitchell Hall reached over and struck Fretwell on the head with his pistol, knocking him unconscious from the train. Meanwhile four of the robbers were still searching Campbell and Freeman who were still standing with their hands up. Harrison Gibson shouted: "Give it to them," and at point blank he shot Freeman in the side and as he fell cried out, "Jack, I'm done for" and then he struggled to hold onto the edge of the car as Lesley Fahley pumped five bullets into him with his automatic pistol. At that point all of the blacks began firing into the body of Freeman and then James Foster opened fire on Campbell.

Campbell was shot three times as he fell over the edge of the car before he grabbed a ladder and with bullets whizzing over his head in the dark, he let go and rolled end over end down the embankment. The man lay half conscience and bleeding in the ditch until he staggered up to the track where he tried to make his way back to Nihil. Campbell's strength finally gave out after about a half a mile and he started a fire on the tracks out of some of his personal letters and pieces of scrap wood. A passing train crew picked up Campbell along with the unconscious Fretwell and the dead body of Freeman. Conductor Ed Voaght stopped the train at Franklin where he telephoned Musselshell County Deputy

Sheriff Robert V. Jennings stationed at Ryegate. Deputy Jennings and a couple of men from Ryegate drove to Cushman by moonlight after the headlights on their Model "T" had given out.

At Cushman the posse arrested five of the murderers just before their train pulled away and from there Deputy Jennings and G.T. Bennett drove the five prisoners to Judith Gap where a mob had gathered with the intention of lynching the black men. After quieting down the leader of the mob, Officer Jennings took his prisoners to White Sulphur Springs where the telegraph wires were kept busy for about an hour when another arrest was made at Judith Basin and the last fugitive was apprehended in Mobridge, South Dakota. After hearing the evidence from a large number of witnesses the coroner's jury rendered a verdict that Michael Freeman came to his death from gunshot wounds received at the hands of Harrison Gibson and he implicated Henry Hall, Leslie Fahley, Julius Foster and Mitchell Hall as his accomplices. A week later the wife of Foster, whom Claude Campbell positively identified as the man who had shot him on the train came to Montana from Chicago to assist in the defense.

Harrison Gibson and Julius Foster, the primary shooters were tried first and found guilty of first degree murder and a couple of days later Roy Bridges and Oscar Rogers were found guilty of second-degree murder, and a week later Henry Hall, Mitchell Hall and Leslie Fahley were all also found guilty of first-degree murder. On Tuesday, January 16, 1917, Judge John A. Matthews sentenced Henry Hall, Leslie Fahley and Harrison Gibson to be hanged on Friday, February 16; Mitchell Hall and Julius Foster were given life, Oscar Rogers drew a fifteen to twenty year sentence and Roy Bridges was assigned a term of from ten to twelve years. Judge Mathews explained that the other four convicted men weren't sentenced to death only because Claude Campbell and Earl Fretwell survived their gunshot wounds.

A constant deathwatch was placed over the three condemned men about thirty days before the execution and Reverend Father Sherf of Ringling and Reverend J.M. Hard of the Episcopal Church at Martinsdale spent considerable time offering the prisoners spiritual comfort. Leading up to the execution it was said that the three doomed men slept far better than the sheriff and the spiritual advisers. The friends of the condemned men including two black ministers from Helena, Reverends H.C. Parsons and Martin made a strong effort to secure executive clemency on the grounds that the murderers were ignorant and irresponsible, but Governor Samuel V. Stewart, who was a strong believer in capital punishment, after a thorough and impartial review of the case declined to interfere with the execution. In his pronouncement the Governor acknowledged that the three condemned men were not highly educated but they deliberately entered upon a career of crime that was sure to bring them into conflict with the law.

Governor Stewart went on to say that he didn't believe the men had specifically planned to kill those particular white men, but they had deliberately armed themselves to rob whomsoever they encountered.

He explained that in the early days of the territory it was infested with road agents committing wholesale murder as they robbed the innocent citizens. These three men were engaged in the same kind of crime and should receive the same punishment after a fair and impartial trial. At first Governor Stewart had questioned whether race had played a part in the prisoners' convictions, but he was later convinced that they were treated as fairly as any white man would have been.

Many people including Father Scherf objected to the execution of the three men because of their poor up bringing and because the hangings would take place within one hundred yards of a school at White Sulphur Springs. He had been the spiritual adviser for the condemned men for about three weeks and he described Fahley as the smartest of the three; Gibson was intelligent but he was always nervous and Henry Hall was reticent and moody. All three men said on numerous occasions that when they went before God, they would speak highly of Sheriff Nagues and his deputies including Undersheriff Bob Menzies and Deputy M.D. Holmes. After being sentenced to death, the prisoners all had admitted their guilt in the murder of the victim at various times but they often squabbled among themselves as to the exact occurrences during the night of the murder.

After sleeping soundly Thursday night the three men were awakened at five a.m. but one of them was allowed to sleep another hour. It was snowing and blowing outside of the jail when the three prisoners got dressed and were baptized and given their last rites by Reverend Hard. It was during this final prayer session with the Reverend that the three prisoners showed any emotion, but they quickly recovered and regained their familiar cool composure. After eating a hearty breakfast the three men rested for a while before the leather straps were adjusted around their waists and the handcuffs secured their wrists. Finally two deputies accompanied each prisoner through the cold and windy dawn from the jail building to the county barn, some one hundred feet with Sheriff George B. Nagues bringing up the rear. The big rolling doors of the barn were thrown open by one deputy as the procession arrived and headed for the stairway to the gallows.

Since it had been nearly eight years that a hanging had taken place in Montana, there weren't any operating gallows available in the state. There was still an ancient scaffold in storage at White Sulphur Springs, which had been built in 1884, but it had never been used but Sheriff Nagues called on Dan Hurd who had helped build the original death machine to salvage what he could of the old relic and devise a makeshift gallows in the county barn. Utilizing the trap hinges and release mechanism from the old gallows, Mr. Hurd installed an eight by four foot trapdoor through the second floor, which provided for a drop of seven feet. The stairway in the barn was narrow and each of the condemned men tugged at their leash while they ascended to the drop. Reverend Hard led the way across the floor to the dangling ropes and the heavy trap, praying as the condemned men each mumbled a prayer.

All three men showed great bravery as they climbed the stairs and took their places over the trap, appearing to be totally indifferent to the proceedings. One of them didn't take his place within the square marked out for him, but after realizing the fact he quietly stepped onto the spot. The Reverend stood at the edge of the drop as the leg straps were quickly fastened; the nooses adjusted and the black caps pulled down by the deputies.

According to the witnesses, Harrison Gibson boasted that, "they can't kill a smile" and he had a broad grin on his face when the black cap was being pulled down. Gibson was the bravest and more of a braggart than the others with his jesting while Fahley was silent and showed some nervousness and Hall faced death with total indifference. After the last cap was pulled down, Sheriff Nagues shouted, "Look out," then at 7:02 he pulled back the lever, and the three men dropped through the trap. Not a word was spoken by anyone in the crowd of onlookers from the time the men marched up the stairs to the scaffold until they were dropped from the trapdoor. According to most of the sheriffs present, the execution at White Sulphur Springs was probably the shortest hanging on record, as the three condemned men had stood on the trap for only about eleven seconds. Except for one of the men biting his lip, none of the men weakened, which made the execution go quickly and only forty-three minutes ticked off from the time Henry Hall, the first in the procession, reached the top of the stairway, until their bodies were placed in coffins and buried.

The trap worked perfectly and there was only a soft thud as the three bodies reached the end of their ropes. Each of their necks were broken, and Dr. A.T. Gilhus pronounced Henry Hall dead in just over four minutes, Fahley's body gave a slight tremor as his muscles relaxed and he was declared dead at the end of five minutes, and Gibson took over eleven minutes to die. The three bodies were cut down after hanging for fifteen minutes, placed in simple wooden coffins, put on a sleigh and hurried to the cemetery where they were buried in the Potter's Field in a single grave, large enough to accommodate the three boxes.

There were reportedly one hundred and fifty invitations sent out but there were only about forty witnesses in the barn including government, state, county and city officers and doctors. Among the spectators was Claude Campbell one of the shooting victims as well as L.A. Cowan of Judith Gap, Sheriff Ed Majors, Deputy U.S. Marshal Groff and Robert V. Jennings, former Musselshell County deputy sheriff of Helena. Mr. Jennings was the deputy that arrested five of the seven men after the murder in October of 1916.

Bad weather in the region had prevented many of the invited guests from attending the hanging and the witnesses returning to Helena after the execution experienced a great deal of trouble getting from White Sulphur Springs to Ringling. A local daredevil, Stanley Smith of Martinsdale snuck into White Sulphur Springs during the hanging and uncoupled the engine from the train, which had brought over most of the spectators of the execution and "took her for a spin." When the passengers and train crew returned to the station the engine was gone and all the engineer and fireman could do was stand next to the abandoned passenger cars and look at each other while the passengers apparently thought the engine had been taken away for some routine business. The train crew finally surmised that the engine had somehow gotten uncoupled and it was slowly rolling back towards Ringling.

Then as the engineer and firemen were getting out a handcar and the sheriff was rounding up a posse to pursue the fugitive engine the crowd heard a whistle and the trail of smoke off in the distance. When the engine slowly backed up to the cars, Stanley Smith stepped down from the cab and greeted the engineer with, "Hello, Bill, didn't care if I took the old two-cylinder out for a little leap did you?" The adventure didn't end there as the train got stalled later in a huge snow drift and the passengers were forced to use sleighs to get to the main line of the Milwaukee.

Postscript:
Claude Campbell eventually settled at White Sulphur Springs and Earl Fretwell worked for the telephone company at Judith Gap and he helped build the road between White Sulphur Springs and Martinsdale. After serving in World War I, Mr. Fretwell returned to Meagher County where he remained until he retired in California.

The only known relatives of Michael Freeman at the time of his death were a wife and child living somewhere in Detroit. What the authorities didn't know was that Michael had a brother living at Shonkin just south of Fort Benton. Eighty-five years later Patrick E. Freeman of Great Falls finally learned the fate of his long-lost uncle. Patrick was only three years, living at Shonkin when Michael Freeman was murdered and the family was never notified. While traveling through White Sulphur Springs in 2002, Mr. Freeman came across the story in a Meagher County history book and then found more information from the museum there and at Harlowton. Patrick Freeman finally visited the final resting place of his uncle in the wind-swept country cemetery in an unmarked grave.

February 16, 1917

Leslie Fahley

Other Name: Leslie Foley and "King Faro"
Location and Gallows: Fahley's life ended at White Sulphur Springs on ***Gallows No. Fifteen: (Feb. 1917)***.
Hanged with: Harrison Gibson and Henry Hall
Description: Fahley was an eighteen-year-old black man and at the time of his arrest he was wearing two pairs of underwear, two suits of clothes and pair of sweaters.
Crime: Murder of Michael Freeman on October 6, 1916, during a commission of a robbery.
Judge: John A. Matthews

Prosecution: County Attorney Hagerman and assisted by William Louis Ford
Defense: Earl F. Angell[9]
Sheriff: George B. Nagues
Distinction: At the age of eighteen, Leslie Fahley was probably the youngest man ever legally hanged in Montana. These three convicted murderers were the last men to be hanged in Meagher County.
Remnants and Relics: The entire barn at White Sulphur Springs where the three men were hanged was later donated to the Nevada City Museum where it is displayed as the "Gallows Barn." An invitation to the triple hanging is presently on display at the Castle Museum at White Sulphur Springs.

At the time of his arrest Fahley didn't know for sure how his name was spelled or how old he was. He had no parents, no relatives; no education whatsoever and absolutely no cares. "Ah don't know how old Ah is, but Ah'm maybe nineteen." When asked where he was born he said, "Well, the first time Ah knowed maself Ah was down in Mississippi." Testimony at the trial revealed that after Gibson had first shot Michael Freeman, Fahley stood over the victim and emptied his automatic pistol into the man's body before throwing him off the moving train.

February 16, 1917

<u>Harrison Gibson</u>

Other Name: "Rain in the face"
Location and Gallows: Gibson and his two partners in crime were hanged at White Sulphur Springs on ***<u>Gallows No. Fifteen: (Feb. 1888)</u>***.
Hanged with: Leslie Fahley and Henry Hall
Description: large black man, about twenty-eight years old
Crime: Murder of Michael Freeman on October 6, 1916, during the commission of a robbery.
Judge: John A. Matthews
Prosecution: County Attorney Hagerman and Special Prosecutor Carl August Linn
Defense: Earl F. Angell
Sheriff: George B. Nagues
Distinction: These three convicted murderers were the last men to be hanged in Meagher County.
Remnants and Relics: The entire barn at White Sulphur Springs where the three men were hanged was later donated to the Nevada City Museum where it is displayed as the "Gallows Barn." An invitation to the triple hanging is presently on display at the Castle Museum at White Sulphur Springs.

Harrison Gibson was considered one of the principal shooters and he was the first to be placed on trial. Because of the eyewitness testimony of Campbell and Fretwell the jury returned a first-degree murder verdict within twenty-four hours. Since the jury did not fix the penalty, nor did they authorize Judge Mathews to do so, the panel was sent back into deliberation and when they finally returned their verdict was the same but this time the jury left the penalty up to the court.

W.B. Rhoades, secretary of the railroad commission, formerly of Marshal, Missouri, the hometown of Gibson, spoke to Governor Stewart on behalf of the condemned man and he presented letters written by prominent white residents of the community. Mr. Rhoades also offered to the Governor petitions signed by hundreds of Missouri citizens stating that Gibson, up to the time he had left home a year or so earlier had a good reputation. Deputy U.S. Marshal Goff, who talked with Gibson during his last night, reported that at one point he said, “Well, I've got to die tomorrow, but I certainly would like to have some possum and watermelon before a die.”

As Sheriff Nagues was strapping Gibson's hands to his sides in the jail, the prisoner mused, “Say, Mistah Sheriff, Ah've got a bad taste in my mouf this mawnin. There's a red apple down in my pocket an Ah'd like jess' one bite before Ah leaves.” The sheriff held the apple up to the man's mouth and Gibson took a bite. After munching it a bit he said, “All right, let's go,” and Gibson started off cheerfully with the other two prisoners to the gallows.

February 16, 1917

Henry Hall

Other Name: “Bama”
Location and Gallows: Like Leslie Fahley and Harrison Gibson, Henry Hall was hanged at White Sulphur Springs on ***Gallows No. Fifteen:***.
Hanged with: Leslie Fahley and Harrison Gibson
Description: Twenty-two-year-old black man
Crime: Murder of Michael Freeman on October 6, 1916, during the commission of a robbery.
Judge: John A. Matthews
Prosecution: County Attorney Hagerman and Special Prosecutor Carl August Linn
Defense: Rufus Hopkins of Lewistown
Sheriff: George B. Nagues
Distinction: These three convicted murderers were the last men to be hanged in Meagher County.
Remnants and Relics: The entire barn at White Sulphur Springs where the three men were hanged was later donated to the Nevada City Museum where it is displayed as the “Gallows Barn.” An invitation to the triple hanging is presently on display at the Castle Museum at White Sulphur Springs.

The Triple Hanging of Frank Fisher, John O'Neil and Sherman Powell.

In 1917, a terrible crime wave had struck Butte and during the April session of Judge John V. Dwyer's court there were forty-one criminal cases heard including eight murders involving nine defendants. After a number of the murder cases resulted in short prison terms and only one receiving a life sentence, Butte Chief of Police Jere J. Murphy made a passionate plea in the local newspapers that hangings were once again needed in Silver Bow County. In his public statement, Chief Murphy pointed out that the Mining City had suffered from an unparallel number of killings and the lenient sentences that the convicted murderers had been receiving was sending a bad signal to the dangerous elements.

Chief Murphy said that even with the triple hanging at White Sulphur Springs the previous year, it had been some eight years since there had been an execution at Butte. He was quick to point out that after those executions crime had diminished and he called for the juries of the county to convict and start fixing the death penalty in murder cases. Prior to 1917, the juries were charged with assigning the degree of guilt to the defendant while the judge decided the penalty. While previously the juries could recommend certain penalties, after 1917, the jury could actually fix the penalty or leave it up to the court to set the sentence.

While the jury in the Frank Fisher and John O'Neil case had left the penalty up to Judge Dwyer to decide, the statement by the chief of police and other public outcries undoubtedly affected his decision. By the time the Sherman Powell case came to trial the attitude of the community was clearly pro death penalty and the jury fixed the penalty at death. Fisher and O'Neil had been convicted of the murder of Thomas Higgins, a miner in October while Powell was sentenced to death for the killing of a fellow railroad worker. The three condemned men were all hanged at the same time on a brand new scaffold, which was built especially for the triple execution. Initially the county commissioners had planned to use the original "Galloping Gallows" of Silver Bow County, which was in storage at the state penitentiary at Deer Lodge after being used to hang inmates, Rock and Hays in 1908 and 1909 but there were questions about its effectiveness.

The ancient scaffold had become the most famous "Galloping Gallows" and after quickly snuffing the life from ten convicted murderers from 1888 through 1906, it had failed to snap the necks of its two final victims at Deer Lodge. When Sheriff John K. O'Rourk decided to use a new death machine he put Undersheriff Jack Melia in total charge of the execution of the three men and the officer planned the new gallows with the help of T.O. Angell[10] of Butte. The men decided to design a drop type gallows, which would accommodate all three of the condemned men at once with a four by eight-foot trap consisting of two doors that separated in the middle, which allowed the men to drop straight through eliminating the possibility of twists, swerving, slipping or losing their balance. The doomed men stood on the trap about two and a half feet apart and the dual doors were opened by pulling a single heavy lever, which tripped two heavy beams supporting them.

The stone stairway leading down to the basement of the new jail building was used as the pit for the gallows and it was about eight feet deep and a ten by ten-foot platform built of heavy timbers was constructed over it. The overhead beam of the scaffold, which supported the ropes, was about seven feet above the trap. The new timbers for the scaffold were delivered to the county jail on January 11, and the carpenters immediately began erecting it along with the high temporary board fence that enclosed the extreme northeast corner of the jail yard.

This particular hanging was the first and only time that the gallows as well as the condemned men were completely concealed until the actual time of their execution. First, a heavy burlap curtain was wrapped around the back and sides of the scaffold and another was placed over the front of the gallows. The condemned men were partially strapped in the jail and then they were marched into the enclosed scaffold where the rest of the restraints were adjusted and the noose and death masks were fitted on the trio. Finally the front curtain was drawn back exposing the condemned men to the witnesses and then the trap was tripped and the men dropped out of sight into the pit below. While there were electric lights in the stairway, they were only used by the physicians to check the bodies for life.

In order to make room for the new gallows the old jail kitchen building, which was a small frame structure against the north wall of the old jail, was demolished. The new county jail building had a built-in modern kitchen and Albert Rouleau, the jail cook, had already transferred his headquarters into the new building. O'Neil and Fisher were both able to watch the workmen erect the scaffold from their cell window of the old jail building but Sherman Powell's cell wasn't situated that afforded him a view. O'Neill was in the same cell occupied twelve years earlier by Miles Fuller before he was hanged, and James Martin who met his end on the gallows in 1904. That particular cell was located in a part of the jail that was then referred to as the "witness quarters." Fisher and O'Neil passed the time awaiting their execution by playing checkers in the evenings and following baseball scores during the summer months. The gallows was tested the day before the execution by placing three dummies, corresponding to the three men's weight, and when the trap was tripped it released smoothly and the heavy beam supporting the five hundred and fifty pounds didn't even shudder.

For obvious reasons the three condemned men weren't in the least bit interested in the New Years Eve celebrations of 1918, especially Sherman Powell who spent the evening writing to Governor Sam V. Stewart asking the top executive to look into his case and requesting that his sentence of death be commuted. The letter was reportedly well worded and prisoner used most of the jail personnel as character references as the staff considered him a model prisoner. The only guest to visit Fisher and O'Neil was their attorney, John A. Groeneveld who later reported that the prisoner's attitudes hadn't changed since their convictions, and they showed no sign of being afraid of their fate.

Despite the obvious preparations for their execution the three condemned men displayed remarkable fortitude. They woke up each morning at eight o'clock, got dressed, washed up and ate a hearty breakfast while visiting with their guards. The prisoners received the best attention from the sheriff's force and they were furnished with any kind of foods they desired. The day before their trip to the gallows they had ham and eggs for breakfast, steak for their noon meal and again a steak for their dinner. Since their incarceration the trio was never interested in reading and within a few days of their execution they had lost all interest in current magazines and daily newspapers.

Several organizations had distributed petitions and met with Governor Stewart to have the men's sentences commuted including the woman's group of "The Good Government Club" of Butte, and the district court clerk's office of Silver Bow County made a special plea for the life of Sherman Powell. All three men had hopes of commutation until the last minute but on their last night on earth the three prisoners rested remarkably easy, according to members of the sheriff's office. The staff stated that, "the prisoners were completely fatigued from an arduous day of uneventfullness and idleness." All day long they had waited anxiously for Governor Stewart to save them from the gallows. On the eve of the execution Governor Stewart denied the application for commutation of sentence made in behalf of the three men and in his statement he pointed out that the laws of the state of Montana provided for capital punishment and he had taken an oath to protect the laws.

The Governor pointed out that the petitions were solely based on the disapproval of capital punishment and he referred those people strongly against the death penalty to take their arguments to the state legislature. For those arguing that other guilty men of Silver Bow County who had gotten off with life terms, the Governor explained that if others had been inadequately punished, there should be no more miscarriage of justice in the county. Some of the cases that Governor Stewart had referred to were of Jack Rowan, who twenty-five years earlier had shot at a bartender but missed and killed another man walking into the saloon. He was condemned to death but his sentence was later commuted to life imprisonment and he was eventually pardoned if he promised that he would never do it again.

Another was Jake Shaffer, a black man who had killed another black in a quarrel and he was convicted of first-degree murder and sentenced to death but the Supreme Court ordered a new trial for him. Shaffer was again found guilty and sentenced to be hanged but by the time he was given another chance for a trial all of the witnesses had disappeared and the man's case was eventually dropped. While waiting to be hanged for murder, Bill Demsey got away in a mass jailbreak and he was never re-captured. Charles Lennox also cheated the gallows for killing a railroad man near Silver Bow with James Martin when he escaped with other prisoners in another jailbreak. While Martin was recaptured and eventually hanged, Charles Lennox was never caught.

The sheriff and his staff kept the Governor's decision from the condemned men until the following morning when they were totally devastated by the news. At first Powell trembled violently and Fisher and O'Neil were totally dejected. While Fisher at first blasphemously refused all spiritual advice, he welcomed religion when word came down that the governor wouldn't interfere with the executions. Powell and O'Neil were both baptized at a Catholic Mass held at the jail on the day before their execution by Reverend Father James Franchi, chaplain of the St. James Hospital. Father Franchi and Father F. X. Leschner worked with the two doomed men until the moment of their deaths.

The trio slept in rather late and then ate a substantial breakfast of boiled eggs, toast, grapefruit and coffee. They had a pleasant last day, Fisher reading the morning papers while Powell and O'Neil lounged around. Early in the afternoon a steaming turkey dinner, presented by the Silver Bow Club was brought into the jail and Joe Dudley, the club chef served the condemned men and he took particular pains to see that the dinner was prepared to suit their individual tastes. The three prisoners were very appreciative of the fine meal and after eating the condemned men passed away the time in idleness and visiting with scores of visitors and curiosity seekers. The supper hour found the doomed men still with a good appetite and they again ate heartily.

Towards midnight a solemn spirit had settled over the entire courthouse and large groups of people had gathered in front of the building. The jail yard had a surreal appearance with its yellow glow from the many incandescent lights and directly above the scaffold was a high-powered lamp that caused weird shadows over the scene. With a heavy coating of snow, the jail yard appeared particularly dejected and besides the approximately one hundred witnesses invited to the affair, the prisoners in both the new and old jails had gathered at their cell windows early that morning to await the event. Initially, Sheriff O'Rouke had planned to be very liberal in allowing as many spectators to view the execution as possible, but he had a change of heart after realizing the potential size of the crowd. When it was reported that all of the streets surrounding the county jail were packed with people trying to get admittance to the execution yard the sheriff realized he could never control such a crowd. The gates to the jail yard were secured and the entire grounds were under guard by the deputies, city police and the Washington Coast Artillerymen with fixed bayonets and only about three hundred witnesses were allowed to attend.

Among the visiting sheriffs and other officials witnessing the hanging were: Cascade County Sheriff Louis Kommers, W.E. Splann and Homer Robertson of Great Falls; Deer Lodge County Sheriff C.L. Hartsell, Jefferson County Sheriff T.L. Locker, Lewis and Clark County Sheriff T.J. Majors, Madison County Sheriff C.W. Hungerford, Meagher County Sheriff George B. Nagues, Missoula County Sheriff J.T. Green, Powell County Sheriff Mullen and Stillwater County Sheriff Edward B. Fellows.

Also attending the hanging were Valley County Sheriff C.W. Powell, Sheriff Lee B. Anderson and C.N. Sargent of Bozeman. Another of the visiting officers was Sheriff Cyrus K. Wyman of Beaverhead County who on April 21, 1920, was shot down in cold blood by Albert Yeik. The murderer of the sheriff was hanged at Dillon on August 26, 1921.

In an effort to limit the time that the prisoners would have to be in the cold air, most of the straps were placed on the men while they were in the jail. After being strapped around the waists the trio was assembled in the corridor of the jail and two deputies were assigned to each prisoner. Frank Fisher was the first man strapped up and he was positioned near the outside door in his shirtsleeves, no collar or tie and bareheaded. Fisher asked for a cigarette and one was lighted and placed in his mouth. He stood calmly smiling as he nodded to the many deputies he had grown to know over the many months. His arms were bound with heavy webbing from his waist to above his elbows making it difficult for him to shake hands with the guards bidding him good-bye.

After O'Neil was bound he joined Fisher at the end of the corridor where he smiled and muttered "God bless you," to the bystanders. Powell at first seemed to be the most courageous of the three and when their death warrants were being read in their cells Fisher and O'Neil appeared a bit unnerved just before they exited the jail. When Powell was secured the procession led by Sheriff O'Rourk and Father Franchi walked through the jail door and onto the upper landing of the steel stairway leading from the second floor down to the jail yard below.

This was the first time that Powell had seen the jail yard and when he saw the men curiously gazing up at him he stopped to take in the macabre scene. He then looked at the scaffold, which with its fresh lumber under the many lights startled him momentarily and he collapsed against the brick wall of the building. Within a second the man had recovered and with the help of the deputies Powell continued down the steps. By the time he reached the yard there was a faint smile across his face. Fisher continued to smoke his cigarette and smile as the trio passed through the large crowd of witnesses where there were many "good-bye" and "God bless you'" heard.

Without faltering the three men walked the fifty feet to the scaffold and up the short flight of stairs to the gallows and then they passed from view behind the burlap curtain. It took several men to bind the feet of the prisoners, adjust the nooses and then place the black masks over each of their heads. Undersheriff Melia, who had bound the men's arms in the jail, again took charge of securing their feet on the gallows. Fisher continued to smoke right up to the end and he didn't relinquish the butt until the black cap was being pulled over his face.

When everything was ready, the front cover of the gallows was removed exposing the condemned men and the hangman's ropes to the crowd for the first time. Evidently the noise of the curtain shocked Powell and he fainted into the arms of the deputies assigned to him and while the officers held him in position the trap was sprung and the three men disappeared below the platform.

Undersheriff Melia had used the scientific method of calculating the length of the drop for each man based on their individual weights, height and general condition. Powell weighed 223 pounds and he was given enough rope to drop six feet, eight inches; Fisher dropped six feet, six inches, as he weighed 155 pounds and since O'Neil weighed in at 135 pounds he was given the longest drop of three men falling seven feet, three inches.

After the trap fell the ropes became taut and there was scarcely a quiver from any of the bodies. Fisher was pronounced dead after two minutes, a minute later O'Neil was dead and Powell had passed a moment later. Several minutes later the undersheriff untied the ropes and the bodies were lowered into undertaker baskets and placed in the basement of the new jail. After examining the bodies, Doctors Dan J. Donahue, J.D. Freund and Philip J. McCarthy declared that the necks of the three men had been broken and their windpipes severed.

The following morning, Sheriff O'Rourk and his men rested after the great strain of the previous few days and then they began the work of dismantling the scaffold that afternoon. Before it was stored away the apparatus it was given a heavy coat of preserving paint and this version of "Galloping Gallows" was eventually used to hang Monte and William Harris in a double hanging on April 20, 1923, Roy Walsh on Valentines Day, 1925, Anthony Veteran on October 1, 1926, and finally George Hoffman on August 29, 1933.

Sheriff O'Rourk confiscated the dead men's clothing and immediately after the hanging the souvenir hunters began slicing up the ropes into suitable sizes as memorials of the event. Thousands of the curious people who didn't get a chance to witness the execution filed through the Daniels & Bilboa Undertakers to view the body of Fisher and the M.J. Walsh Undertakers to see the bodies of Powell and O'Neil.

Frank Fisher was the first to be buried and his funeral took place on the afternoon of January 16, in the undertaker rooms of Daniels & Bilboa, the service was simple and consisted of a few passages read from the Bible by Reverend E.J. Groenveld. No other vehicles accompanied the hearse to Mountain View Cemetery where Fisher's remains were interred. Fisher's parents had asked that the body of their son not be sent to Cincinnati, Ohio and they refused to come out to Butte for the services. The funeral for the two Catholics, O'Neil and Powell took place at the M.J. Walsh Undertakers and Reverend Father F.X. Leschner, assisted by Father Franchi conducted the gravesite services in the Holy Cross Cemetery.

January 14, 1918

Frank Fisher

Other Name: Frank Fletcher
Hanged with: his partner in crime, John O'Neil and another murderer, Sherman Powell
Location and Gallows: The three convicted murderers were hanging in the jail yard of the Silver Bow County Courthouse and they were the first three men executed on ***Gallows No. Sixteen: (Jan. 1918): "Galloping Gallows" No. Five***.
Description: Fisher was rather tall, thirty-five years old and originally from Hamilton, Ohio.
Crime: Fisher and John O'Neil were convicted for the murder of Thomas Higgins on September 3, 1916.
Judge: John V. Dwyer
Prosecution: Silver Bow County Attorney Joseph R. Jackson and deputies, Nick A. Rutering and Frank Riley
Defense: William G. Sullivan; Alexander Levinsky; Alf C. Kremer and Tuoy; John A. Groeneveld
Sheriff: John K. O'Rourk
Relics and Remnants: The gallows, which was used to hang Fisher, O'Neil and Powell, went on to execute another five convicted murderers and in 1933, the gallows were returned to Butte where it is currently in storage in the basement of the Silver Bow County Courthouse. Because the scaffold is being stored with possible hazardous material the ancient death machine is not available for viewing.

Thomas Higgins was on his way home at about nine o'clock on the evening of September 3, 1916, when he spotted two unmasked highwaymen, Frank Fisher and John O'Neil robbing J.P. Sullivan and he rushed to his rescue. O'Neil turned his gun on Higgins and told him to throw up his hands, but instead of complying he ran towards Park Street shouting for the police. While Fisher stayed and covered Sullivan near the old Revival Tabernacle on the corner of Porphyry and South Wyoming Streets, O'Neil chased after Higgins, firing as he ran and one of the bullets struck the victim in the foot but he kept on running and the bandit finally gave up. While Higgins' wound wasn't considered serious at first, infection set in and he died of blood poisoning on October 1.

The Fisher and O'Neil case was delayed several times including when their first appointed counsel, William G. Sullivan withdrew and the defendants were going to hire their own attorneys. Eventually Judge Dwyer assigned Alexander Levinsky to defend Fisher and he appointed Daniel McGrath to represent O'Neil. Finally the murder case went to trial on March 29, 1917, and the following Silver Bow County residents were sworn in as jurors:

John L. Peterson	W.H. Nettle	Joseph Plunkett
A.W. Stecker	Joe Krinatz	Ed O. Reese
W.J. Tallon	Frank Peterson	O.D. Holmes
David D. Jones	Ed Dunleavy	David Gennara

Frank White of the Butte Police Department testified that he escorted the defendants to the St. James' Hospital on the evening of the shooting and Tom Higgins positively identified John O'Neil as the man who had shot him on the street. Dr. Langdon who was present at the time of the Higgins' statement was called to confirm the policeman's testimony. On the second day of the trial Traffic Policeman Phil Prilja told the court how he had arrested the two suspects on West Park Street on the night of the crime and he also testified that he was present at Higgins' identification of O'Neil at St. James' Hospital.

At their trial there was no real evidence presented against Fisher and he would have surely beaten the rap but he insisted on taking the stand where he incriminated himself. At six o'clock p.m. on the evening of March 30, 1917, the case was given to the jury and at nine p.m. they returned a first-degree guilty verdict. The sentence was delayed for two weeks when the defense attorneys filed for separate new trials and once again when members of the defense team were called out of town. Finally on May 5, Judge Dwyer sentenced Fisher and O'Neil to death on Friday, June 29, and neither man showed any signs of emotion as O'Neil had previously told his attorneys that he preferred death over life in prison. Undersheriff Melia and Deputy Noonan escorted the two condemned men back to the old jail where they were placed in new cages in the lower corridor. The other prisoners were moved from that portion of the old facility and Fisher and O'Neil were stripped of their clothes to make sure they didn't have anything to break jail or to take their own lives.

Sheriff O'Rourk assigned Deputies Riley, Quigley and Kinley to deathwatch duty over the condemned men. While Fisher had been regarded by the other prisoners as one of the most unruly inmates in the jail, it was O'Neil who became a braggart and troublemaker after the two men were placed in their death cells. After receiving his sentence of death, Fisher became meek and kept to himself while O'Neil began boasting that he would go to the gallows courageously. Attorney John A. Groeneveld was brought in to help with the appeals for Fisher and O'Neil and after various motions the date of execution was scheduled for December 14, 1916, and when the district court denied a new trial for the two men and the Supreme Court affirmed the lower court decision they were finally re-sentenced to be hanged on January 14, 1918.

The total expenses involved in the arrest and conviction of Fisher and O'Neil was estimated at about fifteen hundred dollars including about four hundred dollars each for the cost of the trial and the care of the prisoners and the remaining seven hundred dollars going for the additional salaries for the death watches and the expense for a copy of the transcripts for the appeal to the Supreme Court. The undertaking bill for the three men was estimated between two hundred and five hundred dollars.

Fisher's partner, John O'Neil threatened to return as a ghost to haunt a Butte police officer that had testified against them. Read about the incident under John O'Neil (January 14, 1918).

January 14, 1918

John O'Neil

Other Names: Richard Ray Gullich
Hanged with: his partner in crime, Frank Fisher and another murderer, Sherman Powell
Location and Gallows: O'Neil and the other three men were hanged in the jail yard of the Silver Bow County Courthouse and they were the first three men executed on ***Gallows No. Sixteen: (Jan. 1918): "Galloping Gallows" No. Five***.
Description: O'Neil was a twenty-six-year-old small man originally from Webb City, Missouri
Crime: O'Neil and Frank Fisher were convicted for the murder of Thomas Higgins on September 3, 1916. (See: Frank Fisher for story of crime)
Judge: John V. Dwyer
Prosecution: Silver Bow County Attorney Joseph R. Jackson and deputies, Nick Rutering and Frank Riley
Defense: William G. Sullivan; Daniel McGrath; John A. Groeneveld (See: Frank Fisher for the description of the trial)
Sheriff: John K. O'Rourk
Relics and Remnants: The gallows, which was used to hang O'Neil, Fisher and Powell went on to execute another five convicted murderers and after it was used for the last time in 1933, the gallows were returned to Butte where they are currently in storage in the basement of the Silver Bow County Courthouse. Because the scaffold is being stored with possible hazardous material the ancient death machine is not available for viewing.

After being born in Missouri, John O'Neil moved to New York City as a young boy where he found work as an elevator boy and later as a porter at several clubs in the city. O'Neil left New York and headed west where he lived in several cities including Chicago until he finally landed in Bisbee, Arizona. After working only twenty-eight shifts in a mine there he took a freight train to Butte. At the Mining City O'Neil met Fisher and the two men started their career of crime.

From the time of his arrest, O'Neil refused to give his true name in order to save his family, as he would rather die a thousand deaths than bring shame to his mother who he considered the best women in the world. Eventually O'Neal told the officers that his real name was Richard Roy Gullick and that he had been born in St. Louis and later moved to St Paul. Almost immediately after being placed in his death cell O'Neill began causing trouble with the jail staff. At first he began throwing out his meals threatening to cause problems until he received proper food and then he attacked the local newspapers, claiming that they had been responsible for his conviction and sentence of death.

While O'Neil paced up and down in his cell yelling and complaining, Fisher sat in the rear of his cage with his head buried in his hands. O'Neil left behind three letters with Father Franchi with instructions to make them public after his death, one to the public and the press; another was to his mother and the third to his father. In his public letter O'Neil insisted on his innocence stating he was a victim of circumstances and announced that he would die with a clear conscience. To his parents and family he said good-bye and said he was sorry that he had disgraced them. He swore to them that he was innocent and prayed that he would she them in heaven.

On the day of the execution Patrolman Philip Prilja, one of the officers who had testified against Fisher and O'Neil, called on the men at their cell to say good-bye and to make peace before the condemned men. As he approached the prisoners, Frank Fisher spat in the officer's face while O'Neil cussed him out and neither man ever forgave him. At that point Prilja lost his temper and started calling the two men names and told them that they deserved to be hanged. He told them he was glad he "got them" and said that Powell, the Negro, was the whitest man of the trio to die that day.

After Officer Prilja had left the jail, O'Neil told the deathwatch, John Leshy that if his ghost could come back it would surely return to haunt Prilja. "If I can come back I will make his life miserable. I will dog his steps in the lonesome watches of the night; my spirit will be with him when he sleeps and in the daytime. I will make him rue the day that he crossed my path, if there is such a thing as the spirit of a man coming back to haunt the living." A short time after O'Neil had made his threat he was led out to the scaffold. When later told about the threat, Officer Prilja said that he had run afoul with many criminals and that every one of them had bore him a grudge, and all that ghost business didn't worry him a bit.

Whether Officer Philip Prilja[11] was haunted or just unlucky, his life ended brutally about three years later when in March of 1921, Mike Burzan shot him down in front of a crowd of people on Arizona Street. In September of 1918, the over aggressive officer apparently beat Burzan while arresting him near the Northern Pacific Depot and Prilja was later found guilty of first-degree assault and received a sentence of from one and a half to three years at the state penitentiary.

Before Officer Prilja had begun his sentence at Deer Lodge however, Governor Stewart pardoned him, which reportedly outraged Mike Burzan. Determined to deal out justice with his own hand, the embittered man waited at the door of his pool hall on the south side of Park Street for Prilja to pass by. As the officer walked passed the doorway of Burzan's business the enraged man stepped out; caught up with his victim, placed his left hand on Prilja's shoulder and then he opened fire with his automatic revolver shooting the four times in the head. The shooting was apparently considered warranted as Mike Burzan was tried and eventually acquitted of the charges.

January 14, 1918

Sherman A. Powell

Hanged with: Frank Fisher and John O'Neil

Location and Gallows: Powell and the other three men were hanged in the jail yard of the Silver Bow County Courthouse on ***Gallows No. Sixteen: (Jan 1918)***

Description: During his incarceration Powell was the largest and most powerful inmate at the Silver Bow County jail. The twenty-nine-year-old Black man reportedly had a chest measuring forty-eight inches while his neck was twenty inches around.

Crime: Murder of another black man, Joseph H. Montgomery on April 8, 1917

Judge: John V. Dwyer

Prosecution: Silver Bow County Attorney Joseph R. Jackson and deputies, Nick Rutering and Frank Riley

Defense: James H. O'Flynn and assisted by Edward F. O'Flynn

Sheriff: John K. O'Rourk

Distinctions: Sherman Powell was the first and only black man hanged in Silver Bow County. He was also the first man convicted of first-degree murder in Silver Bow County where the jury had fixed the death penalty. As a side note, the entire jury later petitioned to the Governor for Powell's sentence to be commuted to life imprisonment.

Relics and Remnants: The gallows, which was used to hang Powell Fisher and O'Neil went on to execute another five convicted murderers and after it was last used in 1933, the gallows were returned to Butte where they are currently in storage in the basement of the Silver Bow County Courthouse. Because the scaffold is being stored with possible hazardous material the ancient death machine is not available for viewing.

Powell was a porter for the Great Northern Railroad and he had worked on the same dining car with his murder victim. In the Butte yards the two porters were playing cards in a dining car when a quarrel broke out between Powell and Joseph Montgomery who was a cook. When the game broke up Montgomery went to sleep on a cot inside the car and after midnight Powell broke into the dining car with a butcher knife and slashed Montgomery's throat. Detectives Larkin, Powell (no relation) and Morrison along with Lieutenant Dwyer arrested Sherman Powell about an hour later in a noodle parlor on Murray Street.

Two days later Coroner Lane conducted a hearing where Sherman Powell was named as the murderer of J.H. Montgomery of Great Falls. The prisoner claimed that the victim had pulled a gun and he killed him in self-defense. There was no weapon of any kind found near Montgomery's body while at the time of Powell's arrest he was carrying a revolver, which had been recently fired. At first the prisoner told the authorities that his friends were trying to raise the money for an attorney but eventually Judge Dwyer assigned the defendant counsel and on Saturday, April 28, 1917, he pleaded not guilty to the charge of murder. Powell's trial opened on May 21, 1917, when the following jury was sworn in:

J.R. Wharton (f)	John Kellett	Dave D. Lewis
William Thomas	H.M. Probst	Nick Roman
Ed McNamee	James Sennett	William Rowe
John Stenson	Claude V. Hammond	Fred C. Stafford

(f) Foreman

Dr. P.H. McCarthy told the court how the victim's neck had been cut clear to the spinal cord and that death was probably instantaneous. Other than the fatal wounds, Jack Daniels, the undertaker testified that there was no sign of a struggle on the body of the dead man. At nine o'clock on the evening of May 22, 1917, Foreman J.R. Wharton handed the verdict to Clerk Frank Leahy who announced that the jury had found Sherman Powell guilty of first-degree murder and they had fixed the punishment at death by hanging. This was the first time that a jury had fixed such a penalty in Silver Bow County history. Powell reportedly took the verdict coolly and he was returned to the jail without showing any emotion.

In sentencing Powell to death, Judge Dwyer broke away from the old precedent of scheduling hangings on Fridays and ordered the original execution for Monday, July 23, 1917. Before the sentence was pronounced Attorney James O'Flynn told the court that he had filed a notice for a new trial, and since his client was destitute he asked that a transcript of the testimony be furnished free of charge. After granting the request for the transcripts, Judge Dwyer proceeded in passing sentence, which Sherman Powell accepted without any emotions. Because he considered himself one black man who wasn't yellow, Powell later told Deputy Whalen that it was a tough sentence, but he was prepared to have his neck broken as long as he could first see a Methodist minister.

While Powell said that a fair-minded jury had given him a fair trial and that his attorneys made a good fight, he said that he was a victim of circumstances at a time when the people of Butte were demanding hangings. Without making any judgment on Powell's crime and execution, he may have been correct about the mood of Butte at the time, as another black man escaped the gallows after murdering a fellow black man after a pool game at Billings in October of 1916. What concerned Powell the most was his poor mother living in Canada who he had been the sole support of for the past nine years.

When Powell was ordered to the death cell there was some concern that the other doomed prisoners, Fisher and O'Neil would object to having a black man locked up in the same section of the jail. The authorities were reportedly surprised when the two white men immediately began socializing with Powell as he was being placed in a cell above them, proving that their similar death sentences obliterated any color line. The only thing that Fisher and O'Neil objected to about Powell was the same thing that all the inmates of the old jail did, that of the black man's terrible snoring that kept them all awake at nights.

Powell had high hopes for a commutation of sentence from Governor Sam V. Stewart because the jurors who had found him guilty and the entire sheriff's department had recommended it. While Fisher and O'Neil were troublesome inmates, Powell was considered the best and most obedient prisoner ever confined in the Silver Bow County jail.

On New Year's Eve, Sherman Powell wrote a well-worded letter asking Governor Stewart to consider his case, and if possible commute his sentence to life. On January 7, 1918, Sherman Powell received a letter back from the Governor, which greatly brightened his outlook and he expected to be saved from the gallows until the last.

While there was never a doubt about Powell's guilt of the murder, he was known to be peaceable and he had never caused any trouble before. Before his execution Powell said good-bye to the jailers and he thanked them for their kindness. He also wrote to the judge and the jurors telling them that he bore no ill will towards any of them and entrusted a letter with Undersheriff Melia to be mailed to his mother at South Colchesten, Ontario Canada. It was a short note expressing his disappointment that his sentence wasn't commuted and contained a newspaper clipping describing the efforts made by the citizens of Butte to save his live along with a copy of the petition was also included in the correspondence.

April 12, 1918

Juan Cuellae

Other Names: Juan Quarro

Location and Gallows: Juan Cuellae was hanged inside the county jail at Billings from the custom-built ***Gallows No. Seventeen: (April 1918)***.

Description: Thirty-seven-year-old unmarried Mexican national

Crime: Murder of Police Officer Enos M. Nelson on the evening of December 16, 1917.

Judge: Charles A. Taylor

Prosecution: County Attorney James L. Davis

Defense: M.J. Lamb

Sheriff: Stone W. Matlock

Distinction: Cuellae was the first Mexican national to be legally executed in Montana as well as the last man hanged in Yellowstone County.

In February of 1933, while cleaning out a huge safe, which for years had been kept in the booking room of the police headquarters at Billings, officers found some grim relics of an old crime of that city. Inside of an old basket were a police uniform cap and a strand of hemp rope. The cap belonged to Officer Enos Nelson a brother of Dr. Cedric H. Nelson who was shot down in cold blood and soon after his killer did a "shadow dance" from the end of the rope inside the county jail.

The stiff visor of the dead officer's cap showed the hole where the bullet had passed through the man's head, which ended his life and the name of the murderer was Juan Cuellae who had come to the United States from Mexico in about 1910, and had lived in Montana his last five years. He had worked as a farm laborer in the beet fields of Yellowstone County and as a section hand on the Northern Pacific Railroad.

On the evening of December 16, 1917, Cuellae and several other Mexicans were drinking at the Little Terrace Saloon on Minnesota Avenue near South Twenty-Seventh Street when they got into a fight with bartender, Carl M. Flagg who had refused to serve them more drinks. The men left with Cuellae who was wearing a heavy fur overcoat but he soon returned without the coat with five or six other men demanding to be served. When the bartender refused the order Cuellae whipped out a .32-caliber automatic pistol as the other patrons of the bar rushed for the exits. Mr. Flagg was standing beneath an American flag at the time and he put up his hands and invited the Mexican to go ahead and shoot. Apparently influenced by the large flag in the background, Cuellae backed out of the door, keeping his pistol on the bartender. When the Mexican left the premises, the bartender telephoned the police while one of the patrons said that another man had already gone for help.

A few moments later Night Patrolman Enos M. Nelson walked into the Little Terrace and he quickly arrested three of the Mexicans and telephoned police headquarters for the patrol wagon. When Sergeant W.L. Terrell and Motorcycle Patrolman Patrick Bakke arrived with the van, Officer Nelson turned over his prisoners and told the offcers about the incident before going after the Mexican gunman who had fled into the alley. Moments later a black woman on an errand had observed Cuellae crossing the alley holding an object behind his back and the woman had hardly finished crossing the alley when she heard the four or five gunshots ring out and saw the patrolman fall. After first shooting Officer Nelson in the forehead, Cuellae then fired four more shots into the patrolman while he was on the ground. The shooting of Officer Nelson took place in the same block where William Brooks had shot and killed his wife in November of 1898, and the murderer was later hanged at Billings on November 24, 1899.

The patrons in the Little Terrace presumed that Officer Nelson had shot the Mexican but they soon learned that the patrolman was dying. Other patrolmen on the south side beat heard the shots and several rushed to the scene of the shooting where Patrolman Lawson found Patrolman Nelson bleeding profusely from his wounds in the alley. It was later learned that Cuellae had hid behind a low fence in the alley after the shooting and then left after Nelson was removed. Word that Patrolman Nelson had been mortally wounded by a Mexican spread across Billings like wildfire and within thirty minutes a crowd of about two hundred citizens swarmed the police station begging Chief Talgo to let them assist in the capture of the desperado. Every available policeman was called to duty and assigned to different sections of the city and each officer was accompanied by a number of deputized civilians, eager to avenge the shooting of one of the most popular police officers of the force. Within an hour the patrol wagon returned to the station with eight Mexicans picked up in various sections of Billings, mostly on the south side.

Just before midnight, a call came into the station for the patrol wagon at Fourth Avenue North and Thirty-second Street. The call was made by two girls for a couple of young men, Wilbur Jefferies and Walter Loomis who had seen a Mexican on their way home and they were trailing the suspect. The patrol wagon, driven by Patrolman Pat Bakke and carrying Sergeant W.L. Terrell and Chris Jensen, a civilian garage operator, turned onto Montana Avenue at Thirty-Second Street and passed Cuellae and the two men following him. Jensen jumped off the wagon when he saw the automatic in Cuellae's hand and took cover behind a tree just in time before he was struck by the Mexican's bullet. A pitched gun battle ensued in which Officer Bakke was wounded in the foot and the Mexican was brought down by Sergeant Terrell with two loads of birdshot to the abdomen from his sawed off shotgun. Cuellae was originally identified as Juan Martinez and he was placed in the patrol wagon and taken to the police station while Officer Bakke was sent to the old St. Vincent's Hospital on Division Street.

In another room at the hospital the life was slipping away from Officer Nelson as the physicians attempted to remove the bullets from the officer's head and side, but it was later determined that the man was beyond help and he died shortly after Officer Bakke's arrival. The wounded Cuellae was also taken to the same hospital about midnight, but when word got out that Patrolman Nelson had died a mob began gathering and talking of a lynching. Chief Talgo knew that he had to get his prisoner to the county jail to protect him from the enraged crowd so he called Herman Smith, the county coroner to bring his hearse to the hospital. After he was drugged with morphine to keep him quiet, the prisoner was placed in a wicker basket used to transport dead bodies, placed in the hearse and then slipped out under the noses of the mob. The coroner's hearse drove past Smith's undertaking shop and then took the back streets to the county jail.

The following night a mob of about a hundred angry men stormed the Yellowstone County jail in an attemptt to lynch Juan Cuellae and after they had battered down the front door of the jail, Sheriff Stone W. Matlock and his deputies held the lynch mob at bay until the police officers arrived to disperse the crowd. A rain of lead from the county officers was reportedly poured into the door as it was being battered in by the mob, but miraculously no one was shot. After that initial violence he prisoner remained safely in the jail except for the two-block trips to and from the courthouse during his trial and conviction.

It was determined that Cuellae and other Mexican workers on the railroad section crew had sworn vengeance on Billings police officers, Shultz and Nelson, who they had nicknamed, "crooked neck" and the "short fellow." Shultz and Nelson had patrolled the beat on the south side of the tracks including Minnesota Avenue where several saloons were located where the Mexicans congregated. Nelson and Shultz had arrested Cuellae and other members of the section crew on at least one occasion for vagrancy, drunkenness and the disturbance of the peace. Thirty-seven-year-old Officer Nelson was a native of Billings and the son of former Police Magistrate Nelson and the businesses of Billings closed down for the officer's funeral and practically the entire town paid homage to the fallen patrolman.

Cuellae was arraigned before Judge Taylor on January 18, 1918, when he pleaded not guilty and the court assigned M.J. Lamb to defend him. The accused murderer once again pleaded not guilty on February 4, and his trial was set for the unlucky thirteenth day of the month. While waiting for his trial Cuellae shared a cell with Father F.X. Holinberger, the former Catholic priest who had been jailed on suspicion of being a member of a German espionage organization. The Mexican's trial opened at 9:30 in a jammed courtroom and the following jury wasn't drawn until after four that afternoon:

H.L. Gervais	John Eck	J.E. Rehard
Cornelius H. Frey	Thomas Murphy	William Cox
C.C. Sanderson	Ernest A. Mangler	Thomas C. Barnes
John E. Sadring (f)	Frank Martz	George Coon

(f) Foreman

The defendant appeared somewhat emaciated from the two months of confinement when Deputy Burns brought him into the courtroom. When he first was seated he quickly glanced around with nervous eyes perhaps fearing violence from the large mob of spectators. His demeanor quickly changed to indifference and his eyes became riveted at his feet as his boney hands rested loosely on his knees. The prisoner wore a dark Mackinaw coat that was apparently several sizes too large and a dark soft shirt without a necktie, black-buttoned shoes and a cap. The defendant needed a haircut badly and his tangled black hair partially covered his ears and a shock fell over his eyes after he removed his cap.

Cuellae paid little attention to the jury selection until the prosecutor asked one of the perspective jurors if he had anything against capital punishment. When the man assured the prosecutor that he had no qualms about imposing the death penalty Cuellae was seen twisting his cap with his nervous fingers and darting sharp glances at the juror who had spoken. On the second day of the trial Cuellae testified on his own behalf and practically clinched the state's case when he admitted firing twice at "some man" as he was approached in the dark alley. A murmur of surprise was heard in the packed courtroom as the defendant made his statement through his interpreter. Although the entire courtroom gasped with astonishment at Cuellae's admission he showed no sign that he realized the importance of the statement. The prosecution had hoped to wring out such an admission from the defendant during cross-examination but they didn't expect the defendant to volunteer the information while he was being questioned by his own defense attorney.

When the defendant was called to the stand the small Mexican rose from his chair somewhat unsteadily and then he shuffled to the witness chair where he appeared bewildered and uncertain of what was expected of him. After he and the court appointed interpreter, George

Serna were both sworn in, Cuellae told the court that he had been born in Mexico and that he had lived in the United States for eight years, the last five in Montana. After leaving the Little Terrace Saloon, Cuellae knew he was being followed and he turned and fired at a man who he thought was attacking him. When the prosecution presented the .32-caliber Colt Automatic revolver, Cuellae identified the weapon as the one he was carrying on the night of the shooting and the one he fired at the man in the alley. The prosecution then presented Officer Nelson's gun, still in its scabbard and showing no sign that it had been fired.

Before Cuellae's surprise admission, Defense Attorney Lamb had tried to cause reasonable doubt by saying that another Mexican by the name of Soto, who resembled the defendant, had actually killed the police officer. When that failed, the defense called area farmers J.P. Zeman, W.T. Ruggles, Alex Gries, J.C. Price, G.C. Baffington and T.C. Rickard who all testified that Cuellae had been a hard and honest worker. After deliberating for just thirty minutes on February 15, the jury notified the court that they had a verdict and within an hour Deputy Burns returned with the prisoner. Cuellae's face was reportedly pale and he swallowed hard when the jury foreman handed the death message to the judge who in turn gave it to Deputy Clerk of Court Lorin T. Jones. As the clerk rose to read the verdict there wasn't a sound from the spectators and the defendant sat leaning forward with his eyes fixed on the floor. Cuellae sat clutching his cap with both of his hands, his feet were together and his knees wide apart.

Clerk Jones announced, "We the jury find the above defendant Juan Cuellae, guilty of murder in the first degree, as charged in the information herein filed, and fix the punishment at death." Judge Taylor then announced that Cuellae would be sentenced at nine o'clock Monday morning, February 18. A hushed murmur arose from the large crowd while Cuellae, who reportedly understood just enough English to get the general idea, maintained the same indifference attitude and he remained seated until Deputy Burns tapped his shoulder to leave. The officer and his prisoner disappeared through the rear stairway and they made their way back to the jail. On the way back to the jailhouse the deputy asked the prisoner if he understood what the verdict meant. "Yes," the Mexican replied, "I die tomorrow morning."

The following Monday morning the convicted murderer was formerly sentenced to be hanged on Friday, April 12, 1918, and Cuellae received it without flinching and Sheriff Matlock had already been besieged with requests for invitations for the hanging. Later that day the Mexican told Captain Richard Guest of the local Salvation Army that he wanted to warn boys and young men to stay away from alcohol and modern motion pictures. He told Mr. Guest that he had left his family, including his wife to come to the States and when he said that he heard that his father, his wife and infant child had all died the authorities made an effort to locate the rest of his relatives.

Two weeks before the hanging, Cuellae was moved from the "bull pen," where he was confined with the other prisoners and placed in a separate cell on the ground tier in the southeast corner of the jail. The sheriff assigned two deathwatches, Deputy Williams and District Court Bailiff W.H. Piper to watch over the prisoner and during that time he was frequently visited by the Reverend J. Philip Anshutz, pastor of the Episcopal Church. Cuellae's last day started like any other with a hearty breakfast but this time he was dressed in a new dark suit provided by Yellowstone County. After breakfast Cuellae received a haircut and a shave, and then met with Father Raymond and Reverend Anshutz. Cuellae smoked many cigarettes during the day while he sat on the edge of his bunk in what appeared to be deep thought. While Father Raymond would not divulge what had been confessed to him by the prisoner the reverend said, "The law made no mistake in sentencing Cuellae to death."

The doomed man retired at about 9:30 that night and he was awakened at about three in the morning to get dressed in his new suit and Reverend Anshutz visited his cell where he received the prisoner's last confession. The prisoner was then offered a meal, but he ate very little and when he asked for a cigarette one of the deputies handed him a full pack. The condemned man sat quietly in his cell until Deputy Burns tapped lightly on the barred door and motioned to the guard to bring the prisoner forward. Reverend Anshutz walked beside Cuellae as he mounted the four steps leading up to the platform within the jailhouse. There a pair of steel handcuffs was fastened to his wrists and behind his back; the black hood was adjusted and the knotted noose was placed about the man's neck. Other than slightly supporting Cuellae because his knees were getting a bit weak, there wasn't anything for the two deputies stationed on both sides of the prisoner to do.

The scaffold consisted of a platform built out over the top rail of the second floor of the cells and the trap operated on hinges and was secured by a two-by-four with a long lever, which was released by the hangman who stood on the platform with the Cuellae. Since Sheriff Matlock was unable to secure a hemp rope, an ordinary five-eighths inch manila variety was used and it was suspended from an iron hook secured to the ceiling. The sheriff gave the signal just after four a.m. and the trap was released dropping Cuellae like a stone and after coming to a sudden halt with a creak of the rope the body twitched for a moment, then it hung limp with the head drooping far to one side.

Dr. J.D. Burrett and E.G. Balsam stepped forward, placed a stethoscope to Cuellae's heart and after a few moments they pronounced him dead. After hanging for a while the body was cut down and carried to a nearby cell to await the arrival of the undertaker. While Sheriff Matlock had sent out over fifty invitations the execution was only witnessed by between twenty-five and thirty officials and citizens.

Postscript:

Like former sheriff, George Hubbard who hanged William Brooks at Billings in 1899, Sheriff Matlock eventually became a jailer at the Yellowstone County Jail and seventeen years after he had hanged Cuellae at Billings in 1918, he guarded convicted murderer Henry Zorn while he was being temporarily housed at the Billings jail. Zorn was eventually returned to Miles City where he was hanged in April of 1935.

(Endnotes)

[1] Dr. Bertha Mackel was the first female physician to testify in a murder trial in Montana and her testimony had to be approved by the defense before it was offered.

[2] Juror Theodore Loveland was also listed as Theophilus G. Lovell.

[3] Juror James Prichard was also listed as James G. Prichett.

[4] R.S. Price had the contract to build the scaffold in White Sulphur Springs in 1884 to hang Joseph Hanna. "Rocky Mountain Husbandman" 8/28/1884, p3

[5] Prosecuting Attorney Walker later helped with the unsuccessful defense of Tony Vettere who was hanged in October of 1926.

[6] Sheriff Graham would later be called on to construct the gallows and stockade at Missoula for the hanging of Joe Vuckovich in February of 1922.

[7] Phoebe Lang and her family settled in the wild country on the Thompson River in the 1890's and lived there all her life. While Mr. Stollfuss never knew why his grandmother, Mrs. Lange was in Kalispell at the time of the LeBeau trial or why she had attended the sentencing but the woman told him about the sentencing on several occasions. Personal story by Chouteau County Clerk and Superintendent of Schools Larry Stollfuss, October of 2006.

[8] In an interview many years later Earl Fretwell recalled that only seven of the nine black men were involved with the murder and robbery. "Meagher County, An Early-Day Pictorial History 1867-1967" Meagher County Historical Society

[9] Earl F. Angell was born at Washington D.C. in 1890 and attended law school at Georgetown University. Angell where he graduated in 1913. In October of that same year Angell moved to Helena, Montana where he was admitted to the Bar. In 1916 he located at White Sulphur Springs where he was appointed as City Attorney and eventually he was elected as Meagher County Attorney in 1918 as a Democrat. "History of Montana" by Tom Stout Vol.2, p616

[10] Mr. Angell operated a hat factory at 21 East Broadway Street in Butte

[11] Philip Prilja was born in Montenegro and was thirty-five at the time of his death. He had come to the United States at age seventeen and a year later he was living in Butte. His last eleven years were spent as a Butte policeman and he was about to be reinstated on the force at the time of his murder. "Brady Citizen" 3/28/1921

Legal Hangings of the Roaring Twenties
(September 1920 through November 1929)

September 3, 1920
Alfred Lane

Location and Gallows: Lane was hanged at Forsyth in Rosebud County and he was the first man executed with ***Gallows No. Eighteen: (Sept. 1920): "Galloping Gallows" No. Six***. A description and complete history of this scaffold or any other can be found in the "Montana Gallows" chapter.
Description: The thirty-six-year-old quarter-breed Indian had dark complexion and a quiet manner
Crime: Murder of Harry Theade on April 26, 1920, near Hathaway.
Judge: George P. Jones
Prosecution: County Attorney Sam Crawford
Defense: Felkner F. Haynes of Forsyth
Sheriff: Henry Grierson
Distinction: Although a Lynch Mob had hanged Henry Hoefner at Forsyth in April of 1912, this was the only legal execution in Rosebud County.
Relics and Remnants: After being used to hang six other convicted murderers the famous Rosebud County "Galloping Gallows" that first executed Lane, eventually was sent to the state penitentiary at Deer Lodge where it is on display in the museum of the Old Montana Prison Complex. Another relic of the Lane case is the noose portion of the hangman's rope, which is also the property of the Old Montana Prison Museum at Deer Lodge.

A financial transaction, which had gone bad, resulted in the first and only legal execution in Rosebud County when the body of Harry Theade was found in the cellar of Alfred Lane's cabin near Hathaway on the morning of April 30, 1920. Lane had been renting the house from and working on the ranch of a Mr. Ben Benson who was a foreman for the Northern Pacific Railroad. Theade and Lane were said to have been friends and partners, and they had just returned from Miles City where they had trouble cashing a number of small checks.

Lane, who was raised in Chicago and had been living near Hathaway for about four years apparently had given a number of checks to his friend that didn't clear at Miles City, which put Theade in a financial bind as well as being embarrassed in front of the local residents. Twenty-three year old Harry Theade had lived in the county all of his life and he was very popular with all of the residents of the county. Evidently Theade went to Lane's place to confront him about the checks and he was killed.

After the young homesteader had been missing for three or four days Mr. Benson and Larry Rice investigated the Benson house where Lane lived alone. Lane hadn't reported for work for Mr. Benson and on the door of the house the renter had left a signed note saying that he was at the Webber Ranch, some three miles away. Benson and Rice entered the house where they found the body of Theade, which had been dead for at least three days.

The remains were found in the cellar under the house and the trap door in the floor was closed when the men entered the residence. It was reported that there was one wound in Theade's left shoulder and another in the right side, just above the abdomen. The position of the body and the markings on the floor indicated that the murdered man had struggled about before death had finally ended his suffering.

After leaving another neighbor, Arthur Lott to watch over the body, the two men went to call Sheriff Henry Grierson and the Rosebud County coroner. On the way they passed Alfred Lane on horseback as he was heading to his home but as they approached he veered off the road and took a southward route. As Rice and Benson continued down the road, Lane doubled back to his place where he found Mr. Lott standing by.

Mr. Lott ordered Lane to halt but the suspect took a parting shot with his 30-30 Winchester and then rode off. Sheriff Grierson wired for assistance from Custer County and Undersheriff Milligan and Deputy Bob Ogilvie went to Hathaway with the bloodhounds from the Industrial School at Miles City. In the meantime Sheriff Grierson organized a large number of well-armed men at Forsyth and started out after the suspect.

The fugitive remained at large a couple of days in the hills outside of Hathaway before sneaking back into town on foot to break into the West Mercantile on May 1, 1920. Lane entered the store through a side window and made off with some bacon, coffee, beans, sugar and a few other small articles. Before leaving the store, he wrote a note saying, "I am sorry to have to do this, Mr. West, but it is my only means of securing food. If I had time I would like to fix up your window."

Following the store robbery, the bloodhounds, two pups and a well-trained older dog, followed the trail of the fugitive for seven miles until the rain destroyed the scent. The officers continued to follow the tracks to where Lane had changed his shoes and made his escape. According to John Burgess, who was familiar with the country south of Hathaway, the only way the fugitive could be flushed out would be with a "rabbit drive" with hundreds of men. Besides being rough country, the ground was covered with small pines and cedars along with many holes that a man could easily hide in.

Finally on Tuesday, May 4, 1920, with only three rounds of ammunition remaining and with little food, shelter and nerve, Lane surrendered to Captain Sam B. Roberts. Lane later told the authorities that the posse had gotten terribly close to his position and that a couple of the riders nearly stepped on him in the brush. He said that he wasn't able to secure any assistance from the outlining ranchers and that life in the badlands was unbearable, with fires almost impossible to make because of the wet wood.

At his crowded arraignment before Judge James Read, Alfred Lane appeared very comfortable, as he pleaded not guilty to the charges. Standing in a slouching position, with one shoulder higher than the other he took in the proceedings without displaying displeasure, uneasiness, fear or regret. Lane was then transported to Miles City immediately after the hearing for safekeeping, as there were rumors that a "special organization was going to make an informal call on the prisoner sometime later that night."

Lane's trial opened on July 21, 1920, with self-defense being the plea but the evidence including the fact that the victim had been shot three times couldn't sustain it. After being out for an hour on the evening of July 22, and only deliberating for thirty-five minutes the jury found Lane guilty of murder in the first degree. At two o'clock on the next day, Judge Jones explained the state statutes concerning first-degree convictions and then sentenced Lane to death on the gallows on September 3.

The defendant was unmoved by the pronouncement and he scarcely moved a muscle or displayed any facial expression when he thanked the court for the sentence. The condemned man's behavior and attitude after being sentenced was described, as being remarkable and he never whimpered during his forty days in his death cell. No appeal was ever made for a new trial or executive clemency in Lane's behalf.

When asked later why he had shot the third round into Theade's body, Lane replied, "He was making such a noise that I thought I would stop his yelling." By 1920, The State of Montana along with the rest of the nation had been experiencing one of the worst crime waves and most of the citizens of the state were happy with how fast Alfred Lane was put on trial, convicted and how short the time was between sentencing and his execution.

As the new scaffold was being constructed inside the jail building on Wednesday, September 1, Lane remarked to Sheriff Grierson with a smile, "I notice you're moving in the rest of my furniture." After Lane ate a heavy supper he sat up late on his last night and he was willing to discuss any subject other than his hanging or the crime. Many folks in the community dismissed the theory that the motive of the murder had been over a forty-dollar check and they thought the dispute had been over a woman at Miles City.

The condemned man got dressed in a new suit while he talked with the Catholic priests, Fathers Trigoly and George E. LeDoux as the sheriff opened the cell door and told him the hour had come. It was said that Lane received the death warrant as calmly as he would have listened to a call for breakfast. The morning stars were giving way to the dawn and the blushing eastern horizon announced the approach of another day as Lane walked up the steps of the gallows as steady as the tick of a giant clock. After repeating the prayers of Father LeDoux and smiling to the priest, Lane said good-bye to the county attorney and sheriff. He said that he bore no grudge and he asked forgiveness, saying he wanted to leave the world with no enemies behind.

The self-confessed murderer continued to smile as the rope was being adjusted about his neck and the death mask finally covered his face. At 4:25 a.m. Sheriff Grierson pulled the lever that released the trap door, breaking Alfred Lane's neck and after six minutes he was pronounced dead. Immediately after the physician's verdict the remains were buried in the first cemetery in Forsyth, which was located at the southeast corner of Spruce and Cliff Streets. There were about forty spectators at the hanging including Sheriff Middleton of Custer County and the sheriff from Big Horn County.

Postscript:
Alfred Lane's parents were living somewhere in the East, but he never told the authorities where they resided. It was reported that he wrote to a brother earlier, telling him about his fate and to never let their parents know how he had died.

The famous gallows that Sheriff Grierson had built at Forsyth for the hanging of Alfred Lane was eventually used to execute Glenna Bolton and Joe Reagin at Hysham in 1923; Henry Zorn and George Criner at Miles City both in 1935, Frank Robideau at Columbus in 1938, and finally Lee Simpson in 1939, at Ryegate.

The Rosebud County "Galloping Gallows" was later sent to the state penitentiary at Deer Lodge and when the original prison closed in 1979, the ancient scaffold was erected in the old auditorium where it is still on display at the Old Montana Prison Museum. The hangman's rope may have been cut up for souvenirs as only the noose remains today and is also on display at the Old Montana Prison Museum at Deer Lodge.

August 26, 1921
Albert Yeik

Other Names: C.A. Davis; C.D. Neshisser; Albert Yek
Location and Gallows: Albert Yeik was hanged behind the jail at Dillon on ***Gallows No. Nineteen: (August 1921).***
Description: At the time of his execution Yeik was twenty-nine years old but he looked ten years older with his baldness and low sloping forehead. According to penitentiary records he was born at Red Oaks, Iowa; stood five feet, eight inches tall and weighed 155 pounds. He had a slim build with blue eyes, auburn hair with a sandy complexion. Yeik was listed as being Catholic, a single ranch worker, with good teeth, slim nose and a five-inch scar inside of his right forearm and an anchor tattooed on his left arm.
Crime: Murder of Sheriff Cyrus King Wyman at Monida on April 21, 1920.
Judge: Joseph C. Smith (brother of Governor Robert B. Smith)
Prosecution: County Attorney T.E. Gilbert and assisted by W.G. Gilbert of the firm of Rodgers and Gilbert.

Defense: William J. Cushing and C.W. Robinson of Dillon
Sheriff: Dan Mooney
Distinction: Yeik wasn't the first man hanged for murdering a Montana lawman, but he was the first man executed for killing a county sheriff and the last person to be legally put to death in Beaverhead County.
Relics and Remnants: A souvenir piece of the hangman's rope and an invitation to the Yeik execution is at the Gallatin County Historical Society Museum at Bozeman.

After a cowboy arrived in Monida on the evening of April 20, 1920, he made a bed for himself in the barn at the rear of the Summit Hotel. The next morning Delmar Torp, who was employed at the hotel, discovered the man and immediately recognized the man's Richardson saddle as belonging to his father. The boy immediately telephoned his father at Idaho Falls, Idaho with the information and the man called Dillon asking Sheriff C.K. Wyman to arrest the man at Monida.

The rancher from Idaho reported that the man was C.A. Davis and that he had stolen the saddle from him and the horse from another man. Sheriff Wyman arrived in Monida that same day on the 11:40 Oregon Short Line train and he walked to the Monida Hotel where the suspect was having lunch.

Wyman was fifty-three years old, serving his second term as the sheriff of Beaverhead County and he was married with an eighteen-year-old daughter. The lawman had gained fame in November of 1904 as a former deputy sheriff at Philipsburg when he killed the notorious Frank "Kid" Brady who had been terrorizing the country. When he first campaigned for the Beaverhead sheriff position he used the novel approach of walking through the county from ranch to ranch and house to house becoming personally acquainted with all of the miners, ranchers and farmers.

At the Monida Hotel, the sheriff tapped his man on the shoulder and informed C.A. Davis, actually Albert Yeik that he was under arrest. Even though he was warned that the suspect was a bad man, the sheriff evidently didn't take the necessary precautions as the fugitive offered no resistance or questioned the charges but only asked if he could get his coat from the barn. The officer agreed and two men left the hotel together and entered an alley towards the barn with Yeik in the lead. As the two men were turning to the rear of the building and were partially concealed from view, Yeik turned and fired his automatic pistol point blank twice into the officer's body.

The first bullet entered the sheriff's abdomen, entering the fifth rib and came out the back and as Sheriff Wyman pressed both of his hands to his body and bent over the assailant fired a second time, the bullet severing the sheriff's left thumb and entered above the liver and then it ranged downward and lodged in the pelvis. The fact that the victim's thumb had been shot off and the bullet ended up in the sheriff's pelvis proved that the second shot was fired as he was falling to the ground.

Yeik then ran to the corral, mounted his horse and raced out of the alley as James Robbins, a clerk at the Monida Mercantile having heard the shots, took a rifle from the store's stock and fired a number of rounds at the fleeing killer. One of the bullets glanced off a fence posts and inflicted a flesh wound on horse's jaw making it unmanageable and Yeik dismounted and headed over the train tracks returning fire all the way. While running along the railroad grade Yeik slipped off his chaps and hid them behind one of the telephone poles.

Meantime another Monida resident had been watching the drama through a pair of binoculars and noticed Yeik take refuge in an abandoned cabin on the E.F. Price Ranch about a mile and a half west of town. William W. Knott, James Robbins William Miller and Delmar Torp of Monida followed the gunman to the lonely cabin and kept their man held up with a steady stream of rifle fire.

Word of the slain sheriff was telegraphed to both Undersheriff Otto C. Gosman at Lima and Deputy Dan Mooney at Dillon and a special train was arranged to carry a posses to Monida. After being directed to the cabin by the observer, the one hundred-and-fifty-man posse then carefully made their way across the snow-covered field. Several members of the posse took up a position at a barn, which was about a hundred feet from the man's hideout and from the roof they began firing into the cabin. When there was no return fire, a number of men ran to the cabin with burning brands to set the shack on fire, but instead they tried to draw out the fugitive by breaking out the window.

Yeik was hiding in the cellar of the building and he wouldn't come out without the insurance of the sheriff's protection against a lynching. While at Monida he had made friends with two local dogs and both had followed him to the Price cabin and one of the animals was wounded during the shooting and it began to howl. It was later discovered that Yeik had choked the animal to death by using a noose made from a piece of rope, and then he stabbed it through the heart with his pocket knife just to keep it quiet. Finally the murderer surrendered after being assured that he would be protected from a Lynch Mob.

The murderer was first taken to Monida where he was placed under guard at the hotel and since feelings ran so high throughout the area and the residents were out to lynch him, Deputies Mooney and W.D. Ross along with J.W. Carney snuck the prisoner through a window of the establishment during the dark of night and took a freight train. As a large crowd of enraged citizens were meeting both the passenger and freight trains as they pulled into the station at Dillon, the officers and their prisoner left the freight in the stockyards and then hurried on to the county jail.

According to the deputies, Yeik slept on the freight all the way to Dillon and he wasn't in the least bit remorseful over the killing of the sheriff. He was housed in a double cell at the jail where he reportedly ate and slept well but spoke very little. At his arraignment, Yeik gave his name as C.A. Davis and he claimed that he had been hunting rabbits at the time the sheriff was shot and killed.

When arrested Yeik wore a pair of khaki trousers, black fur chaps, a woolen shirt, leather vest, large "forty-gallon" black hat, new woolen underwear, silk socks and a pair of good walking shoes. He was carrying twenty-six cents and strapped to his saddle was a raincoat and a mackinaw coat. He had a 30-30 Winchester rifle with nine shells, which had been hammered down, turning them into dum-dum bullets and a few days later Yeik's .32-caliber automatic revolver was located, along with five cartridges.

Records of the state penitentiary showed that Albert Yeik had been first convicted at Miles City for burglary in 1910, and then at Blaine County in June of 1913, for grand larceny and sentenced for three years as prisoner No. 4242. On November 4, 1913, Yeik escaped from the prison road camp in Flathead County and he was recaptured in June of 1914, in Oregon.

After having another year tacked on to his sentence for the escape, Yeik escaped from another work camp at Warm Springs in April of 1916, with only forty days left on his term by stealing two horses. Four days later he was recaptured at Big Hole and he finished out his additional term for that violation. As soon as he was released Yeik was again convicted of grand larceny at Deer Lodge County and he served until March 21, 1920. Yeik apparently assumed the name of C.A. Davis, from a cellmate of his at Deer Lodge.

After being released from prison in March of 1920, Yeik stole a saddle and a horse at Idaho Falls, and another horse from a railroad camp before burglarizing two homes at Dubois. He was also suspected of robbing a pool hall and a general store there and less than a month later he murdered Sheriff Wyman. Shortly after his initial hearing he began pretending he was insane by repeating ordinary phrases and counting imaginary chickens. In another attempt to prove his insanity, Yeik tore his bed to shreds and ripped out the electrical wires in his cell. The prisoner also tried a hunger strike for a day but his pains overtook him and he always ate heartily afterwards.

When Yeik's trial opened on May 17, 1920, the defendant continued his constant mumbling with an occasional yell and it was necessary for an officer to sit on each side of the prisoner to keep him in his chair. He would usually sit with his head in his hands, his hair matted and unkempt and because of his violent and unmanageable appearance Yeik was given a wide berth as he was brought in or taken out of the courtroom. After a day and a half the jury was finally selected and it was made up of the following citizens:

James D. Harrison	David Ingram	John H. Brundage
Robert L. Robertson	William Christensen	J. Robert Morton
George V. Patterson	Morton J. Robertson	William Rosenbaum
Martin Pierson	H.H. Soper	C.V. Garland

After the prosecution had built quite a case against the defendant, the defense attorneys tried to present facts to show that their client was insane at the time of the crime. When Yeik took to the stand he refused to answer any questions posed at him and the lead defense attorney took the witness chair and testified that he had never been able to hold a rational conversation with his client.

The courtroom was filled to capacity and overflowing into the doorways as well as the halls when the case was given to the jury on May 19, and after forty-five minutes they returned a verdict of guilty and fixed the punishment at death.

On May 24, 1920, Judge Smith sentenced Yeik to hang on the morning of June 25, and as the court made his pronouncement there were large beads of sweat seen on the convicted man's forehead. After returning to his cell Yeik broke down and asked that his mother not be informed of his fate, but that request wasn't honored.

That evening he was placed in a new cell with plenty of bedding and a three-man deathwatch was placed over him. Yeik's appetite was very good and on any given breakfast he would eat a porterhouse steak, four eggs, six hotcakes with syrup, bread, butter and coffee. During his stay at the county jail Yeik was never sick and he always appeared cheerful. His only visitors were his brother William and his spiritual adviser Reverend Father Fole.

Card playing was Albert Yeik's favorite diversion and he often played with the other inmates of the jail as well as his guards. He always sat up close to the bars of his cell where the cards were tossed to him as another prisoner dealt them out and bets were exchanged and the mythical pot would sometimes amount to ninety dollars or more. The prisoners had their own lingo such as, "You better settle out of court if you haven't got a better case," or "No, I'll fight the case in court."

Whenever a new prisoner was brought into the jail he was arraigned in the "Kangaroo Court" on a charge of breaking into the Beaverhead County jail without the consent of the inmates. The fines assessed out of any funds in the custody of the sheriff were turned in to the tobacco fund for the prisoners. Yeik ended up presiding over the mock court, where the prisoners were brought to the bars of his cage.

The condemned man wore a pair of dark glasses during those mock trials and in the murky light of the cell the glasses gave him a ghastly appearance. Yeik conducted his court with regular procedure and remained serious throughout the mimic trials, admonishing the prisoner that it was against jail etiquette to enter such a place without proper preliminaries.

On June 14, 1920, Yeik's attorneys secured an appeal to the Supreme Court and his life was preserved for another year before the high court denied the appeal on June 27, 1921, and Judge Smith re-sentenced Yeik to be hanged between the hours of three a.m. and six a.m. on August 26, 1921. Yeik reportedly showed no emotion at his second sentencing but he accused Judge Smith and the Supreme Court of not granting him a fair and impartial trial.

During Yeik's stay at the county jail, Deputy Dan Mooney was elected to the office of sheriff, replacing interim Sheriff Grossman. After the re-sentencing of Yeik, Governor Joseph M. Dixon was petitioned for executive clemency but the public didn't show much support for the action because the majority of the folks were disgusted by the nature of the murder. While Governor Dixon commuted the death sentences of Steve Bryne and Theodore Chronopolous awaiting execution at Silver Bow County, he decided not to interfere with in the Yeik case.

Just three days before the hanging, William Yeik, the brother of the prisoner made a personal appeal to the Governor in an attempt to save his brother's life and since the condemned man had refused to talk about his life; his brother told what details he knew about his sibling's life. As a boy, Albert was just an ordinary youngster and he was never in any kind of trouble and at the age of thirteen he reportedly ran away from home like many other boys seeking their fortune and he stayed away for four years.

At seventeen Yeik returned to Minnesota where he found his mother bed ridden and he became a model son, staying home and caring for her. As time past his mother's health improved and Albert's longing for adventure began to increase. While his mother begged her son to remain, an older man convinced Yeik to leave home and to come out West.

Yeik's family heard nothing of the young man for twelve years until the letter came from the wandering man with the awful news of his fate. William Yeik came immediately to Dillon where he assisted his brother in every way he could, supplying the funds to carry his brother's case to the Supreme Court at quite a sacrifice to himself personally.

William Yeik remained with his brother during his last week and he didn't go back home until Albert's body was buried at Dillon. Besides his invalid mother and brother, Yeik was survived by two sisters and all of his family members except for his mother were aware that he had been hanged.

The prisoner passed his last night playing cards with Deputy Sam Ditty, Undersheriff Bill Ross and Police Chief Charles E. Nelson. He ate a midnight meal of fried chicken, French fried potatoes and he visited with his attorney, C.W. Robinson and his brother. At three o'clock in the morning he listened intently as Sheriff Dan Mooney read the various court orders, which demanded the death penalty and the condemned man commented that he would surprise the people of Dillon by dying like a man.

Only a limited number of invitations were issued for the hanging and no women or children were allowed to witness the execution. Deputies had cleared an entire block around the jail and no boys under the age of twenty-one were permitted on any of the surrounding rooftops or even to be seen at upstairs windows before the hanging. Among the witnesses to the hanging were Sheriff Wyman's father, Alphonso Wyman of Philipsburg and his two brothers, Henry and Forest.

As the clock in the tower of the courthouse tolled 4:30, Deputy Sam Ditty led Yeik from his cell flanked by Sheriff Mooney and Undersheriff Ross and followed by Father Gallagher of Butte. The gallows had been constructed in advance but it wasn't erected until the day before the hanging in a small enclosure between the courthouse and the jail. Some reports have stated that Yeik was executed at the same location as Harding in 1887, but old timers who were around for both of the hangings said that they were at two different places.

At about four a.m. the invited guests were seen entering the enclosure, which was accessed through the front door of the jail and the electric lights, which were especially strung up for the hanging were switched on and the flickering illumination on the gallows added a weird somberness to the already quiet crowd. After surveying the scene, Yeik turned to the sheriff and jokingly commented, “You’ve got quite an audience; you must be going to pull off a grandstand performance.”

There was reportedly a slight breeze that rippled through the cool morning stillness; there was a faint haze that covered the surrounding mountains, and only the crow of an early rising rooster disturbed the quiet of the still-sleeping city. The execution enclosure in the courtyard had been walled off from the curious eyes by a fourteen-foot wooded fence.

While about a hundred and fifty men gained entrance with their special printed invitations hundreds of others jockeyed for positions at various knothole viewpoints. Among the invited guests were Sheriff Larry Duggan, Undersheriff Dale O. Robinson of Silver Bow County, Sheriff C.L. Beal of Deer Lodge County, Deputy Brown of Philipsburg, Undersheriff Wilson of Yellowstone County, Sheriff Charles C. Esgar and Deputy Marble of Gallatin County.

Yeik wore a pair of dark trousers and a black pullover sweater along with a slight smile on his face as he mounted the six steps to the gallows without assistance. The condemned man maintained his smile and co-operated with the deputies as the harnesses were fitted around his body. When the noose was placed around his neck, Yeik requested that the five-eighths inch Manila rope be loosened a bit and then he recognized Chief Nelson in the crowd he gave him a wink. After the police chief returned the wink the condemned man moistened his lips, took a deep breadth and in a clear and audible voice, which was heard clearly throughout the enclosure, he proclaimed, “I am going to die like a dead game sport. That’s all. Goodbye.”

The condemned man then shook hands with Sheriff Mooney and Undersheriff Ross, and as he was reaching for the hand of Deputy Ditty, who had guarded him for the past seventeen months, he said, “Good-bye Sam, God Bless you and I wish you all the luck in the world.” He then requested a final adjustment to the knot on the noose and then he shouted out: “Let ‘er go!”

As a deputy was binding his legs, Yeik looked down to see that he was standing squarely on the trap and then his hands were fastened behind his back and the black hood lowered over his head. The trap was designed to be was sprung by a rope, which passed under the gallows, through the fence and into a tent where the executioner, the identity of whom was never made public was concealed. At 4:47 a.m. Sheriff Mooney gave the signal and Albert Yeik fell through the trap with a quick jerk followed by a dull sickening thud.

Watching from the window of the sheriff's office, less than five feet from the gallows was Alphonso Wyman, the eighty-five-year-old father of the slain sheriff. Not once during the execution did his aged eyes leave the murderer's body and when the noose snapped taut, he reportedly lowered his head into his hands and he remained quiet for several minutes.

Eight minutes after the trap had dropped, Drs. R.H. Ryburn of Dillon and Buchen of Wisdom pronounced Albert Yeik dead and at five o'clock the rope was cut and the body was lowered into the pit. The remains were taken to the Brundage Undertakers where many folks visited to look at the dead man with the cynical smile still present on his face. Father Gallagher conducted the funeral at eleven a.m. and the remains were later interred in Potter's Field at Mountain View Cemetery.

By nine a.m. on August 27, 1921, the massive gallows that rose thirteen feet in the air and, which required two days to be constructed by Dillon carpenters, Art Wimple and Jay Holtz were removed along with the high board fence and the pit beneath the trap was filled in. The gallows were stored away at the Beaverhead County Fairgrounds, but know one knows what ever happened to the massive timbers. The hanging site itself was eventually paved over and it was part of the rear parking lot.

February 17, 1922
Joseph Vuckovich

Other Names: Gjuro I. Wukecvich; Joe Wines

Location and Gallows: When Joseph Vuckovich was hanged behind the jail at Missoula he was the last victim of ***Gallows No. Nine: (Feb. 1888): "Galloping Gallows" No. Three***. Although the original timbers of this most famous of all Montana gallows were deemed inadequate for the Vuckovich hanging, the original weight and pulleys were used in the Missoula execution.

Description: Vuckovich was a thirty-three-year-old Serbian from the Balkans who stood five foot, eight inches tall and he weighed about 140 pounds. The prisoner had gray eyes, dark complexion and smooth shaven face with two gold false teeth that filled the upper fronts.

Crime: Murder of Mrs. Jerry Shea, and mother of two on February 12, 1921

Judge: Theodore Lentz

Prosecution: County Attorney John L. Campbell and assisted by Edward C. Mulroney

Defense: James L. Wallace

Sheriff: George A. Cole

Distinction: Vuckovich was the last man in Montana to be hanged on a Jerk-Type Gallows.

On the early morning of February 12, 1921, a thirteen-year-old boy saw Joseph Vuckovich, using the alias Joe Wines, walking east on North First with twenty-four-year-old Mrs. Jerry Shea. Near the Burkhart

Grocery Vuckovich forced the woman off the sidewalk while shouting in her face. Moments later a shot was heard and the man was seen running west on North First by Mrs. William C. Cates. Incidentally her husband, William Cates was later convicted of killing a revenue agent and he was scheduled to be hanged at Missoula in 1933, but his sentence was eventually commuted to life in prison. Edwin Anderson, a switchman for the Northern Pacific was one of the first persons to reach Mrs. Shea and he called the police and ambulance from the office of the Stone-Ordean-Wells Company.

Vuckovich had been dealing in moonshine in the area and he was known to have had several affairs with area women. Several years earlier he was forced to leave Darby after having relations with a woman and then threatening her before being run out of Hamilton for the same reason. The neighbors said that Mr. Shea knew that Vuckovich had been hitting on his wife but he was confident of her loyalty and so he took no action. Vuckovich and another Serbian, Peter Kossich were arrested on January 25, 1921, by Police Chief William J. Moore following a disturbance at the Jerry Shea house where Vuckovich had slapped Mrs. Shea around. He then took her two daughters, ages five and three as far as the gate of the front yard before jumping into a car with Kossich and driving around the block.

Chief Moore noticed that the suspect was carrying a gun as he drove by and when they didn't stop the officer fired into the car, whereas Vuckovich tossed out the weapon and they stopped the vehicle. The two men were later released because Mrs. Shea wouldn't press charges against the two but Patrolman Alex D. Ross later arrested Vuckovich on a charge of bootlegging, but he was released after spending a few days in the city jail. As a routine procedure, Jerry Shea was brought in for questioning but he was quickly released and because of prior confrontations with the victim, Joe Wines, or Joseph Vuckovich was the primary murder suspect.

The day after the murder, E.C. Henry of Grant Creek reported that a man had robbed him at his ranch after taking him in out of the cold and giving him something to eat. Mr. Henry said that while he went to Missoula to buy groceries the man matching the description of Vuckovich had run off with food items and some clothes including a dark woolen shirt, woolen trousers, vest jacket with the initials, "E.C.H.," lambskin coat and a black soft-brim cowboy hat. Mr. Henry also told the Missoula authorities that Vuckovich had mentioned that he was heading for Butte. By then Undersheriff Henry Clemens had sent out a description of the suspect to every peace officer within two hundred miles of Missoula and Deputy Alva C. Baird had discovered that Vuckovich had traded a rifle for an automatic pistol at a local pawnshop several days before the killing of Mrs. Shea.

Following up on a sighting by Conductor Ike Harpster of the Butte bound train, on February 16, 1921, Special Deputy Sheriff Harry P. Phillips and Signalman L.J. Lafferty came across Vuckovich walking up the tracks about five miles west of Bearmouth. The men found a .32-

caliber automatic pistol in the prisoner's coat pocket but he didn't resist. The man confessed that he had shot Mrs. Shea to Deputies Phillips and Barney Wheeler as they were bringing him back to Missoula on the train and he explained to the officers that when he got mad he really got mad. After confessing, the prisoner said that once he had left the Henry Ranch in Grant Creek he went over into the Rattlesnake Creek country and then made his way to Bonner where he spent Sunday night, February 13. Monday morning he continued eastward for about twenty miles from Missoula where he spent the night.

During the day Vuckovich was kept in the upstairs cell with the other prisoners but he was kept in his own cell at night. The wall of Vuckovich's cell was covered with pictures of female motion picture stars and on a shelf above his bunk there was a Hyacinth flower, which had been a present from a woman visitor. On another shelf there were two Christmas cards displayed and beside his bed was a photo of his cousin, Mike Vuckovich, who was a commander in the Serbian Army. The prisoner had another cousin in the service of the Serbian government and a sister, Mary who lived at Butte at the time of his incarceration.

When Joe Vuckovich was arraigned on February 24, 1921, he plead not guilty to the charge of murder and after examining eighty-eight men of Missoula County the following jury was seated on March 22, 1921:

John D. McCormick	Thomas L. Bisson	A.E. Dahlberg
George W. Reeves	John McCulloch	Ira Allport
Lucien J. Croonenberghs	Charles Lindborg	Albert B. Kimball
Clayton E. Sanborn	Henry C. Kath	Jacob Barer

The defense wouldn't let Vuckovich testify on his own behalf trying instead to get the medical officials to testify that Mrs. Shea may have shot herself and when that didn't succeed they tried to convince the jury that her husband had done the dirty deed. In the end, the jury wasn't convinced and after deliberating for three hours they returned a guilty verdict. The defendant appeared to be unmoved by both the verdict and Judge Lentz's sentence of death.

Following the sentencing, a deathwatch was placed on Vuckovich, which was made up of Henry DeKraay, Thomas Bishop and Ike Abernathy.[1] But on December 31, 1921, the county commissioners after reviewing their budget voted unanimously to lift the deathwatch over the condemned man while his case was pending before the Montana Supreme Court. After the high court affirmed the district court's decision in the first week of January of 1922, Judge Lentz ordered the clerk of court to set the Vuckovich case for ten o'clock on January 10.

There were reportedly marked changes in the prisoner's appearance since his arrest. When first placed in custody Vuckovich had a ruddy complexion and a vigorous physic and by January of 1922, his color was sallow and he had lost weight. His spirits were still good and he had always steadfastly maintained his innocence but while Judge Lentz briefly reviewed the case, Vuckovich was quite pale and he was trembling and working at his handcuffs nervously.

When Judge Lentz asked if the defendant had any reason why sentencing shouldn't be passed Defense Attorney Wallace formerly declared that the court was without jurisdiction; that Vuckovich's conviction had not been affirmed by the Supreme Court; that the defendant's constitutional rights had been overridden and if executed it would be without authority. After listening to the defense attorney, Judge Lentz again asked the defendant if he had any reason why he should be sentenced and Vuckovich stepped forward and in broken English he said that he was innocent and that he didn't get a fair trial.

After listening to the defendant, Judge Lentz sentenced Vuckovich to be hanged on Friday, February 17, 1922, and for the third time in less than a year a deathwatch was ordered for the condemned man and the guards assigned this time were Thomas Bishop, Henry DeKraay and D.R. Mills. The condemned man was confident that his friends would come to his aid by raising the necessary funds to carry his case to the United States Supreme Court.

The Reverend Jesse Lacklen of the Methodist Church caused quite a stir at Missoula on Sunday, January 15, 1922, when in his sermon he declared that no man should ever be hanged and he urged for reform in how our country punished its prisoners. He questioned the jury that had convicted Joe Vuckovich and implied that he wasn't given a fair trial. Within days the jury published a letter of their own in the "Missoulian" defending their actions and then condemned the Reverend for calling for strict law enforcement against his pet issue, prohibition while taking a soft stance on violent crime. The jurors pointed to examples where Reverend Lacklen had called for restricted rights for bootleggers while he claimed that murderers were treated harshly.

Meanwhile Sheriff George A. Cole began the preparations for the execution and after witnessing several hangings in the Philippine Islands during the Spanish American War along with being present for the execution of Louis Mott at Missoula in March of 1904, the sheriff decided to use a jerk-type scaffold and to have a stockade erected once again just south of the jail in the courtyard. The sheriff ordered the stockade be built to extend from the street to the courthouse and then south to the sidewalk and he had originally planned to use the same scaffold that was used for the Mott hanging but after a close inspection of the death machine at Deer Lodge he decided to use the weight, trap release and the pulleys of the ancient 1889 gallows but ordered new timbers be assembled at Missoula.

On January 30, 1922, former sheriff, David Graham, then a general contractor living at 315 East Cedar was granted the contract to build both the stockade and the new scaffold for the execution. As sheriff of Missoula County in 1906, Mr. Graham had witnessed the hanging of Miles Fuller at Butte and he was familiar with the ancient scaffold, which was later used in the Mott execution. The ten-foot board fence enclosed the south door of the jail on Pine Street on the southeast corner of Woody and it extended eastward across the driveway to the Missoula County

Courthouse and then along the sidewalk west to a line even with the west side of the jail.

Since the all important hardware of the original 1889 Gallows were used, the scaffold was most likely built from the same plans of the ancient death machine, which stood about twelve feet tall and it resembled a simple child's swing with its two uprights and a heavy crossbar. The lumber for the stockade and the gallows was delivered to the jail yard on January 31, 1922, and the following day the condemned man began hearing the saws and hammers of the carpenters.

Due to the fact that the ground was frozen solid it was necessary that small bon fires were started to thaw the soil for the digging of the four main postholes and it was reportedly quite a sight to see small children playing around the dancing flames of the five or six small fires while men were carrying lumber and Mr. Graham barking orders in the jail yard. While the carpenters were preparing the scaffold and stockade, a "Missoulian" reporter called on the condemned man on February 2, 1922, where Vuckovich was seen on his folding cot playing the card game of "Pedro" with Special Deputies Tom Bishop and DeKraay. The prisoner told the reporter that while he knew what all the sawing and hammering meant, he didn't think he would hang.

The prisoner was very friendly and with his pleasing manner he was considered one of the most popular men at the jail. The newspaperman stated that while Vuckovich seemed quite polite, his sharp black eyes suggested that the Serbian had a quick and bad temper. According to his deathwatches, the man turned into his jailhouse blankets at ten o'clock each night and he slept soundly and his appetite was always good and the only complaint he had was understandable, the boredom of prison life.

There wasn't anything to do in his cell but play cards and read and Vuckovich wasn't much of a reader since he only had one year of schooling and that was when he was a young boy in Serbia. He could read and write English fairly well, which he had picked up along the way while working but he never learned a trade and he was a common laborer while working mainly in the Bitterroot Valley for Walter L. Moody of Chicago.

Joseph Vuckovich came to the United States in 1907, when he was nineteen from Belgrade, Serbia where he was born on November 16, 1888. He said that his parents were religious and the family walked three miles to attend the Greek Orthodox Church. According to the prisoner, he started working at age ten on the family farm of forty acres, which raised grapes and other fruit. He had two sisters and two brothers that all remained in Europe and the prisoner never knew if his mother was still living, as his letters back home had never been answered.

During his time in jail at Missoula, two cousins from Wyoming were the only family members to visit Vuckovich and while his family seemed to have abandoned him, some of his friends and acquaintances along with many curious strangers called on him every day. Along with visitors the prisoner received a great deal of mail, letters from cranks as well as people showing a morbid interest in his fate. During his confinement for almost a year, Vuckovich lost about seven pounds and he became quite pale since he was only allowed to exercise in a small corridor in the jail.

Meanwhile the defense attorneys argued before Federal Judge George M. Bourquin in Helena on January 25, 1922, that Vuckovich should be released from jail on a writ of habeas corpus. Ronald Higgins of the District Attorney's office argued against the motion while James L. Wallace stated that the remittance filed by the Montana Supreme Court affirming the district court's decision was invalid because only three commissioners[2] of the high court had signed it.

When they lost their appeal in the Federal Court, the defense appealed to the U.S. Supreme Court, not only on habeas corpus proceedings but because one of the jurors in the case was not a citizens of the United States, as required by law; that the bullet used in evidence was removed from the murder victim's head after the body was exhumed from the grave and the remains were not properly guarded.

An eighteen-year-old girl from the Bitterroot Valley called on the jail with her mother during the first week of February and filed a news story with the "Missoulian." In her news story the young women reported that she was first given a tour of the facility including the woman's ward, which she described as being much cleaner and more comfortable than the men's quarters.

The young reporter was introduced to the sheriff's wife and Mrs. Cole showed her the jail's kitchen, which was said to have been the "cheeriest place" in the facility. The spic and span kitchen was under the care of Mrs. Cole and her assistant, Mrs. Jones and the women explained how and when the prisoners were fed and that Vuckovich wasn't given a knife or fork and that Mrs. Cole personally fed him.

Mrs. Cole said that she didn't want Joe to be hanged and she certainly didn't want her husband to do it, but she conceited that because it was his job, she expected him to carry out the execution. The reporter described the sheriff's wife as a very kind person who showed her emotion for the men she cared for and she explained that she had been horribly affected by the sound of the workers constructing the scaffold, and she didn't think a man could be sentenced to death on purely circumstantial evidence. When the young woman met with the prisoner he was dressed in neat clothes and his hair was well brushed. As she met him in the corridor the other prisoners respected their privacy and they fell back to their own cells.

Mrs. Cole and the reporter followed Vuckovich into his cell along with one of the deathwatches and he offered the young woman the only chair in the cell while he sat on the cot with Mrs. Cole. When the reporter commented on all of the pictures, posters and news clipping on the cell wall, the deputy explained that Vuckovich was allowed to paint the wall and he had placed the items on it as it dried. Vuckovich had a pleasant talk with the two women and as the reporter was leaving she said that she would send him other newspaper articles for his collection.

Although the United States Supreme Court held that the defense should proceed on a writ of error, the attorneys announced that their funds were exhausted and they weren't able to legally stop the execution. By February 4, 1922 the condemned man had sent cablegrams to Montenegro and to Serbia and several telegrams to the Serbian embassy at Washington D.C. and to a man named Vuckovich living in Minneapolis.

While the officials at Missoula couldn't read the contents of the cables, each one of the messages contained the date February 17, 1922, and signed Guro I. Wukecvich, the true name of the prisoner. Also by then the stockade was half finished and Sheriff Cole had sent out the invitations for the execution and returned from Deer Lodge with the three-hundred some-pound weight and the other necessary hardware for the scaffold.

In a final effort to save the life of his client, Vuckovich's attorney sent a telegram to Governor Joseph M. Dixon asking for a reprieve sighting the forty-five hundred Missoula County residents and some twelve hundred other state citizens who had signed petitions requesting the top executive commute the prisoner's sentence to life in prison. One of the signers of the petition was William Matlock who had served with Vuckovich in the county jail and who had recently been acquitted of a murder charge. He said that Vuckovich was every inch a gentleman and in the five months he was in lock up with the man he never once said a bad word about anyone.

Although Governor Dixon had earlier commuted three death sentences at Butte during his administration he refused to commute Vuckovich's appointment with death. Vuckovich carefully clipped out the news article about the Governor's decision and after filing the memento with the others in his collection, the condemned man spent the rest of the evening as he often did, swapping stories with his deathwatch.

To limit the crowds of visitors at the jail, Sheriff Cole issued orders forbidding admission of the curious folks and only admitted friends of the condemned man including Reverend Father Broeckert of St. Francis Xavier and Reverend Henry H. Kumnick, pastor of the Evangelical Luthern Church who made regular semi-weekly visits to the county jail. All the preparations for the execution had been completed by February 9, 1922, and it was necessary to keep the stockade locked at all times to prevent the children from swinging on the ropes and climbing the timbers of the gallows.

Two days before the scheduled execution, Sheriff Cole and Deputy James Teevan carefully inspected the gallows including the drop and the pulleys. About the time the rope was being stretched with heavy sandbags, a married woman reportedly came to the jail requesting to see the death machine. After a few minutes inside the enclosure with the gallows the woman ran into the sheriff's office where she cried horribly and then without saying a word she mysteriously ran out of the jail. There was much speculation that she had been just another of the many women who the infamous woman-killer had known or she was possibly just a sensitive person who had felt sorry for the condemned man.

The day before the hanging County Attorney Campbell spent about two hours with the condemned man who had asked the prosecutor to intercede on his behalf with the governor. All he wanted was a reprieve from the top executive so that he could have time to appeal to the Board of Pardons and Mr. Campbell told the prisoner straight out that he honestly believed that he was guilty and that he should die for his crime. Without the assistance from the prosecuting attorney, Vuckovich sent his boyhood friend, George Chekovich of Butte to the telegraph office to send a message to the Serbian Diplomatic Consul at Washington D.C.

At about 11:30 p.m. Al Hultman of the Grill Café brought in a big meal for the condemned man, which included cream of tomato soup, a whole chicken with cream gravy, peas in butter, sliced tomatoes, celery, green onions, radishes, French fried potatoes, cheese, apple pie a-la-mode and topped off with a number of cigars. During his last evening the prisoner wrote many letters to his relatives and friends in Serbia and then he made arrangements with George Chekovich concerning the disposal of his remaining property and his burial at the Serbian Cemetery at the mining city.

Besides George Chekovich, who was allowed to spend most of the evening with Vuckovich, the condemned man had several visitors during the day including the Reverends Jesse Lacklen, and H.H. Kumnick and Father Joseph Stack. Joe Vuckovich wrote and placed an advertisement in the "Missoulian" thanking his many supporters who had signed the petition to save his life and the day after his death George Chekovich accompanied his remains to Butte.

While the prisoner spent his last night sleeping, the scaffold was again being inspected and tested and armed men were patrolling around the new stockade made of shiny yellow boards on the south end of the jail yard. Vuckovich was awakened from a sound sleep just an hour before the execution and it was said that he was the calmest person in the jail. Vuckovich refused any narcotics to calm his nerves and other than a small drink of whisky after his evening meal he wasn't administered any stimulants.

Soon after five o'clock in the morning the doorbell of the jail began to ring and a steady stream of special deputies were admitted to handle any possible trouble and at half past the hour George Chekovich arrived to say good-bye to his friend as a priest was giving Vuckovich counsel and the death warrant was being read to him. As he left his death cell the prisoner told the officers: "Good morning Boys," and then he greeted the two hundred witnesses outside with, "Good morning everybody."

With his arms and wrists bound with heavy straps, Vuckovich walked firmly without assistance to the gallows as the Marsh Undertakers hearse was parked just outside of the front doors of the county jail and about one hundred and fifty people were surrounding the stockade trying to get a peek at the execution. Many other folks observed the hanging from trees and nearby rooftops and the crowd, which was made up of many women was said to have been very quiet and respectful.

Inside the enclosure there were at least fifty armed men to prevent problems during the execution by any of Vuckovich's friends or countrymen and other guards with weapons were stationed at the courthouse windows where they would have clear shots at any attackers. Meanwhile inside the stockade there were cries of, "Down in front" from several of the witnesses and the spectators nearest to the scaffold knelt down. In all, there were nearly two hundred witnesses in the enclosure including Martin Hutchens, the editor of the "Missoulian"

Deputy Teevan strapped Vuckovich's ankles together and after Sheriff Cole had placed the noose around the prisoner's neck, Vuckovich said, "I pray to God and Jesus Christ that they may get the one who got me into this, and take him and punish him in the fire. Of course, I am losing my life as innocent as any man that was here."

After Reverend Kumnick offered a prayer and the condemned man repeated the last rites of the Lutheran Church, Deputy Teevan tied the black hood around the prisoner's head and a moment later, at 6:11 a.m., the trap was sprung. The 320-pound weight catapulted the condemned man two feet off the ground and after ten and a half minutes the county physicians pronounced Joseph Vuckovich had died of strangulation.

Double Hanging of Glenna M. Bolton and Joseph B. Reagin February 10, 1923

In the late fall of 1921, Joseph B. Reagin and Glenna M. Bolton were two young men who were running around and looking for trouble in the Horse Creek country, which is in the southern part of Treasure County near the Big Horn County line. Some of the residents suspected that the boys were trying to start a moonshine-still and needing startup funds they decided to burglarize the residence of Mrs. Nancy Gambol near the McRea Post Office while she was visiting her relatives in Missouri. After battering down the front door of Mrs. Gambol's house, Bolton and Reagin stole bedding and other household articles including some dishes and utensils.

To cover up their crime the boys built a big fire in the cook stove; opened the door of the fire box and stuck a chunk of wood into the fire and rested the other end on a wooden chair. They then poured kerosene into a wash-pan and set it on the floor so that when the wood chunk burned off, it would fall into the fuel and set the shack on fire. The plan didn't work and Jess Gambol, checking on his mother's things, discovered the broken door and reported the incidence to Treasure County Sheriff Jess Cunningham. Since Reagin and Bolton were considered rough necks and wild boys, they were of course suspected of all the crimes in the neighborhood including the burglarizing of Mrs. Gambol's place.

On December 9, 1921, Treasure County Sheriff T.J. Cunningham, Undersheriff Irving Keeler and Jess Gambol went to Glenn Bolton's house on Horse Creek about thirty-five miles south of Hysham. After being admitted into the home they spotted a bedspread that belonged to Mrs. Gambol and the officers noticed other items as well but they didn't possess a search or an arrest warrant. Mrs. Glenn Bolton was bedridden in the house with a broken leg and so the sheriff told Deputy Keeler to remain in the house to keep an eye on the stolen items while he returned to Hysham to secure the proper warrants on the excuse of getting a doctor for the woman's wound. It would take the sheriff until the following morning to return to the ranch and Deputy Keeler was settling in when Sam Pope stopped by for a visit.

After the sheriff had gone, Glenn Bolton left the house under the pretense of getting some camphor from a neighbor for his ailing wife while Reagin was at the home of Bolton's mother, Amanda J. Bolton, some three miles away. At about dark Glenn met with Reagin at the Brazille Water Gap as he was returning to his home with the medicine and the two men planned to stage a hold up to rob the deputy of the stolen goods in order to clear themselves. They returned to Amanda Bolton's home where they secured a large handkerchief and a piece of material for a mask and then went to Glenn's residence. They agreed that Reagin would wait until Bolton had time to enter the house and inform his wife and Sam Pope of the plan so they wouldn't be unduly excited.

Bolton entered the house at about ten o'clock that night and Joe Reagin soon followed him wearing a mask over his face and armed with a revolver. The Bolton cabin was a one-room affair but it was partitioned off with a canvas curtain that separated it in half. As Reagin entered the house he cocked his .45-caliber Frontier model six-shooter and ordered everyone to throw up their hands.

Everyone complied with the order except for Undersheriff Keeler who was sitting with his legs crossed and his hands locked over his knees. Apparently the officer recognized Reagin's voice and when he put his foot down and was about to say something, Reagin shot and killed him. Reagin then gathered up the stolen items and burned them and then he took the deputy's gun as well as Bolton's weapon and then fled on horseback into the nearby mountains. Bolton told Sam Pope that they would tell the authorities that a short man with whiskers and riding a gray horse had committed the murder.

Sheriff Cunningham organized a posse of about a hundred men including Sheriff C.E. Thompson and Undersheriff Denver Sherman of Rosebud County and the sheriffs of Custer and Big Horn Counties to trail the fugitive into the Sarpy country of Big Horn County. Three weeks earlier Reagin had gotten into a fight and he had received knife wounds to the neck and head and the posse was given orders to shoot on sight at a man with a white bandage around his head.

After evading arrest for twenty-four hours, Reagin snuck back to the Mrs. Amanda Bolton place under the cover of darkness for food and news on the third day and after knocking on the door and hearing unfamiliar voices the murderer jumped on his horse and made a break for it when posse members, William E. Williamson, Philip Isaac and W.J.

Noble bolted from the house. Williamson ran a meat market at Hysham and it was his idea to watch the Bolton place, thinking sooner or later Joe would be looking for something to eat. While riding off, Reagin was shot just above the knee by Williamson's 30-30 and he fell from his horse.

Undersheriff Denver Sherman, Williamson and Noble loaded the prisoner into a car and they escorted Reagin to the county jail at Hysham and then on Sunday morning Glenn Bolton was arrested at his home and charged with being an accomplice in the murder of Officer Keeler. Bolton admitted that even after he and Sam Pope had been deputized by the undersheriff to help guard the stolen items, he warned Reagin that the deputy was in the house. When asked by the authorities why he hadn't warned the deputy, Bolton said he didn't dare cross Reagin.

At the preliminary hearing held on Monday, December 12, Joe Reagin pled guilty to the charge of murder while Bolton said that he was innocent. The men were scheduled for separate trials and Felker F. Haynes of Forsyth was assigned to represent Bolton and the firm of Young and Young of Forsyth was appointed to defend Reagin who with his counsel changed his plea to innocent.

After their trials, Reagin and Bolton were placed in adjoining cells and they were considered model prisoners and other than an occasional quarrel, the two men were friendly to each other during their long confinement in the county jail. Bolton's repeated assertion that he had nothing to do with the killing of Undersheriff Keeler seemed to enrage Reagin, who freely admitted to the shooting and charged Bolton of making all of the plans.

On Tuesday afternoon, January 2, 1923, Reagin and Bolton made their last appearance in court when they were re-sentenced to death by Judge George Horkan. The two prisoners were brought into the courtroom, Reagin walking with a slight limp from his leg wound, by Philip Isaac and W.E. Williamson who had become sheriff and undersheriff of Treasure County. Sheriff Philip Isaac assumed office in January of 1923, and one of his first official duties was the hanging of Bolton and Reagin. Even before becoming sheriff, Mr. Isaac had taken part in the case, as he was in on the arrest of Reagin and was one of the twelve jurors that found him guilty of murder.

Sheriff Isaac borrowed the scaffold from Rosebud County, which had been used to hang Alfred Lane in September of 1920, and the gallows was erected and tested several times inside the high-fenced enclosure behind what was the courthouse building, later Irv's Place. The stairs, which went up to the back door of the saloon were utilized as the steps to the gallows, which was built to accommodate only one man at a time. The noise caused by the carpenters erecting the scaffold just outside the jail on Monday, February 5, 1923, aroused the curiosity of the prisoners and at first Bolton became very nervous but eventually the two condemned men weren't concerned about the activity.

Mrs. Emily Reagin never failed her son and she worked day and night trying to save Joe. Reagin's sister, Mrs. Filmore of Casper,

Wyoming made a last ditch effort to convince Governor Joseph Dixon to intervene in the executions and although he had played an instrumental role in their prosecution, no one tried harder to secure a reprieve from Governor Dixon to save the lives of Bolton and Reagin than State Attorney General Wellington D. Rankin.

The two condemned men didn't give up hope that the Governor would commute their sentence until Sheriff Isaac read the death warrants to them at 2:50 a.m. Friday morning, February 10. During their last afternoon and evening the two prisoners were visited by their mothers and sisters and they spent most of their last hours in Bible study and playing music on their harmonicas.

Just before daylight on Friday, and after receiving a prayer from Reverend G.B. Nye of the Hysham Presbyterian Church, Bolton was the first to make the trip to the scaffold. Bolton showed no evidence of nervousness as he accompanied Sheriff Isaac, Undersheriff Williamson and Reverend Nye around the jail building, and then up the stairs to the gallows. As a light snow was whitening his bared head, Bolton faced the assembled crowd and thanked the officers for their courtesy during his year in jail, and for their kindness to his mother and sisters. After the black hood was drawn over his head the trap was sprung at 3:41 a.m. and at 3:49 Drs. J.C.E. Hagen and F.M. Alexander of Hysham and Dr. Colton of Forsyth pronounced him dead.

Moments after Glenn Bolton was pronounced dead, Reagin also asked to be prayed for by the minister and then he told new County Attorney C.L. Harris that they had just hanged an innocent man, claiming that he had lied about the whisky and the signal. During Reagin's trial he said that Bolton had supplied him with moonshine whisky and that he was intoxicated at the time of the shooting. He also claimed that Bolton had signaled him to enter the house before the murder by lighting a cigarette.

Ten minutes later Reagin was taken to the scaffold accompanied by the same officers as fast as his crippled knee would permit and after making a remark about the snowstorm he took his place under the noose without fear or nervousness. When asked for any last words he only said, "I hope to meet all you men on the other side of the blue. So long." As the black hood was being pulled down he shouted: "Good bye, men" and then at 3:54 a.m. the trap fell and Joe Reagin was pronounced dead sixteen minutes later.

As Reagin left the jail on the way to the gallows he handed a statement to County Attorney Harris stating his prayer that other young men would avoid guns and alcohol that got him in to trouble and broke his mother's heart. Bolton presented his final statement to his attorney and he asked that it be published several days after his death, in it he explained that the scheme was Reagin's idea and that he didn't want any violence at his house. Bolton wrote that he thought the job would be a little bogus hold-up where Reagin could get his stuff back and the problem would simply go away. He said he was terribly sorry that Deputy Keeler was killed and sorry for his family. He concluded by forgiving everyone including Reagin and asked for forgiveness.

Postscript:
Undersheriff Irving Keeler's 45-caliver government automatic revolver was never found after Joe Reagin took it from him. Joe later told the authorities that he had buried it under a pine tree a short distance from the Bolton house when he was on the run from the posse. Some locals think that someone found the weapon and merely didn't report it.

Speaking of weapons, Former Treasure County sheriff, Orville Campbell eventually got possession of the pistol, which was used by Joe Reagin in the shooting death of Deputy Keeler and he described it as a bird's bill handled, nickel-plated double-action Frontier model 45-long Colt. He said it had an eight-inch barrel and it was the type carried by the U.S. Cavalry in the early days.

February 9, 1923
Glenna Martin Bolton

Location and Gallows: Bolton was hanged in the Treasure County jail yard at Hysham and he was the second man hanged on ***Gallows No. Eighteen: (Sept. 1920): "Galloping Gallows" No. Six***.
Hanged With: Joseph B. Reagin
Crime: Conspiracy with Joe Reagin to rob Undersheriff Irving Keeler during which the officer was murdered by his co-conspirator on December 9, 1921.
Judge: George A. Horkan
Prosecution: County Attorney E.D. Greys and assisted by State Attorney General Wellington D. Rankin
Defense: Felker F. Haynes of Forsyth
Sheriff: Philip Isaac
Relics and Remnants: The noose and shackles used in the hanging of Glenn Bolton and Joe Reagin are on display at the Treasure County Museum at Hysham. The gallows used in the executions is now on display at the museum at the Old Montana Prison Complex at Deer Lodge.

The biggest mistake in Bolton's life was taking in Joe Reagin into his family's home. Glenn had accepted stolen cattle from Reagin and eventually assisted his guest in the burglarizing of Mrs. Gambol's home and taking items for his own use. The trial for Glenn Bolton started Monday morning, January 9, 1922, and the jury was made up of:

M.C. Almond	Clyde Edenfield	F.L. Baker
James Eason	M.A. Williams	Fred Heyneman
Julius Reisner	Jeffery Dinsdale	John Bishop
Roy Ward	R.C. Shuey	Henry M. Vander Pauwert

Joe Reagin was the primary witness against Bolton telling the court that the defendant had planned the hold up of Deputy Keeler. Reagin told the jury that at the McRea Store Bolton had told him that he and his brother had cut logs for old lady Gambol and that they weren't paid for their work. The witness said that the defendant encouraged him to break into the old lady's place and steal bedding and other items for the coming winter. Reagin said that he had taken bedding to both Glenn's place and to his mother, Mrs. Amanda Bolton.

After the officers had discovered the stolen items at Bolton's house, Reagin and the defendant told Amanda Bolton to destroy any of Mrs. Gambol's items she still had. Reagin told the court that while Bolton's mother was helping him with his mask, Glenn suggested that he keep one of the stolen quilts to use while he was hiding out in the hills.

Testifying in his own behalf, Bolton reportedly displayed a lack of memory concerning specific details and he apparently left a bad impression with the jury. It took only three hours for the jury to return a guilty verdict with a penalty of death and Judge Horkan sentenced Bolton on Monday morning, January 16, 1922 to be hanged with Joe Reagin. The men's sentences were stayed when their cases were appealed to the Supreme Court, Reagins's bid for a new trial was denied on October 19, 1922, and they affirmed Bolton's conviction as well on November 13. The law allowed the defendants fifteen days after the judgment of the Supreme Court to file for a rehearing; the Attorney General had ten days in which to file an answer and the Supreme Court could then render a decision without argument. Once the court affirmed the lower court's decision the county attorney then had to request re-sentencing.

February 9, 1923
Joseph B. Reagin

Location and Gallows: Reagin was hanged immediately following Glenn Bolton's execution in the Treasure County jail yard at Hysham on ***Gallows No. Eighteen: (Sept. 1920): "Galloping Gallows" No. Six***.

Hanged With: Glenna M. Bolton

Description: Reagin was a twenty-two-year-old quarter breed Indian who stood six feet tall and weighed about160 pounds

Crime: Murder of Undersheriff Irving Keeler at the Bolton Ranch about thirty-five miles southwest of Hysham on December 9, 1921.

Judge: George A. Horkan

Prosecution: County Attorney E.D. Greys and assisted by State Attorney General Wellington Rankin

Defense: Young and Young of Forsyth and Gwinn and Maddox

Sheriff: Philip Isaac

Relics and Remnants: The noose and shackles used in the hanging of Glenn Bolton and Joe Reagin are on display at the Treasure County Museum at Hysham, as a reminder of the days gone by. The gallows used in the executions is now on display at the museum at the Old Montana Prison Complex at Deer Lodge.

Reagin was born in Oklahoma and he was reared there until he was about fifteen years old, when he moved to Montana. From time to time he resided in Texas, New Mexico, Washington, Wyoming and California, and while in the Golden State he committed grand larceny and was captured and convicted. After his release from prison he returned to Montana where he worked near Hardin until the fall of 1921, and then he moved to Treasure County where he worked a few days for Mr. Dowlin near the McRae Post Office. Joe moved in with the Bolton's, and because they didn't have sufficient bedding to accommodate Reagin, he stole bedding from Mrs. Gambol at the suggestion of Glenn. Reagin on several occasions went out on the range and killed and butchered a steer to replenish the food supply of the Bolton household.

Reagin's trial began Thursday morning, January 5, 1922, and it was presided over by Judge George A. Horkan. State Attorney General Wellington D. Rankin assisted County Attorney E.D. Gerye in both the Reagin and Bolton case and because it was the first murder trial of the county, Clerk of the Court Muri was aided by the county treasurer, J.D. Clark. The jury for the Reagin trial was made up of the following Treasure County residents:

H.S. Klingeman	Axel Olson	C.R. Stoll
Phil Isaacs	Carol Kimball	Frances Owens
George Nutter	Leslie Williams	Archie Wilson
Oli Muri	Harry Winfrey	Anton Kenney

Because of the bullet wound to his knee, the defendant was forced to recline in a cot during the trial and his mother, Mrs. Emily Reagin of the Crow Agency and sister, Mrs. Elizabeth Filmore were constantly by his side. Coroner A.O. Warnica and Sheriff Cunningham testified how they found Officer Keeler's body and County Attorney C.L. Harris told the court how Reagin had confessed to the killing of the deputy after his arrest.

When it was time to testify in his own behalf, Reagin's cot was placed next to the jury box and he said that he had known the Bolton's for about five years. He said that after moving to Montana he and Henry Pope had killed cattle to help feed the Bolton's as well as other area families. The defendant also admitted that he and two other boys had stolen a Ford automobile in Oklahoma to take a joy ride and he had also served time for grand larceny there.

Although he admitted killing Undersheriff Keeler, Reagin said it was Bolton's idea and that the shooting was an accident explaining that while he was holding the revolver he didn't realize he was pressing the trigger. The defense tried to place the major blame on Bolton to make him appear more culpable than Reagin in an attempt to mitigate his sentence. The case went to the jury at four o'clock Saturday afternoon, January 6, 1922, and they returned at nine p.m. with a guilty verdict and a recommendation for death. At ten o'clock Saturday morning, January 14, Reagin was carried into the courtroom on his cot and after Judge Horkan denied a motion by Attorney Guinn for a new trial the defendant was sentenced to be hanged at sunset on Monday morning, February 20, 1922. Reagin was depressed when he first received the news about the Supreme Court's decision but he cheered himself up by stating, "While there is life there is hope."

Double hanging of Monte and William Harris April 20, 1923

About midnight on Thanksgiving, November 24, 1921, Earl McCoy, alias, Clyde Miller, George Beach, Monte Harris and William Harris, (not related) went to the side door of the Harrison Avenue Hotel at Butte and knocked for admission. All four of the men and another conspirator had been recently released from the State Penitentiary at Deer Lodge before they decided to rob the hotel.

Cyril "Sut" Schilling, the proprietor, opened the door and he was confronted by William Harris pointing a revolver at him. Schilling reportedly said: "For God's sake don't shoot and you can have anything in the house." Paying no attention to the man's plea, William Harris shot and killed Schilling and as their victim lay dying on the floor the bandits calmly went through his pockets and then stepped over his body and entered the barroom of the hotel where there were several holiday parties in progress.

In the dancehall the gunmen ordered the men and women to line up against the wall where they were robbed of their money and jewelry. One of the bandits announced that since they had already killed one man, it didn't matter how many more people they killed. One of the robbers used a pair of pliers to twist a diamond from a woman's ring and in all, the bandits got away with about fifteen hundred dollars worth of cash and jewelry. Ross McGrew who was staying at the hotel heard the shot and slipped out of the rear entrance to call the police as the criminals were making their escaped in an automobile. Within minutes automobiles full of police and members of the sheriff's department were tearing down Harrison Avenue to the scene of the crime.

The officers spent the rest of the night rounding up the usual suspects and sifting through their alibis and releasing them. Finally about five o'clock on the following afternoon the officers discovered that Monte Harris had been recently released from the penitentiary and he was linked with a house at 2205 Wall Street. Deputies Jack Kelly, William Curran and "Doc" Porter arrived at the house where the suspects were all arrested and the residence was searched. The officers found William Harris carrying a .41-caliber Colt's revolver, Earl McCoy had .38-special Colt revolver and two fully loaded .32-caliber automatics were found in a dresser drawer. Somehow the deputies missed another .38-caliber revolver that one of the suspects had slipped under the seat of the patrol car, on the way to the county jail.

It was learned later that the Harrison Hotel holdup and murder had taken place because the bandits had abandoned their original plans of robbing a bank at Whitehall and then the holding up the Holland Ice Rink at Butte. The criminals had staked out the ice rink because the large crowds had impressed them and they were anticipating a big haul from the Thanksgiving Day receipts of the business.

Their plans required five men, four to guard the crowd while the fifth man held up the box office. On Thanksgiving Day however, Edwin A. Graham, alias Neil Mulcaster had been ill for a number of days so the other four hold-up men milled over the situation at their cabin until dark and then decided to take the ice rink anyway. By the time they had arrived at the rink the manager had already left and the criminals figured he had taken the day's receipts with him. After discussing the matter the four bandits then decided to rob the Harrison Hotel.

After their arrest it was learned that the suspects had carried out several other crimes in the area including plundering several private homes and isolated businesses and the five holdup men were also suspected in two attempts to rob the Westside Dairy earlier in November of 1921. After the failed attempts at the business, Sheriff Larry Duggan had stationed a special deputy at the dairy but the holdup men never came back.

William Harris and Ed Graham were quite well educated and like Monte Harris they were reportedly from good families, the former being from St. Louis and his father was a supply sergeant at Camp Louis. Earl McCoy at first refused to divulge any personal information while George Beach said he was originally from Cincinnati, Ohio. In those days Butte was a dangerous place and while the five suspects were being held there was at least three other suspected murderers in lockup at the county jail.

At first it was believed that Monte Harris, the local Butte boy had been the shooter, and the fact that the popular victim had befriended the young murderer along with the cold-blooded nature of the crime made it difficult to appoint attorneys for the gang members. Finally Judge Lynch had to use the power of the court in securing the suitable counsel. Each of the criminals had prior records and they had all recently been released within a few days from the State Penitentiary under the recommendation of Warden Potter.

The five men asked for and received separate trials, and both the Harris boys were found guilty of murder in the first degree and they were sentenced to death. (See individual profiles for Bill and Monte Harris below for details of their trials) Although McCoy and Beach were also convicted of first-degree murder, they were each sentenced to a life term at the state penitentiary. McCoy, who was an army veteran, and Beach apparently felt fortunate to keep their lives and they didn't appeal their sentences while Ed Graham turned state's evidence and he received a light sentence in the county jail for co-operating with the authorities and was eventually released and was allowed to leave the state.

While awaiting their trials, Monte and William Harris along with their friend and accomplice, Earl McCoy was involved in an attempted prison break on January 4, 1922. After receiving a tip that there were saws in the jail from Earl Hawkins, who had been finishing a ninety-day sentence for drug use, Deputy Jack Duggan inspected cell number seven where the three men were housed and found that two of the three-quarter inch round iron bars had been cut clean through just under the crossbeam, some fourteen inches from the floor.

Since the cuts were so near the crossbar they might not have been detected if the officers hadn't received the tip. After a painstaking search, the jailers located the saw and a small piece of a file secreted away in the ceiling of the cell. After being detected, the prisoners nonchalantly owned up by saying the chilled steel bars of their cell cut like a piece of wood. While the trio admitted that they had cut the bars they never did tell the officers how they obtained the saw, which was an ordinary twelve-inch blade that ironworkers used. The blade was quite rusty and it was caked with soap, which was used as a lubricant during the cutting of the bars.

Undersheriff Dale O. Robinson said that the prisoners had worked fast as the cells were inspected hourly during the night and more frequently by day. The officer explained that merely cutting through the cell bars wouldn't have freed the prisoners, as they would still be secured inside the corridor. Robinson suggested that the prisoners had probably planned on gaining their freedom the same way that six prisoners had escaped from the county jail in 1903. The prisoners, including James Martin who was eventually recaptured and hanged in1904, had access to the corridor where one of the men had faked an illness and the others jumped the jailer as he unlocked the door.

The ease by which the cell bars had been cut made the jailers uncomfortable and it caused quite a stir among the county commissioners of Silver Bow County who immediately called for an investigation. They were under the impression that the company that had built the jail had assured them that the bars used were casehardened chilled steel, which were supposed to be guaranteed to be tool proof.

The Polly Jail Company was notified and after reviewing the warranty it was explained to the commissioners that the round bars of the individual cells were made of Bessemer Steel, which could be cut but the cage bars of the corridor surrounding the cells were constructed with a core of tool-proof steel. Around the core of special steel there was a layer of tool-proof steel, a layer of iron, another band of steel and then finished with a layer of iron. Both the ceiling and floor of the corridor was constructed out of tool-proof steel.

This attempted jailbreak in 1922 caused the sheriff's office to introduce new procedures in handling the admissions of new prisoners and starting on January 6, 1922, every new prisoner at the Silver Bow County Jail was stripped naked and searched along with every article of his clothing was thoroughly gone over. While some jails issued prison garb, at that time the prisoners in the Butte facility wore their own clothing.

These new procedures proved valuable when Roy Walsh arrived at Butte from Boulder after attempting to break jail there in June of 1923. Before assigning Walsh a cell at the Butte facility, the jailer was conducting the routine strip search when the officer found a piece of heavy pipe that the prisoner had removed from the washbowl in his cell at Boulder in his trousers. Walsh was convicted of first-degree murder but he successfully escaped from the Boulder Jail in October of 1923, only to be recaptured in April 1924, and eventually hanged on

Valentine's Day, 1925.

Other rules that had been initiated to prevent the smuggling in of weapons and tools at the Butte jail were that prisoners had to communicate with their visitors through walls of fine mesh screen so that not even a sewing needle could be passed. There had been earlier cases when a female visitor had slipped a watch-spring saw to an inmate from her mouth as they kissed. After the attempted jailbreak by McCoy and the Harris boys, the jailer was instructed to never open the door to the corridor without being accompanied by at least one armed deputy outside of the cage with orders to shoot to kill if necessary.

After loosing their individual appeals for new trials, Attorneys Earl E. Blodgett, Charles E. O'Neill and Hanley teamed up and made a joint effort to save the Harris boys. By March first, 1923, the Supreme Court had already ruled against the two doomed prisoners, first on an appeal and the second time in a rehearing. By March 2, the county attorney had asked the court for re-sentencing and the two prisoners, not kin but related in crime, and two separate juries agreed, were brought before Judge Lynch the next day to hear that they would be hanged by the neck until they were dead between two o'clock and eight on the morning of April 20, 1923.

On the way back to the jail, Monte told Sheriff Duggan, Undersheriff Robinson and Deputy Charles Erb, "Well, that's all until the Big Show," referring to their execution. Bill Harris remained quiet as they were walking but Monte continued saying that they still had forty-seven days, which he considered a long time. The prisoners appeared to be in good health, neatly dressed and they both reportedly went through their final sentencing without a tremor.

After the re-sentencing, Sheriff Duggan announced that in order to limit the number of spectators at the execution it would take place within the walls of the county jail and he would utilize the gallows that was used for the triple hanging of Fisher, O'Neill and Powell in 1918. Since the 1918 scaffold would require modifications in order to be used within the jail building, Sheriff Duggan called on Mr. T.O. Angell, the man who had drawn up the original plans for the killing machine to direct the construction of the gallows.

The finished scaffold was placed in the northwestern end of the jail building on the third floor nearly directly above the cells of the condemned men. It was designed so that the doomed men would fall into the foyer near the entrance of the jail and a curtain of canvas was used to conceal the drop of the bodies where the physicians would examine the remains.

Also on the day of the re-sentencing, Sheriff Duggan went before the county commissioners asking for authorization to establish a deathwatch and the following day he was informed that the county would not pay for the additional guards, making it the first time in history of the county that a deathwatch was not placed over a condemned prisoner or prisoners. In most cases it was customary to employ a three-man deathwatch so that at least one special guard would be with the doomed man or men twenty-four hours a day from the time of sentencing up to their execution.

The Harris boys were locked in cells on the north end of the jail while the other prisoners were confined in the south corridor and every half hour a jailer walked along the corridor, which divided the north from the south tier of the cells. While the gallows were not visible to the inmates, the sounds of the carpenters' hammers must have sent chills down the spines of all the inmates of the jail, particularly the Harris boys.

With twenty-five days left, the two condemned men remained in good spirits in front of the jailers and their visitors and they received frequent visits from members of the Salvation Army, Lutheran, Congregational and Catholic Churches but at first they seemed to be impressed with the Christian Science faith. Monte was the most talkative of the pair and he generally served as the spokesman while Bill Harris just smiled and nodded his agreement.

With all other avenues closed to them, a commutation of their death sentence to life in prison was their only hope of survival. Monte Harris was quick to point out the Byrnes and Chronopolous case of a year earlier when Governor Joseph M. Dixon saved them from the gallows. The Governor commuted their sentences because two other men charged with the same murder were given life sentences. The Harris' were confident that they would also cheat the gallows as their case was almost identical with the earlier case since a couple of their associates in crime had gotten off with life terms and most importantly, the same Governor was involved.

In the meantime the prisoner's attorneys and friends along with local churches with the Christian Science Church leading the way, were distributing petitions for clemency and many citizens quickly signed them including five of the jurymen that had found the prisoners guilty. The most important signature at the time however, was that of Judge Lynch who had signed the death warrants of both convicted murderers. The two death warrants were identical except for the dates of their convictions, and they covered the normal format, ordering the sheriff to keep the prisoners in a safe place until the time of execution and then goes on to describe the history of the appeals, the Supreme Court denials, etc. Finally the warrants described how, where and when the execution was to take place.

After struggling whole-heartily for Monte Harris, his client, Attorney Charles O'Neill sent a number of petitions to the state capital and with many more coming in from Great Falls and other locations, he was feeling confident just ten days before the scheduled execution. With Bill Harris and his attorney riding the coattails of the young popular Butte boy, they were quite confident that the Governor would follow his precedence that he had established in the Byrnes-Chronopolous case. The defense attorneys pointed out that in his commutation for Byrnes and Chronopolous, Governor Dixon wrote that it was discriminating and unfair when they were sentenced to death while two others received life.

In a public-relation "bomb" the newspaper reported that because of the age-old custom of granting condemned men almost anything they wished for short of liberty, Monte and William Harris were being given illegal drugs. The newspapers reported that each evening the two drug addicts got a "shot each" and one of the deputies was quoted as saying: "If these men are held under sentence another thirty days there won't be enough left to hang. Whether it is from nerves or because of their supply of drugs, the two men are actually wasting away." The officer pointed out that Bill Harris had lost most of the weight and he said that his cheeks had fallen as though he had lost his teeth.

The newspaper articles implied that the sheriff had authorized the drug use in order to keep the prisoners "together until the day of execution." The public was aware of the fact that both of the condemned men were drug addicts and they were aware that the sheriff's department had frustrated the many attempts of Monte's friends to smuggle drugs into the jail for the pair, but they became outraged when they heard that Sheriff Duggan was in fact supplying narcotics to them.

The following day in a statement to the press, Sheriff Duggan strenuously denied that he or any of his deputies had ever given the condemned man narcotics as a means of "bracing" them up. The sheriff pointed out that both of the prisoners were showing drastic signs of worry as their execution date grew nearer but he reiterated that neither he nor his staff had ever administered to or given any prisoner in the county jail narcotics of any kind. He explained that the county physician visited the men in their cells each night and whether or not he administers narcotics to any of the prisoners is entirely up to the doctor. It is entirely within the rights of the physician to prescribe narcotics to the prisoners who require stimulants.

About a week before the execution the two doomed men for the first time since their incarceration began displaying strong emotions. William Harris refused for the first time to speak with the reporters and while Monte Harris was still confident that he would cheat the gallows he had become more moody. On April 12, 1923, Governor Dixon announced that he had declined to grant executive clemency and he reiterated his position the next day after he had received more petitions from Earl "Mickey" Gordon representing the labor organizations of Great Falls. Monte Harris told the visiting reporters that they would keep the faith until six o'clock on the eve of their execution, after that, they would just have to figure on "going down."

The condemned men spent the last few days discussing their cases with their attorneys, studied with their Christian Science advisor, visited with friends and discussed their chances of a commuted sentence with the newspapermen. Monte would often joke about having such a long time before their fateful day and one of their great highlights was getting a letter from Earl McCoy at the penitentiary, which they received about once a week. The condemned men told the reporters about a group of prison guards at Deer Lodge that had paid a visit at the Silver Bow County Jail. The peniteniary guards had told the Harris boys that McCoy was deeply affected by the impending executions of his friends. Monte also shared with the newspapermen that Graham, one of their cohorts who had gotten off because he had co-operated with the authorities, was back in St. Louis playing in the cabarets and having a great old time. Monte said that he had gotten the news from a girl in Butte who had recently received a letter from Graham.

While Monte laughed and joked with his visitors, Bill Harris had become quite nervous and become very white from being out of the sun for so long. With just a couple of days left, Bill became more talkative instead of his normal role of a smiling listener as Monte chatted with interviewers. Bill told the reporters that he was far from his relatives in British Columbia and he hadn't wanted to burden his parents with his troubles. While most people knew that the Canadian family had clearly deserted him, Bill tried to justify their absence at his time of need by saying he hadn't told them about his predicament. He often stated that if his family had known he was in trouble they would have come to Montana in a minute.

Monte had many friends who called on him every day and over time they had adopted Bill as one of their own and the most regular visitor was Monte's sixty-two-year-old adopted mother who visited the boys every day. The little old lady had been at the side of her son and his friend every day since they were arrested except for one day when she was ill and another when she went to Helena to personally speak with the Governor. On top of her grief over her son's troubles, her husband had died just three weeks before Monte's scheduled execution.

In the mother's absence, six Butte women including a seventy-eight-year-old matron who had taken an interest in the case visited the doomed young men. The women clasped hands of the two prisoners through the bars while the oldest lady wept and prayed for them. In the meantime preparations had begun in the basement of the courthouse where the gallows were being prepared and a few days later the scaffold was assembled.

Members of the Salvation Army who held Sunday services for all the inmates of the county jail also made a special visit to the cells of the two condemned men who had been loosing weight. Even though their appetites were good, Bill Harris dropped some thirty pounds while Monte had lost nearly twenty pounds during their incarceration. Days before their hanging the boys had given up their beadwork because they couldn't control their nerves but they really enjoyed their chicken dinners followed with cake and ice cream. The guards said that the prisoners slept well but generally they had little to do with the other men in the adjoining corridor and the only inmates that the Harris' spoke with were Harry "Fat" Allen, Charles Paulson, alias "Baldy" Roberts, who were both locked up on murder charges.

Two days before the scheduled double hanging, Sheriff Duggan visited the condemned men and told them of his trip to the capital where the Governor informed him that there wasn't the slightest chance of his interfering with the court order. After speaking with the sheriff, Monte sat in his cell with his arms hanging loosely across his knees and said that it was all over and Bill in the next cage nodded his agreement.

Members of several religious denominations visited the two men along with many other people including their friends who spoke to them through the prisoner's "box" at the side of their cells. Since there was no hope for the prisoners, the sheriff allowed them the privilege, which wasn't accorded to the other prisoners, of uncensored mail and the letters that Monte and Bill Harris had sent to the Governor were not inspected before they were mailed.

From unofficial sources it was learned that William Harris had written the Governor saying that as he was about to mount the scaffold for his crime he felt he had made peace with his Maker. Harris explained that he had shot Mr. Schilling accidentally as the victim had struck his weapon with his elbow. The condemned man went on to warn the Governor that if he allowed Monte Harris to be executed he would surely be judged a murderer himself when he met the "bar of eternal justice."

While Monte spent his time in reading, and walking about his cell, William Harris generally was on his cot with his eyes closed. At about four o'clock in the afternoon of the day before his trip to the gallows, Monte Harris called for the sheriff and asked the officer for the name of the Catholic priest who had visited them before. The sheriff immediately sent for Reverend Father J.S. Faley of St. Patrick's Church who later said that Monte didn't know if he had ever been baptized and so the priest conducted the services. Monte kept the priest's rosary, went to confession, and received Holly Communion.

Monte and Bill Harris eventually turned away the two representatives of the Christian Science Church who had been calling on them for several weeks and about the same time the two men were embracing the Catholic religion a reporter was calling on the mother of the murder victim who lived in a brick home in the center of the city. When asked for her response, the tall full-figured woman pressed her hands to her breast and said she wanted them hung. After staring at the interviewer with a frown she said that while she didn't want to witness their deaths, she wanted them hung and then the elderly woman burst into tears and closed the door.

About eight o'clock on the eve of the execution, Governor Dixon telephoned Judge Lynch who was in Harlowton where he had been holding court, stating that he would commute the sentence for both men to a life sentence if the judge approved it. Judge Lynch reportedly told the Governor that as judge, he had performed his duty when he sentenced them to death, and that his honor must do his duty as he saw fit. After that conversation Governor Dixon notified Monte Harris' attorney, Charles O'Neill stating that he would not interfere with the execution.

Mr. O'Neill called the sheriff at 8:45 and informed him about the Governor's decision, and said that the execution would have to go forward. At that point the two condemned men asked to see Deputies William Curran, "Doc" Porter and Jack Kelly, the three officers who had arrested them at the Wall Street house and in a poignant moment the prisoners told the officers that they didn't have any hard feelings against them as they were only doing their jobs. The Harris boys shook the hands of each of the officers and then the deputies returned to their stations near the gallows.

At eleven p.m. Governor Dixon formerly announced to the Associated Press at Helena that he had finally decided not to interfere with the decision of the law. Monte Harris was still allowed to send a final appeal to the Governor by telegraph before Sheriff Larry Duggan and Deputy Jack Duggan went to "Death Row" where they read the death warrants to the men, as they stood erect in their cells. After paying his last respects to his prisoners, the sheriff told the reporters that other than their one attempt to break jail, the Harris boys had been model inmates at the jail. They had never gotten into quarrels with the other prisoners; they didn't bear any hard feelings against anyone, and they had always been friendly with the jailers.

The sheriff said that the doomed men had always spoken freely with him and his staff and they had never been caught in a lie. There appetites had remained good and Monte Harris had ordered their evening meal, which was especially delivered from the Silver Bow Club. The special meal consisted of a mushroom omelet, two cups of Boston coffee, French fried potatoes and hard rolls.

At midnight the sheriff asked the prisoners if they would like a last meal and the men ordered Boston coffee, a Spanish omelet, including a ham and egg and clubhouse sandwich. By midnight all of the legal formalities had been completed and the sheriff and his deputies once again tested the gallows and ropes. Drs. C.E. Emery, P.E. Cane, Herbert A. Mailett and Dan J. Donahue along with representatives of the sheriff's offices of Madison, Deer Lodge, Cascade and Jefferson Counties were gathering in the sheriff's office where there was a great deal of uneasiness and tension among the officers and the prisoners alike. Sheriff Duggan had originally scheduled the execution at precisely two o'clock but he delayed the hangings for an hour at the request of Monte Harris.

The gloom was not totally confined to the jail as the normally happy and carefree city of Butte reportedly was a bit sober on the eve of the double hanging. People passing along Alaska Street looked nervously at the square brick county jail building with its huge lion-headed gargoyles and the gigantic ferocious looking beasts guarded the structure with their teeth and wrinkled foreheads. From the chimney of the jail a thin trail of colorless gas arose as if it might have been the spirits of the two condemned men as they went into eternity. About a quarter to three the large canvas curtain over the scaffold was raised for the first time exposing the death machine to the waiting visitors. A few minutes later the great iron door of the jail opened and the sheriff appeared and informed the waiting reporters that Monte wanted to make a statement.

Monte read from his two-paged statement telling the reporters of his early years and that he had always played square stating that he had made thousands of friends in the underworld but none of them had aided him during his time of need. Monte said he held no animosity against anyone and he wished everyone all the best. He finished by proclaiming that he was absolutely innocent of the murder of "Sig" Schilling and announced publicly that Bill Harris had taken full responsibility for the man's death.

Harris said that Governor Dixon has commuted every foreigner in Butte that had been sentenced to die and yet he was allowing two white boys to go to the gallows. Finally he asked God to bless and protect his mother and asked that his good friends also be blessed. He thanked Sheriff Duggan, Undersheriff Robinson and Deputy Johnnie Duggan for being true blue with them. Bill Harris simply thanked the reporters and then walked back to the end of his cell corridor for a final drink of water.

As Monte was still visiting with the reporters, Bill suddenly declared that he wanted to send some of his things to his friends and he quickly entered his cell and began autographing a book. He handed the novel to Sheriff Duggan and told him to give it to a girl named Bernice and then he grabbed a small bible, which he instructed the officer to present to Pearl. This seemed to really excite the prisoner and he sat down on his bunk and began hastily signing other books in his cell and as he glanced at the many floral wreaths and plants, which had been arranged against the steel walls of the corridor, he asked for one of the white roses. One of the flowers was pinched off and when it was handed to the prisoner, Bill carefully placed it in the buttonhole of his shirt.

Sheriff Duggan walked up to Bill and handed him a string of Rosary beads and told him that he had owned them for a long time and he wanted the prisoner to have them. The condemned man thanked the officer as he placed them over his head and then he arranged the beads around his neck. Bill Harris appeared complacent and Monte was nervous as they spent their last minutes watching the progress of the hour hand as it crawled slowly towards the death hour of three. Fathers J.C. Meehan and Faley were in the cell with the men when the clock struck three o'clock and Sheriff Duggan announced that the "law would now exact its toll." Other officers entered the cells with packages containing the restraining straps, which had been purchased for the convicted murderers, Byrnes and Chronopolous before Governor Dixon had commuted their sentences.

Bill tossed his half-smoked cigarette onto the floor of his cell and he carefully crushed it with his foot before he let his arms drop to his sides. Undersheriff Robinson then stepped forward with the straps and began adjusting them around Harris' body near the shoulders and another one around his arms. Deputy Jack Duggan was in Monte's cell waiting with his straps while the prisoner was finishing autographing his books for his friends. Monte then asked the officer if he could write one last note to their friend Earl McCoy and after quickly finishing the letter he handed the note along with a letter for his mother through the bars to Butte Assistant Chief of Police Mike O'Donnell.

In the meantime Undersheriff Robinson released Bill's hands so he could grab a handful of silver coins, and after stepping across the corridor he tossed them through the bars into the cells of other convicted murderers. Earlier, Bill had instructed Deputy Curran to deliver six silver dollars to a female prisoner by the name of Vera White. He then entered Monte's cell and with his partially free right hand he grasped his friend's hand and said, "We've been pals in life, Monte, we'll stick together in death."

Bill suddenly appeared unconcerned when he noticed that the reporters were watching them and the condemned man turned to the crowd of newspapermen and told them not to write any bunk about him weakening or getting emotional. As Bill was telling the crowd that he would go down like a man, the straps were being tightened on him and they were being placed on Monte as well. After their final farewell to the officers, the prisoners began to move in a silent procession towards the gallows.

There was a stillness over the jail corridor, which wasn't even broken by faint whispers of the awaiting witnesses that had assembled near the scaffold. The only sounds heard were the rattling and clinging of the heavy iron doors and the footsteps over the floor grating. William Harris and Undersheriff Robinson lead the way followed by Sheriff Duggan and Fathers Faley and Meehan followed by Monte Harris accompanied by Deputies Duggan and Dan "Paddy" Holland. Finally they reached the cement floor where they passed through an aisle and entered the foyer over looking the crowd of witnesses. Bill Harris was pale and he remained tight-lipped and stared straight ahead while Monte was looking around until he caught a glimps at the scaffold.

After seeing the gallows for the first time, Monte's face had a look of despair and with wild eyes he began glancing into the faces of the spectators below and even though he was clearly shaken, he didn't falter in his step. Bill walked without hesitation or assistance up the slight incline to the scaffold and he took his place under the heavy beam and noose. A second later he was joined by Monte as the witnesses rushed forward to get into better positions. As the leg straps were being secured, Bill stared straight ahead and over the little crowd but Monte took advantage of the situation to once again protest his innocence. He also expressed his love for his mother and he shouted out a reminder to Officer Mike O'Donnell to deliver his letter to the woman.

A single light bulb suspended directly above the heads of the condemned men, which accentuated the chalky appearance of their appearance. The men had earlier been told in their cells that black masks would be placed over their heads after the nooses had first been placed around their necks. Deputy Duggan placed the rope around Monte's neck as Undersheriff Robinson adjusted Bill's noose behind his left ear. As the noose had settled around Monte's neck he quickly turned his head to see if the same procedure was being carried out for his companion and it was reported that a strange almost startled expression came over his face when he looked over at Bill who was staring straight ahead without a tremor.

Monte then faced the crowd once again and in an apparent attempt to lighten the mood he asked Deputy Duggan to make sure he did a good job of placing the knot behind his left ear. As Monte was still speaking the deputy pulled a black handkerchief from his pocket, which was the signal to the sheriff that all was ready, and the chief officer pushed a button and somewhere in the basement of the jail an electric buzzer sounded to the unknown executioner who worked the lever, which released the trap. The Harris boys were caught totally by surprised as they were dropped to their deaths while they were still waiting for the black hoods to be placed over their heads.

The bodies of the two men dropped out of sight behind the canvas curtain and the death ropes were still swaying as the other canvas curtain was dropped, once again obscuring the gallows from sight. So quickly and quietly was the execution pulled off that many of the witnesses weren't aware that it had occurred. Minutes later the crowd filed out of the jail as the five attending physicians went behind the curtain to examine the bodies, which were hanging, toes pointed down, barely two feet from the floor of the jail. The doctors reported that the necks of both men had been broken and they were declared dead after seven minutes. Officers Robinson and Duggan cut the ropes and thirty minutes later Undertakers Quirk and Treglown of the Duggan Undertaking establishment took charge of the remains.

Sheriff Larry Duggan had intended to carry out his disagreeable task as quietly as possible and to prevent the congregation of large crowds he had ordered a number of his deputies as well as city policemen to patrol outside of the jail. There were small crowds of curious people outside the jail and while many of them left the scene when it was announced that the execution had been completed, some hung around for a glimpse of the bodies as they were being removed by the undertakers.

Meanwhile Assistant Chief O'Donnell honored his promise to Monte Harris by personally delivering a letter to the dead man's mother living in a dilapidated house at 207 Curtis Street. When he and two fellow officers arrived at the Harris residence at about 3:30 in the morning they found the elderly lady being comforted by a neighbor woman. Officer O'Donnell told the bent-over woman that it was all over and then he handed her the letter from her son and the woman shouted, "Oh! My dear Boy" and then she staggered to her bed and fell upon it.

Postscript:

Later that day hundreds of curious people visited the Duggan Undertaking Chapel to get a glance of the remains of Bill and Monte Harris. By noon, hundreds of the morbidly curious had passed through the viewing room until the family and friends of the two boys requested that no more spectators could view the remains. Arrangements had first been made to send Bill Harris' body to Big Timber for burial but the priests prevented the action by stating that the two boys had embraced the Catholic faith and so they held mass for them and they were interned in the church cemetery.

The pen with which Judge Lynch had signed the death warrants of Bill and Monte Harris was offered to the younger sister of "Sut" Schilling, the murder victim, but she reportedly drew back in horror and said, "I would not want it. It would remind me of my brother's death. I want to forget. I am not interested in what may happen to his murderers. Their fate will not change matters with us. My brother is dead, nothing can change that. We are not seeking vengeance."

April 20, 1923

William "Bill" Harris

Other Names: William "Slim" Lemmox

Location and Gallows: The hanging of Monte and William Harris at Butte was the second multiple execution on ***Gallows No. Sixteen: (Jan. 1918): "Galloping Gallows" No. Five***.

Hanged with: Monte Harris (not related)

Description: The six-foot, twenty-four-year-old William Harris was a youthful looking slender man with hard gray-blue eyes, which gave him a curious looking expression. Both Bill and Monte Harris were drug addicts.

Crime: Cold-blooded murder of Cyril "Sut" Schilling on Thanksgiving night, November 24, 1921.

Judge: Jeremiah J. Lynch

Prosecution: Silver Bow County Attorney and his deputy, Leslie B. Sulgrove

Defense: Earl E. Blodgett and Fred E. McCraken assisted by Frances Silver and Charles O'Neill

Sheriff: Larry Duggan

Relics and Remnants: The gallows, which was used to hang the Harris' eventually, hanged a total of eight convicted murderers and after its final victim in 1933, the scaffold was returned to Butte where it is currently in storage in the basement of the Silver Bow County Courthouse. Because the scaffold is being stored with possible hazardous material the ancient death machine is not currently available for viewing.

Bill Harris was originally from Vancouver, British Columbia, Canada before he was sent to the Montana State Penitentiary from Flathead County on a burglary charge. He was received at the prison on August 21, 1918, but he escaped from Deer Lodge three months later but he was quickly recaptured. Governor Dixon had commuted his robbery sentence at Deer Lodge on October 6, 1921, with the condition that he was returned to Canada. His three other partners in crime had also been recently released from the state prison by the executive clemency board.

William was the first of the four men tried and his case, No. 5836 began on February 20, 1922, before Judge Lynch. The Silver Bow County courtroom had a high ceiling and it was lighted from above by stained glass skylights and from the east by a triple window through which the Continental Divide of the Rocky Mountains could be seen. On the south side of the room sat a high bench on which sat the bald and mustached Judge Lynch.

The judge was alert and stern and he made ruling after ruling in an even calm voice. The hard-working stenographer, Flurry Sullivan was seated at a flat-topped desk, which was piled with stacks after stacks of notepaper of jottings, and she struggled to hear the mumbled, low-voiced responses of the witnesses who at times only nodded their heads to the questions. The stenographer had to be able to interpret the replies of men to whom English was often their second language.

In those days, during high-profile cases like murder trials, the courtroom was often crowded with artisans, merchants of all kinds, professional men, miners as well as idlers, some with a look of interest on their faces, others with a bored expression. Some of the men were present because they had been called while others were there in hopes that they would witness something exciting. Although William Harris was said to have been from a well-to-do family in Canada, none of his family attended his trial and they apparently declined to contribute to his defense.

While the attorneys were examining the prospective jurors Harris sat motionlessly besides his four attorneys, E.E. Blodgett and Fred E. McCraken representing him directly and Frances A. Silver and Maurice J. English who had been assigned to defend Harris' alleged associates in the murder assisted. Despite the defendant's youthful appearance the sheriff didn't take any chances and he assigned Deputy Piskolich, the giant of the sheriff's staff to sit directly behind the accused man.

It was said that when Bill Harris got mad his whole face transformed with his nose turning up and wide white lines formed on either side of his snarling mouth. When being escorted to and from the courtroom Harris was handcuffed to the giant deputy and it was all he could do to keep up with the long strides of the large guard.

While the county attorney began the trial by reading the charges against Harris the defendant became clearly nervous and the right corner of his mouth twitched violently and veins in his head grew large and he began taking large breaths. He was seen clutching his hands on his lap while his face went through contortions and by the second day of his trial William Harris was clearly showing signs of the tremendous mental strain he was under.

The courtroom was jammed each day with spectators along with a few women including Mrs. Schilling, the widow of the victim and his mother, both wearing black in mourning. The first two days were devoted in trying to secure a jury, the defense questioning the prospective jurors heavily on the legal provision that the testimony of an accomplice in a crime is not sufficient to convict unless the testimony was supported by other evidence of the type, which was strong enough to convict by its self. The questions for the jurors by the prosecution were brief and dealt primarily with how the panelists felt about capital punishment.

Among the many prospective jurors who were excused were several who couldn't speak English and a number of other men because they had already formed an opinion about the case and one man who said while he believed in capital punishment, he wouldn't be able to vote for it.

The defendant sat motionless with one knee crossed upon the other and he slightly swayed his foot as he viewed the impaneling of the jury with an impression of indifference. Finally shortly after five o'clock that evening the following jury was placed in the custody of the bailiff, Deputy Dan O'Donahue:

Leslie Hastie	J.J. Manley	Henry Umhang (f)
J.J. Harrington	John Keating	Peter Raffery
Thomas Leehy	S.J. Carson	Louis Becktell
Henry J. LaReu	Steve Kremer	Fred C. Burgdof

(f) Foreman

As the bailiff was escorting the jury out of the courtroom, Harris looked back at the spectators and he glanced at Mrs. Schilling but the widow merely turned her back on the defendant. Because she was a witness for the prosecution the widow wasn't allowed in the courtroom the following day when she testified against Harris. After closing arguments, Judge Lynch instructed the jury that because the murder took place during a robbery, second-degree murder and manslaughter didn't apply, and that the panel could either convict the defendant of first-degree murder or acquit. When the jury retired to deliberate many of the curious spectators who had sat through the trial kept their seat in the belief that the panel would return a quick verdict. Among those who remained seated was the silver haired mother of Cyril Schilling and the widow of the victim along with her ten-year-old son who sat between the two women.

While most of the people believed that the jury wouldn't be out long, no one anticipated that the jurors would return as quickly as they did and only thirty-four minutes had elapsed between the time the jury left the box and when the verdict was read at 4:49 on the afternoon of February 27, 1922. After deliberating for only about twenty minutes the jury found William Harris guilty of first-degree murder and they fixed the penalty at death.

The defendant had a sickly pallor look on his face as his eyes followed the piece of paper containing the verdict from the hands of the foreman to those of the judge and after recording the verdict in his log, Court Clerk Peter Tobin rang out the fateful words that doomed the defendant to the hangman's noose. After the verdict was read the court ordered the jury be polled and then Attorney Fred McCraken leaned over and whispered to his client and Harris forced a smile on his face as the veins in his neck were noticeably throbbing.

After Judge Lynch announced that he would formerly pronounce sentence at ten o'clock on the morning of March 13, Harris was quickly returned to the jail where he joined Assad Juhray on "Death Row." Harris was the fourth condemned murderer that had been confined to death cells during that year, two having their sentences commuted to life and sent to Deer Lodge and Juhray who was convicted of murdering Hugh Gibson in September of 1920, at his residence.

Steve Bynne and Theodore Chronopolous had been sentenced to death for the murder of Sylvester J. Prenatt in his home while attempting to steal a load of liquor. Governor Dixon eventually commuted the sentences of two men and when Harris arrived on "Death Row" Juhray was also expecting to be saved by the top executive officer of the state. A spirit of moroseness quickly fell over Bill Harris and he seldom spoke to anyone including fellow prisoners who considered him cold and aloof. The court costs for the nine-day trial of William Harris paid by Silver Bow County included jury fees of over fifteen hundred dollars and another two hundred dollars for attorney fees for the defense.

Judge Lynch postponed the original sentencing day of William Harris to allow his attorneys additional time to prepare for an appeal for a new trial and even with the delay, the lead defense attorney, Earl Blodgett opposed the sentencing on March 18, 1922, but the court stated that the nineteen days had been sufficient. Before he was ordered to stand by the judge, Harris had been engaged in a laughing and smiling conversation with one of the many guards who were scattered about the courtroom as thick as plums in a pudding.

Harris was seated in the jury box while he was awaiting sentencing along with August Becker, convicted of assaulting his daughter and George Beach, one of Harris' accomplices in the Schilling murder. When called by the judge he stood up in the box and placed his long index finger of his left hand over the railing and he listened attentively to the judge. In a mild and low voice Judge Lynch began to pronounce sentence on Harris, pausing a bit just before delivering the words that meant death to the prisoner and observers said that the court's pronouncement seemed more like a prayer than a death sentence.

On March 21, 1922, Judge Lynch signed William Harris' death warrant, which fixed his hanging between three o'clock a.m. and ten o'clock on the morning of May 12, 1922. The general mood of the county jail was greatly improved when on March 23, Assad Juhray received word that the Governor had commuted his death sentence to life imprisonment but it dampened once again on March 25, when Monte Harris was sentenced to die along with Bill.

The closer to his execution the more nervous and talkative Bill became and instead of his normal role of a smiling listener as Monte Harris chatted away, he began telling the reporters about his relatives in British Columbia and how he didn't wanted to burden them with his troubles. Bill finally wrote a letter to his family and two days before his execution he was found in his cell holding a photo of his mother and sobbing.

Harris told the guards that his family in Canada didn't have any money to help in his defense but while Monte's mother traveled to Helena with representatives of the Butte YMCA to meet with the Governor, some of Bill's family members had reportedly made a visit to England. William Harris had won the respect of his jailers with his chilled-steel nerves by never complaining during his seventeen-months in jail and although he had deep tired lines in his face from the terrible strain, he still showed great courage and bravery. Although he stood up squarely and smoked a cigarette as he talked with the reporters, there was a trace of despair creeping into his voice.

Bill explained to one reporter that he had done many things wrong over the past twelve years, many of them illegal, but he had never been a rat. He said everyone had to go sometime and tonight when he walked to the gallows he would go like a man. At the time very few people knew that Billy had tried to save the life of his friend, and while Monte Harris had written a twenty-seven-page letter to the Governor appealing for his life, William not only refrained from making a personal appeal for himself and destroying any chance of saving himself, he wrote to the top executive, taking all the blame for the murder to save his companion's life.

Harris' last words to the interviewer were that he hoped that his case would be an example to other young men and then he leaned up to the cell bars and gazed straight into the eyes of the reporter and said that booze and dope had put him into the hangman's noose. He said that he appreciated what everyone had done for him and he forgave those who had wronged him and then he pointed to Monte in the next cell and told the interviewer that he had gotten the bum deal. As for himself he had given up all hope after his trial and conviction and said that the rumors that the Schilling crime had been planned in the state penitentiary were not true. He explained that they all ended up at Butte together where they were broke and desperate. Bill said that the gang had no intentions of staying in the Mining City and they intended to head for Tijuana after the holdup.

William spent most of his last thirty minutes in his cell writing a letter to his mother in which he asked that he buried in Montana an at the prisoner's request Sheriff Duggan didn't disclose any other information in the correspondence. Harris didn't disclose much information about his family and the officers did not press him when he said he preferred not to talk about his relatives. After his death, the small photograph of his mother, his dearest possession was found in William Harris' pocket and perhaps as the trap on the grim and forbidding platform dropped, the doomed young man's final thoughts went back to the times he spent on his mother's lap.

April 20, 1923

Monte Harris

Other Names: "Monte Blue"
Location and Gallows: The hanging of William and Monte Harris at Butte was the second multiple execution on ***Gallows No. Sixteen: (Jan. 1918): "Galloping Gallows" No. Five***.
Hanged with: William "Bill" Harris (not related)
Description: Monte was a small young man about twenty-two years old

and he had a rather slender build. Both Monte and Bill Harris were drug addicts.

Crime: Cold-blooded murder of Cyril "Sut" Schilling on Thanksgiving night, November 24, 1921.

Judge: Jeremiah J. Lynch

Prosecution: Silver Bow County Attorney and assisted by his chief deputy, Leslie B. Sulgrove

Defense: M.D. Kelly along with Charles E. O'Neill and assisted by Earl E. Blodgett and Frances A. Silver

Sheriff: Larry Duggan

Distinction: Monte was the first native-born Butte man to be hanged in Silver Bow County.

Relics and Remnants: The gallows, which was used to hang the Harris boys, eventually executed a total of eight convicted murderers and after its final victim in 1933, the scaffold was returned to Butte where it is currently in storage in the basement of the Silver Bow County Courthouse. Because the scaffold is being stored with possible hazardous material the ancient death machine is not currently available for viewing.

Monte Harris lost his parents when he was a young child and he was adopted by the sister of a well-known Butte businessman and he attended local schools in the Mining City. Although he had been raised in a good family he had been in considerable trouble and had quite a police record under his alias of "Monte Blue." While he had a reputation as being a petty thief, the authorities at Butte had never considered him especially dangerous. Chief of Police Mike O'Donnell reported that once Detective Mitchell had shot Monte in the heel while he was trying to escape after breaking into a Butte store.

After initially arresting Harris, Detective Mitchell took him to the Oxford Hotel where he was going to call for a patrol wagon. While in the hotel, Harris broke away and the detective followed the fugitive for about two blocks before ordering him to stop and then shooting him in the foot. The shooting took place on North Main Street at about five o'clock in the afternoon in front of several bystanders.

At the hospital Monte shook the detective's hand and reportedly told the officer that he was a good shot and he was glad he wasn't aiming at his head. Harris was later taken to the county jail but he eventually was transferred to the county hospital at the poor farm where he managed to escape after his heel had gotten better.

Several weeks later he was arrested for a minor offense at Great Falls and apparently being glad to be rid of him, the Silver Bow County authorities made no effort to have him returned to face the local charges. Not long afterwards, Monte was caught in the act of burglarizing a bakery at Billings and from there he was sent to the State Penitentiary on May 21, 1921. Six months later, Warden Potter paroled Monte Harris and he returned to Butte just before the Schilling murder.

At first it was believed that Monte was the shooter and the fact that he had been friends with Mr. Schilling outraged the people of Butte and the court found it difficult to appoint an attorney for the local boy.

Over objections of the county attorney, Monte Harris had first asked for bail, which the court had fixed at thirty thousand dollars on December 4, 1921, but the prisoner couldn't raise the necessary funds. Both Monte and Bill Harris were drug addicts and while they were confined at the county jail there were several attempts to smuggle drugs to them by the local boy's friends.

The week before Monte's trial he became quite ill with the flu and Dr. Dan J. Donahue had to treat him before the hearing opened on Tuesday, March 7, 1922, and after the regular jury venire had been exhausted the court was continued until Thursday. Along with those prospective jurors who weren't selected because they didn't understand English; had already formed an opinion or opposed capital punishment there were a few others who weren't considered for other reasons. Among these other disqualified men was the clerk of the court, J.F. Driscoll, Steve Kristy who was near death at a Butte hospital after having recently killed his wife and attempted suicide and W.H. Pearth who had died the night before the trial opened.

During the process of selecting the jury the courtroom and both hallways were jammed with prospective jurors who stood for over an hour while the jury commission and the clerk patiently checked them off of their list. There was an age limit of seventy years of age for prospective jurors and they were paid four dollars a day for their services. When the accounting of the names had been concluded, Judge Lynch ordered them to "hold up your hand," and a forest of palms went skyward.

After the oath was administered, the judge told them to take their seats, causing a big laugh in the courtroom, as there were only enough seats for about half of the prospective jurors. Judge Lynch corrected himself by saying, "I mean those who can find a seat then take it." The judge then stated the grounds on which a juror could be excused and then he said that he would listen to their valid excuses and immediately a long wriggly line, three abreast formed in front of the judge's bench and extended into the hallway.

Every excuse known to the court was presented including insufficient knowledge of the English language, business pressures, sickness in the family and personal illness. After politely listening to each and every personal story, the judge ordered them to take their places with the rest of the men, and after a short deliberation the court announced the names of those who were excused.

Finally by late Thursday night the attorneys had concluded their examinations of the prospective panelists and the following jury of Silver Bow County residents was selected:

Edwin B. Scott	John Karn	Pat O'Tool
H.F. Bartell	William J. O'Neill	Frank Benoit
J.R. Wall (f)	Edwin Walsh	W.H. Neavy
Collin McGibbon	Fred Lemke	Charles Mudro

(f) Foreman

Monte was neatly dressed in a black and white checkered suit with a silk shirt while he sat with his attorneys, M. D. Kelly and Charles O'Neill. The young defendant was newly shaven and sported a fresh haircut and like William Harris and Earl McCoy he sported a black Fedora hat, which was believed to have been shared by the three men. While William Harris was found guilty and assigned the death penalty a jury found Earl McCoy also guilty of first-degree murder but asked that he serve life at the state penitentiary. It was presumed that the jury was more lenient on McCoy because he had been a veteran of World War I, and after taking the stand in his own defense the little man was considered a very loyal person.

Monte took the witness stand in his own behalf and told the court that he been been raised at 211 South Arizona Street at Butte and later he worked at the Gagnon, Original, Badger, Speculator, High Ore and Colorado mines. He said that he had also been employed at two hotels as a bellhop and as a waiter and that he had been sentenced to a one to three year term at the state prison for burglary and when he was paroled after six months on November 11, 1921, he returned to Butte where he ran into William Harris.

William had been a barber at the penitentiary barbershop and he used to give the defendant his haircuts and shaves. Bill Harris took the defendant to 2346 Silver Bow Street to visit Ed Graham and then they all spent the night at Monte's room on the Dora Block. The following day Monte met with his rich uncle who gave him some money while Graham and Bill Harris rented the room on Wall Street. While on the witness stand, Monte admitted that he was a member of the Wall Street gang and that they had planned to rob the bank at Whitehall and also considered robbing the Holland Skating Rink.

The largest crowd to attend any of the trials dealing with the Schilling murder case turned out to hear the fate of their hometown boy, Monte Harris and the last day of his trial was delayed by ten minutes when the defendant reportedly slept in. The instructions to the jury by the judge were similar to the ones given in the McCoy case when the court stated that if the men were out to rob, and if a murder followed, all who participated in the crime were equally guilty of murder in the first degree. The jury was told that it was not to concern itself with the question of the guilt or innocence of the other men charged but merely with the guilt of Monte Harris.

The case was given to the jury at 2:59 on the afternoon of March 13, 1922, and at 3:49 the bailiff rushed into the courtroom to notify Judge Lynch that a decision had been made and by four o'clock the jury was back in their box. The officials expected a quick verdict and Harris wasn't returned to the jail and he and his guards waited in the courtroom for the verdict.

The crowd of spectators only shifted around a little while the jury was out and those fortunate enough to have a seat remained in them watching the clock and speculated among one another when the verdict would be in. Monte himself was reportedly cool and collected and he appeared as if he was a mere spectator instead of the main attraction to the drama. The defendant's face was like a statue as he watched the jury file back into the room and he didn't appear to be at all interested when the guilty verdict was announced.

The defendant seemed to have been in complete control of his feelings and there was not even a change in his color as the jury was polled and each one of the men stated: "Guilty." It was later learned that the jury had taken three ballots to determine the man's fate, the first stood at eight for hanging, one for a life sentence and three men wanted to leave the punishment up to the judge. The second ballot was nine for hanging and three to leave it up to the court and the third vote was unanimously for the death penalty.

Immediately after the verdict the defense asked for two weeks to prepare for sentencing and they were granted until ten o'clock on the morning of March 25, 1922. There was a murmur throughout the courtroom and there were obviously mixed feelings among the audience with some men being pleased with the verdict while some of the women in the crowd were crying and showing pity for the boy. The estimated cost of the three trials of the Harris boys and Earl McCoy was about twelve thousand five hundred dollars for the juries, witnesses, attorney fees, salaries of the deputies and other costs.

Monte Harris reportedly looked like a pitiful juvenile delinquent when the judge asked him to stand up for his sentencing and although Judge Lynch ordered him to death he didn't name the date and time of the execution as he apparently wanted to allow the defense time to prepare an appeal and if they failed, the Harris' would both be hanged on the same day, originally set for May 12, 1922. The arguments for a new trial for Monte Harris eventually took place on Saturday, April 29, 1922, but the motion was overruled.

Six days before his execution, Monte wrote his final appeal to Governor Joseph M. Dixon in a twenty-seven-page letter reviewing his life pointing out the circumstances that had befallen him as a young child. It was learned that the Governor had come very close to pardoning Monte after considering the hand-written letter from Bill Harris stating that he had killed Schilling and because of all the support from Butte and Great Falls. Monte explained to his friends and reporters that the worst hours of his imprisonment was when he was visited by the weeping women who came to pray with him. He said it gave him the "jimmies" when respectable old ladies broke out crying as they talked to him.

Monte told of one old lady who said that she and her friends had held a two-day prayer session for him and as he said that gesture hurt him, he glanced down and was silent for several seconds. The condemned man was particularly worried about his mother and he said, "If they hang me Friday morning it will kill her." Then in an attempt to brighten the mood, Monte spoke of more pleasant visits and pointed to the row of potted flowers on a shelf in his cell and said, "We don't even know most of the people that sent them."

From his cell Monte made a statement to reporters detailing his life and he said that narcotics had been the curse of his world. In his typewritten story he emphasized that it was his contact with houses of vice, which started him down the rode of crime and his eventual downfall. He made it clear that his adoptive mother had done her best to prevent him from straying but circumstances had gone against him explaining that because her husband was an invalid and unable to work, Monte found himself working for his family at a young age. He sold papers after school, and after quitting his classes in the eighth grade he became one of the youngest messenger boys in Butte. Mrs. Harris didn't approve of Monte working as a messenger as those young men were allowed into the "Red Light" districts of Butte without any restrictions.

After running the streets as a messenger for a couple of years Monte became a bellhop in the Thorton, Finlen and the Butte Hotels where wide open gambling and other vice was rampant. Besides his regular salary, Monte usually made from fifteen to fifty dollars a day in tips and after giving his mother four or five dollars a day he found himself with lots of money in which to get in trouble with. When he was older Harris went to work in the mines and started to make real money but the lure of making even more money he began riding racehorses for Mr. Howard of Helena. Monte managed to save some of his money and he started a taxi service in 1916 and by 1917, he had moved his business to Great Falls where he expanded into message services as well.

Young Monte was doing well in Great Falls and he eventually bought the Turkish Bath Parlor where he began associating with older businessmen including the manager of the top restaurant in town and the secretary of the union. Unfortunately for Monte, both of those successful men were also heavy users of opium and by 1921, Monte was in his words: "insane with drugs." In his statement, Monte took issue with the newspapers portraying that Mr. Schilling had befriended him, when actually he didn't allow young people, sometimes under-aged persons in his establishment unless they paid for their drinks.

Harris said that poor Mr. Schilling could have helped the young people out more if he and other tavern owners had refused young people from patronizing their drinking establishments. Thirty minutes before his march to the gallows Monte Harris sent the following message to the newspapermen: "My dying message is this: I thank all my friends who have been good to me. I forgive all my enemies. I die in peace with my God."

In the poor part of Butte in an old tumbledown building a little, bent, gray-haired old woman sat with her arms folded on her lap. The woman's hands were rough and thick from years of labor and they were wrapped in her apron as she rocked gently to and fro as she stared down at the worn carpet. That was how a reporter found Mrs. Harris, the adopted mother of Monte when he visited her with news that a total of eight of the jury in Monte's trial had signed the petition in an attempt to save her son from the gallows. After hearing the news, the woman's face lit up as she exclaimed, "Oh, thank God!" and then she choked with emotion before she stood up and began walking hurriedly back and forth in the little bedroom. When the man cautioned Mrs. Harris not to get her hopes up too high, the old woman said that her son had never given up hope so she would keep the faith.

Mrs. Harris told the man that her real son and Monte had kept the news of his arrest from her so she wouldn't get sick from worry and she had only known about Monte's trouble for six months and just two month before his scheduled execution her husband died. As a neighbor women tried to comfort her, Mrs. Harris screamed out that she was all alone and she said that they couldn't take her son's life too. "For twenty-nine years I lived over there," Mrs. Harris said as she pointed to Mercury and Arizona Streets and she said that it wasn't her foster son's fault.

She explained that from his bedroom window her young son good see the scenes of the "Red Light" district of Butte, which in the wide-open days was known as the "Twilight Zone." She said there wasn't any other place in the United States that could duplicate the tinsel-decked vice, which flaunted its abbreviated skirts, its paint and drunkenness in front of the public.

Postscript:

After his execution it was pointed out that Monte Harris had once been the young mascot of the Arizona Street Fire Station at Butte. As the story goes the firemen had noticed the little black haired toddler playing in the yard of the little house across the street from the firehouse and about three years later when Monte was about eight years old he would wander over to the station and visit with the lounging firefighters. Monte eventually became the official mascot of the company and all of the members loved the little boy.

In 1923, pictures of the executed murderer still adorned the walls of the fire station and in one photo the youngster was standing proudly with a group of firemen. Another picture showed Monte alone smiling, probably at the group of firemen who were standing around as the photographer snapped it and Fire Chief Fred Martin said it was hard to believe that it was the same kid.

July 18, 1924

Seth Orrin Danner

Location and Gallows: Danner was hanged inside the Gallatin County jail at Bozeman from the built-in scaffold, ***Gallows No. Fourteen: (March 1912)***.

Description: Danner had Cherokee blood and he was unusually large and powerful standing six feet, three with broad proportions.

Crime: Robbery and murder of Mr. and Mrs. John Sprouse at Central Park on November 14, 1920.

Judge: Benjamin B. Law

Prosecution: County Attorney E.A. Peterson assisted by State Attorney General Wellington D. Rankin

Defense: former county attorney, Justin M. Smith

Sheriff: James Smith

Distinction: Danner was the first man executed with a built-in gallows and the last person hanged in Gallatin County.

Relics and Remnants: The jail building and the gallows used in the execution of Seth Danner are still standing and the facility now houses the Gallatin County Historical Society Pioneer Museum at Bozeman.

During the fall of 1920, Seth Danner and his wife Iva were working on a threshing crew at Britton, South Dakota where they met and became friends with John and Florence Sprouse of Mobridge, South Dakota. After the harvest, the four agreed to drive to Bozeman to look for work, Mr. and Mrs. Sprouse traveling in one car and the Danner's and their children in another vehicle, a converted truck. They traveled Highway 10, the famous "Yellowstone Trail" until they reached Central Park on the Gallatin River, where they decided to make their camp in a strip of forest next to the river and about seventy-five feet from the main highway. They set up their tents side by side on a little rise and while they could be seen from the road the nearby farmers and ranchers paid little attention to the transients.

It was an ideal spot for a camp and instead of moving after a day or two the couples remained at Central Park about a month while they hunted, fished and trapped. A few hunters and fishermen visited with the campers as they passed along the river and they later testified that there were two men, two women, three children along with a small dog. On the evening of November 14, 1920, the two men went fishing on the river and sometime later Danner returned with some fish, but Mr. Sprouse wasn't with him. When Mrs. Sprouse became anxious about the whereabouts of her husband and began hounding Danner he picked up a small camp axe and struck her on the side of the head. The attacker then tied a cord tightly around the woman's throat and then dragged her into the Sprouse tent.

Mrs. Danner stood and watched the murder in shock and then Seth reportedly threatened her with death if she ever talked about the incident. By then it was quite late and the couple went to bed in their tent but later that night Danner left the tent and didn't return for a couple of hours. The next morning he pulled back the flap of the Sprouse tent and showed his wife the two bodies of both Mr. and Mrs. Sprouse. That night Danner buried the two bodies in a hole he had dug next to their tent and then covered it with rocks and brush.

Later the couple drove both cars to Three Forks where they eventually settled and sold the Sprouse vehicle to Jake Devore. The local folks didn't think anything of it when the campers had broken camp and left except that they had left the dog behind to fend for itself.

Danner found employment as a mechanic at the Avery Garage at Three Forks and he eventually began illegal activities in Gallatin County including bootlegging. After being arrested for grand larceny, Danner was placed on parole and he was forced to move to Bozeman for work. Mrs. Iva Danner had tried to convince her husband to confess the murders but each time he had threatened her and finally on June 7, 1923, the woman called on Deputy Pierce Elmore who was stationed at Three Forks. The deputy naturally believed Mrs. Danner wanted to talk to him about her husband's recent arrest or her recent divorce action against Seth but the officer was both amazed and skeptical when she said that her spouse had murdered two people in the fall of 1920.

When Deputy Elmore asked the woman why she had waited three years before reporting the murders, Mrs. Danner insisted that her husband had threatened to kill her if she went to the authorities. Because her husband was on probation and in Bozeman she felt safe to talk and although the deputy was far from convinced that the woman was telling the truth, Mrs. Danner insisted that he check the campsite. The deputy went to Central Park where he easily found the old campsite and he poked around a bit but he couldn't find any evidence of such a crime. Deputy Elmore was convinced that Mrs. Danner had cooked up the wild story in order to help her divorce proceedings but after again talking to the persistent woman he decided to take her to Bozeman in order to speak with Sheriff James Smith. The sheriff wasn't anymore inclined to believe the woman than his deputy, but of course the story would have to be investigated.

Mrs. Danner was nervous and looked at her clasped hands as she told the officers that her husband had killed the man and wife over their money but she couldn't say how much money the Sprouse's had and the officer felt it was hard to believe that a couple of auto-tramps would have enough money with them to tempt anyone to murder them over.

On June 8, 1923, Sheriff Smith along with Coroner E.W. Harland and Deputies Howell and Elmore took Iva Danner to Central Park to look for the remains of the murder victims. Since there was more moisture in June than in the fall, many of the small hollows along the river held small puddles and in one such depression the woman insisted was the location that her husband had buried the bodies. Following Mrs. Danner instructions, Sheriff Smith began poking about in the foot or more of water and muck when he suddenly dislodged some sort of object, which proved to be a human leg.

The gruesome find obviously proved that at least one body had been buried in the hollow and after the men began using picks and shovels they discovered the badly decomposed remains of Mr. and Mrs. Sprouse, both bodies were fully clothed except for the man's boots, which had been removed. An examination showed that the top of the man's head had been blown off with a shotgun and the woman's skull had two indentations on it.

The physician said that neither blow was sufficient to cause death and the woman may have been buried alive. Mrs. Danner was placed in protective custody; Seth Danner was arrested and their three girls, ages three to eight were placed in the custody of the Child and Animal Protective Home at Helena. Later that evening Mrs. Danner made a sworn statement to County Attorney E.A. Peterson that her husband had shot and killed John Sprouse with a 20-guage shotgun and then he murdered Mrs. Sprouse to silence her.

When Danner was taken into custody he didn't know what the charges against him were until shown a copy of the newspaper describing the alleged crime. He did admit having been in the camping party but he immediately denied any knowledge of the murders and he ridiculed the idea saying that his wife was framing him because she was getting tired of him. Danner presented a story that Mrs. Sprouse had been married before and her former spouse had killed her and John Sprouse.

Meanwhile the day after Danner was arrested Mrs. Danner formally filed for divorce, alleging cruelty and at first the husband said that he wouldn't fight the action, citing that it was the reason she had accused him of the ridiculous charges of murder, but by the end of June his attorney was fighting the decree, which would block her from testifying against her husband.

Danner's relationship with his wife was so confusing in the narrative that even the lawyers had trouble unraveling it. Danner and his present wife were first cousins and they were married at Dillon, Montana on December 23, 1916, and she was a sister of his first wife who died in Fairport, Kansas in 1913. Another bazaar fact was that his first wife had been married to Bert Danner, an uncle of Seth and the father of Iva Danner. When Bert Danner died, Seth married his uncle's widow and became Iva's stepfather when she was less than five years old. At the time the couple was married in 1916, Iva was fifteen years old and only weighed about eighty pounds.

At his arraignment Danner entered the courtroom smoking a cigarette and for the first time he appeared nervous. When presented with the charges, he once again placed the cigarette in his mouth and glanced over the papers. The judge apparently ignored the breach of etiquette and asked Danner if he had an attorney or if he had the money to hire one. To both questions Danner answered "No," and that he was not guilty of the charges. The prisoner said that he was the son of Amos Danner and Aldrea Cool and he was born and raised at Rooks County, Kansas. The accused man maintained that the former husband of Mrs. Sprouse probably killed the couple if in fact they were even dead pointing out that the remains hadn't yet been positively identified.

When first incarcerated, Danner ate well and laughed and joked with the other prisoners as well as the jailers. He sang at times, and he was permitted to use a banjo but at night he was heard pacing up and down in his cell. After his initial arraignment Danner became quite solemn but when he recovered from his nervousness he assumed his attitude of indifference, his appetite returned and he smoked heavily and read magazines, which the jailers brought in for him. The prisoner exercised by swinging by his hands from the top bars of his cell and he took delight in listening to the comments of the other prisoners about his muscular development resembling that of World Heavyweight Champion Dempsey.

Danner's trial for his life began on October 22, 1923, when the following jury was selected:

L.W. Watson	Burton Thompson	C.L. Watkins
Ralph Newkirk	W.J. Booher	W.J. Heaston
E.C. Warwood	Leonard Hinson	Ralph Bates
A.B. Carter	A.F. Dawes	E.H. Dean

On the second day of the trial the defense astounded the prosecution when it informed the court that the defendant waived any right, which might have prohibited a wife from testifying against her husband. This action led the way for Danner's wife to take the stand and prompted a severe warning by Judge Law concerning the safety of the court. Because the courthouse was fifty years old, the judge interrupted the trial to warn the audience that they were at their own risk as the walls might fall in at any moment. The judge later ordered the sheriff and the bailiff to prevent additional people from crowding into the courtroom, and again he warned the spectators of the fire department's dire warnings.

Iva Danner told the court of her family's gypsy life along the mountain streams of North and South Dakota and Montana where she cooked fish and wild game that her husband caught with line, rifle and trap. With tears in her eyes she explained that she was married just two days before her first child was born and during their first few years of marriage she had only lived five months inside of a house, the rest of the time they lived in tents or under the open skies. The breathless crowd listened as Mrs. Danner described how her husband brutally killed Mrs. Sprouse by striking her twice with an axe and then strangled her with a cord before burying her and her husband just a feet away from the Danner tent.

The prosecution presented the camp axe, shotgun and the skull of Florence Sprouse as well as statements signed by the defendant stating that he had not seen Mr. and Mrs. Sprouse since they left South Dakota, and yet witnesses saw them camped together at Central Park. Members of the Sprouse family including the sixty-five-year-old mother of the victim, Mrs. Alpha Sprouse identified personal items belonging to her son including his guns, watches and other family keepsakes, which were later found in the Danner household.

At first the defense was going to have Danner testify on his own behalf but eventually they only offered his formal statement that Mrs. Sprouse had killed her own husband while he was checking his traps after she had found out that he had been carrying on an affair with Iva Danner. Then when the wildly jealous Mrs. Sprouse came after Mrs. Danner at the camp the defendant's wife killed her with the axe. Danner claimed that he had been fishing at the time of the murders and when he returned to camp his wife told him what had happened and together they searched for and found the body of Mr. Sprouse.

The defendant said that he and his wife buried the bodies and that his oldest daughter had witnessed the killing of Florence Sprouse. He claimed that his wife was framing him because she was interested in another man and she wished to get rid of him. Danner's counsel then tried to prove that Mrs. Danner had a history of being promiscuous and that Seth Danner had married the unwed pregnant child in order to protect her honor. Attorney Smith told the jury that Seth Danner had agreed to help conceal the bodies in order to protect his young wife.

When the defense put Danner's eleven-year-old daughter from another marriage on the stand the under-nourished and sick child broke down when she was being questioned about the Central Park camp in 1920. Danner had earlier said that if his daughter were allowed to testify she would clear him of the murder charge but in a dramatic move, he walked over to the witness stand and with tears in his eyes he took his child in his arms. In what was his first display of emotion, Danner gently shook his daughter's hand and comforted her and after smiling at her father the girl left the courtroom.

While Danner never did take the stand in his own behalf, he was seen occasionally whispering to his attorney about the various testimonies offered. He had lost most of his healthy color and he looked in poor health as the result of his long confinement. Danner asked to be clean-shaven before entering the courtroom each day explaining that there might be a lot of women present and he didn't want to look like a bum to them.

In his closing argument, Defense Attorney Smith stressed the inadequate motive for the murders presented by the prosecution of an old car and a few dollars and Danner's version was far more probable. After seven hours of deliberation and four ballots the jury apparently chose to believe Iva Danner and they returned a first-degree murder verdict against Seth Danner on October 26, 1923. The defendant did not look at the jury as they filed into the courtroom at 11:20 that evening or afterward as he walked to the jail without any sign of concern as he was escorted by four deputies.

While the verdict of guilt had been reached on the first ballot, the difference of opinion arose from the question of the degree and the punishment. On November 17, Judge Law sentenced Seth Danner to be hanged but he didn't set the date of execution since the defense had filed intentions for a new trial. The judge eventually sentenced Danner to be hanged on January 11, 1924, but at the last minute Mr. Smith filed an appeal to the Supreme Court for a new trial.

On May 26, 1924, the Supreme Court denied a new trial for Danner and within days his demeanor had changed from a happy spirit to a person who was less talkative and preferred to be left alone. His re-sentencing was delayed as Judge Law had spent several weeks in Virginia at the bedside of his sick father but when he returned he set the fateful day for July 18, 1924. At his re-sentencing, the prisoner didn't show any interest in the proceedings, which reportedly only lasted about five minutes. Upon returning to his jail cell the prisoner told the jailer that they would only have to feed him until the eighteenth and the deathwatches were set for eight-hour shifts and they guarded Danner in the rear cell of the jail.

As the weeks past by the prisoner was allowed visitors and he was presented with a cake adorned with candles on his birthday. As petitions were being circulated to be presented to the Governor, Danner's former wife and new husband left Montana and relocated at Seattle. Observers reported that the condemned man was more perturbed about his wife divorcing him than the more serious murder charges, which he would pay for with his life. The prisoner grew more and more nervous and unsettled almost by the hour and he was seen constantly running his fingers through his hair, pounding on his chest and slapping his knees as he walked up and down and back and forth in his cell like a wild animal in a cage.

Meanwhile extra platforms were erected on each side of the built-in death trap to accommodate the officers and those extensions were re-enforced with iron pipes secured from the ceiling to the basement floor. About a week before the execution Sheriff James Smith received a new rope from a specialty cord manufacturer and it was described as having a silken texture and it was guaranteed to stand a strain of a drop of over one thousand pounds for a distance of six feet.

Two days before his execution, Danner told a reporter from the "Bozeman Daily Chronicle" that he never felt better in his life and while in the death corridor he expounded on his philosophy of life. He said he didn't want any pity because he was better off than anyone, as he knew when he would die while everyone else wasn't aware of when they would go. He assured his visitor that he had made peace with his God and he wasn't afraid to die and while he was happy and looking forward to his end, he felt sorry for the officers saying, "I pity the officers who have to bump me off." He explained that the deputies and jailers had been good to him and that they felt bad about what they had to do. Danner wanted to be brave for the officers and he promised that he wouldn't weaken at the end.

Danner said that during his fifteen months of incarceration he had time to reflect and considering everything, life wasn't very promising for him anyway, pointing out that the world was in such a state of turmoil referring to the news reports that there wasn't any peace anywhere on earth. The prisoner continued by trying to show pity for his visitor saying that he and the rest of society would be left behind with such a life to look forward to.

Danner then pointed out his physical condition saying that he felt better than he looked and again said he wasn't afraid to die and remarked, "That I have been in tighter boxes than this in my life time, and my luck has always been with me." When the visitor was about to leave Danner shook his hand and said: "I'm the happiest man on earth and I having nothing to worry or fear; I will within a short time be among the blessed."

During his last day the prisoner partook of two hearty meals and just before midnight he ate again. The prisoner's noon meal consisted of roast beef with a salad and strawberries, for his late night meal the prisoner again had roast beef and then he talked and smoked constantly with his guard. Since his conviction, Danner had spent a great deal of his time studying the Bible and discussing the scriptures with his visitors and deathwatches.

Members of the Salvation Army visited Danner weekly but he finally accepted the Catholic Church during his last week of life and Father A.D. Leitham, pastor of the Holy Rosary Church of Bozeman became his advisor and confessor. Danner spent the day before his death quietly in his cell and he spent considerable time with Father Leitham and Father Joseph Blaere of St. Mary's Church at Livingston who prepared him for his fate and shortly before midnight on July 17, the prisoner was baptized.

While the priests were with the prisoner, Sheriff Smith and his men prepared the scaffold, which had been built in a small room at the county jail that was built in March of 1912. The officers dropped a black covering over the scaffold to completely hide the apparatus from the witnesses until it was being used and the sheriff didn't have invitations to the execution printed up and he apparently notified the witnesses individually.

Besides the two Catholic priests and the members of the sheriff's department, Deathwatch Sil Bragg, Undersheriff Orville Jones and Deputies E. Max Howell, Roscoe C. Holland and D. Pierce Elmore the witnesses from Gallatin County included John C. Holland, Thomas S. Kirk, John M. Arnold, L.E. Fuller, M.F. Getchell, David T. Powell, A.R. Williams, M.B. Bond, T.L. Tillery, O.L. DeVore, A.I. Poor, W.H. Everson and Dr. Joseph Piedalue. Other persons present at the hanging were Gallatin County Attorney E.A. Peterson, Salvation Army Captain Fred Stevens, Park County Sheriff James McClarty and his deputy, Clarence Gilbert.

Danner maintained his apparent indifferent attitude and he never showed any signs of breaking down under the strain and he declared that he had made peace with God and that he would go to the gallows with a clear conscience and would go to Heaven. He said that he was comforted by the fact that it would all be over in a fraction of a second, while those left behind would have to live in a state of uncertainty about their death.

Danner was clearly disappointed on the morning of his execution when County Attorney Peterson handed him a letter that he had received from the prisoner's former wife, which read in part: "Seattle, Washington, July 15, 1924. Dear Mr. Peterson, In reply to your letter, would say that I am well. I have never been in the hospital. I have never been sick since I left Three Forks. Now, my husband (James Troglia) and I have been in Seattle for some time. He is working in a bakery. Mr. Peterson, you can tell Seth that I will meet him in Heaven; that we are all trying to go to the same place; that I hope that he don't do there what he has done on earth." She finished her letter by asking Mr. Peterson if Seth had ever spoken of her.

After Undersheriff Orville Jones read the death warrant to the prisoner the march to the gallows began and when Sheriff Smith, the guards and two priests appeared at the door of his cell at about two a.m. Danner arose from his chair and quickly fell in between two guards and the procession passed down the jail corridor. Danner smoothed back his long black hair with both hands; threw his head back and stuck out his chest as he walked through the long corridor towards the death chamber.

One deputy entered the small room ahead of the procession and he raised the black curtain, which had hidden the scaffold. Sheriff Smith, Deputy Howell and Deathwatch Sil Bragg accompanied Danner up the concrete stairs to the railed balcony and the trap door, which was on the west side of the room. The condemned man stepped without hesitation upon the steel trap at 2:04 a.m. and for eleven minutes he faced the small crowd of sixteen residents of Gallatin County.

The prisoner seemed paler than usual but while some of the witnesses displayed tears and moist eyes, Danner's composure was described as being calloused. Father Leitham handed a crucifix to the prisoner and the man pressed it to his lips and handed it back to the Reverend Father. After he had secured Danner's arms, knees and ankles, the sheriff asked him if he had a statement to make and the doomed man replied, "I bear no malice to anyone. I have made peace with my Savior and will go to Him with the assurance that I am fully prepared. I hope that all of you will follow my example. I have nothing more to say, Good-bye."

As Danner stood on the trap awaiting his final exit one observer later said that the paleness of his face brought out the cruel lines that revealed his true character. The reporter recalled a story that the condemned man had told him illustrating that he took pleasure in seeing others suffer. Danner told the reporter that when he was in a snowball fight as a young boy he said they were all having fun and they were all trying to get the better of the other team.

Danner found a doorknob and he packed it into a snowball and threw it at one of the other kids and the concealed medal ball struck the lad near his eye and he was knocked out. Danner said that he returned home years later and he saw the fellow he had hit in the fight and according to the prisoner the man was crippled and he had never recovered from the terrible blow to the head.

While Sheriff Smith was adjusting the noose and the black cap many of the witnesses reportedly turned their heads away and after a moment of complete silence the trap was sprung at 2:15 a.m. and Danner's body dropped about six feet. The body quivered for about sixty seconds and four minutes later the county physician pronounced Seth Danner dead. After being allowed to hang for ten minutes longer, the body was cut down and Dr. Piedalue announced that the cause of death was the rupturing of the spinal cord between the base of the skull and probably the fifth cervical.

The doctor said that both jugular veins had swollen until they almost burst and the rope had cut the skin from ear to ear. The body was placed in a black coffin inscribed with "At Rest" and a silver crucifix and it was turned over to Funeral Director H.F. West for burial. Internment was made at three o'clock that morning in the northwest section of the Catholic Cemetery at Bozeman with Father Leitham giving the burial services in both Latin and English while Father Blaere held a flashlight for the reading. The dim light reportedly gave the scene a strange mood, as the faces of twenty-three spectators for the services were barely visible.

Danner's sisters, Mrs. Lucy Marlow of Coffeyville, Kansas and Mrs. Mabel Moody of Newberry, Oregon had made a desperate eleventh-hour appeal to Governor Joseph M. Dixon in an unsuccessful attempt to save their brother's life. When all hope was gone, Seth Danner had asked to be photographed before his execution and he requested that Sheriff Smith send a copy to his loyal sisters.

As was customary, the identity of the executioner who had released the trap was unknown even to the two men assigned the task. Two separate ropes led from the gallows, one going to the basement while the other went harmlessly into an adjoining room. At a given signal from the sheriff, both ropes were pulled and the trap was sprung, only one of the ropes was actually attached to the release mechanism and neither man knew who had pulled the fatal trigger.

Postscript:
At the time of the execution there were only two other prisoners at the county jail, Tony Schwemmer and Harvey Walton, a black man from Manhattan and it was reported that during the hanging the two men buried themselves in the bedding of their cots. While there were no women present at the execution one particular lady was inside the jail and reportedly claimed that she had observed the hanging. That same unidentified woman reportedly followed Danner's dead body to his grave where she later planted flowers.

Iva Danner died a few years later and there were persistent rumors that the woman had made a deathbed confession that she and not her husband had killed Florence Sprouse at Central Park in 1920. While Iva's confession was impossible to prove, Seth Danner's sister later reported that his former wife had told her that she still loved him and that she wouldn't live long after his execution. Mrs. Moody had visited her sister-in-law at Three Forks while Danner was on death row and she noticed the woman was still wearing Florence Sprouse's coat, which had been taken immediately after the murders. Evidently it didn't bother Iva Danner to take comfort from the murder victim's coat.

In 1982, the Gallatin County Historical Society began renovating the old county jail and eventually established a museum in the old building. Some of the residents of Bozeman including Sally Lytle who has cleaned the museum believe that the spirit of Seth Danner is still present in the old jailhouse where he was hanged. Lytle has cited several unexplained events, which have occurred late at night while she was working. She has claimed that her cleaning supplies have mysteriously disappeared while working on the first floor only to reappear on the second floor and she also said that certain electric outlets have gone dead while she was vacuuming only to be found in perfect condition the next day. Although Sally claims she feels Danner's presence in the building from time to time, she has never felt threatened by the spirit and she believes that the spirit is only displaying his sense of humor and is only having fun with her.

February 14, 1925
Roy Walsh

Other Names: Albert Wallace Schoonover, Albert Bell, Roy Mason and Donald Stewart

Location and Gallows: When Walsh was hanged at Boulder he became the sixth man to be executed on ***Gallows No. Sixteen: (Jan. 1918): "Galloping Gallows" No. Five***.

Description: The twenty-two years old Walsh stood six foot tall, weighed two hundred pounds and had a medium build, hazel eyes, dark brown hair and medium complexion

Crime: Murder of Albert Johnson at his store at Renova in the Jefferson Valley on the night of June 26, 1923.

Judge: Lyman H. Bennett of Virginia City

Prosecution: County Attorney Howard A. Johnson assisted by former county attorney, James Kelly of Butte.

Defense: John E. Elliott of Butte

Sheriff: John W. Mountjoy

Distinction: Walsh was the last man hanged in Jefferson County and many of those who knew him believed that he was nearly a genius even though he had little formal education.

Relics and Remnants: The gallows, which was used to hang Walsh, eventually executed a total of eight convicted murderers and after its final victim in 1933, the scafold was returned to Butte where it is currently in storage in the basement of the Silver Bow County Courthouse. Because the scaffold is being stored with possible hazardous material the ancient death machine is not available for viewing. While the scaffold can't be seen at the Mining City, the bullet that killed Albert

Johnson is on display at the Jefferson County Courthouse at Boulder.

On the evening of June 26, 1923, fifty-year-old Albert Johnson, the proprietor of the general store at Renova on the Northern Pacific was reading a newspaper when there was a knock at the side door of his business. Thinking that it was a neighbor, who was calling late for some small purchase, the cautious merchant peered through the partially opened door but he saw a large man wearing a mask and carrying a rifle.

As he was bolting the entrance to his business he was shot through the door and the 30-30-caliber bullet struck Johnson in the windpipe and he reeled backwards as his assailants ran off. A moment later a dark automobile with its curtains drawn over the windows roared away as Johnson tried to use the telephone for help but the holdup men had taken the precautions of cutting the phone lines to prevent outgoing calls from being made.

With the faint drumming of the get-away car still in the air, the badly injured merchant made his way through the darkness toward the home of his neighbor, O.W. Severtson who called the sheriff at Boulder and a doctor from Whitehall. Dr. L.R. Packard arrived at Renova accompanied by Fred Fessenden, Marshal Waldo and Elroy Moulton, and after administering first aid the doctor accompanied the wounded man to Butte. It was probably because Al Johnson was an old-timer of the west, possessing the belief that people were honest, which cost him his life at Murray Hospital at Butte some twenty-four hours later.

Johnson's chest was full of wood splinters from the door and his vocal cords were destroyed rendering him practically speechless and therefore he couldn't provide many details about his attackers. While being propped up on his cot at the hospital to allow easier breathing from his wound he was able to write down answers to questions by Deputy County Attorney Emigh. Johnson didn't know who had shot him and said he only saw one man at the door. The authorities were never able to recover a wallet, which Mr. Johnson reportedly carried on his person that was known to contain from five hundred to one thousand dollars.

After being notified, Boulder County Sheriff John W. Mountjoy and Undersheriff M. B. Knight went to Renova where they found that any footprints or other clues at the crime scene had already been obliterated by the many citizens of the little town passing into and out of the store after the shooting. After questioning the folks the officers received word from one woman that she heard a vehicle speed off immediately after the shooting and Sheriff Mountjoy took up the trail of an automobile, which had badly worn tires leading to the main highway towards Butte.

Meanwhile the Silver Bow sheriff's office had been notified and they were also on the lookout for the get-away vehicle. The tracks of the car were easily followed towards Butte and the large Cadillac was found at about 9:15 on the morning of June 28, 1923, between two houses near the Parrot Smelter. An examination of the vehicle quickly convinced Silver Bow County Deputies Jack Duggan and Dennis Lowney that it was the stolen car stolen from Butte wholesaler, Charles Youlden. The officers found a large red Mackinaw coat and a complete set of tools used by burglars in the stolen vehicle.

Deputy Duggan pointed to one of the nearby houses and announced that it was the home of one Arthur Hughes, a suspected car thief. The authorities quickly arrested seventeen-year-old Arthur "Mickey" Hughes, a miner from Butte while he was having breakfast at his mother's house at 516 East Park Street. Hughes was taken to the Butte city jail and finger printed as he denied anything to do with the shooting. At first Hughes was a tough nut to crack but according to Sheriff Mountjoy after a few hours of grilling he finally admitted he had been at Renova the previous night, but he denied being involved with the shooting. The Butte officers knew that Hughes had been working with a partner and the red Mackinaw jacket found in the Cadillac was too large to fit the younger man.

Later at the county attorney's office Hughes asked the stenographer to tear up his previous statement and then he confessed to having participated in the holdup attempt but he named Roy Walsh as the shooter. In Hughes' statement he said that after knocking at the door, Walsh peered through the window to determine the location of Mr. Johnson as he came to the door. Walsh then stepped back a few steps and leveled his rifle and fired through the door.

That afternoon rancher, Jack Lank noticed a stranger in one of his fields about a mile west of Cardwell while he was looking for some of his cattle. When he started for the man, Mr. Lank said the stranger disappeared in the brush along the river bottom. In an isolated cabin on his property, the rancher discovered it had been occupied and in the nearby bushes he located a Buick automobile. There was a 30-30 rifle with four shells in the magazine on the rear seat and the rancher slipped his little finger into the muzzle and determined that the weapon had been recently fired.

Having heard about the shooting at Renova, Mr. Lank called Sheriff Mountjoy who instructed him to sound the alarm among his neighbors and try and find the suspect. By the time the sheriff and Undersheriff Knight arrived at Jefferson Island a posse of ranchers and local businessmen armed with Winchesters and shotguns had already surrounded a clump of willows and they were squeezing the suspect. Sheriff Mountjoy called out, "Come out of there if you want to keep a whole hide!"

As Deputy Knight was beating the brush the posse heard a shout of, "All right, I'll give up" and Walsh emerged from the thicket. Mr. Lank quickly identified him as a farmhand that he let use his old cabin several months earlier. When Lank stated that he thought the young man had left the country, Walsh answered that he had, but he came back to look for work. Then the rancher commented that it was funny that a man looking for work could be driving such a fancy automobile.

Trying to shake the suspect into confessing, Sheriff Mountjoy told the men to cut out the small talk and then he told Walsh that he had been caught with the goods and Hughes was back in Butte talking his guts out. To the sheriff's surprise, not a single muscle in Walsh's face indicated any shock or fright and the suspect only sneered and said he didn't know what the officer was talking about. The prisoner was first taken to Whitehall where he identified himself as Roy Mason and he said he knew a Roy Walsh but he was at Butte.

The ruse didn't last long as several people at Whitehall recognized him as Roy Walsh and the suspect made the sullen trip to Boulder quietly refusing to talk about the killing. He refused to believe that Arthur Hughes had made a statement against him, believing the story of the confession was an attempt by the officers to get him to talk. When the party arrived at Boulder, Walsh took one look at the county building and said, "Call this a jail?" with a sarcastic grin.

A check with the motor vehicles registrar at Deer Lodge showed that the Buick had been stolen and the arrest of Hughes and Walsh on murder charges led the authorities to uncover several other stolen automobiles from the Butte area during the last few weeks. Meanwhile County Attorney H. Johnson questioned Walsh at Boulder but he wasn't able to get anything out of the prisoner concerning the murder so they held him for the stolen vehicle.

The sheriff posted a special guard posing as a man arrested for bootlegging in an adjoining cell to Walsh's in an effort to pick up some evidence against the suspected murderer. While the stool pigeon didn't learn anything about the murder he did tip the guards off about a planned jailbreak by Walsh. A search of the prison's cell by the deputies uncovered a key carved from a piece of discarded hardwood, which was found to easily open the cell door and in less than a week Walsh had made a second attempt to escape by wrenching a piece of angle iron from his cot to try and force the lock.

While he was frustrated over his failures, the prisoner remained an egotist and he announced that there wasn't a jail strong enough to hold him and he ridiculed the Boulder jail and boasted that it couldn't hold him for long. After the failed attempts to break jail and the prisoner's threats, Sheriff Mountjoy decided to move Walsh to the Silver Bow County Jail for safekeeping. Before assigning Walsh to a cell at the Butte facility, the jailer was required to make a routine search of all new prisoners and as Walsh was removing his clothing one of the officers discovered a piece of heavy pipe, which he had removed from the washbowl in his cell at Boulder in the prisoner's pants.

Albert Johnson was well known throughout the state, having come to Montana in about 1891, and having served with distinction in the United States Army during the Spanish-American War. Mr. Johnson was extremely popular at Renova and he usually supplied the free ice to make the ice cream for the annual Fourth of July picnics. Besides his brother, Morgan of Anaconda who eventually took over the business at Renova, Johnson was survived by a daughter who could not be located and two sisters, Mrs. Arvilla Sellers of Goodrich, Texas and Mrs. Mary Becraft of El Dorado Springs, Missouri.

The funeral of Al Johnson was held on Saturday, June 30, 1923, at the home of his brother at 409 Cedar Street at Anaconda and he was later buried at the Hill Cemetery at the Smelter City. Roy Walsh was held in strict seclusion at the jail at Boulder and he was not told of Mr. Johnson's death in the hopes that he would be more likely to make a statement. On June 29, 1923, Walsh finally broke his sullen silence and he confessed to firing the shot, which resulted in the death of Albert Johnson.

Walsh not only told the authorities that he had done the shooting, he said that he had deserted his companion, Arthur Hughes as he tried to flee the scene. He stated that the two men had participated in several robberies and that Mrs. Sara Hughes, the mother of Arthur was aware of their activities and had covered and protected them. Walsh's confession was made in the presence of Sheriff Mountjoy and Undersheriff Knight and after it was put down in writing and signed by the prisoner, it was sworn before a notary public.

Based on the statement by Walsh, which corroborated in many details Hughes' confession, Boulder County Attorney Howard Johnson filed first-degree murder charges against both men on Monday, July 2, 1923. While Hughes stated that Walsh first knocked on the door; then peered through the window and then shot through the door, his partner claimed that they both carefully planned that Arthur be on one side of the building to prevent Johnson's escape while he knocked on the other door. Walsh said that he stumbled over a box as he was going around the building and that he looked through a window to see if Johnson had heard the commotion. He claimed that his rifle accidentally discharged as his hand got tangled up in a vine next to the building.

Without waiting to learn if he had hit Mr. Johnson, Walsh said that he jumped the fence and ran back to the stolen car that they had parked nearby and then he drove past the store and crossed the nearby bridge into Madison County. About two hours later he drove back to Renova in an effort to find his partner, but after seeing the Jefferson County patrol cars he turned around and drove the car into a swamp where he abandoned it and the sheriff and the posse later captured him. The prisoner said that the reason for the attempted robbery was to raise funds so that he and Hughes could go to Seattle as the law was closing in on them at Butte.

Another motive for the crime presented was a confrontation, which Walsh reportedly had with Mr. Johnson a few months earlier concerning a delinquent bill that the defendant had at the store. Days later Walsh was seen pressing his face against the store window and stating: "I'll get you one of these days, Johnson." It was also determined that Walsh had been sentenced to the Washington State Reformatory at Monroe in 1918 on a grand larceny charge under the name of Albert Bell, where he escaped less than two years later.

Defense Attorney John Elliott, who handled the defense of both Hughes and Walsh, announced that he would prove that his clients didn't kill Mr. Johnson but a third party who was hiding outside as the ill-fated pair were going to rob the store. To prove his theory, Elliott announced a week prior to Walsh's trial that he planned on subjecting his client to a new scientific method for telling the truth, using the drug Scopomalin or "truth serum."

At that time the use of Scopomalin had been proven successful at San Quentin on convicts and it was scheduled to be used in a criminal case at Chicago on not only a defendant but on witnesses as well.

The defense arranged for Dr. R.E. House of Ferris, Texas, and the foremost authority on Scopomalin to administer the drug upon Walsh. After Dr. House agreed to come to Montana, the defense attorney notified Walsh's family and friends about the large fee required to bring in the well-known medical professional responsible for the experiments at San Quentin. While Dr. House was willing to come to Montana, time became an issue and the defense asked for a continuance on the grounds that he didn't had enough to prepare with Hughes at the Boulder jail and Walsh at Butte.

On July 17, 1923, just four days before the scheduled trial of Roy Walsh, Judge Lyman Bennett denied the continuance, which would have postponed the hearing until the next term of court. The refusal by Judge Bennett also prevented the Walsh trial to be the first to use of the truth serum drug in a Montana murder case as both Hughes and Walsh had signed affidavits signifying their willingness to submit themselves to the drug. Unable to secure a continuance, the defense then requested a change of venue on the grounds that the murder case had aroused widespread interest and attention especially in Jefferson County. In denying the motion, Judge Bennett said that he was convinced that there weren't strong enough feelings against the defendants to make him believe they wouldn't get a fair trial in Jefferson County.

For the first time since their arrest Hughes and Walsh were brought together on Friday, July 20, for the latter's first day of trial on Saturday, July 21, 1923. The prisoners were brought into the courtroom handcuffed and accompanied by Sheriff Mountjoy, Undersheriff M.D. Knight and another deputy and Mrs. Sarah Hughes sat with the defendants at the defense table and vehemently defended "her two boys," as she called them.

Archie Hughes was the woman's youngest son and he had suffered from infantile paralysis, which had impaired his facial features. The woman reportedly said that, "If Archie Hughes hangs; he has a brother in the British Army to whom certain officials of Jefferson County will have to answer to." When asked about the charges of her son and Walsh stealing cars, Mrs. Hughes said, "What of it, lots of people steal cars," and then she stated that a woman in Butte had induced the boys to steal autos.

Mrs. Hughes threatened to reveal the Butte woman if she didn't offer financial aid for the boys' defense and the mother also claimed she knew the real killer of Mr. Johnson. The woman said it was a man the Renova merchant had help send to the state prison some ten years earlier and that the convict had sworn he would "get" Johnson some day. When the trial began, Attorney Elliott alleged bias and prejudice against his clients among the citizens of Jefferson County and he filed an affidavit concerning Sheriff Mountjoy remarking that if Walsh and Hughes weren't quickly taken to jail at Butte, a trial would not be necessary implying that the citizens would have lynched them.

John P. Shea of Butte testified that ha had visited with several men at Renova and Whitehall all displaying angry feelings toward the defendants and one of the men had told him that there were a number of men in the northern part of the county that had said they would perjure themselves to get on the jury so that they could vote to hang the accused. On the stand Sheriff Mountjoy said that while he did hear indirectly that there might have been a lynching, he believed the defendants would be able to get a fair trial at Boulder.

The undersheriff confirmed the sheriff's views as well as W.W. Severtson, the neighbor of the victim at Renova who said that he hadn't heard much talk about the case and he believed it would be easy to get a fair jury. Even County Attorney Johnson took the witness chair and told the court that he had traveled throughout the county and he had found no indications that there was bias or prejudice against the two accused men. He denied making the statement that if the prisoners were released the county would be saved the expense of a trial.

Sheriff Mountjoy and his staff exercised the utmost care to prevent an escape but on various occasions the prisoners were caught in the act of trying to break out. One morning the sheriff entered their cell and found that during the night Walsh and Hughes had tried to burn their way out through the roof using an electrical wire. By stripping the wire of an electric light they managed to burn through some of the tin roofing. On another occasion the special deputy, posing as the arrested moonshiner was asked to come in on a plan to break the heavy iron lock on the cell door and the officer was offered five hundred dollars if he could get through the lock and then keep quiet about it.

Although it was predicted to take several days to select a jury a panel was obtained during the first morning of the trial. Actually the jury was secured in record time and not a single man called for duty was against the death penalty and out of thirty-four men called, the attorneys only questioned eighteen before the following jury was selected:

Jedson Shankoltzer	Antone Anderson	Thomas Johnson
Charles Perry	Theodore Schuley	Martin Jensen
Henry Sanborn	Henry Madison	J.T. Baker
Joe Nugent	G.W. Stride	unknown

For the first time Walsh displayed any signs of nervousness and he was allowed to sit with his attorney without handcuffs. According to testimony, Walsh and Hughes had planned the robbery at Renova while they were stopped at Cedar Hill and they arrived at Johnson's store between ten and eleven o'clock on the evening of June 26. When they arrived at Renova, Mr. Johnson was talking to another man so the robbers waited until he had left and then Walsh took up his position in a clump of bushes on the east side while Hughes watched the west side of the building.

Although the defense tried to get Walsh's earlier confession thrown out, Judge Bennett allowed the evidence to be heard and after listening to hours of arguments the judge ruled that the defendant's statement made three days after his arrest that his rifle accidentally discharged into the door of the Johnson store would be admissible.

Walsh was the only witness for the defense and on the stand he showed no sign indicating that he was engaged in a crucial fight for his life. He told the court that Sheriff Mountjoy had told him following his arrest that things would go better for him if he gave a clear statement and he was made to believe that if he made a "clean breast" of the night of the murder that certain leniency would be shown him. The prisoner also claimed that the sheriff didn't advise him of his constitutional rights to counsel or that any statements made might be used against him.The rest of that day' session was taken up with arguments whether or not the sheriff had made promises in order to secure a confession from the defendant.

In Walsh's written confession he swore that he and Hughes were going to use the stolen money to travel west to Missoula and Seattle with the Cadillac they had stolen. He said they hadn't any real plans other than to hang around the store until Johnson was alone and then stick him up. Walsh said that he didn't want to hurt the man, but figured they would have to tie him up. Walsh had made their two masks from an old shirt and Hughes was to hold Johnson up with his 32-claiber six-shooter while he took the cash and other provisions from the store.

The plan went bad when Walsh tripped over a box outside of the door and when he crouched down by the vines the rifle in his right hand caught on something and accidentally discharged into the door. After the gun discharged Walsh said he jumped over a fence and ran to the railroad tracks and to his car. He finished his written and signed statement by stating that no promises had been made to him and he was making the statement because he knew that the authorities would find out about the facts anyway from Hughes and others.

Sheriff Mountjoy was grilled on the stand by the defense concerning his means of obtaining Walsh's statement and when asked if he had asked the defendant for a statement or informed him of his right to counsel the officer said he did ask the prisoner for a statement and he didn't think he told the accused that he could have a lawyer present.

When asked if he informed Walsh that any statement he made might be used against him Sheriff Mountjoy answered he believed he had. When he was finished with the sheriff, Attorney Elliott called County Attorney Johnson to the stand and when he asked the prosecutor if he had told the defendant he couldn't have an attorney until July 9, Assistant County Attorney Kelley objected to the questioning and it was sustained.

Finally Judge Bennett ruled that the point in question was whether or not the inducement was sufficient to cause a false admission and he concluded that Walsh's statement was in the nature of a confession and not an admission. During these arguments it should be noted that the jury was excluded from the courtroom. The next day the trial was threatened by the sickness of juror, Martin Jenson of Grace who suffered with a high fever while in the jury box and the hearing was recessed for a few hours for the man to rest.

The following day on the advice of the physician who was attending the sick juror, Judge Bennett ordered a continuance of the trial until the following day, Thursday, July 26. Although Mr. Jenson was able to find his seat with aid and said that he could go on, the judge feared that the juror may relapse and his condition might result in the dismissal of the jury, which would call for a re-trial of the case. Martin Jenson greatly benefited from the recess and when court convened the following day there were no further delays in the trial.

During Friday's testimony a gun expert testified that gunpowder marks found at the scene showed that the barrel of Walsh's rifle was closer to the door than the vines, which the defendant had claimed caused the accidental discharge of the weapon. Attorney Elliott decided not to call Arthur Hughes to the stand and Walsh was recalled to the stand and he said that he was a twenty-two-year-old mechanical engineer and inventor. He claimed he didn't know anything about the murder and that he didn't make the false confession and swore he did not sign the statement.

Walsh had contradicted himself, after admitting that he had accidentally fired the shot that killed Mr. Johnson he then denied that he had made that admission. He also tried to introduce a story that as he stood in front of the door a bullet from a gun held in the hands of another man whizzed by his head and struck Mr. Johnson. Walsh may have implied that the victim's missing money was the motive for the killing and he even named the man but he was a prominent man of Renova and he had an airtight alibi on the night of the murder and his name wasn't published.

In his final argument, Special Prosecutor James Kelly exclaimed, "There sits the biggest desperado in the state. Gentlemen of the jury, it is the rope or nothing." The case was given to the jury and three hours later, at 11:20 p.m. Friday night, July 27, 1923, they returned a guilty verdict and they fixed the penalty at death. Walsh took the verdict without a trace of emotion and he later jokingly remarked to the sheriff that the jurors made it "short and sweet" but he would never swing.

Although Judge Bennett had scheduled formal sentencing for Walsh on Friday, August 3, the defendant was granted a reprieve until October 1, 1923, in order for his attorney to file a motion for a new trial. Walsh appeared to be unconcerned and extremely confident that he wouldn't be hanged, saying that he had been in just as tight places at least six or eight different times before.

While waiting for the jury to return to the courtroom, Walsh sprang another surprise on his guards when as he was sitting with Sheriff Mountjoy and Undersheriff Knight the prisoner said, "I'll bet I can unlock these bracelets." As the officers smiled unbelievingly down at him, Walsh reached to his side pocket and produced a small key, which had been fashioned out of a handle of a spoon with a nail file as his only tool. After placing the improvised key into the lock of his handcuffs they slipped off of his wrist and dropped to the floor.

Hughes began to feel guilty as it was largely due to his confession that the authorities were able to pin Walsh to the crime in the first place, and on July 28, 1923, he refused to plead guilty to the second-degree murder charge he had negotiated for. After hearing of the prisoner's decision, County Attorney Johnson told the seventeen-year-old boy he only had once chance to take the plea and Hughes asked the prosecutor to give him until August 2, the day before Walsh's sentencing to make up his mind.

The next day Hughes said that he would accept the second-degree deal instead of going to trial, only to once again change his mind. Eventually going against his mother and his lawyer's advice, Hughes accepted the deal and received a life sentence at Deer Lodge, which probably eliminated any chance for a new trial for Walsh. Any animosity Walsh felt towards his young friend had seemingly vanished and the two men were seen laughing together and jesting with their guards while they played cards and drawing cartoons in jail.

Hughes often said that he had gotten the worst deal, because he didn't think Walsh would hang and said that Walsh was too smart for the law and that he would take bets that he would never swing. Sheriff Mountjoy also realized that Walsh was a clever fellow and he assigned three deputies, working in eight-hour shifts to watch over the two prisoners twenty-four hours a day. Even with the extra precautions it was discovered on August 11, that Walsh had devised a cutting tool to burn through the steel bars of his cell.

A piece of copper wire attached to a small piece of carbon was found hidden in the men's cell after the guards noticed the lights at the jail were flickering. The appliance, which was powered by a light socket, was taped so that the operator wouldn't receive a shock as he attempted to cut the bars by the arching electricity. The wire used had been used in the cell for the inmates to hang their clothing on while the carbon was evidently obtained from a dry battery.

According to Jailer John H. Williams the search of the cell also revealed a hole had been started in the floor of the cell and in the past, letters had been intercepted by the guards from Walsh asking friends to help him to escape including smuggling in a gun or to slip a couple of hack saw blades in a can of tobacco and bring it to the jail.

Before being transferred to Deer Lodge where he was to serve an eighteen to thirty-six year sentence, Hughes made a "hard luck" statement saying that he should have never talked to the authorities, who gave him a life sentence and would be the death of his pal, Roy Walsh. Hughes explained that he thought the cops had the goods on them so he talked and with hindsight the young convict realized that if he had kept quiet they would both be free. The only remorse expressed in his statement was the mess he had gotten the boys into and his mother said that Archie had been a fool to accept the plea deal and thought her son should have fought the charges like Walsh had done. Hughes said that he accepted the deal not because of a fear of the rope but he was afraid of getting life.

Contradicting his original confession, Hughes said that he never actually saw the shooting at Renova and he didn't know for sure who had killed Johnson that night. He collaborated Walsh's story by admitting he was on the other side of the store building at the time of the shooting and after the shooting he heard Walsh go over the fence and his friend never once admitted that he had shot Mr. Johnson. Hughes said that if he had known the facts he would have never confessed, but the sheriff had his jacket, which was found in Walsh's car and made out that he new the score. The young man confessed to all the auto thefts in the Butte area and he also claimed that his mother was aware of their activities.

After the departure of Arthur Hughes to the state prison, Roy Walsh was held alone at the ancient gray stone jail and he was awaiting the motion for a new trial that was to be heard by Judge Bennett on Monday, October 22, 1923. If Judge Bennett overruled that motion on that day, Walsh was going to be sentenced to death. The boasting by Walsh and the prediction of Hughes appeared to have come true when the prisoner escaped from the Jefferson County Jail at Boulder.

Walsh's escape from the Boulder jail

At about 7:30 on Saturday morning, October 20, 1923, Undersheriff Knight went to the condemned man's cell to see if he was ready for breakfast and according to the officer, Walsh didn't often eat breakfast and he didn't get up until about noon. Finding the key in the usual hiding place the officer entered the corridor and noticed that Walsh appeared to be asleep in his bunk.

When Officer Knight entered the cell to awaken the prisoner he discovered that the blankets had been rolled up to appear to be a body and Walsh was gone. Special Deputy Aaron Smith claimed that he had looked in on the prisoner several times and he believed that the form on the cot was the prisoner. The deputy was immediately accused of assisting Walsh in his escape as both the sheriff and the undersheriff said it was impossible for a prisoner to get to the key from his cell and the door couldn't be unlocked from the inside.

This would be a good place to explain the operation of the Jefferson County Jail in 1923. As was the case in most Montana counties, part of the sheriff's compensation package was that living quarters were furnished for him and his family in an adjoining residence. Sheriff Mountjoy and his family occupied the sheriff's quarters along with Mrs. Mountjoy's father, Mr. Lou Foreman and while Walsh was being housed at the jail at Boulder, Undersheriff Knight also had his own room where he slept while a deathwatch was stationed in the corridor.

While Walsh had been found with various keys he had fashioned out of would and pieces of iron from his bunk, the sheriff and the county attorney were convinced that the escape was certainly an inside job. Walsh had been confined in a small cell and two padlocks enclosed in boxes released a steel bar, which opened the heavy door. As Deputy Smith was on watch at the time of the escape, he was formerly charged on three counts of aiding the prisoner. The deputy hotly denied helping the prisoner escape saying that he had gone on duty to relieve Lester McNeil without talking to Walsh, as he appeared to be sleeping.

The deputy said he had called out to the prisoner two or three times but Walsh didn't answer and the officer thought nothing of it as the prisoner had often refused to answer the guards. County Attorney Johnson charged that money from the missing wallet of Mr. Johnson had been hidden and it was probably used to bribe the deathwatch to help him escape between six and eight o'clock p.m. Undersheriff Knight had possession of the keys and from eight o'clock to midnight the officer was at his home leaving Deputy Smith alone with the prisoner.

It was reported that Walsh had left the facilities in a hurry, not putting on his underwear and he was wearing only a blue serge coat, a pair of overalls and white tennis shoes, leaving a vest, an extra pair of pants and the rest of his personal effects behind. Tracks made by the tennis shoes were found outside the jail door and they were traced across a vacant lot to the Boulder River where they disappeared in the brush on the timbered mountainsides.

After the escape, the Jefferson County authorities immediately notified the entire state and wanted posters were quickly plastered all over bearing a photo and description of Roy Walsh. In the meantime a two hundred and fifty dollar reward was offered for his capture, dead or alive and the lawmen suspected that Walsh had friends on the outside waiting with a car and other provisions. The home of Mrs. Sara Hughes was examined for possible signs of the fugitive but none was found and the mother of Archie Hughes was plainly jubilant and when asked if she had seen the fugitive she answered in the negative, but added, if she had she wouldn't tell the authorities.

Two days following the escape the authorities called in the bloodhounds from the state prison at Deer Lodge and armed posses continued their search of the country while other officers guarded roads and railroads. Sheriffs in other counties where Walsh and Hughes were known to have operated in their automobile stealing escapades also helped out in the search and while the Jefferson County authorities were searching for the fugitive, Deputy Aaron Smith sat in the same cell, which Walsh had earlier escaped from. Originally from the Ozark Mountains in Missouri, the forty-six-year-old Smith had lived in the Boulder area for twenty-three years, he was married and he had three children.

On October 24, 1923, Walsh's attorney appeared in Judge Bennett's court with a motion for a new trial for his client and when the case was called the defendant of course was absent but the hearing went on and all of the proceedings were observed and the motion was submitted. The court scheduled October 30 as the date Judge Bennett would render his decision and on that day the judge denied a new trial for the fugitive and he set November 10, 1923, as the date for Walsh's formal death sentence. By the end of October of 1923, the convicted murderer had seemed to have vanished from the surface of the earth and with no other clues or leads the Silver Bow County authorities were keeping Walsh's associates in Butte under surveillance in case he returned to the Mining City.

Meanwhile Sheriff Mountjoy continued to send out telegrams throughout Montana as well as the Dakotas, Minnesota, Illinois and other eastern states. For weeks the sheriff was busy following up tips, which all proved false until a report of a Buick being reported stolen from a Mr. Ballin at Melrose peeked his attention because during his confinement in the county jail Walsh talked a good deal about automobiles and it was clear that the Buick was his favorite make.

The small town of Melrose, just south of Butte was located on the main road toward Salt Lake City and Sheriff Mountjoy developed a theory that the fugitive had driven the stolen vehicle south. In December of 1923 the sheriff's theory was confirmed when a former Butte friend of Walsh spotted him at Reno, Nevada in the stolen Buick. Because of nasty rumors and accusations concerning the integrity of the sheriff and his staff, Sheriff Mountjoy decided to track down his man himself.

Re-capture of Walsh

Following Walsh's escape from Montana, Sheriff Mountjoy traced Walsh from Las Vegas to California and then finally to the Mexican border. The sheriff later said that there were times that he felt like giving up but then a clue would pop up and it would revive his enthusiasm and one of those times occurred in February of 1924, when it was learned that Walsh was held on a charge of petty larceny at San Diego, California under the name of Don Stewart.

By the time the Montana sheriff received word of the arrest in California the fugitive had been released and the same Buick automobile that Walsh had stolen from Montana gave him away at San Diego when the fugitive paid for the legal services of his lawyer there with a bill of sale for the car. Sheriff Mountjoy made a hurried trip to San Diego where the attorney, P.M. Andrews informed him that a Don Stewart had already left town with his Buick to Missouri. The sheriff returned to Montana where the attorney at San Diego later informed him that he had received word from Stewart in Missouri concerning the sale of his Buick and a dealer was handling the transfer of the vehicle.

Sheriff Mountjoy immediately notified the Missouri authorities to pick Stewart up and hold him for Jefferson County and on May 2, 1924, Sheriff Mountjoy was surprised when his office received word from the Missouri State Prison at Jefferson City notifying that they were holding a man by the name of Don Stewart answering the description of Roy Walsh. Don Stewart, Convict No.26593 was arrested on a theft charge in Armstrong, Missouri and the authorities there were holding the stolen Buick belonging to Mr. Ballin of Melrose, Montana.

The sheriff sent Walsh's fingerprints to the authorities in Missouri to confirm the prints of Don Stewart and a day later Warden John C.

Crawford at Jefferson City reported that the Bertillion measurements and fingerprints of Roy Walsh and Donald Stewart, who was serving a two-year sentence for burglary were identical. Sheriff Mountjoy and his undersheriff left for Helena on Monday, May 5, 1924, to secure extradition papers and then they left for Jefferson City the following morning to bring back their long lost prisoner.

At first the Missouri authorities didn't inform Walsh that his identity had been learned but when "the jig was up" he told the other convicts at the prison shop where he was working that he didn't have long to live. Without hesitation he shook hands with each of the prisoners and told them he had escaped from a Montana jail. When Sheriff Mountjoy confronted his man at the Missouri prison on May 9, he said, "Well, Roy, your vacation is up." "Guess your right, sheriff," Walsh answered with a grin but he reminded the officer that the rope wasn't around his neck yet.

The Montana sheriff met with Missouri Governor A.M. Hyde in St. Louis on May 10, where he received the requisition papers for the prisoner's return to Boulder and the papers automatically pardoned Walsh of his Missouri offense, clearing his extradition to Montana. The Montana officers left Jefferson City with their prisoner on Sunday, May 11, and while en route Walsh wore an Oregon boot, which was a heavy leather belt with attached handcuffs that Sheriff Mountjoy had borrowed from Sheriff Larry Duggan of Silver Bow County.

The party arrived at Butte on Wednesday morning where Roy Walsh was placed in the county jail until three p.m. when they boarded the Great Northern for Boulder. A curious crowd of spectators including a number of Walsh's friends had gathered at the Silver Bow County jail to watch the prisoner, escorted by Sheriff Mountjoy, Undersheriff Knight and Sheriff Duggan into an automobile, which carried them to the train station.

Walsh was placed in his old cell in the Jefferson County jail on May 14, and the following day Judge Bennett announced that counsel would be appointed to represent the prisoner and that he would pronounce sentence on May 16. Walsh came back to Montana wearing a light gray suit and cap and spoke freely about his escape and time on the run as he hoped that he would receive clemency from the gallows by explaining how he escaped from the county jail at Boulder. He told reporters that the major reason he had escaped from Boulder was to get even with the man at Renova who he still claimed had killed Mr. Johnson but when things got too hot in Montana he felt it best to leave the state.

The prisoner said that he escaped early Saturday morning, October 20, 1923, and his escape wasn't discovered until a day later and he declared that he had fashioned a wooden key from a spoon and gained his freedom from his cell when the special guard had turned his back for a short time. From there he went upstairs to the unoccupied cells and then cut his way out of the roof of the jail. Walsh stated that he received no outside aid and while he was hiding out in the upstairs of the jail he overheard the sheriff questioning Deputy Smith about the escape.

Walsh said he waited in the attic for a while and then he return to one of the vacant second-floor cells to sleep part of the night and the following night he escaped through a hole he had cut in the roof. He was about to climb down the roof of the jail when he discovered that Mrs. Mountjoy was hanging clothes in her yard and he hung suspended from the roof until she returned to her house. From the jail yard Walsh made his way to a milk shed in Boulder where he was again almost discovered when a man came in to milk a cow. He hid in the darkness of a corner of the building and he was about to leave again when another person came into the barn to care for a small calf.

After leaving Boulder, Walsh said he walked through the mountains to Butte where he hid out for a day and a half and was given food from Mrs. Hughes. The fugitive then walked to Divide and then to Melrose where he spent several days in and around a garage. Walsh fashioned a key to the door of the garage and then stole the Buick, which later brought about his undoing ten days after breaking out of jail.

Driving the car, Walsh went through Idaho, Utah and then from Nevada to California where he hung out at San Diego and got into trouble in December but he escaped into Mexico when Sheriff Mountjoy came to California. Since the sheriff was getting close to his trail, Walsh left California and drove through the southwestern states and stole some new tires for his Buick in Oklahoma. The prisoner said that he was heading for Illinois where he had hoped to go straight and make a new start.

In Missouri he broke into a cabin at Armstrong where he stayed for several days eating up the food stores but when the Buick became mired in some mud he was forced to abandon it with a farmer, saying he would be back to reclaim it. In the meantime he was arrested by a local marshal who was on the verge of letting Walsh go when a couple of deputies discovered two guns in his luggage and he was arraigned and sentenced in March of 1924, to the two-year term at the Missouri State pen. While serving at the Missouri State Prison he knew that his true identity would eventually be learned so he tried to be placed on the prison farm where he could easily escape.

On Friday morning, May 16, Roy Walsh was brought into district court before Judge Bennett for his formal sentencing and the day before the judge had informed him of his rights and had appointed James E. Murray of Boulder to represent him. While waiting for his sentencing Walsh displayed various moods, at times being optimistic of his chances of escaping the gallows and at other instances he sat dejected and despondent. While talking with his guards the prisoner appeared to be in good spirits but when he was left alone he was said to be gloomy. Judge Bennett quickly sentenced the convicted murderer to be hanged on June 16, 1924 between the hours of four o'clock in the morning and four in the afternoon.

While Attorney James E. Murray had been assigned the case, he withdrew from the case when Mr. Elliott arrived and conferred with the prisoner and filed notice of the prisoner's intention to appeal the case to the Supreme Court. After sbeing entenced Walsh walked calmly back to the jail handcuffed to Undersheriff Knight where he picked up a magazine and read it on his bunk. Walsh again expressed that he wanted to explain in detail just how he managed to escape from the Boulder jail provided the death penalty was reduced to life imprisonment.

When Walsh had been discovered at the Missouri prison, the Jefferson and Silver Bow County authorities at first scoffed at the stories that the escaped prisoner had engineered his escape alone and made his exit from his cell with a wooden key. After hearing Walsh's story of his escape, Sheriff Mountjoy told the newspapermen, "You can quote me as saying that Walsh's story of his escape is ridiculous." On May 22, Sheriff Mountjoy, County Attorney Johnson and others were examining the jail and the cell doors in an attempt to determine the plausibility of Walsh's story when the prisoner said: "Give me a piece of hard wood and a knife and I'll show you how I got out."

The piece of wood, a knife and the padlock were given to Walsh and he sliced a thin piece of the material and fitted it into the padlock and then from memory he marked off spaces for the six teeth of the key. While he was working Undersheriff Knight told the prisoner, "Don't cut yourself," causing a laugh from the crowd but Walsh quickly formed the small stick into a key. It took Walsh about an hour to form the key with a deep hole at the end, which he fashioned with a small piece of wire and after trying it several times and trimming the wooden teeth the tumblers in the lock turned and it finally opened with a click.

As the startled crowd stood there silently, Walsh told them with a smile, "Leave me alone with theses tools for half an hour and I'll be out." While Walsh was working he had told the officers that Deputy Aaron Smith had only aided him by giving him several articles, which enabled him to make two wooden keys and an apparatus that he used to reach the locks from inside of his cell. The prisoner explained that he had obtained an impression from the padlocks when he was allowed out of his cell to exercise in the corridor and he said that he had made adjustments to his keys several times just days before his escape.

Walsh said that Deputy Smith had given him the key to the corridor door, which he traced onto a piece of paper before returning it to the officer and he was able to unlock the cell padlocks by attaching the key to pieces of pliable strips of iron from his bed and with a piece of broom handle he was able to turn the key and slide the bar, which secured the door. He said that the corridor lock was manipulated with some heavy string and without a key to the remaining door to the jail Walsh considered going through the residence of Sheriff Mountjoy but he abandoned that plan when he heard voices in the house.

Any skepticism of Walsh's escape story vanished when he told the officers that he had broken part of his wooden key in the corridor door when he relocked it in October of 1923, and upon an investigation of the keyhole a small piece of wood was indeed found in the mechanism. The piece of wood was removed from the lock and it matched perfectly with the chunk missing from the wooden key that Walsh had carefully hidden in an out-of-way place at the jail before leaving the jail.

It didn't take much more convincing for Sheriff Mountjoy to realize that his prisoner was too much for his county jail and he made arrangements to have Walsh transferred to the Montana State Penitentiary at Deer Lodge. It was a good idea economically as well since after reimbursing the state, Jefferson County saved about four hundred and fifty dollars a month by keeping Walsh at the prison because of the extra costs in deathwatch salaries.

After learning of his imminent transfer to the state penitentiary, Walsh planned another escape attempt and it wasn't discovered until after the prisoner's removal to the prison at Deer Lodge. On searching Walsh's cell a gag was found made from a blanket torn into strips and a devise to automatically close the cell door, which was fashioned out of the rubber belt of his suit. It was learned from the other inmates at the jail that Walsh had planned to overpower the guard and after securing the officer make his escape to Idaho.

Apparently the plan was that Undersheriff Knight, who had been on guard day and night, would enter the cage to feed the prisoner; the cell door would automatically close thereby surprising the officer and Walsh would jump the tired man, tie him up and gag him. After making his escape from the jail Walsh had planned to steal another car this time one belonging to E.J. Walton of Boulder and then dumping it after driving to the Snake River country. Evidently Walsh was transferred to the state penitentiary before he was able to execute his plan.

At the state prison at Deer Lodge Walsh was considered a model prisoner and although he was given the same privileges as the other inmates he made no attempt to escape. He was given the regular hour of exercise each morning and afternoon; he ate with the other prisoners and he was allowed to attend the show on Sunday, although a guard sat next to him. Although Walsh had never given the prison officials any trouble, they kept a special watch over the man and he was housed in the new cell house, which was one of the strongest in America at the time where the guards could easily see inside of his cage. At Deer Lodge Walsh always ate well and his cool and quiet demeanor remained the same as it had been at the Boulder jail.

In an eleventh-hour effort to save his friend's life, Hughes made a statement from the state prison swearing that he had shot Johnson and not Walsh. Hughes believed that since he was already under sentence his statement would do him no harm but it could save his friend from the gallows. Although the basis of his appeal was weak, the change in Hughes' story most likely helped Walsh's motion for an appeal and his execution was postponed until after the Supreme Court hearing in October of 1924.

On October 29, Jefferson County Attorney Johnson, Sheriff Mountjoy and Flurry Sullivan, Butte court stenographer went to Deer Lodge to take statements from both Roy Walsh and Hughes concerning the new revelation. The officers spent about two hours with Walsh and Hughes but the two men's statements were reportedly hopelessly in conflict. The Supreme Court heard the arguments for Walsh's appeal for a new trial on Friday, October 31, and on Tuesday, December 23, the high court affirmed the judgment of the district court. Because Judge Bennett was out of the state, the re-sentencing hearing was postponed until January of 1925.

For his re-sentencing at Boulder on Monday, January 12, 1925, Walsh was transferred from the Deer Lodge prison on Sunday while his attorney was preparing a petition that was later circulated and eventually presented to Governor John E. Erickson. Copies of the appeal for executive clemency circulated at Butte and all points in Jefferson County including Renova where the crime took place. While climbing into the car at Deer Lodge, Walsh remarked that he was taking his last automobile ride to his old cell at Boulder.

Sheriff Mountjoy and Undersheriff Knight escorted Walsh first to the sheriff's office at Butte to obtain the hangman's straps, which had been last used for the double hanging of Bill and Monte Harris in April of 1923 and then the officers and their prisoner ate at a café in Butte before driving to Boulder. While the condemned man had given up any hope for his life he never showed any sign of nervousness and he was talkative and he was seen laughing and joking with the officers while they ate their meal. The prisoner said that he would be soon with St. Peter, and that he would become sheriff up there jokingly offering Sheriff Mountjoy the job of being his undersheriff, saying that he was a good officer.

When he was back in his old cell at Boulder, Walsh removed his light gray suit coat and carefully hung it up in the cage that still had all of the "fixtures" left behind by the amateur mechanical engineer. The prisoner was placed under a twenty-four-hour rotating watch made up of Lester McNeil, Ed McAuley and E.J. Watson. The law provided that hangings were not to take place before thirty days or after sixty days from the date of sentencing but that provision had already elapsed in the Walsh case and his re-sentencing that Monday was merely an order "redirecting" the sheriff to hang the prisoner anytime after the pronouncement.

On Monday morning, January 12, 1925, in a crowded but hushed courtroom, Judge Bennett sentenced Walsh to be hanged, not on Friday the thirteenth, but instead on a Saturday, Valentine's Day, February 14. Walsh, handcuffed to Deputy John Williams, stood erect and without a tremor listened calmer to the sentence, "hang by the neck until dead" than most of the curious spectators.

Long before the prisoner was escorted from the jail, a scattered crowd loitered in the lobby and stairs of the Jefferson County Courthouse. About a half dozen women, some with their children were among the crowd watching for the arrival of Walsh when suddenly there was a hush as someone said, "Here he comes." Across the snow-covered and icy courthouse lawn walked the tall and muscular Roy Walsh in new overalls and a flannel shirt flanked by Deputies John Williams, Ernest Sumner and Ed McAuley. The crowd hurried into the courtroom and was seated as Walsh walked in glancing at the crowd and smiling. He sat before the bench for about ten minutes while the courtroom was as quiet a tomb waiting for the appearance of Judge Bennett

When the judge ordered Walsh to stand, the prisoner stood straight as a soldier and he faced the court. Judge Bennett reviewed the case including the recent Supreme Court decision and then he asked if the prisoner had any legal reason why sentence shouldn't be rendered. Walsh said that he didn't see why Hughes got off with a prison term while he had to take such "the heavy end."

After receiving his sentence Walsh and the guards quickly left the courtroom but before leaving he smiled at a couple of women who were weeping over the prisoner. As he was walking back to the jail with his guards he jokingly remarked, "He might as well have made it for the thirteenth. I was born on that date and I might as well die on the same one." While sitting in his chair with his feet propped on a table Walsh told a reporter that he was ready for the end and he finished by saying: "I'm ready to let 'er go."

The day after Walsh was re-sentenced to be hanged Representative E.N. Joffray of Jefferson County introduced a bill in the house providing that all executions take place at the state prison. The immediate purpose of the measure was to save Jefferson County the expense in connection with the hanging of Walsh and the people of the county from the stigma of another hanging in their community. Silver Bow County Representative Kinville also introduced a like measure giving the warden the responsibility for the hangings and that only twelve witnesses would be allowed to witness the executions.

Several other state representatives argued how recent executions had caused a financial burden on their counties and Representative Lincoln of Flathead County explained how the execution of Fred LeBeau in 1909 had broken down Sheriff O'Connell and was ultimately blamed for the death of the officer's wife who had befriended the condemned man. But after a long and impressive argument of how the measure would be a great disadvantage to the city of Deer Lodge by Representative Keely of Powell County, House Bill Number 62 was soundly defeated on January 21, 1925.

After Walsh's trial in 1923, Sheriff Mountjoy intended to use the scaffold, ***Gallows No. Eight: (March 1887): "Galloping Gallows" No. Two*** that had been stored away in the basement of the county jail, gathering dust since the execution of William Pepo nearly twenty five years earlier but he later decided to use the ***Gallows No. Sixteen: (Jan. 1918): "Galloping Gallows" No. Five*** as it was considered more humane. About the same time that the sheriff was bringing Walsh back to Boulder from Deer Lodge a truck from Butte was hauling the gallows, which had executed the two Harris boys in April of 1923, to its next job at Boulder.

The freestanding scaffold was erected just a few feet from the window of the jail and after seeing the structure Walsh began telling some grim jokes about the death machine. The carpenters completed the scaffold on February 9, and Walsh was the sixth victim of the second

"Galloping Gallows" of Silver Bow County, having already executed Fisher, O'Neil, Powell, and Monte and Bill Harris. The condemned man said that he was sorry about what happened to Mr. Johnson, but his greatest regret was his recapture after his escape. While he blamed himself for his recapture he was proud of his ability to travel from Boulder, Montana to California on only four dollars.

In an effort to save his client's life, John Elliott tried to secure as many signatures as he could on the petitions before presenting them to the Governor and on February 3, the attorney declared that Morgan Johnson, the brother of the slain man was even willing to sign the petition, but the next day Johnson emphatically denied ever agreeing to sign a petition to save the life of the convicted murderer of his brother.

In a telephone conversation with an "Anaconda Standard" reporter, Morgan Johnson said, "I certainly will not sign the petition, and I will be in Boulder the morning of February 14 to see the hanging." After the failed publicity stunt Mr. Elliott drove to Helena on February 10, to hand deliver the petitions to Governor Erickson personally. While his attorney was working hard to save his life, Walsh maintained his calm indifferent attitude depending on luck, which had generally played a hand for him.

Meanwhile at Boulder two local clergymen, the Reverend Father James Franchi, rector of the Roman Catholic Church and Reverend E.C. Smith of the Methodist Episcopal Church visited the condemned man in order to tend to his needs but Walsh had declined spiritual assistance. Walsh talked with the clergymen on other subjects other than his impending death on the gallows and within three days of his execution the prisoner was still eating and sleeping well and staying up late each night talking with his guards.

When Governor Erickson announced that he would issue his decision on February 12, 1925, Roy Walsh said that it would be his big day and then jokingly announced that they should give the Governor ten more days to decide. He had high hopes and said, "Why shouldn't an innocent man be hopeful?" He maintained his innocence keeping to his version that an unknown "third party" had killed Johnson in his store at Renova.

The condemned man didn't write any farewell letters to relatives, as he didn't know the whereabouts of his mother and he didn't want her to know about his predicament anyway. A few days earlier he had received a letter from an aunt in Wisconsin, which he quickly answered, and he later told his guards that he was sorry she had learned of his trouble. The only correspondence that the authorities had received on behave of Walsh was from his stepfather just before his trial in 1923, stating that the boy had been kicked around as a child and he never really had a home.

Because of special requests from Butte, Governor Erickson postponed his decision about the Walsh case until February 13, the day before the execution and the action buoyed prisoner's hope of moving back to Deer Lodge instead of mounting the gallows waiting for him in the Jefferson County jail yard. The appearance of a couple of deputies in his cell after they had put the "finishing touches" on the gallows the evening before reminded the condemned man of the other possibilities. With his typical humor he remarked, "If you fellows don't quit monkeying with that thing out there somebody's going to get hurt on it some day."

Dr. C.L. Clifford, pastor of the Mountain View Methodist Church of Butte visited Walsh and while he said the condemned man made no reference to his predicament, he had been reading the Bible at times. Walsh had been impressed with Reverend Clifford after hearing a sermon he had given earlier using him as the subject and the prisoner opened up to the minister. According to his life story that he had related to Reverend Clifford, Walsh said he was born near Milwaukee and his father had deserted the family when he was a baby. His mother kept the two children a son and daughter for about six months before turning Roy, whose real name was Albert W. Schoonover over to her parents.

Walsh never did say anything more about his sister but he said he lived with his grandparents for a number of years before his mother came for him. The family roamed through South Dakota, Montana and Idaho before his mother married a man at Missoula. Roy moved with the family to Seattle where at the age of nine he was working in a woolen mill and when his mother left, instead of remaining with his stepfather, Walsh ran away and went to work on a ranch until he was fifteen. He later went to work for a lumber camp and then he kicked around until he arrived at Butte at the age of eighteen.

The condemned man found that he had many new friends from Butte since his time of trouble and he had received several boxes of homemade candy, while people of Boulder had supplied him with pies, cakes and candy. While Walsh was a big eater and his cell was well stocked with baked delicacies the prisoner rarely asked for anything special. Sheriff Mountjoy had offered him anything for his last meals but he usually ordered eggs, and in large quantities. On his final trip to Helena to meet with the Governor, Attorney Elliott dropped by the jail at Boulder to discuss matters with his client and then the two men shook hands Good-bye. After visiting with his attorney, Walsh slept very little Thursday night, which he spent playing cards with one of his guards.

Walsh learned the meaning of "Black Friday" when Sheriff Mountjoy went to his cell about three o'clock on the afternoon of Friday the thirteen to hand him a telegram from Governor Erickson denying the petition for commutation of sentence. The prisoner read the telegram without any visible emotion or a word and soon afterwards he asked for some writing paper and for several hours he wrote to relatives and friends, bidding them good-bye and then he wrote a long statement in which he urged other boys to avoid the pitfalls that he had fallen in.

In the more than a thousand words, his rambling statement went on to praise horses and their faithfulness to mankind. He met with reporters later, telling them that he had gone that far, he figured he could go the rest of the way and about that time the sheriff came in with some other visitors and Walsh asked, "When's my party coming off?"

"About two o'clock," answered the sheriff.

For dinner Friday night Walsh ate several eggs with potatoes, milk and a lot of pasties, which adorned the shelves of his cell. About seven o'clock the barber came at the prisoner's request and shaved him and while the man was trimming his beard, Walsh joked with him and urged him to "doll me up as pretty as possible, because I want to make a good appearance. First impressions are so important." A girl from the valley called on the doomed man later and she urged him to call a clergyman and he yielded to her pleadings and called for Reverend E.C. Smith. Mr. Smith instantly responded and he remained with Walsh until about eleven o'clock that night.

Friday evening Walsh maintained his semi-jovial attitude until late that night when a dog outside the prison walls howled dismally. At that, Walsh lifted his head and with a sinking heart he announced, "That means someone is going to die." Father Franchi joined Reverend Smith in assisting the condemned man and after midnight the newspapermen were allowed a final interview with Walsh who said he was going with a good will, but claimed he was innocent. In the jail yard the witnesses were shivering while a light snow was falling, which made the scene even more gruesome and the dim rays of the two electric lights above the scaffold threw shadows eerily here and there.

When the sheriff and Deputy Williams went for Walsh at his cell at 1:30 a.m. he was calmly eating an orange and his feet were propped up on his table. The sheriff asked the prisoner if he was ready and Walsh answered in a calm voice, "I guess so, Johnny." "Here are the doctors, who will give you something for your nerves. How are they" asked the sheriff. "They seem pretty good," answered Walsh with a smile, "To hell with it, I don't need any of it. I'll have plenty of nerve." Walsh finished his orange, wiped his hands on a paper sack and then he stood up and then Deathwatch George Smith reached over and shook hands with the prisoner. Walsh told the guard to tell the girls thanks for the pies and cakes they had sent.

Walsh walked briskly out of his cell between Sheriff Mountjoy and Deputy Williams and at the door to the jail yard they stopped where the officers adjusted the straps to his arms while the condemned man looked on with his patented smile. Recalling his previous journey with the sheriff, Walsh said, "Am I going back to Missouri?" as the party continued to the gallows with the prisoner walking erect and seemingly unconcerned as he mounted the steps with a firm step.

The doomed man watched the officers curiously as they adjusted the rest of the straps around his legs and arms. Undersheriff Dale O. Robinson of Silver Bow County and Sheriff James Smith of Gallatin County assisted on the scaffold and the spectators, including Park County Sheriff Clarence Gilbert were gathered below and to the east of the gallows. Unlike other recent hangings there were no large crowds hanging around outside the enclosure and the town of Boulder was quiet that night.

After the sheriff had adjusted the noose around Walsh's neck he asked if the condemned man had any final words and he answered with, "Well, gentlemen, I am leaving you, I have no malice and no ill will against anyone. I wish you all good luck." The sheriff sounded a buzzer and the unknown hangman pulled the lever and at 1:43 a.m. the heavy trap door fell and Roy Walsh's body dropped like a stone into the pit, which was hidden from the spectators. Some witnesses later explained that when Walsh hit the end of his rope it sounded like a sack of coal dropping on a cement floor and six and one-half minutes later Drs. D.E. Rainville and G.L. Routledge of Boulder pronounced that the man's neck had been broken and life was extinct.

Walsh had fulfilled his reputation for nerve and gameness to the very last and his dead body was lowered into a cheap rough casket and taken to the J.E. Wild Undertakers across from the courthouse where a few curious people went to observe it including Aaron Smith, the guard that was charged with aiding the prisoner's escape. After the funeral ceremony, officiated by Reverend E.C. Smith and witnessed by a small group of curious spectators, the sheriff and his deputies helped bury the remains of Roy Walsh in Potter's Field on the old Jefferson County Poor Farm south of Boulder, which later became part of the John Heide Ranch.

Postscript:
The case against Aaron Smith of helping Walsh escape in October of 1923, was dismissed in April of 1925, and Arthur Hughes served several years of his life sentence before he was released and reportedly was successfully rehabilitated and became a solid citizen. He liked Deputy John Williams who later became sheriff of Jefferson County and he returned to Boulder a number of times to visit the officer.

October 1, 1926
Anthony "Tony" Vettere

Location and Gallows: When Vettere was executed inside the county jail building at Butte he became the seventh man hanged on ***Gallows No. Sixteen: (Jan. 1918): "Galloping Gallows" No. Five***.
Description: The forty-five-years-old Italian had a black mustache, stood five foot, eight-inches tall and he weighed about one hundred and fifty pounds,
Crime: Convicted of the shotgun murder of Antone Favero, and he was also accused of killing Joseph Ciccarelli, who was shot as he was talking with Favero in Meaderville on November 22, 1925. It was also believed that he killed John Deriana at East Butte, three-quarters of an hour after Vettere murdered Favero and Ciccarelli. Before the murders, Vettere was suspected of firing five shots at Angelo Gucciono during his rampage along with holding up Frank Rossi. In all, Anthony Vettere was probably responsible for leaving eighteen children fatherless.
Judge: Jeremiah J. Lynch

Prosecution: County Attorney Tim E. Downey and his deputy, Nick A. Rutering
Defense: Maxwell S. Galasso and Thomas J. Walker[3] handled the appeal
Sheriff: Larry Duggan
Distinction: Vettere was the last man to be hanged in Yellowstone County and he was the only legally executed person in Montana who had to be physically restrained and carried to the gallows.
Relics and Remnants: The gallows, which was used to hang Vettere, eventually executed eight convicted murderers and after its final victim in 1933, it was returned to Butte where it is currently in storage in the basement of the Silver Bow County Courthouse. Because the scaffold is being stored with possible hazardous material the ancient death machine is not available for viewing.

At seven o'clock on the evening of November 22, 1925, Angelino Gucciono was walking along Casey Street in Butte with Lina Marsetti after a date when Anthony Vettere fired twice at them from the doorway of his cabin, which he was renting from the Marsetti family. The couple ran away and took refuge in the Marsetti house and after breaking several windows of the house the shooter was confronted by Frank Rossi before leaving the scene.

While Miss Marsetti remained at her home, Gucciono ran to the Northern Pacific depot where he reported the incident and then took a cab to the Sheriff's office. Mr. and Mrs. Marsetti and their daughter clung together in fear in the house as Vettere broke windows and threatened to shoot into the residence. When Deputy Duggan arrived at Vettere's cabin at 10 Casey Street he found a revolver with two discharged shells but before he could begin his search for the suspect he received word of another shooting at Meaderville.

Shortly after they stepped from the home of Antone Favero at 210 Main Street of Meaderville at about 9:40 that same Sunday evening, miners, Favero and Joseph Ciccarelli were shot down in the yard. Fifty-year-old Ciccarelli was killed instantly at the scene but Favero, 52, was rushed to Murray Hospital at Butte where he died before midnight.

The first at the scene was Favero's son and Sam Lazzari and they found the boy's father semi-conscious and saying he had been shot. Antone Favero was transported to the hospital and soon after Sheriff Larry Duggan and his son Chief Deputy Jack Duggan arrived at the scene followed by Coroner Holland who after examining the body of Ciccarelli ordered it to be taken to the Duggan Undertakers.

While the officers were busy working the crime scene on Main and Wing Street the news was phoned into the sheriff that another man had been shot to death on the East Butte viaduct that crossed Silver Bow Creek about a quarter of a mile away. The first report was of a rumor that the man who had shot Favero and Ciccarelli had committed suicide but when the officers arrived at the scene they found the body of a middle-aged man on his back, wearing a mackinaw coat and work clothes near the northwestern corner of the viaduct.

In the dead man's pockets was found a loaded revolver and identification indicating that the man was John Deriana and the people nearby recognized him as "John the watchman." One of the spectators who knew the slain man went to the Deriana home and returned with the thirteen-year-old daughter of the watchman who identified her dead father.

The officers went to the Deriana home on the edge of the flats just north of East Butte where they informed the mother of eight youngsters of the death of her husband and with a baby in her arms the woman told the authorities that she didn't know of any reason why her husband would be killed. Mrs. Deriana's six-year-old son, Nick, mournfully told friends who came to the house: "Well, I guess I can't go to school anymore, I'll have to go out and work."

John Deriana was born in Austria and he came to the United States in 1907 where he lived in East Butte for fifteen years before his death. He was an industrious man who worked very hard to support his large family. The Deriana family was well known and popular in the community and during Christmas of 1924, the neighbors knowing that some of the children might go without, took up a collection so that the children would have a good holiday.

Back at the Ciccarelli home, neighbors gathered to comfort the bereaved family, and Joe's wife was completely distraught. Fourteen-year-old Joe and Lucy, 15, held up bravely and they informed the authorities the probable motives for the killing of their father and they speculated who the murderer was. Joe and Lucy Ciccarelli explained that Tony Vettere had been a former boarder at their residence when they lived at 126 Main Street in Meaderville about two years earlier and the children described the man as a heavy drinker, who caused trouble at the home by getting fresh with their mother and he was ordered to leave.

After Vettere left the Ciccarelli home he repeatedly attempted to move back in and he was arrested four times for threatening and annoying the family. Eventually after a disturbance outside the Ciccarelli home the family had Vettere arrested and he was ordered to leave town or pay a peace bond. Vettere moved on to Basin where he found work in a mine there and he spent his spare time target shooting before once more returning to the Mining City.

Undersheriff Robinson and Deputies Duggan and Byers started after Vettere when they came across a section crew that said they had seen a man answering to the fugitive's description crossing the flat in the vicinity of Timber Butte. The officers followed the man's trail for about five miles until their car became stuck in the snow and they continued on foot about eight miles south of Butte when they saw a man behind Timber Butte and they chased him into a gully where they caught him a small depression.

Vettere had a copy of the morning paper describing the murders of the previous night in his pocket and when he was arrested he admitted that he had shot at the young couple. In a statement to the county attorney Vettere also admitted that he had taken a shotgun to

Meaderville on Sunday but he claimed it was well after the time of the shootings had taken place and he swore he didn't know anything about the killings.

After holding an inquest over the deaths on Wednesday, November 25, 1925, the coroner's jury returned separate verdicts that Anthony Vettere was responsible for the shooting deaths of both Favero and Ciccarelli. Witnesses testified that the suspect was seen with a shotgun in the vicinity of the murder scene, and Jack Favero, second son of the victim, said that their dying father told them that Vettere had done the shooting. The deputies testified that they found shotgun shells at Vettere's home, loaded with the same type of shot that physicians had removed from Favero's body and the suspect reportedly didn't testify at the hearings as he was unable to speak or understand English, but he was explained his constitutional rights in Italian by the deputy county attorney.

Anthony Vettere was born in Italy in 1880, and he came to America on September 11, 1908, leaving a wife and son in his homeland. He took out citizenship papers at Butte in November of 1920, and he was employed as a section hand for the Northern Pacific Railroad. While living at Meaderville, Vettere worked at the Black Rock Mine and he generally got drunk every evening after work and he would usually get in a dispute with someone.

On December 5, 1925, Vettere was arraigned for the murders of Favero and Ciccarelli and Attorney M.S. Galasso was assigned as his counsel. The defendant entered a not guilty plea on December 7 and his attorney requested a continuance for six or seven weeks in order for him to have more time to work with his client who couldn't speak English and other witnesses to build a defense. Mr. Galasso also believed that a delay would calm the community's clamor for a hanging and felt that his client suffered from mental disease and should be properly evaluated.

The Vettere trial opened on February 15, 1926, and most people couldn't recall when a homicide had attracted as much interest as this case. Each day the courtroom was packed with spectators and scores of people stood throughout the entire procedure. On the first day the defendant arrived at the courtroom on the third floor of the courthouse dressed in a plain gray suit and handcuffed to Deputy Tony Harris.

Vettere spent very little attention to the proceedings and he spent most of his time pressing the crease and flicking off specks of dust from his hat. While Vettere was only being tried for the murder of Antone Favero, both his widow and Mrs. Ciccarelli were dressed in black and sat near the railing where they paid closes attention to the proceedings including the selection of the following jury:

Harry A. Kinney Jr.	John Zurfluh	Samuel Binder
Thomas Coughlin	George F. Vogel	S. Gotterdam
Victor Anderson	Dennis Sullivan	I.W. Genzberger
P.J. Angove	Thomas Elliott	George Heawood

On the stand and through an interpreter, Vettere proclaimed his innocence even though he said he didn't remember what he had done that day. The other twenty-four defense witnesses were called to try and prove that the defendant was suffering from mental disease, while the state called their own old-time residents of Butte who testified that the defendant had seem perfectly sane. The case went to the jury at 2:45 on February 23, 1926, and they returned a guilty verdict at five o'clock.

About two hundred people remained seated in the courtroom and standing around the corridors until the first-degree verdict was reached and Vettere acted more like one of the spectators than a defendant during the trial, only playing with his hat while the verdict was being read. The county later reported that the trial cost nearly twenty-one hundred dollars and the expenses were broken down as, jury expense twelve hundred and sixteen dollars, witnesses five hundred and thirteen and meals for the jury came to three hundred and twenty-five dollars.

When Attorney Thomas J. Walker and Vettere's cousin visited the jail during the second week of March of 1926, the prisoner displayed for the first time any emotion since his arrest. After getting Vettere's signature on a pauper affidavit, which permitted the court to authorize public funds for his appeal, the condemned man talked for a moment in Italian with his cousin and then he broke down and wept freely. For quite awhile the doomed prisoner continued talking as he paced back and forth on the floor and wiped the tears from his eyes.

While the jury had recommended the death sentence, they left it up to the court to decide Vettere's fate and Judge Lynch initially was to pronounce sentence on March 6, 1926, but he granted a one-week continuance. On Saturday, March 13, he ordered the execution to be on Friday, May 7, 1926, and like every other occasion when Vettere had appeared in the courtroom, the sentencing hearing was packed with mostly Italians. Vettere's attorney immediately announced that he would file for a new trial and the prisoner's cousin, Joe Vettere was instrumental in raising the funds for the appeal. After the sentencing the condemned man only smiled and shrugged his shoulder as he was being led out of the courtroom.

After Vettere's initial sentencing, Silver Bow County had two men on death row, the defendant and twenty-one-year-old Louie Won, convicted the previous fall for the murder of Peter Pavicle on West Mercury Street. The two doomed men had been in adjoining cells and up to that point they were both considered obedient prisoners and while Vettere's appeal was about to begin, the Supreme Court was currently reviewing Won's case. The basis for a new trial for Vettere was an invalid juror and the admission of the victim's final statement but on July 2, 1926, the Supreme Court denied the appeal. A week later the defense petitioned for a new hearing on the grounds of insanity through alcohol but it was also denied.

After both condemned men's appeals had failed, the jailers said that the two prisoners had become more moody. Won ate well and did everything he was told and he never asked for favors but Vettere was reportedly moody, sometimes appearing frivolous and talkative with other prisoners and at other times he was silent and morose.

A hand-fashioned knife of remarkable strength and sharpness was taken from Vettere several weeks earlier and he explained that it wasn't to be used as a weapon but to help in his escape. The knife had been made from the handle of a spoon, fitted with a hand-made wooden handle and it was sharpened by tediously rubbing it on the concrete floor. While the first weapon was found in Vettere's bunk the guards later confiscated another homemade knife that they found under the casement of his cell.

On July 20, 1926, Judge Lynch re-sentenced both prisoners to be hanged together on August 27, 1926, and while Louis Won was dressed in a nice blue suit; bowed his head slightly as tears came to his eyes, Vettere was in his usual well-worn suit and work shirt without a tie and was loud and rowdy. At that point Mr. Galasso asked Judge Lynch for a hearing before a jury to determine whether his client was sane but the court denied the petition. After his sentencing, Vettere wrapped his head with clothes, remained unshaven for three months and destroyed everything he came in contact with. His erratic behavior worsened as the hanging drew nearer and Vettere kept asking for Judge Lynch, but he could never be reached.

On August 24, Governor John E. Erickson granted reprieves for Vettere and Louis Won who were both scheduled for a double hanging, the former man's reprieve was until October 1, to permit his case to be heard before the Supreme Court, which was in recess at the time. The Supreme Court had upheld Vettere's original conviction but his attorney asserted that his client had become mentally ill since his trial and the district court refused to grant a sanity hearing. The gallows, which had already been erected earlier inside the jail were removed and again placed into storage.

Although he had but a few weeks to live, Tony Vettere never seemed to be overly concerned and he took a leading role in directing the daily talkfest among the inmates. The biggest pastime of the vagrants, burglars, murderers and other criminals at the jail was to converse on various topics that were brought up. The jailers reported that Vettere would sometimes hide in his cell and then he would playfully jump out and yell "Boo" at the guards and at other times he claimed to be Santos Santonio and told the jailers that Tony Vettere had shot his best friend, Mr. Favero. Both Louis Won and Vettere were fed the regular prison fare and the two condemned men were also given a piece of pie with their meals.

On September 13, the board of pardons approved Governor Erickson's recommendation that the death sentence of Louis Won be commuted and the news, while making the Chinese national understandably exuberant, it served to make Vettere even more volatile. He immediately claimed that he was sick; that his head hurt, and then his entire body pained him. A couple of days later before Louie Won left for the state prison he said to Vettere: "Good-bye, Tony, good luck."

Vettere, who had earlier congratulated the Chinese man, didn't reply, but only shrugged his shoulders.

On September 15, Mr. Galasso was pleading to have the Supreme Court listen to a sanity hearing for his client on the grounds that the county sheriff had asked for such a proceeding. On September 22, the high court announced that Vettere would not be granted a sanity hearing and since Governor Erickson's original reprieve expired on October 1, Judge Lynch ruled that the condemned man didn't require re-sentencing and that he would be executed after midnight of September 30.

Sheriff Duggan consulted with Attorney Timothy Nolan who informed him that he believed that the prisoner would have to be re-sentenced before he could be legally hanged. While the sheriff and Judge Lynch were trying to agree upon the date and time of the execution, Vettere sat in his cell and only shrugged his shoulders when questioned about his appeal or the debate over his execution date.

When questioned by an interpreter who used a mixture of Spanish and Italian, the prisoner stated that he considered it unjust that Louie Won was able to escape the noose and he couldn't. While he was speaking with the interpreter the prisoner wore trousers and an undershirt and smoked a pipe. His wiry black beard completely covered the lower part of his face extending to his eyes, one of which was usually half closed and he spoke nervously and paced the floor of his small cell, occasionally folding and unfolding his arms.

The question of when Vettere would be executed was still a complicated issue in the records of Montana jurisprudence and the following day a new wrinkle was added when the condemned man began a hunger strike. While the condemned man didn't make an announcement of his strike in so many words, he abruptly refused to take any food offered to him. Besides not partaking of food, the prisoner refused to speak with anyone and he only indicated that he was ill.

On September 23, Montana Attorney General L.A. Foot announced that some time after ten days the district court of Silver Bow County was required to set a day for the execution of Vettere but Judge Lynch disagreed with the ruling and he reiterated that he did not believe it was necessary for him to re-sentence the convicted murderer. County Attorney Tim Downey concurred with the judge's opinion and Vettere's counsel, having decided to suspend the fight on behalf of his client stayed out of the issue all together.

The next day the Attorney General announced that Vettere's last day on earth would be September 30, 1926, explaining that Governor Erickson's reprieve postponed the condemned man's execution, "Until October 1, 1926" and he advised the officials of Silver Bow County that the reprieve merely delayed the sentence therefore it was unnecessary to set a new date. This statement, which aligned the Attorney General with Judge Lynch and County Attorney Downey, helped clear up the most complicated capital punishment case in the county and perhaps the state of Montana.

The following day Sheriff Duggan told the press that he would soon decide if he would ask for a sanity hearing but he would also proceed with the preparations for the execution. In another announcement the sheriff said that the prisoner had broken his hunger strike by eating an egg and a piece of meat. On Monday, September 27, Sheriff Duggan formerly requested the court to grant Vettere an examination of his sanity saying that he didn't know if the prisoner was sane or not as he was no expert on such matters. The sheriff said he did know that he didn't want to execute a man while there was still a question of his mental condition.

Sheriff Duggan explained that while Dr. H.A. Bolton of the state hospital had reported to Governor Erickson concerning the prisoner, the Silver Bow officials were not informed of the results. The sheriff was certain that there was ample time before the scheduled execution on Friday to answer the sanity question and according to section No.1205 of the criminal code, if a sheriff believed that a man under sentence of death was insane he could recommend a sanity hearing and if the prisoner was deemed insane at a hearing he could not be legally executed. According to the sheriff, Vettere had become a real freak show at the jail with his hair and beard becoming long, ragged and unruly. Most of the time the prisoner wore a red bandana handkerchief tied around his head because he was always complaining that his head hurt.

Although Judge Lynch denied the sheriff's request for a jury sanity hearing, he ordered that Silver Bow County Physician Dan J. Donohue and Dr. Bolten, superintendent of the Warm Springs Mental Hospital visit the prisoner on September 28. The judge himself accompanied the two physicians to the county jail and all three men agreed that Tony Vettere was sane. Along with Drs. Bolton and Donohue, Dr. Ungherini of Butte and Dr. Weare of the state hospital at Warm Springs had earlier diagnosed Anthony Vettere sane. With that settled, Sheriff Duggan ordered new ropes for the condemned man.

Vettere was poorly clad at the time of his arrest and he had worn overalls during his eleven months in jail and on September 29, the county furnished him with a suit of black clothes, but because he was in the habit of tearing up everything, the sheriff decided to save them to bury him in. During the condemned man's final day he wore a rough flannel shirt and a pair of overalls when he called for the sheriff to tell him, "My heart is clean, I don't kill anybody."

While speaking to the sheriff, Vettere viciously struck his chest and eventually began speaking unintelligently. The prisoner asked the sheriff in a calm voice if he would bury his remains near where he had lived by the Northern Pacific depot and without warning Vettere suddenly began shouting then he cried for a moment and then he started to laugh in a wild and weird tone for several minutes.

Later five Italian friends called on Vettere at his death cell and they talked vivaciously for several minutes and then the prisoner burst into tears and he began to laugh again. As soon as his friends left the condemned man wrapped himself in a gray blanket and laid down on his cot. He refused to be shaved and his three months growth of beard gave him a fierce-looking appearance as if he were a Mediterranean pirate of the Middle Ages. At six o'clock a sumptuous dinner prepared by the chef of the Silver Bow Club of soup, relishes, fried chicken and various vegetables was sent to the condemned man's cell and Vettere ate quickly and he apparently relished what was probably the most elaborate meal he had ever had.

During the afternoon and early evening hundreds of people including many women and boys stopped by the jail on Alaska Street to view the gallows, which was last used to hang Roy Walsh in February of 1925. The scaffold was placed in the foyer near the front door of the jail and about eighty feet from the tier of cells where Vettere was locked up and in the same spot where the Harris boys had met their death. Like the previous execution, a runway was constructed from the main floor of the jail up to the platform.

A day earlier one women spent several minutes feeling the heavy hemp rope and she was especially intrigued by the regulation hangman's knot. During previous executions, Silver Bow County utilized persons outside of the sheriff's office to spring the trap and Jack Favero the son of one of Vettere's victims was willing to do the job for the county. Jack and his younger brother, Martin both had expressed their desire to witness the execution, and that the boy's mother had said that it would be good for the two boys.

The Reverend Father Gilmer, chaplain of St. James Hospital visited with Vettere on Tuesday afternoon and the two men spoke in Italian. The condemned man had previously refused to see the priest but on his last day he welcomed the spiritual adviser kindly and Father Gilmer returned again between six and seven o'clock. Vettere refused to speak to reporters and he told his jailers that he would kill the next newspaperman he saw.

The prisoner's voice had become hoarse after all of his yelling and cursing but he didn't seem to be nervous as he ate his meal and he spent most of the day brooding and when he slept he curled up in a blanket. While the workers were oiling the hinges and testing the trap on the gallows, the guards in an effort to spare the feelings of the condemned man shut a heavy steel door that separated the cells from the rotunda of the jail.

After Father Gilmore left, Vettere started writing three letters, one to the Italian Vice Consul, another to his cousin Joe and the third to another man. He stood in the corridor of his cell leaning on a shelf and quickly wrote, sheet after sheet and then stopped and began awkwardly folding them. After placing the letters on the shelf he climbed like a monkey up the bars and tried to look out of the window of the jail and then he began singing an Italian ballad, which he sang in a carefree manner. A woman and two men, friends of Vettere called on him late in the evening and they spoke through the bars of his cell and after bidding them farewell and good-luck, the prisoner spent the remainder of the night alone shouting incoherently and pacing in his cell.

A little white cat that roamed the jail corridor always seemed to change Vettere's mood and he enjoyed petting and playing with the animal. The condemned man on several occasions had promised Undersheriff Robinson, Deputy Duggan and Jailer John Shea that he would cause no trouble on the scaffold saying, "I'll go easy; I want to die. I'll be singing." Although Vettere went through his moments of calm and periods of rage the rest of the jail was reportedly in deathly silence.

The guards said that the usual chatter of the other inmates was missing as it was on the evening before the execution of the Harris boys in 1923. Earlier Vettere had asked for his attorney and when Mr. Galasso arrived the prisoner grasped his hand and thanked him earnestly for his services and at first the prisoner spoke calmly as he smoked but when his visitor tried to encourage the prisoner to put on the suit the county had provided the condemned man began shouting the only thing he wanted was his freedom.

Since the county commissioners had refused the expense of a deathwatch, the sheriff along with Jailer Shea and the other deputies checked the death cell every half hour and at one point the prisoner said, "I am try to write but no can think, my head she hurt to think. I want to see my cousin, Joe Vettere; I want to see the Judge Lynch." Sheriff Duggan explained that he had sent for the judge but he was unable to get in touch with him. He also told the prisoner that Joe Vettere was a patient at a local hospital and he wasn't able to come to the jail. At first Vettere turned away in disgust, but then he suddenly turned and stuck his hand through the bars and shook the sheriff's hand.

As Undersheriff Robinson entered the man's cell to read the death warrant Vettere pulled out a three-foot piece of pipe from his blankets and attacked the officer and then tried to fend off the other deputies with a knife he had been hiding. The undersheriff barely escaped the flying pipe, which had been torn from the cell plumbing and Vettere chased after him before retreating down the aisle between the cells swinging the three-quarter inch iron club and flourishing his knife. Vettere had a white cloth wrapped around his head; his face almost covered with his black beard as he was threatening to kill every man there and he was yelling for Judge Lynch so that he could kill him as well.

Then the maniac began shouting "Viva Mussolini, Shoot me. I don't care, but no hang me up." When Sheriff Duggan ordered the prisoner to drop the bar, Vettere shouted, "Not by damn sight, I kill." Deputy Jack Duggan took a long pole used to lower the windows and from an adjoining cell he tried to grasp Vettere's weapon, which only infuriated the prisoner and he began striking his bar so hard that he bent it. "I got a knife too. I got a knife," and then the prisoner displayed the handle of a spoon inside his waistband. Deputy Rockefeller quickly pulled the lever closing the corridor and because no one could get near the crazed man, Sheriff Duggan ordered teargas.

Undersheriff Robinson quickly returned with several bombs containing the potent gas and he started the fumes towards the cursing slayer and the fiend retreated back into the west end of the corridor and then he began beating the plumbing from the wash sinks. As the streams of hot and cold water were gushing all over the cells Vettere continued to shout obscenities and striking at the officers with the pipe. As the gas began to take effect, the prisoner ran back into his cell where more chocking gas was sprayed and the pipe dropped from Vettere's hands and he covered himself in his bedding.

As the other thirty prisoners were yelling, screaming and coughing from the effects of the gas, Deputies Shea and Byers with eyes and noses running from the teargas rushed in and subdued the prisoner and then dragged him to the south end of the jail, where the windows had been opened to clear the air. While the officers applied the arm and leg straps to the prisoner while he was half conscious on the floor, the other prisoners were allowed into the main corridor.

The gas only temporarily disabled most of the inmates but one of the other prisoners was rendered unconscious for several hours. Vettere was dragged half way to the door leading to the scaffold where Undersheriff Robinson finished reading the death warrant, the Governor's message refusing clemency and the other required documents to the prisoner. During the reading Vettere stood slumped over and supported by Deputies Duggan and Byers and only groaned during the reading as he was just coming out of the effects of the gas.

When Officer Robinson finished the reading in the gas-filled room, the big door to the gallows was opened and the procession consisting of Vettere, the undersheriff and Deputies Duggan, Piskolich Rockefeller, Byers and McBride marched on. The prisoner was told to walk but he only groaned and his limp body had to be shuffled aimlessly along for the twenty-five feet to the gallows where Undersheriff Robinson quickly slipped the noose over Vettere's head.

Vettere's last words were only curses and he refused to stand upright on the gallows and the deputies were forced to hold him up over the trap door and at 12:28 a.m. the deputies stepped aside and Anthony Vettere dropped out of sight and six minutes later Drs. Donohue, O'Rouke, Herbert A. Maillett and J.F. Lhotka pronounced him dead. The physicians reported that the fall had not broken the man's neck and he had died from strangulation. After the doctors signaled that the man was dead, Deputy Duggan cut the rope and the body fell to the cement floor.

The small crowd at the jail that witnessed the execution was strongly affected by the unprecedented struggle that preceded the hanging, which they could hear going on the other side of the heavy steel door. The doctors and Father Gilmore and the Reverend J.C. Meehan occupied the pit into which Vettere dropped to his death and the remains were sent to the Duggan Funeral Chapel where about two thousand people poured in to view them.

Within thirty minutes after the condemned man had been hanged men, women and children were lined up at the undertaking establishment to look at Vettere's body as it lay on a cushion in a room shared with a dead miner. That evening Dr. Mailett removed the brain of the murderer on the orders of Sheriff Duggan and with permission of the prisoner and the following day Dr. I.E. Dobos, pathologist at St. Jame's Hospital reported that the brain of Vettere showed no sign of insanity. According to the physician the executed murderer's brain was not abnormal in any way and there was no damage from injury or disease found. Dr. Mailett concurred by reporting that the brain weighed the same as an average man's organ and it was well developed.

The friends of Anthony Vettere took up a collection and they paid for his burial in the Holly Cross Cemetery and many of his countrymen accompanied the body to his grave sight and the pallbearers were Joe Verand, Frank Duranti, Carl Mittino, Frank Albo, Dominico Dalmuto and Peter Notti.

May 20, 1927
Ferdinand Schlaps

Location and Gallows: Schlaps was hanged in the Roosevelt County jail yard at Wolf Point from ***Gallows No. Twenty: (May 1927)***.

Description: The nineteen-year-old German-Russian was slightly under average height, and while appearing a bit slow, he never seemed to be vicious or mean. The young man was described as having an ordinary appearance with very fair complexion with blond hair combed straight back.

Crime: Murder of Antone F. Geisler and his wife, Ludmilla on their farm near Homestead on the afternoon of May 1, 1926.

Judge: Spurgeon E. Paul

Prosecution: County Attorney Hugh N. Marron assisted by his deputy, Arlie M. Foor

Defense: Erick Moum of Poplar, assisted by his law partner, R.M. Morford and Howard M. Lewis of Plentywood was brought in to help with the appeal

Sheriff: John H. Anderson

Distinction: While there had been three victims of Lynch Mobs at Poplar in 1884, this was the last hanging and the one and only legal execution in Roosevelt County.

Wanting Mr. Geisler's automobile for a road trip, young Ferdinand Schlaps went to the man's house on Saturday, May 1, 1926, and got a shotgun and four shells, because he said later that he wanted to be able to shoot his victims a second time, and then shot and killed Tony Geisler and then his wife Ludmilla.

Schlaps had gone to work for Tony Geisler at his ranch near the town of Homestead on April 5, 1926, at an agreed wage of fifty dollars per month. Ludmilla Geisler lived on the ranch with her husband and the young farmhand roomed at the house and ate with the couple. Mr. and Mrs. Geisler had only been married for about ten months and before her marriage Ludmilla had been a nurse back in Texas. A week or two before the tragedy Schlaps conceived the idea of killing the couple in order to get their Ford automobile and money so that he could return to Ashley, North Dakota.

At about two o'clock on the afternoon of May 1, 1926, Schlaps and the thirty-eight-year-old Tony Geisler were in the barn harnessing the horses for work in the field and twenty-eight-year-old Mrs. Geisler was in the house getting ready to attend a school program at Homestead. Schlaps later said that he told Mr. Geisler that he was going to the house for a drink of water, and at the house he got the farmer's Stevens12-guage single-shot shotgun and some shells, telling Mrs. Geisler that he was going hunting.

With the loaded shotgun Schlaps returned to the barn where he shot Mr. Geisler in the left shoulder and side, while trying to aim at the man's heart. As his victim was struggling on the ground Schlaps put another shell in the weapon and shot him in the head. The young man reloaded the weapon as he was walking towards the window on the south side of the house where he observed Mrs. Geisler standing in the bedroom. The murderer shot the woman through the window and as she was hollering for help Schlaps reloaded the shotgun and entered the house.

The murderer went to the bedroom where the woman had been but she had gone to Schlaps' room where she was hiding behind a curtain. When discovered the dying woman begged for her life but Schlaps took aim and nearly blew her head off with a shot to her neck. The man then dragged Mrs. Geisler's body down to the barn and then picked up the empty shells and threw them into the creek. The murderer then got a pail of water and mop and washed up the blood and after cleaning the house Schlaps found about twenty dollars in a trunk and then he went down by the barn and covered the oats in the wagon with a blanket to protect it from the horses and cattle. Then he went to the barn and took the harnesses off the horses and turned them loose.

The murderer gave the cattle water and completed a few other chores on the place before he took the Ford out and filled it with gasoline. Schlaps waited until dark and then he loaded the two bodies into the sedan and drove towards Homestead until he reached the bridge over the Big Muddy River. After throwing Mrs. Geisler's body into the river, Schlaps was interrupted when he saw a car coming his way so he drove the Ford off the bridge; turned off the lights, waited along the riverbank until the other vehicle passed and then he dropped Tony Geisler's body into the stream. When he was done with his gruesome task Schlaps drove to Homestead where he remained about an hour and a half before staying overnight at his mother's home.

The next morning while Schlaps was washing the blood out of the Ford sedan, a neighbor of the Geisler's discovered their bodies hung up on some debris in the river and after removing them from the water he notified the Sheridan County authorities at Plentywood. Sheriff Salisbury and the coroner went to Homestead where they examined the bodies and naturally the suspicion fell on the victim's hired hand who was seen the night before driving their car.

Sheriff Salisbury and the county attorney found Schlaps at his mother's home and when asked about Mr. and Mrs. Geisler he told the officers that he had taken Tony and his wife to Poplar where they were going to a hospital. When the sheriff found blood on Schlap's clothing and other stains in the Geisler automobile the murderer broke down and confessed that he had killed the couple.

One of Schlaps' brothers said that Fred could never do something like that alone and he was convinced someone must have told him what to do. Fred Schlaps picked up on the remark and then told the officers that a stranger, an older man, had come to the Geisler place and killed Tony and then the man gave him twenty dollars to shoot Mrs. Geisler and dump the bodies.

After further questioning, Schlaps' first story fell apart and he finally told the officers that he had planned to kill both Tony and his wife for their car and traveling money to drive to North Dakota. The young man said that he had no trouble with Mr. and Mrs. Geisler in fact they had been very good to him but the desire for the new car and the need to get back to North Dakota was stronger than his friendship for the victims.

Fred had come to Montana from Ashley with his mother and siblings after his father had died a few months earlier and he volunteered to take the authorities over to the crime scene and re-enact the tragedy and recover the empty shotgun shells from the creek. He said he was sorry about killing Mrs. Geisler after she had pleaded for her life and then he signed the written confession. Sheriff John H. Anderson and County Attorney Hugh N. Marron went to Plentywood on Monday, May 3, and returned to Wolf Point with Schlaps on Tuesday.

Four days after the grisly murders, the bodies of Antone F. Geisler and his wife were shipped to Shiner, Texas at the direction of Ludmilla's father. Geisler was from Germany and it was believed that the couple had become acquainted through correspondence while he was working on the big Schnitzler Farm at Froid, Montana and they were married in Texas. Tony Geisler and his wife by all appearances were a happy couple and a good team, being thrifty, industrious and on the road to prosperity as well as looking forward to the birth of their first child. An uncle of Mrs. Geisler living at Powderville, Montana sent his oldest son to look after the murdered couple's ranch until it could be disposed of.

After Schlaps had made several oral confessions and a written statement saying that he had planned the double murder for some time, Roosevelt County Attorney Marron filed first-degree murder charges in the justice court of Judge Charles Gordon. The county attorney reported that there was nothing in Schlaps' conversation or action that suggested he had a diseased mind.

The prisoner appeared rational, fully aware of what he had done and he was sorry for what had happened. Schlaps was slow, and the questioning had to be framed in simple terms and words for him to comprehend like when Mr. Marron asked him what his nationality was, he said he didn't know what he meant and when asked if he had felt pity for Mrs. Geisler, Schlaps told the sheriff that he felt sorry and tears came to his eyes. Despite his confessions and detailed accounts of the crime

Fred Schlaps pleaded not guilty at the preliminary hearing on May 13, 1926.

The Ferdinand Schlaps' trial for the murder of Ludmilla Geisler was the first murder trial in Wolf Point and it was held in the spacious and beautiful Palm Room of the Sherman Hotel. The county board had selected the location because its size was better suited than the regular courtroom at the courthouse. The hearing began at one o'clock on Thursday afternoon, July 8, 1926, and it was presided over by Judge Spurgeon E. Paul with Attorney Erick Moum of Poplar for the defense and County Attorney Hugh N. Marron handling the prosecution. People from all parts of the county were in attendance including the defendant's mother and two of his brothers. By the second day the following jury had been sworn in:

A.E. Huseby	John Kopitzke	Sid Scourey
Sam Wagaman	J.R. Clutter	Nels Sorenson
John Haagenson	Albert Lee	Cecil G. Perry
Paul Arndt	Andrew Harbo (f)	A.M. Hanson

(f) Foreman

The young defendant was dressed in a green and black woolen blazer and overalls and his face seldom moved and his gaze was generally directed at the floor. The defendant showed very little emotion during the proceedings except when hanging and the death penalty were spoken of and Schlaps' eyes seemed to get large and his lips tightened.

During the trial the defense made an effort to show that their client wasn't normal mentally because of an injury to his head while he was a youngster and Christina Schlaps, the mother of the defendant, testified that her son had been severely ill when he was six years of age; that he didn't talk as much as the other children; then when he was about ten he was sick with the flu and in 1925, he fell from a horse breaking his arm and hurting his chest. She said that her son had constantly complained about headaches and that he had difficulty learning his catechism.

Fred Schlaps was the only witness for the defense, which had conceded that he had committed the murders but they hoped his testimony would convince the court of his insanity. Schlaps proved to be a poor witness for the defense, and as the questioning went on he replied more readily and he could recollect events from several years earlier. When the defendant was questioned about the murder his testimony was nearly the same as his earlier written confession.

The heat and tedium of the long days didn't lesson the public interest in the fifteen-day-long trial and the courtroom was reportedly packed every day and the unusual length of the trial brought about an unavoidable financial burden on Roosevelt County. Finally at 11:15 Friday evening, July 23, 1926, the case was placed in the hands of the jury and the court was adjourned until ten a.m. the following day.

Judge Paul instructed the jury that only children under the age of seven, idiots, lunatics and insane persons were not legally responsible for their acts. The court said that if they found a verdict of murder in the first degree the punishment could be fixed at either death or life imprisonment or it might be left up to the judge. If second-degree murder was found the penalty might not be less than ten years with the lowest maximum sentence of twenty years.

Early Saturday morning the jury sent word that they had arrived at a verdict and when all the necessary parties were present the court was convened and Andrew Harbo, the foreman handed the verdict to the bailiff and Clerk of the Court Thomas R. Forbes read the following: "We, the jury, duly empanelled and sworn, do hereby find the defendant guilty of murder in the first degree and fix the punishment at death."

Several of the jurors later said that it was not easy to impose the death sentence, but in view of the evidence and the instructions, they couldn't do anything else. They also stated that only one ballot was required to reach the unanimous decision and all of the jurors were convinced that Schlaps was sane and was mentally capable of knowing right from wrong.

On August 11, Judge Paul sentenced the prisoner to be hanged on September 25, 1926. As the handcuffed prisoner was being brought over from the jail he struggled with the officers and when he was brought into the courtroom he slumped down into his chair as if he had already been condemned to death. His eyes stared at the floor his face chalky and swollen from weeping and he held a handkerchief over his lips with his handcuffed hands.

Judge Paul's voice betrayed him twice with emotion as he sentenced the young man to death and Defense Attorney Eric Moum asked for a ninety-day stay of execution while a transcript of evidence was made. The judge said that he would take the motion under advisement but he stated that the law gives the defense sixty days from the date of the appeal and that the transcript could be made in a week or two. After the verdict was read, the prisoner appeared hopeless as the spectators filed out of the courtroom and he was helped to his feet.

After relatives of Schlaps had raised funds, Howard M. Lewis of Plentywood was retained to assist the defense and the appeal to the Supreme Court stayed the execution. Roosevelt County officials reported that the trial had already cost about ten thousand dollars and had consequently put the general fund into the red until the tax collections that fall. Many of the citizens of the county were upset that the defense was adding to the bill by taking advantage of the rights offered to a convicted person.

The defense argued Schlaps' case before the Supreme Court on February 24, 1927, stating that the court had erred by admitting evidence about Tony Geisler's body and for not allowing the testimony of the defendant's mother concerning his mental condition. The high court ruled that it was universally accepted in a case of a double homicide that all the evidence was introduced. The Supreme Court went on to rule that the defendant's mentality was immaterial as long as he was aware of right and wrong and on March 29, 1927, the high court affirmed the decision of the district court. Following the Supreme Court decision, Judge Paul re-sentenced Schlaps on April 13, 1927, to be executed on May 20 and when the defendant was brought before the judge he had the same demeanor that he had characterized since his arrest. The defense announced after the sentencing their intentions to appeal the case to Governor John E. Erickson.

On May 19, 1927, the day before the execution, Governor Erickson refused to interfere with the execution stating that because the murders were so brutal and if capital punishment was ever justified it was in the Schlaps' case. Since there had been a question concerning the prisoner's sanity, the Governor ordered Dr. H.A. Bolton, superintendent of the state hospital at Warm Springs and his assistant, Dr. Johnson to examine the prisoner's condition and the physicians later reported that the condemned man's condition was normal although he had a low IQ, but he knew the difference between right and wrong.

A few hours before his execution, Schlaps was taken to the dining room of the woman's section of the jail where he was served a specially prepared roast chicken dinner with dressing, bread and butter, pickles, coffee, cream pie and a bottle of malt. His deathwatch and the reporter from the "Wolf Point Herald" sat with the condemned man as he ate his last meal. Schlaps appeared cheerful and he talked freely with the reporter about being saved by his religion and that he was heading to a better place explaining that he had been baptized into a Protestant church earlier that day and Reverend Sidney A. Walker would remain with him until the end.

Sheriff Anderson and Undersheriff Charles Council had gone about their grim duties of preparing for the execution with the utmost care, having the gallows framed and ready to set up several weeks in advance. The eighteen-foot tall fence was built the width of the jail building, which was about seventy feet long and while Sheriff Anderson and his men were preparing for the execution of Fred Schlaps, Captain Charles A. Lindbergh was getting ready for his epic flight across the Atlantic, and while he was on his way to Paris the young Montanan walked to the gallows.

The prisoner walked firmly to the scaffold and as soon as Sheriff Anderson and Deputy James A. Boyd assisted Schlaps onto the platform the doomed man made a short farewell speech saying that he was sorry for what he had done and that he was convinced that his Maker would forgive him and then he said, "Good-bye world." As the black cap was slipped over his head the youth repeated several times, "Good-Bye world, Oh Jesus." Two ministers were offering a prayer when at 12:10 a.m. the trap was sprung. The suspended body made a few convulsive movements of the legs and after about seventeen minutes later the three physicians present pronounced Ferdinand Schlaps dead.

The large crowd of witnesses including most of the jury and officials from Roosevelt and the surrounding counties maintained almost complete silence during the execution, and the only sound heard was the splatter of the cold rain, which was being driven by an east wind. When the body was eventually cut down, it was placed in the undertaker's basket, which had been stored in the pit beneath the gallows and the following day many people viewed the body at Clayton's Undertaking Parlor at Wolf point.

Ferdinand Schlaps body was turned over to his mother and his remains were buried on Sunday, May 22, 1927, in the Wolf Point Cemetery. Mr. and Mrs. Doty of the Pentecostal Mission conducted the services and the mission's choir furnished the music. Mrs. Schlaps and her other children along with other relatives were present at the services on that rainy afternoon.

November 6, 1929

Rollin Davisson

Location and Gallows: Davisson was hanged inside the county courthouse at Livingston on the built-in scaffold, ***Gallows No. Twenty-One: (October 1929)***.

Description: The forty-four-year-old Rollin Davisson was described as being a tall, thin man who appeared to be emaciated by disease.

Crime: Murder of Police Chief Peter Holt and Officer Martin Zollman in City Hall on August 21, 1929.

Judge: B.E. Berg

Prosecution: County Attorney Elbert F. Allen assisted by Deputy County Attorney E. Patrick Kelly[4] and former County Attorney Fred L. Gibson

Defense: Daniel Yancy

Sheriff: Clarence Gilbert

Distinction: Davisson was the third and last man hanged in Park County.

This crime was one of the most shocking murders in the history of Montana and it was provoked when Chief of Police Peter Holt refused to intervene over a dispute involving fifty cents. Rollin Davisson, armed with his 9-mm German Lugar in a holster strapped to his leg concealed beneath a pair of woolen trousers entered the office of Chief Holt at about nine o'clock on Wednesday morning, August 21, 1929.

In the office at the time was J.P.V. "Trapper" Evans, a local curio dealer and pioneer resident of Montana; Traffic Officer Martin Zollman seated across the table from the chief and leaning against the wall reading a magazine. The chief himself was seated at his usual position at his desk when without warning Davisson entered the office and fired point-blank at Holt, whom had only enough time to remove his glasses from his eyes before a bullet passed through his heart.

In true fashion of a public servant who was willing to risk his own life to assist a fellow officer in trouble, Traffic Officer Zollman jumped from his chair and also received a bullet to his heart but before dying the officer was able to take the assassin to the floor. In the struggle, Davisson clubbed Zollman over the head jamming the action of the revolver before the murderer tried to fire the weapon at City Treasurer Robert Bailie and "Trapper" Evans.

The seventy-year-old "Trapper" Evans clutched Davisson's throat in a vise-like grip and began chocking him while watching Officer Zollman die next to him. Knowing his own limitations, Mr. Evans began yelling for help and Fireman Clyde Neal came down from the fire station upstairs and grasped a cinder block, which was used as a doorstop and struck Davisson several times over the head.

Fireman Neal did not know "Trapper" personally, and because he was on top of the other man, it was his first inclination to lay the older man out but he sensed the sincerity of the older man's screams of, "kill him! He has already killed Holt and Zollman and will kill us if given the chance." The heavy blows from the large block was still insufficient to knock Davisson unconscious but he was rendered dazed enough so that the men could disarm him.

About that time Sheriff Clarence Gilbert arrived at city hall and took the man bleeding from the scalp wound into custody and transported him to the county jail. That afternoon County Physician J.E. Stuart dressed and stitched Davisson's wounds and the prisoner was eventually booked without bail on first-degree murder charges. Although the feelings against Davisson were at a high pitch, Sheriff Gilbert declared that he did not fear violence from the citizens of Livingston and Park County.

Attorney Frank Arnold was first to be appointed to defend Davisson, but because of his longtime friendship with the two policemen, he asked to be relieved and Judge B.E. Berg assigned the firm of Gibson and Smith. Attorney Vard Smith also requested his firm be excused from such service on much of the same reasons as was given by Attorney Arnold. Judge James F. O'Connor was then appointed by Judge Berg but after three or four days the attorney decided it would be impossible for him to represent Davisson and finally Attorney Dan Yancey was called upon, and after weighing the matter, he decided that every defendant deserves a defense and he assumed the task.

Chief Holt was killed with a bullet that is referred to as a "dumdum" round, which expands on contact and after piercing the upper left lung of the officer it then tore into his heart. Rollin Davisson and Chief Holt had known each other for many years having served together in the army while they were stationed at Yellowstone National Park. Peter Holt came to Yellowstone Park with Company "D" Sixth Cavalry in 1892, and after his discharge in 1897 he became a government scout. Holt along with James Morrison journeyed into the mountains of the park and captured two buffalo calves to produce a sturdier strain of animals in the Lamar River herd.

In 1903, Holt accompanied President Theodore Roosevelt as a scout and guide in charge of the pack train for the chief executive's camping trip into the Absaroka Mountains. Police chiefs of Butte, Missoula, Helena, Bozeman and Billings, all in uniform formed a guard of honor for the funeral of Chief Peter Holt and they accompanied his body to the Mountain View Cemetery at Livingston.

The bullet that entered Martin Zollman pierced his heart and then exited his body after going through one of his his kidneys. Officer Zollman was the son of a Luthern minister and he later became a first class pilot in the U.S. Air Corps and remained an officer in the Army Reserves while being a flight instructor. Zollman later joined the Livingston police department and became one of the state's most fearless officers.

Over the years Martin Zollman ran a flying school at Helena and on various occasions he was called on to make passenger flights as well as test flights for airplane manufacturers. At the Northern Pacific depot at Livingston, the local American Legion sent the body of Officer Zollman to his home in Milwaukee where it was buried with full military honors. The children of Livingston raised funds to have a wreath of flowers placed on the fallen officer's grave at Milwaukee and the Montana city later named the municipal airfield "Zollman Field."

Davisson was "cashiered" from army service shortly before the soldiers were relieved from duty at Yellowstone National Park and he and another soldier were going through court martial proceedings for stealing chickens at Gardiner but the officers decided instead to just pay them off and discharge them. After leaving the army, Davisson left the area and he wasn't heard from until he returned to Livingston in 1927. For a number of months Davisson had been a laborer at Livingston and he was receiving food and shelter from a charitable organization during the previous winter.

The day before the murders, Davisson had gone to city hall to ask Chief Holt to intercede in a labor dispute that he had with a local employer. Davisson had expected five dollars for the job and the employer had only paid him four dollars and fifty cents. In his usual "fatherly" way of offering advice, Chief Holt recommended that Davisson show the employer that he was too big of a man to quarrel over fifty cents and recommended that he just accept the payment and call it square.

Rollin Davisson's trial for the murder of Police Chief Holt opened Monday morning, September 16, 1929, and the small courtroom was never able to accommodate the huge number of people who wanted to witness the trial. The prisoner was barely recognizable to the local observers as he was dressed in a brand new suit, shirt, shoes, and with a fresh shave and haircut. The defendant listened to the proceedings and reportedly paid particular attention to the jury selections and after two days the following Park County jurors were sworn in:

George Shepard	S.C. Johnson	Fred Bassett
R.W. Lucas	H.M. Davidson	Earl H. Brown
Stephen J. O'Rourke	C.W. Enoch	Glen Overfelt
Bert Goudy	Elmer Lee	Sam Stofer

On Wednesday, September 18, after the state had rested its case, Attorney Yancey shocked the courtroom by trying to introduce into evidence several legal documents, letters and other items to substantiate the defense's claim that Davisson was incompetent. The prosecution objected, stating that the defendant's letters were self-serving and were irrelevant and would be an illegal presentation. The prosecution pointed out that Montana law did not permit an alleged insane man to take the stand to prove his own insanity.

The following day Rollin Davisson took the stand and testified that he had been admitted into insane asylums in Missouri and at Las Vegas, New Mexico. He was admitted in New Mexico for getting into a fight where he nearly killed a man and later managed to escape from the institution before coming to Montana. The defendant said that he had an outbreak of syphilis in 1914, which the defense intended to prove was part of the cause of his insanity.

Davisson described his background and then he admitted that he had killed the two officers at city hall and he didn't expect to get away with it. The defense presented witnesses trying to prove Davisson was in fact insane but their testimonies along with the fact that the defendant had been incarcerated in two state institutions for the care of mental patients failed to convince the jury that the murderer was unable to know the difference between right and wrong.

Thirty minutes after being given their instructions from the judge, the jury returned with a first-degree murder verdict and placed the burden of affixing the penalty to the court. Davisson was unmoved by the jury's verdict as he had told the deputies that he had predicted a guilty vote. Except for the continual twisting of his fingers, which for the most part was unseen by most people in the crowded courtroom the defendant sat unmoved during the final arguments of the lawyers.

Sheriff Gilbert had also known Rollin Davisson at Yellowstone Park years earlier when the officer was a mailman and the prisoner was serving as a soldier. One time on the way back to his cell at the jail, Davisson commented to the sheriff that he never thought the day would come when he would swing from a rope and that his old friend would be his executioner.

Although nobody knew how long the jury would be out, not a single person left the crowded courtroom in anticipation of the verdict. While the court proceeded with another murder case the audience only appeared casually interested while they were waiting for the main attraction. No one was surprised when the knock on the door of the jury room was quickly heard as most of the crowd had expected a first-degree verdict. The records of the clerk of the court indicated that the Davisson trial cost the county approximately one thousand three hundred and seventy-two dollars, which included the one hundred dollar fee paid to the defense attorney.

Davisson told the deputies that he had developed a real hatred towards former county attorney Fred Gibson who assisted in the prosecution and in so many words said that he would certainly take care of him if he were ever free. When told of the threat, Attorney Gibson said that he didn't doubt it in the least because while he was making his final arguments to the jury, the prosecutor looked over to the defendant and when the two men's eyes met, the attorney became convinced that

Davisson knew the difference between right and wrong and that he was a mean and brutal man.

A day or two after the trial the "Livingston Enterprise" received a letter from Samuel Davisson at Priscoe, Missouri, the father of the Park County prisoner requesting copies of the papers carrying the story of the trial, verdict and the sentence. Mr. Davisson included a book of stamps and twenty-five cents to cover the cost of postage and the letter was reportedly well written and indicated it was from someone who was well educated and well refined.

Besides his father's letter, a brother of the defendant arrived at Livingston in mid-October to visit the prisoner. Roy Davisson said that his brother, Rollin left home at age fifteen and he had caused his family much sorrow since. He said that he believed that his brother had received a fair trial and although he was sorry that his brother was to be hanged he truly understood why.

On Wednesday, September 25, 1929, Judge Berg sentenced Rollin Davisson to be hanged on October 30, which was just ten weeks to the day from the time of the two murders. After his sentencing, Davisson was placed into the section of the jail on the second floor known as "Condemned Row" and Sheriff Gilbert immediately set a rotating deathwatch over the prisoner consisting of Thadeous Pound, Walter Peterson and Jens Jenson.

On his way to his new cell Davisson walked across the trap door of the built-in gallows and the condemned man's cell faced the place of execution and from there all of the preparations were always in sight. While in his cell Davisson only stared down to the floor and Sheriff Gilbert said that he wanted his prisoner's right to privacy to be respected and he ordered the deathwatch not to discuss their conversations with the condemned man.

Although Davisson was raised a Baptist he eventually affiliated with the Evangelical Church and still later he claimed to have taken the necessary vows for membership in the Catholic Church, only to return to the Baptist Church. In the last few years leading up to his execution Davisson had disavowed all religion and he declared that he would go to his death without clerical assistance. On the eve of the execution, Davisson asked no special favors except to reiterate his request that no member of the clergy be called to console him before his death.

The sheriff dropped in on the condemned man just about every day to find out what he wanted to be served for his meals and every effort was made to give him anything he wanted in the way of fruit along with his three good meals a day. Davisson maintained his even disposition and he enjoyed discussing anything foreign and domestic except his case. The prisoner talked with the deathwatch and read a great deal from the better grade of magazines, which were furnished him by the staff.

Davisson began reading a particular series, "The Planet of Peril" by Otis Adelbert Kline in the "Argosy" magazine, which was a twenty-five-chapter story starting on July 20, 1929. It was about a planet infested with bad men and full of fights, narrow escapes and gunplay from sea monsters, and other hard individuals. The jail was missing issues of August 17 and 24, and so a request went out to the public for missing copies in order that the condemned man would be able to finish the story before his execution and immediately after the request had gone out the jail was besieged by at least a dozen copies of the wanted issues.

Rollin Davisson's cell habits had become quite routine and shortly after dark he would normally remove his clothing and retire to his bunk and the officers at the county jail described him as a model prisoner who talked little, kept to himself and ate well, gaining seven pound since his incarceration. The condemned man's only real request was that his parents not be asked to bare the expense of shipping his body back to Missouri saying he wanted to be buried in Montana.

While this was the first and only hanging that Sheriff Gilbert had officiated he had witnessed two other executions in Montana, as a deputy he was present when Seth Danner paid for his crime in July of 1924, and later he saw Roy Walsh drop in February of 1925. There was only a one in a thousand failure rate in ropes but Sheriff Gilbert still ordered two hangman's strands, which was quite customary to insure that if one failed the other one could be used.

One of the ropes was used to test the built-in gallows by fastening one end to the eyelet in the ceiling above the scaffold and when the platform in the floor was tripped the weight would fall within a few inches of the floor below. The hangman's rope used to hang Davisson was different from the ordinary rope bought from the local hardware store, as its texture was soft and very pliable.

Meanwhile Sheriff Gilbert made arrangements with Silver Bow County Sheriff Angus B. McLeod to borrow the hangman's straps, which were kept in a trophy closet at the county jail at Butte that housed other grim items such as loaded rifles and pistols, tear-gas bombs and miscellaneous knives and other weapons taken off of prisoners. The leather straps used for the Davisson executions had also been used to hang Roy Walsh in 1925, and then Tony Vettere in 1926.

By October 29, 1929, all the details for the executions had been completed, the rope having been stretched to full length and the trap was oiled and thoroughly tested. The built-in gallows was on the second floor above the entrance to the sheriff's office on the ground floor and less than fifteen feet from the condemned man's cell. The gallows was near the railing and the trapdoor, which was operated by a lever that resembled an automobile gear shift, was designed to fall by its own weight and in a fraction of a second.

With only twenty hours before the execution, Governor John Erickson granted a stay until November 6, so that he could thoroughly review the transcripts of the trial and other pertinent information before considering a possible commutation of sentence. When told of the Governor's action the condemned man didn't display any enthusiasm, and the sheriff believed that Davisson was so sure of his fate that the delay only increased his ordeal. Davisson told his brother that he couldn't see any reason for asking for an appeal or for a stay of execution from the Governor.

On November 4, Governor Erickson declared that the judgment of the district court was proper and that he would not interfere with the execution and copies of the Governor's decision were sent to Davisson's attorney, Judge Berg and to Sheriff Gilbert. The sheriff didn't notify the condemned man until the following day and the prisoner expressed his displeasure that a delay had been caused saying, "I would rather be dead than spend the rest of my life in the pen."

After receiving word from the Governor, Judge B.E. Berg set a precedent by naming the exact hour for Davisson's hanging of seven o'clock on Wednesday morning, November 6, 1929. Park County authorities announced that the court's action was the first time in Montana history that a specific hour was set instead of a range of time in which the sheriff could decide the fate of the condemned man.

While on death row Davisson had pretty much what he wanted and he particularly enjoyed oranges, apples and bananas. The meals at the jail were prepared in the kitchen by a prisoner who had become quite an expert culinary artist and although the condemned man had the choice of chicken, the finest steak or any other delicacy for his last big meal, he only ordered the regular daily prison meal but he did ask for a piece of cake and milk. After the evening meal Davisson read a magazine and then he went to bed at nine o'clock and slept like a log all night with the exception of when he was snoring so loudly that he woke himself up. He reportedly turned to his deathwatch, Jailer Jen Jenson and said, "Call me at 5:30 in the morning. I don't want to miss any of the details of this party."

On his last morning Davisson was asked if he wanted breakfast but he refused saying: "What in the hell do I want to eat for? What good will it do me?" Except for his evening meal the night before the only indulgence the doomed man consumed were the cigarettes, which he smoked incessantly from the time he woke up until the officers were adjusting his death straps. A nice blue serge suit with a vest, shirt and collar was prepared the week before for the prisoner and it had been stored in a closet at the jail until it was needed.

At six o'clock the doors of the courthouse were locked to the public and the forty-eight witnesses arrived in twenty-six automobiles and each man was checked off the invitation list by Police Chief Frank Olson. In the sheriff's office some four-dozen men discussed previous hangings and how well the condemned men had died. Among the witnesses were Sheriff Brannin of Sweet Grass County, R.W. Swenson of the "Butte Daily Post," and Ray Conger with the "Bozeman Chronicle." Others in attendance were Charles Cartnel, R.A. Shannon, Ed L. Nowells, Charles R. Bridgeman, W.H. Flint, C.B. Wilcutt, F.B. Nickerson, Andrew Botterud, Jerry L. Moran and jurymen Earl H. Brown and C.W. Enochs.

While Sheriff Gilbert and Jailer Vern Meigs stood by, Deputy Vinackle read the death warrant to the condemned man at 6:55 and then Davisson walked the few steps to the scaffold where he faced the witnesses while the straps were being adjusted. After his knees were strapped together the deputies helped the prisoner turn and face eastward. When asked if he had any last words Davisson answered, "Nothing, except that I want my body buried in Montana. None of my folks are entitled to my body. They have never given me any consideration."

Sheriff Gilbert asked, "Are you ready Rollin?" and in a quiet tone Davisson answered, "Yes, all ready." The death mask was placed over the prisoner's head, the rope adjusted around Davisson's neck and the sheriff repeated, "Are you ready, Rollin?" "Yes" replied the doomed man, "all ready, Clarence." Sheriff Gilbert then pulled the lever at seven a.m. and Rollin Davisson's body fell through the floor and out of sight.

Witnesses near the scaffold later said that they heard Davisson's neck snap and three minutes later County Physician J.E. Stuart and Dr. Paul Greene pronounced the man dead. After the rope was cut, Coroner G. Walter Selby took charge of the body and it was loaded in a hearse parked at the east end of the jail. In the dim light of that November morning the body was transported to the Mountain View Cemetery where the tarp was removed from the grave that had been dug eight days earlier.

Moments later the rough box with Davisson's remains was lowered without ceremony into the grave and it was covered with earth. Sheriff Gilbert and Coroner Selby returned from the cemetery at exactly 7:35 a.m. and the sheriff later said that he had not wanted the duty of hanging a man, but since he had the duty to perform, he ought to perform it as best he could. Coroner Selby was in charge of Davisson's funeral and he reported that the burial costs was forty-five dollars.

(Endnotes)

[1] Before becoming a deathwatch over Vuckovich, Ike Abernathy served as Sheriff Houston's deputy when Missoula County hanged the four Indians in December of 1890.

[2] Because of the congestion and legal workload of the Montana State Supreme Court a commission made up of sitting District Court Judges was established in early 1921 to help examine pleadings, write decisions and other legal functions for the high court. Great Falls Tribune 12/22/1921, p4

[3] Defense Attorney Walker had previously headed up the prosecution team against Miles Fuller who was hanged in May of 1906.

[4] E. Patrick Kelly was a very popular figure in Montana sports having left his home at Big Timber to attend Dartmouth where he was a star quarterback in 1908 and 1909. In 1912 Kelly transferred to the University of Montana where he was starting quarterback for the Grizzlies in 1912 and 1913. While starring on the football field, Kelly was part of the first graduating class of the University Law School. The football star continued to be active in Montana sports acting as referee and even was the head official for the 1921 Bobcat-Grizzly Game.

The Last Hangings in Montana
(August 1933 through September 1943)

August 29, 1933
George Hoffman

Location and Gallows: The hanging of Hoffman took place inside of a machine shed at Choteau and he was the last man executed on ***Gallows No. Sixteen: (Jan. 1918): "Galloping Gallows" No. Five***.
Description: At the time of his execution Hoffman was described as being fifty-two years old and balding.
Crime: Murder of George Burrell during an attempted robbery on September 20, 1932.
Judge: R.M. Hattersley of Conrad
Prosecution: County Attorney Bert I. Packer and assisted by along with Chief Deputy Cascade County Attorney Art Jardine and Arthur Dean of Great Falls
Defense: F.J. Rigney of Cut Bank
Sheriff: Newly elected, J.C. "Shell" Billings
Distinction: Hoffman was the last man hanged in Teton County and his executioner; Sheriff Billings was the first sheriff in the United States to officiate over an execution in the same county in which the crime was committed since the other states had outlawed the practice. By 1933, all the other states in the Union had changed their statutes requiring that all capital punishments be carried out at their state penitentiaries.
Relics and Remnants: The hangman's noose, black cap and hand restraints that were used for the execution of George Hoffman along with murder weapons, the lead pipe and telephone cord are all on display at the Choteau Old Trail Museum in Choteau. The gallows, which was used to hang Hoffman, executed a total of eight convicted murderers and after it was last in at Choteau, the scaffold was returned to Butte where it is currently in storage in the basement of the Silver Bow County Courthouse. Because the scaffold is being stored with possible hazardous material the ancient death machine is not available for viewing.

George Hoffman arrived at Choteau from Bynum on September 9, 1932, and he had taken up residency at the Beaupre House with no money and little prospects of finding work as an itinerant barber. By September 20, he was flat broke and hadn't eaten for two days when he had heard that George Burrell, the owner of the Cigar Club was in the habit of carrying his daily receipts on his person. Later that evening Hoffman noticed that the crippled storeowner was alone in his store, and that was when he decided to rob the man.

At about eleven o'clock that evening Hoffman entered the adjacent barbershop and obtained a piece of telephone wire and a section of iron pipe about eighteen inches long and about two inches in diameter. After entering the cigar store and when Mr. Burrell's back was turned, the intruder struck him at the base of the skull with the pipe and while the victim was on the floor Hoffman removed the money from the cash register behind the counter. When returning from behind the counter, Hoffman noticed the man was still moving and he wrapped the telephone wire tightly around the neck of the semi-conscious man.

Hoffman returned to the barbershop where he replaced the pipe and then went back to his room at the Beaupre House where he hid the stolen money except for two five-dollar bills and three silver dollars. The murderer then went out and bought a pint of whisky and returned to his room and drank it. The next morning after giving his landlady a blood stained five-dollar bill, Hoffman went out for breakfast at eight o'clock where his waitress told him about the murder.

On Wednesday morning, September 21, 1932, Jess W. Davis discovered the body of his fifty-two-year-old employer as he was opening the store. The body of George Burrell had been dragged behind the counter of the popular cigar store and gambling house and feelings ran high and many citizens joined in to assist the authorities as they began rounding up the strangers in town. Since Hoffman had only been in town for a short time he was taken in with the sweep and his lame explanation of his newfound wealth led the officers to search his room at the hotel where the chambermaid, Mrs. Clyde Darby found a sock under the bathtub containing thirty-five dollars in paper and forty-four silver dollars.

Teton County Sheriff J.L. Collins ordered the suspect be taken to Great Falls for safekeeping and while en-route Hoffman confessed to the robbery and murder to the deputies including Undersheriff J.L. "Shell" Billings. At Great Falls the prisoner repeated his confession for Cascade County Stenographer Harriet Jewett to record and to Teton County Attorney Bert I. Packer and Cascade County Deputy County Attorney Art Jardine.

Although he had confessed to the crime twice in the presence of witnesses he still refused to sign the written copy of his statement. Meanwhile fingerprint expert, Walker B. Carroll of Great Falls was called to Choteau where he found and photographed prints on the cash register and other items at the cigar store, which matched those of the suspect.

Hoffman was reportedly born at Little Falls, Minnesota in about 1880 but he had lived in Montana since his early twenties having operated a barbershop at Gardiner from 1908 until 1916, when he cut hair at Wilsall. He sold his business there in 1920, and moved on to Hunters Hot Springs before working at various shops at Livingston, Great Falls, Missoula, Kevin, Oilmont, Bynum and Shelby.

George Hoffman's trial opened on November 28, 1932, and after Judge R.M. Hattersley denied a request for a change of venue the following jury was selected from men living outside of Choteau:

John Mathison	Edward R. McLean	Marcus Johnson
Jacob H. Gutshall	Louis Semington	Truman J. Oliver
Jens C. Lindholm	P.N. McCrorie	Sam Luinstra
Lee Weesner	John Depner	David Svenby

Throughout the trial the courtroom was filled every day and Hoffman reportedly remained calm while his attorneys tried to prove that he had been insane from drinking liquor. R.B. Thompson, editor and publisher of the "Pondera County News" at Conrad testified that he had known the defendant since 1917, and he told the court that the defendant had become a heavy drinker during that last few years. He further stated that Hoffman was not himself when he drank excessively.

The jury retired for deliberation at 12:15 p.m. Saturday December 3, and they returned at 3:30 with a guilty verdict with a recommendation for the death penalty. Observers in the courtroom said that when the verdict was read, Hoffman seemed totally unmoved by the jury's decision and the large crowd didn't cheer but talked among themselves.

At 9:30 Tuesday morning Judge Hattersley granted a hearing on December 28, 1932, for a new trial on the grounds that the defense had discovered new evidence. After that hearing the judge sentenced George Hoffman to be hanged on January 28, 1933, and the defense appealed to the Supreme Court, and while the high court postponed the original date of execution it eventually denied the appeal and Hoffman was then re-sentenced to be hanged before daybreak on August 29, 1933.

Teton County hadn't hanged a man since William Pepo in April of 1900, and the county officials found themselves without a gallows. To save the expense of building a new scaffold the county commissioners decided on an "economical hanging" by borrowing the "Galloping Gallows" from Silver Bow County. A truck transported the death machine the two hundred and fifty miles to Choteau where new sheriff, J.C. "Shell" Billings reported that Hoffman showed little interest in the preparations for his hanging.

The trap-type gallows was set up in a spacious tool shed with a high ceiling, which was located about one hundred yards from the county jail. A fenced walkway, covered with canvas was also erected between the jail and the shed to protect Hoffman from the eyes of the thrill seekers as he marched to his death.

George Hoffman's three brothers, John of Columbia Falls, Henry of Lewistown and Louis of Augusta appealed to Governor Frank H. Cooney in Helena for executive clemency but the request was declined. Finally, Mrs. F. J. Rigney, the wife of the defense attorney appealed to the Governor on day before the scheduled execution because her husband was too ill to make the trip. Governor Cooney once again refused to interfere with the execution saying: "Mrs. Rigney presented the best arguments she could, but I consider this murder the most brutal in Montana of any of which I have knowledge."

The condemned man went to bed at eleven p.m. after a quiet day in his cell writing what were called "character sketches" of his deathwatches. Hoffman ate well on the day before his execution but he refused to eat, visit with relatives or speak with Reverend Father J.F. Schulte before his trip to the gallows.

After reading the death warrant to the prisoner in his cell, Teton County Undersheriff E.L. Carver along with Deputy Joe Urgin and

Cascade County Sheriff Ed Shields escorted Hoffman from the county jail to the machine shed where the gallows was waiting. Showing no fear, Hoffman walked firmly up the thirteen steps to the platform on the scaffold.

Not a single word passed from Hoffman's lips from the time he left the jail until his death on the scaffold and the officials offered the customary black cap to the prisoner twice but each time he turned his head away. When one of the officers dropped the cap, Sheriff Billings sprung the trap before the hood had fluttered to the platform.

At 4:40 a.m., before the early morning sun fell on the roof of the tool shed, George Hoffman plunged to his death and eight minutes later he was pronounced dead by County Physician Howard W. Bateman and Dr. R.T. O'Neill. Former Teton County Sheriff Thomas Joseph Dellwo and Police Chief C.R. Dawley of Great Falls were among the one hundred and fifty witnesses of the execution at Choteau.

Hoffman was very angry that his eighty-two-year-old mother, Mrs. Mary Hoffman was told of his situation after he had tried so hard to conceal it from her. Until just a few days before his execution his relatives had told his mother that he was in California but some unknown person informed Mrs. Hoffman in time so that she could visit her doomed son twice before his death. In the only written statement left by the condemned man he wrote, "There's only one person on earth lower than me and that's the one who told this affair to my mother."

The body of Hoffman remained in the city morgue for five days before it was finally buried in the Potter's Field at Choteau at the expense of the county since none of his family members claimed the remains.

Postscript:
With the hanging of George Hoffman, Teton County Sheriff J.C. Billings became the first sheriff in the United States to officiate over an execution of a condemned man in the same county in which the crime was committed since the changes in laws of the various states. The distinction, which Sheriff Billings held wouldn't remain long however, as there would be five more legal hangings in Montana after the Hoffman case.

April 24, 1935

Henry John Zorn

Other Names: Henry John Miller; Henry J. Brown; Henry Doyle
Location and Gallows: Although this was the first legal execution in Custer County, Zorn was the fourth man hanged from ***Gallows No. Eighteen: (Sept. 1920): "Galloping Gallows" No. Six***.
Description: Zorn was a well-built man who stood five foot, two inches tall and weighed about 128 pounds. The twenty-six year-old man had dark brown hair and dark eyes.
Crime: Murder of Lester C. Jones, faculty member of the State Industrial School during a robbery attempt on Sunday, August 12, 1934.

Judge: S.D. McKinnon
Prosecution: County Attorney Rudolph Nelstead and assisted by Judge George W. Farr
Defense: I.W. Choate, trial counsel; T. Leo Boland, Joseph J. McCafferty, interim appellate attorneys and Maxwell .S. Galasso who handled the appeal
Sheriff: Edgar "Tuffy" Taylor
Distinction: Henry Zorn was the first man legally hanged in Custer County.
Relics and Remnants: The gallows used to hang Henry Zorn is now on display at the museum at the Old Montana Prison Complex at Deer Lodge.

On August 12, 1934, Lester C. Jones was found dead on the floor of the superintendent's office of the Montana State Industrial School. The son-in-law of A.C. Dorr, the superintendent of the school had been shot twice, the first striking him in the flank and the second round pierced his heart. There was evidence of a terrible struggle with blood on the desk and a turned over telephone indicated that the victim had made an effort to call for help before he died. From fingerprints found at the scene, Sheriff Edgar "Tuffy" Taylor focused his search on one Henry John Miller, alias Zorn, alias Doyle who had served a term at the state penitentiary for robbing the same institution in 1929.

After the initial alarm went out about the murder, three youths were picked up at Billings as they were stealing rides on the North Coast Line but after being finger printed and spending a couple of days in the jail the three were sent on their way. While Zorn was on the loose there were several false sightings of the fugitive by railroad personnel at Livingston and at Butte and a rancher in the Powder River Country.

While the search continued for the fugitive, Zorn's own brother reportedly volunteered to help locate the suspected murderer in the rough Powder River country where he had worked during the summer months. Meanwhile Tom Jones buried his son, Lester at Miles City and the services were attended by many people including Sheriff C.S. Patterson of Forsyth.

Wanting the suitcase he had left at a Billings hotel before he left the state, Henry Zorn sent a letter from Grand Forks and then a telegram from Hillsboro, North Dakota to Claude Kyle with instructions to have the black case shipped to him by express to Minneapolis. Through the diligent work of Yellowstone County Sheriff Everett M. Birely, the communication between the two men was discovered and the Montana authorities notified the Minnesota officers and the suspect was arrested on August 18, 1934, when he came to the express office for his suitcase.

The Minneapolis police later reported that Zorn's Bertillon Measurements (an early form of identification used by law enforcement before fingerprinting)[1] matched those of a Henry Doyle who had served a prison term in Minnesota for burglary and was later imprisoned for entering the United States illegally.

Sheriff Taylor and Davy O'Connor, the probation officer for the industrial school brought Zorn back to Montana on the Milwaukee Railroad where it stopped at Roundup. Meeting them at the station was A.C. Dorr, the father-in-law of the murder victim, County Attorney Rudolph Nelstead, Custer County Undersheriff Harold B. Cross, Fred Griffith, the court reporter of Miles City and John J. Popovich, former sheriff of Musselshell County and investigator for the Alcohol Bureau. Because there had been talk of a lynching at Miles City, the authorities decided to take the prisoner to Billings for safe-keeping.

On the morning of August 23, 1934, Henry Zorn made a verbal confession of the murder at the Yellowstone County jail in the presence of the above officers as well as Billings Police Chief Val Lechner and D.H. Dickason, an agent with the Department of Justice from Butte. That afternoon Zorn signed the twenty-page typewritten version of his statement. He explained that he had decided to rob the school at Miles City because he knew the ends and outs of the operation and he was familiar with Superintendent A.C. Dorr's office and where he kept the money. Zorn said that he robbed the institution because he was down and out, and on account of the poor treatment he had received at the school in the past.

Zorn said that he came to Billings from Butte on Friday, August 10, and after leaving his suitcase at a hotel he left for Miles City the following night on a freight train to Forsyth. At Forsyth, he caught the Northern Pacific No. 4 train to Miles City and he arrived there at about eleven o'clock Saturday night, August 11, and then he walked straight down the tracks to the Industrial School.

The prisoner explained that all he had on him at the time was a flashlight, his little revolver and a pair of dust goggles, which he wore while he rode the rails. As he walked along the tracks he picked up a couple of railroad spikes, which he had planned to use to pry open the roll-top desk at the school office.

While he was trying to get into the safe, Zorn said he was surprised when the lights suddenly came on in the office. Jumping behind the door, the robber tried to elude detection but Lester Jones accosted him and the two men struggled. According to Zorn he and Jones had been friends at the school and he said that he pleaded with the man to let him go. When the bigger man refused, Zorn threatened him with his revolver but according to the prisoner, Jones told him that he didn't have the guts to shoot and then he rushed the intruder. Zorn said that he was surprised by the attack and the weapon was fired in the excitement, the first shot going wild, the other two rounds struck the victim, killing him instantly.

Zorn said that he left the scene of the crime at a little after midnight and he caught an eastbound freight. At Terry, Montana the train was stopped and searched but Zorn had managed to get off without being detected and then he walked about a mile ahead of the train where he got back on as it was pulling out of town. The fugitive remained on the train until it reached Fargo, North Dakota where he boarded a Great

Northern freight heading back to Montana but when he learned that there was an intense manhunt underway for him he took the first freight back to Minneapolis.

Many people said that Henry John Zorn was more of a victim of circumstances than a confirmed criminal noting that when he was only eleven years old he and his five siblings were taken away from their mother at Malta because she couldn't provide or handle them. Zorn's two sisters were sent to the Girls Home at Helena and he and his three brothers were placed in the industrial School at Miles City.

The school at Miles City was described as being an elaborate ranch house with a big school nearby and at the time young Henry Zorn stayed at the facility only boys were housed there and they were separated by age. The boys spent half of their days in formal schooling and the rest of the day they worked in jobs at the institution. The farm on the school grounds produced all the food required to feed the boys throughout the winter.

The Industrial School had a creamery, a laundry, butcher shop and splendid dormitories along with training departments, which included shoe making, tailoring and printing. It wasn't all work for the lads however, as the institution had an excellent scout troop, which met weekly and it held summer camps in the National Forests and the local Elks sponsored various activities for the boys. The school also maintained baseball and football teams, which Zorn reportedly was a talented halfback.

The Salvation Army along with the Methodist, Presbyterian, Episcopal and Catholic Churches at Miles City were represented on the campus.[2] During his six years at the school, he made two escape attempts, the first with several other boys and according to Zorn after their capture they were all welcomed back with forty lashes applied to their bare bodies. The next time was in April of 1926, when Zorn made it all the way to Minnesota where under the name of Henry Miller, alias Henry Dole he was sent to the State Reformatory at St. Cloud after being convicted of four counts of burglary in Carver County.

In November of 1926, D.H. Knickerbacker, state parole officer for Minnesota notified President Dorr at Miles City that Zorn had been sentenced to the state reform school for ten years and Mr. Dorr, who had taken an interest in the young man at the school, made arrangements with the authorities in Minnesota to have the boy transferred back to Miles City to serve out his sentence as long as the prisoner promised to stay away from their state for ten years.

The president of the Industrial School took custody of Zorn in June of 1929, and A.C. Dorr quickly got him a good job on a farm in Rosebud County. When he later lost his paycheck gambling at Miles City, Zorn stole money from the school and he was sent to the state penitentiary at Deer Lodge for a five-year term in October of 1929. In January of 1930, Zorn wrote Mr. Dorr at the school saying that he was sorry and asked for another chance to straighten out his life. When released from prison he was deported to Canada through Sweet Grass,

Montana in December of 1932, since he had been born in that country and had never become an American citizen.

Zorn illegally returned to the United States and he was arrested in January of 1933, and served in the Yellowstone County Jail from February 19, 1933 through April 8, when he was taken to Great Falls where he was sentenced to eighteen months at McNeil Island, Washington before being once again deported to Canada on June 26, 1934. Four days later immigration authorities again arrested him at Eastport, Idaho but he escaped from the officers the very next day.

After first re-entering Canada, the fugitive entered the United States at Minnesota where he stole enough money to purchase a .22-caliber revolver for what he said was for "self protection." After leaving Minnesota he returned to Montana where he first traveled to Butte to visit his mother and family and then he went to Billings before going to Miles City where he murder Mr. Jones at the state school.

Zorn was brought from Billings to Miles City on Tuesday, September 4, 1934, for his preliminary hearing where he declared that he was penniless and therefore Judge S.D. McKinnon appointed Mr. I.W. Choate as his counsel and then scheduled his arraignment for that Thursday, September 6, at ten a.m. The prisoner was brought back to Miles City on Thursday when he entered a "not guilty" plea in district court. Judge McKinnon ordered Clerk of the Court C.A. Lindeberg to draw names for the jury and scheduled the trial to begin at 9:30 on the first of October.

On Monday, October 1, 1934, the district court trial began and at that time the prisoner declared that his true name was Henry John Zorn. Throughout the three-day trial the courtroom was filled with spectators including the victim's parents, Mr. and Mrs. Thomas Jones and the defendant's mother Mrs. Josephine Adams of Butte. Zorn showed little or no emotion during the proceedings while his mother reportedly broke down on several occasions. The following twelve men were finally sworn in to sit on the jury:

R.S. Weimer	E.G. Bentley	C.F. Meier
H.A. Pahrman	Leonard B. Cumming	William H. Blum
G.D. Schindler	Charles W. Henridnett	E.C. Vial
P.J. Ginther	George H. Fowler	J.R. Calvin

The prosecution's key witness was Claude Kyle, a Billings auto mechanic who testified that Henry Zorn told him and Stanley Johns in his hotel room on August 10, 1934, that he was going to Miles City to burglarize the office of the industrial school. Kyle also said that the defendant wanted to borrow his high-caliber handgun for the job but he didn't give it to him. The witness also testified that he saw Zorn's 22-caliber revolver when he removed it from his suitcase and placed it in his pocket and confirmed it was the same weapon that was found on the defendant at the time of his arrest. Kyle then told the court that Zorn had written and telegraphed him from North Dakota asking him to send his suitcase to Minneapolis.

Captain H.A. Peradeau of Minneapolis, one of the arresting officers testified that the 22-caliber pistol found on Zorn had been wrapped in a handkerchief and he said that the prisoner had thirty-seven shells in one of his pockets and when he was taken into custody he gave his name as Brown. Sheriff Taylor told the jury that when he was bringing the defendant back to Montana, the defendant asked him if there had ever been a hanging in Custer County.

When Sheriff Taylor told the defendant that there had never been a legal execution in the county, Zorn reportedly said, "There's always going to be the first one, and I guess I'm it." The sheriff also told the court that Zorn told him that he had planned to rob the school at Miles City and then described the subsequent scuffle with Jones and his escape during which he lost his flashlight, cap and goggles.

Judge McKinnon finally acquiesced to the state's request of allowing the jury to visit the murder scene at the school and Sheriff Taylor accompanied the panel while Deputy William Cahill and the jurors were instructed not to talk among themselves while on the outing. Of course Zorn and his attorneys were also allowed to accompany the jurors and the officers to the Industrial School. The defense only offered a single witness, that being the defendant's mother who testified about her son's disadvantages.

Mrs. Josephine Adams of 712 E. Mercury Street, Butte told the court that her son was born on March 11, 1909, at Gravelburg, which was in Saskatchewan, Canada. The witnesses said that when her husband, Frank Zorn was on the run from the Canadian authorities the family moved to Malta, Montana where he abandoned her with her six children. After her son Henry got into trouble he was sent to the reform school at Miles City on December 13, 1920, and because of a terrible elevator fire at Malta her other three sons eventually were sent there. Mrs. Adams explained that she later moved to Butte where she was a seamstress at a government subsidized mattress factory.

When the defense rested its case, Judge McKinnon gave the jury its instructions and final arguments were completed Wednesday afternoon and while the defense admitted to the killing they asked that Zorn be found guilty in the second degree with a penalty of life instead death. While acknowledging his client's guilt, Mr. Choate told the jury that it would do no good to "make another hallowed grave."

The jury was given the case at three o'clock on the afternoon of October 3, 1934, and two bailiffs were sworn in to accompany the panel to their quarters. Five hours later the jury returned to the courtroom to receive additional instructions from the judge concerning the defendant's confession. The courtroom remained filled with patient spectators until it was clear that the jury wouldn't report until later that night.

At 11:30 that night the jury announced that they had made their decision and messengers were sent to the prosecutors and defense attorneys and others who were connected to the case and the defendant received the report with the same indifference he had displayed during the entire trial. During his trial the defendant had reportedly listened carefully to the witnesses and on some occasions he was seen wiping tears from his eyes with his shackled hands during some touching testimonies but when he was being escorted into the courtroom, Zorn seemed oblivious of the large crowd waiting to hear the verdict.

The jury returned a first-degree murder verdict but they left the question of death or life imprisonment up to the court and at ten o'clock in the morning of the following Saturday, Judge McKinnon referred to the defendant's criminal record and after pointing out that all but one of the jurors voted for the death penalty, he sentenced Henry Zorn to be hanged on Wednesday, November 14, 1934. While Henry Zorn's body shook as the judge announced the death sentence his mother, Mrs. Adams sobbed hysterically.

As the convicted murderer was being returned to his cell the crowd slowly filed out of the courtroom, with tears in the eyes of some of the women. Downstairs in the main hall, Mrs. Adams was still crying hysterically over her son's fate and a couple of officers escorted her to a quiet and private room where she could sit down.

Mrs. Edgar Taylor, the wife of the county sheriff spoke sympathetically with the distraught mother and the two women discussed the case as the crowd was slowly leaving the courthouse as if they expected further developments to occur, which could change the sentence of the young man. Finally after the prisoner was safely secured in the jail and the officers of the court were carrying out the business of the district court the spectators went home.

Wearing the shackles, which he wore throughout the trial, Zorn was returned to Billings to await his execution and the prisoner's cell at the Yellowstone County Jail was near the entrance of the lower floor known as the "Bull Ring." Immediately after his sentencing he had little to say to the reporters, though he had always been a surly and defiant little guy but soon after he began speaking freely as he paced back and forth in his narrow cell.

The prisoner was still wearing the same trousers and shirt that he had been wearing the day he was arrested in Minneapolis and while he was talking with the reporter, Zorn fumbled with a small object that probably was a brown button. When he was asked about an appeal, Zorn said with a smile, "Appeal?" and as he shrugged his shoulders he asked "With what?" "I haven't any money. The state gave me a lawyer so you know what kind of trial I got." The prisoner's tone of voice wasn't bitter but merely displayed the acceptance of his fate.

Zorn explained that nothing had ever gone right for him, referring to his run-ins with the immigration authorities as being a joke since he had spent his entire life in the states except for when he was born in Canada. Zorn's formal education ended his sophomore year in high school but somewhere along the way he learned to play the saxophone and clarinet. He claimed that he had acquired a saxophone while serving at McNeil's Island and he was planning to get a job with an orchestra but he was forced to pawn it off at Portland after running out of money.

When the conversation turned to the murder, the prisoner's boyishness instantly turned into a mask of hate and he emphatically stated that the prosecution's accusation that he had shot Jones in the back was a "God Damn Lie." Then he shrugged his shoulder and said, "But I guess they proved I did." He was also very bitter against Claude Kyle who had betrayed him to Sheriff E.M. Birely of Billings and as the reporter was leaving he asked the prisoner if he could send him some cigarettes or a newspaper. Zorn told the man that he didn't smoke and with a boyish smile he said he could do his last thirty-eight days easy enough. While waiting for his first scheduled execution, Zorn embraced his childhood religion of Catholicism and he spent his time writing letters.

By the middle of October of 1934, Mrs. Adams was actively campaigning at Butte to save her son's life, being committed in securing an appeal on the grounds that her son hadn't received a fair trial. While she and her daughter finally managed to engage Charles F. Juttner of Butte to launch an appeal, it was T. Leo Boland, Joseph J. McCaffert and Maxwell S. Galasso who eventually represented her son.

Meanwhile Zorn wasn't allowed visitors except for his family, legal counsel and his spiritual advisers. America was truly a dangerous place while Zorn was serving on death row and while his mother was trying to arrange for his appeal Charles "Pretty Boy" Floyd was being shot and killed at Wellsville, Ohio. Mrs. Adams, I.W. Choate and Mrs. Elizabeth Kennedy and C.F. Juttner of Butte called on the Governor on November 8, 1934, with more than six thousand signatures on petitions asking for a commutation of sentence or a respite but on Sunday, November 11, Governor Frank H. Cooney announced that he had decided not to intervene with Zorn's execution.

On November 12, Zorn was photographed in the sheriff's office at Billings before Custer County Undersheriff Cross, Miles City Sergeant Prochnow and John Skinner drove the prisoner to the Miles City jail to await his November 14, execution. After being fitted with a twenty-pound Oregon Boot, Zorn gathered up his personal possessions, which were a new bible, a few letters and a few toilet items and they started for Miles City.

Sheriff Taylor secured ***Gallows No. Eighteen: (Sept. 1920): "Galloping Gallows" No. Six*** and it was secretly brought to Miles City where it was erected south of the city airport and just north of the Yellowstone River. Before Henry Zorn's case there had been five murderers sentenced to death in Custer County but they all had successfully cheated the gallows.

Four Indians were convicted of murdering "Catfish" Sandy, a pioneer of the county while he was fishing on the Yellowstone River and they hanged themselves with their own moccasin strings. Dan Lahey was sentenced to hang for the murder of a deputy sheriff at Coulson, which died out when the city of Billings came along and he swallowed a powerful narcotic and died in his cell before the executioner could do his duty.

In an attempt to prevent her son from being the first man to be legally hanged in Custer County, Mrs. Adams drove four hundred and fifty miles from Butte to Miles City with T. Leo Boland and John Sprangler in an old dilapidated truck. At four o'clock on the morning of her son's execution, she arrived at the Custer County Jail where she awoke Sheriff Taylor and demanded to see her son. The mother and son reunion reportedly brought tears to the most hardened law officers at the jail who figured it was going to be their last before his execution.

After securing her son's signature on a form she and Attorney Boland had brought with them from Butte they filed it with the clerk of the court, which initiated an automatic appeal to the Supreme Court. Once the paperwork was filed, which constituted an immediate stay of execution, Sheriff Taylor was directed by County Attorney Nelstead to stop the preparations for Zorn's hanging on November 13, 1934. Then following a conference with I.W. Choate of Miles City, Mrs. Adams announced that the attorney would be withdrawing from her son's case and that she would return to Butte to raise the necessary funds to retain another lawyer for the appeal to the Supreme Court.

Meanwhile Sheriff Taylor was frantically trying to notify all of the people he had invited to witness the hanging including Teton County Sheriff J.C. Billings who he wanted to assist him because he had recently hanged George Hoffman at Choteau in 1933. Others who had to cancel the trip to Miles City were, Judith Basin County Sheriff Lester Black, Fergus County Sheriff Guy Tullock, Cascade County Sheriff Guy Palliago and former sheriff, Bob Gordon of Great Falls as well as Lewistown Chief of Police Art Baker and newspaperman, J.W. Hanley of Lewistown.

The day after his stay of execution, Thursday, November 15, Zorn was reportedly visibly relieved as the workmen dismantled the gallows near his cell and it was returned to Forsyth. Eventually Zorn was returned to Billings and the supporters of the condemned man tried just about everything to save his life including falsely reporting that his night jailer, Yellowstone County John Alevizakes had said that the prisoner was clearly insane and that he shouldn't be executed. Jailer Alevizakes as well as the day watch, Stone W. Matlock denied making the statement on several occasions before and after the execution. In another one of those twists of fate, seventeen years earlier Stone Matlock, then sheriff of Yellowstone County, was in charge of the hanging of the Mexican, Juan Cuellae in April of 1918, for the murder of a Billings police officer.

Zorn's mother managed to raise funds through subscriptions in order to retain the services of Joseph J. McCafferty of Butte but after his withdraw from the case, Butte attorney, Maxwell S. Galasso who had unsuccessfully defended Tony Vettere, filed the necessary briefs for a motion before the Supreme Court. After hearing the case however, the Supreme Court affirmed the decision of the district court and Zorn's last chance of escape from the gallows vanished on April 18, 1935, when Governor Cooney, while vacationing on the west coast, informed Acting Governor W. Elmer Holt, he would take no action to stay the condemned man's execution.

After threats had been made, the Lewis and Clark County Sheriff's office placed an armed escort to protect Acting Governor Elmer Holt and his wife from being harmed or kidnapped by friends and supporters of Henry Zorn. On the day before the execution, Mr. Holt and his wife had been out of town and on their return to their hotel in Helena they were followed for several blocks by a delegation of Butte men who had tried to get the legislature to intervene in the Zorn case.

Inside the hotel lobby, Acting Governor Holt and his wife were accosted and some onlookers later said that one man told the acting executive that he better hear them out, or "You'll be sorry if you don't." It was also learned that other members of the delegation had called on other occupants of the hotel in an attempt to locate the Governor's room. While sheriff deputies headed off the Zorn supporters at the hotel, Mr. and Mrs. Holt were snuck out through the back of the building where they were driven away by two deputies.

When the Rosebud County scaffold was returned to Miles City for the second time it was erected inside the northeast corner of the jail building where the condemned man only needed to walk thirteen paces from his second tier cell door to reach the trap. The scaffold allowed for an eight-foot drop and a black garment was stretched around the lower portion of the gallows so the dead body couldn't be seen by the fifty or more witnesses who were crammed into the small isle between the rear wall of the cells and the outer wall of the jail.

The condemned man started his last full day in good spirits at the Yellowstone County Jail and the first thing he asked for was a shave and haircut and Jailer Stone Matlock and Undersheriff Clem Sage escorted the prisoner to room on the first floor where a barber was waiting. Although Zorn was still hopeful for a reprieve from the Governor, he stepped into the barber's chair and told the man that this was going to be the last time he'd be shaved by a barber.

That afternoon Zorn said good-bye for the last time to the jailers at Billings and then he lumbered down the sidewalk with a clumsy Oregon Boot fastened to his right leg. As the prisoner was getting into the waiting automobile to transport him back to Miles City, Zorn told his former handlers at Billings that he was "a gonner" with a big smile.

The condemned man made that final trip to Miles City with Custer County Deputy Sheriff Bill Cahill, Walter Prochnow, fingerprint expert attached to the Miles City Police Department and a civilian by the name of L.C. Davis. A second squad car occupied by Stillwater County Sheriff Jack Benjamin, Yellowstone County Sheriff W.E. Boley, Undersheriff Sage and Billings Police Chief Val Lechner followed the car with the condemned man.

In his death cell at Miles City, Zorn made a statement stating: "I want to say as my final word that I am going out with no revenge or hatred or bitterness for anyone. I know I am going to a better world. I want to thank the people of Montana for their loyalty and interest in my behalf. I have no bitterness or hatred in my heart for anyone. I am going with a clear conscience." Zorn said publicly that his mom was a "good mother," and that she was also grateful for the effort made on his behalf.

Petitions to commute the man's sentence were being circulated right up to the day before the execution like the one at Great Falls where Zorn supporters argued that the young defendant had been so scared to death of being lynched if set free, that he didn't offer much of a defense, and because of his destitute situation he wasn't able to show that the murder wasn't premeditated.

All day long before the execution Sheriff Taylor was receiving telegrams from several parts of the state requesting that the hanging be postponed. Among the last minute attempts to save the condemned man's life was a telegram from Charles Davidson, county attorney of Cascade County and Leo Boland, of the "Henry Zorn Defense Committee" of Butte.

For his last dinner, Zorn had a T-bone steak, shoestring potatoes, mixed vegetable salad with dressing, coffee and a pudding dessert, which was served in his cell. Zorn's mother was with him constantly and at 9:30 p.m. they were each served pie and coffee in his cell. At about midnight Reverend George Reid, pastor of the Miles City Methodist Episcopal Church, and Sheriff Taylor escorted Zorn's mother out of the jail crying and nearly hysterical.

After his mother had left, the prisoner sat down and wrote several letters and then he talked with Reverend Reid and although Zorn was raised a Catholic, and had embraced that religion before his first scheduled execution, he asked that Reverend Reid stay with him before he went to the gallows. Mr. Reid had taken a deep interest in saving the condemned man and he had accompanied a delegation to Helena to speak with Governor Cooney for executive clemency. During his last thirty minutes of his life, Zorn seemed a little nervous but he still declined any sedative drugs to calm him down and before leaving his cell he made his last statement, which was, "I am going out with no revenge or hatred or bitterness for anyone."

Zorn walked the fifteen feet to the scaffold calmly and before mounting the platform he shook hands with his guards and told them good-by. He displayed no emotion except that he trembled a bit before mounting the scaffold and then he clenched his fists and quickly opened them several times while he stood on the platform. The jail was filled to capacity with witnesses and a large crowd had gathered outside of the building but there were no demonstrations reported. The three or four county prisoners had been transferred to the city jail during the hanging but among the witnesses was Tom Jones, long-time rancher, Miles City businessman and father of Zorn's victim, Lester Jones.

Witnesses from Billings included, Special Officer W.E. Wilson, Patrolmen Ed Leckie and Harry Rafn who had attended grade school with the murder victim at Miles City for several years before he moved to Billings and later joined the police department. Zorn's sister left Butte Tuesday afternoon for Miles City but because her train didn't arrive until 3:45 a.m. she was too late to say good-by to her brother. Another disappointed person who missed the hanging was a Miles City High

School student who wanted to witness the hanging for a school project but he wasn't allowed to attend.

Before the hood was placed over the doomed man's head, Sheriff Taylor asked Zorn if he had anything to say and the young man shook his head with a slight smile. The sheriff again offered Zorn a chance to speak and he was met with another shake of the head but the prisoner's smile had diminished. The sheriff adjusted the shackles on the prisoner and the hood and noose was then placed over Zorn's head by Undersheriff Cross assisted by Teton County Sheriff "Shell" Billings and Judith Basin County Sheriff Lester Black who was representing the Montana State Sheriffs' Association as their president. An unknown executioner tripped the trap at 1:27 a.m. and fourteen minutes later Custer County Physician A.R. Varco and Dr. M.R. Snodgrass of Miles City pronounced Henry John Zorn dead.

Postscript:
The mother of Henry Zorn stayed with friends at Miles City until she claimed her son's body and she returned it to Butte where it was buried on Saturday April 27, 1935. Sheriff Birely reportedly kept Zorn's small black suitcase in his office at the Yellowstone County Jail as a memento.

October 16, 1935

George Criner

Other Names: George Herman; James Edward Johnson
Location and Gallows: Six months after the execution of Henry Zorn, ***Gallows No. Eighteen: (Sept. 1920): "Galloping Gallows" No. Six*** was returned to Miles City for the hanging of George Criner.
Description: Criner was a big powerful thirty-six-year-old black man who stood six foot, one inch tall with copper-hued features.
Crime: Murder of his live-in girl friend, Mrs. Marie Allsup, a black woman and seventy-six-year-old Police Sergeant, James Fraser on August 7, 1935.
Judge: S.D. McKinnon
Prosecution: County Attorney Rudolph Nelstead
Defense: W.B. Leavitt
Sheriff: Edgar Taylor
Distinction: Criner was the last person legally hanged in Custer County and the second man to be sentenced to death without a jury trial. There were three other men who went to the gallows without a jury trial, George Rock in 1908; Frank Robideau in 1938, and Philip Coleman in 1943.
Relics and Remnants: The gallows used to hang George Criner is now on display at the museum at the Old Montana Prison Complex at Deer Lodge.

While apparently crazed with drink, George Criner went home on August 7, 1935, and tried to take a diamond ring from his girl friend, Marie Allsup and while fighting with the woman he beat her with an iron poker and then slashed her several times with a pocketknife. Custer County Physician A.R. Vargo later testified that he had counted at least twenty knife cuts on the dead woman's body. Hearing the commotion, a neighbor, Mr. M.E. Hanrahan called the police from his home in what was at that time the Negro section of Miles City. George Thomas, a black youth was outside when the police officers arrived and he later heard a shot coming from inside the Criner home.

Veteran Police Officer James Frazer, accompanied by Chief of Police Joseph Sullivan who was off duty and unarmed at the time, answered the alarm at the little house at 320 South Fourth Street and as the two men started to enter the house, Criner wrestled Fraser's gun away and shot him in the top of the head and seriously wounded the chief with a wild shot as the officers were running from the house.

Even with an injured hip the police chief managed to make it to a neighboring house where he phoned for help and when Sheriff Edgar Taylor and his men answered the call, Deputy Bill Cahill fired a rifle shot into the air, which brought Criner out of the house without resisting. At the time of his arrest the prisoner gave his name as George Herman and he was only wearing striped coveralls, which were unbuttoned and exposing bare skin.

Sheriff Taylor found the house in a shambles with Officer Frazer dead near the entrance and Mrs. Allsup lying on her back under a bed in the bedroom. The woman was rushed to the local hospital where she died the following morning and after Dr. A.R. Vargo, the county physician had performed autopsies on the two victims he called for a coroner's jury where George Thomas, Sheriff Taylor, Deputies Williams and Cahill were questioned.

When the hearing was completed it was found that Officer Frazer and Mrs. Allsup were both killed by George Criner and a day later, crowds of curious people visited the murder scene at Miles City where they found blood smeared on the floor and walls of the bedroom. The little house showed signs of a terrible struggle where a light socket was torn out, shelves torn off the walls and furniture was in disarray. A mattress had been dragged to the floor and the bed sheets and blankets were scattered about the house.

Shortly after the shooting a large mob had assembled outside the Custer County jail demanding that the murderer be given up to them for lynching and after about an hour the crowd then demanded that four of their number be permitted into the jail to inspect the facility to insure that the prisoner was in fact there. When the sheriff staff admitted the four civilians into the building it was determined that Criner wasn't at the jail but the officers didn't disclose where the prisoner was taken.

Because of possible mob action, Criner had been rushed to Billings for safekeeping at the Yellowstone County jail where he later made a full confession to Sheriff Taylor, Custer County Attorney Rudolph Nelstead, Undersheriff H.V. Cross and George N. Vinton of Baker where he was the court clerk for Judge Stanley E. Felt.

At his arraignment on Thursday, August 15, 1935, Criner said that his real name was James Edward Johnson and then he pleaded not guilty to the first-degree charges and Judge S.D. McKinnon appointed

W.B. Leavitt as his attorney. Soon after his preliminary hearing, Criner was over heard saying that he sure wished he wasn't there.

On August 22, the authorities once again returned Criner to Miles City from Billings where he pleaded guilty to first-degree murder and Judge McKinnon ordered the prisoner be returned on September for a hearing to determine the degree of his punishment. Judge McKinnon opened the hearing on September 3, and he heard from several witnesses about the case including the defendant the only person called for the defense.

The thirty-six-year-old black man told the court that he was born in Waco, Texas and again he said that his real name was Johnson but that he had adopted the name George Criner when he was thirteen. He came to Montana when he was a young man and while living at Whitefish he enlisted into the army during the war in Europe. Criner was sent overseas with the Ninety-Second Division of the Eight-Hundred and Fifteenth Pioneer Infantry, which was an all Negro Regiment with white officers. After the war Criner returned to Montana where he settled in Havre and worked as a cook at a café and as a bootblack at a barbershop. It was while he was working at the barbershop that he first met Mrs. Allsup who was married to Thomas Allsup, a clerk for the Great Northern Railroad at Havre.

Mrs. Marie Allsup eventually left her husband and her four children to follow George Criner to Miles City in the spring of 1935, and the woman received a divorce in July, just a month before her murder. After hearing the evidence in the case, Judge McKinnon sentenced the prisoner to death on Wednesday, September 4, 1935, specifically for the murder of Mrs. Allsup.

Other than taking a long deep breath after the pronouncement by the judge, Criner showed little emotion as he stood before the court and after his sentencing the prisoner was returned to Billings where he was a cellmate to another accused murderer, eighteen-year-old Ralph Scott who allegedly killed another teenager at a sheep camp near the Musselshell River. No appeal was ever made for Criner and there was no movement undertaken to ask Governor Frank H. Cooney for a reprieve or commutation of his sentence.

On Sunday, October 13, 1935, the gallows frame was erected again in the northeast corner of the Custer County jail just two cells away from the condemned man. The scaffold was built to allow for an eight-foot drop and like the Henry Zorn execution, a black garment was stretched around the lower portion of the gallows. While the scaffold was being installed, Criner was transferred to the city jail but on his return he was placed in the same cell that Zorn had once occupied. Criner wanted to inspect to gallows to see how it was made and how it worked but his request was denied. On Tuesday Criner ate a chicken lunch and for his last meal he was served a medium-rare T-bone steak.

Reverend Walter G. Smith of the Baptist Church remained in the death cell with Criner from eight o'clock of the evening before the hanging until he was led to the scaffold helping the man with his final statement and to give him final consolation. In his statement, Criner wrote, "Just a few lines to you as I depart of this world. I want you to know that I regret and I am sorry for what I have done. I am not sorry because I have to go, but for the wrong I have done to others. I am not afraid to die. Do not forget the Lord; to you all good-bye."

Since his sentencing on September 4, Criner had crossed off each day on a calendar that he kept in his cell and on Tuesday night he marked off the final square of the calendar with a pencil and told the officers that he had never been in trouble before and that a lot of people would really be surprised to see the jam he was in.

Before going to the gallows the prisoner dressed himself in a gray suit and a white shirt with an open neck. The witnesses from Billings included Sheriff W.E. Boley, Undersheriff Clem Sage, Patrolmen Harry Rafn, James Hirst and James Smith along with Sheriff Frank Blackburn of Cody, Wyoming. The witnesses were all crammed into the small isle between the rear wall of the cells and the outer jail wall.

At the scaffold Sheriff Taylor asked for silence so Criner could speak and the condemned man spoke in a firm voice, "It is just this, I am sorry for what I have done. Although I am not sorry that I am leaving this world because I feel I am going to something better. I hope you will always pray though life because you don't know what way you will be called out. A few minutes before this happened if anyone had told me that I would be here, I would have said they were crazy. But remember, anything can happen to anybody. You can walk out on the street and die of heart trouble. Or you can go out on the street and get run over. I think that will be all."

After applying the shackles, Undersheriff Cross then placed the black hood over the condemned man's head, the trap was sprung at 1:14 a.m. and Criner was pronounced dead fifteen minutes later. Criner's remains were buried later that day in the Miles City Cemetery at the head of the grave of Marie Allsup.

Postscript:
While Criner's service as a war veteran was recognized, and the federal government paid the burial charges, no military rites were performed over his grave. Criner's last request was that thirty-two dollars and fifty cents, the only money he had in the world, be used to purchase a headstone for the grave of Mrs. Mary Allsup. Criner's cellmate at Billings, Ralph Scott was eventually found guilty of murder but because of his young age, Judge Ford sentenced him to life in prison.

January 15, 1938
Franklin Robideau

Other Names: Joseph Liberty, Frank Johnson
Location and Gallows: Robideau was hanged in the Wess Handy Warehouse at the corner of Diamond Street and First Avenue North in downtown Columbus and he was the sixth victim of ***Gallows No. Eighteen: (Sept. 1920): "Galloping Gallows" No. Six***.
Description: Fifty-five-year-old Latin-American with a slight build
Crime: Murder of husband and wife, Mike and Frieda Kuntz on November 26, 1937
Judge: Benjamin P. Harwood
Prosecution: County Attorney P.H. Heily
Defense: M.L. Parcells and E.A. Blankner
Sheriff: Frank Murphy
Distinction: Robideau was the only person legally hanged in Stillwater County although in 1896, a sheepherder by the name of Gottleib Heide was found dead from a bullet wound in the county with traces of a rope burn around his neck.[3] Robideau was also the third man to be sentenced to death in Montana without a jury trial. In 1908, George Rock pleaded guilty to first-degree murder, George Criner did the likewise in 1935, and Philip Coleman would do the same in 1943.
Relics and Remnants: The hangman's rope with its five-knot noose that was used to hang Robideau remained stored in the black muslin execution cap in a closet at the sheriff's office for many years before it was finally placed on display at the Stillwater County Museum at Columbus. Also at the museum is the 38-caliber murder weapon, leg weights, which were used on Robideau, an invitation to the execution and a number of large crime-scene photographs used during the trial. The gallows itself was stored at Columbus until they were sent to Ryegate in December of 1939, for the execution of Lee Simpson and finally the Rosebud County version of a "Galloping Gallows" was erected in the old auditorium building and is on display at the museum of the Old Prison Complex at Deer Lodge.

On November 27, 1937, five-year-old Larry Kuntz, bleeding and dazed from a terrible head wound stumbled into Mike Vissor's Wheat Basin Grocery Store exclaiming: "They killed my momma and papa." Before the child could identify his parent's killer he lost consciousness and he was rushed to the Columbus Hospital. The farmers quickly notified the authorities and the bodies of Mr. and Mrs. Mike Kuntz were found in the elevator that had been managed by the murdered man.

When the injured young boy hadn't identified Frank Robideau at the store, the murderer decided to further deflect suspicion from himself by accusing a couple of "Okies," a husband and wife who had just arrived in town looking for work. Robideau reinforced his accusation by telling the sheriff that he had seen them near the elevator on the evening of the murders.

Unfortunately for the murderer, the young couple whose name was Downard had an airtight alibi for the night of the crime, and the next morning from his hospital bed, little Larry Kuntz pointed his finger at Frank Robideau and told Sheriff Frank Murphy that it was him who had killed his parents and gave him his beating. The sheriff arrested Robideau for the murder of Mr. and Mrs. Kuntz and locked him up in the sandstone jail located behind the courthouse and Harold Nordahl later described how County Attorney Heily, Sheriff Murphy and Undersheriff Jack S. Benjamin had grilled the accused man until he finally confessed.

Mr. Nordahl explained that while they didn't hurt Robideau physically, they just didn't give him anything to eat or drink and kept at him until he finally broke down. After the undersheriff fingerprinted the suspect he was later transferred to the Yellowstone County jail for safekeeping and while dressed in an old shirt and no strings in his shoes, he showed no emotion as he retold to Albert Thomas, Earl Wilson of the Yellowstone County sheriff's office and Coroner O.R. McColley about shooting to death the thirty-five-year-old grain-elevator manager, Mike Kuntz and his wife, Frieda along with the beating of their five-year-old son Larry.

According to Robideau's confession, on Friday, November 26, 1937, he went to the Occidental Grain Elevator, a short distance from Columbus and wanted to get paid for the one hundred and eighty bushels he had delivered there. Mike Kuntz tried to explain to the farmer that not all of the proceeds from his crop could be paid to him and reminded him that since he was farming on land owned by a Mr. Keselhieum of Billings he owed a third of the payment to his landlord. At first Robideau told the authorities that Kuntz wouldn't pay him for his grain and he even threatened to kill him and his family.

The prisoner said he feared for his life and the safety of his family so he killed Mr. and Mrs. Kuntz out of self-defense. Eventually Robideau told the authorities that before he left the elevator he had forced Kuntz into writing several checks to him and then he warned the manager not to say anything to anyone. Mr. Kuntz had been cautioned by the former elevator manager about the risks of confronting or quarreling with farmers with encumbered grains.

On the evening of the murders, the Kuntz family had planned to attend a party at the home of Ted Lugent, and when Robideau noticed their car heading towards Columbus he assumed that the elevator manager was on his way to report him to the sheriff. The frantic farmer ran down to the road just in time to flag down the Kuntz vehicle and climbed into the rear seat of the automobile. It was determined that they drove down the county road (Columbus-Molt Road) a little ways when Robideau ordered Mr. Kuntz to return to the elevator.

When he refused, Robideau shot Mike Kuntz in the back of the head and then Mrs. Kuntz lunged at her husband's murderer and she began grabbing and biting him until the farmer shot her through the heart. Robideau told the officers that after killing Mr. and Mrs. Kuntz he figured he might as well kill the boy too and so he began pistol-whipping him. After striking the boy several times, so severely that a piece of the wooden gunstock was imbedded in the youngster's skull, Robideau said he couldn't finish the boy off because the child reminded him of his own son.

The murderer then drove the car back to the elevator where he parked it inside and out of sight. Robideau then locked up the elevator and placed "Closed" signs on all of the doors. The prisoner told the officers where he had hidden the gun and at midnight Sheriff Murphy found the 38-caliber Smith and Wesson revolver and a box of cartridges buried in a hole a few feet west of the prisoner's house.

Stillwater Coroner O.R. McColley conducted an inquest at three o'clock on Monday afternoon, November 29, 1937, with the following jury members:

W.E. Boston	Roy Jones	R.L. Duba
W.H. Hillstead	P.F. Morrison	P.E. Hegland

After hearing the testimony from the three witnesses, Sheriff Murphy, Undersheriff Benjamin and Dr. W.P. Smith, the panel returned a verdict that the deceased, Mr. and Mrs. Kuntz met their deaths by a gunshot wound inflicted by Frank Robideau. The report stated that Mrs. Kuntz was shot through the heart and her husband was shot in the head, the bullet entering behind the lobe of his right ear and then it shattered his spinal cord.

A brother of the victim, Valentine S. Kuntz, took the bodies of Mr. and Mrs. Kuntz back to Richardton, North Dakota where the couple had been born and raised before they lived at Beulah, North Dakota and later transferred to Montana to open the Occident Elevator at Wheat Basin. Mike Kuntz was born on January 26, 1903, and his wife, Frieda Hammerschmidt Kuntz came into the world on September 18, 1910.

The fingerprint report from the FBI revealed that Robideau's real name was Joseph Liberty and that he was involved in a murder with his younger brother in the state of New York. The then twenty-one-year-old Joseph Liberty and his eighteen-year-old brother, George shot and killed David Varno, 60 and seriously wounding his younger brother Noel in their cabin near West Beekmantown in Clinton County, New York.

In 1910, the two young men were sentenced to twenty years to life at Dannemora Prison after being convicted of the second-degree murder at Plattsburg. At first Robideau denied any connection to the crime but later he asked permission to be the first to inform his wife about his past record. In the presence of Sheriff Murphy and Undersheriff Benjamin Robideau told his wife about the jam he had gotten in back in New York.

He told his wife that after serving two years at Dannemora Prison he became a trusty and was assigned to Auburn Prison on November 13, 1920, as a cook on a road gang. Apparently Robideau got wind that he was going to be replaced as cook on the gang and so he escaped at Montezuma, New York on July 25, 1922, and ran off to New York City where he found work as a long shoreman and cook.

Traveling west to Pittsburgh, Robideau worked on a road-paving job and then found employment at a box factory. When it appeared that the authorities were getting on to him, Robideau moved out West in

1923, where he worked in the oil fields in Wyoming. His brother, George Liberty remained at Dannemora where he took educational courses and he was paroled from prison shortly after Robideau's escape from Auburn.

After moving to Montana in about 1928, Robideau worked for B.S. Dowler near Broadview and then for the Campbell Farming Corporation near Hardin. While working for John Melby in Stillwater County, Robideau, who was using the name, Frank Johnson, left for what he said was a special "short-time job" in Wyoming and sometime later he returned to the Columbus area using his new name of Frank Robideau, which at the time he claimed he had gotten legally changed while in Wyoming.

John Melby later recalled another incident while the killer worked for him prior to the Kuntz murders in which Robideau had been out all night and he returned early the next morning dog tired and claiming that he had been robbed at Billings and he had to walk back to the ranch. Come to find out, a Billings taxi driver had been murdered that same night on Poly Road in the general direction of the Melby Ranch with a .38-caliber bullet, the same round Robideau used on the Kuntz family years later. Mr. Melby oftened wondered if Robideau had killed and robbed that taxi driver and then walked home to his place.

Robideau married the daughter of a prominent rancher and he started a farm in the Wheat Basin area and by November of 1937, he had three children and was expecting a fourth when he fell on hard times along with other area farmers when they experienced crop failure for three straight years. Along with most everyone else in the area, Robideau got into heavy debt and he owed just about everybody in Columbus.

On Friday afternoon, December 3, 1937, Frank Robideau was brought before Judge Benjamin P. Harwood at Columbus to enter his plea and since the prisoner had no money or property in which to hire an attorney, the court said that one would be provided. After explaining that there were only three practicing attorneys in Stillwater County, the county attorney along with M.L. Parcells and E.A. Blenkner, the judge appointed both of the lawyers to defend Robideau. After a short conference with his attorneys Robideau entered a plea of not guilty to the charge of first-degree murder.

The defendant entered a new plea of guilty in Case No.292 in district court on Saturday, December 11, and then on the following Wednesday, while not denying their client's confession or guilt the defense entered a plea of mercy because of the defendant's many trials and tribulations of dry-land farming including poor prices, grasshoppers and hail that had left his family destitute.

The defense contended that Robideau's wife and children were suffering from malnutrition and they were experiencing hunger pangs during the Thanksgiving season. The attorneys went on and explained that creditors had repossessed much of his farm equipment and the defendant had frantically tried to find work in order to supplement his farm income. County Attorney Heily countered the defense by calling a number of witnesses to describe the horrible murders.

The prosecution presented large photographs of the crime scene, which were taken by Yellowstone County Deputy Sheriff Albert Jansen and a telegram from the Department of Justice stating that the handwriting on the sign, which was attached to the door of the elevator matched the samples of the defendant. While the attorneys presented their positions in the case, Robideau remained seated and kept his eyes on the floor.

The Stillwater County courtroom was packed and the hallway was filled during the hearing and even more people came to hear the sentencing of Robideau. After about thirty minutes, Judge Harwood ordered Robideau to stand and then he sentenced the double murderer to be hanged at Columbus on Saturday, January 15, 1938. The defendant showed no emotion as Sheriff Murphy and Undersheriff Benjamin escorted him back to the jail.

Section No.12103 of the revised codes of Montana stated that, "A judgment of death must be executed within the walls or yard of a jail, or some convenient private place in the county. The sheriff of the county must be present at the execution, and must invite the presence of a physician, the county attorney, and at least twelve reputable citizens, to be selected by him; and he shall, at the request of the defendant, permit such priest or ministers of the gospel, not exceeding two, as the defendant may name, and any persons, relatives or friends not to exceed five, to be present at the execution, together with such peace officers as he may think expedient, to witness the execution. But no other persons those mentioned in this section can be present at the execution. Nor can any person under age be allowed to witness the same."

At the time of his confession, Robideau said that he needed the money because his wife was expecting their fourth baby and on the day before Christmas, 1937, Mrs. Robideau gave birth to their daughter at the hospital at Columbus. In another the twists of fate, it was learned that Mrs. Kuntz, the victim of the death ride on the day after Thanksgiving had earlier offered to be Mrs. Robideau's midwife.

There were a couple of scaffolds available to Sheriff Murphy at the time but he elected to borrow the Rosebud County portable gallows from Sheriff George Burns who had the death machine in storage since it was last used to hang George Criner at Miles City in October of 1935. The scaffold was transported by truck to Stillwater County where Joe Mann of Columbus was hired to construct the gallows in the warehouse.

Prior to his execution, Robideau was being held at the Yellowstone County jail at Billings and on the evening before the hanging Stillwater County Undersheriff Benjamin was detailed to bring the prisoner back to Columbus. As the condemned man began his last stroll from the murder cell to the jail office at Billings, Robideau reportedly told the authorities that, "If I'm going to croak, I might as well die happy." He then asked a deputy for a drink of whisky stating he really needed a "good one."

When Robideau was securely handcuffed to Yellowstone County Undersheriff Ed O'Donnell, he was given his whisky and the iron-bar jail door was swung open. The men walked to the awaiting sheriff's car where O'Donnell and the prisoner hurried into the back seat along with Yellowstone County Sheriff Dan Stephenson. Deputy Sheriff Jansen sat up front with Dan McCarthy, a newspaper reporter along with Undersheriff Benjamin who drove back to Columbus.

There was quite a mob around the Billings jail and the sidewalks and curbs were full of spectators trying to get a last look at the condemned murderer and as the car sped from the city limits of the Magic City Robideau said: "I suppose there will be a big mob at Columbus too. They're all coyote hunters. When they get me in the trap, they'll all go home." The condemned man asked Undersheriff O'Donnell, who had been a daily visitor of the prisoner during his last week at Billings to exchange jokes to kill time on the way to Columbus.

The hour and fifteen minute trip from Billings to Columbus was rather pleasant for the occupants of the vehicle because of Robideau's sense of humor. After one of the officers was giving Undersheriff Benjamin a hard time about how slowly the sheriff's car was traveling Robideau quipped, "Yes, let's get there and get the thing over with."

One time during a brief lull in the conversation the condemned man said, "I'll flip a coin with anyone to see if they want to change places with me. You know when I knock at St. Peter's door tonight. I'll say my name is Deputy Albert Jansen. And when St. Peter says that you don't belong here, then I'll say my name is Undersheriff Ed O'Donnell" and when Robideau said that he would then be told go to the other gate everyone in the car broke out laughing.

Occasionally during the trip Robideau became serious like the time he told how hard it was on him the last time his wife and children visited him and he concluded the story with an up beat note by repeating his statement of: "If I'm going to croak, I might as well die happy." He told the officers that his conscience was clean and if taking his neck pleased the people it's alright. "I'm going to walk right up to the scaffold and take it like a man. I'm going to do my part, you do yours. I'm not the first man to be hung and I'm not the last one."

As the car was passing Park City the officers gave their prisoner a cigar, and Sheriff Stephenson lighted it for him. "Well, this is my last smoke. I'll never ask you for another cigar." At about 12:45 the caravan started up the Columbus Hill and when the lights of the city were visible Robideau was telling the officers how Reverend H.S. Tool of Columbus had told him that he was a brave man.

Turning to the reporter Robideau said, "Now I want you to write a good story about me. I'm coming back down here tomorrow night and read that story. If it's not a good one, I'm going to haunt you tomorrow night." The men then began singing "My Wild Irish Rose" as the lead car passed the lead automobile as the motor caravan entered the city limits of Columbus under the moonlight. According to Mr. Nordahl, a local restaurant prepared the last meal for the condemned man and he was also given a couple shots of whisky before the execution.

There were dozens of automobiles parked near the main entrance of the warehouse of Wess Handy's Columbus Machinery Company, which was the only building in town big enough for the hanging. "Surely a lot of people around here," Robideau said as the patrol car drove between the lines of law enforcement personnel made up officers from several counties along with state highway patrolmen. At 1:08 a.m. the men stepped from the vehicle and a minute later Robideau was standing a foot away from the thirteen steps leading up to the scaffold.

The doomed man had joked with Undersheriff Benjamin days before about the steps being made of gold and he even joked about using an elevator instead of using the steps up to the scaffold. While standing in front of the steps the undersheriff handcuffed the prisoner's hands behind his back and then he placed the two straps around Robideau's waist over his green poka-dot shirt and blue coat. Robideau's face became a bit pale, but he still asked the undersheriff if he wanted to flip that coin and then he laughed and said "Well, good-by boys."

Undersheriff Benjamin and Deputy Paul Rosean led Robideau up the steps and seconds later the prisoner made his last remarks: "About all I wish to say is that if you have any sympathy to show, direct it to my wife and family. I don't need it." The black hood was then placed over his head and the rope was adjusted tightly around his neck. When the undersheriff snapped his fingers at 1:10 a.m. the trapdoor dropped and Robideau disappeared from the platform. Drs. A.V. "Old Doc" Blackstone and W.F. Smith reported that the man's neck was broken and about sixteen minutes later he was pronounced dead. Another witness, Dr. Swanson reported that Robideau's neck wasn't broken and that he had choked to death. Later that day Frank Robideau was buried in Mountainview Cemetery at Columbus.

On the evening of the hanging it was reportedly the busiest night in Columbus' history up to that point. The local bars did a bang-up business and the so-called non-public hanging got out of hand as well. Judge Harwood had specified that the sheriff only invite twelve reputable citizens and up to five relatives or friends of the defendant including any priests to witness the hanging along with enough peace officers to carry out the execution. "But no other person than those listed shall be permitted at the execution."

Things really got out of hand and reportedly over six hundred curious people gathered around the shed and three hundred and seventy-five folks were crowded inside when the trap was sprung including Undersheriff Carl Ferrington and County Attorney Lewis D. Glenn of Harlowton, James Law, Horace Wyman, Thomas Lee, Matt Fuchs, S. Kotan, John Pirrie, Mark Whetstone and one woman, Florence Bowie of Columbus who was reportedly dressed like a man.

Postscript:

Mrs. Robideau and her children moved away from Columbus and ironically the grain company eventually paid the widow of the hanged murderer the money, which had been the cause of the brutal crime in the first place.

After the death of his parents, Larry Michael Kuntz went to live with his grandmother, Mary Hammerschmidt at Richarton, North Dakota during the school year and he spent the summers on the farm of his Uncle Val Kuntz. After graduating from the Abbe Assumption High School he attended Gonzaga University at Spokane and then Larry retuned to Fargo where he earned a degree in pharmacy. After working as a druggist at Richarton for a number of years he eventually moved to Washington State where he got married and raised a family.

In the summer of 1956, Larry Kuntz returned to Columbus for a visit and he attended a community picnic there. In an interview, Larry said that due to his religious upbringing he didn't believe in capital punishment for any reason and although he had wished he had his parents, he was blessed with wonderful relatives who loved and cared for him. He concluded by saying; "I'm happily married, have a nice family and a good profession. I enjoy my work and my life."

December 30, 1939
W. Lee Simpson

Location and Gallows: When Simpson was hanged in the Golden Valley County Courthouse yard at Ryegate, he was the last man executed on ***Gallows No. Eighteen: (Sept. 1920): "Galloping Gallows No. Six***. A complete history of this scaffold and others can be found in Chapter Seven: "Montana Gallows."
Description: The fifty-one-year-old stout rancher had risen from a common mine laborer to becoming one of the most prosperous stockmen in Golden Valley County.
Crime: Murder of Undersheriff Arthur "Buzz" Burford on April 14, 1938.
Judge: William L. Ford of White Sulphur Springs
Prosecution: County Attorney Nat Allen assisted by Special Prosecutor Wellington D. Rankin of Helena
Defense: A.G. McNaught of Roundup and assisted by George Hurd of Great Falls
Sheriff: Elmer J. Dolve
Distinction: While there was an unknown rustler lynched sometime in the 1880's in the Twin Coulee region, the execution of Simpson was the only legal hanging in Golden Valley County. Simpson was also the last man hanged in Montana for the murder of a law enforcement officer.
Relics and Remnants: The hangman's noose and black cap used in the Simpson execution along with Sheriff Dolve's bullet-riddled hat are available for viewing at the Golden Valley County Court in Ryegate. The gallows used to hang Simpson is now on display at the museum at the Old Montana Prison Complex at Deer Lodge.

In the early spring of 1938, newly elected County Attorney Nat Allen brought a court action to recover goods wrongfully seized against Lee Simpson over a mare and a colt stolen from H.K. Gibbs. When Simpson wasn't able to get his neighbor, Art Lewis to alter a bill of sale for the animals he tried to substitute a scrub colt for the purebred but Sheriff Elmer J. Dolve wasn't fooled.

Finally in a last resort Simpson decided to hide the evidence and on the morning of March 4, 1938, Sheriff Dolve and Rancher Gibbs drove up to the Lee Simpson home place, which was known as the Sahara Ranch in search of the black mare and her colt. Besides the Sahara Ranch, Simpson owned two other spreads in the area, the Twin Coulee and the Mountain Ranch, which was located over the divide of the Snowy Mountains. After carefully looking over the horses on the home ranch, the sheriff asked to inspect the stock on the Twin Coulee Ranch, which adjoined the Sahara Ranch. When the three men drove down to the other ranch they found the fine black mare in a corral with several other horses but the colt was nowhere to be seen.

Simpson insisted that he had no idea how the mare ended up in his corral and said he didn't know anything about the colt. There was no love lost between the two ranchers and when Gibbs asked where his colt was Lee Simpson immediately took offense. The powerful Simpson was quick tempered especially with anyone smaller than he was and Sheriff Dolve had to step in between the ranchers to prevent a fistfight. Mr. Gibbs said that there had been too much rustling going on and he made it clear that he wanted his colt back.

The sheriff turned to Simpson and told him if he had the animal he had better turn it over but Simpson only laughed and said that he hadn't seen the colt but suggested that the coyotes might have gotten it. Later that afternoon while Mr. Gibbs was collecting his mare, Sheriff Dolve returned to Ryegate where he and County Attorney Allen discussed the recent cases of horse and cattle thefts and Mr. Gibbs' accusations of Lee Simpson stealing his horses. In the meantime Simpson demonstrated his style of problem solving by calling his two cowpunchers, Harry Dunwald and Roy Harmon to the ranch house where he fired them both on the spot. When they protested, the rancher let off all of his steam by going into a rage and then kicking the men off his ranch without paying them their wages. Dunwald and Harmon went to Ryegate where they were overheard threatening to get even with their former employer.

Simpson quickly replaced the fired hands with Bob and Gerry McDonald, two brothers of a family of six boys and two girls who lived with their widowed father, Aaron McDonald on the outskirts of Ryegate. Simpson knew the McDonald boys well as their brother, Richard "Slats" McDonald was working on his Mountain Ranch and he was engaged to his seventeen-year-old daughter, Elizabeth.

Twenty-one-year-old Bob McDonald and his eighteen-year-old brother Gerry had known Mr. Simpson all of their lives and they both liked him. One of the first jobs Simpson assigned the boys was to ride by night to a hidden ravine on his property and retrieve a black colt and take it to the Jess Sterling Ranch. After telling the boys that he wanted to keep the animal under wraps until he could get a good price for it, he asked the McDonald brothers to tell Mr. Sterling that it was their horse. True to their word, the McDonald boys followed their orders and they didn't tell anybody about the incident except for their brother Richard.

Shortly after he had hired the McDonald boys in April of 1938, Simpson found one of his calves had been killed and butchered on his place. Simpson took great delight in calling Sheriff Dolve about the incident on his ranch after the officer and Gibbs had implied that he had been doing the rustling. With the McDonald brothers, Sheriff Dolve backtracked from the butchered carcass to where they discovered a set of distinctive tire imprints in the soft mountain dirt, which the officer photographed. It was eventually determined that there was only one truck in the area with those particular tires and it had been used recently by Roy Harmon and Harry Dunwald.

Shortly after being arrested by Sheriff Dolve, Harmon and Dunwald confessed and they were both given stiff prison terms at Deer Lodge. Simpson was quite jubilant since the convicted rustlers made him out as a victim; deflected any blame of horse stealing away from him and he still had possession of Mr. Gibbs' prized colt. Then on April 8, 1938, Simpson received a shock when he opened a letter from Deer Lodge containing the arrest warrant for the arrest of Harmon and Dunwald, which he had initiated with "Best Regards," scribbled across it. According to Mrs. Simpson, on the evening her husband received the letter from Deer Lodge he acted like a frantic animal, which was in a trap and she later told the authorities it was on that night when her husband swore that he would never go to prison for stealing a colt and then he made a list of all the people that linked him to the stolen animal.

A few days later Simpson reportedly told Rye Schmittou, an old acquaintance of his at Lavina that he was planning to kill Art Lewis, H.K. Gibbs, F. Loughlen, Fred Metzger, Earl and Carl Simpson and "them boys" for trying to frame him of stealing a colt and a mare. When Mr. Schmittou asked if "them boys" were the McDonald brothers, Simpson replied that he had made a good guess. Simpson then told his friend that the McDonald boys had stolen the horses and they were hiding them and he also implicated the boys of slaughtering some of his cattle as well.

On April 13, 1938, Tom Biggerstaff of Lewistown, the manager of the Production Credit Association for the Ryegate District received a call from Simpson stating that someone had rustled his sheep and some of the animals that the association had an interest in had been scattered. The rancher asked Mr. Biggerstaff to come out to his place at once and figure his loss and to make out a check for his losses. That same day Sheriff Dolve received a letter from Simpson about the stolen sheep and asking the officer to come out and take care of the situation.

The next morning Mr. Biggerstaff, accompanied by Hall Clements, another man working for the association, left Lewistown and made their first stop at Simpson's Mountain Ranch where they were met by Richard McDonald and his father, Aaron McDonald who asked the two men for a ride to the Sahara Ranch where he wanted to visit his other two sons. When the three men arrived at Simpson's place Mr. McDonald placed the rifle he was carrying in the barn as the other fellows were walking towards the house.

Lee Simpson met the men angrily with a high-powered rifle and he wanted to know why McDonald had placed his rifle in his barn. When Aaron McDonald told him that he had only wanted to keep the weapon dry while he visited with his sons the angry rancher said that the two boys were out in the hills and then he ordered him to get his rifle and told all three of the men to get the hell off of his property.

While leaving the property the three men met Simpson's sheepherder and they stopped to warn him that his employer was in a terrible mood. It was then that they learned from the herder that none of the sheep had been scattered and the flock had only suffered a normal winter loss. Aaron McDonald was willing to give Simpson the benefit of the doubt and he blamed the rancher's ugly disposition that day to alcohol but the businessmen from Lewistown decided to report the threats to the authorities at Ryegate.

At Ryegate the two men told their story to County Attorney Allen who offered to take legal action if they were willing to sign a complaint and even when the two men refused to sign, since the county attorney had previous problems with Simpson over the Gibbs' colt, Mr. Allen still notified the sheriff's office. Undersheriff Arthur "Buz" Burford, who doubled as deputy county treasurer as well, immediately called Sheriff Dolve at Roundup and the top law enforcement officer said that he would go directly to the Sahara Ranch on his way back to Ryegate. Mr. Allen drove Deputy Burford who had only been an officer for about a month and a half, along with Albert "Lank" Corcoran in his car to Lavina where they met the sheriff.

From Lavina the two vehicles proceeded to the Wesley Johnson Ranch, which was about four miles from the Sahara Ranch and because of the prosecutor's earlier trouble with Simpson, the officers thought it would be best if the sheriff and his deputy went to the ranch alone where they only expected to find the rancher drunk and obstinate. At about three o'clock on the afternoon of April 14, 1938 Sheriff Dolve and Deputy Burford left the others at the Johnson Ranch and drove on to the Sahara Ranch.

Sheriff Dolve's brand new .45-caliber automatic revolver, which he had never fired before was on the front seat of the patrol car as the officers parked in front of the gate leading to the Simpson house. The sheriff stopped Mrs. Simpson as she was coming from the barn but she cried out that her husband was sick and that she couldn't talk just then. The woman reportedly pushed by the officers crying out to her husband as the sheriff ran after her.

As the sheriff approached the front porch there was a blast in the officer's face and he hurled onto the lawn; rolled to the rock wall and scaled over it with revolver in hand. From his position along the wall, Sheriff Dolve knew that he was safe from Simpson who was standing on the porch of the two-story house but he was still open to fire from the second-story windows. He ran around the corner of the house and then proceeded across a small creek and up a small ravine where he took shelter in some rocks.

Snuggling into the rocks the sheriff once again heard the crack of the rifle along with two pops from Deputy Burford's .38-caliber handgun. When Sheriff Dolve peered over the rocks he noticed his oficer flat on his back with his gun still in his hand and as Deputy Burford waved at the sheriff indicating that he was unhurt, a rifle blast came from an upstairs window of the house and the sheriff's hat went flying off and the officer was slightly burned as the hot lead passed through his hair.

For the remainder of the afternoon Simpson continued to keep the officers with their handguns at bay by shooting through the sheriff's car and knocking chips from the rocky outpost held by the sheriff with his .30-30 rifle. At one point the sheriff snuck behind the house and tried opening a rear window but all the entry points were secured. Then through hand signals the two lawmen agreed that at dusk the sheriff would cover the house with fire, as the deputy would try to drive the car away for reinforcements.

When the sheriff began firing the deputy immediately jumped into the vehicle but before he could turn the key Simpson's rifle cracked into the driver and Burford cried out as he fell from the car with both legs shot clean through. No sooner had the deputy tumbled onto the ground that there was another rifle shot and his body jerked from the impact of the bullet. Lee Simpson then left the house and ran to his milk shed from which he again shot the wounded deputy.

Knowing he was a sitting duck, Deputy Burford somehow pulled himself up and took shelter behind the wheels of the front of the patrol car when suddenly the silhouette of Mrs. Simpson wearing a white dress presented a ghostly appearance in the darkness as she walked to the patrol car and glanced down at the fallen deputy. True to the code of the Old West, neither side fired a shot until the woman was safely back inside the house but then Simpson charged into the open towards the crippled deputy.

With only five rounds left, the sheriff left the safety of the rocks and he started to trade shots with the crazed rancher. Simpson was like a wild-eyed animal as he shouted: "Come and get it, you damn coyotes. Come and get it." As the sheriff inched in closer firing his unfamiliar automatic in an attempt to save his deputy, a bullet ripped through his coat. The sly rancher faked that he was shot and when the sheriff moved in closer he shot and this time grazed the skin of the officer's arm. At that point Simpson and the sheriff both ran out of ammunition; the rancher ran into the house and after seeing the lifeless body of his deputy, the lawman ran back to the Johnson Ranch.

As he was retreating to the Johnson place, one wonders if Sheriff Dolve had thought about what had happened to Sheriff Jesse Garfield in December of 1920, shortly after the establishment of Golden Valley County. With a bullet hole through his hat and a wound to his arm, it might have been natural for Sheriff Dolve to recall that Jesse Garfield was the county's first elected sheriff and he himself was fatally wounded while he was attempting to arrest another demented farmer in the Ryegate region.

After defying the county authorities the disgruntled farmer barricaded himself in his cabin and mortally wounded Sheriff Garfield as he approached the man's residence. In January of 1921, the county commissioners appointed the dead officer's widow, twenty-eight-year-old Mrs. Ruth Garfield as sheriff of Golden Valley County, making her the first woman sheriff in Montana.[4]

An hour later several cars of heavily armed and angry ranchers from Ryegate, as well as Roundup were on their way to the Sahara Ranch. With the powerful spotlight from Highway Patrolman Charles Dell's car on the house and the posse's rifles leveled for action, Officer Dell and Sheriff Dolve drove up to the front gate and recovered the body of Deputy Burford. At the Weir Mortuary House at Roundup it was determined that the deputy had been shot eleven times with high-powered bullets and several times with .22-caliber rounds.

A bullet hole had entered Officer Burford's skull above the left ear and it exited near the right ear, producing a large opening, from which brain matter had exuded. There were bullet wounds found above and below the left collarbone; another five wounds were in the victim's chest and there was one in his left arm. There were bullet wounds in his left knee joint and two in his right leg and a large powder burn on Burford's Stetson hat indicated that the killer had placed the muzzle close to the officer's temple before finishing him off.

The posse stormed the house at about four o'clock in the morning but only found Mrs. Simpson who said that her husband had escaped at about eleven p.m. well before the posse had arrived. The woman said that after her husband returned to the house for more ammunition he sent her outside with a lantern to determine if the deputy was dead and if Sheriff Dolve had indeed left.

When the woman told her husband that the coast was clear the rancher took a .22-caliber revolver from a holster on the wall and went out side and it was later determined that after Simpson stood over the helpless deputy and mocked the pleas of the wounded man he blew the officer's brains out. The authorities also noted that the McDonald brothers had been noticeably absent during the gun battle and they weren't sure if they were with the fugitive rancher or not.

County Attorney Nat Allen believed that Simpson had been hiding something from Mr. Biggerstaff earlier that morning and the rancher had apparently believed that Sheriff Dolve and Deputy Burford were sent out to arrest him that afternoon. The county attorney also suspected that Simpson might have gone to Lewistown where his children were attending school and he instructed Musselshell County Sheriff Jess Burns to take Mrs. Simpson to Roundup. Mr. Allen then conducted a search of the Sahara Ranch just before dawn where a .38-caliber revolver, 12-guage shotgun, .30-30 Winchester and a .30-caliber Remington were found along with various types of ammunition.

The muzzle of Officer Buford's weapon was jammed with dirt and it was found under his body and the officers also found the discarded .22-caliber rifle, which Simpson had first used in the assault before it reportedly had jammed after he first missed the sheriff near the front porch of the house. It was learned that the weapon wasn't Simpson's but it actually had belonged to the McDonald boys.

Along with the weapons, the authorities found shoes and a bloodstained shirt, which had been partially burned in a pile of ashes in the back yard. Once more the question was asked, "Where were the McDonald boys?" why had they let Simpson use their gun, and did the bloody and partially burned shirt found behind the house belong to one of the missing lads?

After thanking the other members of the posse for their help and telling them they could go home, Sheriff Dolve got into his bullet riddled Dodge sedan; started the motor; switched on the only headlight that wasn't shot out, and with a weary smile he said, "I'm going after Simpson." A few hours later Sheriff Dolve received word that Lee Simpson had turned himself in to Fergus County Sheriff Guy Tullock and Musselshell County Undersheriff Frank Otten at Roundup.

According to Sheriff Tullock, Simpson had stayed at a Lewistown hotel under an assumed name and after visiting with his children he turned himself in and told the Fergus County officers that he had killed Deputy Burford in self-defense, saying that when he went out to check on the officer the undersheriff became crazed and tried to shoot him. Simpson said that he was afraid to go to Ryegate claiming that the Golden Valley officers would surely kill him and since his teenage daughter and nine-year-old son were living at the home of Floyd Nayor while attending school at Roundup, he wanted to be surrounded by his wife and children when he turned himself in to the authorities.

The Golden Valley County lawman arrived at the Lewistown jail just as Simpson was in the act of signing a full confession of how he had killed Deputy Burford when Sheriff Dolve interrupted the signing by asking the prisoner why he had killed Gerald and Robert McDonald. Simpson began laughing and he exclaimed that he had never killed a man except for Burford and that was in self-defense. He said that the McDonald brothers had left his ranch and they had skipped the country. Sheriff Dolve accused Simpson of killing the two McDonald brothers and trying to throw suspicion off him by accusing the boys and others of stealing his stock.

The sheriff explained that Simpson had acted defensively when Mr. McDonald had asked about his two sons and he was obviously threatened when the officers came out to his place. While he was telling Simpson that he would hang for the murder of his best friend and deputy, Art Burford, Sheriff Dolve draped the partially burned bloodstained shirt of nineteen-year-old Gerald McDonald around the prisoner's neck and shoulders. When the sheriff said that the shirt was found in an ash pit behind the Simpson house the murderer quickly tore the shirt away in horror as if it were a poisonous snake.

At first Simpson adamantly stated that the McDonald boys weren't dead but they were hiding out in the mountains after they had stolen horses from his ranch and that they had fled once he found out about their crimes. After three hours of questioning without effect, Sheriff Tullock tried another approach by asking Simpson how he would feel if his own son had been murdered and his body left where the coyotes and rats could get at it.

The sheriff explained that all Mr. McDonald wanted was a chance to bury his two boys and the prisoner was told that he was already in big trouble over the death of Deputy Burford and he should think of his own children. Simpson's face reportedly twisted and for a short time he fought the urges to confess but finally he broke down and told the whole story. Simpson's eyes narrowed and then he said that he had killed the two boys in self-defense claiming that when he was alone with Bob McDonald at the old Cantrell Ranch he confronted the young man about them stealing his cattle.

According to Simpson, the boy ran for the rancher's gun in the truck but he managed to take the weapon from Bob and then shot him. The rancher then said that Gerry McDonald was in the barn when he confronted him about the rustling and the ranch hand came at him with a pitchfork. Confronted with the deadly weapon, Simpson said he grabbed an axe and killed Gerry and hid his body in a stack of straw. The prisoner then told the officers that on Sunday night he ordered his wife to help him load Gerry's body into the truck with the remains of Bob and they took them into the rim rocks behind the Roundup Country Club. Simpson said that when Sheriff Dolve and Deputy Burford were driving up to his place he believed they had found the bodies of the McDonald brothers and they were coming for him.

A posse of more than two hundred men searched the rim rocks near Roundup where they found the bodies of the McDonald boys buried in their underwear, one in a shallow grave covered with a slab of rock and the other was hidden in a crevice covered with brush. The autopsy report discredited Simpson's story of self-defense when it was determined that Bob McDonald was shot in the back and his brother was killed by a blow to the back of the head with an axe.

Another damning fact for Simpson was a list found on the prisoner of sixteen names, which he had described as "Rats," with Sheriff Dolve listed at the top. Also included on the list were the entire McDonald family of four, Rancher H.K. Gibbs, Peter Jensen, Chris Dunwald, Percy Badgett, Clarence Evans, W.A. Lewis, Fred Metzger and Carl Simpson, a nephew of the murderer. Next to the names of Gerald and Robert McDonald were large check marks and when asked about the list, Simpson with out elaborating said that he had a grudge against one of them and he had planned to kill them all. He finished by stating that he was sorry he was only able to get two of them and he later mentioned that he had intended on killing everyone in the Emory community "from A to Z."

On Friday April 15, 1938, Coroner E.R. Fouts impaneled an inquest over the remains of Undersheriff Arthur Burford made up of the following men:

Dan H. Corcoran	William H. Milne	Sam Clark
Byron Corcoran	John A. Slayton	Dan Corcoran

The jury found that Officer Burford "came to his death as a result of gunshot wound or wounds as inflicted by one W.L. Simpson on the fourteenth day of April, 1938, and that said gunshot wounds were inflicted by W.L. Simpson by criminal means." The bodies of the McDonald brothers were taken to the Weir Funeral Home at Roundup and later buried at Ryegate. A few days after the shooting the bullet-riddled body of Deputy Burford was also laid to rest in the Ryegate Cemetery after one of the largest funerals ever held in Golden Valley County.

Shortly after confessing on Saturday, April 16, Simpson tried to commit suicide by slashing his wrists with a jagged piece glass from a large drinking glass, which he had broken. Before he weakened from shock, Simpson tried to write a note with his own blood, which only said, "The result of a frame-up through my wife and..." Sheriff Tullock found the prisoner in a pool of blood but by the time the physician had arrived at the Fergus County jail the wounds had coagulated and the bleeding had alreadystopped. Eventually the wrist that had bludgeoned Gerald McDonald with an axe, and the hand that raised the rifle that killed Robert McDonald and the trigger finger, which murdered Deputy Burford became infected and Simpson's right arm had to be amputated at the elbow.

On Wednesday evening, May 4, Sheriff Dolve along with Dan Corcoran Sr., A.W. Thiel and Albert Corcoran went to Lewistown and returned Simpson to the Golden Valley County jail at Ryegate. The triple slayer had not yet been officially arraigned due to the prisoner's infected hand and Judge William Ford's order that Simpson be hospitalized. The sheriff made arrangement with the State Penitentiary at Deer Lodge to house his prisoner at the prison hospital where his right arm was amputated. In the meantime fifty-year-old Mrs. Gertrude Simpson who was being held in the Musselshell County jail at Roundup was arraigned on first-degree murder charges but Judge Ford later released her on five thousand dollar bail.

After his release from the prison hospital at Deer Lodge, Simpson only spent two days at the Golden Valley County jail at Ryegate when Judge Ford ordered that he be moved to the Musselshell County jail at Roundup. After conferring with Golden Valley County Physician Dr. E.R. Fouts of Ryegate and Dr. G.A. Lewis of Roundup, the judge ruled that the Musselshell County facility could provide better medical attention to the prisoner.

The court order also provided that two special deathwatches be placed on Simpson at the jail at Roundup and that the prisoner would be required to pay the expense for the additional guards. Simpson was taken to the Roundup jail on May 29, and his two doctors stated that their patient would have to receive medical care for at least two months before he could stand trial.

On the fourth of July, Lee Simpson was finally charged with the murder of Deputy Arthur Burford in the Golden Valley County courtroom at Ryegate and County Attorney Allen used the Gibbs' colt case, the Harmon and Dunwald calf-butchering incident, and the murder and cover up of the two McDonald brothers to establish a motive for the murder of the deputy.

Mr. and Mrs. Lee Simpson hired A.G. McNaught of Roundup as their defense counsel and he prevented anyone from speaking with the woman and he asked for a further delay in Mr. Simpson's trial because of his weak physical condition. Judge Ford scheduled the Simpson trial for July 18 and Sheriff Dolve immediately made arrangements to have the defendant returned from the Roundup jail.

Defense attorney, A.G. McNaught with the help of George Hurd of Great Falls successfully pushed back the trial and in September 1938, the proceedings were further delayed when it became difficult to obtain a jury from the sparsely settled ranch and farm community because so many residents had heard about the case and they had formed an opinion. Finally the Simpson trial began on September 6, 1938, with the following jury:

W.H. Northey (f)	C.M. Brovold	Axel Johnson
J.B. Brown	Carl Fulkerson	John J. Neuharth
Henry Bukoskey	Dan T. Hart	Melvin Rasmussen
Gunnar Birdsing	Frank Schanz	Edward Olson

(f) Foreman

Golden Valley County commissioners hired Wellington D. Rankin, one of the leading criminal prosecutors in Montana to assist their new county attorney and the two tried to paint Lee Simpson as a sane, deliberate and fiendish killer with the instincts of a wolf that didn't fear death. They brought in psychologists who testified that Simpson probably would have tried to kill all sixteen persons on his "death list" especially if he had gotten away with his first two murders.

The prosecution argued that Simpson went into his violent outburst after receiving the copy of the arrest warrant from the two convicted cattle thieves at Deer Lodge and he decided to kill the McDonald boys because they knew about Gibbs' stolen colt. Simpson's next step was to call in the insurance men to confirm his accusations that the boys had stolen stock from him.

Because of the overwhelming evidence against their client, the defense introduced testimony to indicate that Simpson had feared arrest for the deaths of Gerald and Robert McDonald when he opened fire on Sheriff Dolve and Deputy Burford. They made it clear at the preliminary proceedings that Simpson had plead innocent because he was insane at the time he committed the murders.

The trial was postponed the following week when Simpson was found unconscious on the floor of his cell with a cut on his forehead and after the county physician along with Doctors E.C. Person and Lewis of Roundup had dressed Simpson's wound the deputies found evidence that the prisoner had climbed up to the top of his cell and intentionally fallen. When court resumed, Defense Attorney Hurd explained to the court that Simpson had come to Montana from Missouri several years earlier when he first took out a homestead and worked in the coalmines near Roundup.

Mr. Hurd stated that Simpson had suffered a mental disorder in 1937, and it had evolved into paranoia, which eventually caused him to commit murder. Elizabeth Simpson, the defendant's sixteen-year-old daughter testified about several incidents in her home during the past two years and how her father had changed. Mrs. Simpson testified that her husband's parents had lived with them on their ranch and that they both became totally insane before their deaths. She claimed that she hadn't been involved with the murders but because she had become terrified of her husband's mental state she helped with the cover up.

After a seventeen day trial the jury found Lee Simpson guilty on September 23, 1938, and fixed the penalty at death. On Tuesday, September 27 Judge Ford formerly sentenced Simpson to be hanged and then granted the defense until December first to present a bill of exceptions. While Judge Ford denied a motion for a new trial for Simpson, the wealthy rancher appealed his case to the Supreme Court on the grounds that one of the jurors was permitted to sit on the panel after he had admitted that he had already formed an opinion; that lay witnesses were permitted to testify for the prosecution regarding the defendant's sanity and the remarks made to the jury by Special Prosecutor Rankin was prejudicial.

The case was argued before the Supreme Court on October 3 and on November 18, 1938, the high tribunal found no errors in the record and affirmed the district court judgment. In summing up their decision, the Supreme Court declared, "The defendant's attitude may be described as akin to the old proverb: The Guilty Fleeth When No Man Pursueth." Simpson's defense team re-submitted the case to the high court and when it refused to re-hear his appeal his only chances of escaping the gallows was either executive clemency from the Governor of Montana or taking his appeal to the United States Supreme Court.

In order for the highest court of the land to hear the case, a point of federal law had to be raised and while the contention that a juror had been improperly impaneled could be asserted as having violated Simpson's constitutional rights, apparently the case wasn't strong enough or the Ryegate rancher's resources were not sufficient to pursue it. On Friday, December 1, Judge William L. Ford re-sentenced him to be hanged between two and eight on the morning of December 30, 1939.

When asked by Judge Ford if there was any legal objection why the sentence shouldn't be pronounced, Simpson stated, "I don't think its right I should be hung." His attorneys immediately made preparations to ask the Governor for a commutation of sentence for their client but Governor Roy E. Ayers denied Simpson executive clemency.

Meanwhile Sheriff Dolve mailed out invitations for the execution to virtually every county sheriff of the state and on December 27, 1939, the scaffold was traveling towards Ryegate from Columbus on Train No. 264, with Conductor Ed Streble in charge with the crew of Engineer George Eaton, Fireman Ernest Stein and brakemen, John Martin and Clayton Ogden. The sixty-foot square courthouse yard was bordered on two sides by buildings and the other two by a twenty-foot tall stockade fence, which was constructed out of rough bridge planks. The gallows, which had been last used to hang Frank Robideau in January of 1938, at Columbus were reassembled piece by piece under the direction of the regular night jailer.

Housed in the one-room jail at Ryegate, the condemned man was unable to hear the workers building the stockade and setting up the gallows and after being away for two days, Simpson asked the night jailer where he'd been and the officer without hesitation explained what he had been doing. During the days leading up to the execution, the little town of Ryegate of about three hundred residents in 1939, paid little attention to the construction of the enclosure on the north side of the courthouse yard but shortly before the fateful hour the streets of the county seat were jammed with automobiles.

A large crowd numbering in the hundreds milled about in the tiny lobby of the courthouse, laughing and joking just a short distance from Simpson's small cell. The condemned man had spent much of his last day writing letters and visiting with the Reverend E.L. Mills, Baptist minister of Roundup and church worker, Mrs. Rose Williams. On the table in the county commissioner's room in the northeast corner of the courthouse was a length of stiff, new one half-inch hemp rope, which had been removed from the hangman's rope.

Nearby on the same table was a bar of soap, which had been rubbed thoroughly over the hangman's knot to insure that it would slip better around the victim's neck. A hangman's knot had already been tied at one end of the rope, but two visiting sheriffs, both of whom had previous experience as executioners, retied the noose, not in the traditional thirteen-loop variety but with seven instead. A window of the courthouse had been removed and four temporary steps were built up to the sill and another eight steep steps led to the platform of the gallows.

At no time did the prisoner lose his composure that he had maintained since the jury called for the mandatory death sentence. At times Simpson had shown some remorse and he wept one other time when his children visited him for the last time before they and their mother went to Warrensburg, Missouri prior to the execution. When asked about his preference for his last meal Simpson said, "Bring me what you have regularly," and he was served chicken, dumplings, mashed potatoes and apple pie.

At 1:30 a.m. the courthouse was cleared and thirty minutes later the stockade was opened and several highway patrolmen checked for invitations and searched each of the witnesses to ensure that no guns or cameras were taken into the enclosure. At 2:10 a squad of visiting sheriffs, deputies and other officers marched out of the courthouse and surrounded the gallows. Before leaving his cell, Simpson shook hands with County Attorney Allen and he said that he had no hard feelings. Almost to the last moment Simpson had clung to the faint hope that Governor Ayers would save him.

Dressed in dark trousers and a gray shirt, Simpson stepped directly from a courthouse window and with a prayer book clutched in his hand he walked cowardly to the gallows steps. With his arms bound to his sides with rawhide straps, Simpson climbed to the scaffold supported by two peace officers and followed by Reverend Mills. Park County Deputy Sheriff Verne Meigs of Livingston and Undersheriff Dan Corcoran of Ryegate followed the procession.

At the request of the condemned man, Reverend Mills offered a brief prayer and then Sheriff Dolve asked the crowd to remain silent in order for Simpson to speak his last words. "I want to praise God I am being taken out of this world of sin tonight and I feel confident that you people will meet us all up there. God Bless you all. Pray for my loved ones. That is all." The next thing uttered by the prisoner was, "Don't choke me," as the sharp points of the hemp rope pricked his bare skin as Meagher County Sheriff Mike Bergen adjusted the strand snugly around his neck.

Finally after the leg straps were fastened above Simpson's knees and the long black hood was pulled over his head, the signal was given to Sheriff Dolve and at 2:14 the trap was sprung. Witnesses said that for a fraction of a second the strapped and hooded body of Lee Simpson stood all alone on the trap with an officer on each side gently holding a sleeve of the doomed man's shirt with their fingertips.

The crowd of about five hundred witnesses stood in silent awe under the black and cold winter night's sky as they gazed on the grim scene, which was barely illuminated by two small light bulbs. The silence was broken by the terrible crash of the falling trap and the crowd surged forward to look through the holes and openings in the canvas screen to get a glimpse of the hanging limp body.

Simpson's body dropped to the end of the seven-foot rope and out of sight beneath the screened off trap while the four officers silently peered down through the trap. The rope hung straight and motionless like a plumb line and the tense silence was finally broken when one of the deputies on the gallows announced, "It's a good, clean job." Sixteen minutes later Lee Simpson was pronounced dead by Dr. E.R. Fouts, county coroner and Dr. A.A. Bennett of Roundup.

Several visiting sheriffs assisted the local officers with the execution and among the many witnesses were two members of the Great Falls police department and three highway patrolmen from the Cascade County district. A number of private citizens of Golden Valley County as well as neighboring counties were also inside the plank-walled enclosure to watch Simpson die for his crime of murder.

Earl Simpson, the brother of the hanged man ordered Roundup mortician, Fay Roberts to conduct a private service in the New Miners Cemetery at Roundup. The grave had been dug in advance and to insure the privacy of the service, Mr. Simpson had even withheld from the mortician the day of the burial and gave him only one-hour notification.

Postscript:
In February of 1940, Judge William L. Ford died of a heart attack and two months later Judge W.C. Husband dropped all charges against Mrs. Gertrude Simpson. The woman's murder trial was originally set for September 26, 1938, but it was put off until October when it was postponed indefinitely. She was never prosecuted in connection with the murders or for her involvement in the cover up and she eventually took her two children to Missouri where she reportedly taught school.

September 10, 1943
Philip J. Coleman

Other Names: "Slim"
Location and Gallows: Coleman was hanged inside the Missoula County Jail from the last hangman's scaffold ever built in the state of Montana, ***Gallows No. Twenty-Two: (Sept. 1943)***.
Description: Coleman was a tall, slim twenty-five-year-old black man.
Crime: Murder of Mrs. Rosalyn Pearson in her home at Lothrop on July 25, 1943.
Judge: Albert Besancon
Prosecution: County Attorney Fremont W. Wilson
Defense: Leon L. Bulen and former county attorney Edward T. Dussault
Sheriff: Robert D. MacLean
Distinction: Along with being the last legal execution in Missoula County, Coleman's hanging was the last to take place in the State of Montana. Coleman was the fourth and last man to be sentenced to death in Montana without having had a jury trial. In 1908, George Rock pleaded guilty to first-degree murder charges, George Criner did likewise in 1935, followed by Frank Robideau in 1938. Coleman also had the distinction of being quickest man legally hanged in Montana, having only lived forty-eight days from the time of his crime until his march to the gallows. The Indians, Pierre Paul and La La See defied the gallows the longest, having been on the run and in custody for a total of one thousand two hundred and ninety-eight days each before they were eventually hanged for their crime in 1890, also in Missoula.
Relics and Remnants: The gallows, which was used to hang Philip Coleman, is being held at the Historical Museum at Fort Missoula.

Friday, July 23, 1943, forty-nine-year-old Northern Pacific Railroad Section Forman Carl W. Pearson hired Philip J. "Slim" Coleman of St. Louis and thirty-nine-year-old Louis Brown of Herington, Kansas as section hands at Lothrop. The two men became friends on the job and on Saturday they decided to hitchhike the thirty miles to Missoula for drinks and to roll some dice. They got as far as Alberton where they did their drinking at a small bar and hatched a plan to rob the section foreman back at the camp. Both men later laid the blame on each other, Brown claiming "Slim" had forced him to participate in the crime and Coleman accussing his companion of coming up with the plan.

Early Sunday morning, July 25, 1943, Coleman and Brown went to the Pearson home with a story that the latter was ill and when Mr. Pearson met the men in the front yard with a flashlight and a bottle of aspirin; Coleman reached into the grass, picked up an axe and struck the unsuspecting man in the head. The two men then entered the dimly lit house where they found the half-awake Mrs. Rosalyn Pearson and after asking the woman where their money was, Coleman struck her with his fist.

After being slashed with a large knife Mrs. Pearson pointed to where the money was kept and then with her three-year-old daughter, Judie Lee lying asleep in a nearby bed, Coleman killed the woman by stabbing her several times. With the woman dead, "Slim" ordered his companion to get their bags from the bunkhouse and meet him back at the Pearson house but instead Brown got the bags and ran down the railroad tracks, which ran along the county road. When he saw Coleman coming up the road in the Pearson car, Brown hid in the weeds until he drove past and about twenty minutes later a freight train came along and the man left the bags and took the train to Missoula.

Shortly after eleven a.m. Sunday morning, seven-year-old Richard Pearson went to Mrs. Vera Winsper's house crying and told the woman that his daddy was lying in the garden and his momma wouldn't wake up. After discovering the tragic seen at the little boy's home, the neighbor lady reported the heinous crime to Sheriff Robert D. MacLean in Missoula and he and Coroner Ella Stucky immediately went to the scene. The family-ration books and an empty billfold found on the floor of the bedroom indicated to the sheriff that the motive had been robbery.

The victims were prominent citizens of the area having come from Bozeman in 1938, Mr. Pearson was a veteran of World War I and he had worked for the railroad for twenty years and was a member of the Masons. Mrs. Pearson was an active member of the Methodist Church at Alberton and an officer of the Eastern Star. The family's oldest child, thirteen-year-old son, Ray was visiting his grandparents in Livingston at the time of the murder.

Sheriff MacLean quickly sent out an alarm to the authorities across Montana as well as the surrounding states to apprehend the two black men involved with the murder and within five hours the Missoula police department had located the Pearson car abandoned at the Northern Pacific stockyards in Drummond. At six o'clock that same evening Louis Brown was arrested in front of the Western Hotel in Missoula with blood on his clothes and two nickels and three dice sewn into the cuff of his pants. Before being placed in solitary confinement at the county courthouse, Brown said that he knew nothing of the double murder and he claimed that the blood on his clothes was his own from a wound that was inflicted by Coleman.

Finally on Monday, July 26, 1943, Brown broke down under interrogation and gave the details of the brutal killing, for which he placed the blame on Philip Coleman and he asserted that he had been forced to take part. In the meantime Granite County Undersheriff Charles Popich arrested Coleman at Drummond while he was hiding on a westbound Milwaukee freight train.

When Sheriff MacLean and his deputies arrived at Drummond for their prisoner, Coleman was laying on a cot boasting that he could bust out of that jail in twenty minutes. On the way back to Missoula the prisoner admitted to having served time in various institutions including Washington State where he served fourteen months at Monroe Reformatory and six months at the penitentiary at Walla Walla.

Coleman was taken to the State Penitentiary at Deer Lodge for safe keeping before being returned to Missoula and ushered into the crowded courtroom in handcuffs and under heavy guard. After admitting killing Mrs. Pearson, Coleman told the officers he wanted "to get it over with as soon as possible." Judge Cloyde E. Comer set Friday, July 30 as the time for Coleman to enter his plea before Judge Albert Besancon, and on that day Coleman failed to enter a plea to the murder of Mrs. Pearson while Louis Brown retracted his earlier statement that he had witnessed the killing of the woman. Meanwhile the victims, Mr. and Mrs. Carl Pearson were being buried at Livingston.

Arraignment in the case was continued until Monday, August 2, 1943, at ten a.m. when Judge Besancon appointed Leon Bulen and former county attorney Edward T. Dussault to defend Coleman. Both lawyers accepted the appointment but made it clear that they were consenting only because of the ethical requirements of the legal profession. After Coleman was remanded to the custody of the sheriff, the defendant was returned to the court of Judge Comer for his indictment on first-degree murder charge in the murder of Carl Pearson and set the arraignment for ten a.m. on August 4.

According to a sworn statement made by Coleman, County Attorney Wilson had met with him and said that he would recommend a ninety-nine-year sentence to the judge if he would plead guilty. Coleman stated that Mr. Wilson explained that the "old boy," referring to the judge, had never hung a man that had pleaded guilty and that same evening the prosecutor again assured Coleman that he would stick to his word and said that if the trial went before a jury he would surely hang. According to the defendant's statement, no one else was present during his conversation with the county attorney and he didn't tell his attorneys about the deal until after he was sentenced to be hanged.

Over the weekend Coleman was held in "the hole" of the sheriff's office at the county courthouse where he spent his time reading magazines and sleeping. Developed pictures taken a day or two after their arrest arrived at the sheriff's office and they illustrated the different nature of the two prisoners. The camera captured Coleman smiling while Brown's face showed definite signs of strain and mental stress.

Although Coleman had received letters from various lady friends, neither prisoner asked to notify friends or relatives about their predicament. While Coleman was charged and scheduled for separate hearings for the two murders, his partner in crime, Louis Brown was held at the county jail but he hadn't yet been charged for the killings.

On Monday morning, August 9, in an atmosphere, which was described as being electric from the suspense of a mixed crowd of spectators, Philip Coleman pled guilty of killing Mrs. Pearson and with little emotion he admitted to the cruel murder in a clear voice as he stood before Judge Besancon with his hands manacled. Before hearing the man's plea the judge granted the defense council an hour to confer with their client as the crowd in the courtroom waited in suspense. After the guilty plea, Judge Besancon announced that he would pass sentence on Coleman at 2:30 that same afternoon.

An hour or two after pleading guilty of murdering Mrs. Pearson in district court, Philip Coleman preferred charges against Louis Brown in the murder of Mr. Pearson. While in the county attorney's office, Coleman gave a detailed thirty typewritten paged statement charging that Brown had been the planner of the robbery of the Pearson's, which ultimately led to the killing of the man and wife at the isolated section station at Lothrop. He said that he had played "sick" in order to entice Mr. Pearson from his house and that it was Brown who bludgeoned the man to death in the small Victory garden.

Coleman's charges against Brown were filed with Justice of the Peace Ralph L. Starr and the magistrate denied the motion by County Attorney Wilson that the complaint be dismissed without prejudice in order that Brown may be charged later in the district court. The county attorney believed that Coleman's charges against Brown was an effort on his lawyer's part to clear him of the state's charge that he had also killed Mr. Pearson.

Mr. Wilson said that the action was an attempt by the defense council to clear Coleman and to embarrass the state's case against him. The prosecutor explained that the complaint charged that Brown alone was the slayer of Mr. Pearson instead of charging Coleman as an accomplice and he feared that it may be superfluous and may even clear the charges against the man who had earlier pleaded guilty to murdering Mrs. Pearson.

At 2:30 that afternoon County Attorney Wilson presented witnesses who testified to the circumstances of the murder of Mrs. Pearson along with her bloodstained nightgown and photographs taken after the murder. The list of witnesses called by the prosecution included Sheriff MacLean, Undersheriff George Bukovatz, Coroner Ella Stucky, Assistant Coroner Alvin Lister, R.M. McKay, Deputy Charles Popich of Granite County, who had arrested Coleman at Drummond and R.A. Shannon, special agent of the Northern Pacific Railroad.

Louis Brown was also called to identify a tobacco pipe with fine carvings belonging to Coleman, which was found on the blood-soaked bed where Mrs. Pearson was found murdered and after Brown had answered a few of the county attorney's questions, Judge Besancon halted the testimony, saying: "The court cannot permit the witness to incriminate himself even if he raises no objection to testifying." All of Brown's testimony was then ordered to be stricken from the court record.

Mr. Lister and Dr. Fred H. Lowe presented the most dramatic testimony when they identified the bloodstained, lace-trimmed satin nightgown as the garment that Mrs. Pearson was wearing as she lay across her bed. The courtroom was deathly silent as the garment was unrolled but the defendant didn't display any sign of emotion indicating that he had no remorse or any other feelings of the brutal act that he had admitted to. Dr. Lowe testified that he found between ten to twenty-one stab wounds, two of them in the heart, others in the abdomen, breast, chest and face. He described the body when found as being covered with and her hair matted down by dried blood as well as blood oozing from her wounds.

In summary, County Attorney Wilson asked the court to sentence the defendant to death and if he was allowed to live, that he serve ninety-nine years in prison. Replying to Mr. Wilson's recommendation, Judge Besancon stated that the law mandated that the death penalty be demanded when both deliberation and premeditation had been admitted. The judge said that both had been established by the statements of the defendant and that the court had no recourse other than to invoke the death penalty.

Judge Besancon then sentenced Philip Coleman to be hanged on September 10, 1943, and as Sheriff Mclean escorted the him from the courtroom the prisoner remarked, "To hell with him," referring to the judge and he later told a reporter that he had figured all along that he would hang for the crime to which he had confessed and said he wished it was all over with. Coleman also said that he had been treated kindly while in custody and he told the interviewer that he probably would have been lynched back at St. Louis. While being convinced that he would have been lynched, he also commented, "that he would have preferred it."

When asked if the sight of the bloody nightgown made him feel that he had committed a monstrous offense, Coleman said that he knew he had done wrong and that he figured all along that he would hang. He said that he had come to his fate through his own doing saying, "I've had a chance to make something of myself and to do right, but I just didn't take it." The condemned man said that he had family in St. Louis as well as in Montana and Washington but he wouldn't say who or where they were. He said that he was married to an Indian girl from Arlee and that he had two small children living about ninety miles from Missoula.

Later Mr. E.T. Dussault summed up their case for Coleman by saying that generally when a defendant pled guilty and threw himself on the mercy of the court, he was offered some consideration. The defense attorney pointed out that he and Mr. Bulen had permitted their client to plead guilty, because the evidence presented had convinced them that they couldn't have cleared him of the charges if brought to trial.

When the county attorney continued to state that the defense attorney's action in charging Louis Brown with first-degree murder with Coleman as the complainant was unethical, Mr. Dussault and Mr. Bulen referenced Section 11729, of the Montana Code: "Every person who has reason to believe that a public offense has been committed and that a certain person has committed such offense, must make complaint of such person before a magistrate of the township in which the offense was committed, or if there be no magistrate in such township, before the nearest magistrate."

Coleman was again asked if he felt any remorse for the murder of Mrs. Pearson, and he said that he was sorry, but being sorry does no good. He explained that he had killed the woman with a large butcher knife, which was never found and he couldn't remember what happened to it but he didn't throw it into the river as many had suggested. The condemned man stated that he drank a bottle of one hundred and fifty-one-proof rum on the evening of the murder and that he was very high at the time.

The condemned man said that if he had accepted the ride to Glendive that some white friends had offered he would have escaped. When it was suggested the authorities would have eventually caught up with him anyway, Coleman said that he would have gone back to the hills of Mississippi and explained that there were a lot of wanted black men hiding out there and it wasn't safe to look for fugitives in that region.

Sheriff MacLean received the blueprints of ***Gallows No. Sixteen: (Jan. 1918): "Galloping Gallows" No. Five*** on Sunday, August 22, 1943, and then he hired a local carpenter to build a custom scaffold just inside the main door of the cellblock of the ancient county jail. The carpenter made a special trip to Butte to get a first-hand glimpse of the killing machine and to take measurements of the scaffold. Like the old gallows of the Mining City, the Missoula County scaffold was constructed of six by six-inch timbers, which were secured with large bolts.

The condemned man's cell on the second tier was only a few feet from the gallows but Coleman was reportedly as unconcerned about its construction as he was when he was apprehended for the murder. According to Sheriff MacLean, Coleman was a quiet and courteous prisoner and he took his showers on Sunday mornings and he usually danced on the concrete floor in the corridor

The day before his execution, Coleman requested that "The Missoulian" print a statement correcting a reporter's article that the prisoner wasn't sorry about his crime. Coleman made it clear that he had said that he was very sorry for everything, and for all the grief he had caused. The condemned man also said that he didn't have any hard feelings that Louis Brown's life was spared and he had to die for the same crimes. Although Coleman had refused the services of a black clergyman after his arrest, he eventually asked for spiritual advice and Reverend Father Henry L. Sweeney baptized him as a Catholic on Monday, September 6, 1943.

Despite the fact that he had received a message from Governor Sam C. Ford advising him that nothing could be done, and after Coleman had a fruitless personal telephone call with the Governor, he still hoped for a last minute miracle to save him. With no hope left and after a fine chicken dinner, Coleman expressed a willingness to get things off of his chest and a court reporter was called to the jail. Coleman confessed to committing twenty-three murders since he was a boy of fourteen at St. Louis but he only dictated the accounts of eight killings. He bragged of being a triggerman for a gang in Missouri where he said he killed three people in one week but he provided no names or dates.

Coleman also confessed that he killed "Devil" Moore with a hammer in East St. Louis when he was only fourteen years old and then he told the officers that in 1939, he strangled a Mexican by the name of Ventez to death and buried the body under a house in Stockton, California. He claimed that he committed a murder at Lackawanna, New York and he killed another Negro in Canada. Coleman admitted that he killed a white girl by the name of "Tullie" in May of 1943, at Seattle and sank her body into Puget Sound.

He said that he had also killed a man in Seattle but he wouldn't describe the case because it involved a prominent black man there. Finally Coleman admitted killing A.J. Walton, the eighty-one-year-old black man who was fatally beaten with a hatchet in Helena on July 3, 1943. He convinced the officers of his involvement with the murder by accurately describing the wounds he had inflicted and he said he killed the old man for money but he only found twelve cents on the body.

The condemned man told Sheriff MacLean that a black man by the name of Jack L. Williams was serving a long prison term at Walla Walla, Washington for an assault on a man that Coleman said that he had committed. Sheriff MacLean reported later that he had received a letter from Williams from the Washington State Penitentiary saying he was serving time for a crime committed by Philip Coleman.

A few hours after confessing his other murders, Coleman ate another meal of oysters and then he put on a new blue suit with dark blue trousers, which had been provided by the county. At seven o'clock Sheriff MacLean read the death warrant to the condemned man in his cell and the prisoner told the officer that he had no objections of him having to carry out his orders of the court. Coleman smiled and shook hands with the sheriff and the deputies and he wished them all well.

Moments later Coleman was shackled and he walked briskly to the gallows and while his white teeth glistened as he smiled in his cell with the officers, he was very solemn as he stepped to the gallows with Father Sweeney. The man looked sharp in his new suit and shoes, which reportedly gleamed in the dim light of the corridor as they marched to the deathtrap.

Sheriff MacLean and Undersheriff Bukovatz were on either side of the prisoner and on the scaffold Deputies Clark Davis, Henry Roseth, Frank Bond, Ed Perry and Ray Hamilton joined them. Coleman greeted the officers and the small handful of witnesses and with a firm voice he said he was sorry for what he had done and that he was ready to meet his maker.

Deputy Davis placed the noose around the man's neck, pulled down the black hood and at 7:09 a.m. the sheriff pushed a button on the platform in the corridor of the gray brick county jail, which flashed a light below where three men pushed handles, one of which released the trap. At 7:21 the physicians pronounced the slim high school-educated Philip Coleman dead. After the hanging, Coleman's body was interned in the St. Mary's Catholic Cemetery where it was marked with a simple slab marker.

Postscript:

The hanging of Philip Coleman was the quickest legal execution in Montana history having only taken forty-eight days from the time of the crime to the springing of the trap. Although County Attorney Wilson claimed they had absolute proof that Coleman had killed both Mr. and Mrs. Pearson, the formal charges for the murder of Carl W. Pearson were dropped against the dead prisoner on September 13, 1943.

Howard Toole and Randolph Jacobs were appointed to represent Louis Brown and on August 12, 1943, he entered a plea of guilty to the charge of second-degree murder and he was sentenced to life imprisonment at Deer Lodge. According to state law, after serving twelve years of a life sentence, an inmate was eligible for parole for good behavior and Louis Brown was paroled on April 16, 1958.

According to George Bukovatz of Butte, U.S. Marshall and former undersheriff of Missoula County, after the execution of Philip Coleman the gallows was dismantled and stored in the courthouse basement and in 1951, the scaffold was loaded on a truck and sent to Toole County for an execution but the condemned man's sentence was eventually commuted.

Over the years the location of the Missoula gallows became unknown, the Toole County authorities saying it had been returned while officials in the Garden City declared they had no idea where it was. Finally in February of 1963, the old scaffold was located in a dusty pile of lumber in the cannery building of the Missoula County Fair Grounds and they have been held at the Historical Museum at Fort Missoula since 1975.

(Endnotes)

[1] Prior to the nineteenth century, identifying criminals often involved dismemberment or forced marking by either by scarring or with tattoos. When civilizations eventually wouldn't allow such barbaric means, law enforcement found itself without a way of identifying criminals. Photography helped but they were difficult to file and they could easily be ineffectual when the outlaws grew beards and from the effect of age. In the 1870's Alphonse Bertillon came up with a system of taking measurements of body parts including the skull, foot length and left middle fingers. By 1893 New York State had implemented the Bertillon System and by 1900 it was being used by seventeen other states and Canada. (From New York State's Bureau of Identification website)

[2] Description of Montana Industrial School at Miles City, "Missoulian" 2/5/1922, p1 Section 2

[3] "They Gazed on the Beartooths" Jim Annin Vol. 2, p198

[4] "Fallow County Times" 1/24/1921

The Gallows of Montana

The Trap Gallows used to hang John Burns at Missoula in December of 1892
"Weekly Missoulian" 12/21/1892

A Miners' Court at Bannack ordered the first scaffold built in the Territory of Montana for an execution in August of 1863, and the following year four suspected road agents were hanged from the same gallows by the Original Vigilantes. Although the first man-made gallows was used in 1863, it was twelve years later before another such device, which also served as symbols of a formal justice system, was constructed in the Territory.

In the meantime, not counting the four road agents executed on the first gallows, at least sixty-seven men were hanged without legal authority by the Miners' Courts, Original Vigilantes, Lynch Mobs and various chapters of "Hometown Vigilantes." By our count, there were eventually a total of twenty-two gallows used in Montana from August

1863 through September of 1943. These twenty-two death machines claimed the lives of seventy-six men, less than a third of the total men hanged in Montana.

We have classified the scaffolds used in Montana into three major groups, "Trap," "Jerk" and the "Hoist-Type" Gallows. There were forty-four hangings in Montana utilizing the trap or drop method, twenty-seven men were jerked to their deaths and five died on the simplest form. These three groups are further separated into sub-categories of "Freestanding," "Galloping," "Conversions," "Custom Built or Adaptations" and "Built Ins."

A number of the killing machines started out as a freestanding scaffold and used for a particular outdoor hanging; then they became a "Galloping Gallows," which was transported to other executions and eventually converted to operate inside of a jail building. A few county authorities had the foresight to have gallows built into the jail buildings for future hangings. Along with classifying the twenty-two gallows we have also tried to describe them in as much detail as possible along with a history of the executions and the final disposition of the scaffolds.

Accept for the very first scaffold, which was designed to be permanent and therefore available for additional executions, the rest of the scaffolds were designed for a specific hanging and not used again. In fact nine of the twenty-two gallows were constructed for a single hanging and there was a fifteen-year delay between executions on another scaffold. By the time the eighth scaffold was constructed there had been twelve legal hangings over the same number of years and because of its simple construction and operation it was probably designed for multiple use.

Simple Hoist or Drop Type

This form of gallows originated in Europe as a transitional scaffold from a tree to the more complicated system, which used a trapdoor in a raised platform and an overhead beam. The simple Hoist or Drop-Type gallows consisted of two large posts, permanently embedded in the earth, with a strong crossbeam from which the hangman's rope was suspended or thrown over. Like a "Hangman's Tree," this man-made death machine could be used by either hoisting the victim up by the hands of several men or the hangman's noose could be first secured to the overhead beam and the condemned man merely dropped to his death from a horse, wagon or other support or trap.

As far as we have determined, there was only one of these gallows used in Montana, although there had been another simple scaffold erected earlier at Virginia City but it was never employed for an execution. Like its earlier predecessors, the Hangman Trees, Montana's earliest scaffold was used both as a "Hoist" and "Drop" gallows. This simplest form of a Hangman Gallows, which was built at Bannack, is credited with taking the lives of five men from August of 1863 to October of 1864, including the man responsible for its construction, Sheriff Henry Plummer.

Victims of the Hoist-Type Gallows:

John Heron (8/25/1863)
Buck Stinson (1/10/1864)
Ned Ray (1/10/1864)
R.C. Rawley (10/30/1864)
Sheriff Henry Plummer (1/10/1864)

Trap or Drop Type

While most Montana residents along with other states and territories in the West still approved of capital punishment and in particular hanging, by 1875, they didn't want a permanently standing reminder of it. When a gallows was needed in Lewis and Clark County in August of 1875, the only scaffold generally thought of at that time was the "Trap" or "Drop-Type."

The first man executed in England by the "Drop" was reportedly Earl Ferrers on May 5, 1760, making this one of the oldest forms of gallows in the world. After Ferrers' arms were secured with a black sash a noose was placed around his neck and on a signal he fell though the opening in the suspended platform.

Executions in the United States and Montana on the Trap Gallows weren't very different from those of ancient England. The Trap-Type Gallows used in Montana generally consisted of a scaffold of two uprights and crossbeam with a suspended platform beneath, which had a trapdoor directly under the hangman's noose.

While most of the judges in Montana observed the ancient rule of sentencing condemned men to be hanged on Fridays, the tradition of utilizing thirteen steps to the gallows wasn't always followed. If questioned, some Montana executioners might have said, "Why quibble over a step or two?"

The condemned man with the noose around his neck would then be dropped through the trap and ideally his neck would be broken in the fall. During the eighteenth and the first half of the nineteenth century in America the standard drop was generally utilized, which was around four to five feet. A drop of that distance, while not always sufficient to break the condemned man's neck, it caused enough force and impact to usually knock him unconscious and he would die quietly by strangulation.

There weren't any problematic hangings recorded in Montana but the correct drop was critical and a larger man dropping too far could result in decapitation like the execution of Tom "Black Jack" Ketchum in April of 1901, at Clayton, New Mexico. An insufficient drop usually ended in a slow death by strangulation like the terrible execution described by Warden Duffy at San Quentin in California. The warden explained that the condemned man fought at his restraints while wheezing and whistling while he struggled for air.

Warden Duffy observed blood oozing through the black cap as well as the victim's urine and faeces dropping to the floor while witnesses were passing out and throwing up. It reportedly took ten minutes for the condemned man to finally die and when he was taken down it was found that his face had been badly mutilated by the noose. The man's face was purple with his eyes protruding and his tongue was swollen and hanging from his mouth.

By the Twentieth Century the executioners in the United States were employing a formula, which had been developed by the U.S. Army to calculate the fatal drop according to the condemned man's weight, height and physique. In general, the heavier the man, the shorter the drop and conversely the lighter individual required a much longer drop.

The force of the calculated drop combined with the proper positioning of the hangman's knot below the victim's left ear was designed to break the prisoner's neck and cause instant unconsciousness, followed by a quick death. If the drop was too short the spinal cord may not be severed while too much of a drop may result in decapitation. In an attempt to eliminate either of these results the "Drop Distance Table" shown below was eventually established.

DROP DISTANCE TABLE

Person's Weight	Required Drop	Person's Weight	Required Drop
120 or less	8' 1"	170	6' 0
125	7' 10"	175	5' 11"
130	7' 7"	180	5' 9"
135	7' 4"	185	5' 7"
140	7' 1"	190	5' 6"
145	6' 9"	195	5' 5"
150	6' 7"	200	5' 4"
155	6' 6"	205	5' 2"
160	6' 4"	210	5' 1"
165	6' 2"	220 and over	5' 0"

More men were hanged on the Trap-Type Gallows than any other system in Montana. In all, forty-four men were executed on this type of scaffold from August of 1875 to September of 1943. Ten of the sixteen Territorial executions were conducted on the Trap-Type Gallows and they were used exclusively until 1881 when the first Jerk-Type Scaffold was employed.

The Trap Gallows fell out of favor during the latter years of the Territory because the simpler Jerk-Type scaffold was more economical to build. After statehood the Trap System was used primarily during the first five years and then it once again gave way to the simpler Jerk-Type.

Of the thirty-nine men executed in Montana during the Twentieth Century, twenty-five were hanged with a Drop-Type Gallows and because they were perceived to be more humane, they were used for the last fifteen hangings. The following are the convicted murderers who were hanged through a trap.

Victims of the Trap-Type Gallows:

William Wheatley (*) (8/13/1875)
William Sterres (*) (10/28/1875)
Michael McAndrews (3/1/1878)
Francois Robert (*) (10/31/1878)
Joseph Koble (10/6/1879)
Orlando Marsh (10/6/1879)
Peter Pelkey (2/4/1881)
Henry Furhmann (5/2/1883)
Ah Yung* (8/16/1883)
John Clark* (12/27/1883)
Antley* (12/19/1890)
La La See* (12/19/1890)
Pascale* (12/19/1890)
Pierre Paul* (12/19/1890)
John Burns* (12/16/1892)
Robert Anderson (**) (7/13/1894)
John Osnes (7/13/1894
Calvin Christie (12/21/1894)
Thomas Salmon (**) (1/27/1899)
Frederick LeBeau (4/2/1909)
Leslie Fahley*** (2/16/1917)
Harrison Gibson*** (2/16/1917)
Henry Hall*** (2/16/1917)
Frank Fisher (***) (1/14/1918)
John O'Neil (***) (1/14/1918)
Sherman Powell (***) (1/14/1918)
Juan Cuellae**** (4/12/1918)
Alfred Lane (***) (9/3/1920)
Albert Yeik (8/26/1921)
Glenna Bolton (***) (2/9/1923)
Joseph Reagin (***) (2/9/1923)
Monte Harris (***) (4/20/1923)
William Harris (***) (4/20/1923)
Seth Danner + (7/18/1924)
Roy Walsh (***) (2/14/1925)
Anthony Vettere (***) (10/1/1926)
Ferdinand Schlaps (5/20/1927)
Rollin Davisson + (11/6/1929)
George Hoffman (***) (8/29/1933)
Henry Zorn (***) (4/24/1935)
George Criner (***) (10/16/1935)
Frank Robideau (***) (1/15/1938)
Lee Simpson (***) (12/30/1939)
Philip Coleman**** (9/10/1943)

Unless otherwise noted, the gallows were a freestanding scaffold with a suspended platform and an overhead beam from which the condemned was suspended after he fell through the trap.

* The traditional freestanding gallows with the traditional thirteen steps
(*) Galloping Gallows
** Converted from trap to jerk-type
*** Traditional freestanding trap adapted for an indoor hanging
**** Trap custom built to be used in the jail
\+ Built-In Gallows

Built-in Trap Gallows

Three Montana counties, Cascade, Gallatin and Park had built-in gallows installed in their jail buildings but only two, the ones at Bozeman and Livingston were ever used to take a life of a convicted murderer. Seth Danner was hanged inside the jailhouse at Bozeman in July of 1924, and Rollin Davisson was executed at Livingston in November of 1929. Both executions were described as well done, and while we don't know how long it took for Danner to die, it only took three minutes for Davisson to expire, making his the second fastest hanging death on record.

Although the built in gallows in the Cascade County Jail at Great Falls was never used, it came close in the 1980's when Pondera County made arrangements to utilize the facility to hang Duncan McKenzie who was convicted of kidnapping and murder in 1975. While there was very little preparations required for the hanging of McKenzie at Great Falls, the prisoner during his many years on death row at the county jail at Conrad had put on a huge amount of weight, and in some people's view, for the purpose of cheating the gallows. The condemned man had gotten so large that he was unable to walk and when it was feared that he would suffer decapitation on the scaffold the hanging was cancelled.

The Duncan McKenzie case was instrumental in the State Legislature's move to change the capital punishment statutes of the state, which provided that lethal injection would be the means of execution and all executions in the state would be conducted within the walls of the State Penitentiary. After eight separate sentencing dates and twenty years on death row, Duncan McKenzie was finally executed by lethal injection in May of 1995, at Deer Lodge.

Jerk-Type Gallows

Over the years this form of scaffold was also referred to as the "New York Gallows," "Drop Weight," "Sudden Suspension," "Jerk Up" or the "Patent Weight System." Which ever name was used, the system utilized a heavy weight dropping from a platform, which jerked the condemned man off of his feet, which was intended to snap his neck either from the initial lift or the rebounding fall.

According to some records, the Jerk-Type gallows was first used in the United States to hang William E. Udderzook in West Chester, Pennsylvania in 1874, but it wasn't utilized in Montana until May of 1881 when it took the life of John Douglas at Virginia City. Initially the hangman's rope was merely thrown over a beam and the victim was jerked up when the weight was dropped as was the case in the Douglas hanging but eventually the gallows were constructed utilizing a series of two or more pulleys attached to the underside of the overhead beam through which the rope ran from the hangman's noose to a large weight.

In some cases elaborate mechanisms were used to release the weights from their perch and many styles of enclosures were constructed to conceal both the weight and the executioner from the witnesses. The various county authorities used a number of different items for the heavy drop including sheets of tin, window irons or weights, scrap and custom molded lead. In an effort to keep the identity of the executioner anonymous they were stationed inside of an enclosure and at times more than one man would be hidden so that no one would no which person had actually cut the cord.

Some Montana sheriffs would have a small hole dug directly beneath the noose to increase the distance between the crossbeam and the ground, giving them an extra twelve inches before the victim's toes touched the ground. In at least one case the condemned man was placed on a platform, which was then pulled away after the weight was dropped having the same effect as a hole dug in the ground.

For many years the "Jerk Type" Gallows were very popular because of their simple design and low cost of construction but shortly after the Twentieth Century they were perceived to be less humane than the traditional Trap Scaffolds. Our research, however, indicates that on

Sketch of the Jerk-Type Gallows used in the hanging of Joseph Allen at Helena in 1899
"Anaconda Standard" 9/12/1899

average, death was actually quicker on the Jerk-Type Gallows but their reputation was harmed by a number of high-profile hangings.

While Montana used the Jerk-Type Gallows for the last time in February of 1922, to execute Joseph Vuckovich, the state of Connecticut used the system up until 1926, when Gerald Chapman was hanged.

Victims of the Jerk-Type Gallows:

John Douglas (5/27/1881)
Thomas Harding* (3/25/1887)
John Hart* (2/10/1888)
Martin Scott* (2/17/1888)
George Bryson* (8/9/1889)
Harry Roberts* (8/23/1889)
Thomas King* (6/6/1890)
Joseph Hurst** (3/30/1900)
William Pepo* (4/6/1900)
Daniel Lucy* (9/14/1900)
James Fleming* (9/6/1901)
Clinton Dotson* (4/4/1902)
James Martin* (2/23/1904)
Louis Mott* (3/18/1904)

(Victims of the Jerk-Type Gallows continued)

Clay Pugh* (7/1/1895)
Joseph Cadotte* (12/27/1895)
William Biggerstaff* (4/6/1896)
William Gay* (6/8/1896)
Joseph Allen* (9/14/1899)
William Brooks** (11/24/1899)
William Wallace (3/18/1900)
Herbert Metzger* (5/5/1905)
Lu Sing* (4/20/1906)
Miles Fuller* (5/18/1906)
George Rock* (6/15/1908)
William Hayes* (4/2/1909)
Joseph Vuckovich* (2/17/1922)

*Galloping Gallows
** Galloping Gallows converted from trap scaffold

Conversions (From Trap-Type to a Jerk-Type Gallows)

There has been at least one occasion where a sheriff has converted a Trap-Type Gallows into a Jerk or Lift-Type Scaffold to hang a man in his jurisdiction. In this particular case the sheriff had recently witnessed an execution in other county and he apparently gained a preference for the jerk variety. After the scaffold had been converted it remained a Jerk Gallows and it was used again by another sheriff.

For the hanging of William Brooks In November of 1899, Yellowstone County Sheriff Hubbard ordered the Trap-Type scaffold built at Livingston in 1894, to hang execute Robert Anderson be converted to a Jerk Type Gallows. This conversion was relatively simple as only the two uprights and the crossbeams were needed from the original scaffold and then pulleys were installed to the underside of the overhead beam. In March of 1900, the converted gallows was used for the last time to hang Joseph Hurst at Glendive.

"Galloping Gallows"

To be considered a "Galloping Gallows," the scaffold or the vital components of the contraption had to be used to hang men in at least two different jurisdictions. For the execution of Francois Robert at Virginia City in 1878, only the all important trap mechanism was transported from Helena and only the pulleys and drop weight was sent from Butte to Missoula for the Joseph Vuckovich hanging in 1922.

Of the six known "Galloping Gallows" used in Montana, three were of the trap variety, two were Jerk Type and one started out as a drop but it was converted to a jerk-up gallows. Although more men met their fate on a drop scaffold, the jerk-type variety of "Galloping Gallows" was used to hang twenty-five convicted murderers while twenty-two were executed through a trap.

Individual Gallows History

The following are the descriptions, histories and lists of victims of the twenty-two gallows used in Montana. These individual scaffold profiles have been numbered in chronological order by either when they were constructed or used. Scaffolds that were used for hangings in other counties have also been assigned an individual "Galloping Gallows" number. To better identify these individual scaffolds and to track the various "Galloping Gallows" used in Montana these "Identification Numbers" are utilized throughout the chapters dealing with legal hangings.

These Gallows are described by type, location and include as much detail as is available. If the gallows were used for more than one hanging, or employed as a "Galloping Gallows," the changes and alterations made to the original design are described if known. Besides type, location, and the description of the scaffold, if a particular gallows was unique in any way this "Distinction" is also noted.

The most complete history possible of the scaffolds is provided and while very little is known about many of the Montana Gallows, in some cases the designer, contractor, carpenters and even the painters of the individual death machines have been identified. Lastly the final disposition of the gallows is included if known as well as the location of any remnants of the scaffold.

Gallows No. One: (August 1863)

Type: Simple hoist or drop type
Location: The first gallows to be used for a hanging in Montana was located in Hangman's Gulch, which ran at right angles to Bannack's lone street. The scaffold stood between fifty and seventy-five yards from where the Meade Hotel later stood at Bannack.[1] The notorious Sheriff Plummer originally built the scaffold for the execution of Peter Heron in August of 1863, and within eleven months the gallows was used to hang four other men including the sheriff himself.
Description: The gallows stood about ten feet tall and consisted of two large posts embedded about three feet in the earth with a sturdy twelve-foot crossbeam from which the hangman's rope was suspended. The victim could be hanged by securing the rope to the overhead beam and dropped or hoisted up from the ground.
Distinction: Technically this was the second scaffold constructed in Montana but it was the first to take a man's life. John X. Beidler and Dick Sipe[2] built the first gallows at Virginia City in July of 1863, for the execution of Buck Stinson and Haze Lyons but the scaffold was never used as the judgment of a Miners' Court was overruled by a vote of the miners.
Remnants and Relics: Although the scaffold was chopped down in 1865, two chunks of the support posts, each about three feet long still exist today. One piece of gallows is on display at the Beaverhead County Museum at Dillon while the other has a home in the Masonic Grand

Lodge of Montana at Helena.

Victims: **Peter Heron** (8/25/1863) Miners' Court
Sheriff Henry Plummer (1/10/1864) Original Vigilantes
Ned Ray (1/10/1864) by the Original Vigilantes
Buck Stinson (1/10/1864) by the Original Vigilantes
R.C. Rawley (10/30/1864) by the Original Vigilantes

While Heron was dropped from the back of a wagon, Ned Ray and Buck Stinson were hoisted up "Naval Fashion and Sheriff Plummer was dropped from the shoulders of several Vigilantes while others held the rope taunt.

A few months after the hanging of R.C. Rawley the Vigilantes of Bannack, as a joke, had warned a local drunk Cornishman by the name of Davey Morgan, that he had better mend his ways or he would meet the same fate as Henry Plummer. Apparently Old Davey took them seriously and under the cover of darkness one night in 1865 he chopped the famous gallows down.

The next day, after again getting himself drunk, Morgan began admitting to the deed, bragging that the Vigilantes wouldn't be able to hang him now. This was the same Davey Morgan that was caught in the cabin looking over the dead bodies of Plummer, Ray, Stinson and "Dutch John" with a lighted match in January of 1864. Unfortunately whisky finally got the best of Old Davey Morgan and he eventually died at the insane asylum at Warm Springs.[3]

The story of the ancient gallows didn't end there however as time, weather and souvenir hunters all took a toll on the stumps of the old gallows. Then when the stumps became a hazard to the local children as they slid down the nearby hillside on their sleds they were eventually cut off at ground level.

In 1942, the Dillon Mason Lodge No. 16 formed a committee made up of Harry C. Graves, Dale Tash, S.P. Meade, Fielding H. Graves and W.F. Shaffner to locate the gallows and in July the men traveled to Bannack. From his recollections of when he was a youngster sledding near the stumps, Harry Graves was able to point out the general location and the old relics were indeed found by the party among the sagebrush and the following year Dale Tash removed them and took them to the lodge at Dillon.[4]

The two stumps, which were about three feet long, were kept at the lodge at Dillon until the opening of the Beaverhead County Museum when one of the ancient remnants of the famous gallows was donated to its collection. The Dillon lodge apparently loaned the remaining stump to the Grand Lodge at Helena, which displayed it for a while and over the years has claimed the relic as their own. It reportedly is presently in storage in the basement at the lodge at Helena.[5]

Gallows No. Two: (Aug. 1875): "Galloping Gallows" No. One

Type: Trap
Location: This scaffold was originally built inside a high-fence enclosure at Helena for the first legal execution of Montana Territory, that of William Wheatley in August of 1875.
Description: Prior to 1875, the only other scaffold used in the territory had been a Hoist-Type Gallows at Bannack where five men were hanged. A Miners' Court had ordered the execution of John Heron in 1863 and the Original Vigilantes hanged Sheriff Plummer, Ned Ray, Buck Stinson and R.C. Rawley the following year.

By the time Lewis and Clark County Sheriff Seth Bullock was ordered by the District Court to construct the first gallows to be used in a legal execution in Montana, the Helena chapter of the "Hometown Vigilantes" had already hanged at least twenty-one suspected criminals. Thirteen of the victims of the local vigilance committee had been hanged from the limb of the famous "Hangman's Tree" in Dry Gulch.

Because the basic design of the Hoist-Type Gallows was meant to resemble the branch of a tree, Sheriff Bullock probably wanted to distance his form of legal justice from the mob mentality of the vigilance committee. The "Hometown Vigilantes" were known to either pull their victims up the tree by their necks or drop them off the back of a wagon where they broke their necks when they reached the rope's end.

In 1875, the state-of-the-art scaffold in the American West was the "Free Standing Trap-Type Gallows," which is normally portrayed in western movies with a suspended platform complete with a trapdoor from which the condemned man fell through and was hanged from the tall overhead beam.

The first Gallows used in Montana had a fourteen-foot square platform supported by timbers and standing about eight feet off the ground, which probably accommodated the traditional thirteen steps. The two large upright posts on each side of the platform supported the heavy crossbeam, which was about fifteen feet off the ground and seven above the platform.

The hangman's noose was suspended directly over the three-foot square trapdoor, which was supported on one side by hinges and the other by two heavy lips at the end of an iron rod. On the platform there was a lever that was connected to the iron rod, which was held in place by a small cord. When the cord was cut the lever flew back, which permitted the rod to turn and release the trapdoor. The rope was given enough slack so that the doomed man would fall about four feet, which was generally sufficient to break the neck of a normal sized man.

Victims: **William Wright Wheatley** (8/13/1875) Helena
William H. Sterres (10/28/1875) Helena
Francois Joseph Robert (10/31/1878) Virginia City
Peter Pelkey (Friday 2/4/1881) Helena
Henry Furhmann (5/2/1883) Helena

Apparently for the hanging of Frank Robert, U.S. Deputy Marshal James H. McFarland decided not to utilize the platform, crossbeam and support posts of the Lewis and Clark County scaffold but only borrowed the vital trap mechanism. The Virginia City gallows was probably of the same design to better utilize the protruding lips of a heavy rod and lever.

Gallows No. Three (March 1878)

Type: Trap
Location: This gallows was erected in an enclosure in the yard of the Jefferson County Jail on the hill at Radersburg, which is presently in Broadwater County.
Description: Jefferson County Sheriff Allen M. Easterly ordered the scaffold and enclosure built for the execution of Michael McAndrews on March 1, 1878. While there is no description of this scaffold we have determined that it was of a Trap-Type variety and it was most likely modeled after Helen's ***Gallows No. Two: (August 1875): "Galloping Gallows" No. One***.

Perhaps the crucial trigger and trap mechanism of the Helena scaffold was again used at Radersburg as it was to Virginia City in October of 1878, for the hanging of Frank Robert. There is an outside chance that the Helena scaffold was used at Radersburg but the habit of transporting entire Gallows apparently didn't start for another eight years when the entire ***Gallows No. Eight: (March 1887): "Galloping Gallows" No. Two*** was sent from Dillon to Helena for the execution of John Hart in 1888.

Victim: **Michael McAndrews** (3/1/1878) Radersburg

Gallows No. Four: (September 1879)

Type: Trap
Location: In the jail yard at Fort Benton
Description: While we have no detailed description of this gallows we know it used a trapdoor, which was secured with a heavy staple, which was released when a lever was pulled.
Distinction: Although Wheatley and Sterres were originally sentenced to be hanged together in 1875, but when that didn't occur, this scaffold at Fort Benton was the first to be used for a multiple legal hanging in Montana when Koble and Marsh were executed in 1879.

Victims:
Joseph K. Koble (10/6/1879) Fort Benton
Orlando Marsh (10/6/1879) Fort Benton
John Osnes (7/13/1894) Fort Benton

Gallows No. Five: (May 1881)

Type: Jerk
Location: In the Madison County jail yard at Virginia City
Description: After being charged with the execution of John Douglas in May of 1881, Sheriff Marshal Plantler decided to utilize the Jerk-Type Gallows or "Patent Weight System" as it was known then. The sheriff's decision to use the new style of scaffold was considered the most novel idea since the days of the Vigilantes when out of necessity the executioners used every thing from trees, buildings and fence posts.

The scaffold consisted of a beam suspended about twelve feet off the ground on two uprights, over, which the hangman's rope passed. From the noose, the rope ran into a high, upright box in the corner of the stockade where a 250-pound weight, which was suspended about six feet off the ground along with the unknown executioner.

The condemned man stood on the ground below and slightly to one side of the beam; the noose was placed around his neck leaving about three feet of slack. When the weight was released from its perch the doomed man was jerked into the air, which either broke the man's neck on the way up or on the way back down.
Distinction: This was the first Jerk-Type gallows used in Montana and another such scaffold wasn't used until six years later.
Victims: **John B. Douglas** (5/27/1881) Virginia City

Gallows No. Six: (August 1883)

Type: Trap
Location: Inside the Missoula County Jail yard at Missoula
Description: It was reported that since Sheriff Charles W. Berry wasn't able to secure adequate plans for the building of a scaffold he designed the gallows to hang convicted murderer, Ah Yung himself from scratch. The gallows was erected inside of an enclosure behind the Missoula County Jail.

Sheriff Berry had an eight-foot square platform built eight-feet off the ground so it probably utilized the traditional thirteen steps. With a railing built around the platform the gallows was said to have looked like a judges' stand at a horse racing track. Over the platform however there was a hefty crossbeam erected to support the hangman's noose and enough rope to allow for a drop of about six feet. Directly beneath the crossbeam was a trap door, which was hinged on one side and supported with a crossbar, made of iron. By an ingenious design, the trap was released when the sheriff pulled a lever on the platform.
Victims: **Ah Yung** (8/16/1883) Missoula

Gallows No. Seven: (December 1883)

Type: Trap
Location: Inside the Gallatin County Jail yard at Bozeman
Description: This sturdy pine scaffold at Bozeman stood eighteen feet tall and the entire structure with its braces was twenty foot square. The platform was probably twelve foot-square and since it was about nine feet off the ground it probably had the customary thirteen steps, which were said to have been on the south side of the gallows. The five-eighth inch manila hangman rope was rigged to provide for a drop of seven feet.

Although there was already a twelve-foot brick wall around the jail yard, Sheriff Blakely still ordered a large canvas to be spread around the scaffold to hide the gallows and the doomed man from the prying eyes of unauthorized spectators.

Distinction: This particular scaffold was built specifically for the execution of one convicted murder but it was used to hang another murderer. Carl Adolphson had the distinction of sitting in his jail cell while another man; John A. Clark was executed on the gallows built for him.

Victim: **John A. Clark** (12/27/1883) Bozeman

Gallows No. Eight: (March 1887): "Galloping Gallows" No. Two

Type: Jerk
Location: This gallows was originally set up behind the old Beaverhead County Courthouse for the execution of Thomas Harding in March of 1887.
Description: Beaverhead County Physician H.D. Pickman[6] of Dillon has been credited with designing this Jerk-Type gallows, which at the time was referred to as the "New York" Style Gallows. This was only the second time that this type of gallows was ever used the Montana Territory, the first time being for the execution of John Douglas at Virginia City in 1881. Along with designing the death machine, Dr. Pickman also served as one of the attending physicians at the hanging of Harding.

The scaffold consisted of a six-by-six inch beam resting upon two twelve-foot pine wood posts, which were placed ten feet apart. Two pulleys were attached to the top beam where the rope ran from the hangman's noose to a weight, which originally was a 290-pound box of sheets of tin.

The large weight was suspended from two to four feet off the ground and supported on top of an iron shelf, which was held up by only a small cord. This weight was concealed along with the executioner inside of an enclosure constructed of rough-pine boards near one of the upright posts. Illustrations of the gallows indicate that the uprights were supported at their bases and the entire scaffold was generally attached to one or more of the tall walls of the execution enclosure.

The system was designed to jerk the condemned man off the ground when the heavy weight dropped after the executioner cut the small cord. Sometimes the authorities had a small hole dug beneath the noose in order to increase the distance of the drop to compensate for the stretch in the rope and this depression would then be covered with boards and often a patch of carpeting would be placed over the wood. If the doomed man's feet didn't clear the ground after rebounding back to earth, the officers would simply pull the boards away adding another foot or so. Instead of a hole, some sheriffs had a platform built from which the condemned man would be launched. If the rope stretched unexpectedly, the platform would be pulled away.

The scaffold originally designed by Dr. Pickman went on to execute a total of ten men, and in 1889, the Dillon physician's design was copied to construct ***Gallows No. Nine (Feb 1888): "Galloping Gallows" No. Three*** at Butte. The second gallows was responsible for the deaths of another thirteen convicted murderers across Montana and while the doctor only appears to have been present at one execution, he was ultimately responsible for devising the means of causing the legal deaths of twenty-three men. When one considers that of the seventy-one legal hangings conducted in Montana, Dr. Pickman's design has been credited with over thirty-two percent of all the sanctioned executions.

Like Drs. Joseph Guillotine and Richard Gatling before him, Mr. Pickman's intentions were well meaning. Dr. Guillotine was described as a kind man who merely wanted to design a more humane means of executing criminals and Mr. Gatling had hoped that his revolutionary weapon would help end the Civil War.

When he agreed to design the scaffold for the execution of Thomas Harding in 1887, it is certain that Dr. Pickman wanted to come up with the most humane hanging device possible. What's more, the good doctor most certainly didn't have any idea that his design would be responsible for so many human lives.

Distinction: This was the first Jerk-Type "Galloping Gallows" used in Montana and it was credited with having hanged the second most legally condemned men in the Territory and State.

Victims: **Thomas H. Harding** (3/25/1887) Dillon
John Patrick Hart (2/10/1888) Helena
George Duncan Bryson (8/9/1889) Boulder
Thomas A. King (6/6/1890) Boulder
Clay Pugh (7/1/1895) Boulder
Joseph Cadotte (12/27/1895) Fort Benton
William Biggerstaff (4/6/1896) Helena
William Gay (6/8/1896) Helena
Joseph Allen (9/14/1899) Helena
William Pepo (4/6/1900) Choteau

The gallows was again set up in the Lewis and Clark County Jail yard at Helena for the execution of the Cree Indian by the name of Godas who had been convicted of murdering seventy-two-year-old John Embody in his cabin along the Dearborn River in 1887. While waiting for the Supreme Court to hear his case, Godas escaped from the Helena jail and went to the Northwest Territory where the mounted police captured him. The high court eventually affirmed the ruling of the district court and Godas was re-sentenced to hang on March 8, 1889 but Governor Preston Leslie saved him from the scaffold by commuting his sentence on the day before his execution.[7]

After the Bryson hanging in 1889, the gallows was disassembled and the giant timbers of the scaffold were placed into storage at Boulder where they were again employed to take the life of Thomas King the following year. Then in 1895, Sheriff Gilliam of Jefferson County brought the scaffold out of storage for the execution of Clay Pugh. After witnessing the hanging of Pugh at Boulder, Chouteau County Sheriff George B. McLaughlin had the gallows transported to Fort Benton for the hanging of Joseph Cadotte in December of 1895.

When faced with a potential double hanging in his jurisdiction, Lewis and Clark County Sheriff John Henry Jurgens also attended the execution of Clay Pugh at Boulder in July of 1895, and he later had the ancient gallows transported back to Helena in 1896, for the hanging of William Biggerstaff in April of 1896, and William Gay in June of that same year.

The design of the contraption was such that the gallows could be assembled in two or three hours and it was again brought out of the basement of the Lewis and Clark County Jail to execute Joseph Allen in September of 1899. After attending the Allen hanging at Helena, Teton County Sheriff William D. Hagen made arrangements with Lewis and Clark County Sheriff Davidson to use the tried and tested gallows to hang William Pepo at Choteau in 1900. The county commissioners hired the services of Charles Wymer of Choteau to construct the enclosure in the jail yard and to assemble the infamous gallows. After the successful hanging of Pepo the scaffold was returned to Boulder.

In 1925, Jefferson County Sheriff John Mountjoy considered using the ancient gallows to hang Roy Walsh but instead he borrowed the newer ***Gallows No. Sixteen: (January 1918) "Galloping Gallows" No. Five*** from Silver Bow County. After being used to hang Pepo the old scaffold was eventually returned to Dillon where it reportedly remained in storage gathering dust until the heavy timbers of the scaffold were used in the construction of a new coal bin at the rear of the courthouse.

Gallows No. Nine: (Feb. 1888): "Galloping Gallows" No. Three

Type: Jerk
Location: First used between the Deer Lodge County Courthouse and Jail at Deer Lodge to hang Martin Scott in 1888.
Description: When faced with the responsibility of executing a convicted murderer at Deer Lodge, Sheriff Coleman attended the John Hart hanging at Helena in 1888 in order obtain hands-on experience. Apparently while at Helena Sheriff Coleman was impressed with ***Gallows No. Eight: (Mar. 1887): "Galloping Gallows" No. Two*** and he secured the plans of the scaffold, which Dr. Pickman had originally drawn up in 1887.

Sheriff Lewis Coleman of Deer Lodge County and Silver Bow County Sheriff Lloyd decided to go in with each other on the building of the gallows after they had witnessed the execution of Hart at Helena in February of 1888. Evidently both counties invested in the new gallows, which were built at Butte, but after the hanging of Martin Scott at Deer Lodge the scaffold returned to the Mining City and they became the property of Silver Bow County.

Like the gallows it was modeled after, the new scaffold consisted of a six-by-six inch beam resting upon two twelve-foot pine wood posts, which were placed ten feet apart and when assembled it resembled a child's swing set. Two pulleys were attached to the underside of top crossbeam where the rope ran from the hangman's noose to the large weight, which was concealed along with the executioner inside of an enclosure constructed of rough-pine boards near one of the upright posts. The weight itself was supported atop a projecting iron shelf, which was suspended about two feet off of the ground and held by only a small cord. The noose was suspended from the center pulley on the crossbeam and the condemned man was jerked upward and to one side when the weight was released.

After the Martin Scott hanging the gallows was used for twelve more executions across Montana. Besides being first used at Deer Lodge, four men each were hanged on this scaffold in Silver Bow and Powell Counties, and the gallows was transported to Missoula, White Sulphur Springs and Bozeman for other hangings.

This tried and true killing machine was used in ten straight executions between 1900 and 1909. While the ancient scaffold was never again re-assembled entirely after the1909, execution of William Hayes at Deer Lodge, the all-important weight, trap release and the pulleys were used for the efficient hanging of Joseph Vuckovich at Missoula in February of 1922.
Distinction: With its thirteen victims, this particular "Galloping Gallows" was the top killing machine in the Territory and State and it was used in more executions than any other man-made scaffold in Montana and equaled the record for hangings on the famous "Hangman's Tree" at Dry Gulch near Helena.

Victims: **Martin Luther Scott** (2/17/1888) Deer Lodge
W.H. "Harry" Roberts (8/23/1889) Butte
Daniel Lucy (9/14/1900) Butte
James Fleming (9/6/1901) Deer Lodge
Clinton Dotson (4/4/1902) Deer Lodge
James Martin (2/23/1904) Butte
Louis Mott (3/18/1904) Missoula
Herbert Metzger (5/5/1905) White Sulphur Springs
Lu Sing (4/20/1906) Bozeman
Miles Fuller (5/18/1906) Butte
George Rock (6/15/1908) Deer Lodge
William Hayes (4/2/1909) Deer Lodge
Joseph Vuckovich (2/17/1922) Missoula

Gallows No. Ten: (December 1890)

Type: Trap
Location: First built for the multiple hanging of the four Indians at Missoula in December of 1890, and it was also used to execute John Burns in 1892.
Description: When the four Indians, Pierre Paul, La La See, Antley and Pascale were sentenced to be hanged, Missoula County Sheriff William Houston had just two months to come up with a Gallows to execute them in December of 1890.

Sheriff Houston contacted the authorities at Cook County, Illinois who had executed four anarchists in November of 1887, for the murder of several Chicago policemen. Apparently Cook County Sheriff Seth Hanchett was very cooperative as he obviously provided plans, sketches and advice concerning the huge gallows as well as presenting Sheriff Houston with the four hangman's ropes used in the 1887 execution.

Fireman R. S. "Bob" Mentrum, who later became the fire chief at both Missoula and Anaconda and then state fire marshal was hired by Missoula County to and build the scaffold. While the Cook County Gallows[9] was built inside the jail building at Chicago, Mr. Mentrum's design was for a freestanding scaffold erected in the jail yard.

The gallows consisted of two upright timbers mortised to a crosspiece lying on the ground, and at the top, fifteen feet above the lower crossbeam, another beam, which was about twelve feet long was mortised and bolted into the uprights. About three feet up the upright timbers there were braces securing them to the ground reportedly making the structure strong enough to hoist a locomotive.

The huge platform of the Chicago gallows was accessed from the second tier of the cells but for the Missoula scaffold Mr. Mentrum constructed stairs utilizing twelve risers with the traditional thirteenth step being the twelve-foot square platform itself. Judging from sketches of the Chicago gallows, the huge trapdoor was nearly seven feet wide and extended about four feet to the edge of the platform.

When released, the large trap on the gallows dropped forward towards the witnesses providing an unobstructed view of the hanging bodies. Four heavy iron hinges supported the trapdoor on one side and it was held up on the other by a strong rope, which passed through pulleys underneath the platform. In order to conceal the trap mechanism the entire platform was skirted except for in front of the trap.

Mr. Mentrum designed the trap to drop when a small cord was chopped when the sheriff stepped on a button on theway down the stairs. The hangman ropes passed through individual noose bolts, which were fastened to the underside of the crossbeam and then they were secured to the two uprights. Mentrum was called in to rebuild a smaller version of the gallows in 1892, for the hanging of John Burns.

Distinction: This scaffold has the distinction of being the largest ever constructed in Montana and it was used for executing the most men at the same time, four in 1890.

Victims: **Pierre Paul** (12/19/1890) Missoula
La La See (12/19/1890) Missoula
Antley (12/19/1890) Missoula
Pascale (12/19/1890) Missoula
John Burns (12/16/1892) Missoula

Gallows No. Eleven: (July 1894): "Galloping Gallows" No. Four

Type: Originally built as a Trap Type in 1894, but it was converted to a Jerk-Type Scaffold for the November 1899, execution of William Brooks at Billings.

Location: Originally built at Livingston in 1894, for the hanging of Robert Anderson.

Description: The sturdy scaffold stood eighteen feet tall and with a twelve-foot square platform standing nine feet off the ground it provided for an eight foot drop and probably had the traditional thirteen steps.

Victims: **Robert Anderson** (7/13/1894) Livingston
Thomas Salmon (1/27/1899) Red Lodge
William Brooks* (11/24/1899) Billings
Joseph Hurst* (3/30/1900) Glendive

*Hanged after it had been converted to a Jerk-Type Gallows

Gallows No. Twelve: (December 1894)

Type: Trap

Location: Originally built in the Flathead County Jail yard at Kalispell for the execution of Calvin Christie in December of 1894.

Description: No description has been found of this particular scaffold other than that it utilized a trapdoor. The same man who built the original gallows for the Christie hanging re-built the scaffold for the LeBeau execution.

Distinction: This scaffold was used for both of the legal hangings in Flathead County.

Victims: **Calvin Christie** (12/21/1894) Kalispell
Frederick LeBeau (4/2/1909) Kalispell

Gallows No. Thirteen: (March 1900)

Type: Jerk Type
Location: Fergus County Jail yard at Lewistown
Description: For the execution of William Calder and Eli Fisher at Lewistown in May of 1899, Sheriff Thomas M. Shaw ordered the simplest of the gallows, the Jerk-Type scaffold and large enough for the double hanging. The finished gallows, which was finally used to hang Calder in March of 1900, consisted of three beveled six by six-inch black timbers and a crossbeam supported twelve feet off the ground by the two uprights. Four wood and steel pulleys like the ones found in barns to hoist hay were attached to the bottom of the crossbeam, which the two ropes were to pass to hang the two condemned men.

When Fisher gained a new trial and was saved from the gallows, only two of the four pulleys were utilized for the Calder execution and the rope was allowed thirty inches of slack. To insure against error in rope length or stretch, a hole was dug beneath the noose, which was covered by three large boards. The board covering was about three feet wide and it had a rope attached to it so that it could be easily pulled away if needed. The 308-pound weight, which consisted of a box of scrap metal, was held at the left of the scaffold by a pin that was released by Fergus County Sheriff Shaw who was hidden behind a sheet of canvas.

In 1905, Meagher County Sheriff Sherman had considered using the Lewistown scaffold for the execution of Herbert Metzger at White Sulphur Springs before learning that it had been damaged during the construction of the new Fergus County Courthouse. Sheriff Sherman eventually used the tried and true ***Gallows No. Nine: (Feb 1888): Galloping Gallows" No. Three*** and the timbers of the Lewistown gallows were never used again.

Victim: William Wallace Calder (3/16/1900) Lewistown

Gallows No. Fourteen: (March 1912)

Trap: Trap
Location: Built in the Gallatin County Jail
Description: While the other gallows of the state were typically built or borrowed just before the scheduled execution, the gallows, which was used to hang Seth Danner in July of 1924, was a built-in feature of the Gallatin County Jail, which was opened in 1911. The scaffold was built in a small room in the jail and the steel trap was on a railed balcony at the top of a concrete staircase.

About five months before the execution, Sheriff Smith was allowed to have extra platforms erected on each side of the built-in death trap to accommodate the officers and these extensions were re-enforced with iron pipes secured from the ceiling to the basement floor. To prevent the witnesses below from seeing the death machine before the hanging, the trap was covered by a black curtain and a deputy entered the room and raised the curtain just as Danner and the other officers entered. The balcony where the condemned man was dropped was only large enough to accommodate Sheriff Smith and two guards along with the prisoner.

As was customary, the identity of the executioner who released the trap, which killed Seth Danner was unknown even to the two men, assigned the task. Two separate ropes led from the gallows, one going to the basement while the other went into an adjoining room. At a given signal from the sheriff both ropes were pulled and the trap was sprung. Only one of the ropes was actually attached to the release mechanism and neither man knew who had pulled the fatal trigger.

Relics and Remnants: A newer facility eventually replaced the old jail building at Bozeman, which now houses the Gallatin County Historical Society Pioneer Museum. Another building with a built-in gallows still in existence is the former Cascade County Jail at Great Falls.

Victim: <u>**Seth Danner**</u> (7/18/1924) Bozeman

<u>Gallows No. Fifteen: (February 1917)</u>

Type: Trap

Location: Inside the large barn belonging to the Meagher County Jail at White Sulphur Springs.

Description: To accommodate the three condemned men at one time, a four by eight-foot heavy trapdoor was cut through the upper floor of the jail barn, which provided for a drop of seven feet.

Because of a hiatus of nearly eight years without a legal hanging in Montana, there weren't any operating gallows available in the state when three black men were sentenced to hang in Meagher County in February of 1917. There was an ancient scaffold at White Sulphur Springs, which had been built by R.S. Price and Dan Hurd to hang Joseph W. Hanna or "Toe String Joe" in 1884, but the prisoner managed to escape from the jail on the night before his scheduled execution. Hanna was eventually located at Crawfordville, Indiana, but the county commissioners didn't want to go through the expense of returning him to Montana.

The old trap-type scaffold was again erected to execute Charles J. Wooster in 1892, but he also managed to cheat the old gallows by hanging himself in his cell. The first man to be sentenced to hang in Meagher County, the Chinaman, Henry Lee managed to cut his way out of the log jail with another prisoner before the sheriff had even gotten started on a gallows. After an inspection of the untried ancient gallows, the timbers of the scaffold were found to be warped out of shape and so another killing machine had to be brought to White Sulphur to execute Herbert Metzger in May of 1905.

The thirty-three-year-old and derelict gallows remained silent and forgotten in county storage until 1917, when Sheriff George B. Nagues called on his resident gallows builder, Dan Hurd to salvage what he could from the ancient relic and devise a makeshift gallows inside the barn of the Meagher County Jail. Utilizing the trap hinges and release mechanism from the old gallows, Mr. Hurd built the eight by four-foot trap on the second floor, which provided for a seven-foot drop.

There was a narrow stairway leading up to the upper floor of the garage where the three prisoners took their places on squares marked

on the four by eight-foot trap and just forty-three minutes ticked off from the time they had reached their assigned spots until their bodies were placed in coffins and buried in the local Potters Field.
Relics and Remnants: The entire barn where the executions took place was eventually donated to the museum at Nevada City and is displayed as the "Gallows Barn."
Victims: **Leslie Fahley** (2/16/1917) White Sulphur Springs
Harrison Gibson (2/16/1917) White Sulphur Springs
Henry Hall (2/16/1917) White Sulphur Springs

Gallows No. Sixteen: (Jan. 1918): "Galloping Gallows No. Five

Type: Trap
Location: Originally built in the Silver Bow County Jail yard.
Description: In January of 1918, Silver Bow County found themselves in the same predicament that Meagher County had faced the year before, multiple condemned men to execute with no available gallows. Since the county's famous, ***Gallows No. Nine: (February 1888) "Galloping Gallows" No. Three*** had been retired after the hanging of William Hayes at Deer Lodge in April of 1909, Silver Bow County Sheriff O'Rourk found himself in need of a new scaffold to execute Frank Fisher, John O'Neil and Sherman Powell.

The sheriff put Under Sheriff Jack Melia in charge of the execution including coming up with the design and the construction of the new killing machine. Deputy Melia enlisted the help of T.O. Angell who ran a hat factory at Butte at the time to draw up the plans for a new Trap-Type gallows.

In order to make room for the gallows, the old jail kitchen building, which was a small frame structure against the north wall of the old county jail building, was demolished. The new timbers for the scaffold were delivered to the county jail on January 11, 1918, and the carpenters immediately began on the gallows and the high temporary board fence to enclose the extreme northeast corner of the jail yard. The new gallows was tested the day before the execution by placing three dummies, which closely corresponded with the three condemned men's weight. When the trap was tripped it reportedly released smoothly and the heavy beam supporting the five hundred and fifty pounds didn't even shudder.

The new gallows was originally built over the stone stairway leading down to the basement of the new Silver Bow County Jail, which acted as the pit for the gallows. The stairway was about eight feet deep and the ten by ten-foot platform built of heavy timbers was constructed over it. There were thirteen steps leading to the platform and the sturdy overhead beam, which supported the three ropes, was about seven feet above the trap.

The four by eight-foot trapdoor consisted of two doors that separated in the middle. This split-door design eliminated the possibility of the condemned men from twisting, swerving, slipping or loosing their balance as they dropped. The doomed men stood on the trap about two and a half feet apart and by pulling a single stout lever the dual doors were opened when two heavy supporting beams were tripped.

When Sheriff Duggan decided to hold the execution of Monte and William Harris inside the jail of the Silver Bow County Courthouse, he needed to convert the old 1918, freestanding Gallows for the indoor hangings. For the modifications of the scaffold, the sheriff called on Mr. T.O. Angell who had drawn up the original plans of the gallows to erect the death machine for the double hanging and he and his crew prepared it in the basement of the Silver Bow County Courthouse.

The scaffold was then placed in the northwestern end of the third floor of the jail building above the cells of the condemned men and it was designed so that the doomed men would fall into the foyer near the main entrance.

Distinction: The execution of Fisher, O'Neil and Powell was the first and only time that the gallows as well as the condemned men were concealed from the witnesses until the actual time of their hanging.

Relics and Remnants: After its last victim in 1933, the gallows was returned to Butte where it is currently in storage in the basement of the Silver Bow County Courthouse. Because the scaffold is being stored with possible hazardous material the ancient death machine is not available for viewing.

Victims: **Frank Fisher** (1/14/1918) Butte
John O'Neil (1/14/1918) Butte
Sherman Powell (1/14/1918) Butte
Monte Harris (4/20/1923) Butte
William Harris (4/20/1923) Butte
Roy Walsh (2/14/1925) Boulder
Anthony Vettere (10/1/1926) Butte
George Hoffman (8/29/1933) Choteau

Gallows No. Seventeen: (April 1918)

Type: Trap

Location: Set up inside the Yellowstone County Jail to hang Juan Cuellae in 1918.

Description: The scaffold was a short distance from the condemned man's cell at the county jail and it consisted of a platform built out over the top of the second floor handrail. There were four steps leading up to the platform where the trap operated on hinges and it was secured by a two-by-four with a long lever attached to it. The executioner, who stood next to the condemned man, released the trap and the deed was done. The ordinary five-eighth inch manila rope was suspended from an iron hook that was secured to the ceiling of the jail.

Victim: **Juan Cuellae** (4/12/1918) Billings

Gallows No. Eighteen: (Sept. 1920): "Galloping Gallows" No. Six

Type: Trap
Location: While this particular gallows was constructed as a freestanding scaffold in September of 1920, for the execution of Alfred Lane inside of the Rosebud County Jail Building at Forsyth, it was adapted twice to fit inside the Miles City jail.
Description: There were thirteen steps leading up to the platform of the original gallows, which was constructed of heavy timbers. The timbers were bolted together for easy take down and re-assembly. In some cases a canvas covering was wrapped around the platform in order to conceal the victim's body after it had fallen through the trap.
Relics and Remnants: While this isn't the only surviving gallows in Montana, it is the only scaffold in the state that is assembled and on display. Currently the scaffold can be viewed in the old auditorium of the old state penitentiary and is part of the prison museum.
Victims: **Alfred Lane** (9/3/1920) Forsyth
Glenna Bolton (2/10/1923) Hysham
Joseph Reagin (2/10/1923) Hysham
Henry Zorn (4/24/1935) Miles City
George Criner (10/16/1935) Miles City
Frank Robideau (1/15/1938) Columbus
Lee Simpson (12/30/1939) Ryegate

Gallows No. Nineteen: (August 1921)

Type: Trap
Location: Inside a small enclosure between the Beaverhead County Courthouse and the jail. The door of the jail opened into the execution enclosure and members of the murdered man's family witnessed the hanging from inside the sheriff's office through the windows.
Description: This massive scaffold stood thirteen feet tall and it required two days to be constructed by Dillon carpenters, Art Wimple and Jay Holtz. The scaffold was built in advance of the execution and was erected the day before the hanging over a large pit, which was dug in the jail yard. There were six steps leading up to the gallows and the trap was sprung by a rope, which passed under the scaffold, under the fence of the enclosure and into a tent where the executioner was concealed from the public. Several electric lights were especially strung up around the gallows, which reportedly added a weird somberness to the quiet crowd.
Victim: **Albert Yeik** (8/26/1921) Dillon

After the execution of Albert Yeik in 1921, the gallows was placed into storage at the Beaverhead County Fairgrounds, but know one knows for sure what ever happened to the huge timbers. The hanging site itself was eventually paved over and was part of the rear parking lot of the county courthouse.

Gallows No. Twenty: (May 1927)

Type: Trap
Location: Inside of an enclosure built next to the Roosevelt County Jail.
Description: Sheriff John Anderson and Under Sheriff Charles Council of Roosevelt County went about the grim task of preparing for the hanging of Ferdinand Schlaps several weeks before his scheduled execution on May 20, 1927.

The structure was approximately twelve feet high and consisted of two upright timbers each supported by two brace planks each and the platform itself. The large crossbeam, from which the rope was secured, sat atop the two uprights and there were six steps leading up to the platform.

Normally when such a short platform was used a pit was dug beneath the gallows to accommodate a longer drop and Sheriff Anderson and his deputies also had an eighteen-foot fence built around the jail yard to conceal the execution.

Victim: **Ferdinand Schlaps** (5/20/1927) Wolf Point

Gallows No. Twenty-One: (October 1929)

Type: Trap
Location: This built-in gallows was about fifteen feet from the death cell of the Park County Jail building.
Description: The first courthouse built at Livingston in July of 1896, didn't include any prison facilities and county inmates had to be housed at the city jail. Sometime after the second courthouse was built a double-door trap gallows was installed in the floor of the second story of the building. The trapdoor was located next to the door leading into the jury room just above the entrance to the sheriff's office, which was on the ground floor. The trap was perfectly level with the floor and very few people of Livingston had ever noticed it unless they had served on a jury and passed over it while going to and from the jury room.

To accommodate the hangman's noose, an eyelet was installed in the ceiling of the jail directly above the gallows and the trapdoor was designed to drop by its own weight and it was operated with a lever, which looked like a gearshift of an automobile of the 1920's. The jail building was eventually demolished in the 1970's and replaced with a new courthouse structure. There are two jail buildings still standing in Montana, which has a built-in gallows, the former Cascade County Jail and the one at Bozeman, which is presently the home of the Gallatin County Historical Society Pioneer Museum.

Victim: **Rollin Davisson** (11/6/1929) Livingston

Gallows No. Twenty-Two: (September 1943)

Type: Trap
Location: Built in the Missoula County Jail building
Description: When Philip Coleman was sentenced to be hanged at Missoula on September 10, 1943, Sheriff Robert MacLean had less than thirty days to prepare for the execution. The sheriff wanted the deed to be carried out inside of the county jail and on August 22, he received the blueprints of the famous Silver Bow County ***Gallows No. Sixteen: (Jan. 1918): "Galloping Gallows" No. Five***. The sheriff hired a local carpenter to build the custom scaffold just inside the main door of the cellblock of the ancient jail.

After first reviewing the blueprints, the carpenter made a special trip to Butte to get a first-hand glimpse of the gallows and to take measurements of the scaffold. Like the ancient gallows of the Mining City, the Missoula scaffold was constructed of six by six-inch timbers, which were secured with large bolts. A button on the platform controlled the trap, which was located just a few feet from the condemned man's cell, and when pushed a light flashed below in the corridor of the gray brick jail where three men pushed on handles, one of which actually released the trap.

Relics and Remnants: According to George Bukovatz of Butte, U.S. Marshal and former under sheriff of Missoula County, after the execution of Coleman the gallows was dismantled and stored away in the courthouse basement. In 1951, the scaffold was loaded onto a truck and sent to Toole County for an execution there but the condemned man's sentence was eventually commuted. Over the years the location of the Missoula County gallows became unknown, the Toole County authorities saying that the apparatus was returned while officials in the Garden City claimed that they had no idea where it was. Finally in February of 1963, the missing scaffold was located in a dusty pile of lumber in the Cannery Building of the Missoula County Fair Grounds and they have been held at the Historical Museum at Fort Missoula since 1975.
Victim: **Philip Coleman** (9/10/1943) Missoula

(Endnotes)

[1] Information provided by F. Lee Graves through personal interviews with his grandfather, Harry C. Graves as well as Dale Tash and Elvin Thompson.

[2] According to Virginia Rowe in her "Vigilante Woman" the man helping X. Beidler was Richard Todd.

[3] "Bannack, Cradle of Montana" F. Lee Graves

[4] Writings of Fielding H. Graves in the "Plummer File" Beaverhead County Museum, Dillon, MT.

[5] Information from F.L. Graves

[7] "Helena Daily Herald" 3/8/1889, p5

[8] "Silver State" 4/7/1909 reported that the scaffold was built in Butte in 1888 and Scott was the first victim.

[9] The Cook County Gallows were built in 1887 for the hanging of the four anarchists, August Spies, Albert Parsons, George Engle and Adolph Fischer for the murder of seven Chicago policemen during the Haymarket Riot in 1886. The gallows eventually hanged a total of eighty-six men before being retired in June of 1927. They remained in storage for fifty years until Mike Donley purchased them for an undisclosed amount in 1977 for his "Wild West Town" amusement park located northwest of Chicago. The ancient gallows were auctioned off for over sixty-eight thousand dollars in December of 2006 to the Ripleys Museum. "Seattle Times" 12/8/2006

Extra-Legal Hangings

Hanging of Wilson and Compton from the famous "Hangman's Tree" near Helena in 1870
Photo by Madame M.A. Eckert: From the collection of the Montana Historical Society, Helena

Illegal or "Extra-Legal"

Those who refused to consider the hangings conducted by the various groups of Vigilantes and Lynch Mobs as illegal often referred to these executions as "Extra-Legal." There were a total of one hundred and sixty-four "Extra-Legal" or illegal hangings between 1862 and 1913, and we have grouped these executions into five categories: Miners' Courts, the Original Vigilantes of Bannack and Virgnia City, the various chapters of "Hometown Vigilantes" across the Territory, Lynch Mobs and the "Cowboy Stranglers" of 1884.

The following victims are listed below by date, name, location, type of executioners and a brief description of the hanging. A more detailed history of the different types of "Extra-Legal" hangings of Montana as well as the individual cases will be available in "Hanging Around the Big Sky Book Two: Extra-Legal Hangings"

Executions Conducted by Miners' Courts

Colonel Wilbur Sanders arguing during the Ives' Trial in 1863
From the "Anaconda Standard" 12/15/1895

Most Miners' Courts generally dealt with mining matters such as the length of a mining claim and the time allowed a miner to "lay over" without having his claim legally "jumped" by another prospector. Common sense was the law of the mining camps and the miners were expected to work their claim as long as there was running water to operate. No man was required to operate his claim if it couldn't be worked on account of high water, snow or frozen ground. Besides these natural disruptions, mining laws were also established to protect a prospector's claim from being jumped while he was out fighting Indians, out hunting for food or if he was sick. The miners' judge had jurisdiction over all matters civil and criminal, regardless of the dollar amount or the character of the offense.

Without jails[1] in the early gold camps the Miners' Courts obviously were limited to what types of punishments they could sentence on a convicted criminal. The Miners' Courts and later the Vigilante groups found that they could only hang, whip, brand or banish their victims. When there was a question between hanging, whipping or branding, a committee would sometimes be appointed to determine such punishment. While Miners' Courts are often criticized today and are sometimes described as being capricious mobs that inflicted harsh punishments on mere whims, the records indicate otherwise and in Montana this form of authority only hanged eleven men.

August 26, 1862

C.W. Spillman

Location: Gold Creek near Garrison Junction
Description: Spillman was described as being a large, fine looking man.
Crime: Horse Stealing
Distinction: Spillman was the first man reportedly hanged in what later became Montana as will as being the first man executed for stealing a horse. He also had the distinction of being the first man to be sentenced to death by a Miners' Court in Montana Territory.

August 25, 1863

John "Peter" Heron

Other Names: Peter, "Pee" Horan; Peter Herring; Haron
Location: Heron was hanged on **Gallows No. One: (August 1863)** on the outskirts of Bannack. (See Chapter Seven: "Gallows of Montana")
Description: Heron was a native of St. Louis, Missouri
Crime: Heron shot and killed his mining partner, John Lawrence Keeley.
Judge: Judge B.B. Burchett.
Sheriff: Henry Plummer
Distinction: Peter Heron was the first man hanged in Montana on a gallows and he might have been the first to receive religious counsel before his execution. This is also the first hanging where an attending physician was called on to pronounce the executed man's death. In many writings this execution has been described as a legal hanging.

December 21, 1863

George Ives

Location: Ives was hanged from a log beam that was suspended between two cabins about two hundred yards from the center of Nevada City.
Description: Ives was about twenty-seven years old and he was described as being a good-looking man who stood six feet tall with blue eyes and light complexion. When most men wore beards to their waist, Ives remained clean-shaven and was dressed in black along with a soldier's overcoat and he always covered his head with a white felt hat. Over a short span of two or three years George Ives was transformed from being an honest, hardworking young man to a hardened cold-blooded criminal who was absolutely fearless.
Crime: While Ives was a well-known road agent having conducted several holdups including the first robbery of a stage between Virginia City and Bannack with Frank Parish and Bill Bunton he was eventually hanged for the murder of Nicholas "Dutchman" Tiebolt. Ives was implicated as well in the robbery south of Stone's Ranch in November of 1863, with "Whiskey Bill" Graves and Bob Zachary.
Miners' Judge: Don L. Byam of Nevada City was selected as the judge and a miner named Wilson of Junction was assigned to assist him.
Prosecuting Attorneys: The outlaws had hired all of the lawyers in the area to defend George Ives and at first there was no one brave enough to prosecute the case. At that point the miners of Nevada City wanted to hold the trial without lawyers but then Colonel Wilbur F. Sanders of Bannack insisted that the accused should have counsel and that he would prosecute the case. The citizens agreed to Sanders' offer and they selected a miner by the name of Major Charles S. Baggs to assist him.
Defense Attorneys: Harry Percival Adam Smith who had gotten other outlaws off, was assisted by James M. Thurmond, Colonel Wood of Georgia, Alexander Davis and L.F. Ritchie
Court Officers: William Young Pemberton and W.H. Patten were selected as clerks of the court, Robert Hereford, the miners' sheriff of Nevada City was made the chief executive officer of the court and Adriel B. Davis, the miners' sheriff of Junction was assigned to assist him.
Distinction: Over the years this well known hanging has been credited to the Vigilantes but the committee hadn't yet been organized.

February 17, 1864

John Doe, Murderer

Location: Virginia City in Madison County
Crime: Murder
Jurisdiction: People's Court of Virginia City
Judge: Judge Alexander Davis or John Lott
Distinction: This was the only hanging ordered by a People's Court, which differs from the normal Miners' Court in that it was conducted with more standard rules of conduct instead of the "hit-or-miss" procedures used by the miners. Although the two forms of justice had

differences, their similarities were arguably greater and there for this case is included in this section.

June 7, 1865

John Keene

Other Names: Bob Black, John Kean
Location: Murderer's Tree, later known as Hangman's Tree in Dry Gulch at Helena
Crime: The notorious John Keene shot and killed the equally tough Harry Slater through the head on July 6, 1865, while he was sitting on the steps on Bridge Street in downtown Helena.
Miners' Court Judge: Stephen Reynolds
Distinction: Keene had a number of distinctions; he reportedly committed the first murder in the young mining camp of Last Chance Gulch, a Miners' Court tried him but the Hometown Vigilantes were charged with his execution. The unlucky Keene was also the first man to be hanged on what became the famous "Hangman's Tree."
Relics and Remnants: The skull of John Keene was on display at the Montana Historical Society until 1984, and because of later state statutes it was removed from the collection by order of the Montana Preservation Burial Board.

March 12, 1866

Leander W. Johnson

Location: Johnson was hanged from a limb of a tree in Deer Lodge.
Description: The man was said to have been a very neat young man and described as being strong and energetic.
Crime: Johnson was charged with the theft of a steer in the spring of 1866 but the animal eventually showed up after the man was hanged.
Distinction: Not only was Johnson innocent of the crime for which he was hanged, the crime was never committed.

April 20, 1866

J.L. Goones

Other Name: Sam Gowan
Location: Goones was hanged from a tree in German Gulch, sixteen miles west of Butte.
Crime: Goones was hanged for the attempted murder of Hugh "Jack" Dowd who eventually recovered.
Miners' Court Judge: Green Campbell
Distinction: J.L. Goones was the second man hanged in Montana for just wounding his victim. James Brady was hanged by the Original Vigilantes in June of 1864, even when his victim survived.

May 18, 1868

George Ballou

Other Names: George Blue

Location: Ballou was hanged at Reynold's City in what was originally Deer Lodge County but now Powell County.

Crime: Murder of saloon owner, John Gordon on May 17, 1868

August 16, 1868

John Varley

Location: Varley was executed at the head of Dry Gulch near Beartown in what was then a part of Deer Lodge County but presently in Granite County.

Crime: Highway robbery of Julian Guezala on August 12, 1868.

September 2, 1871

Baker

Location: From a butcher's hoist near Keatingville, not far from Radersburg in present day Broadwater County.

Crime: The murder of Dr. Mann at Keatingville on September 2, 1871.

October 31, 1871

John Doe, Chinaman

Location: Mining camp of Henderson Gulch in Granite County

Description: Chinese national

Crime: This man was accused of breaking through the rear door of the camp store at Emmetsburg in the gulch and he was later caught with about three hundred and fifty dollars of the stolen money. The result of the vote of the miners was reportedly nineteen "ayes" and eighteen "nays" and therefore the execution was ordered.

Distinction: Last recorded hanging victim of a Miners' Court in Montana.

Victims of the Original Vigilantes of Bannack and Virginia City

While it was hoped that the execution of George Ives by the miners in December of 1863, would reduce crime in the mining camps, it only served to infuriate as well as galvanize the criminal element. Many of the better-known outlaws openly threatened the honest citizens who had taken part in the hanging of Ives and most of the miners in the area were afraid to talk about the criminal activity in fear that they would wind up dead.

Out of these threats and for self-defense, a "Committee of Safety" or "Vigilance Committees" were established at Virginia City and Bannack. The organization came easy with the leadership and experience of many of the miners who had come from Denver where a similar movement had cleaned up the town, following the example set by the San Francisco Vigilantes. Some of the leaders from Colorado included Paris S. Pfouts, Captain James Williams, Adriel B. Davis, John S. Lott and his brother, Mortimer.

January 4, 1864
George W. Brown

Other Names: "Missouri" Brown
Hanged With: Erastus "Red" Yeager
Location: Brown and Yeager were hanged from a cottonwood tree on the J.B. Lorraine Ranch, which was near the Dempsey's Stage Station not far from Beaverhead Rock in Madison County.
Description: Brown was a twenty-six-year-old native of New York.
Crimes: Committing perjury at the George Ives trial, obstructing Vigilante Justice by warning Alex Carter and in general for lying to the Vigilantes. All of these actions were considered "obstructing Vigilante Justice" and were all punishable by death.
Distinction: George Brown was the first victim of the Original Vigilantes.

January 4, 1864
Erastus Yeager

Other Names: "Red"
Hanged With: George W. Brown.
Location: See: George W. Brown, 1/4/1864
Description: The thirty-two-year-old-old Yeager had a slight build standing about five foot five with dark red hair.
Crime: "Obstructing Vigilante Justice" when he warned Alex Carter and other road agents at Deer Lodge.

January 10, 1864
Henry Amos Plumber

Location: Sheriff Plummer was executed at Bannack with his two deputies, Ned Ray and Buck Stinson.
Description: Granville Stuart described Henry Plummer as being of medium height with a fair complexion. He was about twenty-five years old at the time of his death and he was very polite and genteel.
Crimes: Operating a gang of road agents that robbed and murdered countless individuals in Beaverhead and Madison Counties.
Distinction: Plummer was the first and only elected officer ever hanged in Montana, a fact that might be jokingly regretted by many voters of today.
Relics and Remnants: An approximate three-foot section of one of the upright posts of the gallows on which Plummer was hanged along with Buck Stinson and Ned Ray can be found at the Beaverhead County Museum at Dillon and another similar piece is at the Grand Mason Lodge at Helena. In the collection of the Montana Historical Society at Helena is a shotgun, which belonged to Henry Plummer, possibly the weapon that Granville Stuart had repaired. According to Amede Bessette who donated the weapon, the notorious sheriff had used it to shoot and kill a gambler.

January 10, 1864
Edward S. "Ned" Ray

Other Names: Ed Wray
Location: Ned Ray was executed in Bannack along with Sheriff Henry Plummer and Buck Stinson. Ray was still struggling after Plummer and Stinson had been hanged and he finally strangled to death after the Vigilantes grabbed his freed arm and jerked his fingers from between his neck and the rope.
Description: Ned Ray was a tall, rather slender man and about thirty-five years old at the time of his execution. The New York native usually wore a full suit of cream-colored buckskin, which was liberally trimmed with fringe around the collar and on the bottom. His broad brimmed slouch felt hat partially covered his carrot colored red hair that fell in long and straggly locks to his shoulders. Ned Ray reportedly had a bad foot, which was caused by a gunshot wound he had received during his escape from San Quentin Penitentiary in California. Ray was described as being a soft-spoken man that even the smallest children were comfortable with.
Crime: In his confession to the Vigilantes, "Red" Yeager had named Ned Ray as "council room keeper" or master-at-arms for the Plummer organization. Ray was wanted in Salt Lake City for various crimes and in Montana Territory he was suspected of attempting to rob a man named Leroy Southmayo with Buck Stinson.
Relics and Remnants: An approximate three-foot section of one of the upright posts of the gallows on which Ned Ray was hanged along with Henry Plummer and Buck Stinson can be found at the Beaverhead County Museum at Dillon and the other one is at the Mason Grand Lodge at Helena.

January 10, 1864
I.N. "Buck" Stinson

Location: Stinson was executed at Bannack with Sheriff Henry Plummer and Ned Ray.
The knot in the rope apparently slipped under Stinson's chin and it took several minutes for him to die from strangulation.
Description: It was said that no one would ever call Stinson a coward or handsome. He had large sunken eyes, an upturned nose with a bulging forehead and a slightly protruding chin. He was a well-built man with a light complexion and he kept himself clean-shaven. Although he was a barber by trade, he wore his own hair long and down to his shoulders.
Crimes: Buck Stinson was executed for numerous murders like the killing of "Old Snag," a friendly Bannack or Lemhi Shoshone Indian chief who was just walking through town, and for the gunning down of the only honest lawman in Bannack at the time, Deputy Dillingham with the help from fellow road agents, Haze Lyons and Charlie Forbes. Stinson was also involved in many robberies including the attempted holdup of a man named Leroy Southmayo with Ned Ray.

Relics and Remnants: An approximate three-foot section of one of the upright posts of the gallows on which Buck Stinson was hanged along with Henry Plummer and Ned Ray can be found at the Beaverhead County Museum at Dillon and the other one is at the Mason Grand Lodge at Helena.

January 11, 1864
Joseph Pizanthia

Other Names: "The Greaser"
Location: Before determining if the mortally wounded Pizanthia was dead the angry crowd hanged him from a neighboring clothesline pole at Bannack.
Description: Mexican national
Crime: After the execution of Henry Plummer and his deputies, Ned Ray and Buck Stinson the executive committee of the Original Vigilantes decided to rid Bannack City of its remaining bad characters. At the meeting it was pointed out that one of the men on Red Yeager's list was a young man who had worked at the Rattlesnake Ranch by the name of "Spanish Frank." According to some of the aroused citizens, Frank was living in a small cabin up stream from the Thompson Store.

After successfully executing five members of the dreaded road agent gang, the Vigilantes may have become both over zealous and over confident when they turned their attention on who they thought was "Spanish Frank," but the target of the committee was actually another Mexican by the name of Joe Pizanthia. Although Pizanthia was executed because of a case of mistaken identity, the Vigilantes managed to justify their actions claiming that the Mexican had a reputation of being a robber and a murderer as well associating with members of Plummer's gang at his cabin.

January 11, 1864
John Wagner

Other Names: "Dutch John"
Location: Wagner was hanged in the carpenter shop at Bannack where the bodies of Henry Plummer and Buck Stinson were being kept after their execution.
Description: "Dutch John" Wagner was a German immigrant who was described as being a giant of a man, standing well over six foot tall with dark and swarthy features.
Crime: Wagner had once dreamed of being a horse dealer but he took up crime instead as he was hanged for highway robbery.

The Hanging of Five Road Agents at Virginia City

After first surrounding Virginia City the various committee members of the mining camps of Alder Gulch captured George Lane, Jack Gallagher, Boone Helm, Frank Parish and Haze Lyons. After questioning the prisoners the Vigilantes hanged the outlaws in an unfinished building.

January 14, 1864

George Lane

Other Name: "Clubfoot George" and "Reel Footed George"
Location: Hanged with Jack Gallagher, Boone Helm, Frank Parish and Haze Lyons in an unfinished building at Virginia City.
Description: Lane was a small man who hobbled around awkwardly because he had been born with a muscular paralysis, which prevented his one heel from touching the ground. He was forced to walk on the ball of his right foot and leaned heavily on a cane with each step.
Crime: Lane was accused of marking coaches carrying valuable shipments for the road agents to rob.
Relics and Remnants: Virginia City Mayor Frank Walker kept George Lane's clubfoot in a showcase at city hall until he left office and the relic moved to Walker's "Club Saloon." The gruesome relic was kept in a glass case for many years at Warden's Soft Drink Parlor in downtown Virginia City before it moved in the 1920's to the City Museum located in the Thompson-Hickman Memorial Building.

January 14, 1864

Jack Gallagher

Location: Hanged with "Clubfoot George" Lane, Frank Parish, Boone Helm and Haze Lyons in an unfinished building at Virginia City.
Description: Thirty-year-old Jack Gallagher was a tall, well-built man who was one of Sheriff Henry Plummer's deputies assigned to Virginia City. Jack wore a handsome blue cavalry coat, which had been trimmed with beaver fur. While waiting to be executed Jack and Boone Helm got into a friendly argument over Gallagher's warm coat. Boone accused Gallagher of never giving him anything, and Jack answered back that his disgruntled friend wouldn't need such a warm coat where he was going anyway.
Crime: In his position as a deputy for Sheriff Henry Plummer Gallagher was able to facilitate crimes including the murder of Deputy Dillingham.

January 14, 1864

Boone Helm

Other Names: "Cannibal"
Location: Hanged with "Clubfoot George" Lane, Jack Gallagher, Frank Parish and Haze Lyons in an unfinished building at Virginia City.
Description: At the time of his execution Helm was about forty years old with a medium build. He had hard features and it was said that he wasn't very intelligent looking. Boone Helm was reportedly deadly with both his revolver and his large Bowie knife and it was fortunate for the Vigilantes that his right arm was in a sling when they confronted him

out side of the Virginia City Hotel. Helm was quite a jokester and he was described as being very energetic, a superb marksman and horseman.
Crime: While Helm was never accused of any crimes in Montana he confessed that he was a fugitive from justice.

January 14, 1864
Frank Parish

Location: Hanged with “Clubfoot George” Lane, Jack Gallagher, Boone Helm and Haze Lyons in an unfinished building at Virginia City.
Description: Parish was about twenty-five years old and quite crippled having lost portions of both feet and hands after freezing them the previous winter. When the Vigilantes captured Parrish he was shopping in a general merchandise store at Virginia City for the Rattlesnake Ranch Stage Station for his Indian wife who prepared meals for the passengers.
Crime: Highway Robbery and providing food and shelter for known criminals

January 14, 1864
Haze Lyons

Hanged with: “Clubfoot George” Lane, Jack Gallagher, Frank Parish, and Boone Helm in an unfinished building at Virginia City.
Description: Lyons was described as a handsome young man.
Crime: Lyons was convicted earlier by a Miners’ Court of gunning down Deputy Dillingham in cold blooded but was released after playing on sympathy of the miners.

January 16, 1864
Steven Marshland

Other Names: Steve Marsten, Marsden or Morrison
Location: Near the cabin of George Raugh in the Big Hole country.
Description: Marshland was reportedly a college graduate from the east who had fallen in with bad characters. It was reported that Marshland had come to the mining camps of Montana with the same party as “Dutch John” Wagner, “Red” Yeager and Bob Zachary in August of 1863.
Crime: In November of 1863, Mel Forbes and Milt Moody along with John McCormick were carrying seventy-five thousand dollars in gold dust and fifteen hundred in paper money and other freight on their three-wagon train. During the holdup Wagner was suspected of holding a shotgun on the drivers while Marshland dismounted and was looking for the cash when Mr. Forbes shot him in the chest. Marshland fell to the ground, staggered to his feet, fell again, rose and then ran toward the timber, abandoning his horse, weapons and supplies.

January 19, 1864
William Bunton

Location: Bill Bunton was hanged behind his saloon at Deer Lodge from a beef windlass that was suspended from the crossbeam of Lewis

Demorest's corral gate.

Description: At the time of his death, Bill Bunton was thirty-five years old and he stood about six feet, two inches tall. He was intelligent looking and wore a fine looking mustache, which he took great care of. He was from Osborne, Missouri just east of St. Joseph along the Hannibal and St. Joseph Railroad.

Crime: In his confession "Red" Yeager named Bill Bunton as the number-two man in Plummer's gang. Bunton was also reportedly involved in the first stage robbery between Virginia City and Bannack in 1863, with George Ives and Frank Parrish. Apparently Bunton was acting as a frightened passenger on the stage when he was ordered out of the coach to throw down the treasure box and to drive the stage to town.

January 25, 1864
John Doe, Horse Thief

Location: Hanged from an extended log of a cabin, which was about five miles up Rock Creek of the Clark Fork River.

Description: young man

Crime: suspected of being a horse thief.

January 25, 1864
Cyrus Skinner

Location: Skinner was hanged with Alex Carter and Johnny Cooper at Hell Gate near present day Missoula.

Description: Thomas Dimsdale described Skinner as being a well-built but not handsome looking man with knife scars on his face and arms. The saloonkeeper reportedly stood about five foot nine inches tall with dark hair and gray eyes. Skinner would often wear his shirtsleeves rolled up exposing several tattoos of women and ship anchors on his bulging biceps while tending bar.

Crime: Skinner was suspected of plotting the robbery and massacre of the Magruder party on the Nez Perce Trail. While Skinner never made a confession to any crime, the group of Vigilantes reportedly offered abundant proof of his criminal character including running a promiscuous saloon where several men had been killed including a friendly old Bannack Indian. After Buck Stinson shot down the Indian named "Old Snag," Cyrus Skinner scalped the fallen Indian and proudly displayed the trophy at his saloon. In 1915, the scalp of the old Indian was later seen hanging in a bank at Salt Lake City.

January 25, 1864
Alexander Carter

Location: Carter was hanged with John Cooper and Cyrus Skinner at Hell Gate near present day Missoula.

Description: Alex was about forty-one years old and he was described as being a tall man with a big frame.

Crime: Before his execution George Ives told his executioners that Alex

Carter had murdered Nicholas Tiebolt. While claiming that he had killed the young Dutchman in self-defense, he did confess that he had helped steal the victim's mules. At the time of his arrest Carter was very curious about the news of the mining towns and about the Vigilante activities. When told who had been hanged thus far he commented that they hadn't executed an innocent man yet.

January 25, 1864
Johnny Cooper

Location: Cooper was hanged after Alex Carter and Cyrus Skinner were executed by torchlight at Hell Gate near present day Missoula. Because of his injuries from a gun fight with Alex Carter the day before, Cooper was hauled to the corral on a sled.
Description: Johnny was originally from New York and he was the nephew of Cyrus Skinner.
Crime: Cooper was reportedly one of the lieutenants of Plummer's gang and one of the Vigilantes testified at his hearing that he had murdered a man in Idaho but had escaped from the law by coming to Montana. Cooper was also accused of trying to rob C.A. Broadwater in the Deer Lodge Valley with George Ives and the same two road agents tried to rob William Babcock near Virginia City.

January 25, 1864
Robert Zachary

Location: Zachary was hanged at Hell Gate from a pole that was leaned up against the fence of Mr. Higgins' corral near the edge of town. According to Dimsdale, Bob Zachary was hanged from the same pole that was used to execute Alex Carter earlier that morning.
Description: The only description we have of this outlaw is that he was twenty-eight years old and the only clothes he owned were the ones he was wearing.
Crime: Zachary was hanged for various crimes including holding up of the Oliver's stagecoach in November of 1863, with George Ives and "Whisky Bill" Graves.

January 25, 1864
George Shears

Location: Shears was hanged in Mr. VanDorn's barn in the Frenchtown Valley, which later became the property of J.R. Latimer, and then James Caldwell and eventually part of the Deschamp Ranch.
Description: At the time of his execution Shears was reportedly twenty-one years of age.
Crime: Shears was hanged for various crimes as a road agent for the Plummer gang.

January 26, 1864
William Graves

Other Names: "Whisky Bill"
Location: Graves was hanged from a pine tree[2] near Fort Owen in the Bitterroot Valley. A rope was secured to a limb and to Graves' neck and he was placed upon a horse behind one of the Vigilantes.
Description: Graves, a native of Massachusetts had "ferret eyes" and at the time of his death was reportedly about forty-five years of age and wore a soldier's overcoat. The outlaw was described by Thomas Dimsdale as having a sulky personality and he could be a dangerous savage when provoked.
Crimes: "Whisky Bill" was executed for various crimes including the holding up of Oliver's stage south of Stone's Ranch in November of 1863, with George Ives and Bob Zachary.

February 3, 1864
William Hunter

Location: Hunter was hanged from a large cottonwood tree about twenty miles above present day Three Forks.
Description: Bill Hunter always carried a Colt's revolver and he was described as being rather good looking with average intelligence. He was about twenty-four years old, wore a moustache and was said to have been somewhat vain and very fond of his decorative dress. When executed, Hunter was dressed in an old Army overcoat and "foxed" trousers decorated with leather strips. During those days it was quite common for men to wear buckskin patches on the knees and on the seat of their trousers along with strips of the leather down the seams as well as around the bottom of the pant leg.
Crime: Hunter was a close friend of George Ives and he vigorously lobbied to get him acquitted after his conviction. He was considered one of the best shots in Virginia City and according to some he could whirl around and place twelve shots into the crown of a hat. In one particular case a Virginia City businessman recorded the serial numbers of six hundred dollars worth of currency he was sending to his family in the east. Jack Gallagher was seen with four hundred dollars of the bills and he along with Hunter and Haze Lyons spent them at various saloons, gambling and dance halls in Virginia City. Along with being a road agent, Hunter was also implicated in the murder of a Mormon.
Relics and Remnants: Maintenance workers uncovered the body of Bill Hunter and his skull is on display at the Gallatin County Historical Museum at Bozeman.

March 10, 1864

John Alfred Slade

Other names: Slade often went by Captain, Joseph and some of the old timers called him "Charlie."

Location: Slade was hanged from a beef scaffold from the crossbeam of the front gate of the Elephant Corral in Daylight Gulch, which is a tributary of Alder and.

Description: Slade was born in Virginia and raised in Clinton County, Illinois where he belonged to a highly respected family. Slade moved to Missouri as a young man and served during the Mexican War where he quickly earned a reputation of being a tough frontiersman. Slade was a kind-hearted gentleman, loving husband and a loyal friend, but when he was drunk he could be an uncontrollable sadistic bully.

Crime: After one of Slade's drinking sprees Sheriff Jeremiah M. Fox of the People's Court of Virginia City was ordered to arrest him and he came in peacefully and paid his twenty-five dollar fine. A few days later he was again brought before the judge for the same offense. The second time the fine was doubled and while he paid the fifty dollars he apparently wasn't affected as he continued to be brought to the court and the fines kept doubling. When the fine eventually amounted to four hundred dollars he told Judge Davis that he didn't have that amount with him and he would bring it in the next time he came to town.

Slade came to town several times afterward and never offered to pay the large fine, but his drinking soon got him in trouble again. Sheriff Fox once again escorted Slade and some of his friends to the court and when the officer was reading the warrant against the men, Slade quickly drew a cocked Derringer and pointed it at Judge Alexander Davis' heart. Slade exclaimed that not only wasn't he going to pay the four hundred dollar fine or recognize the court's authority he would hold judge personally responsible for his safety. He threatened the judge that if any member of the Vigilantes laid a finger on him he would come back and "blow his heart out."

While Slade and his friends were spouting off to the judge, Colonel Wilbur Sanders left the building and quickly called for an emergency meeting of the vigilance committee where they sentenced the dangerous character to death for "High Treason, for inciting others to rebellion, and for seeking to overthrow our form of government."

June 15, 1864

James Brady

Other Names: James Bradley

Location: Brady was hanged from a beef or cattle hoist on the edge of Nevada City in front of about a thousand spectators.

Description: Brady was described, as being a young man from Iowa who was pleasant, open hearted and generous except for when he was drinking.

Crime: Attempted murder of a man named Lynch or Murphy

Summer of 1864

John Doe, Horse thief

Location: From a tree in the corner of what later became the George D. Thomas Ranch about two miles south of Manhattan.
Crime: Stealing horse in the Virginia City area

September 17, 1864

John Dolan

Other Names: John Coyle, "Hard Hat," "The Hat" and John Dalam
Location: Dolan was hanged from the same butcher's hoist at a slaughter yard at the foot of the hills, about a half mile northeast of Nevada City, which was used to execute James Brady three months earlier.
Crime: Stealing seven hundred dollars worth of gold nuggets from James Redmond of Nevada City and being suspected of spying for a gang that robbed a stagecoach heading for Salt Lake City.

October 30, 1864

R.C. Rawley

Other Name: R.C. Reighley or Rawleigh: N.C. Hawley
Location: This man was hanged on the scaffold at Bannack, which was originally built for the execution of John Heron in August of 1863, and later employed to hang Henry Plummer and his two deputies in January of 1864.
Description: Rawley was said to be a good-looking man and when not intoxicated he was a first class worker. he reportedly lost both of his feet after they were badly frozen during the winter of 1863, and he hobbled around on two wooden pegs and crutches.
Crime: Complicity to various crimes conducted by Plummer and his gang of road agents and threatening to expose the members of the Vigilantes.
Distinction: Rawley had the distinction of being the last man hanged on ***Gallows No. One: (August 1863)***.
Relics and Remnants: An approximate three-foot section of one of the upright posts of the gallows on which R.C. Rawley was hanged can be found at the Beaverhead County Museum at Dillon and the other one is at the Mason Grand Lodge at Helena.

September 27, 1865

John Jackson

Other name: John Jones
Hanged with: John Morgan
Location: From a large hay frame about a half mile from Virginia City
Crime: Horse stealing
Description: Jackson was an intelligent looking man and he accepted his sentence without hesitation.

September 27, 1865
John Morgan
Hanged with: John Jackson near Virginia for horse stealing
Description: Morgan was reportedly an old vicious ruffian and the old marks on his back from a whipping he had received earlier in Colorado from a vigilance committee for committing an unnatural crime proved it.

September 25, 1867
Charles Wilson
Location: Wilson was hanged in a little ravine behind the stone quarry near Virginia City
Description: Wilson was said to be of medium size, and in his thirties.
Crime: According to Henry N. Blake, who was practicing law in Virginia City at the time, Wilson was accused of using his knowledge of the operations of the Wells Fargo Company to pass pertinent information concerning stagecoaches leaving Virginia City for Salt Lake City.
Distinction: Charley Wilson was the last victim of the Original Vigilantes.

Victims of the Hometown Vigilantes

A constant stream of miners and others poured into Montana Territory and settled in the various mining camps and later the cattle towns across the territory. The good citizens were soon followed by the bad elements and eventually the honest residents began to organize vigilance committees to protect the people and property of the new settlements. With the effective examples set by the earlier Original Vigilantes of Virginia City and Bannack, other mining camps and communities across Montana Territory that were faced with growing crime rates and inadequate justice systems either real or perceived, recognized the value of organizing local "Hometown Vigilante" organizations.

Many of these "Hometown Vigilante" organizations were quickly organized with the help and leadership of some of the old hands who had migrated from Grasshopper Creek and Alder Gulch. Members of the Original Vigilantes have been directly linked with a number of the infant vigilance committees and probably provided both leadership and experience for the execution of criminals at Helena, Diamond City, Gallatin City, Fort Benton, Bozeman, Weeksville, Greenhorn and finally at Miles City.

May of 1864
John Doe, Indian
Location: Hell Gate in Missoula County from one of the hangman poles, which was used by the Original Vigilantes to hang the road agents January.
Description: This Indian warrior was reportedly the son of a Pen d'Oreille Indian chief who was living on the Flathead Reservation.

Crime: The murder and robbery of a Frenchman, and for the attack on another prospector. He was also charged with attempting to cause an Indian uprising against the settlers of Hell Gate.
Distinction: The young Indian was not only the first victim of the Hometown Vigilantes but he was also the first Indian hanged in Montana.

Summer of 1865

Four (4) John Does'

Location: These four men were reportedly hanged from the timbers of a bridge somewhere on the outskirts of Helena.
Crime: While there were no details provided, these four men were said to have been hanged for being bad characters.
Distinction: Since John Keene met his death at the hands of both the Miners' Court and the Helena vigilance committee, these four John Does had the distinction of being the first victims of the Helena Hometown Vigilantes.

July 8, 1865

John Doe

Location: Murderer's Tree, later referred to as Hangman's Tree in Dry Gulch near Helena

On the day of his arrival to Last Chance Gulch, newly appointed Associate Justice Lyman E. Munson noticed a man hanging from the famous tree in Dry Gulch. He later wrote that the Hometown Vigilantes had hanged him the previous evening.

July 30, 1865

Jacob Seachrist

Other Names: Jake Silvie; Silvers
Location: Murderer's Tree, later known as Hangman's Tree in Dry Gulch near Helena
Description: Seachrist was reportedly a native of Pennsylvania and he was hanged in his shirtsleeves.
Crime: Murder of a man near Diamond City and for being a confessed road agent, robber and murderer for twelve years.

September, 1865

Jack Howard

Location: Hanging from a tree at the mouth of Montana Gulch in the Confederate Gulch region near the mining camp of Diamond City
Possible Crime: Most likely suspected of the highway robbery of Mr. J. Hineman on September 11, 1865, near Diamond City.

September 18, 1865
Tommy Cooke

Location: Hangman's Tree in Dry Gulch near Helena.

It was thought that Tommy Cooke had gained his skills as a thief in either California or Boise, Idaho or both before being suspected of a number of robberies at Helena where he was arrested by Deputy Marshal "Quill" Lawrence and held for District Court action.

On the night of September 17, 1865, the Helena chapter of Hometown Vigilantes took custody of the prisoner and apparently held their own trial before hanging Tommy from the Hangman's Tree in the early morning of September 18. Later the stiffened corpse of the thief was discovered swinging in the early morning breeze with a sign pinned to his back stating that he was a pickpocket.

October 3, 1865
Con Kirby

Location: Murderer's Tree, later known as Hangman's Tree in Dry Gulch near Helena.

Crime: Kirby was reportedly another bad case from Boise, Idaho.

October 1865
Two (2) John Doe Road Agents

Location: "Dangling in the air" (assumed from trees) near the Prickly Pear Tollgate some fifty miles from Confederate Gulch.

Crime: These two men may have been suspected of the highway robbery of Mr. J. Hineman at Diamond City on September 11, 1865 (See: Jack Howard, September 1865.)

November 21, 1865
George Sanders

Location: Murderer's Tree, later known as Hangman's Tree in Dry Gulch near Helena.

Crime: A card was attached to Sanders' back stating that he had stolen eighteen hundred dollars from A. Slane.

November 25, 1865
Two (2) John Does

Location: Murderer's Tree, later known as Hangman's Tree in Dry Gulch near Helena.

Crime: Nothing is known about these two men other than the passengers of a stage leaving Helena spotted them hanging from the famous tree.

February 4, 1866
John Doe

Location: This unknown man was reportedly found "stretching a rope" at East Gallatin.

February 5, 1866
Charles Jewett

Location: From a tree on the outskirts of Gallatin City
Crime: Killing a man named Fisher in a bar at Diamond City while he was shooting at another man.

March 2, 1866
James B. Daniels

Location: Hangman's Tree in Dry Gulch near Helena
Description: Daniels was small in stature and wore decorative stitched riding boots.
Crime: Daniels was hanged by the Hometown Vigilantes of Helena for threatening the lives of the witnesses who had testified against him at his manslaughter trial.
Relics and Remnants: Like John Keene who was hanged at Helena in 1865, the skull of Daniels' skull was later found and put on display for many years at the Montana Historical Society until 1984, when the organization removed it from its museum.

June 5, 1866
John Crochet

Other Names: John Trochin; Trosha; "Frenchy"
Location: Hangman's Tree in Dry Gulch near Helena
Description: Thirty-five-years-old Frenchman
Crime: Rolled and robbed Captain John Rogers on May 24, 1866, and suspected of threatening the local Masons.

January 22, 1868
Spaulding

Other Names: Spaulding has often been referred to as only the "Old Kentuckian"
Location: From a butcher's hoist belonging to Ike Millner or perhaps Morrier, in the willows along Fish Creek of Madison County.
Description: Spaulding was reportedly about sixty-five years old and he was presumably from Kentucky.
Hanged with: Spaulding was captured with sixteen-year-old Billy Wilson, but the boy was hanged three days later.
Crime: horse stealing

January 25, 1868
Billy Wilson

Other Names: "Charley"
Over the years Wilson's name had been forgotten and he was often referred to as the "sixteen-year-old boy" who was with Spaulding who was also generally known as the "Old Kentuckian."
Location: On a butcher's hoist in the willows near Fish Creek.

Description: Wilson was a teenage boy who had reportedly run away from his parent's home in Salt Lake City.
Hanged with: While Wilson was captured with Spaulding, the boy managed to escape but he was re-captured and hanged three days later.
Crime: horse stealing

August 24, 1868
William Hynson

Other names: Bill Hinson, Hyman
Location: Hynson was hanged from a temporary tripod gallows at Fort Benton.
Description: Bill Hynson was about twenty-eight years old, and he was reportedly a tall, handsome and muscular Missourian.
Crime: Hynson was a suspected murderer and a known robber. His final crime was of highway robbery for beating up and robbing a man on the levee in front of M.A. Flanagan's Store at Fort Benton.
Distinction: Hynson has the distinction of being in charge of his own execution. When word of a possible Vigilante hanging was purposely leaked to Hynson, he wanted him to take part in the execution. Evidently Hynson believed the intended victim was another desperado in town by the name of John Morgan and he was so willing to participate in the hanging that he asked if he could take charge of the execution by providing the rope, selecting the site and preparing the grave.

January 25, 1870
Ah Chow

Other Names: Ah Chow was commonly called "Jo"
Location: Hangman's Tree in Dry Gulch near Helena
Description: Ah Chow spoke English well, was about thirty-five and he was rather short and plump. He had very prominent cheekbones, which made his face appear very broad and he had a large scar from a hatchet cut between his shoulders.
Crime: Murder of night watchman, John R. Bitzer on January 17, 1870.

The Double Hanging of Compton and Wilson
April 30, 1870
Arthur L. Compton

Other Names: Peter Arthur Compton
Location: Hangman's Tree in Dry Gulch near Helena
Hanged with: Joseph Wilson
Description: Compton was a twenty-six-year-old young man with brown hair, blue eyes and stood about five foot eleven. His face was pock marked and his nose was disfigured when portion of it had been cut off, probably in a fight. The man was originally from Indiana, but he came to Montana from Nebraska in 1869. Compton reportedly drove a bull team out of Salt Lake City where he had been accused of stealing from

between three and eight hundred dollars from a local merchant.
Crime: Assault with the intent to kill and for Highway Robbery of George Lenharth or Leonard on April 27, 1870.
Chairman: Harvey H. English
Prosecuting Spokesman: Judge Robert Lawrence: The judge had been an active member of the Original Vigilantes at Virginia City and not only was he the primary spokesman for the prosecution in the Compton-Wilson case he was also the foreman of the jury as well.
Spokesman for the Defense: George Gifford Symes; newly appointed Associate Justice of the Territorial Supreme Court and District Judge along with District Attorney John Shober.

April 30, 1870
Joseph Wilson

Hanged with: Arthur L. Compton
Description: The twenty-three-year-old Wilson was a small man, standing five feet six inches tall and weighing only one hundred and forty pounds. Aside from a film over one of his eyes, Wilson was described as being "tolerably good looking."

Summer 1870
John Doe

Location: unknown location at Helena

In 1939, Mrs. Mary Valiton claimed that when she was seven years old she witnessed the hanging of Arthur Compton and Joseph Wilson and sometime later her father found a man hanging from a pole of his barn with a card pinned to his back stating he had been a victim of the Hometown Vigilantes.[3]

February 1, 1873
John W. St. Clair

Other name: "Steamboat Bill"
Location: "Steamboat Bill" was hanged at Bozeman from the framework of an abandoned slaughterhouse that appears to have been about the size of a one-car garage.
Hanged With: Jack "Old Man" Triplett
Description: St. Clair was reportedly part Negro and he was considered a tough character.
Crime: Murdered and robbed a Chinese prostitute who had been supporting him at Bozeman.

February 1, 1873
Jack Z.T. Triplett

Other name: "Old Man Tripp" or "Tripp"
Hanged with: John W. St. Clair, "Steamboat Bill" at Bozeman
Description: Old Man Triplett was an old man of about sixty-three years old who drove a two-wheeled cart through Bozeman from which he sold

fish from the Yellowstone River and other wild game meat that he and another man hunted and trapped.
Crime: Murder of restaurant owner, Henry Gilpin on East Main Street.

October 1875
John Doe, Chinaman

Location: In Beaverhead County near the mining camp of Glendale, which was about sixteen miles west of Melrose.
Description: This Chinese national was a known trapper and hunter in the area.
Crime: Behaving improperly with little girls at the camp

July 1881
Bill Jones

Other Names: J.N. Jones
Location: Along the Judith River southeast of Fort Benton in Fergus County. Jones was living on a ranch about ten miles south of Fort Benton with his wife and children when he was caught in mid March of 1881, skinning and preserving hides of cattle he had stolen on Arrow Creek.
Crime: Killing cattle and threatening members of the Fort Benton Hometown Vigilantes.

January 1882
"Tex"

Location: Hanged on the Musselshell River by a stock-protective vigilance committee.
Crime: Stealing horses in the Bozeman area

While we normally list executed rustlers under the category of "Mob Lynching" this particular case was emphatically described as the work of an organized vigilance committee and it has been included here.

Cleaning up of Weeksville of Western Montana
Hanging of "Dick the Diver," "Ohio Dan" and "The Barber."
December, 5 1882
"Dick the Diver"

Other names: "Submarine Richard"
Location: From the balcony of the Weeksville Hotel.
Description: The "Diver" was a short, heavyset and ugly character who was said to have been a former associate of the famous Earp boys in Arizona.
Crime: He was a suspected member of the dangerous Weeksville gang and it was said that he would rob a man of twenty-five cents or two hundred and fifty dollars without question.

January 14, 1883

Joseph Davis

Other Name: "Ohio Dan"
Hanged with: "The Barber"
Location: From a pine tree on the Bert Cleveland Ranch west of Weeksville.
Description: Dan was a large good-looking man who was reportedly quite a ladies' man probably because of his mane of blond wavy hair and deep rolling tenor voice.
Crime: Member of the notorious band of outlaws operating at Weeksville in western Montana.

January 14, 1883

"The Barber"

Other name: "Dick the Barber"
Hanged with: Joe Davis or "Ohio Dan"
Location: From a pine tree on the Bert Cleveland Ranch west of Weeksville.
Crime: This character was known throughout the West and although he was able to make an honest living as a barber, he preferred others to work for his money and he had a dangerous reputation with his razor.

Hanging of Milford Coomes and Billy Smith

March 18, 1883

Milford Coomes

Hanged with: William Henry Smith
Location: The two men were hanged from the lower limbs of two large aspen trees on opposite sides of the Deer Lodge Road about two-thirds of the way between McNally's Stables and the Eleven Mile House near the mining camp of Greenhorn, about twelve miles west of Helena. The ropes used in the hangings were three-quarter inch manila and while the one found around Coomes' neck had the typical "hangman's" knot, Smith was pulled up with a slipknot.
Description: While we have no physical description of Coomes he was described as a mean and quarrelsome man.
Crime: Coomes and Smith reportedly confessed to the burning of H.C. McNally's stable, which caused the total loss of about two thousand dollars.

March 18, 1883

William Henry Smith

Hanged with: Milford Coomes near Greehorn
Description: William Smith was apparently a drunk as he was referred to as a "whisky swizzler." Besides his drinking problem he was reportedly a bit slow or even a scatterbrain. Today, Smith would probably be considered mildly retarded, and in such condition he was reportedly easily talked into committing criminal acts by his friends.

July 25, 1883

William "John" Rigney

Location: Rigney was hanged from a Northern Pacific train trestle located over a coulee at the eastern end of Main Street at Miles City.
Crime: Bill Rigney had been a member of a gang of bad men but he was ultimately hanged for attempting to assault the two daughters of a prominent Miles City resident.
Distinction: Rigney had the unenviable distinction of being the last victim of an organized vigilance committee when he was hanged by the Miles City Hometown Vigilantes. Charley Brown, one of the members of the Original Vigilantes of Virginia City undoubtedly supervised the execution of Bill Rigney.

Mob Lynching

It was pointed out in the introduction that the history of capital punishment coincides with the history of revenge and that revenge is as old as the instinct of self-preservation. If true, then "Mob Lynching" was undoubtedly the most primitive of all forms of revenge where a mob of several dozen to several hundred people took the law into their own hands to avenge a wrongdoing. All it took was an alleged offense ranging from murder, rape and horse stealing to in some cases simple robbery could ignite mob action. Martin Ridge wrote in his article titled "Disorder, Crime and Punishment in the California Gold Rush," which was published in "Montana the Magazine of Western History:" "Lynch Law is the act of doing 'Justice' in an irregular or irresponsible manner, by unauthorized anonymous individuals, in opposition to the regular legally established and open courts."[4]

Of course members of Lynch Mobs were less apt to be detected and therefore prosecuted as long as they took the necessary precautions to protect their identity and avoid congregating openly or officially organize or plan to act again in the future. While the majority of the cases of "Mob Lynching" in Montana have dealt with rape and murder cases, we have included many actions taken against rustlers and horse thieves because rural ranchers and their neighbors generally conducted them. These groups of ranchers might have consisted of only a handful of men, but because they were spontaneously reacting to a crime they are considered in this work as a Lynch Mob.

The exception to our policy of including Mob Lynched stock thieves in this chapter involves the hanging of such criminals during the year of 1884 when the "Cowboy Stranglers" conducted their organized and wide reaching campaign against rustlers and horse thieves. While it is obvious that these bands of self-proclaimed law enforcers didn't hang all the rustlers in Montana during the year of 1884, their action most certainly spurred other parties to stand up against the thieves.

The Lynch Mobs of Montana hanged a total of thirty-nine men from the first one recorded in January of 1865, until the last incident in April of 1913. One obvious well-known lynching omitted in this work was the hanging of Frank Little at Butte in 1917. The hanging of Frank Little was merely a murder of a union activist and it doesn't meet our criteria of being a societal revenge action against a criminal who would under normal circumstances been punished by the legal justice system. Frank Little wasn't executed by a Montana Lynch Mob made up of honest citizens anymore than the Chinaman who was hanged at Butte as part of a Fourth of July Ceremony in 1873. While all Mob Lynching is illegal by definition, they were for the most part accepted in Montana at the time and they have been forgiven over the years because the actions of the mobs were usually over shadowed by the violent crimes committed by the criminals.

January 7, 1865

James Zachariah Fogarty

Other names: Forarty; Fogardy
Location: Fort Owen; Ravalli County
Crime: For the murder of a man named Thomas Wilson or Watson on New Years Eve, 1864, in Emanuel Martin's house near Fort Owen.
Distinction: Fogarty wasn't the first man hanged near Fort Owen or the first to be strung up in what would become Ravalli County, those unfortunate distinctions goes to "Whisky Bill" Graves, executed by the Original Vigilantes in January of 1864. James Fogarty's claim to fame was that he was probably the first victim in Ravalli County and of Montana of a Lynch Mob.

November 13, 1867

James M. Douglas

Location: Red Mountain City in southern Silver Bow County_
Description: twenty-five years old
Crime: Douglas was a noted cattle and horse thief in southwestern Montana Territory.

Spring of 1868

"Lone Rider"

Other Names: "Lone Writer"
Location: Hanged from a tree near the Largent's Store at Sun River in present day Cascade County.
Description: Piegan Indian
Crime: The Indian allegedly killed a man by the name of Clark who was a herder for the Diamond R Freighting Co. and his body was found at his cabin at Sun River about six miles below the Sun River Crossing.

August or September 1871

A man by the name of Hunt

Location: on the West Gallatin River in Gallatin County
Crime: Horse stealing

March 9, 1878

Pete Matte

Location: Matte was hanged from a pine tree in Pine Hollow about a mile and a half south of Stevensville.
Description: Pete was a twenty-one-year-old half-breed who was described as being a wild and reckless lad.
Crime: Ultimately Matte was hanged for horse stealing, which he did a lot of. While Matte had successfully escaped earlier necktie parties by primarily stealing Indian horses he was eventually hanged for stealing stock and his earlier involvement in many other crimes including accessory to a murder.

December 1879
John Doe, Rustler
Location: This suspected rustler was hanged near the South Fork of the Judith River in present day Judith Basin County
Crime: The victim was discovered with a card pinned to his coat marked: "Horse Thief."

Early 1880's
Two (2) John Doe, Rustlers
Location: Presumably hanged from a tree near present day Billings.
Description: These two young men were from back east looking to start a cattle ranch.
Crime: These boys were found with cattle that had a particular brand and they were suspected of stealing the animals. It was later determined that they had purchased the stock.

Late 1880's
John Doe, Rustler
Location: In the Twin Coulee country of Golden Valley County
Crime: cattle rustling

July 4, 1881
Thomas Stewart
Other Names: Brackett E. Stewart; Jack Stewart or Stuart
Location: As Montana Territory were celebrating the Fourth of July with picnics, parties and dancing, Tom Stewart was lynched from a cottonwood tree about one mile southeast of Choteau and about fifty miles northwest of Great Falls.
Description: According to William R. Ralston, Stewart was "the toughest looking character he had ever seen. Stewart had been an Indian interpreter and had lived with the Indians for many years.
Crime: Murder of Mrs. Annie Armstrong and her foreman, Joseph H. Morgan on the Teton River on June 29, 1881. After the robbery and killings Stewart burn down the ranch house in an attempt to destroy the evidence including witnesses, Annie Kehoe and Maggie Housman.

April 1882
"Black Feather"
Location: Near the Teton River in Chouteau County
Description: "Black-Feather" was described as a renegade Piegan Indian and was often in company of his older brother, "Antelope Shirt" who was a convicted horse thief.
Crime: "Black-Feather" was hanged for the murder of Ed Caldwell, a crime that he did not commit. It was later determined that a Frenchman by the name of "Froggy" had murdered Caldwell and he was quickly hanged in the summer of 1882. (See: "Froggy" Summer of 1882)

May 1882
John Doe crewmember of the Riverboat "General C.W. Meade"

Location: Hanged by his fellow crewmembers near a wood yard along the Missouri River near Rocky Point.
Description: Negro
Crime: Killing of another crewmember of the "General C.W. Meade" while en route to Fort Benton.

July 6, 1882
Joseph Harrison

Location: Harrison was hanged from a transom that extended over the door of the Ellis and McKinley General Store at Big Timber.
Crime: The murder of Miss Flora Cutler on July 5, 1882, at the home of Harrison's parents at Sweet Grass.

Summer of 1882
"Froggy"

Location: Near the Teton River in Chouteau County
Description: Frenchman
Crime: "Froggy" murdered his neighbor, Edward Caldwell in April of 1882, for his money. What is more hideous, he apparently allowed an innocent Indian by the name of "Black Feather" to be lynched for the crime. (See: "Black Feather April 1882)

March 6, 1883
John A. Jessrang

Other Name: John Merrill
Location: Jessrang was either hanged from the door of his cell or from the transom that extended over the front door of the jail at Dillon.
Description: Jessrang was born in 1860; he was five foot, ten inches tall; 165 pounds, light brown hair, blue eyes and was missing two of his upper front teeth.
Crime: murder of Victor H. "Dutch Jake" Davidson near Glendale on February 5, 1883.
Distinction: Jessrang was the first man to be illegally hanged at a government building. The second such victim was Jack Brown who was hanged by a Lynch Mob from a window of the Valley County Courthouse at Glasgow in June of 1903.

July 1, 1883
John Doe, Indian

Location: Apparently without a suitable tree for a scaffold, a party of cowboys lassoed an Indian horse thief and dragged him to death at Lewistown. This was a common practice of hanging rustlers in Texas.
Crime: Horse stealing

August 8, 1883

John Doe, Indian

Location: On the Grant Ranch near Dupuyer Creek in present day Pondera County.
Description: Piegan Indian
Crime: Murder of Jimmy Grant after first stealing his wife.

Hanging of a Thief and Two Innocent Victims

Summer 1884

John Doe, Boat Thief and Two (2) Innocent Victims

Location: Near the Poplar River
Lynched With: Two innocent John Doe's who were captured with the thief.
Crime: Stealing of a boat to float down the Missouri River

Between December 4 and 7, 1884

Seven (7) John Doe Indians

Location: In a gulch some twenty to thirty miles east of the Musselshell River. After the incident the region was called "Seven Blackfeet" Coulee or Creek
Crime: Horse stealing

January 27, 1885

Cornelius "Con" Murphy

Other Names: "Red Murphy" "Redding" and John Redmond
Location: Murphy was hanged from the Northern Pacific Railroad trestle about two miles east of Helena.
Description: The Twenty-eight-year-old Con Murphy stood five foot, six inches tall and he weighed about 150 pounds. Con wore his hair short and was described as being very muscular, well developed, quick and wiry. He had freckles; light brown hair, a sandy mustache; straight pointed nose; cold peculiar bluish-gray eyes, red eyelids and a pleasant smile. The outlaw usually wore a black slouch hat with a fancy hatband, a dark coat with blue overalls, heavy red socks and arctic overshoes. Murphy always dressed warmly and he could withstand the severest weather.
Crime: Con Murphy had long been a terror throughout Montana with his robberies, horse stealing and jail breaks along with being suspected of starting a string of fires in Helena including the burning of the St. Peter's Church.

March 26, 1885

Felix Constance and Edward McDonald

Other Name: Felix Constant
Hanged With: Edward McDonald

Location: Hanged from a convenient cottonwood tree about a half a mile upstream from the community of Birch Creek.
Crime: Horse stealing, trying to sell stolen horses and threatening citizens of Birch Creek and Dupuyer.

Hanging of Indians, John Annen and Jerome
March of 1888
John Annen

Other Name: Jonninna or John Mimie
Hanged With: Jerome a.k.a. Slume or Sluth
Location: from a cottonwood across the Flathead River from Demersville
Description: Kootenai Indian
Crime: Annen along with fellow Indians, Jerome and Antley murdered three white prospectors, Daniel MacDonald, Ben Tompkins or Thompson and John Cheley at the Fisher River country in September of 1887. Missoula County authorities eventually captured Antley and he was legally hanged in December of 1890.

March of 1888
Jerome

Other Name: Sluth or Slume
Hanged With: John Annen a.k.a. Jonninna or John Mimie
Description: Kootenai Indian
(See: John Annen, March of 1888)

June 10, 1888
Robert Robinson

Location: At Sun River in newly formed Cascade County
Description: Robinson was a big, burly black man who was described by many as a fiend when he was under the influence if alcohol. He was private in the United States Army stationed at Fort Shaw.
Crime: Murder of Charles McGuire on June 9, 1888, at Sun River.
Relics and Remnants: The old jail at Sun River where Private Robinson was held before his lynching is on display at the Nevada City Museum in Madison County.

July 24, 1891
John Doe, Tramp

Location: From a telegraph pole on Minnesota Avenue at Billings
Description: The man reportedly had the brand of Cain on his forehead.
Crime: Murder of saloon keeper, Joseph Clancy on July 23, 1891, at Billings.
Relics and Remnants: A rare photograph of this lynching is available for viewing at the Western Heritage Center at Billings.

October 2, 1901

James Edward Brady

Other Names: A.J. Lilly and James Edwards
Location: Brady was hanged from a telephone pole on the corner of Main and Lawrence Streets, which was referred to as the Haymarket Square at Helena.
Description: Brady was a heavyset man of about fifty years.
Crime: Assault on five-year-old Hazel Pugsley
Distinction: The Brady incident was the only case where a law enforcement officer was openly and severely disciplined for losing a prisoner to a Lynch Mob. The Lewis and Clark County Grand Jury found that Jailer George Mahrt was incompetent and he was apparently fired.

June 18, 1903

Jack Brown

Other Names: Jack Greybeal and Jack Murray, which was probably his real name
Location: Hanged from a second floor window of the Valley County Courthouse at Glasgow.
Crime: Accessory to the murder of Jailer John "Sailor Jack" Williamson at Glasgow on June 6, 1903, during an escape attempt.
Distinction: Brown was the only known hanging victim in Valley County and only the second man to be illegally executed at a government building. John Jessrang was the first such Lynch Mob victim when he was hanged at the Dillon Jail in 1883.

October 14, 1903

Walter K. Jackson

Location: Jackson was lynched from an electric light pole in front of the Ravalli Hotel at the corner of Second and Bedford Streets.
Description: Jackson was said to have been a twenty-four-year-old black man.
Crime: Jackson was convicted in a court of law of the sexual assault and murder of six-year-old Alfonso Giles Buck of Stevensville on August 13, 1903. The murderer was sentenced to be hanged on October 13, but his attorneys successfully delayed the execution, which outraged the people of the Bitterroot Valley.
Sheriff: Joshua Pond
Relics and Remnants: The half-inch hangman's noose, which was reportedly used to lynch Jackson, is presently held in the collection at the Montana Historical Society at Helena.

April 18, 1912

Henry "Harry" Hoefner

Location: Forsyth
Description: Thirty-year-old German from New York City

Crime: Murder of twenty-seven-year-old Mrs. William Merrill at Joppa on April 15, 1912.

April 4, 1913
J.C. Collins

Location: Hanged from a telephone pole at Mondak in Sheridan County
Description: Collins was a black man about thirty-four years old
Crime: Murder of Sheriff Thomas A. Courtney and Undersheriff Richard Burmeister near Mondak on April 4, 1913.
Distinction: Collins was the last known victim of a Lynch Mob in Montana.

Victims of the "Cowboy Stranglers"

The Stranglers on the Move
Sketch by Thorndike: "Anaconda Standard" 7/21/1901

The famous "Cowboy Stranglers," often referred to as "Granville Stuart's Cowboys" only operated during the year of 1884, and have been unofficially credited with at least forty-seven executions, more than any other extra-legal category. For the purposes of categorizing the hangings in Montana we have listed the executions of horse thieves and cattle Rustlers before and after 1884, as cases of "Mob Lynching." While it should be obvious to everyone that the "Cowboy Stranglers" couldn't have possibly executed every horse thief in 1884, their actions most certainly spurred other Lynch Mobs, large or small to do away with thieves.

The work of the "Cowboy Stranglers" had been so fast and deceptive that even by the 1920's reporters could only find a few old-timers willing to speak up, and even then it was hard to piece the facts together. While several of these witnesses claimed that they had actually seen the first man hanged by the "Stranglers," some of these so-called "first men" weren't the same men, nor were they executed in the same locations or even on the same day. These discrepancies lead us to believe that some of these old-timers were just bragging or there were actually several vigilance groups going on simultaneously.

April 1884
Five (5) John Doe, Rustlers

Location: Near Granville Stuart's (DHS) Ranch in Fergus County
Crime: Horse stealing

June 27, 1884
Narcissus Lavardure

Location: Hanged at two o'clock in the morning from a large outspreading branch of a cottonwood tree near a cattle camp on the Judith River in Fergus County
Description: Narcissus was a good-looking twenty-five-year-old half-breed Indian
Crime: Horse stealing

July 3, 1884
Bill "Sam" McKenzie

Location: About two miles below Fort Maginnis
Description: Scotch half-breed Indian
Crime: While McKenzie was a known horse thief, the crime for which he was hanged was for the theft of a small gray mare that was a family pet.

Hanging of Two Outlaws near Fort Maginnis
July 3, 1884
John Doe, Murderer and a John Doe, Thief

Location: About two miles west of Fort Maginnis between the military outpost and the mining camp of Maiden.
Hanged With: John Doe, Thief
Crime: Murder
These two men were found hanging from a tree, one marked as a murderer and the other a thief.

July 4, 1884
"California Ed" and Two (2) John Doe, Rustlers

Other Name: "California Jack"
Location: Ed was hanged from a cottonwood tree at the mouth of Lodge Pole Creek on the Musselshell River in present day Garfield County.

Hanged With: Two John Doe, Rustlers
Crime: Horse stealing

July 4, 1884
Hanging of William "Billy" Downs and Charley Owens
Location: Near his trading post on the Missouri River in the vicinity of the mouth of the Musselshell River, probably in present day Petroleum County.
Hanged With: Charley Owens
Crime: Aiding and abetting horse thieves and for being in possession of stolen horses, cattle and hides.

July 5, 1884
Hanging of Brocky Gallagher and "Red Mike"
Location: North of Rocky Point in Phillips County
Hanged with: "Red Mike"
Crime: Horse stealing

July 1884
Hanging of Silas Nickerson, "Swift Bill" and Orville Edwards after the Bates Point Battle on the Missouri July 1884
Location: Hanged from a pole placed between the roofs of two cabins near Elk Creek in present day McCone County.
Hanged with: "Swift Bill" and Orville Edwards
Crime: Horse stealing

July 1884
Hanging of Charlie Gibbs and Samuel LaFaver
Location: These two men were hanged from the ceiling of the cabin at their wood camp on the Missouri River in Fergus County.
Descriptions: Charlie was between twenty-five and thirty, about six feet tall, with dark complexion and brown eyes. Sam was about the same age as Charlie but he had blue eyes, brown hair and he was rather stout.
Crime: Unknown. So far as their neighbors knew, these two men were honest, hard-working men. Others believed that the two men had been executed for either providing aid or shelter to known thieves or they had threatened to expose the "Stranglers."

July 1884
"Big Mustache Frank" and a John Doe, Rustler
Location: Disappeared in Fergus County with the "Stranglers" and assumed hanged.
Hanged With: His partner, John Doe, Rustler
Crime: Horse stealing

July 1884

Frank Belgrade

Other Names: Frank Belwaux

Location: Belgrade was hanged in Fergus County while he was on his way to Rocky Point.

Crime: Horse stealing

The Largest Single Group of Hangings by the "Cowboy Stranglers"

A total of thirteen men were hanged in the summer of 1884 on Dog Creek in Fergus County.

Twelve John Doe Rustlers And a John Doe, Innocent Victim

Four of the rustlers were half-breed Indians, three were Mexican and one was a two-hundred pound Chinese national. Unfortunately one of the men hanged was an innocent young man who had been on his way to Fort Benton in order to catch a riverboat down river to visit his mother in Iowa. The boy fell in with the bad company and the "Cowboy Stranglers" didn't have the time to confirm his story and he was hanged with the others. After going through the dead boy's possessions they found a letter from his mother along with one hundred and eighty dollars, which confirmed the boy's story.

While running down and stringing up rustlers and horse thieves the "Cowboy Stranglers" apparently took time out to take care of a couple of murderers along the way.

Summer of 1884

"Mugs" Stevens and "Champion"

Location: These men were hanged in what was Meagher County at the time, which at the time included Fergus and a portion of Petroleum Counties. From the facts of the case and history of the "Cowboy Stranglers" the execution probably took place in Fergus County.

Crime: Murder

November 1884

James Costello and Three John Doe Horse Thieves

Location: Near Mingusville, which was renamed Wibaux in 1895.
A report came out of Glendive in the first week of November that the suspected horse thieves were hanged by the vigilantes.

The Work of the Texas "Cowboy Stranglers"

Within two months during the summer of 1884, the twenty-eight Texas cowboys that were rumored to have been hired by the stockmen of Montana cured at least six suspected thieves, four by hanging and two by lead injections. After their first victim, "Half Breed Jack," the Texans split up into seven parties each led by a Montana cowboy and struck out in different directions to earn their "bonus." Along with "Half Breed" Jack, these bands of "Cowboy Stranglers" are credited with the hanging of "Turkey" Williams, "Bronco Charlie" and "Splay-foot" Harnett as well as the shooting deaths of "Scar-Face" Mosley and "Humpy Jack."

Summer of 1884
"Half-Breed Jack"

Location: Head waters of the Yellowstone River in Park County
Jack was reportedly the first victim of the Texas branch of the "Cowboy Stranglers."

Summer of 1884
"Turkey" Williams and "Bronco Charley"

Location: Ten miles above Miles City in Custer County
The Texas "Cowboy Stranglers" hanged these two suspected horse thieves in the Cottonwoods along the Yellowstone about ten miles up stream from Miles City.

Summer 1884
"Splay-Foot" Harnett

Location: Between Miles City and Glendive, probably in Prairie County
After hanging "Turkey" Williams and "Bronco Charley" in the Miles City area the Texas "Cowboy Stranglers" found and strung up Harnett some where in Prairie County.

(Endnotes)

[1] With no jails available, a Miners' Court at Big Timber reportedly lowered a convicted troublemaker down a thirty-foot mining shaft. Food and water was lowered to the prisoner and after serving his sentence a rope was lowered and he was allowed to climb out. "Montana's Golden Anniversary Humorous History, Handbook and 1940 Almanac, Fifty Years of Rip-Roarin' Statehood, Montana Writers' Project" p27

[2] According to the diary of Thomas W. Harris who was working at Fort Owen and farming at the time Graves was "Left swinging to a pine limb."

[3] "Dutton Sentinel" 8/7/1939

[4] "Montana the Magazine of Western History" Vol. 49, No. 3

Hangings by Year

During the years of the Territory of Montana and earlier, from 1862 through 1889, there were only six years when there wasn't a hanging. During that twenty-eight-year period there were a total of one hundred and seventy-four hangings including fifty-seven in 1884, the bloodiest year of all. The year of 1864, was the second most deadly for suspected desperado when twenty-nine were hanged. Statistically there were over six hangings per year during the days of the Montana Territory.

There were seventeen hangings during the remaining years of the Nineteenth Century during statehood from 1890 and 1899, or 1.7 executions per year. During those ten years, three were free of executions while 1890 had five, there were three hangings in 1894 and 1899, two in 1895 and 1896, while 1891 and 1892, had one each.

During the forty-four years of the Twentieth Century there were forty-four hangings averaging only one hanging per year even though there weren't any executions in seventeen years. There were twenty-six hangings during the first twenty years or 1.3 per year; twelve executions during the Roaring Twenties, 1.2 per year and finally six convicted murderers were killed by the noose during the thirties and forties for an average of .42 per year.

Year	Name	Jurisdiction	County
1862			
8/26	C.W. Spillman	Miners' Court	Powell County
1863			
8/25	John Heron	Miners' Court	Beaverhead
12/23	George Ives	Miners' Court	Madison Co.
1864			
1/4	George W. Brown	Vigilantes	Madison Co.
1/4	Erastus Yager	Vigilantes	Madison Co.
1/10	Henry Amos Plummer	Vigilantes	Beaverhead
1/10	Edward S. Ray	Vigilantes	Beaverhead
1/10	Buck Stinson	Vigilantes	Beaverhead
1/11	Joseph Pizanthia	Vigilantes	Beaverhead
1/11	John Wagner	Vigilantes	Beaverhead
1/14	George Lane	Vigilantes	Madison Co.
1/14	Jack Gallagher	Vigilantes	Madison Co.
1/14	Frank Parish	Vigilantes	Madison Co.
1/14	Haze Lyons	Vigilantes	Madison Co.
1/14	Boone Helm	Vigilantes	Madison Co.
1/16	Stephen Marshland	Vigilantes	Beaverhead
1/19	William Bunton	Vigilantes	Powell County
1/25	John Doe, Rustler	Vigilantes	Missoula Co.
1/25	Alexander Carter	Vigilantes	Missoula Co.
1/25	Johnny Cooper	Vigilantes	Missoula Co.

1/25	Cyrus Skinner	Vigilantes	Missoula Co.
1/25	Robert Zachary	Vigilantes	Missoula Co.
1/25	George Shears	Vigilantes	Missoula Co.
1/26	William Graves	Vigilantes	Ravalli County
2/3	William Hunter	Vigilantes	Gallatin Co.
2/17	John Doe, Murderer	Miners' Court*	Madison Co.
3/10	Joseph A. Slade	Vigilantes	Madison Co.
May	John Doe, Indian	Hmtwn Vigilantes	Missoula Co.
6/15	James Brady	Vigilantes	Madison Co.
Sum	John Doe, Thief	Vigilantes	Gallatin Co.
9/17	John Dolan	Vigilantes	Madison Co.
10/30	R.C. Rawley	Vigilantes	Beaverhead

1865

1/7	James Z. Fogarty	Mob Lynching	Ravalli County
6/7	John Keene	Miners' Court	Lewis & Clark
Sum	John Doe	Hmtwn Vigilantes	Lewis & Clark
Sum	John Doe	Hmtwn Vigilantes	Lewis & Clark
Sum	John Doe	Hmtwn Vigilantes	Lewis & Clark
Sum	John Doe	Hmtwn Vigilantes	Lewis & Clark
7/8	John Doe	Hmtwn Vigilantes	Lewis & Clark
7/30	Jacob Seachrist	Hmtwn Vigilantes	Lewis & Clark
9/15	Jack Howard	Hmtwn Vigilantes	Lewis & Clark
9/18	Tommy Cooke	Hmtwn Vigilantes	Lewis & Clark
9/27	John Jackson	Vigilantes	Madison Co.
9/27	John Morgan	Vigilantes	Madison Co.
10/3	Con Kirby	Hmtwn Vigilantes	Lewis & Clark
Oct.	John Doe	Hmtwn Vigilantes	Lewis & Clark
Oct.	John Doe	Hmtwn Vigilantes	Lewis & Clark
11/21	George Sanders	Hmtwn Vigilantes	Lewis & Clark
11/23	John Doe	Hmtwn Vigilantes	Lewis & Clark
11/23	John Doe	Hmtwn Vigilantes	Lewis & Clark

1866

2/4	John Doe	Hmtwn Vigilantes	Gallatin Co.
2/5	Charles Jewett	Hmtwn Vigilantes	Gallatin Co.
3/2	James B. Daniels	Hmtwn Vigilantes	Lewis & Clark
3/12	Leander W. Johnson	Miners' Court	Powell County
4/20	J.L. Goones	Miners' Court	Silver Bow Co.
6/5	John Crochet	Hmtwn Vigilantes	Lewis & Clark

1867

9/25	Charles Wilson	Vigilantes	Madison Co.
11/13	James Douglas	Mob lynching	Silver Bow Co.

1868

1/22	Spaulding	Hmtwn Vigilantes	Madison Co.

1/25	Billy Wilson	Hmtwn Vigilantes	Madison Co.
Sprg	"Lone Rider"	Mob Lynching	Cascade Co.
5/18	George Ballou	Miners' Court	Powell County
8/16	John Varley	Miners' Court	Granite Co.
8/24	William Hynson	Hmtwn Vigilantes	Chouteau Co.

1870

1/25	Ah Chow	Hmtwn Vigilantes	Lewis & Clark
4/30	Arthur L. Compton	Hmtwn Vigilantes	Lewis & Clark
4/30	Joseph Wilson	Hmtwn Vigilantes	Lewis & Clark
Sum	John Doe	Hmtwn Vigilantes	Lewis & Clark

1871

9/2	Baker	Miners' Court	Broadwater
10/31	John Doe, Chinaman	Miners' Court	Granite Co.
Fall	Hunt	Mob Lynching	Gallatin Co.

1873

2/1	John W. St. Clair	Hmtwn Vigilantes	Gallatin Co.
2/1	Jack Z.T. Triplett	Hmtwn Vigilantes	Gallatin Co.

1875

8/13	William Wheatley	Legal Hanging	Lewis & Clark
Oct	John Doe, Chinaman	Hmtwn Vigilantes	Beaverhead
10/28	William H. Sterres	Legal Hanging	Lewis & Clark

1878

3/1	Michael McAndrews	Legal Hanging	Broadwater
3/9	Pete Matte	Mob Lynching	Ravalli County
10/31	Francois Joseph Robert	Legal Hanging	Madison Co.

1879

10/6	Joseph K. Koble	Legal Hanging	Chouteau Co.
10/6	Orlando H. Marsh	Legal Hanging	Chouteau Co.
Dec	John Doe, Rustler	Mob Lynching	Judith Basin

1880's

John Doe Rustler	Mob Lynching	Yellowstone
John Doe Rustler	Mob Lynching	Yellowstone
John Doe Rustler	Mob Lynching	Golden Valley

1881

2/4	Peter Pelkey	Legal Hanging	Lewis & Clark
5/27	John B. Douglas	Legal Hanging	Madison Co.
7/4	Thomas Stewart	Mob Lynching	Teton County
July	Bill Jones	Hmtwn Vigilantes	Fergus Co.

1882

Jan.	"Tex"	Hmtwn Vigilantes	(E. Montana)
April	"Black Feather"	Mob Lynching	Chouteau Co.
May	John Doe, Crewmember	Mob Lynching	Unknown
7/6	Joseph Harrison	Mob Lynching	Sweet Grass
Sum	"Froggy"	Mob Lynching	Chouteau Co.
12/5	"Dick the Diver"	Hmtwn Vigilantes	Sanders Co.

1883

1/14	Joseph Davis	Hmtwn Vigilantes	Sanders Co.
1/14	"The Barber"	Hmtwn Vigilantes	Sanders Co.
3/6	John A. Jessrang	Mob Lynching	Beaverhead
3/18	Milford Coomes	Hmtwn Vigilantes	Lewis & Clark
3/18	William H. Smith	Hmtwn Vigilantes	Lewis & Clark
5/2	Henry Furhmann	Legal Hanging	Lewis & Clark
7/25	William J. Rigney	Hmtwn Vigilantes	Custer County
7/1	John Doe, Indian	Mob Lynching	Fergus Co.
8/8	John Doe, Indian	Mob Lynching	Pondera Co.
8/16	Ah Yung	Legal Hanging	Missoula Co
12/27	John A. Clark	Legal Hanging	Gallatin Co.

1884

April	John Doe, Rustler	Stranglers	Fergus Co.
April	John Doe, Rustler	Stranglers	Fergus Co.
April	John Doe, Rustler	Stranglers	Fergus Co.
April	John Doe, Rustler	Stranglers	Fergus Co.
April	John Doe, Rustler	Stranglers	Fergus Co.
6/27	Narcissus Lavardure	Stranglers	Fergus Co.
7/3	William McKenzie	Stranglers	Fergus Co.
7/3	John Doe, Murderer	Stranglers	Fergus Co.
7/3	John Doe, Thief	Stranglers	Fergus Co.
7/4	"California Ed"	Stranglers	Garfield Co.
7/4	John Doe, Rustler	Stranglers	Garfield Co.
7/4	John Doe, Rustler	Stranglers	Garfield Co.
7/4	William Downs	Stranglers	Petroleum
7/4	Charley Owens	Stranglers	Petroleum
7/5	Brocky Gallagher	Stranglers	Phillips Co.
7/5	"Red Mike"	Stranglers	Phillips Co.
Jul	Orville Edwards	Stranglers	McCone Co.
Jul	Silas Nickerson	Stranglers	McCone Co.
Jul	"Swift Bill"	Stranglers	McCone Co.
Jul	"Big Mustache Frank"	Stranglers	Fergus Co.
Jul	John Doe, Rustler	Stranglers	Fergus Co.
Jul	Charles Gibbs	Stranglers	Fergus Co.
Jul	Samuel LaFaver	Stranglers	Fergus Co.
Jul	Frank Belgrade	Stranglers	Fergus Co.
Sum	John Doe, Rustler	Stranglers	Fergus Co.

Sum	John Doe, Rustler	Stranglers	Fergus Co.
Sum	John Doe, Rustler	Stranglers	Fergus Co.
Sum	John Doe, Rustler	Stranglers	Fergus Co.
Sum	John Doe, Rustler	Stranglers	Fergus Co.
Sum	John Doe, Rustler	Stranglers	Fergus Co.
Sum	John Doe, Rustler	Stranglers	Fergus Co.
Sum	John Doe, Rustler	Stranglers	Fergus Co.
Sum	John Doe, Rustler	Stranglers	Fergus Co.
Sum	John Doe, Rustler	Stranglers	Fergus Co.
Sum	John Doe, Rustler	Stranglers	Fergus Co.
Sum	John Doe, Rustler	Stranglers	Fergus Co.
Sum	John Doe, Victim	Stranglers	Fergus Co.
Sum	"Champion"	Stranglers	Fergus Co.
Sum	"Mugs" Stevens	Stranglers	Fergus Co.
Sum	"Half-Breed" Jack	Stranglers	Park County
Sum	"Turkey" Williams	Stranglers	Custer County
Sum	"Bronco Charley"	Stranglers	Custer County
Sum	"Splay-Foot" Harnett	Stranglers	Prairie County
Sum	John Doe, Boat Thief	Mob Lynching	Roosevelt Co.
Sum	John Doe, Innocent Victim	Mob Lynching	Roosevelt Co.
Sum	John Doe, Innocent Victim	Mob Lynching	Roosevelt Co.
Nov.	James Costello	Stranglers	Wibaux Co.
Nov	John Doe Rustler	Stranglers	Wibaux Co.
Nov	John Doe Rustler	Stranglers	Wibaux Co.
Nov	John Doe Rustler	Stranglers	Wibaux Co.
Dec	John Doe, Indian	Mob Lynching	Garfield Co.
Dec	John Doe, Indian	Mob Lynching	Garfield Co.
Dec	John Doe, Indian	Mob Lynching	Garfield Co.
Dec	John Doe, Indian	Mob Lynching	Garfield Co.
Dec	John Doe, Indian	Mob Lynching	Garfield Co.
Dec	John Doe, Indian	Mob Lynching	Garfield Co.
Dec	John Doe, Indian	Mob Lynching	Garfield Co.

1885

1/27	Con Murphy	Mob Lynching	Lewis & Clark
3/26	Felix Constance	Mob Lynching	Pondera Co.
3/26	Edward McDonald	Mob Lynching	Pondera Co.

1887

3/25	Thomas H. Harding	Legal Hanging	Beaverhead

1888

2/10	John Patrick Hart	Legal Hanging	Lewis & Clark
2/17	Martin Luther Scott	Legal Hanging	Powell County
Mar.	John Annen	Mob Lynching	Flathead Co.
Mar.	Jerome	Mob Lynching	Flathead Co.
6/10	Robert Robinson	Mob Lynching	Cascade Co.

1889

8/9	George Duncan Bryson	Legal Hanging	Jefferson Co.
8/23	W.H. "Harry" Roberts	Legal Hanging	Silver Bow Co.

1890

6/6	Thomas A. King	Legal Hanging	Jefferson Co.
12/19	Antley	Legal Hanging	Missoula Co.
12/19	La La See	Legal Hanging	Missoula Co.
12/19	Pascale	Legal Hanging	Missoula Co.
12/19	Pierre Paul	Legal Hanging	Missoula Co.

1891

7/24	John Doe, Tramp	Mob Lynching	Yellowstone

1892

12/16	John Burns	Legal Hanging	Missoula Co.

1894

7/13	Robert A. Anderson	Legal Hanging	Park County
7/13	John H. Osnes	Legal Hanging	Chouteau Co.
12/21	Calvin J. Christie	Legal Hanging	Flathead Co.

1895

7/1	Clayberg Pugh	Legal Hanging	Jefferson Co.
12/27	Joseph Cadotte	Legal Hanging	Chouteau Co.

1896

4/6	William Biggerstaff	Legal Hanging	Lewis & Clark
6/8	William Gay	Legal Hanging	Lewis & Clark

1899

1/27	Thomas Salmon	Legal Hanging	Carbon Co.
9/14	Joseph H. Allen	Legal Hanging	Lewis & Clark
11/24	William C. Brooks	Legal Hanging	Yellowstone

1900

3/18	William Wallace Calder	Legal Hanging	Fergus Co.
3/30	Joseph C. Hurst	Legal Hanging	Dawson Co.
4/6	William Pepo	Legal Hanging	Teton County
9/14	Daniel Lucy	Legal Hanging	Silver Bow Co.

1901

9/6	James Fleming	Legal Hanging	Powell County
10/2	James Edward Brady	Mob Lynching	Lewis & Clark

1902

4/4	Clinton Dotson	Legal Hanging	Powell County

1903

6/18	Jack Brown	Mob Lynching	Valley County
10/14	Walter Jackson	Mob Lynching	Ravalli County

1904

2/23	James Martin	Legal Hanging	Silver Bow Co.
3/18	Louis H. Mott	Legal Hanging	Missoula Co.

1905

5/5	Herbert Henry Metzger	Legal Hanging	Meagher Co.

1906

4/20	Lu Sing	Legal Hanging	Gallatin Co.
5/18	Miles Fuller	Legal Hanging	Silver Bow Co.

1908

6/15	George J. Rock	Legal Hanging	Powell County

1909

4/2	William A. Hayes	Legal Hanging	Powell County
4/2	Frederick LeBeau	Legal Hanging	Flathead Co.

1912

4/18	Henry Hoefner	Mob Lynching	Rosebud Co.

1913

4/4	J.C. Collins	Mob Lynching	Sheridan Co.

1917

2/16	Leslie Fahley	Legal Hanging	Meagher Co.
2/16	Harrison Gibson	Legal Hanging	Meagher Co.
2/16	Henry Hall	Legal Hanging	Meagher Co.

1918

1/14	Frank Fisher	Legal Hanging	Silver Bow Co.
1/14	John O'Neil	Legal Hanging	Silver Bow Co.
1/14	Sherman A. Powell	Legal Hanging	Silver Bow Co.
4/12	Juan Cuellae	Legal Hanging	Yellowstone

1920

9/3	Alfred Lane	Legal Hanging	Rosebud Co.

1921

8/26	Albert Yeik	Legal Hanging	Beaverhead

1922

2/17	Joseph Vuckovich	Legal Hanging	Missoula Co.

1923

2/9	Glenna Martin Bolton	Legal Hanging	Treasure Co.
2/9	Joseph B. Reagin	Legal Hanging	Treasure Co.
4/20	Monte Harris	Legal Hanging	Silver Bow Co.
4/20	William "Bill" Harris	Legal Hangings	Silver Bow Co.

1924

7/18	Seth Orrin Danner	Legal Hanging	Gallatin Co.

1925

2/14	Roy Walsh	Legal Hanging	Jefferson Co.

1926

10/1	Anthony Vettere	Legal Hanging	Silver Bow Co.

1927

5/20	Ferdinand Schlaps	Legal Hanging	Roosevelt Co.

1929

11/6	Rollin Davisson	Legal Hanging	Park County

1933

8/29	George Hoffman	Legal Hanging	Teton County

1935

4/24	Henry John Zorn	Legal Hanging	Custer County
10/16	George Criner	Legal Hanging	Custer County

1938

1/15	Franklin Robideau	Legal Hanging	Stillwater Co.

1939

12/30	Lee Simpson	Legal Hanging	Golden Valley

1943

9/10	Philip J. Coleman	Legal Hanging	Missoula Co.

* People's Court format

Hangings by County

Lewis and Clark County leads all other counties in hangings with thirty-three with Fergus coming in second with thirty two. While only having twelve hangings total, Silver Bow County conducted the most legal executions with ten. Missoula County followed by nine and Lewis and Clark hanged eight convicted murderers.

Forty present day counties have had hangings within their boundaries and fifteen of them never conducted a legal execution including Cascade. There were ten illegal hangings in Garfield County and they were all conducted in one year, by the "Cowboy Stranglers of 1884." In contrast, all of the hangings Jefferson (four), Meagher (four) and Treasure Counties (two) were legal.

Table indicates victim, date of death, general location of the hanging and the various jurisdictions that had ordered the execution.

BEAVERHEAD COUNTY (established 2/2/1865)

Peter Horen	8/25/1863	Bannack	Miners' Court
Henry Plummer	1/10/1864	Bannack	Vigilantes
Ned Ray	1/10/1864	Bannack	Vigilantes
Buck Stinson	1/10/1864	Bannack	Vigilantes
Joseph Pizanthia	1/11/1864	Bannack	Vigilantes
John Wagner	1/11/1864	Bannack	Vigilantes
Steve Marshland	1/16/1864	Big Hole	Vigilantes
R.C. Rawley	Oct. 1864	Bannack	Vigilantes
John Doe, Chinaman	Oct 1875	Glendale	Hmtwn Vigilantes
John A. Jessrang	3/6/1883	Dillon	Mob Lynching
Thomas H. Harding	3/25/1887	Dillon	Legal Hanging
Albert Yeik	8/26/1921	Dillon	Legal Hanging

BROADWATER COUNTY (established 2/9/1897)

Baker	9/2/1871	Radersburg	Miners' Court
Michael McAndrews	3/1/1878	Radersburg	Legal Hanging

CARBON COUNTY (established 3/4/1895)

Thomas Salmon	1/27/1899	Red Lodge	Legal Hanging

CASCADE COUNTY (established 9/12/1887)

"Lone Rider"	Spring 1868	Sun River	Mob Lynching
Robert Robinson	6/10/1888	Sun River	Mob Lynching

CHOUTEAU COUNTY (established 2/2/1865)

William Hynson	8/24/1868	Fort Benton	Hmtwn Vigilantes
Joseph K. Koble	10/6/1879	Fort Benton	Legal Hanging
Orlando H. Marsh	10/6/1879	Fort Benton	Legal Hanging

(Chouteau County continued)

Black Feather	April 1882	unknown	Mob Lynching
"Froggy"	Sum 1882	unknown	Mob Lynching
John H. Osnes	7/13/1894	Fort Benton	Legal Hanging
Joseph Cadotte	12/27/1895	Fort Benton	Legal Hanging

CUSTER COUNTY (established 2/16/1877)

John Rigney	7/25/1883	Miles City	Hmtwn Vigilantes
"Turkey" Williams	Sum 1884	unknown	Stranglers
"Bronco Charley"	Sum 1884	unknown	Stranglers
Henry John Zorn	4/24/1935	Miles City	Legal Hanging
George Criner	10/16/1935	Miles City	Legal Hanging

DAWSON COUNTY (established 1/15/1869)

J.C. Hurst	3/30/1900	Glendive	Legal Hanging

FERGUS COUNTY (established 3/12/1885)

Bill Jones	July 1881	Judith River	Hmtwn Vigilantes
John Doe, Indian	7/1/1883	Lewistown	Mob Lynching
John Doe, Rustler	April 1884	DS Ranch	Stranglers
John Doe, Rustler	April 1884	DS Ranch	Stranglers
John Doe, Rustler	April 1884	DS Ranch	Stranglers
John Doe, Rustler	April 1884	DS Ranch	Stranglers
John Doe, Rustler	April 1884	DS Ranch	Stranglers
Narcissus Lavardure	6/27/1884	Judith River	Stranglers
Sam McKenzie	7/3/1884	Ft. Maginnis	Stranglers
John Doe, Murderer	7/3/1884	Ft. Maginnis	Stranglers
John Doe, Thief	7/3/1884	Ft. Maginnis	Stranglers
Samuel LaFaver	July 1884	Rocky Point	Stranglers
Charley Gibbs	July 1884	Rocky Point	Stranglers
Frank Belgrade	July 1884	Rocky Point	Stranglers
"Big Mustache Frank	July 1884	Judith Basin	Stranglers
John Doe, Rustler	July 1884	Judith Basin	Stranglers
John Doe, Rustler	Sum 1884	Dog Creek	Stranglers
John Doe, Rustler	Sum 1884	Dog Creek	Stranglers
John Doe, Rustler	Sum 1884	Dog Creek	Stranglers
John Doe, Rustler	Sum 1884	Dog Creek	Stranglers
John Doe, Rustler	Sum 1884	Dog Creek	Stranglers
John Doe, Rustler	Sum 1884	Dog Creek	Stranglers
John Doe, Rustler	Sum 1884	Dog Creek	Stranglers
John Doe, Rustler	Sum 1884	Dog Creek	Stranglers
John Doe, Rustler	Sum 1884	Dog Creek	Stranglers
John Doe, Rustler	Sum 1884	Dog Creek	Stranglers
John Doe, Rustler	Sum1884	Dog Creek	Stranglers
John Doe, Rustler	Sum 1884	Dog Creek	Stranglers
John Doe, Victim	Sum 1884	Dog Creek	Stranglers
"Champion"	Sum 1884	Flt Willow Cr.	Stranglers

(Fergus County continued)

"Mugs" Stevens	Sum 1884	Flt Willow Cr.	Stranglers
William W. Calder	3/18/1900	Lewistown	Legal Hanging

FLATHEAD COUNTY (established 2/6/1893)

John Annen	March 1888	Demersville	Mob Lynching
Jerome	March 1888	Demersville	Mob Lynching
Calvin J. Christie	12/21/1894	Kalispell	Legal Hanging
Frederick LeBeau	4/2/1909	Kalispell	Legal Hanging

GALLATIN COUNTY (establish 2/2/1865)

Bill Hunter	2/3/1864	Three Forks	Vigilantes
John Doe, Thief	Sum 1864	Manhattan	Vigilantes
John Doe	2/4/1866	East Gallatin	Hmtwn Vigilantes
Charles Jewett	2/5/1866	Gallatin City	Hmtwn Vigilantes
Hunt	Fall 1871	Gallatin River	Mob Lynching
John W. St. Clair	2/1/1873	Bozeman	Hmtwn Vigilantes
Jack Z.T. Triplett	2/1/1873	Bozeman	Hmtwn Vigilantes
John A. Clark	12/27/1883	Bozeman	Legal Hanging
Lu Sing	4/20/1906	Bozeman	Legal Hanging
Seth Orrin Danner	7/18/1924	Bozeman	Legal Hanging

GARFIELD COUNTY (established 2/7/1919)

"California Ed"	7/4/1884	LodgePole Ck	Stranglers
John Doe, Rustler	7/4/1884	LodgePole Ck	Stranglers
John Doe, Rustler	7/4/1884	LodgePole Ck	Stranglers
John Doe, Indian	Dec 1884	7 Blackfeet	Mob Lynching
John Doe, Indian	Dec 1884	7 Blackfeet	Mob Lynching
John Doe, Indian	Dec 1884	7 Blackfeet	Mob Lynching
John Doe, Indian	Dec 1884	7 Blackfeet	Mob Lynching
John Doe, Indian	Dec 1884	7 Blackfeet	Mob Lynching
John Doe, Indian	Dec 1884	7 Blackfeet	Mob Lynching
John Doe, Indian	Dec 1884	7 Blackfeet	Mob Lynching

GOLDEN VALLEY (established 10/4/1920)

John Doe Rustler	1880's	Twin Coulee	Mob Lynching
Lee Simpson	12/30/1939	Ryegate	Legal Hanging

GRANITE COUNTY (3/2/1893)

John Varley	8/16/1868	Beartown	Miners' Court
John Doe, Chinaman	10/31/1871	Henderson	Miners' Court

JEFFERSON COUNTY (established 2/2/1865)

George D. Bryson	8/9/1889	Boulder	Legal Hanging
Thomas A. King	6/6/1890	Boulder	Legal Hanging
Clayberg Pugh	7/1/1895	Boulder	Legal Hanging
Roy Walsh	2/14/1925	Boulder	Legal Hanging

JUDITH BASIN COUNTY (established 12/10/1920)

John Doe, Rustler	Dec. 1879	S. Fork	Mob Lynching

LEWIS & CLARK COUNTY (established 12/20/1867

John Keene	6/7/1865	Dry Gulch	Miners' Court
John Doe	7/8/1865	Dry Gulch	Hmtwn Vigilantes
John Doe	Sum 1865	Helena	Hmtwn Vigilantes
John Doe	Sum 1865	Helena	Hmtwn Vigilantes
John Doe	Sum 1865	Helena	Hmtwn Vigilantes
John Doe	Sum 1865	Helena	Hmtwn Vigilantes
Jacob Seachrist	7/30/1865	Dry Gulch	Hmtwn Vigilantes
Jack Howard	9/15/1865	Diamond City	Hmtwn Vigilantes
Tommy Cooke	9/18/1865	Dry Gulch	Hmtwn Vigilantes
Con Kirby	10/3/1865	Dry Gulch	Hmtwn Vigilantes
John Doe	Oct 1865	Prkly Pear Cr.	Hmtwn Vigilantes
John Doe	Oct 1865	Prkly Pear Cr.	Hmtwn Vigilantes
George Sanders	11/21/1865	Dry Gulch	Hmtwn Vigilantes
John Doe	11/23/1865	Dry Gulch	Hmtwn Vigilantes
John Doe	11/23/1865	Dry Gulch	Hmtwn Vigilantes
James Daniels	3/2/1866	Dry Gulch	Hmtwn Vigilantes
John Crochet	6/5/1866	Dry Gulch	Hmtwn Vigilantes
Ah Chow	1/25/1870	Dry Gulch	Hmtwn Vigilantes
Arthur L. Compton	4/30/1870	Dry Gulch	Hmtwn Vigilantes
Joseph Wilson	4/30/1870	Dry Gulch	Hmtwn Vigilantes
John Doe	Sum 1870	Helena	Hmtwn Vigilantes
William W. Wheatley	8/13/1875	Helena	Legal Hanging
William H. Sterres	10/28/1875	Helena	Legal Hanging
Peter Pelkey	2/4/1881	Helena	Legal Hanging
Milford Coomes	3/18/1883	Greenhorn	Hmtwn Vigilantes
William H. Smith	3/18/1883	Greenhorn	Hmtwn Vigilantes
Henry Furhmann	5/2/1883	Helena	Legal Hanging
Con Murphy	1/27/1885	Helena	Mob Lynching
John Patrick Hart	2/10/1888	Helena	Legal Hanging
William Biggerstaff	4/6/1896	Helena	Legal Hanging
William Gay	6/8/1896	Helena	Legal Hanging
Joseph H. Allen	9/14/1899	Helena	Legal Hanging
James Edward Brady	10/2/1901	Helena	Mob Lynching

MADISON COUNTY (established 2/2/1865)

George Ives	12/23/1863	Nevada City	Miners' Courts
George W. Brown	1/4/1864	Beaverhd Rk	Vigilantes
Erastus Yager	1/4/1864	Beaverhd Rk	Vigilantes
George Lane	1/14/1864	Virginia City	Vigilantes
Jack Gallagher	1/14/1864	Virginia City	Vigilantes
Frank Parish	1/14/1864	Virginia City	Vigilantes
Haze Lyons	1/14/1864	Virginia City	Vigilantes
Boone Helm	1/14/1864	Virginia City	Vigilantes

(Madison County continued)

John Doe, Murderer	2/17/1864	Virginia City	Miners' Court*
Joseph Slade	3/10/1864	Virginia City	Vigilantes
James Brady	6/15/1864	Nevada City	Vigilantes
John Dolan	9/17/1864	Nevada City	Vigilantes
John Jackson	9/27/1865	Virginia City	Vigilantes
John Morgan	9/27/1865	Virginia City	Vigilantes
Charles Wilson	9/25/1867	Virginia City	Vigilantes
Spaulding	1/22/1868	Fish creek	Hmtwn Vigilantes
Bill Wilson	1/25/1868	Fish Creek	Hmtwn Vigilantes
Francois J. Robert	10/31/1878	Virginia City	Legal Hanging
John P. Douglas	5/27/1881	Virginia City	Legal Hanging

*People's Court

MCCONE COUNTY (established 2/20/1919)

Orville Edwards	July 1884	Elk Creek	Stranglers
Silas Nickerson	July 1884	Elk Creek	Stranglers
"Swift Bill"	July 1884	Elk Creek	Stranglers

MEAGHER COUNTY (established 11/16/1867)

Herbert H. Metzger	5/5/1905	Wht Sul Spr	Legal Hanging
Leslie Fahley	2/16/1917	Wht Sul Spr	Legal Hanging
Harrison Gibson	2/16/1917	Wht Sul Spr	Legal Hanging
Henry Hall	2/16/1917	Wht Sul Spr	Legal Hanging

MISSOULA COUNTY (established 2/2/1865)

John Doe, Rustler	1/25/1864	Rock Creek	Vigilantes
Alexander Carter	1/25/1864	Hell Gate	Vigilantes
Johnny Cooper	1/25/1864	Hell Gate	Vigilantes
Alexander Carter	1/25/1864	Hell Gate	Vigilantes
Robert Zachary	1/25/1864	Hell Gate	Vigilantes
George Shears	1/25/1864	Frenchtown	Vigilantes
John Doe, Indian	May 1864	Hell Gate	Hmtwn Vigilantes
Ah Yung	8/16/1883	Missoula	Legal Hanging
Antley	12/19/1890	Missoula	Legal Hanging
La La See	12/19/1890	Missoula	Legal Hanging
Pascale	12/19/1890	Missoula	Legal Hanging
Pierre Paul	12/19/1890	Missoula	Legal Hanging
John Burns	12/16/1892	Missoula	Legal Hanging
Louis H. Mott	3/18/1904	Missoula	Legal Hanging
Joe Vuckovich	2/17/1922	Missoula	Legal Hanging
Phillip Coleman	9/10/1943	Missoula	Legal Hanging

PARK COUNTY (established 2/23/1887)

Robert Anderson	7/13/1894	Livingston	Legal Hanging
"Half-Breed" Jack	Sum 1884	unknown	Stranglers
Rollin Davisson	11/6/1929	Livingston	Legal Hanging

PETROLEUM COUNTY (established 11/24/1924)

William Downs	7/4/1884	Missouri R.	Stranglers
Charley Owens	7/4/1884	Missouri R.	Stranglers

PHILLIPS COUNTY (established 2/5/1915)

Brocky Gallagher	7/5/1884	Rocky Point	Stranglers
"Red Mike"	7/5/1884	Rocky Point	Stranglers

PONDERA COUNTY (established 2/17/1919)

John Doe, Indian	8/8/1883	Dupuyer Ck.	Mob Lynching
Felix Constance	3/26/1885	Birch Creek	Mob Lynching
Edward McDonald	3/26/1885	Birch Creek	Mob Lynching

POWELL COUNTY (established 1/31/1901)

* (Hanging took place in what was then Deer Lodge County)

C.W. Spillman	8/26/1862*	Gold Creek	Miners' Court
William Bunton	1/19/1864*	Deer Lodge	Vigilantes
Leander W. Johnson	3/12/1866*	Deer Lodge	Miners' Court
George Ballou	5/18/1868*	Reynolds City	Miners' Court
Martin Scott	2/17/1888*	Deer Lodge	Legal Hanging
James Fleming	9/6/1901	Deer Lodge	Legal Hanging
Clinton Dotson	4/4/1902	Deer Lodge	Legal Hanging
George J. Rock	6/15/1908	State Prison	Legal Hanging
William A. Hayes	4/2/1909	State Prison	Legal Hanging

PRAIRIE COUNTY (established 2/5/1915)

"Splay-Foot" Harnett	Sum 1884	unknown	Stranglers

RAVALLI COUNTY (established 2/16/1893)

William Graves	1/26/1864	Fort Owen	Vigilantes
James Fogarty	1/7/1865	Fort Owen	Mob Lynching
Pete Matte	3/9/1878	Stevensville	Mob Lynching
Walter Jackson	10/14/1903	Hamilton	Mob Lynching

ROOSEVELT COUNTY (established 2/18/1919)

John Doe, Boat Thief	Sum 1884	Poplar	Mob Lynching
John Doe, Victim	Sum 1884	Poplar	Mob Lynching
John Doe, Victim	Sum 1884	Poplar	Mob Lynching
Ferdinand Schlaps	5/20/1927	Wolf Point	Legal Hanging

ROSEBUD COUNTY (established 2/11/1901)

Henry Hoefner	4/18/1912	Forsyth	Mob Lynching
Alfred Lane	9/3/1920	Forsyth	Legal Hanging

SANDERS COUNTY (established 3/1/1906)

"Dick the Diver"	12/5/1882	Weeksville	Hmtwn Vigilantes
Joseph Davis	1/14/1883	Weeksville	Hmtwn Vigilantes
"The Barber"	1/14/1883	Weeksville	Hmtwn Vigilantes

SHERIDAN COUNTY (established 3/24/1913)

C.J. Collins	4/4/1913	Mondak	Mob Lynching

SILVER BOW COUNTY (established 2/16/1881)

J.L. Goones	4/20/1866	German Glch	Miners' Court
James Douglas	11/13/1867	Red Mt. City	Mob Lynching
W.H. Roberts	8/23/1889	Butte	Legal Hanging
Daniel Lucy	9/14/1900	Butte	Legal Hanging
James Martin	2/23/1904	Butte	Legal Hanging
Miles Fuller	5/18/1906	Butte	Legal Hanging
Frank Fisher	1/14/1918	Butte	Legal Hanging
John O'Neil	1/14/1918	Butte	Legal Hanging
Sherman A. Powell	1/14/1918	Butte	Legal Hanging
Monte Harris	4/20/1923	Butte	Legal Hanging
William Harris	4/20/1923	Butte	Legal Hanging
Anthony Vettere	10/1/1926	Butte	Legal Hanging

STILLWATER COUNTY (established 3/24/1913)

Franklin Robideau	1/15/1938	Columbus	Legal Hanging

SWEET GRASS COUNTY (established 3/5/1895)

Joseph Harrison	7/6/1882	Big Timber	Mob Lynching

TETON COUNTY (established 2/7/1893)

Thomas Stewart	7/4/1881	near Choteau	Mob Lynching
William Pepo	4/6/1900	Choteau	Legal Hanging
George Hoffman	8/29/1933	Choteau	Legal Hanging

TREASURE COUNTY (established 2/7/1919)

Glenna M. Bolton	2/9/1923	Hysham	Legal Hanging
Joseph B. Reagin	2/9/1923	Hysham	Legal Hanging

VALLEY COUNTY (established 2/6/1893)

Jack Brown	6/18/1903	Glasgow	Mob Lynching

WIBAUX COUNTY (established 8/17/1914)

James Costello	Nov. 1884	Wibaux	Stranglers
John Doe Rustler	Nov. 1884	Wibaux	Stranglers
John Doe Rustler	Nov. 1884	Wibaux	Stranglers
John Doe Rustler	Nov. 1884	Wibaux	Stranglers

YELLOWSTONE COUNTY (established 2/26/1883)

John Doe Rustler	Early 1880's	near Billings	Mob Lynching
John Doe Rustler	Early 1880's	near Billings	Mob Lynching
John Doe, Tramp	7/24/1891	Billings	Mob Lynching
William C. Brooks	11/24/1899	Billings	Legal Hanging
Juan Cuellae	4/12/1918	Billings	Legal Hanging

UNKNOWN LOCATION

"Tex"	Jan. 1882	Musselshell[1]	Hmtwn Vigilantes
Negro Crewman	May 1882	wood yard[2]	Mob Lynching

(Endnotes)

[1] Hanged along the Musselshell River; placing it either in Petroleum County on the west side of the river and Garfield County to the east.

[2] Hanged at a wood yard near Rocky Point. That would place it either in Petroleum County on the south bank of the river or Phillips County on the north shore.

Hanging Judges of Montana

Judge James M. Clements hearing the Clinton Dotson case in 1901.
"Anaconda Standar" 7/21/1901

While we have an accounting of all the District Court Justices who have legally sentenced men to hang, we have only obtained the names of five judges who presided over Miners' Courts. In all the Miners' Court Judges ordered the deaths of eleven men including seven convicted murderers and one each for attempted homicide, horse stealing, cattle rustling, and burglary. At least one of the victims, Leander W. Johnson, a suspected cattle rustler was hanged an innocent man and the lone burglar hanged was convicted by a nineteen to eighteen vote margin by a jury of miners.

All of the seventy-one men legally hanged were convicted of first-degree murder and after sentencing six to their deaths, District Court Judge Decius S. Wade holds the title of "Top Hanging Judge" of Montana. C.S. Marshall sentenced five convicted murderers; Henry Blake and Dudley Dubose each ordered the deaths of four men, four justices sent three each to the gallows, eight courts each signed two death warrants and twenty-four other judges were responsible for a hanging each.

Judge: (if not otherwise noted they were district court justices) Condemned Man	**Date:**	**County:**
Bennett, Lyman H.		
Roy Walsh	2/14/1925	Jefferson County
Berg, B.E.		
Rollin Davisson	11/6/1929	Park County
Besancon, Albert		
Philip J. Coleman	9/10/1943	Missoula County
Blake, Henry Nichols[1]		
Michael McAndrews	3/1/1878	Broadwater County
Francois Joseph Robert	10/31/1878	Madison County
William Biggerstaff	4/6/1896	Lewis & Clark County
William Gay	6/8/1896	Lewis & Clark County
Burchett (Miners' Court)		
John Heron	8/25/1863	Beaverhead County
Byam, Donald L. (Miners' Court)		
George Ives	12/21/1863	Madison County
Campbell, Green (Miners' Court)		
J.L. Goones	4/20/1866	Silver Bow County
Cheadle, Edwin K.		
Herbert H. Metzger	5/5/1905	Meagher County
Clancy, William D.		
Daniel Lucy	9/14/1900	Silver Bow County
Clements, James M.[2]		
James Fleming	9/6/1901	Powell County
Joseph C. Dotson	4/4/1902	Powell County
Conger, Everton Judson[3]		
Peter Pelkey	2/4/1881	Lewis & Clark County
John B. Douglas	5/27/1881	Madison County
Davis, Alexander (People's Court/Miners' Court)		
John Doe Murderer	2/17/1864	Madison County

DeWolfe, Stephen[4]

W.H. "Harry" Roberts	8/23/1889	Silver Bow County

Donlan, Michael

Miles Fuller	5/18/1906	Silver Bow County

DuBose, Dudley

John H. Osnes	7/13/1894	Chouteau County
Calvin J. Christie	12/21/1894	Flathead County
Joseph Cadotte	12/27/1895	Chouteau County
William W. Calder	3/16/1900	Fergus County

Dwyer, John V.

Frank Fisher	1/14/1918	Silver Bow County
John O'Neill	1/14/1918	Silver Bow County
Sherman Powell	1/14/1918	Silver Bow County

Erickson, John Edward[5]

Frederick LeBeau	4/2/1909	Flathead County

Ford, William L.

Lee Simpson	12/30/1939	Golden Valley County

Galbraith, Thomas J.[6]

Thomas King	6/6/1890	Jefferson County

Galbraith, William J.

Ah Yung	8/16/1883	Missoula County
Thomas H. Harding	3/25/1887	Beaverhead County
Martin Luther Scott	2/17/1888	Deer Lodge County

Harwood, Benjamin P.

Franklin Robideau	1/15/1938	Stillwater County

Hattersley, R.M.

George Hoffman	8/29/1933	Teton County

Henry, Frank[7]

Robert A. Anderson	7/13/1894	Park County
Thomas Salmon	1/27/1899	Carbon County

Horkan, George A.

Joseph B. Reagin	2/9/1923	Treasure County
Glenna Martin Bolton	2/9/1923	Treasure County

Jones, George P.

Alfred Lane	9/3/1920	Rosebud County

Law, Benjamin B.

Seth O. Danner	7/18/1924	Gallatin County

Lentz, Theodore

Joseph Vuckovich	2/17/1922	Missoula County

Loud, Charles H.[8]

William C. Brooks	11/24/1899	Yellowstone County
Joseph C. Hurst	3/30/1900	Dawson County

Lynch, Jeremiah J.[9]

Monte Harris	4/20/1923	Silver Bow County
William Harris	4/20/1923	Silver Bow County
Anthony Vettere	10/1/1926	Silver Bow County

Marshall, C.S. [10]

Pierre Paul	12/19/1890	Missoula County
La La See	12/19/1890	Missoula County
Antley	12/19/1890	Missoula County
Pascale	12/19/1890	Missoula County
John Burns	12/16/1892	Missoula County

Matthews, John A.

Leslie Fahley	2/16/1917	Meagher County
Harrison Gibson	2/16/1917	Meagher County
Henry Hall	2/16/1917	Meagher County

McClernan, John B.

James Martin	2/23/1904	Silver Bow County

McConnell, Newton W.

Patrick Hart	2/10/1888	Lewis & Clark County
George Duncan Bryson	8/9/1889	Jefferson County

McKinnon, S.D.

Henry Zorn	4/24/1935	Miles City
George Criner	10/16/1935	Miles City

Paul, Spurgeon E.

Ferdinand Schlaps	5/20/1927	Roosevelt County

Reynolds, Stephen (Miners' Court)

John Keene	6/7/1865	Lewis & Clark County

Showers, Frank

Clayberg Pugh	7/1/1895	Jefferson County

Smith, D.F.

William Pepo	4/6/1900	Teton County

Smith, Henry C.

Joseph H. Allen	9/14/1899	Lewis & Clark County

Smith, Joseph C.

Albert Yeik	8/26/1921	Beaverhead County

Stewart, W.R.C.

Lu Sing	4/20/1906	Gallatin County

Taylor, Charles A.

Juan Cuellae	4/12/1918	Yellowstone County

Wade, Decius S.[11]

William Wright Wheatley	8/13/1875	Lewis & Clark County
William H. Sterres	10/28/1875	Lewis & Clark County
Joseph K. Koble	10/6/1879	Chouteau County
Orlando H. Marsh	10/6/1879	Chouteau County
Heinrich Furhmann	5/2/1883	Lewis & Clark County
John A. Clark	12/27/1883	Gallatin County

Webster, Frederick C.

Louis H. Mott	3/18/1904	Missoula County

Winston, George B.

George J. Rock	6/15/1908	Powell County
William A. Hayes	4/2/1909	Powell County

(Endnotes)

[1] In 1875 President Ulysses Grant appointed Henry Blake of Virginia City to succeed Justice Francis Servis on the Territorial Supreme Court, making him the first resident of Montana Territory to serve on the high court. Judge Blake was originally from Boston and had studied at Harvard University before starting his practice in the Montana Territory in 1866. Justice Blake remained on the bench until March of 1880 when Judge E.J. Conger replaced him. Judge Blake was again appointed to the Supreme Court when President Benjamin Harrison named him Chief Justice in March of 1889. Blake became the first Chief Justice of the State Supreme Court when he was elected to the bench in November of 1889 and he remained until William Young Pemberton replaced him on January 2, 1894.

[2] Before becoming a district judge, James Clements of Helena assisted in the unsuccessful defense of William Gay who was hanged in June of 1896 and Joseph Allen who was eventually executed in 1899.

[3] Everton Judson Conger of Illinois served in the Union Army during the Civil War and he was in command of the troops that captured John Wilkes Booth, the assassin of President Lincoln. After his appointment to the Territorial Supreme Court by President Rutherford Hayes, Judge Conger arrived in Virginia City with his son on the Overland Company coach on March 1, 1880. Judge Conger retired from the high court in February of 1883 because of ill health from old Civil War wounds and the strenuous duties on the bench.

[4] DeWolfe became an Associate Justice of the Supreme Court when President Grover Cleveland appointed him in 1887 to succeed Judge Galbraith. This made DeWolfe the third citizen of Montana, following Henry Blake and Thomas Bach to be seated on the high court. He remained on the bench until 1889 when he retired to practice law at Butte.

[5] John Edward Erickson was born in Wisconsin in March of 1863 and served as Teton County attorney from 1897 through 1905. After successfully prosecuting William Pepo in 1899, Erickson was elected district judge at Kalispell where he sentenced Frederick LeBeau to hang in 1909. During two separate terms as Governor of Montana, Erickson refused to commute the death sentences of Roy Walsh, Anthony Vettere, Ferdinand Schlaps and Rollin Davisson. Governor Erickson later served as U.S. Senator from 1933 through 1934 before retiring in the Flathead Valley where he died in 1946.

In May of 1887 President Grover Cleveland appointed Newton W. McConnell of Tennessee as Chief Justice of the Territorial Supreme Court, replacing Decius S. Wade. McConnell served until March of 1889 when he went into private practice in Helena.

[6] Judge Thomas Galbraith was one of the first eight district judges elected under the new state constitution in 1889 presiding over the Fifth District, which was comprised of Beaverhead, Jefferson and Madison Counties.

[7] Frank Henry was another of the first elected judges of Montana and he presided over the Sixth District, which was originally was made up of Gallatin, Park and Meagher Counties.

[8] Before becoming a judge, Charles Loud and his partners opened one of the first law firms in Montana. Thise circuit-riding law practice had offices in several communities including Miles City, Red Lodge, Forsyth and Billings.

[9] While Judge Wade has been credited with sending the most men to the gallows, Judge Jeremiah Lynch had sentenced more murderers to death than any other judge.

[10] Judge Marshall was one of the first eight district judges elected after statehood and he presided over the Fourth District, which at the time comprised present day Missoula, Flathead, Sanders, Lincoln, Lake and parts of Powell Counties.

[11] In March of 1871 President Ulysses Grant appointed thirty-six-year-old Decius S. Wade of Ohio to Chief Justice of the Montana Territorial Supreme Court, replacing Henry Warren who had served sixteen years on the bench before retiring in 1887.

Over the many years on the bench Judge D.S. Wade never missed a term of court and he sentenced twelve men to hang, six of whom were successfully executed. Along with the capital cases, Judge Wade sent over five hundred criminals to the penitentiary. "Helena Daily Herald" 12/29/1886.

Individual Hanging Case References

These pages contain the various reference materials used in the individual hanging profiles, which are listed alphabetically. Names in large print are for legal hangings while the others were executed illegally. Individuals are listed by their last name unless they are known only by their nickname. Indian and Chinese names are listed alphabetically as they are pronounced and unknown victims or John Doe listings are grouped by type and date of execution. Dates in parentheses indicate the date of hanging.

Adams, Chris See Calvin Christie

Ah Chow (1/25/1870) Helena Daily Herald 1/18/1870, p3; 1/25/1870, p3; The New North West 1/21/1870; 1/28/1870; Great Falls Tribune 9/2/1934, p12; "Ah Chow" by Bea Jay Block, Birdseye B&B, Helena, MT.

Ah Kee (See Ah Young)

Ah Yung (8/16/1883) Missoulian 8/17/1883; 2/19/1922, p1 Sec 2; 10/15/1933; Helena Daily Independent 3/9/1883, p3; 7/8/1883; 8/17/1883, p5; Weekly Avant Courier 8/23/1883; Missoula County Case No. 555, Microfilm Book #8, pages 1792-1833

Allen, Joseph H. (9/14/1899) Helena Daily Independent 7/26/1898, p8; 7/27/1898, p8; 7/28/1898, p8; 8/8/1898, p6; 8/11/1898, p15; 8/14/1898, p8; 8/16/1898, p5; 8/19/1898, p8; 8/22/1898, p8; 8/23/1898, p5; 11/10/1898, p7; 11/11/1898, p8; 11/12/1898, p5; 11/13/1898, p8; 1/13/1899, p5; 8/24/1899, p8; 9/2/1899; 9/14/1899, p5; 9/15/1899; Helena Semi-Weekly Independent, p5; 9/12/1899, p5; Helena Independent Record 5/25/1995; Great Falls Tribune 7/26/1898, p1; 7/20/1899, p1; 9/12/1899, p1; 9/13/1899, p1; 9/14/1899, p1; 9/15/1899, p1; Anaconda Standard 9/12/1899, p1; 9/13/1899, p1; 9/14/1899, p1; 9/15/1899, p5

Anderson, Robert A. (7/13/1894) Livingston Enterprise 4/28/1894; 5/5/1894; 5/12/1894, p1; 5/19/1894, p1; 5/26/1892, p1; 6/9/1894, p6; 6/16/1894, p5; 6/23/1894, p1; 6/23/1894, p5; 7/14/1894; 7/14/1894, p1; 7/21/1894, p1; 9/22/1894, p5; Great Falls Tribune 7/10/1894, p4; 7/14/1894, p1; 8/2/1903, p9; 8/7/1903, p1; Billings Times 7/3/1894, p8; Billings Gazette 12/7/1897, p4; Midland Empire Farmer 9/2/1935

Annen, John (Indian) (See John Annen)

Antley(12/19/1890) (with Pierre Paul, La La See and Pascale) (See: Pierre Paul

Baker (9/2/1871) New North West 9/9/1871, p2; 9/30/1871, p3; 10/28/1871, p1; Recollections of Tom Moore, written up by Mike Castleberry of Radersburg; "History of Montana" Leeson, p266

Ballou, George (5/18/1868) Montana Post 5/22/1868, p8; "History of Montana" Leeson

"Barber, the" (1/14/1883) (with Joe Davis or "Ohio Dan") Weekly Missoulian 1/5/1883, p1; 1/26/1883; 2/9/1883; Helena Daily Independent 12/20/1882; Anaconda Standard 12/13/1903; Harlowton News 3/13/1924, p9; The Mountaineer 7/9/1928; Redstone Review 4/11/1932; Tribune of Shelby 11/20/1933; Liberty County Forum 12/4/1939

Belgrade, Frank (July 1884) The Ismay Journal 7/11/1927; The Mineral Independent 3/11/1935

Belwaux See Frank Belgrade

"Big Mustache Frank" (July 1884) (with John Doe, Rustler) GF Tribune 10/3/1926, p3 Sec. 2

Biggerstaff, William (4/6/1896) Helena Daily Herald 6/10/1895, p8;

6/12/1895, p5; 6/14/1895, p8; 6/15/1895, p5; 10/15/1895, p8; 10/17/1895, p8; 10/18/1895, p8; 10/19/1895, p8; 10/26/1895, p8; 12/17/1895; 1/8/1896, p8; 2/17/1896, p1, p4; 3/4/1896, p8; 3/5/1896, p8; 4/1/1896, p8; 4/4/1896, p1; 4/6/1896, p1; Helena Weekly Herald 4/9/1896, p6; Anaconda Standard 6/10/1895, p7; 3/24/1896, p1 Sec.2; 4/2/1896, p1; 4/4/1896; 4/7/1896, p1; Neihart Miner 12/19/1895, p1; Billings Gazette 12/7/1897, p4; "Montana the Magazine of Western History" Winter 1963 "The History and Theory of Capital Punishment in Montana" R.O. Raffety

Black, Charles See Calvin Christie

Black, Robert See John Keene

"Black Feather" (April 1882) Weekly Avant Courier 12/11/1884; Forsyth Independent 8/20/1934; "Teton County History" Teton County Historical Society

Blue, George See George Ballou

Bolton, Glenna M. (2/9/1923) (with Joe B. Reagin) Forsyth Times Journal 12/15/1921, p1, p6; 12/29/1921, p1; 1/12/1922, p1; 1/19/1922, p1; 10/19/1922, p1; 10/26/1922, p1; 11/16/1922, p1; Hysham Echo 1/5/1922, p1; 1/12/1922, p1; 1/19/1922, p1; 7/27/1922, p1; 11/16/1922, p1; 1/4/1923, p1; 2/1/1923, p1; 2/8/1923, p1; Billings Gazette 2/11/1923; Great Falls Tribune 12/11/1921, p1; 2/10/1923, p1; 2/11/1923, p4; Bynum Herald 1/16/1922; Kalispell Times 1/27/1938; Supreme Court records, State vs. J.B. Reagin 10/19/1922; State vs. G.M. Bolton 11/13/1922; "Tales of Treasure County" edited by Ruth Carrington

Brady, James (Bradley) (June 15, 1864) Anaconda Standard 12/18/1898; 3/14/1920, p1 part 2; Bynum Herald 3/13/1922; Sumatra Sun 11/10/1924; Silver State Post 1/8/1934; Whitefish Pilot 1/3/1938; Kalispell Times 7/1/1937; "Vigilantes in Montana" Dimsdale; "Vigilantes" H. Birney;

Brady, James Edward (10/2/1901) Anaconda Standard 10/2/1901, p1; 10/3/1901, p1; p4; 10/4/1901, p1; 10/6/1901, p3; 10/17/1901; 10/22/1901, p1; Great Falls Leader 10/2/1901, p1; 10/3/1901, p1; 10/4/1901, p1;

"Bronco Charlie" (Summer of 1884) (Hanged with "Turkey" Williams) Helena Daily Herald 5/8/1889, p2

Brooks, William C. (11/24/1899) Billings Gazette 1/13/1899, p8; 2/7/1899, p3; 2/10/1899, p1; 2/14/1899, p3; 5/23/1899, p1; 10/27/1899, p1; 10/31/1899, p4; 11/7/1899, p3; 11/14/1899, p4; 11/22/1899, p1; 11/24/1899, p1; 2/16/1918, p1; 4/12/1918; Great Falls Tribune 11/24/1899

Brown, George W. (1/4/1864) Bynum Herald 12/19/1921; "Montana Vigilantes" Dimsdale; "Vigilante Days and Ways" Langford; "From Wilderness to Statehood" Hamilton; "Vigilante Victims" Mather and Boswell; "Vigilantes" Birney; "History of Montana" Tom Stout

Brown, Jack (6/18/1903) Great Falls Tribune 6/19/1903, p1; 6/20/1903, p1; 6/22/1903, p3; 7/19/1931, p1, sec 2; Anaconda Standard 6/7/1903, p1; 6/19/1903, p1; 6/17/1905, p1; 6/19/1903, p1; 6/20/1903, p1; Cascade Courier 8/7/1933

Bryson, George, Duncan (8/9/1889) Helena Daily Herald 10/2/1888, p1; 10/3/1888, p8; 10/10/1888, p8; 10/11/1888, p8; 10/15/1888, p8; 11/7/1888, p1; 12/31/1888, p8; 3/11/1889, p5; 5/20/1889; 5/22/1889, p8; 6/27/1889, p4; 7/1/1889; 8/9/1889, p1; 6/6/1890, p8; Helena Weekly Herald 7/25/1889; 8/8/1889; 10/4/1888, p2; 10/18/1888, p7, p8; 3/14/1889, p7; 3/21/1889, p7, p8; 5/23/1889; Great Falls Tribune 6/28/1889, p1; 8/6/1889, p1; 8/9/1889, p1; Butte

Semi-Weekly Miner 8/7/1889, p1; 8/14/1889, p2; The Philipsburg Mail 8/15/1889, p1; Anaconda Standard 6/7/1890, p4

Bunton, William (1/19/1864) Anaconda Standard 12/17/1899; Great Falls Tribune 5/24/1908, p1; Bynum Herald 12/19/1921; The Dillon Examiner; Ekalaka Eagle 5/25/1931; "Vigilantes of Montana" Dimsdale; "Vigilante Days and Ways" Langford; "Vigilante Victims" Mather and Boswell

Burns, John (12/16/1892) Weekly Missoulian 8/17/1892; 9/21/1892; 9/28/1892; 10/19/1892, p3, p4; 10/26/1892, p3; 11/9/1892, p6; 12/21/1892; 2/19/1922, p1, Sec 2; Jefferson County Sentinel 8/25/1892, p1; 12/22/1892; Anaconda Standard 12/17/1892

Cadotte, Joseph (12/27/1895) River Press 12/14/1892, p6; 12/21/1892, p5; 6/19/1895, p5; 7/3/1895, p6; 7/10/1895, p5; 7/10/1895, p5; 7/17/1895, p5; 8/28/1895, p5; 9/4/1895, p5; 9/11/1895, p5; 12/18/1895, p6; 1/1/1896, p5; Missoulian 7/9/1895, p4; 12/28/1895, p1; Great Falls Tribune 10/18/1895, p4; 12/20/1895, p1; 12/28/1895, p1; Anaconda Standard 7/11/1895, p6; 10/18/1895, p1; 12/10/1895, p1; 12/13/1895, p11; 12/20/1895, p11; 12/26/1895, p11; Helena Daily Herald 10/17/1895, p8; 10/18/1895, p1; 12/27/1895, p1; 12/28/1895, p11; 12/30/1895, p11; 1/8/1898, p8; Chouteau County Court Records; Letter of Mollie Sedgwick, May, 1975

Calder, William Wallace (3/18/1900) Helena Independent, 10/6/1898, p1; 10/7/1898, p1; Anaconda Standard 3/13/1900, p11; 3/14/1900, p11; 3/17/1900, p1; Great Falls Tribune 10/6/1898, p3; 10/8/1898, p4; 10/9/1898, p1; 4/2/1899, p1; 3/17/1900, p1; The Billings Time 10/13/1898, p5; 12/1/1898, p5; 12/14/1899, p6; 2/1/1900, p1; Helena Daily Herald 3/16/1900, p1; Helena Daily Evening Herald 4/1/1899, p8; 4/24/1899, p8; Glendive Independent 4/29/1899, p3; Lewistown Democrat, 3/14/1900, p3; 3/21/1900, p2; p3; Carbon County Democrat 3/21/1900, p1; 4/4/1900, p1; 5/2/1900, p8; State v. Calder January 29, 1900, MT. Supreme Court filing; "The Hanging of Billy Calder" by Bill Yaeger

"California Ed" (7/4/1884) Anaconda Standard 8/11/1901, p18; The Mineral Independent 3/11/1935; Judith Basin Star 8/9/1937

"California Jack" See: "California Ed"

"Cannibal" See Boone Helm

Carter, Alexander (1/25/1864) The Stevensville Register 9/16/1918; Dillon Examiner 7/28/1919, p12; Judith Basin County Press 9/8/1924; "Vigilantes of Montana" Dimsdale; "Vigilante Victims" Mather and Boswell

"Champion" (Summer of 1884) (with "Mugs" Stevens) GF Tribune 10/3/1926, p3 Sec 2

Christie, Calvin J. (12/21/1894) Weekly Interlake 5/4/1894, p1; 7/6/1894, p4; 8/3/1894, p4; 8/17/1894, p1; 8/24/1894, p1; 9/28/1894, p1; 10/19/1894; 11/9/1894, p1; 12/14/1894, p1; 12/19/1894, p1; 12/21/1894, p1; Livingston Enterprise 5/5/1894; 12/29/1894, p7; Great Falls Tribune12/20/1894, p3; 12/21/1894, p1; 12/22/1894, p1; Great Falls Leader 12/22/1894, p1; Helena Daily Herald 12/11/1894, p8; "Driftwood from the Flathead" S.V. Frohlicher; "Kalispell Montana and the Upper Flathead Valley" Henry Elwood

Clark, John A. (12/27/1883) Weekly Avant Courier 6/28/1883; 8/16/1883; 9/6/1883; 10/25/1883; 12/27/1883; 1/3/1884; 12/27/1883; 1/3/1884; Bozeman Weekly Chronicle 8/15/1883, p3;

11/7/1883; 1/1/1884, p1; 6/25/1884, p3; Bozeman Daily Chronicle 7/18/1924; Helena Daily Herald 6/23/1883, p2; 11/1/1883, p2; 12/8/1883; 12/20/1883; Rocky Mountain Husbandman 1/10/1884, p2; Livingston Enterprise 6/9/1894, p6; 6/16/1894, p5; 11/3/2003; records of Gallatin County Historical Society

"Clubfoot George" See George Lane

Coleman, Phillip (9/10/1943) Missoulian 7/26/1943, p1; 7/27/1943, p1; 7/28/1943, p1, p5; 7/29/1943, p1; 7/30/1943; 7/31/1943, p1; 8/1/1943, p1; 8/2/1943, p1; 8/3/1943, p1; 8/4/1943, p1; 8/5/1943, p1; 8/6/1943, p1; 8/23/1943, p1; 9/6/1943, p8; 9/9/1943, p10; 9/10/1943, p1; 9/11/1943, p1; 9/14/1943, p10; Great Falls Tribune 7/26/1943, p1; 7/27/1943, p4; 7/28/1943, p9; 7/29/1943, p4; 7/30/1943, p4; 7/31/1943, p4; 8/3/1943, p7; 8/4/1943, p4; 8/6/1943, p4; 9/10/1943, p4; 9/11/1943, p4; 9/12/1943, p1; 6/17/1962; 2/10/1963, p1; Missoula County records, case number 2488; Death Warrant; Return of Death warrant; Court Brief; Coleman's statement; Brown's statement;

Collins, J.C. (4/4/1913) Great Falls Leader 4/5/1913, p3; The Columbus News 7/6/1936; "Sheridan's Daybreak" Magnus Aasheim; "Montana the Magazine of Western History" Vol. 15 Vol. 4, p23; Vol. 16 Vol. 3, p88

Compton, Arthur L. (4/30/1870-with Joseph Wilson) Helena Daily Herald 4/29/1870; 4/30/1870, p3; 5/3/1870, p3; 5/5/1870; 5/6/1870; 3/16/1871, p3; The New North West 5/6/1870; Dillon Examiner 6/21/1920; Great Falls Tribune 4/21.1901, p2, sec 2; 7/28/1920; 9/2/1934, p12; The Nasua Independent, 8/8/1932; Helena Independent Record 10/14/1996, p5A; "We Seized Our Rifles" Eugene Lee Silliman; "Montana the Magazine of Western History" Vol. 28, Vol. 4, p41, p55; Vol.29, No.3, p69; "Indians and Whites in the Northwest" Father Lawrence Benedict Palladino

Compton, Peter Arthur See Arthur Compton

Constance, Felix (3/26/1885) (with Edward McDonald) Sun River Sun 4/2/1885, p1; River Press 4/8/1885, p1; p2; 4/15/1885, p1; 4/29/1885, p2; Helena Daily Herald 4/9/1885; Weekly Missoulian 5/1/1885; The Billings Times 1/6/1930; "Montana the Magazine of Western History" Vol. 15, No. 3, p49; Couteau County Sheriff's Log

Constant, Felix See Felix Constance

Cooke, Tommy (9/18/1865) Montana Post 9/23/1866, p3

Coomes, Milford (3/18/1883) (with William Smith) Helena Daily Herald 3/19/1883, p3; 3/20/1883, Editorial; 3/20/1883; Helena Daily Independent 1/6/1882, p3; 3/20/1883 p3; 3/21/1883, p3; 4/11/1883, p3; 4/18/1883, p3; 4/19/1883, p3; 4/20/1883, p3; "Names on the Faces of Montana," Greenhorn, p126

Cooper, John (1/25/1864) Dillon Examiner 7/28/1919, p12; "Vigilantes of Montana" Dimsdale; "Vigilante Victims" Mather and Boswell

Costello, James (November 1884) (with 3 John Doe Rustlers) Weekly Avant Courier 11/6/1884

Coyle, John See John Dolan

Criner, George (10/16/1935) Billings Gazette 8/8/1935, p1; 8/9/1935, p1; 8/16/1935, p1; 8/23/1935, p1; 9/4/1935, p1; 9/5/1935, p1; 9/22/1935, p1; 10/11/1935, p10; 10/15/1935, p1; 10/16/1935, p1; 10/17/1935, p6; Great Falls Tribune 8/8/1935, p1; 8/9/1935, p1; 10/11/1935, p9; 10/16/1935, p1; Missoulian 10/11/1935, p13; Kalispell Times 1/27/1938

Crochet, John (6/5/1866) Montana Post 6/9/1866; The Helena Weekly Herald 11/8/1883, p2; The Mountaineer 10/1/1928, p2; "Indians and Whites in the Northwest" Lawrence Benedict Palladino

Cuellae, Juan (4/12/1918) Billings Gazette 1/19/1918; 2/4/1918; 2/5/1918, p6; 2/13/1918, p3; 2/14/1918, p5; 2/15/1918, p6;

2/16/1918, p1; 2/18/1918, p3; 2/19/1918, p5; 3/9/1918, p4; 4/2/1918, p3; 4/4/1918, p6; 4/12/1918, p1; 11/10/1934, p1 Sec. 2; Great Falls Tribune 12/17/1917, p5; 12/18/1917, p2; 2/16/1918, p5; 4/12/1918, p3; 4/13/1918, p1; Anaconda Standard 2/16/1918, p11; Pondera County News 2/16/1933; Yellowstone County Court Records

Dalam, John See John Dolan

Daniels, James B. (3/2/1866) Meagher Republican 2/1/1918, p7; The Jordan Gazette 4/7/1919; Dillon Examiner 4/9/1919 p9; Grass Range Review 1/7/1924; Cascade Courier 1/20/1930; Ekalaka Eagle 9/28/1931; Great Falls Tribune 11/1/1931, p4; Big Flat News 11/9/1931; Pondera County News 4/23/1934; "Vigilantes of Montana" Dimsdale; "History of Montana" Sanders; "Montana the Magazine of Western History" Vol. 12, No.1, p31, p34; Vol. 12, No.3, p78

Danner, Seth Orrin (7/18/1924) Bozeman Courier 1/3/1923, p1; 6/13/1923, p1; 6/20/1923, p1; 6/27/1923, p1; 7/4/1923, p1; 7/11/1923, p1; 7/25/1923, p1; 8/22/1923, p1; 8/29/1923, p1; 9/26/1923, p1; 9/26/1923, p1; 10/23/1923, p1; 10/24/1923, p1; 10/31/1923, p1, p6; 11/28/1923, p1; 12/12/1923, p1; 12/19/1923, p1; 12/26/1923, p5; 1/16/1924, p5; 2/6/1924, p1; 5/7/1924, p1; 6/11/1924, p12; 7/2/1924, p1; 7/16/1924, p1; Bozeman Daily Courier 1/10/1924; 2/10/1924; 5/20/1924; 5/28/1924; 6/8/1924; 6/18/1924; 7/10/1924; 7/17/1924; 7/18/1924; 7/19/1924; 7/23/1924; Anaconda Standard 6/9/1923, p1; 6/10/1923, p1; 6/12/1923, p1; 6/13/1923, p1; 6/15/1923, p1; 6/16/1923, p1; 6/19/1923, p4; 6/23/1923, p1; 6/30/1923, p1; 7/19/1923, p7; 8/26/1923, p1; 8/29/1923, p1; 10/21/1923, p1; 10/22/1923, p1, p4; 10/23/1923, p1; 10/24/1923, p1; 10/25/1923; 10/26/1923, p1; 10/27/1923, p1; 10/28/1923, p1; 11/18/1923, p1; 11/27/1923, p1; 11/28/1923, p1; 12/16/1923, p2; 5/20/1924, p1; 5/27/1924, p1; 7/18/1924, p1; Great Falls Tribune 6/9/1923, p1; 6/10/1923, p1; 6/12/1923, p1; 6/13/1923, p1; 6/14/1923, p1; 6/15/1923, p1; 6/16/1923, p1; 6/20/1923, p1; 6/23/1923, p1; 7/1/1923, p1; 10/22/1923, p1; 5/29/1924, p5; 6/10/1924, p4; 7/19/1924, p2; Missoulian 6/23/1923; 6/30/1923, p1; 10/22/1923, p1; 10/23/1923, p1; 10/24/1923, p1; 10/25/1923, p1; 10/26/1923, p1; 10/27/1923, p1; 5/27/1924, p1; 7/18/1924, p1; Harlowtown News 7/5/1923, p4; 7/15/1923, p10; 12/6/1923, p7; Montana Record Herald, Helena, 7/18/1924, p1; Billings Gazette 7/18/1921, p1; 7/19/1924, p1; "True Detective Mysteries"; records of the Gallatin County Historical Society; July 1935; Montana State Supreme Court Records, 5/26/1924

Davisson, Rollin (11/6/1929) Livingston Enterprise 6/5/1929, p8; 6/6/1929, p8; 7/11/1929, p8; 7/24/1929, p8; 8/22/1929, p1, p2, p3, p5, p6, p8; 8/23/1929, p1, p2; 8/24/1929, p1, p2, p3, p8; 8/25/1929, p1; 8/27/1929, p1, p8; 8/29/1929, p1; 8/30/1929, p8; 8/31/1929, p5; 9/4/1929, p3; 9/5/1929; 9/6/1929, p1; 9/7/1929, p8; 9/14/1929, p8; 9/17/1929, p1; 9/18/1929, p1; 9/19/1929, p1; 9/20/1929, p1; 9/21/1929, p1, p2, p3, p5; 9/22/1929, p2, p3; 9/25/1929, p8; 9/26/1929, p1; 9/26/1929, p2, p5, p8; 9/27/1929, p2; 9/29/1929, p5; 10/2/1929, p3; 10/3/1929, p8; 10/9/1929, p8; 10/10/1929; 10/15/1929, p8; 10/16/1929, p8; 10/17/1929, p8;10/20/1929, p2, p8; 10/26/1929, p8; 10/29/1929, p8; 10/30/1929, p1, p5; 10/31/1929, p6, p8; 11/5/1929, p1; 11/7/1929, p2, p8; 11/10/1929, p6; 11/19/1929, p10; 12/27/1929, p6; Great Falls Tribune 8/22/1929, p1; 8/23/1929, p5, p8; 10/3/1929; 11/5/1929, p1; 11/6/1929, p1, p8; 11/7/1929, p5; Billings Gazette 8/22/1929, p1; 8/23/1929, p8; 8/24/1929, p8; 11/5/1929, p9; 11/6/1929, p1; 11/7/1929, p1

Davis, Joseph "Ohio Dan" (1/14/1883) (with "The Barber") Weekly Missoulian 1/5/1883, p1; 1/26/1883; 2/9/1883; Helena Daily Independent 12/20/1882; Anaconda Standard 12/13/1903; Harlowton News 3/13/1924, p9; The Mountaineer 7/9/1928; Redstone Review 4/11/1932; Tribune of Shelby 11/20/1933; Liberty County Forum 12/4/1939

"Dick the Barber" See the "Barber"

"Dick the Diver" (12/5/1882) Weekly Missoulian 1/5/1883, p1; 1/26/1883; 2/9/1883; Helena Daily Independent 3/21/1882, p3; 12/13/1882, p3; 12/20/1882; 12/21/1882, p3; 1/9/1883 p3; 2/2/1883, p3; 2/4/1883, p3; 2/11/1883, p3; 3/16/1883, p3; Anaconda Standard 12/13/1903; Harlowton News 3/13/1924, p9; The Mountaineer 7/9/1928; Redstone Review 4/11/1932; Tribune of Shelby 11/20/1933; Liberty County Forum 12/4/1939

Dolan, John "Hard Hat" (9/17/1864) Montana Post 9/24/1864, p2; Plevna Herald 3/10/1919; The Grass Range Review 12/24/1923; Cascade Courier 6/23/1930; Whitefish Pilot 2/27/1933; "Dimsdale's Vigilantes of Montana" A.J. Noyes; "A Decent Orderly Lynching" Allen

Dotson, Clinton (4/4/1902) Silver State 8/16/1899, p2; 8/23/1899, p2; 8/30/1899, p2; 10/11/1899; 10/18/1899, p2; p3; 10/25/1899, p2; Anaconda Standard 8/12/1899, p3; 8/13/1899, p5; 8/16/1899, p4; 8/17/1899, p4; 8/18/1899, p4; 8/19/1899, p3; 8/29/1899, p1; 8/31/1899, p3; 9/7/1899, p5; 9/8/1899, p4; 9/10/1899, p4; 9/17/1899, p4; 10/5/1899, p4; 10/6/1899, p1; 10/7/1899, p4; 10/8/1899, p5; 10/10/1899; 10/11/1899, p1; 10/12/1899, p1; 10/13/1899, p5; 10/14/1899, p4; 2/22/1901; 2/25/1901, p1; 3/7/1901, p4; 3/9/1901, p5; 3/16/1901, p5; 3/20/1901, p4; 4/17/1901, p5; 4/18/1901, p5; 7/7/1901, p3; 7/8/1901, p3; 7/9/1901, p4; 7/10/1901, p5; 7/11/1901, p5; 7/12/1901, p5; 7/13/1901, p5; 7/16/1901, p5; 7/18/1901, p5; 7/19/1901, p1; 7/20/1901, p1; 7/23/1901, p4; 7/25/1901, p5; 8/1/1901, p4; 8/12/1901, p3; 8/20/1901, p4; 8/26/1901, p3; 9/4/1901, p5; 9/5/1901, p5; 9/15/1901, p4; 12/1/1901, p5; 12/20/1901, p5; 2/25/1902, p1; 3/19/1902, p1; 3/20/1902, p1; 3/25/1902, p1, p11; 3/26/1902, p1; 3/30/1902, p4; 3/31/1902, p1, p8; 4/3/1902, p1; 4/6/1902, p1, p5; 4/9/1902, p1; Helena Independent 8/12/1899, p1; 8/13/1899, p1; 8/16/1899, p1; 8/27/1899, p8; 8/29/1899, p1; 2/23/1901, p5; 2/24/1901, p5; 2/25/1901, p7; 4/5/1902; Missoulian 3/7/1901, p1, p5; 3/15/1901, p3; 9/6/1901, p1; 9/7/1901, p1, p5; Great Falls Tribune 4/5/1902, p1; Harlowton Press 4/25/1918, p7; Dillon Examiner 6/11/1919, p14

Douglas, James (11/13/1867) Montana Post 11/23/1867; "Warner's Montana Territory History" F.W. Warner; "Shallow Diggins" Jean Davis

Douglas, John B. (5/27/1881) Madisonian 4/9/1881, p2; 4/16/1881, p2; 5/7/1881, p2; 5/14/1881; 5/21/1881, p2; 5/28/1881, p2; 8/6/1881, p2; Helens Daily Herald 3/26/1881, p3; 3/29/1881, p3; 4/1/1881, p3; 4/8/1881, p3; 5/16/1881, p3; 5/27/1881, p3 5/28/1881, p3; 5/30/1881, p3; Helena Daily Independent 4/19/1881 p3; 5/31/1881 p3; Advant Courier 4/7/1881 p3; Anaconda Standard 5/4/1902, p29; Midland Empire Farmer 1/24/1938; Madison County court records

Downes, William (7/4/1884) Helena Daily Herald 7/29/1884; Anaconda Standard 8/11/1901, p18; Judith Basin Star 8/9/1937

"Dutch John" See John Wagner

Edward, James See James E. Brady

Edwards, Orville (July 1884) (with "Swift Bill" and Silas Nickerson) Rocky Mountain Husbandman 9/11/1884, p3; Red Stone Review 10/10/1921; GF Tribune 10/3/1926, p3 sec. 2; Judith Basin Star 8/9/1937; "Jordan" Arthur Jordan

Fahley, Leslie (2/16/1917) (with Harrison Gibson and Henry Hall) Judith Gap Journal 9/22/1916, p1; 10/6/1916, p1; 10/13/1916, p1; 10/20/1916, p1; 12/22/1916, p1; 1/12/1917, p1; 1/19/1917, p1; 2/16/1917, p1; 2/23/1917, p1; Meagher Republican 1/12/1917, p1; 1/19/1917, p1; 2/9/1917, p1; 2/16/1917, p1; Helena Independent 2/14/1917, p5; 2/16/1917, p1; 2/17/1917, p1; 2/18/1917, p3; Great Falls Tribune 2/16/1917, p1; 2/17/1917, p11; 2/24/2002; Anaconda Standard 2/16/1917; 2/17/1917, p1; "Meagher County" Meagher County Historical Society

Fields, Robert See Robert A. Anderson

Fisher, Frank (1/14/1918) (with John O'Neil) Meagher Republican 5/18/1917, p5; Flathead Courier 11/26/1917; GF Tribune 1/15/1918, p5; Anaconda Standard 3/21/1917, p9; 3/30/1917, p9; 3/31/1917; 4/8/1917, p9; 4/19/1917, p12; 4/23/1917, p6; 4/29/1917, p9, 10; 5/6/1917, p7; 5/7/1917, p7; 5/8/1917, p10; 5/12/1917, p7; 5/17/1917, p10; 5/18/1917, p8; 1/2/1918, p3; 1/8/1918, p14; 1/12/1918, p8; 1/13/1918, p4, p1 sec. 2; 1/14/1918, p1; 1/15/1918, p1; 1/17/1918, p10; 1/27/1918, p7; 12/19/1925, p6; 2/14/1925; GF Tribune 1/15/1918, p5; 1/21/1968, Sunday Sup.; Montana Record Herald, Helena 1/14/1918, p1

Fleming, James (9/6/1901) Anaconda Standard 2/22/1901; 2/25/1901, p1; 3/7/1901, p4; 3/9/1901, p5; 3/16/1901, p5; 3/20/1901, p4; 4/17/1901, p5; 4/18/1901, p5; 7/7/1901, p3; 7/8/1901, p3; 7/9/1901, p4; 7/10/1901, p5; 7/11/1901, p5; 7/12/1901, p5; 7/13/1901, p5; 7/16/1901, p5; 7/18/1901, p5; 7/19/1901, p1; 7/20/1901, p1; 7/23/1901, p4; 7/25/1901, p5; 8/1/1901, p4; 8/12/1901, p3; 8/20/1901, p4; 8/26/1901, p3; 9/4/1901, p5; 9/5/1901, p5; Helena Independent 2/23/1901, p5; 2/24/1901, p5; 2/25/1901, p7; 4/5/1902; Missoulian 3/7/1901, p1, p5; 3/15/1901, p3; 9/6/1901, p1; 9/7/1901, p1, p5

Fogardy, James See James Z. Fogarty

Fogarty, James Zachariah (1/7/1865) Diary of Thomas W. Harris of Fort Owens; "History of Montana" Leeson; "Montana Genesis" Stevensville Historical Society; Great Falls Tribune, 1/7/1965, p5

Fohrman, Henry See Heinrich Furhmann

Foraty, James See James Z. Fogarty

"Frenchy" See John Crochet

"Froggy" (Summer of 1882) Pondera County News 8/23/1934; Forsyth Independent 8/20/1934

Fuhrmann, Heinrich "Henry" (5/2/1883) Helena Daily Herald 3/7/1883, p3; 3/21/1883; 3/27/1883, p3; 4/30/1883; 5/1/1883, p3;

5/2/1883, p3; 2/16/1888, p3; Helena Daily Independent 12/23/1882, p3; 12/24/1882, p3; 12/27/1882, p3; 12/28/1882, p3; 3/13/1883, p3; 3/27/1883, p3; 3/28/1883, p3; 3/29/1883, p3; 3/30/1883, p3; 3/31/1883, p3 4/1/1883, p3; 5/1/1883, p3; 5/2/1883, p3; 5/3/1883, p3; 5/4/1883, p3

Fuller, Miles (5/18/1906) Anaconda Standard 5/9/1905, p11; 5/11/1905, p10; 5/12/1905, p11; 5/13/1905, p12; 5/16/1905, p8; 5/17/1905, p8; 5/18/1905, p8; 5/19/1905, p1; 5/28/1905, p11; 5/18/1906, p7; 5/19/1906, p7; 1/13/1918, sec 2; 12/19/1925, p6; Great Falls Tribune 5/19/1906, p1; 5/20/1906, p2

Gallagher, Brocky (7/5/1884) (with "Red Mike") GF Tribune 10/3/1926 p3, Sec. 2; Judith Basin Star 8/9/1937; "Forty Years on the Frontier" Granville Stuart: "Montana the Magazine of Western History" Vol. No. 1, Jan.1951

Gallagher, Jack (1/14/1864) Bynum Herald 12/19/1921; "Montana Vigilantes" Dimsdale; "Vigilante Days and Ways" Langford; "Vigilante Victims" Mather and Boswell; "A Decent Orderly Lynching" Allen

Gay, William (6/8/1896) Helena Daily Herald 5/10/1893, p1; 5/13/1893, p1; 5/16/1893, p1; 7/17/1893, p1; 5/19/1893, p1; 5/25/1893, p1; 5/26/1893, p8; 6/6/1893, p2, p8; 6/7/1893, p2; 12/10/1894, p8; 12/11/1894, p1; 12/27/1894, p1; 12/28/1894, p5; 1/12/1895, p6; 9/24/1895, p8; 11/4/1895 p8; 11/5/1895, p8; 11/6/1895, p8; 11/7/1895, p5; 11/8/1895, p8; 11/9/1895, p8; 11/11/1895, p8; 11/12/1895, p8; 11/16/1895, p8; 11/22/1895, p8; 11/29/1895, p8; 12/7/1895, p8; 12/13/1895, p5; 12/19/1895, p8; 1/8/1896, p8; 1/10/1896, p8; 1/21/1896, p5; 3/23/1896, p8; 4/10/1896, p1; 4/16/1896, p8; 5/30/1896, p2; 6/2/1896, p5; 6/4/1896, p8; 6/5/1896, p8; 6/6/1896, p1, p8; 6/8/1896, p1; Anaconda Standard 11/6/1895, p1; 11/7/1895, p2; 11/10/1895, p1; 11/13/1895, p1; 11/29/1895, p11; 12/2/1895, p8; 12/13/1895, p1; 12/13/1895, p1 sec 2; 12/20/1895, p2; 1/11/1896, p11; 3/24/1896, p1, p8; 5/19/1896, p2; Neihart Miner 9/12/1895, p1; 11/14/1895, p1; 12/5/1895, p1; 12/19/1895, p1; 1/16/1896, p8; 1/30/1896, p1; 4/2/1896, p1; 5/28/1896, p5; 6/4/1896, p1; Great Falls Tribune 12/25/1894, p1; 6/9/1896, p1; Billings Times 12/27/1894, p1; Billings Gazette 12/7/1897, p4; Livingston Enterprise 5/13/1893, p1; 5/20/1893, p1; 12/15/1894, p1; 12/22/1894, p1; Interlake 6/12/1896, p1; Winnett Times 4/23/1928

Gibbs, Charles (with Sam LaFaver July 1884) The Ismay Journal 7/11/1927; The Mineral Independent 3/11/1935

Gibson, Harrison (2/16/1917) (with Leslie Fahley and Henry Hall) (see Leslie Fahley)

Goones, J.L. (4/20/1866) Montana Post 5/12/1866 p1; The Townsend Star 9/8/1930

Gowan, Sam See J.L. Goones

Graves, William (Whiskey Bill) (1/26/1864) Semi-Weekly Republican Courier 11/7/1905; Ravalli Republic ("Montana Genesis") 4/23/2003 "Vigilantes of Montana" Dimsdale; "Vigilante Days and Ways" Langford; "Montana Genesis" Stevensville Historical Society; "Vigilante Victims" Mather and Boswell; "Another Man's Gold" Rod Johnson

"Greaser" See Joseph Pizanthia

Greybeal, Jack See Jack Brown

"Half-Breed" Jack (Summer of 1884) Helena Daily Herald 5/8/1889, p2

Hall, Henry (2/16/1917) (with Leslie Fahley and Harrison Gibson) (See Leslie Fahley)

Hamilton, John C. See John Burns
"Hard Hat" See John Dolan
Harding, Thomas H. (3/25/1887) Dillon Tribune 5/29/1886, p8; 6/5/1886, p5; 6/12/1886, p5; 9/24/1886, p5; 11/5/1886, p5; 1/7/1887, p7; 1/14/1887, p5; 1/21/1887, p5; 1/28/1887; 2/4/1887, p5; 2/11/1887, p5; 2/25/1887, p5; 3/18/1887, p5; 3/25/1887, p5; 6/3/1887; 6/10/1887, p5; Helena Daily Herald 12/9/1886; 3/25/1887, p3; 3/29/1887; Dillon Examiner 5/26/1920, p7; 6/9/1920, p9; Montana Newspaper Association 12/29/1930
Haron, Peter See John Heron
Harris, Monte (4/20/1923) Anaconda Standard 1/5/1922; 1/6/1922, p5; 1/30/1922, p3; 2/5/1922, p5; 2/12/1922, p5; 2/19/1922, p11; 3/3/1922, p3; 3/7/1922, p1; 3/8/1922, p3; 3/10/1922, p1; 3/11/1922, p1; 3/14/1922, p1; 3/21/1922, p5; 3/26/1922, p6; 4/2/1922, p5; 4/23/1922, p5; 3/3/1923, p1; 3/4/1923, p7; 3/5/1923, p5; 3/26/1923, p5; 3/29/1923, p5; 4/10/1923, p5; 4/11/1923, p8; 4/13/1923, p1; 4/14/1923, p1; 4/15/1923, p4; 4/16/1923, p1; 4/16/1923, p5; 4/17/1923, p1; 4/18/1923, p5; 4/19/1923, p1; 4/20/1923, p1; 4/21/1923, p1; 12/19/1925 p6; Great Falls Tribune 11/26/1921, p1; 11/29/1921, p5; 12/4/1921, p4; 12/6/1921, p9; 12/7/1921, p4; 2/28/1922, p1; 3/7/1922, p11; 4/15/1923, p7; 4/19/1923, p4; 4/20/1923, p1; 4/21/1923, p2;
Harris, William (4/20/1923) (with Monte Harris) Anaconda Standard 2/21/1922, p1; 2/22/1922, p1; 2/23/1922, p5; 2/24/1922, p1; 2/25/1922, p1; 2/28/1922, p1; 3/3/1922, p1; 3/6/1922, p5; 3/13/1922, p1; 3/15/1922, p3; 3/19/1922, p3; 3/22/1922, p5; 3/24/1922, p5
Harrison, Joseph (7/6/1882) Helena Daily Independent 7/11/1882, p3; 7/26/1882, p3; Billings Gazette 8/26/1934, p1, Sec2; Winifred Times 3/11/1935
Hart, John Patrick (2/10/1888) Helena Daily Herald 10/18/1886, p3; 10/19/1886; 12/22/1886; 5/9/1887, p3; 5/10/1887, p3; 7/20/1887, p3; 11/22/1887; 11/23/1887, p3; 11/25/1887; 11/29/1887, p3; 11/30/1887, p3; 1/24/1888, p3; 1/30/1888, p3; 2/6/1888, p3; 2/9/1888; 2/10/1888, p3; 2/11/1888, p3; 2/16/1888, p3; Great Falls Tribune 2/11/1888, p1; Helena weekly Herald 2/16/1888, p5; Philipsburg Mail 2/9/1888, p2; 2/16/1888, p1; Jefferson County court records
Hartt, John See: Patrick Hart
"Hat" the See John Dolan
Hayes, William A. (4/2/1909) (See: George Rock) Silver State 3/11/1908; 4/15/1908; 4/22/1908, p3; 4/29/1908; 5/20/1908; 5/27/1908; 2/3/1909, p2; 3/17/1909, p1; 4/7/1909, p1; Anaconda Standard 5/20/1908, p1; 5/22/1908, p1; 5/23/1908, p1; 5/27/1908, p1; 5/28/1908, p1; 6/16/1908, p1; 3/15/1909, p1; 4/2/1909; 5/8/1917, p10; Great Falls Tribune 12/4/1908, p5; 11/29/1931; Helena Independent 5/19/1908, p1; Missoulian 5/19/1908, p1; 5/23/1908, p1; 5/27/1908, p1; Kalispell Bee 4/6/1909, p1; Meagher Republican 5/18/1917, p5; Judith Basin County Press 9/11/1933
Helm, Boone (1/14/1864) Bynum Herald 12/19/1921; "Vigilante Days and Ways" Langford; "Vigilante Victims" Mather and Boswell; "A Decent Orderly Lynching" Allen
Heron, John "Peter" (8/25/1863) Twice a week Republican Courier 1/23/1906; Redstone Review 9/30/1918; Forsyth Democrat 5/20/1920, p7
Herring, Peter See John Heron
Hinson, William (See William Hynson)

Hoefner, Henry (4/18/1912) Billings Gazette 4/16/1912, p8; 4/17/1912, p8; 4/18/1912, p4; 4/19/1912, p10; Bonbells Tribune, April 1912; "They came and Stayed, Rosebud County History"

Hoffman, George (8/29/1933) Great Falls Tribune 9/22/1932, p1; 9/25/1932, p1; 10/1/1932, p14; 12/1/1932, p7; 12/2/1932; 12/3/1932; 12/4/1932, p1; 7/29/1933, p5; 8/29/1933, p1, p2; 8/30/1933, 1, p9; 8/31/1933, p5; 9/1/1933, p4; Great Falls Leader 11/28/1932, p8; 12/3/1932, p8; 12/5/1932, p8; 8/29/1933, p1; Missoulian 7/29/1933, p2; Pondera County News 12/8/1932, p1; "Teton County History" Teton County Historical Committee

Horan, Peter See: John Heron

Howard, Jack (9/15/1865) Montana Post 9/12/1865; 9/30/1865; 10/7/1865; "Cowboy Poetry" by D.J. O'Malley

Hunt (Aug or Sept 1871) "History of Montana" Leeson, 266

Hunter, William (2/3/1864) "Vigilantes of Montana" Dimsdale; "Bozeman and the Gallatin Valley" Phyllis Smith; Anaconda Standard 11/12/1899; Dillon Examiner 6/14/1920; Bynum Herald 12/19/1921; Brady Citizen 3/22/1926; Pondera County News 1/11/1932; Historical Society of Montana" Vol. 7, p165;"UM Western/ library" website

Hurst, Joseph C. (3/30/1900) Glendive Independent 12/24/1898, p3; 12/31/1898, p3; 1/7/1899, p3; 1/14/1899, p3; 1/22/1899, p3; 2/11/1899, p3; 2/25/1899, p3; 3/4/1899, p3; 3/11/1899, p3; 3/18/1899, p3; 3/25/1899, p3; 4/29/1899, p3; 6/10/1899, p3; 2/3/1900, p2; 2/10/1900, p3; 2/24/1900, p2; 3/3/1900, p2; 3/10/1900, p3; 3/17/1900, p3; 3/24/1900, p3; 3/31/1900, p3; 4/21/1900, p3; Helena Daily Independent 12/25/1898, p1; 1/11/1899, p5; Helena Daily Evening Herald 3/22/1899; Helena Daily Herald 3/1/1900, p8; 3/5/1900, p8; 3/19/1900, p8; 3/20/1900, p8; 3/21/1900, p8; 3/27/1900, p8; 3/28/1900, p1; 3/29/1900, p1; 3/30/1900, p8; 3/31/1900, p5; 4/2/1900, p8; Great Falls Tribune 12/25/1898, p1; 3/29/1900, p1; 3/30/1900, p1; 3/31/1900, p1; Billings Gazette 1/24/1899, p4; 4/21/1935, p1 Sec 2; Billings Times 1/12/1899, p5; 12/14/1899, p6; 2/1/1900, p1; 3/22/1900, p2; 3/29/1900, p2; Dawson County Review, p1; 3/15/1900, p1; 3/29/1900, p1; 5/31/1900, p1; Lewistown Democrat 3/28/1900, p1; 4/11/1900, p3; Carbon County Democrat 3/28/1900, p1; 4/4/1900, p4; 5/16/1900, p5

Hynson, William (8/24/1868) Montana Post 11/2/1867 p8; 8/28/1868 p6; GF Tribune, 5/10/1901, p3; River Press, 4/2/1975, p9; The Plains Plainsman 11/25/1918; Dillon Examiner 11/11/1940; "Vigilante Days and Ways" Langford

Hyman, William (See William Hynson)

Ives, George (12/21/1863) Anaconda Standard 12/15/1895; Semi Weekly Republican Courier 11/7/1905; Dillon Examiner 2/19/1919, p9; Fromberg Herald 12/6/1920; The Grass Range Review 5/8/1922; Ekalaka Eagle 3/31/1924; 5/25/1931; 3/13/1933; Judith Basin County Press 9/8/1924; 9/13/1924; Brady Citizens 3/22/1926; Eureka Journal 2/6/1928; Great Falls Tribune 8/23/1931, p1 sec. 2; Fallon County Times 1/25/1932; Rocky Mountain American 12/25/1933; Silver State Post 1/7/1935; The Yellowstone 1/6/1935; The Mineral Independent 4/18/1938; Big Timber Pioneer 9/1/1941; "Vigilante Days and Ways" Langford; "Vigilante Woman" Virginia Rowe Towle; "From Wilderness to Statehood, 1805-1900" Hamilton; "Vigilance Victims" R.E. Mather and F.E. Boswell; "A Decent Orderly Lynching" Frederick Allen; "Montana the Magazine of Western History" Vol. 28, No.4, p41

Jackson, John (9/27/1865) Montana Post 9/30/1865; "The Vigilantes of Montana" Dimsdale

Jackson, Walter (10/14/1903) Missoulian 10/14/1903, p1; 10/15/1933, p1; Great Falls

Tribune 8/17/1903, p1; 8/18/1903, p4; 8/22/1903, p4; 8/26/1903, p7; 10/8/1903, p3; 10/14/1903, p1, p2; 10/15/1903, p1, p5; Anaconda Standard 8/18/1903, p1; 8/19/1903, p1; 8/23/1903; 8/26/1903, p10; 9/12/1903, p1; 9/13/1903, p1; 10/8/1903; 10/14/1903; 10/16/1903; Fallon County Times 6/4/1928; "Montana Genesis: A History of the Stevensville Area of the Bitterroot Valley" by the Stevensville Historical Society

Jerome (with John Annen)

Jessrang, John A. (3/6/1883) Helena Daily Herald 10/1/1880 p3; 10/2/1880 p3; 10/4/1880 p3; 7/29/1881; 2/12/1883; 3/10/1883, p3; 3/12/1883, p3; Helena Daily Independent 2/10/1883, p3; 2/11/1883, p3; 2/20/1883, p3; 3/10/1883, p3; 3/13/1883, p3; 3/21/1883, p3; 3/31/1883, p3; Madisonian 6/29/1878, p2; 11/15/1879, p2; 10/9/1880, p2; 8/6/1881, p2; Weekly Avant Courier 3/15/1883; Fort Benton Record 3/17/1883, p3; Weekly Avant Courier 7/26/1883; Dillon Examiner 6/9/1920, p9; Harlowton News 7/12/1923, p7; The Billings Times 3/7/1934

Jewett, Charles (2/5/1866) Montana Post 2/17/1866, p2

John Annen (Indian) (March of1888) (with Jerome) "Early Flathead and Tobacco Plains" Marie C. Shea; "Frontier Days in the Flathead Country" Edward B. McCurdy; Weekly Missoulian 3/21/1888; Helena Weekly Herald 3/29/1888; 4/19/1888; Great Falls Tribune 10/10/1890; "Nuggets to Timber: Pioneer Days at Libby, MT." Libby Pioneer Society and the Libby Woman's Club of 1970; Kalispell, "Montana and the Upper Flathead Valley" Henry Elwood

John Doe (Summer 1865) (with three other John Does) Coffee Creek Herald 10/8/1917

John Doe (Summer 1865) (with three other John Does) Coffee Creek Herald 10/8/1917

John Doe (Summer 1865) (with three other John Does) Coffee Creek Herald 10/8/1917

John Doe (Summer 1865) (with three other John Does) Coffee Creek Herald 10/8/1917

John Doe (7/8/1865) "Pioneer Life in Montana" Judge Lyman E. Munson; Montana Historical Society Contributions, Vol. 5. p200

John Doe (October 1865) (with another John Doe) Montana Post 10/7/1865

John Doe (October 1865) (with another John Doe) Montana Post 10/7/1865

John Doe (November 23, 1865) Montana Post 11/25/1865

John Doe (November 23, 1865) Montana Post 11/25/1865

John Doe (2/4/1866) Montana Post 2/17/1866, p2; "Early History of Gallatin County, Montana" Lina Houston

John Doe (Summer 1870) The Dutton Sentinel 8/7/1939

John Doe, Boat Thief (Summer 1884) (With two John Doe, Victims) GF Tribune 9/26/1926, p1, Sec 2

John Doe, Chinaman (10/31/1871) New North West 5/20/1870; 11/4/1871, p4

John Doe, Chinaman (October 1875) Madisonian 10/9/1875, p2; 10/16/1875, p2; 10/30/1875, p2

John Doe, Indian (May 1864) Missoulian 10/29/1911 p4; Melstone Messenger 8/24/1931; "Forty Years on the Frontier" Granville Stuart; "Shallow Diggins" Jean Davis; "Contributions to the Montana Historical Society" Vol.2, p102

John Doe, Indian (7/1/1883) Weekly Missoulian" 7/6/1883

John Doe, Indian (8/8/1883) The Mountaineer 3/14/1932; Cascade Courier 2/11/1935; "Montana the Magazine of western History" Vol. 3, No. 3, p7; Vol. 52, No. 1, p72

John Doe, Indian (December 1884) (with six other John Doe, Indians) Mineral Argus 11/27/1884; 12/8/1884

John Doe, Indian (December 1884) (with six other John Doe, Indians)

John Doe, Indian (December 1884) (with six other John Doe, Indians)

John Doe, Indian (December 1884) (with six other John Doe, Indians)

John Doe, Indian (December 1884) (with six other John Doe, Indians)

John Doe, Indian (December 1884) (with six other John Doe, Indians)

John Doe, Indian (December 1884) (with six other John Doe, Indians)

John Doe, Murderer (2/17/1864) "A Decent Orderly Lynching" Allen; Diaries of John Grannis and James Morley, Montana Historical Society; Richland County Leader 12/5/1921

John Doe, Murderer (7/3/1884) (with John Doe, Thief) "Montana the Magazine of Western History" Winter 1969

John Doe, Negro Crewmember of the "General C.W. Meade" (May 1882) Helena Daily Herald 5/29/1882; Medicine Lake Wave 11/21/1932; 6/15/1936; The Eureka Mirror, 11/14/1938; "Fort Benton, World's Innermost Port" Joel Overholser; "Packets to Paradise"

John G. Lepley

John Doe, Rustler (1/25/1864) "Vigilantes of Montana" Dimsdale Beehrer's account to A.J. Noyes'

John Doe, Rustler (December 1879) Madisonian 11/8/1879, p2; 11/15/1879, p2; 11/29/1879, p2; 12/6/1879, p2; 12/13/1879, p2

John Doe, Rustler (April 1884) (with 4 other John Doe, Rustlers) GF Tribune 9/19/1926, p1, Sec. 2

John Doe, Rustler (April 1884) (with 4 other John Doe, Rustlers) GF Tribune 9/19/1926, p1, Sec. 2

John Doe, Rustler (April 1884) (with 4 other John Doe, Rustlers) GF Tribune 9/19/1926, p1, Sec. 2

John Doe, Rustler (April 1884) (with 4 other John Doe, Rustlers) GF Tribune 9/19/1926, p1, Sec.2

John Doe, Rustler (April 1884) (with 4 other John Doe, Rustlers) GF Tribune 9/19/1926, p1, Sec. 2

John Doe, Rustler (7/4/1884) (with "California Ed" and another John Doe, Rustlers) Judith Basin Star 8/9/1937

John Doe, Rustler (7/4/1884) (with "California Ed" and another John Doe, Rustlers) Judith Basin Star 8/9/1937

John Doe, Rustler (July 1884) (with "Big Mustache Frank) GF Tribune 10/3/1926, p3 Sec.2

John Doe, Rustler (Summer 1884) (with eleven other John Doe, Rustlers and an innocent John Doe, Victim) Hysham Echo 4/17/1933

John Doe, Rustler (Summer 1884) (with eleven other John Doe, Rustlers and an innocent John Doe, Victim) Hysham Echo 4/17/1933

John Doe, Rustler (Summer 1884) (with eleven other John Doe, Rustlers and an innocent John Doe, Victim) Hysham Echo 4/17/1933

John Doe, Rustler (Summer 1884) (with eleven other John Doe, Rustlers and an innocent John Doe, Victim) Hysham Echo 4/17/1933

John Doe, Rustler (Summer 1884) (with eleven other John Doe, Rustlers and an innocent John Doe, Victim) Hysham Echo 4/17/1933

John Doe, Rustler (Summer 1884) (with eleven other John Doe, Rustlers and an innocent John Doe, Victim) Hysham Echo 4/17/1933

John Doe, Rustler (Summer 1884) (with eleven other John Doe, Rustlers and an innocent John Doe, Victim) Hysham Echo 4/17/1933

John Doe, Rustler (Summer 1884) (with eleven other John Doe, Rustlers and an innocent John Doe, Victim) Hysham Echo 4/17/1933

John Doe, Rustler (Summer 1884) (with eleven other John Doe, Rustlers and an innocent John Doe, Victim) Hysham Echo 4/17/1933

John Doe, Rustler (Summer 1884) (with eleven other John Doe, Rustlers and an innocent John Doe, Victim) Hysham Echo 4/17/1933

John Doe, Rustler (Summer 1884) (with eleven other John Doe, Rustlers and an innocent John Doe, Victim) Hysham Echo 4/17/1933

John Doe, Rustler (Summer 1884) (with eleven other John Doe, Rustlers and an innocent John Doe, Victim) Hysham Echo 4/17/1933

John Doe, Victim) (Summer 1884) (with twelve John Doe, Rustlers) Hysham Echo 4/17/1933

John Doe Rustler (November 1884) (with Jim Costello and two other John Doe Rustlers) Weekly Avant Courier 11/6/1884

John Doe Rustler (November 1884) (with Jim Costello and two other John Doe Rustlers) Weekly Advant Courier 11/6/1884

John Doe Rustler (November 1884) (with Jim Costello and two other John Doe Rustlers) Weekly Advant Courier 11/6/1884

John Doe Rustler (Date Unknown) (with his brother) Anaconda Standard 6/1/1902, p19

John Doe Rustler (Date Unknown) (with his brother) Anaconda Standard 6/1/1902, p19

John Doe, Rustler (Date Unknown) Belt Valley Times 4/15/1929

John Doe, 16-yr-old (See Wilson 1/25/1868)

John Doe, Thief (Summer 1864) Jefferson Valley News 10/28/1935

John Doe, Thief (7/3/1884) (with John Doe, Murderer) "Montana the Magazine of Western History" Winter, 1969

John Doe, Tramp (7/24/1891) Great Falls Tribune 7/25/1891, p1; Billings Gazette 7/30/1891, p1; 11/10/1934, p1 Sec. 2; Winifred Times 6/2/1930; Billings Gazette 4/12/1918; 9/8/1960

John Doe, Victim (Summer 1884) (with another John Doe, Victim and a John Doe, Boat Thief) GF Tribune 9/26/1926, p1, Sec2

John Doe, Victim (Summer 1884) (with another John Doe, Victim and a John Doe, Boat Thief) GF Tribune 9/26/1926, p1 Sec 2

Johnson, Frank See Franklin Robideau

Johnson, Leander (3/12/1866) Montana Post 3/17/1866, 3/24/1866, p1; Anaconda Standard 12/18/1898; Sumatra Sun 11/10/1924; Kalispell Times 7/1/1937

Jones, Bill (July 1881) Madisonian 3/19/1881, p2; 4/30/1881, p2; 7/16/1881, p2; 7/23/881, p2

Jones, J.N. See Bill Jones

Jones, John See John Jackson

Kean, John See John Keene

Kee, Ah See Ah Yung

Keene, John (Bob Black) (6/7/1865) Montana Post 6/17/1865, p2; Helena Daily Herald 9/7/1875; 11/6/1883; 8/10/1889; Hysham Echo 5/3/1922, p7; Fallon County Times 1/25/1932; Philipsburg Mail 6/16/1941; "Vigilantes of Montana" Dimsdale; "Montana the Magazine of Western History" Vol. 2, No.4, p41

King, Thomas A. (6/6/1890) Jefferson County Sentinel 12/5/1889; 1/16/1890; 1/30/1890; 2/6/1890; 3/20/1890; 3/27/1890; 6/5/1890; 5/1/1890; 5/8/1890; 5/29/1890; 6/5/1890; 6/11/1890, p1; 6/12/1890; 7/17/1890; Anaconda Standard 1/29/1890, p4; 2/1/1890; 3/20/1890, p1; 5/3/1890, p1; 6/6/1890, p4; 6/7/1890, p4; Helena Daily Herald 1/13/1890, p8; 1/14/1890, p8; 2/1/1890, p5; 6/6/1890, p8; Great Falls Tribune, 6/7/1890, p1; 6/18/1890, p4; Great Falls Leader 6/6/1890; "Illustrated History of the State of Montana" Joaquin Miller

Kirby, Con (10/3/1865) Montana Post 10/7/1865

Koble, Joseph K. (10/6/1879) (with Orlando Marsh) Fort Benton Record 3/7/1879 p2; p3; 4/25/1879 p3; 5/16/1879 p3; 6/20/1879 p3; 9/5/1879 p2; 9/19/1879 p3; 10/10/1879; Helena Weekly Herald 5/8/1879 p8; Helena Daily Herald 6/18/1879; 10/10/1879, p3; Anaconda Standard 2/17/1897, p9; River Press 4/2/1975, p9; "Montana the Magazine of Western history" Vol. 28, No.4, p41

LaFaver, Samuel (hanged with Charlie Gibbs July 1884) The Ismay Journal 7/11/1927; The Mineral Independent 3/11/1935

La La Chee See La La See

La La See (12/19/1890) (with Pierre Paul, Pascale and Antley) (see Pierre Paul)

Lane, Alfred (9/3/1920) Forsyth Democrat 5/6/1920, p1, p4; 5/13/1920, p3; 7/22/1920, p1; 7/29/1920, p5; 9/2/1920, p12; Miles City Daily Star 5/1/1920, p5; 5/2/1920, p7; 5/4/1920, p5; 5/6/1920, p5; 5/8/1920, p5; 9/2/1920, p5; 9/3/1920, p2, p5; 7/24/1920, p3; Billings Gazette 9/3/1920, p1; 9/4/1920, p1; Great Falls Tribune 9/3/1920, p2; Helena Independent 9/3/1920, p6; 9/4/1920, p1; Fergus County Argus 8/9/1920; "They came and Stayed, Rosebud County History"

Lane, George "Clubfoot George" (1/14/1864) Anaconda Standard 12/18/1898; Bynum Herald 12/19/1921; The Mountaineer 8/22/1927; The Bridger Time 9/8/1941; "Vigilante Days and Ways" Langford; "A Decent Orderly Lynching" Allen

Lavardure, Narcissus (6/27/1884) Mineral Argus 7/3/1884, p1; Daily Yellowstone 7/10/1884; Grass Range Review 5/21/1923; GF Tribune 10/3/1926, p3 Sec. 2; Judith Basin Star 8/9/1937; "Montana Margins, a State Anthology" edited by Joseph Kinsey

Howard

LeBeau, Frederick (4/2/1909) Kalispell Bee 6/23/1908, p1; 7/3/1908, p1; 7/7/1908, p1; 7/10/1908, p1; 7/21/1908, p1; 7/28/1908, p8; 11/27/1908, p8; 12/8/1908, p1; 12/11/1908, p1; 12/18/1908, p1; 12/22/1908, p1; 1/26/1909, p1, p6; 3/16/1909, p1; 3/23/1909, p1; 4/2/1909, p1; Kalispell Journal 6/25/1908, p1; 7/2/1908, p1; 7/23/1908, p1; 11/26/1908, p1; 12/3/1908, p1; 12/10/1908, p1; 12/14/1908, p1; 12/17/1908, p1; 12/21/1908, p1; 1/28/1909, p1; 2/18/1909, p1; 3/22/1909, p1; 3/29/1909, p1; 4/5/1909, p1; Anaconda Standard 6/15/1908, p1; 7/3/1908, p1; 3/25/1909, p1; 4/2/1909, p1; 4/3/1909, p1; Great Falls Tribune 6/19/1908, p4; 6/26/1908, p5; 6/28/1908, p9; 7/3/1908, p5; 7/5/1908, p12; 7/8/1908, p3; 7/29/1908, p5; 3/24/1909; 3/26/1909, p1; 12/16/1908, p1; 12/20/1908, p1; 12/21/1908, p3; 4/3/1909, p1; 4/4/1909, p9; 5/5/1921, p9; 1/23/1925, p2; 6/7/1946, p5; Missoulian 4/3/1909, p1; "Kalispell, Montana and the Upper Flathead Valley" by Henry Elwood; Interview: Chouteau County Clerk of Court and School Superintendent Larry Stollfus

Liberty, Joe See Franklin Robideau

Lilly, A.J See James E. Brady

"Little John" See John Annen

"Lone Rider" (Spring of 1868) Historical Society, Vol. 8, 1917, p149; "A Pictorial History of the Sun River Valley" Sun River Historical Society

"Lone Writer" See "Lone Rider"

Lucy, Daniel, (9/14/1900) Anaconda Standard 7/2/1899; 7/17/1900, p8; 8/2/1900; 8/4/1900, p10;8/15/1900, p8; 8/26/1900, p11; 8/29/1900, p9; 9/6/1900, p8; 9/7/1900, p9; 9/9/1900, p1; 9/10/1900, p8; 9/11/1900, p7; 9/12/1900, p9; 9/12/1900, p10; 9/13/1900, p10; 9/14/1900, p7; 9/15/1900, p1; 9/16/1900, p11, p12, p18; 9/17/1900, p8; 9/18/1900, p10; 2/3/1901; 12/19/1925, p6; Great Falls Leader 9/13/1900, p3; Meagher Republican 5/18/1917, p5; Helena Daily Evening Herald 1/26/1899, p5

Lu Sing (4/20/1906) Bi-Weekly Republic Courier 10/3/1905, p1; 10/6/1905; 10/10/1905; 11/10/1905; 11/14/1905, p1; 11/17/1905; 11/28/1905; 12/12/1905; 3/27/1906; 4/10/1906; 4/13/1906; 4/17/1906; 4/20/1906; 5/1/1906; Bozeman Courier 7/23/1924; Bozeman Daily Chronicle 7/18/1924; Anaconda Standard 4/20/1906; Great Falls Tribune 5/20/1906, p2; records of the Gallatin County Historical Society

Lyons, Haze (1/14/1864) Square Butte Tribune 9/12/1921; Bynum Herald 12/19/1921; "Montana Vigilantes" Dimsdale; "Vigilante Days and Ways" Langford; "Vigilante Victims" Mather and Boswell; "A Decent Orderly Lynching" Allen

Marsh, Orlando H. (10/6/1879) (with Joseph Koble)

Marsden, Steve (See: Marshland)

Marshland, Steven (1/16/1864) Bynum Herald 12/19/1921; Dillon Examiner; "Vigilante Days and Ways" Langford; "Montana Vigilantes" Dimsdale; "Vigilante Victims" Mather and Boswell

Marsten, Steve (See: Marshland)

Martin, James (2/23/1904) Anaconda Standard 7/7/1902, p8; 7/8/1902, p8; 7/9/1902, p9; 7/11/1902, p2; 7/12/1902, p1; 7/15/1902, p7; 7/16/1902, p9; 7/19/1902, p9; 7/20/1902, p9;

7/22/1902, p12; 7/27/1902, p7; 8/10/1903, p1; 8/11/1903, p1; 8/16/1903, p1; 8/25/1903, p8; 12/22/1903, p3; 2/14/1904; 2/18/1904, p8; 2/19/1904, p8; 2/21/1904, p10; 2/22/ 1904, p1; 2/23/1904, p1; 2/24/1904, p10; 2/26/1904, p9; 1/13/1918, sec 2; 12/19/1925, p6; Helena Independent 5/21/1902, p1; 5/23/1902, p1; Great Falls tribune 8/11/1903, p1; 2/23/1904, p1; 2/24/1904, p4; Jordan Gazette 9/29/1919; The Searchlight 10/11/1920

Matte, Peter (3/9/1878) Helena Daily Herald 3/7/1878, p3; 3/19/1878, p3; 4/2/1878, p3; Missoulian 11/13/1921; 2/19/ 1922, p1 Sec 2; Madisonian 3/23/1878, p2; "Early Days in the Sagebrush Country" Clarence Popham; "Montana Genesis" Stevensville Historical Society; Dillon Examiner 11/23/1921, p9

McAndrews, Michael (3/1/1878) Helena Daily Herald 1/14/1878, p3; 1/15/1878, p3; 1/24/1878, p3; 2/2/1878, p3; 3/1/1878, p3; 3/2/1878, p3; Madisonian 9/15/1877, p2; 9/27/1877, p2; 10/20/1877, p2; Anaconda Standard 7/2/1895; "Broadwater County History" by the Broadwater County Historical Society; "Indians and Whites in the Northwest" Lawrence Benedict Palladino

McDonald, Edward (3/26/1885) (with Felix Constance)

McKenzie, Bill "Sam" (7/3/1884) Meagher Republican 3/3/1905; The Ismay Journal 7/11/1927; "Montana the Magazine of Western History" Winter, 1969

Merrill, John See John Jessrang

Metzger, Herbert Henry (5/5/1905) Mineral Argus 5/1/1884; Meagher Republican 12/2/1904, p3; 12/9/1904, p3; 12/13/1904, p3; 3/17/1905, p4; 3/24/1905, p3; 3/31/1905, p3; 4/7/1905; 4/14/1905, p3; 4/21/1905, p3; 4/28/1905, p3; 5/5/1905, p3; 5/12/1905, p3; 5/18/1917, p5; Belt Valley Times 12/6/1904; Anaconda Standard 5/5/1905, p1; 5/6/1905, p1; 4/2/1935, 2; 2/16/1917; Hogeland Herald, 8/3/1931; "Meagher County" Meagher County Historical Society

Miller, John Miller See Henry John Zorn

Mimie, John See John Annen

"Missouri Brown" See George W. Brown

Morgan, John (9/27/1865) Montana Post 9/30/1865; "The Vigilantes of Montana" Dimsdale

Morrison, Steve (See: Marshland)

Mott, Louis H. (3/18/1904) Missoulian 2/21/1903, p1; 2/22/1903, p1; 2/26/1903, p1; 2/27/1903, p1; 2/28/1903, p1; 3/1/1903, p1; 3/3/1903, p1; 3/4/1903, p1; 3/6/1903, p1; 3/5/1904, p8; 3/11/1904, p8; 3/15/1904, p3; 3/16/1904, p3; 3/17/1904, p1; 3/18/1904, p1; 3/19/1904; 2/19/1922, p1 Sec. 2; 10/15/1933, p1; Anaconda Standard 4/10/1903, p14; 12/24/1903, p16; 12/25/1903, p12

"Mugs" Stevens (Summer of 1884) (with "Champion") GF Tribune 10/3/1926, p3 Sec. 2

Murphy, Con "Red" (1/27/1885) Madisonian 9/6/1879, p2; Helena Daily Independent 6/8/1880, p3; Weekly Avant Courier 11/27/1884; Rocky Mountain Husbandman 11/13/1884, p3; 2/5/1885; Helena Daily Herald 2/18/1885; 5/7/1885; The Roy Enterprise 1/7/1918; Harlowton Press 1/12/1918; Northwest Tribune 3/1/1926; Lima Ledger 7/2/1934; Great Falls Tribune, Sec. G, p1; "Montana the Magazine of Western History" Vo. 11 No. 3, p45; Vol. 51 No. 1

Murray, Jack See Jack Brown

Nickerson, Silas (July 1884) (with "Swift Bill" and Orville Edwards) Helena Daily Herald 6/24/1884; Rocky Mountain Husbandman 9/11/1884, p3; Redstone Review 10/10/1921; GF Tribune 10/3/1926, p3 Sec 2; Judith Basin Star 8/9/1937; "Jordan" Arthur Jordan

O'Brien, John See Peter Pelkey

"Old Kentuckian" (See Spaulding 1/22/1868)

"Old Man Tripp" See Jack Triplett

"Ohio Dan" See Joseph Davis

O'Neil, John (1/14/1918) (with Frank Fisher and Sherman A. Powell) Flathead Courier 11/26/1917; Great Falls Tribune 1/15/1918, p5; Billings Gazette 1/14/1918, p1; Meagher Republic 2/15/1918, p7; Brady Citizen 3/28/1921; Anaconda Standard 12/19/1925, p6; 2/14/1925

Osnes, John H. (7/13/1894) River Press 4/11/1894; 4/25/1894; 5/16/1894; 5/23/1894; 6/27/1894; 7/4/1894; 7/18/1894; Great Falls Tribune 4/5/1894, p3; 4/6/1894, p3; 4/7/1894, p1; 7/10/1894, p4; 7/13/1894, p1; 7/14/1894, p3; Great Falls Leader 7/13/1894, p4; Livingston Enterprise 7/7/1894, p7; Helena Weekly Herald 7/19/1894, p7; 12/27/1894, p4; Dillon Examiner 3/2/1921, p9; Winifred Times 9/9/1929; "Fort Benton, World's Innermost Port" Joel Overholser

Owens, Charley (7/4/1884) "Montana the Magazine of Western History" Vol. 1 No.1, Jan 1951

Parish, Frank (1/14/1864) Bynum Herald 12/19/1921; Ekalaka Eagle 5/25/1931; "Montana Vigilantes" Dimsdale; "Vigilante Days and Ways" Langford; "Vigilante Victims" Mather and Boswell; "A Decent Orderly Lynching" Allen

Pascale (12/19/1890) (with Pierre Paul, La La See and Antley) (see Pierre Paul) Missoulian 2/12/1922, p1 Sec 2

Pelkey, Peter (2/4/1881) Helena Daily Herald 9/6/1880, p3; 9/22/1880, p3; 9/25/1880, p3; 12/10/1880, p3; 12/14/1880, p3; 12/15/1880, p3; 12/16/1880, p3; 12/27/1880, p3; 2/3/1881, p3; 2/4/1881, p3; 4/15/1881, p3; 1/7/1883, p3; 2/16/1888, p3; Helena Daily Independent 9/5/1880, p3; 9/22/1880, p3; 9/23/1880, p3; 12/4/1880, p3; 12/15/1880, p3; 2/3/1881, p2; 2/4/1881, p3; 2/5/1881, p3; 4/1/1881, p3; Madisonian 9/25/1880, p2; 2/12/1881, p2; 4/9/1881, p2; "Montana the Magazine of Western History" Vol. 28, No.3, p69; "Indians and Whites in the Northwest" Lawrence Benedict Palladino

Pepo, William (4/6/1900) Anaconda Standard 1/23/1900, p2; 4/8/1900, p1; Helena Daily Herald 3/30/1900, p8; 4/3/1900, p4; 4/7/1900, p1; Great Falls Tribune 3/11/1900, p6; 3/21/1900, p8; 4/1/1900, p7; 4/4/1900, p1; 4/8/1900, p7; Great Falls Leader 4/7/1900, p4; Lewistown Democrat 4/11/1900, p5; Teton County court records

Pierre Paul (12/19/1890) (with La La see, Pascale and Antley) Missoula Gazette 7/2/1890; 7/10/1890; 7/14/1890, p1; 7/15/1890, p1; 7/21/1890, p1; 7/23/1890, p1; 8/5/1890, p1; 8/6/1890, p1; 8/7/1890, p1; 8/21/1890; 12/18/1890, p1; Missoulian 2/12/1922, p1, Sec. 2; Great Falls Tribune 6/26/1889, p1; Anaconda Standard 8/5/1890, p1; 8/6/1890, p1; 8/7/1890; 8/8/1890, p8; 12/20/1890, p1; 3/3/1895, p8; 5/14/1896; Helena Daily Herald 6/25/1889, p8; 6/27/1889, p8; 9/11/1889, p5; 10/12/1889, p5; 10/25/1889, p5; Helena Weekly Herald 9/12/1889; Butte Semi Weekly Miner 6/26/1889, p1; 6/29/1889, p1; Jefferson County Sentinel 11/13/1890; 12/25/1890; Cascade Courier 4/30/1928; The Mountaineer 5/7/1928; Whitefish Pilot 2/21/1938; "Early Flathead and Tobacco Plain" by Marie C. Shea; "Before Kalispell: Demersville, Ashley, Egan, Half Moon, Salish" by Paul Strong; "Frontier Days in the Flathead Country" by Edward B. McCurdy; "Nuggets to Timber: Pioneer Days at Libby, Montana" Libby Pioneer Society and the Libby Woman's Club of 1970

Pizanthia, Joseph (Greaser) (1/11/1864) Mineral County Independent 9/30/1918; The Opheim Observer 12/31/1923; "Montana Vigilantes" Dimsdale; "Vigilante Days and Ways" Langford; "Vigilante Victims" Mather and Boswell

Plummer Amos Henry (1/10/1864) Helena Weekly Herald 2/14/1889, p8; Twice Week Republican Courier 1/23/1906; Harlowton Press 3/3/1917, p7; 4/7/1917, p7; Anaconda Standard 1/27/1918; 1/24/1909, p3; Plains Plainsman 6/10/1918; Redstone Review 9/30/1918; Opheim Observer 12/5/1921; Bynum Herald 12/19/1921; The Opheim Observer 12/31/1923; The Grass Range Review 9/25/1922; 3/3/1924; 9/15/1930; Missoulian 8/5/1927; The Valley Tribune 8/15/1927; The Mountaineer 8/22/1927; 7/9/1928; 9/17/1928; 1/1/1934; Eureka Journal 9/24/1928; Great Falls Tribune 8/23/1931, p1, sec 2; 10/19/1930, p1, sec 2; Fallon County Times 1/25/1932; Billings Times 9/14/1936; Post Falls Advance 9/23/1940; Phillips County News 10/6/1941; Big Timber Pioneer 11/24/1941; "Montana Vigilantes" Dimsdale; "Vigilante Days and Ways" Langford; "Vigilante Victims" Mather and Boswell; "Shallow Diggins" Jean Davis; "A Pictorial History of the Sun River Valley" Sun River Historical Society; "Bannack, Cradle of Montana" F. Lee Graves; "Montana the Magazine of Western History" Vol. 8, No.2, p45; "Bannack Home Page"

Powell, Sherman A. (1/14/1918) (with James Fisher and John O'Neil) Flathead Courier 11/26/1917; Great Falls Tribune 1/15/1918, p5; Anaconda Standard 10/18/1916, p7; 4/9/1917, p6; 4/11/1917, p7; 4/17/1917, p9; 4/29/1917, p10; 5/21/1917, p5; 5/22/1917, p10; 5/23/1917, p10; 5/24/1917, p9; 6/3/1917, p6; 12/19/1925 p6; 2/14/1925

Pugh, Clayberg (7/1/1895) Anaconda Standard 2/16/1895, p4; 2/17/1895, p4; 2/19/1895, p8; 4/11/1895, p1; 4/12/1895, p1; 4/13/1895, p1; 4/14/1895, p1; 4/15/1895, p1; 4/28/1895; 6/27/1895; 6/30/1895; 7/2/1895, p1; 9/8/1895; 10/9/1895; 10/15/1895; 9/16/1900, p18, sec 2; Billings Times 7/4/1895, p4; Helena Herald 2/19/1895, p3; 6/8/1895, p8; 6/27/1895, p8; 6/29/1895, p8; 7/1/1895, p1; Helena Weekly Herald 7/6/1895, p6

Rawley, R.C. (10/30/ 1864) "Dimsdale's Vigilantes of Montana"; "Vigilantes" H. Birney; "A Decent Orderly Lynching" Frederick Allen

Rawleigh, R.C. See R.C. Rawley

Ray, Edward "Ned" (1/10/1864) Redstone Review 9/30/1918; Bynum Herald 12/19/1921; The Opheim Observer 12/24/1923 "Vigilantes of Montana" Dimsdale; "Vigilante Days and Ways" Langford; "Vigilante Victims" Mather and Boswell; "Bannack, Cradle of Montana" F. Lee Graves

Reagin, Joseph B. (2/9/1923) (with Glenna M. Bolton)

Redding See Con Murphy

Redmond, John See Con Murphy

"Red Mike" (7/5/1884) (with Brocky Gallagher) GF Tribune 10/3/1926 p3, Sec 2; Judith Basin Star 8/9/1937; "Forty Years on the Frontier" Granville Stuart; "Montana the Magazine of Western History" Vol. No.1, Jan. 1951

"Reel Footed George" See George Lane

Reighley, R.C. See R.C. Rawley

Rigney, William (John) (7/25/1883) Helena Weekly Herald 7/26/1883, p7; Weekly Avant Courier 8/2/1883; The Jordan Gazette 4/21/1919; Great Falls Tribune 10/28/1901, p11; Dillon Examiner 5/31/1922, p9; Big Timber Pioneer 3/25/1929; Medicine Lake Wave 9/3/1934; Cascade Courier 5/4/1936; Grass Range Review 10/19/1936

Robert, Francois Joseph (10/31/1878) Virginia City Madisonian 10/13/1877, p2; 10/27/1877, p2; 11/10/1877, p2; 1/26/1878, p2; 3/16/1878, p2; 5/25/1878, p2; 8/17/1878, p2; 8/31/1878, p2;

9/13/1878, p2; 9/14/1878, p2; 9/21/1878, p2; 10/19/1878, p2; 10/26/1878, p2; 11/2/1878, p2; 12/25/1880, p2; 2/8/1879, p2; Helena Daily Herald 3/22/1878, p3; 8/31/1878; 9/18/1878, p3; 10/28/1878, p3; 10/31/1878, p3; 11/2/1878, p3; 2/3/1881 p3;

Roberts, Francis See Francois J. Robert

Roberts, W.H. "Harry" (8/23/1889) Helena Daily Herald 5/16/1889, p5; 6/6/1889, p8; 8/16/1889; 8/23/1889, p1; Helena Weekly Herald 6/13/1889, p8; 7/11/1889, p7; 8/21/1889; Butte Semi-Weekly Miner 5/18/1889, p3; 6/5/1889, p4; 6/8/1889, p4; 7/3/1889, p4; 8/2/1889, p3; 8/21/1889, p3; 8/28/1889; Anaconda Standard 9/16/1900, p18, sec 2; 12/10/1916; 12/19/1925, p6

Robideau, Franklin (1/15/1938) The Columbus News 12/2/1937, p1; 12/9/1937, p1; 12/16/1937, p1; 12/23/1937, p1; 12/30/1937, p1; 1/20/1938, p5; 1/27/1938, p1; Great Falls Tribune 11/28/1937, p3; 11/29/1937, p1; 12/25/1937, p9; 11/30/1937, p2; 1/12/1938, p10; Kalispell Times 1/6/1938; 1/27/1938; Stillwater County News 2/21/2001; 3/22/2001; "They Gazed On The Beartooths" by Jim Annin, Vol. 2, p198; Stillwater County case records and death certificates

Robinson, Robert (6/10/1888) Great Falls Tribune 6/11/1888; 6/12/1888, p1; 6/28/1903; Great Falls Leader 6/16/1888, p1, p3; Helena Weekly Herald 6/14/1882, p2; 11/22/1882, p2; Jefferson County Sentinel 6/11/1891; "Sun River Valley Centennial Observance" Sun River Community; "A Pictorial History of the Sun River Valley" Sun River Valley Historical Society, p80, p102, 262; Cascade County Coroner's Report of 6/11/1888

Rock, George J. (6/15/1908) Silver State 3/11/1908; 4/15/1908; 4/22/1908, p3; 4/29/1908; 5/6/1908; 5/13/1908; 6/3/1908; 6/17/1908; Anaconda Standard 5/7/1908, p1; 5/12/1908, p1; 6/1/1908; 6/16/1908, p1; 5/8/1917, p10; Great Falls Tribune 3/16/1908, p5; Helena Independent 5/12/1908, p1; Dillon Examiner 5/25/1921, p9; Meagher Republican 5/18/1917, p5; Judith Basin County Press 9/11/1933; "History, MT. State Prison" by Philip Kent

Salmon, Thomas (1/27/1899) Helena Independent 9/11/1898, p1; 9/14/1898, p1; 12/8/1898, p1; 12/9/1898, p1; 1/28/1899, p1; Helena Evening Herald, 1/23/1899, p4; 1/28/1899, p5; Billings Times, 9/15/1898, p8; 11/24/1898, p5; 2/2/1899, p8; 3/22/1900, p2; Livingston Enterprise 10/29/1929, p8; Cascade Courier 2/19/1934; "Red Lodge, Saga of a Western Area" by Shirley Zupan and Harry J. Owens

Sanders, George (11/21/1865) Montana Post 12/2/1865 p3; Coffee Creek Herald 2/24/1919

Schlaps, Ferdinand (5/20/1927) Wolf Point Herald 5/6/1926, p1; 5/13/1926, p1; 5/27/1926, p1; 6/10/1926, p1; 7/8/1926, p1; 7/15/1926, p1; 7/22/1926, p1; 7/29/1926, p1; 8/12/1926, p1; 4/1/1927; 4/15/1927, p1; 5/13/1927, p1; 5/20/1927, p1; 5/27/1927, p1; Great Falls Tribune 5/18/1927, p4; 5/19/1927, p4; 5/20/1927, p1; Supreme Court records State vs. Schlaps #6070, 3/29/1927; "Wolf point, A city of destiny" Marvin W. Presser

Scott, Martin (2/17/1888) Great Falls Tribune 11/18/1887, p1; 2/16/1888, p1; 2/17/1888, p1; New North-West, Deer Lodge 11/25/1887, p3; 12/9/1887, p3; 12/16/1887, p3; 12/30/1887, p3; 1/6/1888, p3; 1/20/1888, p3; 2/17/1888, p2, p3; Philipsburg Mail

2/9/1888, p1; Helena Daily Herald 2/16/1888, p3; 2/16/1888, p3; 2/17/1888, p3; 2/17/1888, p3; Helena Weekly Herald 2/23/1888, p4; Helena Daily Independent 2/16/1888; 2/17/1888; 2/18/1888; Anaconda Weekly Review 2/23/1888, p2; Anaconda Standard 12/18/1898, p14; Butte Semi-Weekly Miner 2/18/1888; 2/22/1888; "The Silver Empire" Garnet Stephenson

Seachrist, Jacob (7/30/1865) Montana Post 8/5/1865; The Western News 10/21/1918; Meagher Republican, 10/28/1918, p7; "Vigilantes of Montana" Dimsdale

Shears, George (1/25/1864) Bynum Herald 12/19/1921; Melstone Messenger 8/24/1931; "Vigilantes of Montana" Dimsdale; "Vigilante Days and Ways" Langsford

Silvers, Jake See Jacob Seachrist

Silvie, Jake See Jacob Seachrist

Simpson, Lee (12/30/1939) Harlowton Times 4/21/1938, p1; 5/5/1938, p1; 6/2/1938, p1; 7/7/1938, p1; 9/8/1938, p1; 9/15/1938, p1; 9/22/1938, p1; 9/29/1938, p1; 10/13/1938, p8; 10/5/1939, p1; 10/19/1939, p1; 11/23/1939, p1; 12/7/1939, p1; 12/28/1939, p1; 1/4/1940, p1; 2/8/1940, p1; 4/25/1940, p1; Montana Clarion 4/20/1938; 4/22/1993; Billings Gazette 12/28/1939, p7; 12/30/1939, p1; 12/31/1939, p11; Great Falls Tribune 4/16/1938, p1; 4/17/1938, p1; 4/18/1938, p1; 4/19/1938, p2; 12/28/1939, p1; 12/29/1939, p1; 12/30/1939, p2; "Massacre of the Mountain Monster" by Chad Wallin for "Real Detective Magazine"; "Dawn in Golden Valley" Golden Valley County; "16 Marked for Death" by Ernest Cox

Skinner, Cyrus (1/25/1864) Missoulian 10/29/1911, p4; The Stevensville Register 9/16/1918; Dillon Examiner 7/28/1919, p12; Bynum Herald 12/19/1921; "Vigilantes of Montana" Dimsdale; "Bannack, the Cradle of Montana" F. Lee Graves; UM Western/ library website

Slade, Joseph (3/10/1864) Montana Post 1/27/1866, p4; Helena Daily Herald 9/7/1875; Great Falls Tribune 11/16/1902, Sec. 2, p16; 10/20/1945 p1; Twice-Weekly Republican Courier 1/26/1906; Anaconda Standard 8/15/1908 p1; 10/1/1916, p15; 3/20/1920 p1, part 2; 6/20/1920, p1 part 2; Kalispell Bee 9/8/1908 p2; Meagher Republic 10/19/1917 p3; 4/12/1918 p6; The Western News 10/28/1918; Forsyth Democrat 3/20/1919 p3; Bynum Herald 9/22/1922; Opheim Observer 1/1/1923; The Bridger Times 9/2/1924; Brady Citizen 4/12/1926; "Silver State Post 1/8/1934; Phillips County News 12/20/1937; "History of Montana" Tom Stout; "Vigilantes of Montana" Dimsdale; "Vigilante Days and Ways" Langford; "A Decent Orderly Lynching" Allen; Utah State History website

Sluth See Jerome

Smith, William Henry (3/18/1883) (with Milford Coomes)

Spaulding (1/22/1868) (with Wilson 1/25/1868) Montana Post 1/25/1868, p8; 2/1/1868, p8; 5/16/1868; Jefferson Valley Zehry, Whitehall 6/14/1895; Billings Gazette 7/13/1895

Spillman, C.W. (8/26/1862) 9/25/1922 The Grass Range Review, p4; 1/6/1941 The Spirit Lake; "Forty Years on the Frontier" Granville Stuart; "From Wilderness to Statehood, 1805-1900 by J.M. Hamilton; "Shallow Diggins" Jean Davis

"Splat-Foot" Harnett (Summer of 1884) Helena Daily Herald 5/8/1889 p2

St. Clair, John W. (2/1/1873) (with Jack "Old Man" Triplett) Bozeman Avant Courier 2/7/1873, p2, p3; 2/21/1873, p1, p2; Montanian 2/6/1873, p5; 2/13/1873, p4; Republican Courier (Bozeman) 6/13/1911, p6; The Weekly Courier 7/8/1914;"Gallatin County's Heritage 1805-1976" p8;

"Steamboat Bill" See John St. Clair

Stears, William See William Sterres

Sterres, William H. (10/28/1875) Helena Daily Herald 5/3/1875; 5/4/1875; 5/14/1875, p3; 5/19/1875, p1; 5/20/1875; 5/24/1875, p3; 6/11/1875, p3; 6/18/1875, p3; 6/24/1875, p3; 6/29/1875, p1; 7/6/1875, p3; 8/12/1875, p3; 9/6/1875; 9/14/1875, p2, 3; 9/16/1875, p1; 10/9/1875; 10/28/1875 p3; 2/16/1888, p3 Madisonian

5/8/1875; 7/10/1875; 8/21/1875, p2; 9/11/1875; 9/18/1875; 11/6/1875; Medicine Lake Wave 1/7/1918; Denton Recorder 10/20/1919; Glacier County Chief 6/11/1934; "Montana the Magazine of Western History" Vol. 2, No.1, p8, p10; Vol. 20, No.1, p43; "Indians and Whites in the Northwest" Father Lawrence Benedict Palladino

Stewart, Brackett See Thomas Stewart

Stewart, Thomas (7/4/1881) Helena Daily Herald 6/30/1881, p3; 7/1/1881, p3; 7/5/1881, p3; GF Tribune 10/4/1903, p6; Troy Tribune 4/10/1933; Big Timber Pioneer 2/9/1942; "Montana the Magazine of Western History" Vol. 12, No. 3, p21

Stinson, Buck (1/10/1864) Anaconda Standard 1/24/1909, p3; Redstone Review 9/30/1918; Bynum Herald 12/19/1921; "Bannack, Cradle of Montana" F. Lee Graves; "Vigilante Victims" www;

Stuart, Jack See Thomas Stewart

"Submarine Richard" See "Dick the Diver"

"Swift Bill" (July1884) (with Silas Nickerson and Orville Edwards) Rocky Mountain Husbandman 9/11/1884, p3; Redstone Review 10/10/1921; GF Tribune 10/3/1926, p3 Sec. 2; Judith Basin Star 8/9/1937; "Jordan: Arthur Jordan

"Tex" (January 1882) Helena Daily Herald 2/4/1882

Triplett, Jack (Old Man) (2/1/1873) (Hanged with John W. St. Clair)

"Tripp" See Jack Triplet

Trochin, John See John Crochet

Trosha, John See John Crochet

"Turkey" Williams (Summer of 1884) (Hanged with Bronco Charley) Helena Daily Herald 5/8/1889, p2

Varley, John (8/16/1868) Montana Post 8/21/1868, p8; 8/28/1868, p5

Vettere, Anthony (10/1/1926) Anaconda Standard 11/23/1925, p1; 11/24/1925, p1; 11/25/1925, p1; 11/26/1925, p1; 11/28/1925, p1, p5; 12/6/1925, p5; 12/8/1925, p2; 12/11/1925, p6; 1/23/1926, p5; 2/13/1926, p5; 2/16/1926, p5; 2/17/1926, p1; 2/18/1926, p1; 2/19/1926, p1; 2/20/1926, p1; 2/21/1926, p1; 2/23/1926, p1; 2/24/1926, p1; 3/5/1926, p5; 3/13/1926, p12; 3/14/1926, p1; 3/16/1926, p7; 4/8/1926, p1; 7/3/1926, p1; 7/10/1926, p5; 7/17/1926, p1; 7/18/1926, p2; 7/20/1926, p5; 7/21/1926, p2; 7/23/1926, p5; 7/24/1926, p5; 7/26/1926, p1; 7/27/1926, p5; 7/29/1926, p5; 8/10/1926, p5; 8/11/1926, p1; 8/12/1926, p1; 8/13/1926, p5; 8/15/1926, p13; 8/25/1926, p1; 9/13/1926, p5; 9/14/1926, p1; 9/15/1926, p6; 9/16/1926, p1; 9/23/1926, p1; 9/24/1926, p1; 9/25/1926, p1; 9/27/1926, p1; 9/28/1926, p1; 9/29/1926, p1; 9/30/1926, p1; 10/1/1926, p1; 10/2/1926, p2; 10/3/1926, 10/6/1926, p4; 10/9/1926, p4; Great Falls Tribune 11/23/1925, p1; 11/24/1925, p1; 11/26/1925, p1; 8/25/1926, p4; 9/29/1926, p3; 10/1/1926, p1; Montana Standard, p18

Vuckovich, Joseph (2/17/1922) Missoulian 2/13/1921; 2/14/1921, p1; 2/15/1921, p1; 2/17/1921, p1; 2/18/1921; 2/19/1921; 2/20/1921; 2/25/1921; 2/27/1921; 3/21/1921; 3/22/1921; 3/23/1921; 3/24/1921; 3/26/1921; 3/29/1921; 1/1/1922, p2; 1/8/1922, p3; 1/10/1922, p2; 1/11/1922, p1; 1/16/1922, p8; 1/18/1922, p5; 1/26/1922, p2; 1/27/1922, p6; 1/29/1922, p2; 1/31/1922, p1; 2/2/1922, p2; 2/3/1922, p5; 2/4/1922, p2; 2/5/1922, p1; p1, section 2; 2/6/1922, p2; 2/7/1922, p2; 2/8/1922, p2; 2/10/1922, p2; 2/11/1922, p2; 2/12/1922, p1 Sec. 2; 2/13/1922, p1; 2/14/1922, p2; 2/15/1922, p1; 2/16/1922, p1; 2/17/1922, p1;

2/18/1922, p6; 10/15/1933; Great Falls Tribune 12/22/1921, p4; 2/17/1922, p5; 2/18/1922, p1; Missoula City Directory, Davis Graham and Sheriff George A. Cole

Wagner, John (Dutch John) (1/11/1864) Great Falls Tribune 11/16/1902, Sec.2, p2: Mineral County Independent 9/30/1918; Bynum Herald 12/19/1921; The Opheim Observer 12/24/1923; The Augusta News 6/27/1932; "Vigilantes of Montana" Dimsdale; "Vigilante Days and Ways" Langford; "Vigilante Victims" Mather and Boswell

Walsh, Roy (2/14/1925) Jefferson Valley News, Whitehall 7/28/1923; 8/2/1923, p1; 3/13/1975; Anaconda Standard 6/28/1923; 6/29/1923, p4; 7/1/1923, p8; 7/1/1923; 7/4/1923, p1; 7/12/1923, p5; 7/15/1923, p1; 7/16/1923, p8; 7/17/1923, p1; 7/18/1923, p1; 7/20/1923, p1; 7/21/1923, p1; 7/22/1923, p1; 7/24/1923, p1; 7/25/1923, p1; 7/26/1923, p1; 7/27/1923, p1; 7/28/1923, p1; 7/29/1923, p4; 7/30/1923, p1; 8/3/1923, p2; 8/12/1923, p4; 8/25/1923, p1; 9/10/1923, p5; 9/23/1923, p1; 10/21/1923, p1; 10/22/1923, p1; 10/23/1923, p1; 10/24/1923, p1; 10/25/1923, p1; 10/26/1923, p1; 10/27/1923, p2; 10/31/1923, p6; 11/11/1923, p1; 12/9/1923, p14; 5/4/1924, p1; 5/5/1924, p1; 5/6/1924, p1; 5/7/1924, p1; 5/8/1924, p1; 5/10/1924, p1; 5/13/1924, p5; 5/15/1924, p1; 5/16/1924, p1; 5/17/1924, p1; 5/18/1924, p2; 5/23/1924, p1; 12/24/1924, p1; 12/28/1924, p9; 12/29/1924, p5; 12/30/1924, p1; 12/31/1924, p10; 1/10/1925, p5; 1/11/1925, p5; 1/14/1925, p1, p2; 2/1/1925, p1; 2/4/1925, p5; 2/9/1925, p1; 2/10/1925, p1;2/11/1925, p1; 2/12/1925, p1; 2/13/1925, p1; 2/14/1925, p1; 2/15/1925, p1; Great Falls Tribune 6/23/1923, p4; 6/28/1923, p4; 7/1/1923, p1; 7/3/1923, p4; 7/24/1923, p1; 7/25/1923, p2; 7/27/1923, p2; 7/28/1923, p1; 8/2/1923, p1; 8/4/1923, p4; 10/26/1923, p5; 5/4/1924, p1; 5/5/1924, p1; 5/7/1924, p1; 5/11/1924, p4; 5/15/1924, p5; 5/17/1924, p4; 6/14/1924, p4; 10/20/1924, p4; 12/24/1924, p3; 1/6/1925, p1; 1/7/1925, p2; 1/14/1925, p2; 1/23/1925, p2; 2/12/1925, p4; 2/14/1925, p1; Missoulian 10/22/1923, p1; 10/23/1923; 5/15/1924, p1; 5/17/1924, p1; Bozeman Courier 10/22/1924, p4; Harlowton News 6/19/1924, p9; 8/7/1924, p3; Jefferson Valley Collection; "How I Trapped Montana's Boasting Outlaw" by John W. Mountjoy in the "Startling Detective Adventures" magazine Vol. XV, No. 90, January 1936; Supreme Court Records, State vs. Roy Walsh, 12/23/1924

Wheatley, William Wright (8/13/1875) Helena Daily Herald 6/7/1875, p3; 6/9/1875, p3; 6/10/1875, p3; 8/12/1875, p3; 8/13/1875, p3; 8/20/1875; 8/26/1875, p3; 8/27/1875, p3; 2/16/1888, p3; Madisonian 6/12/1875, p2; 8/14/1875; Denton Recorder 10/20/1919; Glacier County Chief 6/11/1934; "Indians and Whites in the Northwest" Father Lawrence Benedict Palladino

Wilson, Bill (1/25/1868) (with Spaulding 1/22/1868) Montana Post 1/25/1868, p8; 2/1/1868, p8; 5/16/1868; Jefferson Valley Zephry, Whitehall 6/14/1895; Billings Gazette 7/13/1895

Wilson, Charles (9/25/1867) Montana Post 9/28/1867, p1; 10/5/1867, p8; "Montana the Magazine of Western History" Autumn, 1964, p39

Wilson, Joseph (4/30/1870) (with Arthur L. Compton)

"Whisky Bill" See William Graves

Wray, Edward See Edward "Ned" Ray

Yeager, "Red" Erastus (1/4/1864) Bynum Herald 12/19/1921; "Montana Vigilantes" Dimsdale; "Vigilante Days and Ways" Langford; "Vigilante Victims" Mather and Boswell; "From Wilderness to Statehood" Hamilton; "Vigilantes" Birney

Yeik, Albert (8/26/1921) Dillon Examiner 4/21/1920, p2; 4/28/1920, p1; 5/19/1920, p1; 5/26/1920, p1; 6/9/1920; 6/16/1920; 5/25/1921, p16/29/1921, p1; 7/27/1921, p1; 8/3/1921, p1, p11; 8/10/1921, p1; 8/17/1921, p1; 10/27/1921; 8/31/1921, p1; Dillon Tribune 4/23/1920, p1; 4/30/1920, p1; 5/21/1920, p1; 5/28/1920, p1; 6/11/1920, p1; 6/18/1920, p1; 9/17/1920, p1; 8/5/1921, p1; 8/9/1921, p1; 8/12/1921, p1; 8/26/1921, p1; 8/26/1964; 8/31/1921, p1; Great Falls Tribune 4/22/1920; 5/20/1920, p4, p14; 8/27/1921, p7; 11/25/1904; Butte Miner 4/22/1920, p1; 4/23/1920, p3; 4/25/1920, p2; 4/26/1920, p6; 5/19/1920, p8; 5/20/1920, p1; 5/23/1920, p12; Anaconda Standard 4/22/1920, p2; 4/24/1920, p9; 4/26/1920; 4/30/1920, p9; 8/3/1920, p3; Missoulian 8/27/1921; "History of Beaverhead County" Beaverhead County Museum Association; "On the North Side of Philipsburg, Montana" Tiny Johnson

Zachary, Robert (1/25/1864); Semi-Weekly Republican Courier 11/7/1905; Missoulian 10/29/1911, p4; "Vigilante Days and Ways" Langford; "Vigilante Victims" Mather and Boswell; "Montana the Magazine of Western History" Vol. 23, No.3, p23

Zorn, Henry John (4/24/1935) Miles City Daily Star 9/5/1934, p1; 9/7/1934, p1; 10/2/1934, p3; 10/3/1934, p8; 10/4/1934, p1; 10/5/1934, p1; 10/7/1934, p1; 10/12/1934, p6; 10/18/1934, p8; 11/13/1934, p1; 11/14/1934, p1; Billings Gazette 8/13/1934, p1; 8/15/1934, p1; 8/16/1934, p1; 8/19/1934, p1; 8/24/1934, p1; 9/5/1934, p1; 10/2/1934, p1; 10/3/1934, p1; 10/4/1934, p1; 10/7/1934, p1; 10/9/1934, p8; 10/12/1934, p9; 10/17/1934, p1; 10/22/1934, p1; 11/9/1934, p1; 11/10/1934, p9; 11/12/1934, p1; 11/13/1934, p1; 11/14/1934, p1; 11/15/1934, p3; 11/25/1934, p2; 12/22/1934, p6; 4/24/1935, p1; 4/25/1935, p1, p14; 4/26/1935, p12; Great Falls Tribune 10/4/1934, p3; 10/7/1934; 11/13/1934, p5, p9; 11/14/1934, p4; 11/15/1934, p3; 4/19/1935, p8; 4/23/1935, p7; 4/24/1935, p1; 4/25/1935, p5, p9; Cascade Courier 5/6/1935; Kalispell Times 1/27/1938

Hanging Victim Index

Individuals are listed by last name first or nickname and in the case of Indians or Chinese nationals, they are indexed by the way they are pronounced.

Ah Chow 580
Ah Yung 86
Allen, Joseph 233
Anderson, Robert A. 161
Annen John (See John Annen)
Antley 134
Baker 564
"Barber the" 582
Belgrade, Frank 595
"Big Mustache Frank" 594
Biggerstaff, William 193
"Black Feather" 587
Ballou, George 564
Bolton, Glenna M. 401
Brady, James 574
Brady, James Edward 591
"Bronco Charlie" 596
Brooks, William C. 244
Brown, George W. 566
Brown, Jack 592
Bryson, George, Duncan 114
Bunton, William 570
Burns, John 152
Cadotte, Joseph 186
Calder, William Wallace 253
"California Ed" 593
Carter, Alexander 571
"Champion" 595
Chow, Ah (See Ah Chow)
Christie, Calvin J. 174
Clark, John A. 89
Coleman, Phillip 525
Collins, J.C. 592
Compton, Arthur L. 580
Constance, Felix 589
Cooke, Tommy 578
Coomes, Milford 583
Cooper, John 572
Costello, James 595
Criner, George 501
Crochet, John 579
Cuellae, Juan 376
Daniels, James B. 579
Danner, Seth Orrin 431
Davisson, Rollin 479
Davis, Joseph 582
"Dick the Diver" 582
Dolan, John 575
Dotson, Clinton 284
Douglas, James 586
Douglas, John B. 77
Downes, William 594
Edwards, Orville 594
Fahley, Lesslie 357
Fisher, Frank 364
Fogarty, James 586
Fleming, James 284
"Frenchy" (See Crochet, John)
"Froggy" 588
Fuhrmann, Henry 82
Fuller, Miles 334
Gallagher, Brocky 594
Gallagher, Jack 569
Gay, William 207
Gibbs, Charles 594
Gibson, Harrison 357
Goones, J.L. 563
Graves, William 573
"Half-Breed" Jack 596
Hall, Henry 357
Harding, Thomas H. 93
Harris, Monte 408
Harris, William 408
Harrison, Joseph 588
Hart, John Patrick 97
Hayes, William A. 346
Helm, Boone 569
Heron, John 561
Hinson Bill (See Hynson)
Hoefner, Henry 591
Hoffman, George 487
Howard, Jack 577
Hunt 586
Hunter, William 573
Hurst, Joseph C. 262
Hynson, William 580
Ives, George 562
Jackson, John 575
Jackson, Walter 591
Jerome 590
Jessrang, John A. 588
Jewett, Charles 579
John Annen 590
John Doe 577

John Doe 577
John Doe 577
John Doe 577
John Doe 577
John Doe 578
John Doe 578
John Doe 578
John Doe 578
John Doe 578
John Doe 581
John Doe, Boat Thief 589
John Doe, Chinaman 564
John Doe, Chinaman 582
John Doe, Crewmember 588
John Doe, Indian 576
John Doe, Indian 588
John Doe, Indian 589
John Doe, Indian 589
John Doe, Indian 589
John Doe, Indian 589
John Doe, Indian 589
John Doe, Indian 589
John Doe, Indian 589
John Doe, Indian 589
John Doe, Innocent Victim 589
John Doe, Innocent Victim 580
John Doe, Innocent Victim 595
John Doe, Murderer 593
John Doe, Murderer 593
John Doe, Rustler 571
John Doe, Rustler 575
John Doe, Rustler 586
John Doe, Rustler 586
John Doe, Rustler 586
John Doe, Rustler 593
John Doe, Rustler 593
John Doe, Rustler 593
John Doe, Rustler 593
John Doe, Rustler 593
John Doe, Rustler 593
John Doe, Rustler 593
John Doe, Rustler 595
John Doe, Rustler 595
John Doe, Rustler 595
John Doe, Rustler 595
John Doe, Rustler 595
John Doe, Rustler 595
John Doe, Rustler 595
John Doe, Rustler 595
John Doe, Rustler 595
John Doe, Rustler 595
John Doe, Victim 595
John Doe, Rustler 595
John Doe, Rustler 595
John Doe, Rustler 595
John Doe, Rustler 595
John Doe, Rustler 595
John Doe, Rustler 595
John Doe, Thief 593
John Doe, Tramp 590
Johnson, Leander 563
Jones, Bill 582
Keene, John 563
King, Thomas A. 127
Kirby, Con 578
Koble, Joseph K. 64
LaFaver, Samuel 594
La La See 134
Lane, Alfred 383
Lane, George 569
Lavardure, Narcissus 593
LeBeau, Frederick 349
"Lone Rider" 586
Lucy, Daniel 274
Lu Sing 329
Lyons, Haze 570
Marsh, Orlando H. 64
Marshland, Steve 570
Martin, James 304
Matte, Peter 586
McAndrews, Michael 58
McDonald, Edward 589
McKenzie, Sam 593
Metzger, Herbert Henry 321
Morgan, John 576
Mott, Louis H. 315
"Mugs" Stevens 595
Murphy, Con 589
Nickerson, Silas 594
O'Neil, John 364
Osnes, John H. 169
Owens, Charley 594
Parish, Frank 570
Pascale 134
Paul, Pierre (See Pierre Paul)
Pelkey, Peter 69

Pepo, William 269
Pierre Paul 134
Pizanthia, Joseph 568
Plummer, Henry 566
Powell, Sherman A. 364
Pugh, Clayberg 180
Rawley, R.C. 575
Ray, Edward "Ned" 567
Reagin, Joseph B. 401
"Red Mike" 594
Rigney, William "John" 584
Robert, Francois Joseph 59
Roberts, W.H. "Harry" 121
Robideau, Frank 505
Robinson, Robert 590
Rock, George J. 339
Salmon, Thomas 230
Sanders, George 578
Schlaps, Ferdinand 473
Scott, Martin 106
Seachrist, Jacob 577
Shears, George 572
Simpson, Lee 512
Sing, Lu (See Lu Sing)
Skinner, Cyrus 571
Slade, Joseph 574
Smith, William Henry 583
Spaulding 579
Spillman, C.W. 561
"Splay-Foot" Harnett 596
St. Clair, John W. 581
Sterres, William H. 51
Stewart, Thomas 587
Stinson, Buck 567
"Swift Bill" 594
"Tex" 582
Triplett, Jack, Z.T. 581
"Turkey" Williams 596
Varley, John 564
Vettere, Anthony 462
Vuckovich, Joseph 393
Wagner, John 568
Walsh, Roy 440
Wheatley, William 47
Wilson, Bill 579
Wilson, Charles 576
Wilson, Joseph 580
Yager, Erastus 566
Yeik, Albert 386
Yung, Ah (See Ah Yung)
Zachary, Robert 572
Zorn, Henry John 490